4th edition

ADVERTISING MANAGEMENT

David A. Aaker
University of California at Berkeley

Rajeev Batra
University of Michigan

John G. Myers
University of California at Berkeley

 PRENTICE HALL, Englewood Cliffs, New Jersey 07632

Library of Congress Cataloging-in-Publication Data

Aaker, David A.
   Advertising management/David A. Aaker, Rajeev Batra, John G.
Myers.—4th ed.
     p.   cm.
   Includes bibliographical references and index.
   ISBN 0-13-014101-1
   1. Advertising—Management.   I. Batra, Rajeev.   II. Myers, John
G.,.   III. Title.
HF5823.A13 1992
659.1—dc20   91–24126
                                    CIP

Aquisition Editor: *Tim Kent*
Production Editor: *Edith Pullman*
Copy Editor: *Sally Ann Bailey*
Cover Designer: *Michele Paccione*
Prepress Buyer: *Trudy Pisciotti*
Manufacturing Buyer: *Bob Anderson*
Supplements Editor: *Lisamarie Brassini*
Editorial Assistant: *Ellen Ford*

The chapter opening quotation on page 116 from the book *HOW TO ADVERTISE* copyright © 1976 by Kenneth Roman and Jane Maas is reprinted with special permission from St. Martin's Press, Inc., and the Julian Bach Literary Agency, Inc., New York, NY. The chapter opening quotation on page 253 from Sidney Levy is reprinted by permission of the *Harvard Business Review*. Excerpt from "Symbols for Sale" by Sidney J. Levy (July-August 1959). Copyright © 1959 by the President and Fellows of Harvard College; all rights reserved. The chapter opening quotations on pages 253, 291, 321, and 439 from David Ogilvy are excerpts reprinted with permission of Atheneum Publishers, an imprint of Macmillan Publishing Company, from *CONFESSIONS OF AN ADVERTISING MAN* by David Ogilvy. Copyright © 1963, 1987 David Ogilvy Trustee. The chapter opening quotation on page 275 is from *PERSONAL INFLUENCE* by Elihu Katz and Paul F. Lazarsfeld. Copyright © 1955 by The Free Press; copyright renewed 1983 by Patricia Kendall Lazarsfeld and Elihu Katz. The chapter opening quotation on page 549 by Bauer and Greyser is reprinted by permission and is from Raymond A. Bauer and Stephen A. Greyser, *ADVERTISING IN AMERICA: The Consumer View*, Boston: Division of Research, Harvard Business School, 1968.

© 1992, 1987, 1982, 1975 by Prentice-Hall, Inc.
a Simon & Schuster Company
Englewood Cliffs, New Jersey 07632

Printed in the United States of America
10 9 8 7 6 5 4

ISBN 0-13-014101-1

Prentice-Hall International (UK) Limited, *London*
Prentice-Hall of Australia Pty. Limited, *Sydney*
Prentice-Hall Canada Inc., *Toronto*
Prentice-Hall Hispanoamericana, S.A., *Mexico*
Prentice-Hall of India Private Limited, *New Delhi*
Prentice-Hall of Japan, Inc., *Tokyo*
Simon & Schuster Asia Pte. Ltd., *Singapore*
Editora Prentice-Hall do Brasil, Ltda., *Rio de Janeiro*

CONTENTS

PREFACE

Advertising is a fascinating subject—"the most fun you can have with your pants on," as Jerry Della Femina once said. Yet it is also perhaps the aspect of marketing where it is most difficult to know for sure what "works," and thus to improve the productivity of marketing and advertising. This book is written with the objective of giving students and practitioners alike the framework and knowledge with which to make more effective advertising decisions, and to communicate some of the excitement and vitality that characterizes the advertising business. Towards this end, the book tries to pull together what we currently know about how advertising "works," and to draw lessons from that knowledge for better advertising decision making.

CHANGES IN THE FOURTH EDITION

This fourth edition of *Advertising Management* has been extensively updated and revised, in part to reflect the biases and perspectives of the new co-author (R.B.). Perhaps the one biggest change is the conceptualization of the various interrelated ways in which advertising influences the consumer's relationship to the advertised brand—the communication of benefit-related information and the creation or modification of attitudes; the association of feelings with the brand; the development of a brand personality; the creation of social norms encouraging consumption of the brand; and the precipitation of buying action. This, we believe, gives a "big picture" perspective on the role of advertising that is both new and unique. Supporting this framework are almost-new chapters on brand personality and the creation of social norms, and a new integrative framework on feeling-oriented advertising.

Another change is the substantial rearranging and resequencing of material. We believe the book's material is now substantially better integrated, with research results brought much closer to the appropriate points of the advertising decision making sequence. The sequence of book chapters itself has been modified, to reflect a strategy/tactics distinction in the two key areas of message decisions and media decisions.

The material in these chapters has, of course, been substantially updated and revised (with some dated or redundant material from previous editions now eliminated). A substantial number of more recent research findings have been woven into the text. Tables and Figures have been updated. Topics now receiving greater attention include the globalization and consolidation of the advertising business, the new and fragmented media environment, identification of target segments, sales promotion, direct marketing, scanner and split-cable data analysis, means-ends chains, co-op advertising, client-agency relationships, principles of good copy, new copy-testing research findings, and ethics in advertising. The media chapters have been almost totally rewritten, so that the reader now has a much better sense of the sources and use of media data than before.

Several new cases have also been added, to provide illustrations of the use of some of the principles discussed in the text, as well as to give the reader practice in applying them.

ORIENTATION AND TARGET AUDIENCE

Despite these substantial changes, the basic thrust of the book remains as in earlier editions. The overriding objective is again to provide an approach to the management of advertising that is sophisticated, thoughtful, and state-of-the-art, while being practical and relevant to "real world" advertising planning, decision making, and control. The book again draws on and attempts to integrate three related disciplines: the behavioral sciences, marketing and advertising research, and management science.

While we do mention industry rules-of-thumb and "received wisdom" at appropriate points, our orientation is clearly one of understanding and applying relevant research. We continue to believe that too many advertising decisions are made wastefully and inappropriately, and that the application of relevant research can contribute substantially to reducing such waste. Having said that, we recognize that advertising is both a science and an art—and while we cannot teach the art of advertising, in our chapters on the creative and production process, we can at least attempt to develop an appreciation for it.

This book is intended for users and potential users of advertising, as well as for those who are preparing for a career in advertising. Previous editions have been used successfully in both undergraduate and graduate courses in advertising, advertising management, communication management, and management of promotions. It has also been used as the basis for training in various leading advertising agencies and marketing organizations. No previous knowledge is assumed, though some familiarity with elementary marketing principles will of course be helpful.

ORGANIZATION AND CONTENT

The book is divided into six parts, with each part except the final one containing an integrative case. Part I describes the field of advertising and the institutions through which advertising "flows," positions advertising within the organization, and introduces advertising planning and decision making. Part II focuses on setting advertising objectives, and presents the concepts of segmentation and positioning. Part III examines the interrelated aspects of message strategy: changing benefit-based attitudes, associating feelings with the brand, developing brand personality, creating social norms, and precipitating action. It leads into these by first presenting some relevant research findings. Part IV discusses tactical issues, those related to actual message execution: designing ads to gain attention, choosing among various creative approaches, writing and evaluating actual copy, testing copy for effectiveness and diagnostics, and producing and implementing advertising— including the topic of how clients and agencies can work together more effectively. Part V moves on to media strategy (setting budgets) and media tactics (allocating budgets). Part VI then returns the reader to the broader environment, looking both at the regulatory environment that impacts advertising and the social environment that it shapes in so many ways.

ACKNOWLEDGEMENTS

We would like to thank the many people who helped significantly to improve this fourth edition of the book. First, Professor Brian Sternthal of the Kellogg School at Northwestern, and Professor John Quelch of the Harvard Business School (and the Harvard Business School Press), for allowing us to reproduce cases. Second, our reviewers, including Boris Becker, Tom O'Guinn, Sharan Jagpal, and Betsy Gelb. They join those who helped us on previous editions, including John Deighton, Julie Edell, David Furse, Ewald Grether, Stephen Greyser, Manoj Hastak, Hal Kassarjian, Trudy Kehret-Ward, Dean Krugman, James Krum, Rich Lutz, Andy Mitchell, William Mindak, Francesco Nicosia, Michael Ray, Allan Shocker, Camille Schuster, Doug Stayman, Debra Stephens, Bill Wilkie, Terrance Witkowski, Henrick Helmers, Don Schultz, Spencer Tinkham, and many others. We also thank Ziv Carmon for his help on the Instructor's Manual. Once again we acknowledge the superb translation effort by Ikujiro Nonaka and Hisashi Ikegami, who translated the book into Japanese, and Roberto Alvarez del Blanco, who translated it into Spanish.

To all these people and others whose efforts and contributions now escape our memory, we offer our thanks. Our faculty colleagues and students at Berkeley, Columbia and Michigan have been a constant source of inspiration and encouragement. Finally, we thank our wives and families for their support and understanding. The book is dedicated to them.

David A. Aaker
Rajeev Batra
John G. Myers

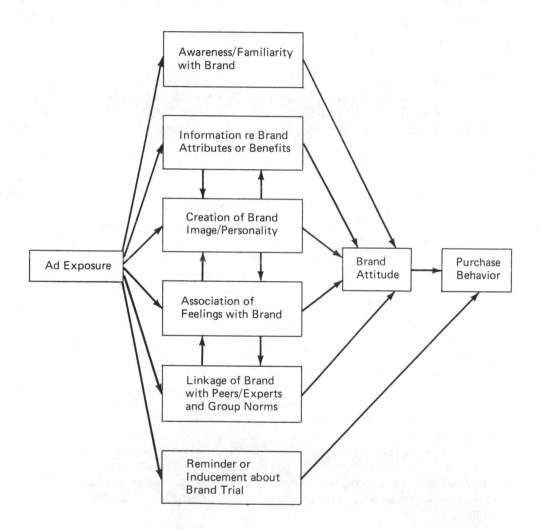

In this book, advertising is seen as influencing consumer attitudes and purchase be-haviors in a variety of interlinked ways. An ad exposure can increase brand familiar-ity, communicate brand attributes and benefits, develop an image and personality for the brand, associate specific feelings with the brand, link the brand to reference groups such as peers and experts, and directly induce action.

1

THE FIELD OF
ADVERTISING MANAGEMENT

The trade of advertising is now so near to perfection that it is not easy
to propose any improvements.

Samuel Johnson, 1760

The competent advertising man must understand psychology. The more
he knows about it the better. He must learn that certain effects lead to
certain reactions, and use that knowledge to increase results and avoid
mistakes. Human nature is the same today as in the time of Caesar. So
the principles of psychology are fixed and enduring. We learn, for instance, that curiosity is one of the strongest of human incentives.

Claude Hopkins, *Scientific Advertising*, 1926

The field of advertising management is made up of a system of interacting organizations
and institutions, all of which play a role in the advertising process. At the core of this
system are advertisers, the organizations that provide the financial resources that support
advertising. Advertisers are private- or public-sector organizations that use mass media to
accomplish an organizational objective. It is the decision to invest resources in purchasing
time or space in such mass media as television, radio, newspapers, or magazines that
basically distinguishes advertisers from nonadvertisers. Advertisers make use of mass
media. Nonadvertisers do not.

Advertising management is heavily focused on the analysis, planning, control, and
decision-making activities of this core institution—the advertiser. The advertiser provides the overall managerial direction and financial support for the development of advertising and the purchase of media time and space, even though many other institutions
are involved in the process. A focal point is the development of an advertising program or
plan for the advertiser. In cases where several different kinds of products or services are
offered by the advertising organization, a separate program may be developed for each.
The resulting advertisement is usually aired or placed several times, and the resulting

schedule of exposures is referred to as an *advertising campaign*. The development and management of an advertising campaign associated with an advertiser's brand, product, or service is thus a major point of departure for advertising management.

In developing and managing an advertising campaign, the advertiser basically deals with numerous institutions, as Figure 1-1 illustrates. The advertising agency, the media, and the research suppliers are three supporting or *facilitating* institutions external to the advertiser's own organization. The agency and the research suppliers assist the advertiser in analyzing opportunities, creating and testing advertising ideas, and buying media time and space; the media, of course, supply the means by which to advertise. Others are, in effect, *control* institutions that interact with and affect the advertiser's decision-making activities in numerous ways. Government and competition are the two most important external control institutions. Most advertisers are affected by a wide range of government regulations concerning their products, services, and advertising. Direct or indirect competitors are usually present and serve as a major external control. What competitors do and how they react is thus an important part of advertising management.

The markets or consumers the advertiser is attempting to reach through advertising can be thought of as yet another kind of external institution that both facilitates and controls advertising. The concepts of *markets* and *consumers* will be used interchangeably to refer to any classification of individuals, organizations, or groups the advertiser is attempting to reach or "get a message to." Examples could be homemakers; electronic engineers; automobile dealers; voters; hospital patients; government officials; or other industrial, retail, government, or nonprofit organizations. Without an existing or potential target for advertising messages, the rationale for advertising would not exist. The consumer is a controlling force, mainly through a whole range of behavioral possibilities,

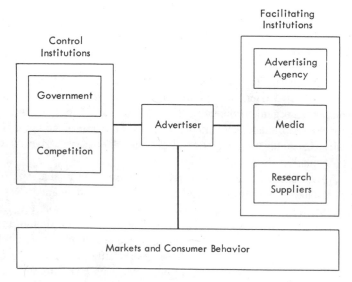

Figure 1-1.   Major institutions involved in the field of advertising management

such as viewing or not viewing, buying or not buying, voting or not voting, and so on. It is the consumer, in this broad sense, to whom advertising campaigns are directed, media are used, advertising agencies create copy, and upon whom advertising research is done. The identification and understanding of markets and consumer behavior is thus also a vital part of advertising management.

In this chapter, background information is presented on advertisers and on the three major facilitating institutions: advertising agencies, the media, and research suppliers. A discussion of several perspectives on the subject of advertising, including the one adopted in this book, follows. The balance of the book, from the perspectives of Figure 1-1, deals, in one way or another, with advertising planning and decision making in the context of markets, competition, and governmental constraints.

THE ADVERTISER

The advertiser is the core institution of the field of advertising management, and expenditures of advertisers provide the basis for estimates of the size of the advertising industry. Expenditures by all advertisers in all media (newspapers, magazines, business papers, television, radio, direct mail, outdoor billboards, and so on) were estimated to be $124 billion in 1989,[1] having increased by 342 percent in the 14-year period after 1975, when they were about $28 billion. Although inflation accounted for much of this growth, it is still impressive. One estimate is that by the year 2000, advertising expenditures in the United States will reach $320 billion and will exceed $780 billion worldwide.[2] It has been estimated that the level of advertising expenditures in the United States has remained stable at about 2.1 to 2.2 percent of gross national product (GNP) for about the last 50 years.[3]

The *Standard Directory of Advertisers*[4] lists 17,000 companies engaged in advertising in a typical year. Most are small, private, or nonprofit organizations utilizing broadcast or print media on a local basis in the immediate region or metropolitan area in which they are located. Even this large figure excludes public service advertisements (PSAs),[5] nonpaid advertisements by nonprofit organizations, and classified advertisements in local newspapers purchased by private citizens. Advertisers utilizing local media, although large in number, do not account for the majority of advertising expenditures. In 1989, for example, local advertising that largely reflects media use by small advertisers accounted for about 44 percent of all advertising expenditures, whereas national advertising, reflecting large-scale users, accounted for the remaining 56 percent.[6]

Small- and large-scale advertisers can be distinguished according to the degree to which they use the facilitating institutions shown in Figure 1-1. Private citizens and many local small-scale advertisers, for example, buy media time or space directly and do not use an advertising agency or the services of a research supplier. The typical large national advertisers will have one or more advertising agencies under contract and will buy numerous types of research services, as well as conduct research on their own. In general, they make full use of the system shown in Figure 1-1, whereas small-scale advertisers, for budgetary reasons, use only parts of the system. Although many of the case examples, models, and research techniques and results presented in this book focus on the full system, and are thus most directly applicable to large-scale advertisers, the underlying principles involved are equally applicable to any advertiser, large or small, profit or nonprofit, and so on.

Advertisers differ according to the markets they serve, the goods and services they produce, and the media they use. In the private sector, advertisers can be distinguished according to whether they are predominantly *consumer, industrial,* or *retail* advertisers. Consumer advertisers are those mainly involved in the manufacture of durable or nondurable goods and services for consumer markets. Industrial advertisers predominantly manufacture and market products for industrial markets, and retailers often advertise locally to attract store patronage. Many large firms, such as General Motors, Kraft General Foods, and Sears service more than one market, which makes attempts to classify advertisers on this basis less meaningful. The media-use distinctions, however, are comparatively clear-cut. Retail advertisers, particularly at the local level, use newspaper advertising extensively. Consumer goods and services advertisers make heavy use of television, radio, and consumer magazines. Industrial advertisers generally make heavy use of trade magazines, business papers, direct mail, and trade shows. Industrial advertising is basically different, because its audience is made up of professionals who are often more willing and able to accept and process detailed information than is an audience made up of members of households.

About 52 percent of all national advertiser expenditures is accounted for by 99 private corporations and the federal government.[7] Table 1-1 shows expenditures for 31 product and service categories in 1989, accounting for over $40 billion. The highest-spending

TABLE 1-1. Product and Service Categories Represented by Top 100 Advertisers, 1989 (millions of dollars)

Rank	Category	Expenditures	Rank	Category	Expenditures
1	Retail	6,028.7	16	Computers, office equipment	667.1
2	Automotive	5,519.9	17	Household equipment	620.9
3	Food	3,897.5	18	Soaps, cleansers	612.3
4	Business, consumer services	3,891.4	19	Sporting goods, toys	610.0
5	Entertainment	2,753.2	20	Jewelry, cameras	403.0
6	Toiletries, cosmetics	2,212.2	21	Building materials	379.7
7	Travel, hotels	2,133.1	22	Household furnishings	357.6
8	Drugs and remedies	1,604.9	23	Electronic entertainment	349.6
9	Beer, wine, and liquor	1,184.6	24	Gasoline, lubricants	341.2
10	Direct response companies	1,150.9	25	Pets, pet foods	275.2
11	Snacks and soft drinks	1,098.7	26	Horticulture and farming	245.7
12	Apparel, footwear	891.1	27	Freight, industrial	149.7
13	Insurance and real estate	868.9	28	Industrial materials	109.8
14	Publishing and media	763.2	29	Business propositions	36.4
15	Cigarettes, tobacco	675.1	30	Airplanes, aviation	18.1
			31	Miscellaneous	331.5
				Total	40,181.1

industries were retail, automotive, food, consumer services, entertainment, toiletries and cosmetics, travel and hotels, drugs and remedies, beer, wine and liquor, and snacks and soft drinks.

The top 10 national advertisers for 1989 are shown in Table 1-2. In 1989, they accounted for over $11 billion of advertising investment, or more than 32 percent of all expenditures of the leading 100 national advertisers, which were $34 billion. Philip Morris (including its subsidiary, Kraft General Foods) was the nation's largest private advertiser, investing over $2 billion in advertising that year. Procter & Gamble was the second biggest U.S. advertiser, spending $1.78 billion. (Outside the United States, Unilever and Nestlé are the other biggest spenders).[8] These are huge consumer packaged-goods companies, and their brands have huge budgets: Philip Morris spent $100 million that year on Marlboro cigarettes, $71 million on Maxwell House coffee, $64 million on Miller Lite beer, $52 million on various Kraft cheeses, and $31 million on Jell-O gelatins and puddings. Procter & Gamble, in turn, spent $90 million on Folgers coffee, $52 million on Tide detergent, $44 million on Oil of Olay, and $41 million on Crest toothpaste. As these figures suggest, mass-marketed consumer products require large advertising budgets.

Since consumer products are bought by virtually every household, most of their budgets are spent on television advertising: almost 60 percent of Philip Morris's advertising and almost 80 percent of Procter & Gamble's total budget went into television (national, spot, cable, and syndicated). Figure 1-2 shows an ad from a campaign for Nestlé. In contrast, a manufacturer of durable goods will typically be more inclined toward print media than will a manufacturer of packaged goods, because a durable product is more complex and requires longer and more detailed copy. Print advertising, especially newspapers, is also more used by retail advertisers. Sears, Roebuck, the third largest advertiser in 1989, spent $150 million in newspaper advertising. Whereas national advertising for retailers such as department stores or food chains is the exception, local advertising is vital. Much local retail advertising features item and price listings, but some retailers take

TABLE 1-2.   Top Ten National Advertisers in 1984 and 1989 (millions of dollars)

	1984			1989	
Rank	*Company*	*Expenditures*	*Rank*	*Company*	*Expenditures*
1	Procter & Gamble	872.0	1	Philip Morris	2,072.0
2	General Motors	763.8	2	Procter & Gamble	1,779.3
3	Sears, Roebuck	746.9	3	Sears, Roebuck	1,432.1
4	Beatrice Cos.	680.0	4	General Motors	1,363.8
5	R. J. Reynolds	678.1	5	Grand Metro PLC	823.3
6	Philip Morris	570.4	6	PepsiCo, Inc.	786.1
7	AT&T	563.2	7	McDonald's Corp.	774.4
8	Ford Motor Co.	559.4	8	Eastman Kodak	718.8
9	K Mart Corp.	554.4	9	RJR Nabisco	703.5
10	McDonald's Corp.	480.0	10	Kellogg	611.6
		6,468.2			11,064.9

Reprinted with permission for *Advertising Age,* September 26, 1985 and September 26, 1990. Copyright Crain Communications, Inc. All rights reserved.

Figure 1-2. An advertisement by a major consumer goods advertiser
Courtesy of Nestlé, Inc.

a broader view and emphasize store image. John Wanamaker, a retail executive in the early 1900s, was among the first to focus on store image, using such headlines as "The quality is remembered long after the price is forgotten."

Nonprofit organizations, such as schools, colleges, churches, hospitals, and libraries, are increasingly making use of local advertising. They have many of the same problems as business firms. They must identify the groups they serve, determine their needs, develop products and services to satisfy those needs, and communicate with their constituencies. This communication can often be done most effectively by advertising. National advertising is also increasing among nonprofit organizations, particularly for fundraising or behavior-change efforts by the major medical associations and such groups as Boy Scouts, Girl Scouts, and the United Way. The federal government was the 36th largest advertiser in 1989, spending $310 million. The largest governmental advertising effort, $100 million, was for military recruiting efforts for each branch of the military services. The postal service spent $45 million.

An interesting new form of advertising, called *advocacy advertising,* began about 1973. Business institutions take a public position on controversial issues of social importance, aggressively state and defend their own viewpoints, and criticize those of their opponents. For example, Mobil Oil ran an ad in the October 23, 1975, *Wall Street Journal* advocating the end of controls on oil.[9] Professional groups, like lawyers, also, for the first time, were legally allowed to advertise their services and thus became yet another type of advertiser.

There are thus dozens of different types of advertisers and an equally large number of forms of advertising, including national, local, consumer, industrial, service, comparative, cooperative, corrective, advocacy, counter, and public service advertising. Each is discussed in various sections of the book.

Role of the Brand Manager

It will be helpful to describe briefly the position of a brand manager because, for many large advertisers, both industrial and consumer, such a position is central to the development of advertising. The brand manager, either directly or through a staff advertising manager, makes the advertising policy decisions and interacts with the agency. The brand manager position has often been compared to the president's position in a small company. He or she is responsible for all marketing aspects of the brand and, internally, draws upon the full range of line and staff resources of the corporation. This includes such departments as sales, new product planning, marketing research, and so on. In many cases, the advertising budget is the most significant expenditure associated with marketing the brand. Externally, the brand manager usually represents the interests of just one brand and oversees the development of the advertising and marketing program for it.

In recent years some large client companies have moved away from traditional brand management organizational structures. Many companies that market multiple brands within the same product category have introduced a higher-level post of "category manager," a person who is responsible for supervising and coordinating the brand managers for individual brands and making sure that competition between the company's own brands does not become unproductive. In Procter & Gamble, for instance, brand managers for Tide and Cheer and other detergents report (through another organizational layer called ad managers) to the category manager for laundry products. The category managers are charged with overseeing personnel, sales, product development, advertising and promotion of their respective categories.[10]

The brand manager role is particularly important in the study of advertising management, even though it is not the only one for which the materials in this book are relevant. Basically, the concepts, models, and decision aids presented here are completely general, even though they are often presented from the viewpoint of a brand manager in a consumer packaged-goods organization. It should also be emphasized that they apply when the object of the advertisement is other than a packaged consumer product; it may be a service, a political candidate, or a government program; or the target of the communication may be other than a consumer, such as an organization, an industrial buyer, a voter, or a client of an organization.

A product or a specific version of a product—a brand—is thus a major reference point for the study of advertising management. We use the term "product" or the term "object" in a general sense throughout the book to refer to the reference point for advertising. It can be something tangible like Green Giant peas, a service like Allstate Insurance, or even an idea like "Just Say No" in an antidrug campaign. As noted, the organizational role most often used to identify the manager of day-to-day advertising operations in a great number of cases is that of brand manager.

FACILITATING INSTITUTIONS

All advertisers, by definition, use some form of media to accomplish organizational objectives. Where significant amounts of media expenditures are involved, the advertiser will also use the services of an advertising agency and one or more research suppliers. Together, these three types of institutions make up the primary facilitating institutions of advertising management. In this section, we present an overview of the role, nature, and scope of these three institutions. Much of the organizational dynamics of advertising management is best understood by observing the role of the facilitating institutions in relation to the advertiser, as shown in Figure 1-3.

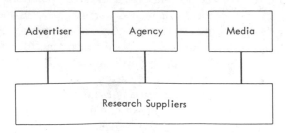

Figure 1-3.   Role of facilitating institutions

First, note that the advertising agency is represented in a position "between" the advertiser and the media. A major role of the advertising agency is the purchase of media time and space. The agency, on the one hand, is interacting with the advertiser and, on the other, with one or more media organizations. A second point to note is the role of research. Although not shown explicitly in Figure 1-3, most large firms, at each of the levels of advertiser, agency, and media, will have their own internal research departments, and each will also be purchasing research data externally from some outside research supplier. The research input to the system is a vital aspect on which many of the formal models, theories, and decision aids presented in this book are based.

Another insight from Figure 1-3 is that a typical advertising campaign evolves from the activities of a project or planning group composed of representatives of the advertiser, the agency, and one or more research suppliers. Basically, many meetings of this group will take place over the course of campaign development. Oral presentations of creative ideas and media plans will be made by the agency representatives. Similarly, research suppliers will make oral presentations on the results of a consumer survey, a copy test, and so on. Much written and telephone communication also takes place during this process.

In the previous section, it was suggested that the brand manager was the major representative of the advertiser's interests. The analogous positions at each of the three facilitating institution levels are the account executive for the agency, the media representative for media, and the project supervisor for research suppliers. Each level of the system is also represented by a professional trade association. For example, the Association of National Advertisers (ANA) represents advertiser interests; the American Association of Advertising Agencies (AAAA) serves the agency component; and associations like the National Association of Broadcasters (NAB), the American Newspaper Publishers Association (ANPA), the Magazine Publishers Association (MPA), the Direct Marketing Association (DMA), and the Outdoor Advertising Association of America (OAAA) serve the major media. The Advertising Research Foundation (ARF) is heavily concerned with the research aspects of the system.

The Advertising Agency

A unique aspect of advertising is the advertising agency, which, in most cases, makes the creative and media decisions. It also often supplies supportive market research and is even involved in the total marketing plan. In some advertiser-agency relationships, the agency acts quite autonomously in its area of expertise; in others, the advertiser remains involved in the creative and media decisions as the campaign progresses.

The first advertising agent, Volney B. Palmer, established an office in Philadelphia in 1841.[11] He was essentially an agent of the newspapers. For 25 percent of the cost, he sold space to advertisers in the various 1,400 newspapers throughout the country. He made no effort to help advertisers prepare copy, and the service he performed was really one of media selection. His knowledge of and access to the various newspapers were worth something to an advertiser.

Although the nature of an agency has changed considerably since Palmer's day, the fixed commission method of compensation is still the one used most often. The basic compensation for most agencies is a fixed percentage of advertising billings, 15 percent, which they receive from the media in which the advertisements are placed. On "noncommissionable" (nonmedia) services (such as preparing brochures and collateral materials), an agency usually marks-up the supplier's invoice cost by 17.65 percent, so that it still keeps 15 percent of the total cost to the client company (of every $100 paid by the client, if the agency keeps $15 and pays $85 to its supplier, it is keeping 17.65 percent of the 85). The fixed commission system has been criticized because it encourages the agency to recommend higher media budgets than may be appropriate, may not relate to the actual amount of work the agency does for the client, and is not linked to the success of the advertising campaign. Thus, many client companies (including IBM, General Foods, R. J. Reynolds, Nestlé/Carnation, and the German detergent giant Henkel) now either pay their agencies a fixed, negotiated dollar fee or some combination of commission and fee.[12] Many companies now also link the compensation to campaign performance, paying the agency a bonus (or a higher commission rate) if the campaign exceeds agreed-to communication goals.[13] The subject of how the success or failure of ad campaigns ought to be evaluated is discussed at length in Chapter 3.

By the turn of the century, agencies started to focus their attention on the creation of advertising for clients. Probably the first agency with a reputation for creative work was Lord and Thomas, which was blessed with two remarkable copywriters, John E. Kennedy and Claude Hopkins. Kennedy believed that advertising was "salesmanship in print" and always tried to provide a reason why people should buy the advertised goods. One of Kennedy's first tasks when he joined Lord and Thomas in 1898 was to recreate an advertisement for a new washer that had relied on the headline "Are you chained to the washtub?" appearing over a figure of a worn, disgruntled housewife shackled to a washtub.[14] Kennedy's advertisement showed a woman relaxing in a rocking chair while turning the crank of a washer. The copy emphasized the work of the ball bearings and the time and chapped hands the machine would save. The cost of the resulting inquiries decreased from $20 each to a few pennies.

Claude Hopkins, who joined Lord and Thomas in 1907, was regarded by many as the greatest creator of advertising who ever practiced the art. One year, soon after joining the firm, he made nearly $200,000 just writing copy.[15] He was particularly good at understanding the consumer and at integrating the advertising into the total marketing effort. His first account was Campbell's Pork & Beans.[16] He discovered, using his own research, that 94 percent of American housewives baked their own beans. Yet the advertisers of the day were focusing on the relative advantages of their own brands compared to competitors'. Hopkins' campaign argued against home baking, reminding housewives of the 16 hours involved in preparing the beans and the probability of ending up with crisp beans on top and mushy beans below. His "primary demand" appeal (getting people to buy the product—any brand) was enormously successful. In response to the competitive reaction, he boldly ran advertisements challenging consumers to "Try Our Rivals Too." He also secured distribution among restaurants and then advertised to the consumers the fact that restaurants had selected the Campbell brand. Hopkins knew the importance of developing an advertising program that was based on consumer desires. In his words, "Argue anything for your own advantage and people will resist to the limit. But seem unselfishly to consider your customers' desires and they will naturally flock to you."[17]

Hopkins also took on the task of advertising the company's evaporated milk, a new product for Campbell.[18] In introducing the brand, Hopkins used a technique on which he often relied. He offered to buy housewives a 10-cent can as an indication of his confidence in the brand. In a single newspaper advertisement that ran in New York for one day only, he inserted a coupon that could be redeemed at a retail store for one can of milk. His idea proved to be brilliant. It provided incentives for people to try the product without tarnishing its image, as a 50-cents-off coupon might have done. More important, it encouraged retailers to stock the brand to satisfy customer demands and to share in the profit represented by the offer. Entering a New York market dominated by another brand, the technique gained for Campbell 97 percent distribution practically overnight. More than 1,460,000 customers redeemed the coupon in the single New York advertisement. The $175,000 cost of the program was recovered in less than nine months, and Campbell captured the New York market.

The agencies grew in size and influence through the years as they demonstrated an ability to create effective advertising. Lord and Thomas grew from less than $1 million in billings in 1898 to more than $6 million in 1910 and to $14 million in 1924.[19] In 1989, Foote, Cone & Belding, the successor to Lord and Thomas, had worldwide billings of more than $3.414 billion.

Table 1-3 shows the top ten advertising agencies in 1989.[20] Billings represent media costs, whereas income is the money retained by the agency, generally around 15 percent of billings. The biggest agency on a worldwide basis in that year was the Japanese agency called Dentsu, with worldwide billings of over $10 billion. Young and Rubicam (Y&R)

TABLE 1-3.   Top Ten Advertising Agencies, 1989 (millions of dollars)

Rank[a]	Agency	World Billings	Gross World Income	Gross U.S. Income	Percent U.S.
1	Dentsu Inc.	10,063.2	1,316.4	NA	NA
2	Young & Rubicam	6,250.5	865.4	409.5	47.3%
3	Saatchi & Saatchi Worldwide	6,049.9	890.0	395.2	44.4%
4	Backer Spielvogel Bates Worldwide	5,143.2	759.8	310.7	40.9%
5	Ogilvy & Mather Worldwide	4,828.0	699.7	305.1	43.6%
6	McCann-Erickson Worldwide	4,772.3	715.5	209.1	29.2%
7	BBDO Worldwide	4,550.0	656.6	373.6	56.9%
8	Hakuhodo, Inc.	4,449.2	585.5	NA	NA
9	J. Walter Thompson Co.	4,407.5	626.4	266.5	42.5%
10	Lintas: Worldwide	3,957.6	593.3	224.9	37.9%

[a]Based on world billings.   NA—Not available.

was next biggest in billings, with over $6.2 billion. Y&R, the largest U.S.-based agency, employed 10,473 people in 1989, in 322 offices worldwide, with about 53 percent of its income being generated in countries outside the United States.

The decade of the 1980s saw a wave of acquisitions and mergers in the advertising agency business, leading to the creation of huge "megagroups." In 1989, for instance, the biggest megagroup was the WPP group, based in London, which acquired (among many others) the Ogilvy and J. Walter Thompson advertising agency groups. (Ogilvy, in turn, owned Scali, McCabe, Sloves, which itself owned Fallon McElligot and the Martin Agency.)[21] In addition to its advertising agency group holdings, WPP Group also owned direct marketing agencies, sales promotion agencies, public relations firms, marketing research companies, and specialized companies concentrating on health, entertainment, recruitment, and Yellow Pages advertising. In fact, while the WPP Group's 1989 advertising billings were over $10 billion, its total revenues (from all sources) were equivalent to $16 billion in billings. Other leading agency megagroups are Saatchi and Saatchi (which owns that agency, plus Backer Speilvogel Bates), the Interpublic Group (owning McCann-Erickson, Lintas-Campbell-Ewald, and Lowe Partners), and Omnicom (owning BBDO and DDB Needham).

There are several reasons for this wave of acquisitions and growth, and the consequent building of worldwide agency networks. First, most client companies are themselves merging, and growing substantially outside the United States, thus demanding larger agency office networks worldwide. Procter & Gamble, for example, already gets 40 percent of its business from outside the United States, a figure expected to grow to 60 percent by the year 2000. This focus on non-U.S. markets is due, in part, to the fact that population—and thus market size—is growing more rapidly outside the United States than within and the fact that the effect of advertising on sales is also greater outside the United States.[22] Such globalization is often accompanied by the growth of "global brands," with similar ad campaigns worldwide. The campaigns for Marlboro cigarettes and Dewar's Scotch whisky, for example, are very similar in concept around the world.[23] Not all brands and ad campaigns can be so standardized, however, and the reader is cautioned to be somewhat critical of the concept of "global marketing."[24]

When companies grow worldwide, the agencies that hope to have a client's business worldwide (or not at all) must therefore create worldwide servicing networks, by owning overseas agencies or creating partnerships with them. McCann-Erickson, for example, now has 144 agencies in 67 countries, and services Coca-Cola in almost all of these markets. It even has a global account director for Coca-Cola in New York, responsible for the agency's work on that account worldwide. In 1989, almost 39 percent of McCann-Erickson's total billings came from Europe, 13 percent from Asia and the Pacific, and 10 percent from Latin America. It should be noted that in addition to the client-derived "demand" for overseas growth, another reason for the agencies' overseas expansion is simply that advertising spending rates are higher overseas than in the United States, since the per capita base levels are usually lower overseas. The volume of total advertising spending outside the United States now roughly equals that in the United States.[25]

The second major reason for the creation of these megagroups is the realization that ad agencies and media advertising are only one part of a client's total communications and marketing mix, which also includes sales promotions, public relations, direct marketing, marketing to minorities, and so on. Since many of these other elements of the mix are, in fact, growing faster than advertising (with advertising dollars often being moved to sales promotions or direct marketing), it makes sense for companies to offer clients not simply media advertising capabilities but these other capabilities as well. The claim is that a client's total communications needs can be better coordinated and served if the client has all these different needs serviced by units of the same megagroup, an idea expressed by phrases such as "complete orchestration" or "the whole egg." Not many client companies appear to have bought into this claim, however, and it appears in hindsight that many of these agency megagroups might have overdiversified, leading to financial strains. The Saatchi & Saatchi group, for instance, which pioneered this concept, has had to sell off many of its holdings in 1989 and 1990. A schematic of the diversified agency megagroup WPP appears in Figure 1-4.

The third reason for the creation of agency holding groups that own several agency networks is to try and avoid account conflict. A client will almost never give an account to an agency that also services a competitor. It is hoped, however, that if the competitor's account is at one of a megagroup's agencies, a potential client will still consider the group's other agency networks, since the different agency networks are supposedly run autonomously.

Obviously, clients do not pick agencies on the basis of size, and servicing capabilities, alone. Creative reputations also matter a great deal. A survey of agency reputations was conducted for *Advertising Age* by SRI Research Center in the last quarter of 1984.[26] A random sample of 300 advertising directors of companies with revenues over $25 million a year selling to the top 20 U.S. markets was interviewed. Six attributes of the agency were identified as most important: (1) creativity, (2) account executives, (3) media, (4) top management, (5) marketing, and (6) research. J. Walter Thompson ranked first on five of the attributes, a reputation distinguished by its across-the-board strength. Ogilvy & Mather, Chiat/Day (now Chiat/Day/Mojo), and Doyle Dane Bernbach (now part of DDB Needham) were perceived as strongest on creativity.

This survey also identified factors considered most important in assessing the strengths of an agency, and those on which agencies were perceived as weak. Figure 1-5 shows the results. Creative talent and knowing the client's business were the two most important "necessary strengths" of an advertising agency. Quality of people was also very important. Not knowing client business, inadequate cost estimating, lack of creativity, poor account executives, and misrepresentation were most frequently mentioned as weak spots.

Agency Organization.   A modern agency employs three different types of people, in addition to those handling administration. The first is the creative services group, which includes copywriters, artists, and people concerned with advertising production. This group develops the advertising campaign, prepares the theme, and creates the actual advertisements. The second is the marketing services group, whose responsibility includes

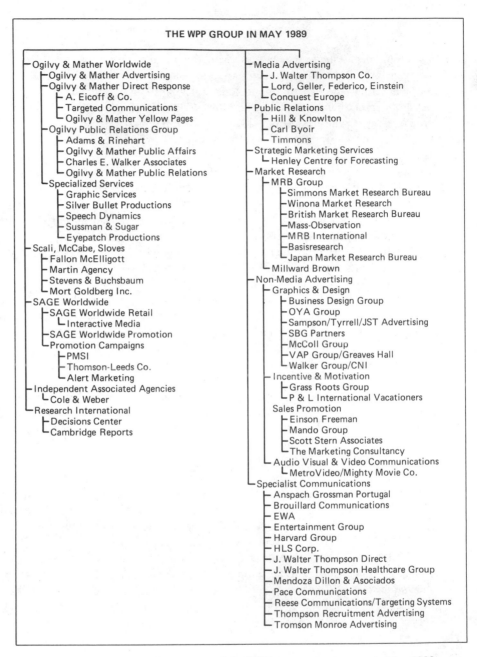

Figure 1-4. The different parts of the WPP agency megagroup, in May 1989

media and market research. This group contains the technical specialists—the psychologists who direct market research efforts and the operations researchers who develop the media buying models. The final major group is the client services group, including

Necessary Agency Strengths

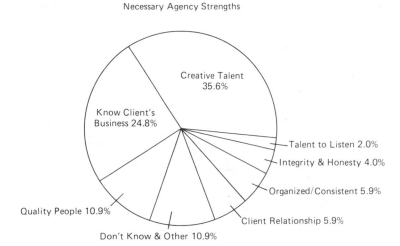

Agency Weaknesses

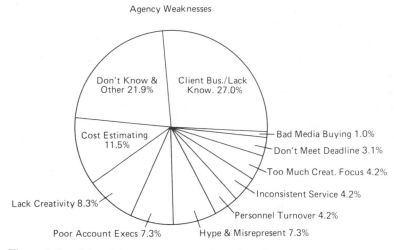

Figure 1-5. Advertising agency strengths and weaknesses

Reprinted with permission from the March 28, 1985 issue of *Advertising Age*. Copyright 1985 by Crain Communications, Inc. All rights reserved.

account executives. An account executive is, in many respects, an agency's counterpart to a client's brand manager. An account executive is responsible for contact with the client. One of his or her important functions is to understand and perhaps contribute to the development of the client's advertising objective and to communicate it to the creative service and marketing service groups. As the advertising campaign is developed, the account executive obtains advice and decisions from the client as they are needed. In addition to these operating groups, there is usually a review board consisting of key agency people who review all campaigns generated within the agency.

In recent years, several agencies have embraced another organizational innovation called "account planning," first developed in the United Kingdom. An account planner is a specialist in consumer attitudes and motivations, often relying on qualitative in-depth research, who works with the account and creative teams in ensuring that the campaign is built with a deep and thorough understanding of the consumer's point of view. In the United States, the Chiat/Day/Mojo agency, which is well known for its creativity, has championed this approach. It is more frequently used (and talked about) by smaller agencies, who wish to show that their creative leaps are also strategically sound. Many of the largest agencies do not have an explicit account planning function, though some of the same work is performed by research specialists working closely with the account; these people are often called "consumer insights" specialists.[27]

The Full-Service Agency and Alternatives.   The dominant type of agency provides a full spectrum of services, including market research, new product introduction plans, creative services, and media purchases, and is termed a *full-service agency.* Alternatives to the full-service agency for large advertisers have recently appeared. Basically, these involve the replacement of the large agency with smaller specialized organizations, perhaps supplemented by a greater in-house client involvement in the process. It is stimulated by the development of organizations that specialize in media purchases (such as Western International Media, or Vitt Media International, which keep about a 3 percent commission) and others that provide only creative services—the "creative boutiques." The perceived need to make advertising and media dollars work harder—by negotiating bigger media discounts and consolidating media buying, and by using smaller agencies that are sometimes perceived to be more creative than the larger ones—have led to these developments. Several client companies and advertising agencies have set up subsidiaries through which media buys are consolidated, and thus made more cheaply, while medium-sized advertising agencies often turn to external media buying companies to benefit from the negotiating clout of these companies.[28]

Magnavox is a firm that has had experience with à la carte buying of advertising services. A Magnavox executive explained the reasoning behind the move, pointing out that the new wave of à la carte advertisers seems to be eliminating many costs related to agency middleman functions, such as account management and marketing and research. Along with the elimination of the full-service agency's overhead factors, this probably knocks off at least one-third of the 15 percent commission that the agency normally collects. The advertiser should be able to obtain the needed services for the remaining 10 percent and, if it does some of the media buying internally, for print, it can come in under 10 percent. The 15 percent agency commission on ad production, research, and other functions that an agency buys outside is also saved.[29]

The American Association of Advertising Agencies has set forth a position paper in which it presents the case for the full-service agency, arguing against "piecemealing." They identified ten advantages of a full-service agency, including centralization of responsibility and accountability, simplified coordination and administration of a client's total advertising program, greater objectivity, sales-oriented creative work, synergistic experience, a stronger pool of talent, and a better working climate.

The Media

The amount of money spent on advertising in the various media from 1935 to 1989 is shown in Table 1-4. Through the years, the largest media category has been newspapers, which carried 26 percent of all advertising placed in 1989. The second largest medium in 1989 was television, which was nonexistent in 1945, with $27 billion. Direct mail was the third largest medium, with expenditures of $22 billion. Thus, direct mail, a medium with low visibility in many respects, garnered more than twice as much advertising revenue as did radio ($8.3 billion). The strength of direct mail is its potential for pinpointing an audience and its capacity to present large quantities of advertising. It is a rapidly growing medium, and we discuss it in detail in Chapter 10. Magazines represent another important medium. Business papers are primarily the trade magazines used by industrial advertisers and others who aim at nonconsumer audiences and, thus, for purposes of classification, could also be considered as magazines.

Media developments have dramatically influenced the thrust of advertising through the years. Perhaps the most significant contribution to advertising was the development of the printing press by Gutenberg in 1438. Forty years later, in 1478, William Caxton printed the first English language advertisement, a handbill for a book of rules for the clergy at Easter.[30] The printing press, of course, made possible newspapers and magazines, the print media on which most advertising still relies.

The first important medium was newspapers. The earliest agencies, in the midnineteenth century, were essentially agents for newspapers. They provided a classic wholesaling function for the newspapers, each of which was too small by itself to sell space directly to the national advertisers. To a large extent, newspapers, particularly the smaller ones, still employ agents to sell their space to national advertisers, although these agents are now organizations distinct from agencies. However, the newspaper is really the domain of the local merchant. More than 80 percent of newspaper advertising is placed at the local level, and the most important newspaper advertisers are local retailers. There were about 1,640 daily newspapers in the country in 1990, reaching 63 percent of all adults (and a higher percentage of those highly educated and with high incomes). The highest-circulation newspapers are *The Wall Street Journal* (1.9 million weekday circulation) and *USA Today* (1.3 million).[31]

For all the attention television has received, it is nevertheless interesting that advertising for television in 1989 was exceeded by newspaper advertising. Furthermore, although the total share of newspaper advertising has declined since the advent of television, the decline has only amounted to a few percentage points. This strength of newspapers comes from their dominant role in local advertising, especially retail.

During the last decades of the 1800s, magazines began to assume increasing importance. In that period, Lord and Thomas concentrated on religious and agricultural periodicals, becoming the exclusive agent for many of them. After the Civil War, a young space salesman, J. Walter Thompson, decided to focus on the general magazine field, particularly the just-emerging area of women's magazines.[32] He provided advertisers with a list of several dozen from which they could choose. His choice of emphasis partly explains the phenomenal early success of the agency that bears his name.

TABLE 1-4. Estimated Advertising Expenditures in Major Media, 1935–1989 (millions of dollars)

	1935	1945	1950	1955	1960	1965	1970	1975	1980	1984	1989
Newspapers	761	919	2,070	3,077	3,681	4,426	5,704	8,442	15,615	23,744	32,368
National	148	203	518	712	778	784	891	1,221	2,335	3,007	3,720
Local	613	716	1,552	2,365	2,903	3,642	4,813	7,221	13,280	20,737	28,648
Magazines	130	344	478	691	909	1,161	1,292	1,465	3,225	4,932	6,716
Business papers	51	204	251	446	609	671	740	919	1,695	2,270	2,763
Television	—	—	171	1,035	1,627	2,515	3,596	5,263	11,330	19,874	26,891
National[a]	—	—	116	810	1,347	2,129	2,892	3,929	8,365	14,819	18,949
Local	—	—	55	225	280	386	704	1,334	2,965	5,055	7,942
Radio	113	424	605	545	693	917	1,308	1,980	3,690	5,813	8,323
National	78	290	332	218	265	335	427	519	935	1,513	2,023
Local	35	134	273	327	428	582	881	1,461	2,755	4,300	6,300
Direct mail	282	290	803	1,299	1,830	2,324	2,766	4,124	7,655	13,800	21,945
Outdoor	31	72	142	192	203	180	234	335	610	872	1,111
Miscellaneous	342	555	1,122	1,793	2,342	2,985	3,848	5,571	10,795	16,775	23,813
Total National	890	1,740	3,260	5,380	7,305	9,340	11,350	15,340	30,435	49,590	68,990
Total local	830	1,100	2,440	3,770	4,655	5,910	8,200	12,820	24,315	38,490	54,940
Grand total	1,720	2,840	5,700	9,150	11,960	15,250	19,550	28,160	54,750	88,080	123,930

[a]The following is the breakdown for television, giving the expenditures for network, cable (national and nonnetwork), syndication, and national and local spot television for 1989:

Network	9,110
Cable (national)	1,197
Syndication	1,288
Spot (national)	7,354
Spot (local)	7,612
Cable (nonnetwork)	330
Total	26,891

Reprinted with permission for *Advertising Age*, April 30, 1980, Part 4, February 16, 1981, May 6, 1985, and May 14, 1990. Copyright Crain Communications, Inc. All rights reserved.

Until television arrived, magazines were the largest advertising medium. With the advent of television, the magazine industry, and particularly the mass-circulation magazines, began to feel the heavy pressure of competition. With the failure of such classic magazines as *The Saturday Evening Post, Look,* and finally *Life,* many began to question the long-term future of the magazine industry. Actually, magazines have considerable strength and vitality despite these visible setbacks. The year that the *Post* stopped publishing, 20 other magazines also merged or closed their doors, but more than 100 new ones appeared.[33] In 1950, magazine circulation was 140.2 per 100 population; 20 years later, it was 170.5 per 100 population and was still growing.[34]

The character of magazine publishing is changing, however. Despite the continued success of the *Reader's Digest* and *TV Guide,* whose circulations are each more than 16 million in 1990, it is a fact that magazines are becoming more specialized.[35] (In 1990, the highest-circulation magazine was actually *Modern Maturity,* with 20 million). Magazines today are aiming at special-interest groups and are often regional in scope. In 1990, there were about 2,100 consumer or farm magazines and about 4,900 business magazines.[36] (Note that media people usually refer to magazines as "books.") As a result of their specialization, the audience is often more specialized and the magazine is therefore desirable to an advertiser who is attempting to reach more specific audiences.

Magazines are innovating and attempting to capitalize on their physical contact with the audience to make their advertisements more effective.[37] Perfumed ink was used as early as 1957 for Baker's coconut in a *Better Homes & Garden* advertisement. Since then it has been used in advertisements for perfume, cologne, vodka, and soap. Recordings, such as Remington's "Music to Shave By," are included in advertisements. They are particularly effective in business advertisements that have a lengthy, detailed story to tell. Actual product samples have appeared in advertisements for Band-Aids, candy, facial tissues, and computer software. Catalogs and other booklets have been included in magazine advertisements. These and other innovations reflect the willingness of magazines to build on their strengths.

Radio emerged in 1922 as an exciting, new, advertising medium. Its coverage of the 1922 World Series established it dramatically as a unique communication medium. The 1930s and 1940s were the golden years of radio. Without the competition of television, the network programs from the soap operas to the major evening shows starring such luminaries as Jack Benny, Eddie Cantor, Fred Allen, and Bing Crosby caught and held the attention of the American people. With the advent of television, however, radio went into the doldrums. But in the 1960s, radio started to make a comeback, finding a useful niche for itself by providing entertainment, news, and companionship, particularly for those in a car or otherwise occupied outside the home. It seemed to serve a purpose in a mobile and restless society. Radio's revitalization has been achieved by such innovations as talk shows, the all-news format, and hard-rock programs, and by such technological innovations as transistors and the "Walkman," which make radios highly portable for people of all ages. Like magazines, radio has become more specialized as stations try to serve well-defined segments of the population. It has been particularly successful in developing a youth appeal. Like newspapers, it is a good medium for local advertisers, who provide radio with more than 60 percent of its advertising. In 1990 there were over 5,000 AM and

5,000 FM stations, plus about 1,700 noncommercial FM stations; while average radio stations only have a 1 percent share of local listenership, radio networks enable advertisers to reach 8 to 9 percent of all U.S. adults at any one time, and up to 75 to 80 percent cumulatively in a week.[38]

Television, delayed by World War II, began in the mid-1940s. In 1948, Milton Berle premiered his show, which was to dominate the ratings during the early years of commercial television. During the first decade of television, the advertiser usually sponsored and was identified with an entire program. This differs from the present practice of having several advertisers share a program. Advertisers were naturally attracted to this new medium because it provided an opportunity for presenting live demonstrations to large audiences. Television grew rapidly during the 1950s and 1960s. The number of homes with television sets in the top 50 markets increased from 6 million in 1950 to 30 million in 1960 and to 40 million in 1970.[39] Today, about 92 million of the 94 million U.S. homes can be reached by television, through the approximately 200 affiliates of each of the big three broadcast networks, the Fox network, and major cable channels like ESPN, CNN, WTBS, USA, Nickelodeon, MTV, and TNN. Each of these cable channels is now available in approximately 50 million TV homes.

The advent of cable television, pay television, video recorders, and video discs promises to bring to television the same level of specialized audiences that magazines now deliver. In 1990, cable TV was in approximately 58 percent of U.S. TV homes. One consequence of these new technologies is the relative decline of the three major television networks (ABC, CBS, and NBC), which have lost audience share to cable channels and independents in homes with cable TV. The network share declined from 91 percent in 1978 to 68 percent in 1989.[40] Another development has been the widespread use of remote control devices to "zap" commercials by switching TV channels whenever ads appear. These new technologies have thus moved us to the era of the "invited commercial," because viewers with the capability of bypassing commercials will only tend to watch commercials that are exceptionally entertaining, informative, or involving. Reaching this audience will require very different approaches to advertising creation and testing. These consequences are discussed at appropriate points later in the book.

Through other developing media technologies, including the ability to specifically "address" each cable TV home from the cable "head," the capability of offering programs to small special-interest audiences is slowly emerging. Further, these "addressable" cable systems are beginning to be tied into systems that, using grocery store checkout-lane scanner data, can create consumer data bases that bring together data on what every household saw in terms of advertising and then purchased in local stores. Clearly, these technologies might someday make possible some very sophisticated targeting of consumers, for it may be possible for advertisers to schedule ad exposures to only those consumers considered most important from either a retention or switching assessment. Also rapidly emerging are new developments in direct-to-home satellite transmission, with the ultimate prospect of reaching world audiences using visual approaches that are not tied to any particular language.

Like the top advertisers and top advertising agencies, there are top media companies. An important characteristic of the media industry is that most of the leading companies are diversified and are large multinational conglomerates spanning all forms of media. Many of them also have significant revenues generated from nonmedia sources as well. These worldwide media giants include Time-Warner, with $8.7 billion in revenues in 1989; this conglomerate owns, among others, magazines like *People* and *Sports Illustrated*, Home Box Office and Warner Amex Cable, Warner books and Warner records, Time-Life books, and the Warner Brothers movie studio. Other companies include the Germany-based Bertelsmann, Italy's Fininvest, Canada's Thompson, Australia's News Corporation (which owns *TV Guide* and Fox broadcasting in the United States), France's Hachette, and the United Kingdom's Maxwell Corporation.

Table 1-5 shows the top ten leading media companies in the United States in 1989, using figures available before the Time-Warner merger. The biggest company was Capital Cities/ABC, with almost $5 billion in U.S. media revenues in 1989. The other two big broadcast networks (CBS and GE's NBC) are also represented in the top five. To understand the media industry, it is important to appreciate that newspapers still dominate all other media in terms of revenue. Among the top ten media companies in 1989, for example, four own mostly newspapers (Gannett, Times Mirror, Advance, and Knight-Ridder). The importance of magazines is reflected in the top group by the Time magazine group of Time-Warner, publisher of *Time* magazine, as well as *Fortune, Life, Money, People,* and *Sports Illustrated.*

Various types of sales promotions can also be considered by the advertiser and represent yet another kind of media. The sales promotion industry has grown rapidly in recent years, faster than advertising expenditures; in 1987, about 65 percent of the total advertising/promotion budgets of packaged goods companies was spent on consumer and trade promotions and only 35 percent in advertising.[41] Like the major media, each form of promotional activity is represented by a professional trade association. Thus, the Promotion Marketing Association of America (PMAA) and the National Premium Sales Executive Association (NPSEA) focus on premiums, promotions, contests, couponing, sampling, price-offs, and cash refunds; the Point-of-Purchase Advertising Institute (POPAI) covers point-of-purchase and aisle display materials; the Specialty Advertising Association International (SAAI) is concerned with specialty advertising, such as imprinted business cards and gifts; and the Trade Show Bureau (TSB) with trade shows. Direct mail, represented by the Direct Marketing Association, is also often included in this category.

Research Suppliers

The final type of facilitating institution is made up of companies that supply research services to advertisers, advertising agencies, and the media. Currently, there are more than 500 firms in the United States[42] that supply all kinds of research information for advertising-planning purposes and for specific decisions, such as copy and media decisions.

The first advertising researchers developed methods for assessing the effectiveness of print advertising. From these early beginnings, research companies have sprung up to provide a wide variety of services to advertisers, ranging from consumer surveys

TABLE 1-5. Top Ten Media Companies, 1989

Rank	Company	Total	1989 MEDIA REVENUES (MILLIONS)					1988-1989 % Change
			Newspaper	Magazine	Broadcast	Cable TV	Other	
1	Capital Cities/ABC, New York	$4,767.0	$ 490.0	$ 376.1	$3,584.9	$ 315.1		3.9%
2	Time Warner, New York	4,575.0		1,855.0		2,720.0		10.5
3	Gannett Co., Arlington, Va.	3,518.2	2,852.0		408.3		$257.9	6.1
4	General Electric, Fairfield, Conn.	3,392.0			3,392.0			−6.8
5	CBS Inc., New York	2,959.9			2,959.9			6.6
6	Advance Publications, Newark, N.J.	2,881.7	1,745.0	841.9		294.8		8.5
7	Times Mirror Co., Los Angeles	2,807.1	2,065.9	305.9	102.8	332.5		4.8
8	TCI, Denver	2,353.0				2,353.0		38.0
9	Knight-ridder, Miami	2,261.8	1,988.4				273.4	8.9
10	News Corp, Sydney	2,203.0	284.0	713.0	700.0		506.0	30.9

Reprinted with permission for *Advertising Age*, June 25, 1990. Copyright Crain Communications, Inc. All rights reserved.

and panels to copy testing, audience measurement, and many others.[43] The progress of the field of advertising research closely parallels the development of each of the major media. The Audit Bureau of Circulations (ABC) was one of the earliest firms to develop the first audits of newspaper circulation in 1914. The notion of auditing circulation quickly spread to magazines, and Daniel Starch, a professor at Harvard University, developed the recognition method for measuring magazine readership in 1919. Later, in 1932, Starch founded the firm of Daniel Starch and Staff, which is still one of the largest supplier firms providing research on print advertising. It is now called Starch INRA Hooper.

Radio research, and broadcast ratings in general, first began in the 1920s, when Archibald Crossley started the Crossley Radio Ratings. The industry expanded greatly during the 1930s and 1940s, as politicians and advertisers realized the potential of radio for reaching national audiences. Frank Stanton, later to become president of CBS, began his career in radio research and, with Paul Lazarsfeld and others, initiated an office of radio research at Princeton University. Lazarsfeld later moved this office to Columbia University to form the Bureau of Applied Social Research.

Television research became one of the numerous specialties of the A. C. Nielsen Company, and it is particularly well known for its television program rating services. A. C. Nielsen, Sr., who founded the company in Chicago, began by developing auditing services of the movement of products through retail stores. This service is an important part of the current range of research services supplied by this company. A. C. Nielsen has become by far the largest research supplier, with $950 million in research revenues in 1989, followed by IMS International, Arbitron/SAMI/Burke, and Information Resources, Inc (IRI). Nielsen's operations extend into many foreign countries, and over 50 percent of its research revenues are generated from operations outside the United States.[44] Table 1-6 shows the largest U.S. research companies in 1989 and their research revenues. Most of the firms shown on the list provide data for advertising planning, implementation, and control purposes. Nielsen, Arbitron, IMS International, and IRI offer syndicated services to which advertisers subscribe on an ongoing basis.

Some companies tend to specialize in either copy testing (ad testing is commonly called copy testing even though it is the whole advertisement that is usually tested, not just the copy) or audience measurement, and provide information most useful for copy and media decision making. In broadcast, Burke Marketing Services, ASI Market Research, ARS, McCollum/Spielman, and the Gallup Organization are well known for their copy-testing services. Among the better known copy-testing services for print advertisements are those of Starch INRA Hooper. Concerning audience measurement, A. C. Nielsen and Arbitron are most prominent in broadcast. Simmons Market Research Bureau is one of the leaders in print audience measurement. Dozens of specialized services, such as Pulse and BAR (Broadcast Advertisers Reports, which monitors advertiser spending rates), are available for media planners. In print, ABC provides basic circulation and other data for magazines and newspapers, and BPA (Business Publications Audit) provides similar information for business, technical, and trade papers. SRDS (Standard Rate and Data Service), Simmons, and MRI (Mediamark Research, Inc.) provide very useful information on all media. Information Resources represents one of the newer forms of

TABLE 1-6. Top Ten Research Companies, 1989[a]

RANK			Research Revenues (Millions)	1988–1989 Percent Change	Research Revenues From Outside U.S. (Millions)
1989	1988	Company			
1	1	Nielsen	$ 950.0	7.5%	$532.0 est.
2	2	IMS International, Inc.	390.0	6.8	214.5 est.
3	3	The Arbitron Co.	238.0	1.7	
4	4	Information Resources, Inc.	136.4	15.9	22.6
5	7	Westat, Inc.	65.7	2.2	
6	8	M/A/R/C, Inc.	53.3	4.3	
7	10	Maritz Marketing Research	46.1	13.6	
8	6	MRB Group, Inc.	44.6	21.3	
9	9	NFO Research, Inc.	43.1	5.4	
10	11	Market Facts, Inc.	39.1	3.4	
		Total	$2,006.3	8.2	$769.1

[a]For some companies, total revenues that include nonresearch activities are significantly higher than those shown in the table. Percent change from 1988 has been adjusted so as not to include revenue gains from acquisition.

Source: Adapted from Jack J. Honomichl, "The Honomichl 50," *Marketing News,* Vol. 24, no. 11, May 28, 1990, p. H4.

marketing research based on supermarket checkout scanners. Their service, called BehaviorScan, has grown rapidly and has now attracted competing companies.

Market research is a significant industry in the United States and is the source of much of the information used in advertising management. Throughout the book, we will show how research information enters at various stages of advertising management and discuss specific services in more detail. Here it is important to gain an initial impression of the diversity and range of such services and to appreciate the importance of their role in advertising management.[45]

PERSPECTIVES ON ADVERTISING

There is an extensive literature on advertising, made up of books, monographs, reports, journal articles, and speeches, most of which have been written since the turn of the century. David A. Revzan of the University of California lists more than 450 books on the subject of advertising written between 1900 and 1969.[46] There are at least six advertising handbooks, eight histories, and several biographical accounts of advertising people. Among recent such assessments are Stephen Fox's *The Mirror Makers* and Eric Clark's *The Want Makers.*[47]

In addition to handbooks and historical perspectives, advertising has been approached through a variety of paths and traditions. These different paths partly reflect the perspectives of such various disciplines as economics, psychology, social philosophy, and management. They also reflect the needs of the audiences to which they are addressed.

Although many of the paths cross and some are ill defined, it is possible and useful to identify some of the main tracks that have been followed through the years.

Several books with an economic perspective, including Roland Vaile's *Economics of Advertising*, were published in the 1920s.[48] The depression of the 1930s increased public concern with the role advertising plays in our competitive economic system. Critics argued that advertising inhibits competition. In this environment, Harvard professor Neil Borden published a classic study of the economic effects of advertising.[49] The evaluation of advertising as an economic force in society has continued to receive attention over the years. A recent book in this tradition is Julian Simon's *Issues in the Economics of Advertising*.[50] The economic perspective tends to deal with aggregate statistics of firms and industries and is concerned with public policy implications.

The writings of sociologists, religious leaders, philosophers, and politicians are also extensive, many reflecting critical views of advertising. Thus, in 1932, Arthur Kallet and F. J. Schlink published *100,000,000 Guinea Pigs*, followed by such works as A. S. J. Basker's *Advertising Reconsidered* in 1935, H. K. Kenner's *The Fight for Truth in Advertising* in 1936, Blake Clarke's *The Advertising Smoke Screen* in 1944, F. P. Bishop's *The Ethics of Advertising* in 1949, and later works like Vance Packard's *The Hidden Persuaders*, Francis X. Quin's *Ethics, Advertising and Responsibility,* and Sidney Margolius's *The Innocent Consumer vs. the Exploiters*.[51] Advertising is a controversial subject about which scholars, intellectuals, and businesspeople tend to form strong and often contradictory opinions.[52]

Another approach to advertising, descriptive in nature, typifies the introductory texts covering the principles of advertising that have appeared from the early 1900s to the present time. They describe such institutions of advertising as advertising agencies and the various media, often from an historical perspective. The relative importance and the operation of these institutions is of central interest. Books of this type often also describe in some detail the physical process of creating advertising—the selection of type faces, the production process, and other practical particulars. The descriptive approach generally focuses on what advertising is in a macro sense and how it works at a detailed level.

Behavioral approaches to advertising can be traced to Walter Dill Scott's 1913 book, *The Psychology of Advertising*.[53] Since then, there has been a steady stream of books firmly tied to the behavioral disciplines, such as D. Lucas and C. E. Benson's *Psychology for Advertisers* in 1930 and, more recently, Edgar Crane's *Marketing Communications*.[54] This approach is largely concerned with the analysis of the communication process, using behavioral science theory and empirical findings. The interest in motivation research in the 1950s and consumer buyer behavior in the 1960s provided impetus to this area of thought. During the past decade, in particular, an enormous amount of progress has been made in using theories and models from psychology, social psychology, and sociology to help understand buyer behavior, the communication process, and the link between the two.

The research tradition in advertising parallels the development of the various media research services discussed earlier. It has also done much to motivate academic work on basic advertising research and studies of advertising effectiveness.

The managerial tradition is really more recent in origin. Perhaps the first book truly devoted to the subject of advertising management was a case book by Neil Borden and Martin Marshall, *Advertising Management: Text and Cases,* published in 1950 and revised in 1959.[55] This book, and the others that followed, approached the subject from the viewpoint of a manager faced with the tasks of preparing an advertising budget, deciding how to allocate funds to different media, and choosing among alternative copy strategies. These books were thus decision oriented and provided a contrast to the principles approach, in which the nature and role of advertising institutions and advertising techniques tended to be the point of emphasis.

Still another approach to advertising, even more recent in origin, is the model-building perspective originating from the fields of operations research and statistics. Although it had early predecessors, it really began in the late 1950s with the development of decision models concerned with allocating the media budget.

The Approach of This Book

This book, like others, will touch on all these traditions, although its main thrust is really to blend the last four. The managerial perspective will largely motivate the book. The focus is on decision making, specifically those decisions that generate an advertising campaign. The book involves an attempt to analyze and structure systematically the various decision areas within advertising and to present material that shows promise of helping decision makers generate better alternatives and improve their decision-making process.

In doing this, the book will draw heavily on the models and theories that have originated from the behavioral disciplines and the more quantitative models that have emerged from operations research and statistics and the research techniques and approaches that underlie each. Our goal will be to extend and organize these models in such a way as to reveal their potential utility to decision makers.

SUMMARY

There are four major advertising institutions with which the reader should be familiar: the advertiser, the advertising agency, the media, and the research suppliers. There is a wide variety of advertisers. Those who are classified as national advertisers spend the largest share of advertising dollars. The balance is spent by local advertisers. Advertisers can also be distinguished by the product type with which they are involved: consumer packaged goods, consumer durables, retail stores, or industrial products, for example.

In most cases, an advertising agency actually creates the advertisements and makes the media-allocation decisions. For this service, it receives from the various media 15 percent of the advertising billings it places. During the 1980s, advertising agencies underwent a wave of acquisitions and mergers leading to the creation of huge megagroups. Reasons for this trend include the high number of mergers in client firms, the rise in other communications mix activities like promotions and direct mail, and the need to reduce client conflict.

Media developments have dramatically influenced the thrust of advertising through the years. The printing press made possible newspapers and magazines, the major media before the advent of the broadcast media, television and radio. Radio in 1922 and television in 1948 provided a new dimension to advertising and sparked a period of growth. Despite the competition of the broadcast media, newspapers continue to be the largest medium, with more than $32 billion in advertising revenues in 1989. Television was second with almost $27 billion, followed by direct-mail advertising's nearly $22 billion. The advent of cable television, pay television, video recorders, and video discs promises to bring television the same level of specialized audiences that magazines now deliver. Increased competition in television has also cut deeply into market share of the major television networks. A wide and diverse group of new telecommunication technologies is having a major impact on broadcast and print media.

Modern advertising management is heavily involved with research, and a sizable industry of research supplier firms has grown up to serve the needs of advertisers, agencies, and the media. Today, over a billion dollars is spent annually on marketing and advertising research, and specialized services associated with each of the major media.

Since the turn of the century, hundreds of books on advertising have been published, most of which can be categorized into different writing traditions. Some are historical and others descriptive in their orientation; still others represent the perspectives of economists, social philosophers, managers, behavioral scientists, and quantitative model builders. As with past editions, this edition of *Advertising Management* is motivated by the managerial perspective, the creative tasks and managerial decisions that generate new advertising campaigns, or guide the management of ongoing campaigns. The book also draws heavily on research and models originating in both the behavioral and quantitative disciplines. A major purpose is to integrate these two model-building traditions to enhance their power and relevance to advertising decision makers.

DISCUSSION QUESTIONS

1. Advertisers are defined as organizations that make use of mass media, whereas nonadvertisers do not. Are there any exceptions to this definition? In what other ways might advertisers and nonadvertisers be distinguished?

2. How will the role of advertising differ when the product involved is a consumer packaged product instead of a consumer durable? How will it differ for a retailer and an industrial advertiser? What part of the marketing program will advertising be assigned to in each case?

3. What similarities and differences would there be between the development of an advertising campaign for the Ford Foundation or the Forestry Service and Procter & Gamble or General Motors?

4. Consider the major institutions of advertising management given in Figure 1-1. Are there others that should be included? Write a brief statement explaining the primary roles of each institution.

5. Do you believe that a company like Procter & Gamble should develop its own in-house agency, thereby keeping the 15 percent commission?

6. What are some of the consequences of the significant number of advertising agency mergers in the 1980s? Discuss and give examples to support your arguments.

7. Examine Table 1-4 for media trends. Why did outdoor media decline between 1955 and 1965? What is its likely future now? Why did total advertising expenditures increase so dramatically in 1950 and again in 1955 and 1984? Why did radio decline in 1955?

8. Consumers will soon be able to purchase prerecorded videodiscs and engage in two-way communications via cable television systems. What are some of the implications of these developments for advertisers?

9. Critics of advertising often wonder why certain advertisements are used. Outline the major research studies and research supplier services that would be involved in developing a major national campaign.

10. Consider the different perspectives on advertising. For each, try to determine what would be regarded as the key issues. What types of experimental evidence would be of the greatest interest to each?

11. What are some of the advertising issues associated with global branding? Discuss the pros and cons of family branding from a global, international perspective.

12. Concerning selecting an advertising agency, what agency attributes would you consider most important in picking an agency for a new Honda sports car?

NOTES

1. *Advertising Age,* September 26, 1990, p. 8.

2. Robert J. Coen, "Vast U.S. and Worldwide Ad Expenditures," *Advertising Age,* November 13, 1980, p. 10.

3. Seymour Banks, "Cross-national Analysis of Advertising Expenditures: 1968–1979," *Journal of Advertising Research,* April/May 1986, pp. 11–24.

4. *Standard Directory of Advertisers* (Skokie, IL: National Register Publishing Company). This directory, one of the so-called Red Books, is published annually by National Register, a subsidiary of Standard Rate and Data Service, and is a very useful reference to information on advertisers. A companion volume is *Standard Directory of Advertising Agencies.* Another useful reference to all aspects of the advertising industry is "Twentieth Century Advertising and the Economy of Abundance," *Advertising Age,* April 30, 1980.

5. The term PSA generally refers to advertisements sponsored by the Advertising Council, Washington, D.C., for federal government and other nonprofit organizations. There are, however, significant numbers of public service announcements donated by media at the local level. None of this national or local advertising activity enters into estimates of the size of the advertising industry given here.

6. *Advertising Age*, May 14, 1990, p. 12.

7. *Advertising Age*, September 26, 1990, p. 8.

8. *Advertising Age*, December 4, 1989, p. S-2.

9. For a book on the subject, see S. P. Sethi, *Advocacy Advertising and Large Corporations* (Lexington, MA: D. C. Heath, 1977).

10. *Advertising Age,* September 25, 1989, p. 6.

11. Maurice J. Mandell, *Advertising* (Englewood Cliffs, NJ: Prentice Hall, 1968), p. 24.

12. *Advertising Age,* May 1, 1989, p. 20.

13. *Business Week,* July 4, 1988, p. 66.

14. Albert Lasker, *The Lasker Story* (Chicago: Chicago Advertising Publications, 1963), pp. 29–31.

15. Claude C. Hopkins, *My Life in Advertising* (Chicago: Chicago Advertising Publications, 1966), p. 172.

16. Ibid., pp. 101–105.

17. Ibid., p. 102.

18. Ibid., pp. 106, 111.

19. Lasker, *The Lasker Story,* p. 38.

20. *Advertising Age,* March 28, 1985, p. 1.

21. *Advertising Age,* May 22, 1989, p. 72.

22. John U. Farley, ''Are There Truly International Products—and Prime Prospects for Them?'' *Journal of Advertising Research,* October/November 1986, pp. 17–20.

23. *Advertising Age,* August 14, 1989.

24. Kamran Kashani, ''Beware the Pitfalls of Global Marketing,'' *Harvard Business Review,* September/October 1989, pp. 91–98.

25. *Advertising Age,* March 6, 1989, p. 4.

26. *Advertising Age,* March 28, 1985.

27. *Advertising Age,* December 11, 1989, p. 28.

28. *Advertising Age,* August 6, 1990, p. 6.

29. ''Advertising That Comes à La Carte,'' *Business Week,* May 1, 1971, p. 46.

30. Mandell, *Advertising,* p. 24.

31. *Leo Burnett Media Costs and Coverage Guide,* 1990.

32. *Advertising Age,* December 7, 1964, p. 32.

33. *Advertising Age,* October 20, 1969, p. 50.

34. *Advertising Age,* April 30, 1980, p. 270.

35. Ibid.

36. *Leo Burnett Cost Guide,* 1990.

37. *Advertising Age,* October 20, 1969, p. 184.

38. *Leo Burnett Cost Guide,* 1990.

39. Ibid., p. 66.

40. *Advertising Age,* April 24, 1989, p. 2.

41. Robert C. Blattberg and Scott A. Neslin, *Sales Promotion: Concepts, Methods and Strategies* (Englewood Cliffs, NJ: Prentice Hall, 1990), p. 13.

42. For information on the marketing and advertising research supplier industry, see *Bradford's Directory of Marketing Research Agencies and Management Consultants in the U.S. and the World* (Fairfax, VA, biennial) and *International Directory of Marketing Research Houses and Services,* published by the New York Chapter of the American Marketing Association. Other useful information is contained in the *Roster of the American Marketing Association.* Recent marketing research texts also provide useful listings. See Donald R. Lehmann, *Market Research and Analysis* (Homewood, IL: Richard D. Irwin, 1979), pp. 138–148 and 161–171, and John G. Myers, William F. Massy, and Stephen A. Greyser, *Marketing Research and Knowledge Development* (Englewood Cliffs, NJ: Prentice Hall, 1980), pp. 101–166.

43. See *Advertising Age,* April 24, 1978.

44. *Advertising Age,* June 5, 1989, p. S-4.

45. See *Advertising Age,* March 17, 1984, pp. M-17ff.

46. David A. Revzan, *Marketing Bibliography,* Parts I and II (Berkeley: University of California Press, 1959). Supplement 1 published 1963; Supplement 2 published 1970.

47. Stephen Fox, *The Mirror Makers* (New York: Vintage Books, 1985); Eric Clark, *The Want Makers* (New York: Penguin Books, 1988).

48. Roland S. Vaile, *The Economics of Advertising* (New York: Ronald Press, 1927).

49. Neil H. Borden, *The Economic Effects of Advertising* (Homewood, IL: Richard D. Irwin, 1942).

50. Julian L. Simon, *Issues in the Economics of Advertising* (Urbana: University of Illinois Press, 1970).

51. Arthur Kallet and F. J. Schlink, *100,000,000 Guinea Pigs* (New York: Vanguard Press, 1932); A. S. J. Basker, *Advertising Reconsidered* (London: P. S. King and Son, 1935); H. K. Kenner, *The Fight for Truth in Advertising* (New York: Roundtable Press, 1936); Blake Clarke, *The Advertising Smoke Screen* (New York: Harper & Row, 1944); F. P. Bishop, *The Ethics of Advertising* (London: Robert Hale, 1949); Vance Packard, *The Hidden Persuaders* (New York: David McKay, 1957); Francis X. Quin, *Ethics, Advertising and Responsibility* (Rome, NY: Canterbury Press, 1963); and Sidney Margolius, *The Innocent Consumers vs. the Exploiters* (New York: Trident Press, 1967).

52. For a business perspective, see Francesco M. Nicosia, *Advertising, Management, and Society: A Business Point of View* (New York: McGraw-Hill, 1974).

53. Walter Dill Scott, *The Psychology of Advertising* (Boston: Small Maynard and Co., 1913).

54. D. Lucas and C. E. Benson, *Psychology for Advertisers* (New York: Harper & Bros., 1930), and Edgar Crane, *Marketing Communications,* 2nd ed. (New York: John Wiley, 1972).

55. Neil H. Borden and Martin V. Marshall, *Advertising Management: Text and Cases,* rev. ed. (Homewood, IL: Richard D. Irwin, 1959).

2

ADVERTISING PLANNING AND DECISION MAKING

Plans are nothing, planning is everything.

Dwight D. Eisenhower

Chapter 1 presented a broad view of the field of advertising management. The advertiser component is the core of the system, and many of the perspectives in this chapter and the balance of the book reflect the advertiser viewpoint. The person most responsible for advertising management in the marketing division of the client company is typically the brand manager, who works with the account executives from the advertising agency. However, the relevant titles will vary by organizational context, and we will henceforth use the more general term, advertising manager.

The major activities of advertising management are planning and decision making. In most instances, the advertising manager will be involved in the development, implementation, and overall management of an advertising plan. The development of an advertising plan essentially requires the generation and specification of alternatives. The alternatives can be various levels of expenditure, different kinds of objectives or strategy possibilities, and numerous kinds of options associated with copy creation and media choices. The essence of planning is thus to find out what the feasible alternatives are and reduce them to a set on which decisions can be made. Decision making involves choosing from among the alternatives. A complete advertising plan really reflects the end results of the planning and decision-making process and the decisions that have been arrived at in a particular product and market situation.

This chapter presents a framework for advertising planning and decision making. It is an elaboration of the advertising system model given in Chapter 1 and expands the advertiser component.

PLANNING FRAMEWORK

The major internal and external factors involved in advertising planning and decision making are shown in Figure 2-1. Internally, situation analysis, the marketing program,

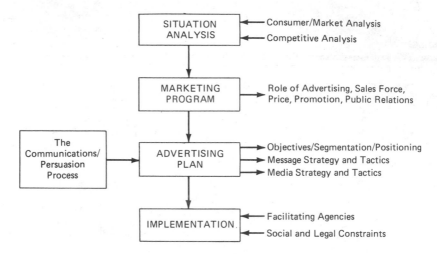

Figure 2-1. Framework for advertising planning and decision making

and the advertising plan are key considerations. As suggested in the diagram, the three legs of advertising planning concern objective setting and target market identification, message strategy and tactics, and media strategy and tactics. However, this advertising plan should flow from (1) the overall marketing program, which places the advertising plan in the context of the other marketing elements (for instance, sales force effort, pricing policies, etc.), and (2) a more general, conceptual understanding of how advertising "works." The marketing plan itself should be developed in response to a situation analysis, based on research. Once developed, the advertising plan has to be implemented as an advertising campaign, in the context of social and legal constraints and with the involvement of various facilitating agencies.

The balance of this chapter addresses each of these factors. First, situation analysis is explained and discussed. Then a brief review of the marketing program and the major parts of the advertising plan is given. This is followed by sections on social and legal constraints and facilitating agencies.

SITUATION ANALYSIS

The planning and decision-making process begins with a thorough analysis of the situation facing the advertiser. Situation analysis involves an analysis of all important factors operating in a particular situation. In many cases, this means that new research studies will be undertaken as well as relying on company history and experience.

AT&T, for example, developed a new strategy for its long-distance telephone services based on five years of research.[1] The research encompassed market segmentation studies, concept testing, and a large-scale field experiment. The field experiment focused on testing a new advertising campaign called "Cost of Visit." An existing "Reach Out" campaign, although successful, did not appear to get through to a large group of people who had reasons to call but were limiting their calls because of cost. Research based on annual surveys of 3,000 residential telephone users showed that most did not know the cost of a long-distance call or that it was possible to make less expensive calls in off-peak periods. Five copy alternatives were subsequently developed and tested, from which "Cost of Visit" was chosen. This campaign was credited with persuading customers to call during times that were both cheaper for them and more profitable for AT&T and, overall, was more effective than the "Reach Out" campaign. One estimate was that by switching $30 million in advertising from "Reach Out" to "Cost of Visit," an incremental gain in revenue of $22 million would result in the first year and would top $100 million over five years.

This example highlights a "situation" in which advertising was undoubtedly a major factor, extensive research was done to study the situation, and large sums of money were involved in both research and advertising. A complete situation analysis will cover all marketing components and involve finding answers to dozens of questions about the nature and extent of demand, competition, environmental factors, product, costs, distribution, and the skills and financial resources of the firm. Table 2-1 provides a listing of topics and relevant questions that need to be answered for each topic.

Situation analysis invariably involves research of some kind. As noted in Table 2-1, for advertising planning and decision making, the principal thrust of research efforts will be on market analysis or, more broadly, the analysis of consumer motivation and behavior with respect to the product, service, idea, or object to be advertised. It is this kind of research that is most important in advertising, and many of the research approaches, techniques, models, and results presented throughout the book pertain to it. Situation analysis can be based on conventional wisdom, managerial experience, or the creative team's inherent imaginative abilities, but current market and environmental conditions—what the situation is now—can only be adequately assessed by research. Such research flows from the company and its agency's research efforts, secondary data sources, and/or is purchased from research suppliers. Several good planning guides are available on situation analysis.[2] Suffice it to say that situation analysis is generally the foundation for any well-developed marketing program, and the cornerstone for an advertising plan.

In many cases, a situation analysis is undertaken from the perspective of the total company or product line and will involve finding answers to dozens of questions including the history of the product, distribution, pricing, packaging, consumer analysis, competition, and many more. While there are many parts to a good situation analysis, two key components are the nature and structure of consumer demand, and the nature of competition.

Consumer and Market Analysis.   As outlined in part B of Table 2-1, a situation analysis often begins by looking at the aggregate market for the product, service, or cause being advertised: the size of the market, its growth rate, seasonality, geographical distribution;

TABLE 2-1. Topics and Questions Involved in Situational Analysis

A. Nature of demand
   1. How do buyers (consumer and industrial) *currently* go about buying existing products or services? Describe the main types of behavior patterns and attitudes.
      a. Number of stores shopped or industrial sources considered
      b. Degree of overt information seeking
      c. Degree of brand awareness and loyalty
      d. Location of product category decision—home or point of sale
      e. Location of brand decision—home or point of sale
      f. Sources of product information and current awareness and knowledge levels
      g. Who makes the purchase decision—male, female, adult, child, purchasing agent, buying committee, and so on
      h. Who influences the decision maker
      i. Individual or group decision (computer versus candy bar)
      j. Duration of the decision process (repeat, infrequent, or new purchase situation)
      k. Buyer's interest, personal involvement, or excitement regarding the purchase (hairpins versus trip to Caribbean)
      l. Risk or uncertainty of negative purchase outcome—high, medium, or low (specialized machinery versus hacksaw blades, pencils versus hair coloring)
      m. functional versus psychological considerations (electric drill versus new dress)
      n. Time of consumption (gum versus dining room furniture)
   2. Can the market be meaningfully segmented or broken into several homogeneous groups with respect to "what they want" and "how they buy"?
      Criteria:
      a. Age
      b. Family life cycle
      c. Geographic location
      d. Heavy versus light users
      e. Nature of the buying process
      f. Product usage
B. Extent of demand
   1. What is the size of the market (units and dollars) now, and what will the future hold?
   2. What are the current market shares, and what are the selective demand trends (units and dollars)?
   3. Is it best to analyze the market on an aggregate or on a segmented basis?
C. Nature of competition
   1. What is the present and future structure of competition?
      a. Number of competitors (5 versus 2,000)
      b. Market shares
      c. Financial resources
      d. Marketing resources and skills
      e. Production resources and skills
   2. What are the current marketing programs of established competitors? Why are they successful or unsuccessful?
   3. Is there an opportunity for another competitor? Why?
   4. What are the anticipated retaliatory moves of competitors? Can they neutralize different marketing programs we might develop?
D. Environmental climate
   1. What are the relevant social, political, economic, and technological trends?
   2. How do you evaluate these trends? Do they represent opportunities or problems?
E. Stage of product life cycle
   1. In what stage of the life cycle is the product category?

TABLE 2-1.   (Continued)

  a. What is the chronological age of the product category? (Younger more favorable than older?)
  b. What is the state of the consumers' knowledge of the product category? (More complete the knowledge—more unfavorable?)
2. What market characteristics support your stage-of-life-cycle evaluation?
F. Cost structure of the industry
  1. What is the amount and composition of the marginal or additional cost of supplying increased output?
G. Skills of the firm
  1. Do we have the skills and experience to perform the functions necessary to be in the business?
    a. Marketing skills
    b. Production skills
    c. Management skills
    d. Financial skills
    e. R&D skills
  2. How do our skills compare with those of competitors?
    a. Production fit
    b. Marketing fit
    c. And so on
H. Financial resources of the firm
  1. Do we have the funds to support an effective marketing program?
  2. Where are the funds coming from, and when will they be available?
I. Distribution structure
  1. What channels exist and can we gain access to the channels?
  2. Cost versus revenue from different channels?
  3. Feasibility of using multiple channels?
  4. Nature and degree of within and between channel competition?
  5. Trends of channel structure?
  6. Requirements of different channels for promotion and margin?
  7. Will it be profitable for particular channels to handle my product?

Source: Adapted from an unpublished note by Professor James R. Taylor of the University of Michigan. Used with permission.

the possible existence of different segments; and trends in all of these aggregate market characteristics.

It is vitally important, however, that the reasons for these aggregate statistics and market trends be understood, and for this the analyst has to examine the attitudes and behaviors of consumers as individuals (or, in some cases, as decision-making groups), as outlined in section A of Table 2-1. Who makes the purchase decision? What benefits are they seeking from the product category? Why are they satisfied or dissatisfied with the different brands? Key aspects of such consumer analysis are discussed later in this book in Chapter 4, where we discuss how markets can be segmented, and Chapter 6, where we discuss different ways of studying the benefits consumers seek in the product category and those they perceive in the competing brands.

Competitive Analysis.   Advertising planning and decision making are heavily affected by competition and the competitive situation facing the advertiser. Competition is such a pervasive factor that it will occur as a consideration in all phases of the advertising planning and decision-making process and the various topics treated in much of the balance of this book. A type of market-structure analysis that involves the development of perceptual maps of a market, for example, attempts to locate the relative perceptual positions of competitive brands. This topic is covered in detail in Chapter 4.

Situation analysis should usually include an analysis of what current share the brand now has (if it is an established brand), what shares its competitors have, trends in these shares, reasons for these trends, what share of a market is possible for this brand, and from which competitors the increased share will come? The planner also has to be aware of the relative strengths and weaknesses—financial, production, and marketing—of the different competing companies, and the history of competitive moves and objectives in the product category. If we spend advertising dollars communicating the fact that our brand has a desired benefit, will certain competitors begin claiming the same benefit, thus eliminating any competitive advantage we may hope to get?

Opportunities for marketing and advertising can also be uncovered using competitive analysis. Is there a "hole" in the market not now being filled by a competitive offering? In other terms, is there a bundle of attributes that a consumer segment desires that some competitor has not yet targeted against? Much research shows that companies that are the first to launch brands that meet unmet needs often have a "pioneering advantage" that later competing entries find difficult to fight.[3]

These types of questions need to be asked and answered not only in the initial stages of developing an advertising plan but through the years in which old campaigns are evaluated and improved. Many companies have initiated their own tracking systems for monitoring competitive advertising, covering the content of that advertising, how much money is being spent, and the media in which these competitive ads appear. We discuss some secondary sources of such competitive information in Chapters 16 and 17, since such competitive spending information is often a useful input into the budgeting decision. A chapter is not devoted to competition in this book because it comes into play throughout most of the topics treated. On the one hand, it is important to look at competition as a precursor to the planning process, and on the other to appreciate that the development of plans and decision making with respect to objectives, budgets, copy, and media all must take into account the competitive factor.

THE ROLE OF ADVERTISING WITHIN THE MARKETING PROGRAM

Advertising planning and decision making take place in the context of an overall marketing program. The marketing program includes planning, implementation, and control functions for the total corporation or a particular decision-making unit or product line. The marketing plan will include a statement of marketing objectives and the spelling out of particular strategies and tactics to reach those objectives. The marketing objective should identify the segments to be served by the organization and how it is going to serve them. The needs and wants of consumers on which the firm will concentrate, such as the needs of working housewives for easily prepared meals, are identified and analyzed in preparing a marketing plan.

There are several marketing tools that can be used to help an organization achieve its marketing objectives. Its product or service can be developed or refined. A distribution network can help match an organization's output with its clientele. Pricing strategy is another marketing-decision variable. The most appropriate way to improve the sales of a brand may not involve promotion or advertising at all, but may involve more extensive distribution, better relationships with the trade, a lower price, or simply better product quality. A brand manager needs to spend considerable time pinpointing the exact source of a brand's poor sales, before deciding that the core problem is inadequate or poor advertising or promotion. For instance, if research data indicate that consumers are trying the brand but are not repurchasing it, it may well be that the firm's advertising is successful (since consumers are trying the brand) but that the brand's product quality needs attention (since people who try the brand do not repurchase it).

The marketing plan thus should be based on the specific problems or opportunities uncovered for the brand by the situation analysis. It should serve as a response to those problems or opportunities, through the allocation of the marketing budget (and the development of specific plans) for various components of the *marketing mix*. The effectiveness of the various elements of the marketing mix with respect to the problems or opportunities should be the factor that determines what share each receives of the total marketing budget. Conceptually, the budget should be divided so that the marginal value of an extra budget increment will be the same in all components of the mix: dollars should be shifted to the area that will produce the higher incremental sales. In evaluating the advertising budget, therefore, it is important to keep in mind that incremental amounts of money put into advertising must be more useful than the same amounts put into distribution or product refinement, or even reduced prices. Chapter 16 is devoted to a discussion of the budget and how the optimal budget level can be determined.

Role of Advertising.   Once it has been determined that a key problem or opportunity for the brand involves its communication with consumers, it should not be immediately concluded that more money needs to be spent on advertising. Advertising is only one part of the *communications mix:* a firm can also communicate with its consumers through the sales force, through publicity or public relations, and through various consumer and trade promotions.

Within this mix, advertising has various strengths and weaknesses. Unlike the high cost of a sales call, which by some estimates now exceeds $225 per call once all relevant costs are considered,[4] advertising is a much cheaper way to reach target consumers (often pennies per exposure), since it uses mass media. Also unlike sales calls, advertising can use complex visual and emotional devices to increase the persuasiveness of the message. However, salespeople can often communicate more complex information (often necessary in industrial or big-ticket purchases) better than advertising can, can tailor the nature of the message much more closely to the message recipient, and are much more likely to "close" the sale, by getting an order.

Advertising is notorious for its inability to actually get the sale: while the effects of advertising in increasing brand awareness and favorable attitudes for the brand are easily documented, effects on sales are harder to find (some reasons for this are discussed in Chapter 3). It is thus often useful, after advertising creates such awareness and brand liking, to supplement advertising with sales promotions (both consumer promotions and trade promotions), which are often more effective in actually getting consumers to try the brand. Such sales promotions may be especially required if research shows, during the situation analysis, that target consumers are aware of the brand and think it has the features they are looking for, but have not gotten around to trying it. This book discusses sales promotions in Chapter 10.

Finally, advertising is also weak in another respect: it is widely perceived as biased. Many consumers often do not trust advertising, and are skeptical about its claims. In such situations, it is often useful for a marketer to try to communicate the message to consumers through media that are perceived as more credible and unbiased, such as editorial endorsements obtained through publicity and public relations campaigns.

Thus, an integral part of the advertising planning and decision-making process is an assessment of the role that advertising is meant to play—as one part of a firm's communication mix, and as one part of the total marketing mix. Once this perspective has been gained, the brand manager must design a marketing and communications plan where the different elements complement each other in increasing the sales for the brand. Although this book deals mostly with advertising management, with some coverage of sales promotions and of public relations, we cannot emphasize enough that an advertising plan can only be developed in the context of a total marketing and communications plan for the brand.

Coordination with Other Elements.   In addition to placing the advertising plan in this total context, the brand manager must also take care to develop a marketing program in which the component parts work in a coordinated, synergistic manner instead of at cross-purposes. For instance, when a firm develops a prestige product with a premium price, it is important that the advertising reinforce that idea of high quality and prestige. This can be done by associating the product with prestigious people, situations, or events. If the advertising objectives are written to encourage the use of advertising copy and advertising media incompatible with a prestige image, the whole marketing program may be jeopardized. Alternatively, when a firm offers a low-priced product, the job of advertising might be to stress the price differential by using hard-hitting copy.

As another example, the role of advertising will also depend on the distribution channel selected. If door-to-door selling is employed, advertising may be used only to introduce the salesperson, or it may not be used at all. If wholesalers, retailers, or other middlemen are employed, different advertising strategies are available. The advertising and selling effort may be primarily directed to either the consumer or the trade. In the former case, the intent would then be to have consumer interest "pull" the merchandise through the distribution channel; in the latter case, distributor margins would get the emphasis, consumer advertising would be less, and the intent would be to "push" it through the channel. Generally, the nature and significance of advertising will differ according to whether the company is stressing a push or pull strategy and whether its distribution strategy is intensive (the use of many outlets to maximize customer convenience), exclusive (the use of a few outlets to maximize retailer interest), or selective (intermediate arrangements).

THE COMMUNICATION/PERSUASION PROCESS

The most important factor to be considered in planning advertising, in addition to a specific marketing plan, is an understanding of the communication/persuasion process. Although much has been researched and written about the effects of advertising and how it works, it is important to appreciate that this is a subject about which there are few definitive answers. There are perhaps as many theories about how advertising "works" as there are people who work in advertising, and it would be impossible to discuss them all here. Some of these theories will appear in later chapters, but we will present two well-known ones here. An appreciation for the processes by which advertising works should be of great value in designing advertising plans that maximize the advertisement's impact on the consumer.

Figure 2-2 shows one simple model of the advertising communication system. Advertising communication always involves a perception process and four of the elements shown in the model: the source, a message, a communication channel, and a receiver. In addition, the receiver will sometimes become a source of information by talking to friends or associates. This type of communication is termed *word-of-mouth* communication, and it involves *social* interactions between two or more people and the important ideas of *personal influence* and the *diffusion of information.*

Source. The source of a message in the advertising communication system is where the message originates. There are many types of "sources" in the context of advertising, such as the company offering the product, the particular brand, or the spokesperson used. A model on source factors is developed in Chapter 12 to show the various dimen-

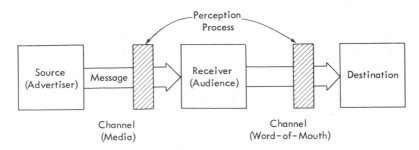

Figure 2-2. Model of the advertising communication system

sions of source effects such as credibility and attractiveness, which are of obvious importance in deciding how best (and through whom) to communicate the advertising message.

Message.   The message refers to both the content and execution of the advertisement. It is the totality of what enters the receiver's perception process. The message execution can be described in a great variety of ways, such as the use of humor and fear appeals discussed in Chapter 12. In later chapters, specific types of television commercials will be discussed and can also be considered ways to think about the advertising message.

Channel.   The message is transmitted through some channel from the source to the receiver. The channel in an advertising communication system consists of the media, such as radio, television, newspapers, magazines, billboards, point-of-purchase displays, and so on. The impact of the communication can be different for different media. For example, an advertisement exposure in *Vogue* magazine can have an effect quite different from exposure to the same advertisement in *Good Housekeeping*. In Chapter 17, this channel effect will be considered in more detail. Word-of-mouth communication represents another channel that is of special interest because it can sometimes play a key role in an advertising campaign; we discuss such effects in Chapter 9. It should be noted that a communication usually has a channel capacity. There is only so much that a receiver will be motivated and capable of processing. Furthermore, there is a physical limit to the number of advertisements that can be shown on prime time. Shortages of available advertising time can be a real problem.

Receiver.   The receiver in an advertising communication system is the target audience. Thus, the receiver can be described in terms of audience segmentation variables, lifestyle, benefits sought, demographics, and so on. A particular interest can be the involvement in the product and the extent to which the receiver is willing to search for and/or process information. It is characteristics of the receiver, demographic, psychological, and social that are, of course, the basis of understanding communications, persuasion, and market processes.

Destination.   The communication model in Figure 2-2 does not stop at the receiver but allows for the possibility that the initial receiver might engage in word-of-mouth communication to the ultimate destination of the message. The receiver then becomes an interim source and the destination becomes a receiver. Word-of-mouth can be a critical part of an advertising program. The reality is that for some products the absence of word-of-mouth communication can be fatal, because it is only the word-of-mouth communication that has the credibility, comprehensiveness, and impact to affect ultimate behavior of a portion of the audience. Furthermore, advertising can actually stimulate word-of-mouth activity. Even when it cannot stimulate it, a knowledge of its appropriateness and power can be very helpful. Chapter 9 will discuss word-of-mouth communication and related concepts of opinion leadership and personal influence.

Note that the communication can have a variety of effects upon the receiver. It can

Create awareness

Communicate information about attributes and benefits

Develop or change an image or personality

Associate the brand with feelings and emotions

Create group norms

Precipitate behavior

Our second model of communication/persuasion processes separates these different effects.

Figure 2-3 provides a simplified representation of this second model, which shows various possible things that can happen after consumers are exposed to the advertisement. First, exposure to the advertisement can create awareness about the brand, leading to a feeling of familiarity with it. Second, exposure to the ad can also result in information about the brand's benefits (and the attributes leading to those benefits) registering with the consumer. Third, advertisements can also generate feelings in an audience that they begin to associate with the brand or its consumption. Fourth, through the choice of the spokesperson and various executional devices, the advertisement can also lead to the creation of an image for the brand, often called ''brand personality.'' Fifth, the advertisement can create the impression that the brand is favored by the consumer's peers, or experts: individuals and groups the consumer likes to emulate. This is often how products and brands are presented as being fashionable. These five effects have the consequence of creating a favorable liking, or attitude, toward the brand, which in turn should lead to purchasing action. Sometimes the advertisement can directly attempt to spur this purchasing action, by serving a reminder function or by attacking reasons why the consumer may be postponing that action.

These two models help us to understand how and why consumers acquire, process, and use advertising information. It is also important at the planning stage to develop a good understanding of where advertising fits into the total pool of information and influence sources to which a consumer is exposed. Understanding information processing invariably leads to the need for understanding a wide range of other important psychological constructs, such as perception, learning, attitude formation and change, source effects, brand personality and image, cognitive and affective response, and social factors such as personal influence. Six chapters in Part III, and two in Part IV, are devoted to these topics, and will be introduced shortly. With this background in the communication/persuasion process behind us, however, let us return to the steps involved in the creation of the advertising plan.

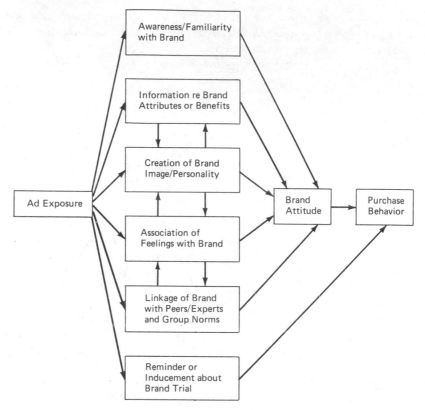

Figure 2-3. A model of the communication/persuasion process

THE ADVERTISING PLAN

As depicted in the flow sequence of Figure 2-1, the advertising plan should only be developed once the overall marketing plan has been created and the role of advertising within it has been assessed. Within the marketing plan, advertising planning and decision making focus on three crucial areas: objectives and target selection, message strategy and tactics, and media strategy and tactics. Every advertising plan will, at a minimum, reflect planning, decisions, and commitments concerning each of these three major components. The broad purpose of advertising management is to develop, implement, and control an advertising plan. Planning as a process involves the generation and specification of alternatives. Decision making concerns the choice of the best alternative. Which strategy alternatives are feasible in a given situation? Which one should be adopted? What media mix will be most effective? These are some of the questions every advertising manager must address.

In an established-brand situation, analysis will involve a retrospective look at what has been done in the past and whether basic changes in the current plan are called for. In new product situations, the manager may be essentially starting from scratch, and each aspect of the plan will require basic new thinking, significant amounts of new research information, and the development of entirely new advertising objectives and new copy and media strategies.

Alternatives with respect to objectives and the target market must first be carefully evaluated and specified. Then copy alternatives must be developed and analyzed with respect to both content (message strategy) and execution (message tactics). The decisions made at this stage take the form of the advertising campaign adopted in the particular situation. Finally, media alternatives need careful specification and analysis and decisions must be made on the how much money to spend (media strategy) and where to allocate it (media tactics). In each case, planning and decision making are involved.

Objectives and Target Selection

The pivotal aspect of any management plan is the development of operational objectives. An operational objective is one that provides useful criteria for decision making, generates standards to measure performance, and serves as a meaningful communication device. Objectives in advertising can be couched in many ways and still fulfill the functions of an operational objective. It is sometimes possible to develop objectives in terms of sales goals. Such goals are desirable because they appear to provide a readily accessible and absolute indication of advertising performance. However, because other marketing variables and competitors' actions can have an important impact on sales, it is often necessary to establish objectives in terms of intervening variables such as brand awareness, image, and attitude. The link between such intervening variables and advertising is more direct. Thus a significant increase in brand awareness can usually be identified with advertising. There are simply few other possible causes. To justify the use of intervening variables, a link must be established between them and subsequent sales. Much of Chapters 3 and 5 of this book will deal with the nature of that link.

An important part of the objective is the development of a precise, disciplined description of the target audience. It is often tempting to direct advertising at a broad audience; the implicit argument is that everyone is a potential customer. The risk is that a campaign directed at too wide an audience will have to have such a broad appeal that it will be of little interest to anyone and thus be ineffective. It is best to consider directing the advertising to more selected groups for which it is easier to develop relevant, stimulating copy. An advertiser need not be restricted to one objective and one campaign. It is quite possible to develop several campaigns, each directed at different segments of the market, or to develop one campaign based on multiple objectives. Chapter 4, also in Part II, looks at different ways of segmenting markets, and in ways to "position" brands to attract specific segments.

Message Strategy and Tactics

The actual development of an advertising campaign involves several distinct steps. First, the advertising manager must decide what the advertising is meant to communicate—by way of benefits, feelings, brand personality, or action content. We call this "message strategy" and devote six chapters in Part III to it. Once the content of the campaign has been decided, decisions must be made on the best—most effective—ways of communicating that content. These executional decisions, such as the choice of a spokesperson, the use of humor or fear or other tones, and the selection of particular copy, visuals, and layout, are what we call "message tactics." Part IV of the book discusses these tactics, as well as other aspects of implementation, such as copytesting, advertising production, and the process of client-agency interaction.

Message Strategy. Part III begins, in Chapter 5, with a research-based discussion of "how advertising works"—and how this knowledge helps shape our decisions on which strategic objectives should be targeted in different situations. Chapter 6 then examines theories of attitude change based on product attributes and benefits. Much of the material draws on recent work of consumer behavior researchers in the area, particularly in extending our understanding of learning, memory, and memory functioning. It focuses on how decisions can be made on which attributes and benefits to talk about in the advertising.

Chapter 7 focuses on theories and research to enhance understanding of advertising that is explicitly designed to generate emotional responses in the audience, such as warmth, excitement, pride, and so on, and "transform" the brand by associating these feelings with it. How should advertisers choose which emotions to evoke, and how can they tell when they have been successful?

Chapter 8 looks at research on brand image and personality. What personality dimensions or traits can brands acquire through advertising? What are the situations when such personality is more important in driving purchase? What is the importance of such personality in creating long-term "goodwill" for a brand? Most importantly, how can advertising (and other marketing mix elements) create such a brand image?[5]

Next, Chapter 9 looks at the processes of social influence and word-of-mouth advertising and examines how advertising can help shape group norms and fashions. In what advertising situations is social influence likely to play a major role? It is often useful to conduct a *personal influence audit,* explained in this chapter as part of a general situation analysis.[6]

Finally, Chapter 10 concludes the section on message strategy with a look at how advertising can be designed that explicitly aims to get consumer buying action. Here, among other things, we look at retail and co-op advertising, direct marketing, and sales promotions, for all of which actual consumer action is the key objective.

Message Tactics. One of the first executional objectives has to be the creation of an advertisement that gains attention, for without that nothing else is possible. In Part IV, Chapter 11 reviews theories of perception processes, in discussing how advertisements can be created that capture and retain the consumer's attention. How can attention best be captured, in an age when thousands of advertisements compete for attention and where consumers can flip television channels with a mere flick of the remote control device?

Chapter 12 then discusses the pros and cons of different kinds of spokespersons, and the kinds of advertising situations when they may be most appropriate. It also examines other decisions on "tone and format," such as the use of fear appeals, humor, comparative advertising, and devices to increase distraction.

The content and tone must eventually be translated into specific advertisements. Throughout the process, decisions have to be made concerning which different copy approaches, scripts, and final advertisements will be used. Chapter 13 examines some of the existing knowledge on the principles of good copywriting for each of the major media (print, television, radio, outdoor), and presents capsule portraits of some of the creative geniuses that have graced the advertising business.

Assessments of what makes for "good" copy are not merely subjective, of course, and several kinds of research-based tests can be used, in the laboratory or in the field, to enable a creative team to check the evolving campaign continually against its objectives. These are discussed in Chapter 14.

Concluding Part IV, Chapter 15 examines how advertisements actually get created, and the client-agency relationship through which this happens. Here, we also present some wisdom on how clients and agencies can best work together to create the most effective advertising.

Media Strategy and Tactics

Whereas message strategy generally concerns decisions about how much to allocate to creating and testing advertising copy, media strategy concerns decisions on how many media dollars to spend on an advertising campaign. Media tactics comprise the decisions on which specific media (television, radio, magazines, etc.) or media vehicles (*"The Tonight Show," Reader's Digest*, etc.) to spend these dollars. Both are covered in Part V.

Media Strategy.   The advertising budget decision, covered in Chapter 16, is closely tied-in with the objectives and target selection decisions discussed in Chapters 3, 4, and 5. Although there are many rules of thumb often used to decide on how much money to spend on advertising, the soundest rules involve beginning with a detailed specification of what a corporation is attempting to accomplish with advertising, and the resources necessary to accomplish them. It is only when the job to be done is well specified that the amount and nature of the effort—the amount of money to be invested in advertising—can be really determined. In Chapter 16 we will examine some of the traditional approaches to the advertising budget decision and contrast them with approaches we recommend.

Media Tactics.   Chapter 17 discusses criteria that apply in the allocation of an advertising budget across media types and within each media type. The media-allocation decision and media planning represent one of the few areas in advertising in which the use of mathematical techniques and computer programs is well accepted. These will be discussed, as will other factors that need to be taken into consideration. One is the type of vehicle audience and how it matches the target audience of the campaign. Another is the ability of the vehicle to enhance the advertising impact, perhaps by creating a compatible mood or setting.

The type and nature of research information required to support media models differs somewhat from the perspectives of research in the case of copy decisions. A media planner is interested in questions concerning the reach and frequency of media alternatives, the effects of various vehicles, and matters involving learning and decay rates over the life of a campaign. Media research is thus a special topic that is treated, along with the sources of media data, in Part V.

The decisions made in this area and in the other areas of objectives and copy constitute the final advertising plan. What should be clear is that advertising plans must all take these three major factors (objectives and target groups, message strategy and tactics, and media strategy and tactics) into consideration and will differ according to the decisions made in each area. The differences between advertising plans stem largely from differences in the external factors and the environmental situations that face advertisers. These external factors shape the advertising plan in many ways, and it is vital that they be analyzed in depth as the planning process proceeds.

FACILITATING AGENCIES

Another external factor identified in Figure 2-1 involves the agencies that facilitate the advertiser and provide the means to advertise. Recall that the nature and role of these types of agencies and institutions were reviewed in Chapter 1. From a situation-analysis viewpoint, the advertiser basically needs to know what kinds of facilitating agencies exist and the nature of the services they can provide. From a planning viewpoint, much local advertising, for example, is done without the services of an advertising agency or a research supplier. A national advertiser, on the other hand, may have under contract many different agencies and research suppliers, each serving one or more brands in a product line made up of several products.

Many advertising decisions involve choices among facilitating agency alternatives. What advertising agency should be chosen? What media should be used? What copy-test supplier will be best for our particular situation? Concerning the question of agency selection, for example, Cagley and Roberts[7] found that the "people factor" tends to dominate in agency selection. Characteristics such as the quality of personnel, reputation, integrity, mutual understanding, interpersonal compatibility, and synergism were very important. The study involved a mail questionnaire sent to 125 companies and ratings on 25 attributes ranging from "critically important" to "not important." Consideration of the facilitating agency factor is woven throughout many parts of the book, with special focus in Chapter 15 on client-agency relations. In addition, the question of choosing a copy-test research supplier is treated at length in Chapter 14, and the question of what media and what media research services to use are the topics of Chapters 16 and 17.

SOCIAL AND LEGAL FACTORS

The final external factor in the planning framework concerns environmental, social and legal considerations. To a considerable extent, these exist as constraints on the development of an advertising plan and decision making. In developing specific advertisements, there are certain legal constraints that must be considered. Deceptive advertising is forbidden by law. However, the determination of what is deceptive is often difficult, partly because different people can have different perceptions of the same advertisements. In guarding against deception, all types of perceptions must be considered. Furthermore, the letter and the spirit of the law on deceptive advertising is evolving rapidly. It is no small task to keep abreast of these developments. One solution is to create bland advertising that is vague and contains little specific information. However, such an approach can result not only in ineffective advertising, but it can lessen the social value of advertising by reducing the amount of useful information that it provides to the audience. Thus, an advertiser who attempts to provide specific, relevant information must be well aware of what constitutes deception in a legal and ethical sense and of other aspects of advertising regulation. Advertising regulation is the subject of Chapter 18.

Even more difficult considerations for people involved in the advertising effort are broad social and economic issues. Does advertising raise prices or inhibit competition? Also, issues such as the appropriateness of the use of sex or fear appeals are being examined. It has been suggested that women and minority groups are exploited in advertising by casting them in highly stereotyped roles. Another concern is that advertising, especially when it is more irritating than entertaining, is an intrusion into an already excessively polluted environment. A whole set of rules is emerging to cover advertising directed at children. These and other similar concerns, particularly those that affect copy and creative strategy, are developed more fully in Chapter 19.

SUMMARY

The predominant perspective of advertising management is that of the advertising or brand manager in the advertiser component of the overall system. The broad purpose of the manager is to develop, implement, and control an advertising plan. His or her major activities involve planning and decision making.

Planning concerns the generation and specification of alternatives, and decision making concerns the choice process. Which alternative should be chosen? Which message or media strategy is best in a particular situation? What copy theme should be used? What media mix will be most effective? And so on. The advertising plan is developed in the context of the company's total marketing program which flows from situation analysis and an assessment of the consumer/market and competitive situation the company is in. Externally, the manager needs to engage in situation analysis with respect to the market conditions that are operating at the time and to assess the consumer/market, competitive, facilitating agency, and social and legal factors that will affect decision making and the development of the plan. Internally, analysis should focus on the overall marketing program and how advertising will interact with the various components of the program. It is vital that the advertising plan be developed so as to mesh with and support the various components of the marketing and communications mix such as personal selling, pricing, public relations, and promotion. The advertising manager also needs to know the major areas of his or her planning and decision-making responsibilities. There are three areas of major strategic importance: objective/segment positioning considerations, message strategy, and media strategy. Planning and decision making are required from each perspective, and the final advertising plan will reflect the various decisions made in each area. Figure 2-1 organized these factors into a planning and decision-making framework for advertising management which is driven by the need for advertising managers to have an in-depth understanding of communication and persuasion processes.

Two views of communication and persuasion processes were presented in this chapter (Figures 2-2 and 2-3), and later chapters will develop others. Cognitive and affective/feeling processes that occur between exposure to advertisements and ultimate buying or consuming behavior are primary points of focus. Exposure can lead to increased awareness and familiarity with the brand, added information on brand attributes and benefits, creation of a brand image or personality, association of feeling with the brand, linkages of brands with peers and experts, and/or reminders and inducements to try or continue using the brand. All can affect brand attitude and ultimately purchase behavior.

Implementation of advertising plans is done with the assistance of many different kinds of external organizations such as production houses, broadcast and print media, advertising agencies, and research supplier companies. These are the "facilitating agencies" that help in bringing advertising into being. Also, implementation takes place in an environment of major social, economic, and legal forces that often serve as constraints on advertising. These too must be understood for effective advertising management.

DISCUSSION QUESTIONS

1. What are the basic differences between planning and decision making in advertising management? How does an advertising plan differ from an overall marketing plan? How do advertising decisions differ from other types of marketing decisions?

2. Outline the major components and considerations that you would include in your advertising plan if you were the brand manager of a brand of gasoline, a major credit card, or a new electronic device for use in business computers. In what ways would the plans differ? In what ways would they be similar?

3. An important internal component to be considered is the overall marketing plan. Provide additional examples of how advertising interacts with the elements of the marketing plan.

4. Using the model in Figure 2-3, explain your reactions to a recent television advertisement.

5. Give an example of how a competitive situation would affect the development of an advertising plan for a museum, an airline company, and a telephone product.

6. Suppose in your assessment of the current advertising plan for your product you decided that the execution of the advertising campaign was fundamentally weak. Which of the facilitating agencies would you look to as a possible source of the problem? Discuss some of the considerations in switching sources in this case.

7. Advertising plans rest on three central planning and decision-making considerations. Name them and give examples of each.

8. Explain the meaning of the term ''message strategy.'' Give an example of three alternative message strategies that might be adopted for a brand of peanut butter. Choose one of the strategies and defend your position.

9. It has been said that an advertising manager lives in an environment of considerable uncertainty. Explain this statement. Do you agree? What are the chief avenues open to reduce uncertainty?

10. It was stated in this chapter that it is often difficult to decide what is deception in advertising and what is not. Do you agree? What rules or principles should an advertiser use in deciding whether or not a message is likely to be considered ''deceptive''?

NOTES

1. Alan P. Kuritsky, John D. C. Little, Alvin J. Silk, and Emily S. Bassman, ''The Development, Testing, and Execution of New Marketing Strategy at AT&T Long Lines,'' *Interfaces*. 12, December 1982, pp. 22–37.

2. See ''Outline for Developing an Advertising Plan,'' in Don E. Schultz and Dennis G. Martin, *Strategic Advertising Campaigns* (Chicago: Crain Books, 1979), pp. 13–16. For a parallel approach which is specific to advertising called ''advertising opportunity analysis,'' see Edward M. Tauber, ''Point of View: How to Get Advertising Strategy from Research,'' *Journal of Advertising Research*, 20, October 1980, pp. 67–72.

3. Gregory S. Carpenter and Kent Nakamoto, ''Consumer Preference Formation and Pioneering Advantage,'' *Journal of Marketing Research*, 16, August 1989, pp. 285–298.

4. The median cost per sales call in 1989 was $225, according to *Sales and Marketing Management*, February 26, 1990, p. 75.

5. John G. Myers, *Consumer Image and Attitude*, (Berkeley, CA: Institute of Business and Economic Research, 1968).

6. A personal influence audit can be usefully done in conducting a situation analysis. See Chapter 9 for procedures involved in conducting a personal influence audit.

7. James W. Cagley and C. Richard Roberts, ''Criteria for Advertising Agency Selection: An Objective Appraisal,'' *Journal of Advertising Research*, 24, April/May 1984, pp. 27–31.

CASE FOR PART I

PROCTER & GAMBLE CO. (A)*

In November 1981, Chris Wright, associate advertising manager of the Packaged Soap & Detergent Division (PS&D) of the Procter & Gamble Co. (P&G), was evaluating how the division could increase volume of its light-duty liquid detergents (LDLs).[1] The excellent growth of Dawn dishwashing liquid since its national introduction in 1976 meant that P&G now manufactured and sold three leading LDL brands, and held a 42 percent share (by weight) of the industry's $850 million in factory sales.

Based on input from the three LDL brand managers that reported to him, as well as his own knowledge of the LDL category, Wright believed there were three major opportunities for volume growth: (1) the introduction of a new brand, (2) a product improvement on an existing brand, and/or (3) increased marketing expenditures on existing brands. In preparation for an upcoming meeting with Bruce Demill, PS&D advertising manager, Wright began evaluating the volume and profit potential of the three options.

Company Background

In 1837, William Procter and James Gamble formed a partnership in Cincinnati, Ohio, so that they could buy more efficiently the animal fats essential to the manufacture of their respective products, candles and soaps. The Procter & Gamble Company, which emerged from this partnership, quickly gained a reputation as a highly principled manufacturer of quality goods. As James Gamble said: "If you cannot make pure goods and full weight, go to something else that is honest, even if it is breaking stone."

In 1890, the Procter & Gamble Company was incorporated with a capital stock value of $4,500,000. This capital allowed P&G to build additional plants, buy new equipment, and develop and introduce new products. Sales volume more than doubled every ten years following incorporation, largely as a result of new product introductions. By 1981, P&G operated in 26 countries. As indicated in Exhibit 1, sales totalled $11.4 billion, of which 70 percent were made in the United States. P&G manufactured 90 consumer and industrial products in the United States and sold the leading brand in 14 of the 24 consumer product categories in which the company competed (see Exhibit 2). One or more of P&G's products were used in 95 percent of homes in the United States—a penetration unequaled by any other manufacturer. P&G had historically grown both by developing

*Copyright © 1983 by the President and Fellows of Harvard College

Harvard Business School case 9-584-047

This case was prepared by Alice M. Court under the direction of Professor John A. Quelch as the basis for class discussion rather than to illustrate either effective or ineffective handling of an administrative situation. Reprinted by permission of the Harvard Business School.

[1]LDLs are defined as all mild liquid soaps and detergents designed primarily for washing dishes.

EXHIBIT 1   Consolidated Statement of Earnings, 1980–1981 ($ millions except per share amounts)

	YEAR ENDING JUNE 30	
	1981	*1980*
Income		
Net sales	$11,416	$10,772
Interest and other income	83	52
	11,499	10,824
Costs and expenses		
Cost of products sold	7,854	7,471
Marketing, administrative, and other expenses	2,361	2,178
Interest expense	98	97
	10,313	9,746
Earnings from operations before income taxes	1,186	1,078
Income taxes	518	438
Net earnings from operations (before extraordinary charge)	668	640
Extraordinary charge—costs associated with the suspension of sale of Rely tampons (less applicable tax relief of $58)	(75)	—
Net earnings	$ 593	$ 640
Per common share		
Net earnings from operations	$ 8.08	$ 7.74
Extraordinary charge	(.91)	—
Net earnings	$ 7.17	$ 7.74
Average shares outstanding: 1981—82,720,858 1980—82,659,861		
Dividends	$ 3.80	$ 3.40

Source: Company records.

products internally and by acquiring companies to which P&G's technological expertise was applied.[2]

P&G executives attributed the company's success in the marketplace to a variety of factors: (1) dedicated and talented human resources, (2) a reputation for honesty that won them the trust and respect of their suppliers and customers, (3) prudent and conservative

[2]P&G acquired the Duncan Hines Companies (manufacturers of prepared cake, cookie, and muffin mixes) in 1956, Charmin Paper Mills (manufacturers of toilet and facial tissues, paper towels, and paper napkins) in 1957, the Folger Coffee Company (manufacturers of ground, flaked, and instant coffee) in 1963, the Crush Companies (manufacturers of Crush, Sun Drop, and Hires Root beer soft drinks) in 1980, the Ben Hill Griffin Citrus Company (manufacturers of concentrated fruit juices) in 1981, and Morton Norwich (manufacturers of pharmaceuticals) in 1982.

EXHIBIT 2   Established U.S. Brands by Product Category, 1981

A. CONSUMER

Laundry & cleaning	Food	Personal care

All fabric bleach:
    Biz (1967)[a]
Cleaners and cleansers:
    #1—Comet (1956)[b]
    Comet Liquid (1976)
    Mr. Clean (1958)
    Spic and Span (1945)
    Top Job (1963)
Detergents/soaps:
    Bold 3 (1976)
    Cheer (1950)
    Dash (1954)
    Dreft (1933)
    Era (1972)
    Gain (1966)
    Ivory Snow (1930)
    Oxydol (1952)
    Solo (1979)
    #1—Tide (1946)
Dishwashing detergents:
    Cascade (1955)
    Dawn (1972)
    #1—Ivory Liquid (1957)
    Joy (1949)
Fabric Softeners:
    Bounce (1972)
    #1—Downy (1960)

Coffee:
    #1—Folger's (vacuum packed & instant, 1963; flaked, 1977)
    Instant High Point (1975)
Oil/shortening:
    #1—Crisco (shortening, 1911)
    Crisco (oil, 1960)
    Fluffo (shortening, 1953)
    Puritan Oil (1976)
Orange juice and other citrus products
Peanut Butter:
    #1—Jif (1956)
Potato Chips:
    Pringles (1968)
Soft drinks:
    Crush (1980)
    Hires Root Beer (1980)
    Sun-Drop (1980)
Prepared Mixes:
    #1—Duncan Hines (cake, 1956; brownie, 1956; snack cake, 1974; pudding recipe cake, 1977; cookie, 1978; bran muffin, 1979)

Bar soaps:
    Camay (1927)
    Coast (1974)
    #1—Ivory (1879)
    Kirk's (1930)
    Lava (1928)
    Safeguard (1963)
    Zest (1952)
Deodorants/antiperspirants:
    Secret (1956)
    Sure (1972)
Disposable diapers:
    #1—Pampers (1961)
    Luvs (1976)
Disposable incontinent briefs:
    Attends (1978)
Hand and body lotion:
    Wondra (1977)
Home permanent:
    #1—Lilt (1949)
Mouthwash:
    Scope (1965)
Paper tissue products:
    Charmin (bathroom, 1957)
    #1—Puffs (facial, 1960)
    White Cloud (bathroom, 1958)
Paper towel:
    #1—Bounty (1965)
Prescription drugs
Shampoos:
    Head & Shoulders (1961)
    Pert (1979)
    Prell (1946)
Toothpastes:
    #1—Crest (1955)
    Gleem (1952)

B. INDUSTRIAL

Finished industrial goods	Unfinished industrial goods
All-purpose cleaning products	Animal feed ingredients
Floor and hard surface cleaning products	Cellulose pulp
Pot and pan washing products	Fatty acids
Cleansers	Fatty alcohols

B. INDUSTRIAL (continued)

Finished industrial goods	Unfinished industrial goods
Commercial laundry products	Glycerine
Coin-vended laundry products	Methyl esters
Hand washing products	
Institutional bar soaps	
Coffee	
Shortenings and oils	
Surgical drapes and gowns	

[a]The date the brand became part of the P&G line is in parentheses.

[b]#1 brands in the category are marked.

Note: Test market brands have been excluded.

management that encouraged thorough analysis prior to decision making, (4) innovative products offering superior benefits at competitive prices, and (5) substantial marketing expertise. The following quotes from company executives and outside analysts emphasize these factors:

> If you leave the company (P&G) its money, its buildings, and its brands, but take away its people, the business will be in real jeopardy—but, if you take away the money, the buildings, and the brands, but leave the people here, we will build a comparable new business in as little as a decade.
>
> Richard R. Deupree, Chairman of the Board, P&G, 1948–1958

> Our predecessors were wise enough to know that profitability and growth go hand in hand with fair treatment of employees, of customers, of consumers, and of the communities in which we operate.[3]
>
> Edward G. Harness, Chairman of the Board, P&G, 1974–1981

> There is no potential business gain, no matter how great, which can be used to justify a dishonest act. The ends cannot justify the means because unethical means, in and of themselves can and will destroy an organization. . . . The total dedication to integrity in every aspect of the business, and the restless, driving spirit of exploration have already been vital to the company's past, and are critical to the company's future.
>
> Owen B. Butler, Chairman of the Board, P&G, 1981–

> . . . Key to Procter & Gamble's continued growth is the importance we attach to research and development . . . if anything, research and development will take on even greater importance in the future.
>
> John Smale, President, P&G, 1981–

[3]As quoted by Oscar Schisgall in *Eyes on Tomorrow* (Chicago: J. G. Ferguson, 1981). All other quotations are drawn from P&G recruitment literature.

Disciplined and consistent, P&G people plan, minimize risk, and adhere to proven principles.

Ogilvy and Mather advertising agency

The secret, in a word, is thoroughness. P&G manages every element of its business with a painstaking precision that most organizations fail to approach.

Fortune

Company Organization

The company comprised eight major operating divisions organized by type of product: Packaged Soap & Detergents, Bar Soap & Household Cleaning Products, Toilet Goods, Paper Products, Food Products, Coffee, Food Service & Lodging Products, and Special Products. As Exhibit 3 shows, each division had its own brand management (called Advertising), Sales, Finance, Manufacturing, and Product Development line management groups. These groups reported directly to the division manager, typically a vice president

EXHIBIT 3   Divisional line management organization

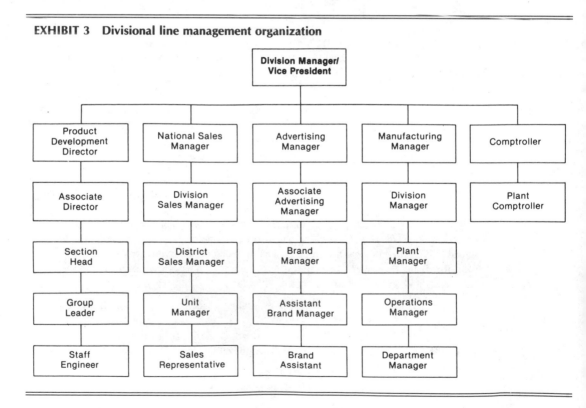

who held overall profit and loss responsibility. The divisions used centralized corporate staff groups for advertising services,[4] distribution, and purchasing.

The Advertising Department was formed in 1930 when P&G initiated its brand management system. This system allowed P&G to market aggressively several brands in the same product category by assigning the marketing responsibility for each brand to a single brand manager. He or she led a brand group that included an assistant brand manager and, depending on the dollar volume and marketing complexity of the product, one or two brand assistants. This group planned, developed, and directed the total marketing effort for its brand. It was expected to manage aggressively the marketing of the brand and to know more about the brand's business than anyone else in the organization.

One of the most important responsibilities of the brand group was the development of the annual marketing plan, which established volume objectives, marketing support levels, strategies, and tactics for the coming year. This plan took approximately three months to develop. It reflected substantial analysis of previous business results by the brand group. Additionally, the brand group solicited input from 6 to 12 internal staff departments and an outside advertising agency. The brand group then recommended a marketing plan, which was reviewed by three levels of management—the associate advertising manager, the advertising manager, and the division general manager. Since the planning process established the marketing plans and volume expectations for the coming year, it was regarded as a key determinant of brand progress. In addition, this process offered the brand groups substantial opportunity to interact with upper management. Details of the planning process are presented in Exhibit 4.

Promotion was based entirely on performance, and all promotions were from within the organization. In addition to their ability to build brand business, brand managers were evaluated on their ability to develop their people. A brand manager who demonstrated excellent management ability was promoted to associate advertising manager, as indicated in Exhibit 3. Associate advertising managers used the skills they had developed as brand managers to guide the marketing efforts of several brands within a division, as well as to further the development of their brand managers. Associates also became involved in broader divisional and corporate issues. For example, the associate responsible for coordinating division personnel policy would evaluate future personnel needs, coordinate recruitment efforts, ensure consistent evaluation methods, analyze training needs, develop a training budget, and work with the Personnel Department to implement training programs.

Each associate advertising manager reported to an advertising manager, who was responsible for the total marketing effort of all of a division's brands. The advertising manager played a significant role in the general management of the division, as he or she was responsible for approving the brand's recommendations for volume objectives, marketing plans, and expenditures. In addition, the advertising manager had responsibility for

---

[4]Advertising services included the following specialized staff departments: TV Commercial Production, Media, Copy Services, Art and Package Design, Market Research, Field Advertising, Marketing Systems and Computer Services, and Promotion and Marketing Services.

EXHIBIT 4   Marketing Plan Development Process

Appropriate number of weeks before plan approved	*Activity or event*	*Purpose*
12	*Business Review*—Assistant brand manager thoroughly reviews brand's and major competition's past 12-month shipment and share results by region, by size, and by form. Key lessons learned and indicated actions for the brand are developed by analyzing influences on brand share, including advertising copy, media weight, promotion, trade merchandising (display, co-op advertising, and temporary price reduction), pricing, and distribution.	To determine what elements of the marketing mix are affecting the brand's business and to develop clear guidelines and actions to improve business results.
8	*Competitive forecast*—Brand group forecasts competitive volume and marketing expenditures for coming year, using input from sales and advertising agency.	To allow brands to gauge level of expenditures necessary to compete effectively.
6	*Preliminary forecast*—Brand manager forecasts brand's volume and share for the coming year, and preliminarily recommends advertising and promotion expenditures.	To allow division and P&G management to preliminarily forecast total P&G volume, expenditures, and profits for the coming year, and the brand to get preliminary agreement to volume objectives and marketing plans.
4	*Promotion review*—Brand assistant thoroughly reviews results of past 12-month promotion plan by region, event, promoted size, and total brand. The document incorporates sales comments, competitive brand activity, and available research to explain possible reasons for success and failure. Plan includes broadscale media effort and testing activities.	To gain preliminary agreement from advertising and sales management to the proposed promotion plan for the coming year.
4	*Media plan*—Advertising agency develops detailed media plan, working with brand manager. Plan includes broadscale media effort and testing activity.	To develop media plan for inclusion in budget proposal.
1	*Budget proposal*—Brand group prepares document and detailing proposed volume share, and marketing plan for coming year. Marketing plan includes detailed media and promotion plans, both broadscale effort and testing activities.	To provide a written record of the proposed plan.

EXHIBIT 4   Marketing Plan Development Process (continued)

Appropriate number of weeks before plan approved	*Activity or event*	*Purpose*
0 (March)	*Budget meeting*—Brand group and advertising agency present the proposed plan to P&G management. The plan can either be approved in full, conditionally accepted provided certain issues raised in the meeting are addressed, or not approved.	To gain management input and agreement to the proposed plans.

approving each of the brands' advertising plans, as recommended by the brand groups and their advertising agencies.[5] All new advertising required the approval of the associate advertising manager and the advertising manager, while significant changes in advertising direction required division manager approval.

Historically, brands competing in the same product category were assigned to different associate advertising managers within a division to assure maximum interbrand competition. Each of the associates promoted the interests of his or her own brand to the advertising manager who then coordinated the most effective and efficient use of limited divisional resources. However, in the fall of 1981, the PS&D Division was reorganized such that each associate advertising manager became responsible for all the brands within a single product category, as shown in Exhibit 5. This change focused authority for key decisions within category groups (e.g., LDLs) at the associate advertising manager level, thus allowing the advertising manager to spend more time on divisional issues. The brand manager promoted the interests of his or her brand while the associate advertising manager assumed responsibility for building the business of all P&G brands in his or her category.

Advertising's Relations with other Line Departments

The brand groups worked closely with the following four line departments in both the development and the implementation of their marketing plans:

Sales.   P&G's consumer divisions employed 2,310 sales representatives and 574 sales managers, who serviced an estimated 40 percent of grocery, drug, and mass merchandise retail and wholesale outlets, accounting for an estimated 80 percent of all grocery and

[5]P&G retained ten leading advertising agencies to work with the brand groups on advertising issues, of which seven worked on the PS&D Division's products. Each LDL was handled by a separate agency. P&G's relationship with most of its agencies was longstanding, and many of the brands had been handled by the same agency since their introduction.

EXHIBIT 5   PS&D Division Organizational Chart—Fall 1981

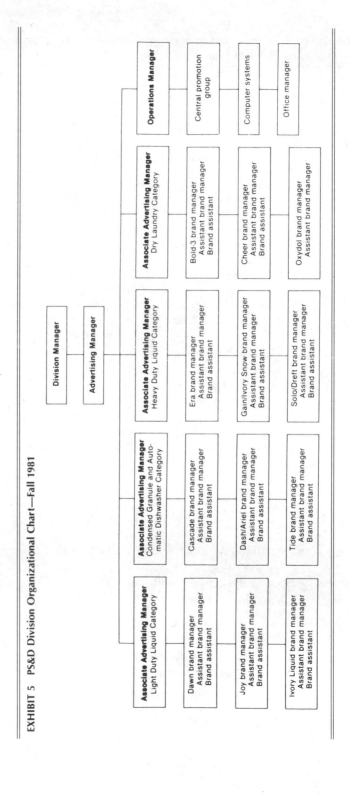

health and beauty aid sales volume.[6] The PS&D Division employed 408 sales representatives and 102 sales managers, who serviced 27 percent of grocery outlets accounting for 75 percent of grocery sales volume. The PS&D sales force did not directly service drug and mass merchandise outlets because of their modest sales potential.

P&G sales representatives were well trained and regarded by the trade as consistently professional. Richard Penner, district sales manager, said:

> Our sales representatives must be experts and professionals in their field. Our customers know that our sales representatives are well-trained professionals whose objective is not only to sell a good, quality product, but whose expertise can show them how to improve overall productivity; people who will bring them business-building merchandising ideas for the next feature or drive, which will reach present as well as new customers, thus increasing overall turnover and profit for the store.

The brand groups and sales force frequently interacted. While the brand groups managed categories and brands, the sales force managed markets and accounts. As such, the sales force provided important perspective and counsel on trade and consumer promotion acceptance, stock requirements to support promotions, competitive pricing and promotion activity, and new product activity. Each brand group worked closely with the sales force to develop the optimal sales promotion plan for their brand together with appropriate merchandising aids. An understanding of the sales function was considered so important to successful marketing planning that each brand assistant was trained as a sales representative and spent three to five months in the field sales force.

Product Development Department (PDD).   Since superior product performance was key to the success of P&G products, each brand group worked closely with PDD to ensure continued improvement of their brand's quality. Fifteen professionals worked exclusively on research and development for LDLs. The PDD continually strove to upgrade product quality or explore new product formulations. If a potential new product was developed, it was extensively tested in consumer and laboratory tests before any test marketing began.

In 1981, P&G spent $200 million on research and development. This spending supported the efforts of about 3,500 employees. Approximately 1,200 were professionally trained staff, and nearly one-third of these held doctoral degrees. P&G had six major research centers, four of which were located in the United States. The PS&D Division spent $30 million on research and development in 1981, which supported the efforts of about 500 employees.

Manufacturing Department.   P&G operated 40 manufacturing plants in 24 states. The PS&D Division utilized 10 of these facilities to manufacture its products. The brand group provided the Manufacturing Department with detailed brand volume estimates (by month, by size, and by form/flavor) to facilitate efficient production, as well as five-year volume

---

[6]Small convenience and corner stores accounted for most of the remaining 60 percent of retail outlets. P&G did not directly service these stores, as they accounted for only 20 percent of all commodity volume (ACV). These stores could, however, obtain P&G products through wholesalers.

base forecasts for capacity planning. In addition, the brand group discussed promotions requiring label or packaging changes with Manufacturing to determine the most efficient production methods. Manufacturing informed brand groups about ongoing manufacturing costs and provided potential cost savings ideas. Interaction between the Advertising and Manufacturing departments was particularly frequent during any new product development process, and included discussions on manufacturing requirements, custom packing options for test markets, and critical paths for production.

Finance Department.   P&G's Finance Department was divided into three major functional areas: Divisional Financial/Cost Analysis, Treasury, and Taxation. Both Treasury and Taxation were centralized groups, while Financial/Cost Analysis was divisionalized and reported to the division manager, as shown in Exhibit 3. Based on volume and marketing expenditure forecasts provided by the brand groups, Financial/Cost analysts developed and fed back brand profit and pricing analyses, as well as profit and rate of return forecasts on new products and promotions. This information was key in helping the brand groups to recommend action which would maximize volume and profit growth.

Advertising Services Department.   Within the department, there were nine staff groups which serviced the Advertising Department. These were Market Research, Art and Package Design, TV Commercial Production, Media, Copy Services, Field Advertising, Marketing Systems and Computer Services, Promotion and Marketing Services, and Advertising Personnel.

P&G's extraordinary depth of staff resources was considered a key competitive advantage. For example, P&G invested an average of $20 million annually on consumer and market research,[7] 10 percent of which was spent on PS&D Division projects. PS&D market research included

1. Market Analysis—including bimonthly syndicated market data that P&G purchased from A. C. Nielsen Co.,[8] as well as selected data purchased from Nielsen, Selling Areas Marketing, Inc. (SAMI), and other suppliers for test markets.
2. Consumer Research—including studies to
   a. Monitor how consumers used products and track consumer usage of, attitude toward, and image of P&G and competitive brands.
   b. Test the performance of current products and possible product modifications under in-home usage conditions.
   c. Evaluate the advertising, packaging, promotion, and pricing of P&G brands. Also, to evaluate the potential of new product ideas using such techniques as concept research and simulated test markets.

---

[7]This $20 million was part of the $200 million the company spent on research and development.

[8]The A. C. Nielsen package that the LDL brands purchased included data on retail shelf movement and share, distribution penetration, retailer feature advertising, special displays, regular and feature prices, out-of-stocks, retail inventories, and percent of brands sold in special packs.

The major strength of P&G's consumer research was the quality of interviewing and consistent methodology among projects. This provided P&G with large data bases of comparable research over several years from which it could establish norms and accurately track changing consumer perceptions and habits. Only a limited amount of the research was actually conducted by P&G employees—most was conducted by outside suppliers, but was closely supervised by P&G market researchers.

Light-duty Liquid Detergents

During the 1940s, most U.S. consumers used powdered laundry detergents to wash their dishes. Research indicated, however, that consumers found these detergents harsh on their hands. In response to these concerns, P&G designed a mild, light-duty liquid in 1949. By 1981, the LDL industry recorded factory sales of $850 million and volume of 59 million cases.[9] The average U.S. consumer had 1.5 LDL brands at home at any one time, used 0.6 fluid ounces of product per sinkful of dishes, and washed an average of 12 sinkful each week. The average purchase cycle was 3 to 4 weeks, and an average household would use over one case of product each year. As Exhibit 6 shows, the most popular sizes in the category were 32 ounces and 22 ounces.

Exhibit 7 suggests that LDL consumption increases, resulting from the growing number of U.S. households,[10] were partly offset by increased penetration of automatic dishwashers (ADWs), as ADW households used one-half as much LDL as non-ADW households.[11] Based on these trends, the LDL brand groups projected category volume growth of 1 percent per year over the next five years.

LDLs could be conceptually divided on the basis of product benefit into three major segments. The performance segment, accounting for 35 percent of category volume, included brands providing primarily a cleaning benefit; the mildness segment, accounting for 37 percent of category volume, included brands providing primarily the benefit of being gentle to hands; and the price segment, accounting for 28 percent of category volume,

---

EXHIBIT 6   Sizes of Dishwashing Liquid Used in Past Seven Days

	SIZE			
	48 oz.	*32 oz.*	*22 oz.*	*12 oz.*
% respondents	13%	30%	42%	15%

Source: Company research.

---

[9]Volume is measured in P&G statistical cases, each containing 310 ounces.

[10]Household growth was a better indicator of LDL volume than population growth, as research indicated LDL household consumption varied only slightly with the number of people in the household.

[11]ADW households still used LDL for pots and pans and small cleanups.

EXHIBIT 7   U.S. LDL Market Influences, 1960–1990

	YEAR			
	1960	1970	1980	1990[a]
% LDL household penetration	53%	83%	90%	92%
% ADW household penetration	5%	18%	36%	44%
Total households (millions)	53	63	79	91

[a]Company estimate.

included brands whose primary benefit was low cost.[12] As Exhibit 8 indicates, the performance segment had experienced the greatest growth in the past ten years. Some LDL brand managers expected the performance segment to continue to grow at the expense of the mildness segment since market research indicated that more consumers rated performance attributes (such as grease cutting and long-lasting suds) as the most important (see

EXHIBIT 8   LDL Market Historic Growth Trends and Projections, 1973–1986

FISCAL YEAR ENDING JUNE 30	VOLUME (000,000 CASES)	MILDNESS[a]	PERFORMANCE[a]	PRICE[a]
Actual				
1973	56.4	44%	19%	37%
1974	57.0	45	20	35
1975	56.4	44	21	35
1976	56.8	43	22	35
1977	56.1	40	28	32
1978	57.8	40	30	30
1979	57.0	39	32	29
1980	58.7	38	33	29
1981	59.0	37	35	28
Projected				
1982	59.4	37%	35%	28%
1983	59.8	36	35	29
1984	60.1	36	35	29
1985	60.8	35	36	29
1986	61.1	35	36	29

[a]As a percentage of category volume.

Source: Company records. Classification and projections were based on collective brand manager judgment.

[12]Price brands were sold to retailers for an average of $7.50 per statistical case versus $17.00 per statistical case for the premium-priced mildness and performance brands.

Exhibit 9). The price segment had been in decline, but was expected to stabilize at its current share level due to increasing consumer price sensitivity resulting from the depressed state of the economy. The LDL brand managers did not expect this segment to grow because most price brands were not a good value, requiring two or three times as much volume to create the same amount of suds as a premium brand. P&G's Ivory Liquid, the market leader, used this comparison in its advertising to persuade consumers that Ivory was a better value.

EXHIBIT 9   Attribute Importance Rating

METHODOLOGY

Respondents were asked to rate the importance to them of LDL attributes on a 6-point scale, with 6 being "want the most" and 1 being "want the least." For example, chart below is to be read: 64% of respondents claimed "Makes dishes shine" as one of the attributes they wanted most in a dishwashing liquid, while 2% of respondents claimed this attribute as the one they wanted least.

% RESPONDENTS

Attribute	6	5	4	3	2	1	No answer	Average rating
Makes dishes shine	64%	16%	7%	6%	2%	2%	3%	5.3%
Has pleasant odor or perfume	40	17	11	10	7	10	5	4.2
Small amount required	70	13	6	5	1	2	3	5.5
Doesn't make skin rough	65	12	7	5	4	3	4	5.0
Is low priced	50	19	10	9	3	4	5	5.0
Is good for hand washing laundry	29	14	9	11	9	23	5	3.7
Does a good job on pots and pans	75	13	4	2	1	1	4	5.6
Does not spot or streak glasses or dishes	67	15	8	3	2	2	3	5.4
Is mild to hands	68	13	5	5	3	3	3	5.2
Makes long-lasting suds	83	12	7	2	2	2	2	5.5
Cuts grease	87	6	2	1	—	1	3	5.8
Is economical to use	72	13	6	4	1	1	3	5.5
Soaks off baked-on or burned-on food	60	17	7	5	2	4	5	5.2
Good for tough cleaning jobs	52	13	8	9	4	9	5	4.8

Source: Company research.

The LDL market was relatively stable with one new premium brand introduced every two and one half years and an average of two price brands introduced and discontinued per year. As Exhibit 10 shows, three companies sold almost 75 percent of LDLs, with P&G holding a 42 percent share[13] of the market, Colgate-Palmolive a 24 percent share,

[13]Share of market is defined as share of statistical case volume.

EXHIBIT 10   LDL Market Shares by Brand and Company, 1961, 1971, and 1981 (shares of statistical cases)

BRAND	SEGMENT	1961	1971	1981
Joy	Performance	14.9%	12.0%	12.1%
Ivory	Mildness	17.5	14.9	15.5
Dawn	Performance	—	—	14.1
Thrill[a]	Mildness/performance	—	2.9	—
P&G		32.4%	29.8%	41.7%
Lux	Mildness	17.3	7.3	3.1
Dove	Mildness	—	4.8	3.1
Sunlight	Performance	—	—	0.7
All other	Price	5.9	1.0	—
Lever Brothers		23.2%	13.1%	6.9%
Palmolive Liquid	Mildness	—	11.7	11.8
Dermassage	Mildness	—	—	3.5
All other	Price/performance	5.5	9.6	8.3
Colgate-Palmolive		5.5%	21.3%	23.6%
All other LDLs	Mainly price— generics and private labels	38.9	35.8	27.8
Total LDL		100.0%	100.0%	100.0%

[a]Thrill was introduced by P&G in 1969. The brand ultimately proved not to provide a needed product benefit and was discontinued in 1975 because of faltering volume.

Source: Company records.

and Lever Brothers, the U.S. subsidiary of Unilever, a 7 percent share.[14] The remaining 27 percent of the market consisted mainly of generic and private label brands.

Total advertising and promotion spending in the category in 1981 was $150 million, over half of which was spent by the P&G LDLs, the balance being spent primarily by Lever and Colgate-Palmolive.

The cost structure for an established P&G LDL is shown in Exhibit 11. Slightly over half of the marketing budget of the P&G LDLs was allocated to advertising, versus only about 40 percent for both Colgate and Lever LDLs. Colgate and Lever sold an estimated 75 percent of their LDL volume to the trade on deal, compared to about half for P&G. Both Lever and Colgate had introduced a single new brand in the past ten years. Dermassage, introduced in 1974 by Colgate, offered a similar benefit to Ivory, mildness to hands. The brand held only a 2 percent share in 1981. Sunlight, introduced by Lever into Phoenix test market in 1980, offered benefits similar to Joy, as a good cleaning, lemon-fresh LDL. The brand had achieved a 10 percent share in the test region after 12 months.

[14]In 1981, U.S. sales of Colgate-Palmolive Company were $5.3 billion and U.S. sales of Lever Brothers were $2.1 billion.

EXHIBIT 11   Cost Structure for an Established LDL Brand

Cost of goods	51%
Distribution	7
Selling and general administration	10
Marketing expenditures	20[a]
Profit	12
Total	100%

[a]Includes advertising, trade, and consumer promotion expenditures.

Source: Company records.

Procter & Gamble's LDL Brands

P&G's three brands in the LDL category, Ivory Liquid, Joy, and Dawn, together accounted for 30 percent of the dollar sales volume and profit of the PS&D Division. While each of the three brands was a different formulation which offered a distinct benefit to appeal to separate consumer needs, they were all marketed similarly. All three brands were sized and priced in line with major premium-priced competition, as indicated in Exhibit 12. Price increases occurred, on average, every 18 months.

In general, the brand managers spent over half of each LDL's marketing budget on advertising, of which 85 to 90 percent was spent on television media and commercial production, and the balance on print. Brands typically held four to six major promotion events each year, each lasting four weeks. Promotions primarily included coupons, price packs, bonus packs, and trade allowances. Consumer promotions typically accounted for at least 75 percent of promotion dollars, while trade allowances made up the balance.

P&G's LDL brands held strongly established market positions as company research results reported in Exhibit 13 reveal. Neither Ivory Liquid nor Dawn had changed its basic product benefits or basic advertising claims since introduction. Joy, however, had undergone two basic changes. It was first introduced as a performance brand, but during the 1960s, as the mildness segment of the market began to grow, it was restaged with a mildness benefit. By the 1970s, Ivory Liquid was clearly established as the major mildness

---

EXHIBIT 12   Ivory, Dawn, and Joy Pricing

SIZE	ITEMS/CASE	MANUFACTURER'S CARLOAD CASE PRICE	MANUFACTURER'S CARLOAD ITEM PRICE	AVERAGE RETAIL PRICE
48 oz.	9	$22.77	$2.53	$2.99
32 oz.	12	21.24	1.77	2.04
22 oz.	16	19.20	1.20	1.46
12 oz.	24	16.08	.67	.84

EXHIBIT 13 LDL User/Nonuser[a] Attribute Association (%)

Respondents Were Asked to Indicate Which One Brand Was Best Described by Each Attribute Phrase	IVORY LIQUID		JOY		DAWN		PALMOLIVE		PRIVATE BRAND	
	Yes	No	Yes	No	Yes	No	Yes	No	Yes	No
Best for mildness	89%	51%	53%	12%	41%	7%	71%	27%	13%	2%
Best overall for getting dishes clean	64	9	78	14	88	15	61	5	18	1
Best for cutting grease	41	6	49	7	96	45	35	4	16	1
Best for removing tough, cooked-on food	47	7	55	10	88	28	41	6	19	2
Best for leaving dishes shiny	44	10	81	45	59	5	40	4	14	1
Gives the best value for your money	74	24	60	4	65	6	55	5	40	7
Makes the longest-lasting suds	79	29	60	10	67	11	50	5	12	1
Has the most pleasant fragrance	43	11	64	35	39	9	35	11	14	1

[a]Brand user was defined as a respondent who reported that brand as her usual brand over the past three-month period.

Note: To be read, for example, 89% of respondents who claimed Ivory Liquid as their usual brand indicated that it was best for being mild to your hands; 50% of people who did not claim Ivory Liquid as their usual brand indicated that it was best for being mild to your hands.

Source: Company records.

brand, and as research revealed that a consumer need existed for a good cleaning brand, Joy was reformulated to provide a performance benefit and restaged.

The brands' individual market positions are discussed in the paragraphs that follow.

Ivory.   Ivory Liquid was introduced in 1957 as an excellent dishwashing liquid that provided the additional benefit of hand care. Its mildness positioning was supported by the heritage of Ivory bar soap, a patented mildness formula, and unique product esthetics—its creamy-white color and mild scent. In 1981, it was the leading brand with a market share of 15.5 percent. Although Ivory's share had declined slightly over the previous five years, it was expected to remain stable over the next five years. Ivory advertising copy featured a mother/daughter comparison to demonstrate its benefit of "young-looking hands." In 1968, the brand added a value claim which stressed the fact that Ivory washed more dishes per penny of product than price brands because of its higher sudsing formula. During 1981, Ivory allocated two-thirds of its advertising budget to the mildness message and the remaining one-third to the value advertising copy. Television advertising storyboards for these two campaigns are presented as Exhibits 14 and 15. The brand was perceived by consumers as the mildest and highest-sudsing brand and had the highest ever-tried level in the category. For this reason, the principal objective of Ivory's consumer promotions was to encourage continuity of purchase rather than to stimulate trial.

Dawn.   Dawn was introduced in 1976 as a performance brand. In two years, it rose to the number 2 position in the LDL category, and by 1981, held a 14.1 percent market share. Dawn captured about 70 percent of its volume from non-P&G brands, with the remaining 30 percent cannibalized equally from Ivory and Joy. Dawn's rapid growth was attributed to its unique position as the superior grease-cutting LDL in the category—a claim that was supported by its patented formula which consumer research provided cut grease better than other formulas. The advertising claim, "Dawn takes grease out of your way," was supported by a powerful product demonstration, as shown in the storyboard presented as Exhibit 16. Consumer research reported in Exhibit 17 indicated that Dawn had the highest conversion rate of all the P&G LDL brands.[15] Dawn's promotion plan emphasized trial with most of the budget allocated to consumer coupons. Its share was projected to increase to 16.5 percent over the next five years. It was expected to take over the leading share position from Ivory by 1985.

Joy.   Joy, introduced in 1949, was the first LDL. Since 1970, it had been formulated to provide a performance benefit, and it was positioned in advertising to deliver "beautiful dishes that get noticed and appreciated." Joy's lemon-based formula, lemon fragrance, and yellow package supported this image. Joy advertising (see Exhibit 18) claimed that it "cleans dishes right down to the shine and isn't that a nice reflection on you." As Exhibit 13 indicates, it was not as strong as Ivory or Dawn. In addition, it had the lowest trial level of P&G's three LDLs. As a result, its promotion plan was trial oriented with par-

[15]The conversion rate was the number of people citing a brand as their usual brand divided by total triers of the brand.

EXHIBIT 14   1981 "Mildness" Ivory TV Storyboard

COMPTON ADVERTISING, INC.
625 Madison Avenue, New York, N.Y. 10022
Telephone: PLaza 4-1100

CLIENT:	PROCTER & GAMBLE CO.
PRODUCT:	IVORY LIQUID
TITLE:	"STOKES"
COMML. #	PGIL 5713
DATE:	10/22/80

TIMING: 30 SECONDS

1. (SFX: MUSIC)
ANNCR: (VO) Can you pick Jean Stokes' hands from her two daughters?

2. LISA: Mom's hands are as young-looking as ours!

3. KATHY: We sing together for charity --

4. MOM: Strictly amateur -- but your hands get noticed.

5. ANNCR: (VO) And Jean does a lot of dishes. What's her secret?

6. LISA: Ivory Liquid!
MOM: And I've told my girls how mild it is.

7. ANNCR: (VO) Lab tests show Ivory Liquid's

8. mildest of all leading brands.

9. And nothing gets dishes cleaner.

10. LISA: I'm going to stay with Ivory Liquid.

11. GROUP SINGS: Ivory Liquid.

12. ANNCR: (VO) Because young-looking hands are worth holding on to.

EXHIBIT 15   1981 "Value" Ivory TV Storyboard

COMPTON ADVERTISING, INC.

625 Madison Avenue, New York, N.Y. 10022

Telephone: PLaza 4-1100

CLIENT: PROCTER & GAMBLE CO.
PRODUCT: IVORY LIQUID
TITLE: "THE KIPPERS"
COMML. #   PGIL 5573   TIMING: 30 SECONDS
DATE: 4/1/80

1. ANNCR: (VO) Is the Kippers' "bargain" brand a better buy than mild Ivory Liquid? Let's see...

2. INT: Let's test your brand against Ivory Liquid with a penny's worth of each.

3. Let's wash some dishes.

4. How are your suds? BOB: I don't have any suds now.

5. INT: How about the Ivory Liquid Mrs. Kipper? BEV: I still have a tubful.

6. INT: Let's scoop some up and compare.

7. Okay what happened? BEV: I did a lot more dishes.

8. What I thought was a bargain isn't really a bargain at all. INT: What's the bargain?

9. INT: What's the bargain? BEV: Ivory is the bargain.

10. It's gentle to my hands, and I can save money.

11. ANNCR: (VO) You don't have to give up

12. mild Ivory Liquid to save money.

B&B

BENTON & BOWLES
909 THIRD AVENUE
NEW YORK, N.Y.
(212) 758-6200

Client: PROCTER & GAMBLE CO.
Product: DAWN
Length: 45 SECONDS (PGDN 6105)
Title: "SLEEPOVER REV/FP"

1. (SFX: KIDS TALKING)
MOM: Lasagna? For break-
fast? DAUGHTER: Oh,
Mom! FRIEND: It's a
slumber party!

2. MOM: O.K. But you will
clean up.

3. DAUGHTER: All that
grease! Yuck!!! Gross!

4. MOM: No, Dawn.

5. DAUGHTER: Ah,
finished!

6. FRIEND #1: Uh-uh, forgot
a glass. DAUGHTER: You
forgot it. You wash it.
FRIEND: After that greasy
pan?

7. DAUGHTER: Try it.
Dawn'll handle it.

8. FRIEND #1: The water
doesn't feel greasy...and
neither do my hands.

9. And this glass looks as good
as the first one you washed.

10. ANNCR: (VO) Look. Add
a half cup of grease to
Dawn dishwater.

11. Dawn breaks up grease,
takes it out of your way.
Helps keep it away.

12. So dishes come out clean.

13. FRIEND: Dawn's great!

14. MOM: So, if lasagna's
breakfast, what's dinner?
DAUGHTER: Corn flakes.
(GIRLS LAUGH)

15. ANNCR: (VO) Dawn takes
grease

16. (SFX) out of your way.

EXHIBIT 17   Current Product Usage[a]

	IVORY	JOY	DAWN
Usual brand	23%	13%	25%
Past 12-month trial	35	30	29%
Ever-tried	58	43	54

[a]An estimated 60–80% of total brand volume was consumed by usual brand users for each brand.

Source: Company research.

ticular emphasis on couponing. Joy's share of 12.1 percent was expected to increase by only 1 percent per year over the next five years.

Exhibit 19 reports factory shipments and market shares for each of the three brands over the past five years, as well as the brands' estimates for the next five years. Exhibit 20 provides a demographic profile of users of each of the three P&G brands, illustrating how each brand appeals to a different consumer segment.

New Growth Opportunities

Wright considered the following three options in evaluating the opportunities for further volume growth on P&G LDLs:

New Brand Introduction.   The success of Dawn led Wright to wonder if another new brand with a distinctive benefit could further increase P&G's LDL volume. Based on the impact of Dawn's introduction and the current strength of P&G's LDL brands, he estimated that a well-positioned new brand could capture at least 60 percent of its share from competitive brands. However, after talking with Manufacturing and PDD, he estimated that a new brand would require $20 million in capital investment to cover additional production capacity and bottle molds.[16] Further, based on input from the Dawn brand manager, he estimated a new LDL brand would need at least $60 million for first-year introductory marketing expenditures.[17]

Wright saw new product potential in all three market segments. First, PDD had invented a new technology for a high-performance product. The formula, called H-80, combined suspended nonabrasive scrubbers[18] with a highly effective detergent system to provide superior cleaning versus other LDLs when used full strength on tough, baked-on foods and parity cleaning versus other LDLs when diluted with water for general dish-

[16]This capital investment per case of estimated LDL volume was lower than the average for new P&G products, since substantial LDL manufacturing facilities already existed.

[17]This estimate was based on Dawn's 12-month introductory marketing plan. Using updated costs, a new brand would require $18 million for media support, $37 million for consumer and trade promotion support, and $5 million for miscellaneous marketing expenses.

[18]The scrubbers were made from the biodegradable shells of microscopic sea organisms.

EXHIBIT 18   1981 "Joy" Advertising Storyboard

Radio TV Reports

41 East 42nd Street New York N.Y. 10017
(212) 697-5100

PRODUCT: JOY DISHWASHING LIQUID   758077
PROGRAM: AS THE WORLD TURNS   60 SEC.
WCBS-TV   1:35PM

1. MAN: Sam. MAN: Joe.
It's been too long.

2. MAN: It sure has. Come on
in. Honey, Sam's here.
WOMAN: How do you do
Captain Randall.

3. MAN: Major Randall now I
hope my phone call didn't
catch you two off guard.
But Joe said, Sam if you're
ever in town --

4. WOMAN: Well of course.
And I hope you stay for
dinner Major Randall. That
is if you don't mind pot
luck.

5. MAN: Oh, don't apologize.
MAN: Sam. Make yourself
at home. Honey, shouldn't
we get out the good dishes?

6. WOMAN: Never mind the
dishes. Ours here look fine.
What about my dress?
MAN: It's just fine.

7. ANNCR: When unexpected
guests drop in one thing you
don't have to worry about is
the way your table looks
when you use Joy.

8. Joy cleans every day dishes
clear down to the shine. And
smells fresh like lemons.

9. Keeps dishes ready for
company, even if you're not.

10. MAN: Sure is nice to get
home cooking.

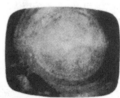

11. And look at that shine.
Looks like you were ex-
pecting company all the time.

12. ANNCR: Lemon fresh
Joy cleans down to the
shine.

13. And that's a nice reflection
on you.

EXHIBIT 19   Shipment and Share Data for LDL Brands, 1977–1986

	SHIPMENTS (MILLIONS OF CASES)			SHARE (% OF LDL CATEGORY)		
	Ivory	Dawn	Joy	Ivory	Dawn	Joy
Actual						
1977	9.1	6.7	6.7	16.3%	11.9%	11.9%
1978	9.0	7.3	6.7	15.5	12.7	11.6
1979	9.1	7.5	6.8	16.0	13.2	12.0
1980	9.1	8.2	6.9	15.5	14.0	11.7
1981	9.1	8.3	7.1	15.5	14.1	12.1
Estimated						
1982	9.2	8.7	7.2	15.5%	14.7%	12.2%
1983	9.3	9.0	7.4	15.5	15.0	12.3
1984	9.3	9.3	7.5	15.5	15.5	12.4
1985	9.4	9.7	7.6	15.5	15.9	12.5
1986	9.5	10.1	7.8	15.5	16.5	12.7

Source: Company records. Projections are based on brand manager's judgment.

washing. Wright believed that such a product could fulfill a clear consumer need, based on consumer research. Since market research indicated that 80 percent of U.S. households scour and scrub their dishes at least once a week, with an average household scouring four times a week, he believed that this product would be valued by a significant percentage of consumers.[19] In addition, the results of blind, in-home use tests, reported in Exhibit 21, were positive.

Second, Wright wondered if he could capitalize on P&G's expertise in the mildness segment to introduce another mildness brand. While the segment was currently declining, he believed there might be potential for a new brand if the mildness benefit could be further differentiated—just as had been done in the performance segment. As Exhibit 22 shows, research indicated that when consumers were asked what improvement they wanted most in their current LDL, more stated "milder to hands" than any other product benefit.

Third, P&G could introduce a price brand. PDD and Manufacturing had told Wright that they could produce a brand with parity performance benefits to existing price brand competition at a cost that would allow them to maintain a reasonable profit. Specifically, the percentage of sales available for marketing expenditures and profit would fall to 14 percent of sales versus the 32 percent of sales available from P&G's current LDL brands. Wright noted that P&G did not currently have an LDL entry in this fragmented segment of the market, characterized by low-share brands with little brand loyalty and substantially lower product quality than the LDL brands P&G currently marketed. He wondered if P&G's marketing expertise could enable the company to capture a significant portion of the price segment with a parity product.

[19]Many consumers used soap-filled scouring pads such as Purex Industries' Brillo pads and Miles Laboratories' S.O.S. pads. Retail sales of such pads approached $100 million in 1980.

EXHIBIT 20 LDL User Demographic Profile (% of total responding households)

	Total LDL households	Heavy LDL users[a]	USUAL BRAND				
			Ivory Liquid	Joy	Dawn	Palmolive	No name/ plain label
ADW usage—past 7 days							
Yes	36%	9%	48%	49%	51%	48%	47%
No	64	90	51	51	49	42	53
Yearly income							
Under $15M	32	46	28	32	35	30	36
$15M–$25M	27	29	27	26	29	27	29
Over $25M	41	25	45	42	36	43	35
Population density (000/sq. mile)							
Under 50	32	39	30	33	38	28	20
50–1999	45	40	45	44	43	46	48
2000 and over	23	21	25	23	19	26	32
Geographic area							
Northeast	22	26	22	23	19	24	36
North Central	28	28	26	27	31	27	31
South	33	35	34	37	35	33	16
West	17	11	18	13	15	16	17

Employment[b]							
Employed	48	37	48	50	49	49	55
Not employed	52	63	52	59	51	51	45
Age[b]							
Under 35	33	39	31	34	38	39	35
35–50	30	25	29	31	30	30	37
51–59	16	15	17	16	15	16	12
60+	21	30[c]	23	19	17	24	16
Number in family							
1–2	40	41	43	38	38	42	28
3–4	44	41	42	45	46	44	50
5+	16	18	15	17	16	14	22

[a]Defined as +15 sinksful per week.

[b]Female head of household.

[c]The heavy LDL user skew toward older respondents may be misleading. Management at P&G believed that, although they washed a large number of small sinkloads, they used a lesser amount of product per sinkload because they tended to live in smaller households.

Note: To be read, for example, 48% of respondents who claimed Ivory Liquid as their usual brand had used an automatic dishwasher in the past seven days.

Source: Company research.

EXHIBIT 21   LDL Category Assessment Four-Week Blind In-Home Use Test of H-80

	H–80 WITH SCRUBBING INSTRUCTIONS	*ESTABLISHED COMPETITIVE LDL WITH SCRUBBING INSTRUCTIONS*
Attribute ratings (%)		
Overall	77%	71%
Cleaning	79	73
Removing baked/burned/dried-on food	73	61
Grease removal	77	72
Amount of suds made	73	69
Mildness	55	63
Odor of product	70	68
Color of product	72	69
Favorable comments (%)		
Unduplicated cleaning	73	65
Cleans well	36	29
Cleans hard-to-remove food	25	15
Cuts grease	34	32
Unduplicated sudsing	49	45
Product color	6	5
Mildness	25	34
Unduplicated odor	45	40
Unduplicated cap/container	8	2
Unduplicated consistency	12	2
Like scrubbing particles/abrasives	12	—
Unfavorable comments (%)		
Unduplicated cleaning	4	9
Not clean well	—	1
Not clean hard-to-remove food	1	5
Not cut grease	3	8
Unduplicated sudsing	9	17
Product color	1	3
Mildness	16	14
Unduplicated odor	10	9
Unduplicated cap/container	2	2
Unduplicated consistency	12	1
Not like abrasive/gritty feel	11	1
Dishwashing information		
Used product full strength for scrubbing	61	52
Used scrubbing implement for tough job	79	85

Note: To be read, for example, 77% of the 425 households who used H-80 rated it as 4 or above on a five-point scale on overall performance.

Source: Company research. Unmarked bottles of H-80 were given to one of two representative samples of LDL users. The other sample group received unmarked bottles of an established competitive brand. Both brands were accompanied by instruction suggesting the product be diluted for general dishwashing but used full strength for tough dishwashing jobs.

EXHIBIT 22   Selected Research Data: Personal Feelings Concerning Dishwashing

1. What is the worst thing about doing dishes?

The time it takes	24%
Having to do them	22
Cleaning pots and pans	15
Scrubbing/scouring	14
Cleaning greasy items	6
Hard on hands	4

2. What is the toughest dishwashing job?

Removal of baked/burned/fried/cooked foods	39
Removal of greasy foods	32
Cleaning of pots and pans	22
Cleaning of skillets	16
Cleaning of casseroles	7
Cleaning of dishes	3

3. What is most disappointing about your current dishwashing liquid?

Nothing	51
Suds disappear	12
Leaves grease	8
Odor	6
Hard on hands	2
Price/expensive	4
Have to use too much	4

4. What improvement do you want the most in a dishwashing liquid?

Milder to hands	11
Do it by magic/itself	10
Eliminate scouring or soaking	9
Cut grease	9
Soak dishes clean	9
Suds never vanish	6
Nothing/satisfied	9

Source: Company research.

Product Improvement on an Existing Brand.   A product improvement on a current brand represented considerably less investment than a new brand and Wright wondered if he would be wiser to introduce the H-80 formula as a product improvement to one of the current LDL brands. While he estimated that the capital costs associated with a product improvement would be about the same as introducing a new product ($20 million), incremental marketing expenditures over and above the existing brand budget would by only $10 million. He wondered which, if any, of his brands would most benefit from this change.

Separately, the Joy brand group was eager to re-stage the brand with a new "no-spot" formula. The formula, considered a technological breakthrough, caused water to "sheet" off dishes when they were air dried, leaving fewer spots than other brands. In addition, the formula reduced Joy's cost of goods sold by about $3 million per year. The brand group estimated this relaunch would cost $10 million in marketing expenses, but would require no capital investment.

Increase Marketing Expenditures on Existing Brands.   Finally, given the low-growth potential of the LDL category, Wright wondered if his overall profits might be higher if he avoided the capital investment and introductory marketing expenses of a new brand or product improvement and simply increased the marketing expenditures behind the existing brands in an effort to build volume. In particular, the brand manager of Ivory Liquid had submitted a request for an additional $4 million to support extra advertising and promotion. Half of the funds were to be used to achieve leadership media levels for Ivory by increasing its current media level from 300 GRPs,[20] which was the average level for major advertised LDL brands, to 365 GRPs. The remaining funds would be used to finance an incremental 20 cents off price pack promotion on the 32-ounce size.

Conclusion

As Wright considered the various options available, he wondered about the time frame for implementation of each option. He knew that he could gain approval for increased marketing expenditures almost immediately if the plan was financially attractive, unless a test market was required, which would delay national approval by six to twelve months. Implementing a product improvement on an existing brand would take about a year, or two years if a test market was necessary, and the introduction of a new brand would require two years plus a year in a test market before it could be expanded nationally. Could he undertake more than one option? What effect would each option have on each of the existing LDL brands? What competitive response could he expect? What were the long- and short-term profit and volume implications of each of the options?

---

[20]A GRP (gross rating point) is a measure of media delivery. Gross rating points equal the percent of viewers reached over a specific period of time (usually four weeks) times the average number of occasions on which they are reached.

3

SETTING
GOALS AND OBJECTIVES

For an advertisement to be effective it must be noticed, read, compre-
hended, believed, and acted upon.

Daniel Starch, 1923

For one who has no objective, nothing is relevant.

Confucius

The pivotal aspect of any management effort is the development of meaningful objectives. Without good objectives, it is nearly impossible to guide and control decision making. Good performance may occasionally occur in the absence of objectives, but it can rarely be sustained. In the past, advertising has often been a free spirit within an organization, operating with little guidance or control. It has been able to resist the discipline of modern management because the actual creative decisions were usually made in another organization, the advertising agency. The challenge today is to bring effective management to the advertising process in such a way as to provide stimulation as well as direction to the creative effort. The key is the development of meaningful objectives. Part II of the book is directed toward this end.

FUNCTION OF OBJECTIVES

Objectives serve several functions in modern management. One function is to operate as communication and coordination devices. They provide a vehicle by which the client, the agency account executive, and the creative team communicate. They also serve to coordinate the efforts of such groups as copywriters, radio specialists, media buyers, and research specialists.

A second function of objectives is to provide a criterion for decision making. If two alternative campaigns are generated, one must be selected. Rather than relying on an executive's esthetic judgment (or on that of his or her spouse), he or she should be able to turn to the objective and select the criterion that will most readily achieve it. One test of the operationality of an objective is the degree to which it can act as a decision criterion.

A related function of an objective is to evaluate results. Thus, another test of objective operationality is whether it can be used to evaluate a campaign at its conclusion. This function implies that there needs to be a measure such as market share or brand awareness associated with the objective. At the end of the campaign, that preselected measure is employed to evaluate the success of the campaign—such success is increasingly how advertising agencies are getting compensated, as was pointed out in Chapter 1.

Sales as an Objective

Advertising objectives, like organizational objectives, should be operational. They should be effective criteria for decision making and should provide standards with which results can be compared. Furthermore, they should be effective communication tools, providing a line between strategic and tactical decisions.

A convenient and enticing advertising objective involves a construct like immediate sales or market share. The ultimate aim of advertising is often to help raise the level of some aggregate measure like immediate sales. The measure is usually readily available to "evaluate" the results of a campaign. There are clearly some situations—mail-order advertising and some retail advertising, for example—when immediate sales are a good operational objective, and others in which they can play a role in guiding the advertising campaign. Chapter 10 will discuss in more detail such situations in which sales or market share make useful objectives.

However, objectives that involve an increase in immediate sales are not operational in many cases for two reasons: (1) advertising is only one of many factors influencing sales, and it is difficult to isolate its contribution to those sales, and (2) the contributory role of advertising often occurs primarily over the long run.

Advertising is only one of the many forces that influence sales, as Figure 3-1 illustrates. The other forces include price, distribution, packaging, product features, com-

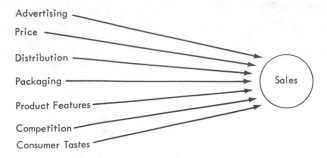

Figure 3-1. Some of the factors influencing sales

petitive actions, and changing buyer needs and tastes. It is extremely difficult to isolate the effect of advertising. Some argue that evaluating advertising only by its impact on sales is like attributing all the success (or failure) of a football team to the quarterback. The fact is that many other elements can affect the team's record—other plays, the competition, and the bounce of the ball. The implication is that the effect of the quarterback's performance should be measured by the things he alone can influence, such as how he throws the ball, how he calls the plays, and how he hands off. If, in a real-world situation, all factors remained constant except for advertising (for example, if competitive activity were static), then it would be feasible to rely exclusively on sales to measure advertising effectiveness. Such a situation is, in reality, infeasible, though for packaged nondurable goods it is possible to run sophisticated field experiments using grocery scanner data that yield fairly accurate estimates of the effect of current advertising on short-term sales (see Chapter 16). For the most part, we must start dealing with response variables that are associated more directly with the advertising stimulus.

The second reason involves the long-term effect of advertising on sales. If we believe that advertising generates a substantial lagged effect on sales, then the impact of an advertising campaign may not be known for certain until an unacceptable length of time has passed. For example, an important contribution of a 6-month campaign might be its impact 12 months hence. Research has estimated that, at least for frequently purchased nondurable goods, the effect of an advertising exposure can take up to 9 months to get dissipated.[1] As Figure 3-2 illustrates, advertising might attract buyers who will be loyal customers for several years, or it might start the development of positive attitudes that will culminate in a purchase much later. To determine this effect from sales data, even in a scanner panel field experiment, it may be necessary to wait far beyond the end of the 6-month campaign. Two problems are created. First, the difficulty of isolating the sales change caused by advertising becomes more severe as the time between the advertising expenditure and the sales response increases. Yet decisions must be made immediately and cannot wait for such data. Second, for more timely and accurate information, variables that respond more quickly to advertising input must be sought.

Thus, advertising objectives that emphasize sales are usually not very operational because they provide little practical guidance for decision makers. No one argues the desirability of a sales increase, but which campaign will (or did) generate such an increase? If an objective does not contribute useful criteria on which to base subsequent decisions, it cannot fulfill its basic functions.

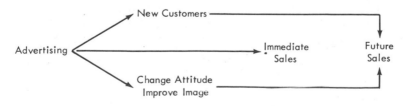

Figure 3-2. Long-run impact of advertising

Toward Operational Objectives

If immediate sales do not form the basis of operational objectives in most situations. how does one proceed? The answer lies in part in three sets of questions. Addressing these questions in a careful, systematic way will often yield useful and effective objectives.

1. Who is the target segment?
2. What is the ultimate behavior within that segment that advertising is attempting to precipitate, reinforce, change, or influence?
3. What is the process that will lead to the desired behavior and what role can advertising play in the process? Is it necessary to create awareness, communicate information about the brand, create an image or attitude, or associate feelings or a type of user personality with a brand?

The first step is to identify the target audience. The specification of the target audience (e.g., upscale buyers of stereo equipment) should be a part of the marketing objectives. However, the segmentation description may need to be refined in the advertising context, that is, those upscale buyers of stereo equipment who have not heard of Bose speakers. We deal with this targeting decision in detail in the next chapter.

The second step involves the analysis of the ultimate desired behavior such as trial purchases of new customers, maintenance of loyalty of existing customers, creation of a more positive use experience, reduction of time between purchases, or the decision to visit a retailer. A part of the analysis should be an estimate of the long-term impact on the organization of such a behavior. What exactly is the value of the desired behavior? For example, the value of attracting a new customer to try a brand will depend upon the likelihood that the customer will like the brand and rebuy it. Companies often call this the "lifetime value of a customer."

The third step involves an analysis of the communication and decision process that will affect the desired behavior. Operationally, this usually involves using advertising-response measures that intervene between the incidence of the stimulus (advertising) and the ultimate behavioral response (certain purchase decisions) that is the focus of the advertising. Such response measures are called *intervening variables* and refer to a wide range of mental constructs such as awareness, brand knowledge, emotional feelings, and attitude. Thus, it might be that the key variable in inducing a new customer to try your brand is to inculcate high levels of brand awareness. The best way to maintain loyalty could be to strengthen an attitude. Even though the end goal is behavioral, the operational objective guiding decision making will often be specified in terms of one or more of such intervening variables. The determination of which intervening variables provide the best link to the desired behavior and which can be influenced economically by advertising is, of course, a challenge.

We start with the analysis of the desired behavior. After turning to the advertising response variables, we will finally discuss the recommended procedures and theoretical frameworks to set advertising objectives.

BEHAVIORAL DYNAMICS

An understanding of market dynamics is necessary to an analysis of the ultimate behavior on which advertising should focus. An increase in sales or, more generally, an increase in product use (if the advertiser were a library or hospital, a sales measure would be inappropriate) can basically come from three sources: (1) from new customers attracted to the brand for the first time, (2) by increasing the loyalty of existing customers, and (3) by inducing existing customers to use more of the product class, either by increased usage or in new situations.

New Customers

Figure 3-3 shows a market divided into three segments. Segment E includes those who now buy our brand, brand A. Some members of segment E will buy only our brand, but many will probably also buy others, because they are either somewhat indifferent about a few brands or because they prefer other brands for some applications and our brand for others. They all buy our brand to some extent. Segment O contains those who buy other brands to the exclusion of ours. Some members of segment O will be loyal to another brand, and others will switch among other brands, but none is a buyer of our brand. Segment N members are not buyers of any brand in the product set. They get along without coffee, computers, lathes, or whatever product is involved.

The focus here is on increasing the size of segment E. One approach is to attract members of segment O to get them to try our brand. In Figure 3-4, Canon typewriters is directing its campaign primarily to members of segment O (the users of IBM typewriters). Such an effort may be difficult if the other brands are performing satisfactorily. However, it can be extremely worthwhile. If a "new trier" likes our brand, he or she could become a customer, a member of segment E for many years. Determining the feasibility of this strategy will depend partly on how difficult this task will be.

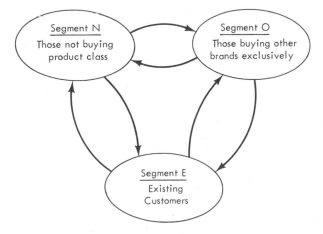

Figure 3-3.   Customer types

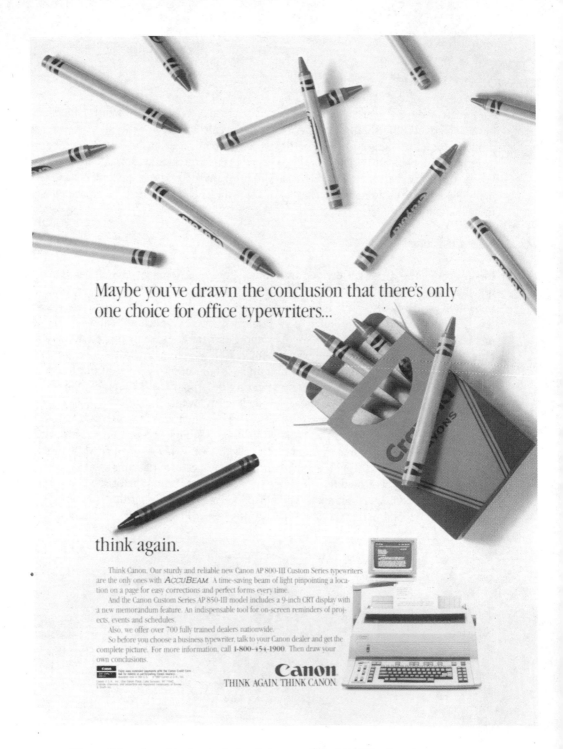

Figure 3-4. An advertisement aimed at users of a competitive brand

Courtesy of Canon U.S.A., Inc. CRAYOLA, chevron, and serpentine designs are registered trademarks of Binney & Smith, used with permission.

Another approach is to attract people from segment N, those not now using the product class. An example of such an approach is the Dannon Yogurt ad shown in Figure 3-5. The intent of that advertisement is to attract those using sour cream as a baked potato topping to a different type of topping that they are not currently using. The cost of obtaining a member from segment N will determine, in part, the advisability of this strategy.

Such an approach, called a *"primary demand"* approach, might be particularly worthwhile to a large firm that already serves most of those buying the product class (such as Dannon Yogurt). The firm in the industry that has the highest market share, the largest distribution, the biggest sales force, and the highest awareness is the one most likely to get the sale from a customer just entering the product category. On the other hand, such a strategy makes much less sense for a smaller firm that runs the risk that the segment N member who is induced to try the product class may buy from a larger competitor. The smaller firm should therefore be content to let the larger firms attract people from segment N, and confine itself to trying to obtain its new customers from segment O (called a *"secondary demand"* strategy). The value of a segment O member will depend, of course, on how large a product-class buyer she or he ultimately becomes and on the share of these purchases eventually obtained by the advertiser.

A defensive strategy is also possible. Efforts could be made to reduce the flow from segment E to segment O. The goal would be to reduce the likelihood that a member of segment E would be tempted to try another brand and would, as a result, eventually stop using our brand. A large firm may also be concerned about customers moving from segment E to segment N. Existing users of the product could drop out of the market altogether. Some people, for example, stop shaving, grow beards, and stop buying any brand of shaving cream or razor blades.

Brand Loyalty

The members of segment E, the existing customers, will, in general, also be buying from competitors. Figure 3-6 shows the brand switching that could occur among existing customers. Some existing customers will be extremely loyal, buying from competitors only rarely if at all. For such customers, the goal would be to maintain their loyalty and repurchase rates, thus reducing the likelihood that they would begin sharing their purchases with other brands and perhaps ultimately move to segment O. Advertising might attempt to remind them of the important features of the brand or to reinforce the use experience. Further, certain consumer promotions, such as premiums requiring multiple proofs of purchases, might also be used.

The Campbell's advertisement shown in Figure 3-7 may be in this category. It provides the opportunity for a user to express loyalty by obtaining a mug that in turn will help to reinforce the usage experience. Other customers may repeatedly switch among our brand and others. It may be possible to convince customers like these to become more loyal. If there are real brand advantages of which they may be unaware, such a task might be feasible. If, however, they are firmly convinced that several brands are equal, the effort may be difficult and costly. As before, the cost of generating the desired behavioral response must be balanced with its worth in terms of future purchase.

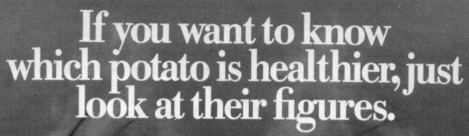

If you want to know which potato is healthier, just look at their figures.

Sour Cream (2 oz.)	
Fat	10g
Calories	104
Cholesterol	20mg
Calcium	56mg
Protein	2g

Dannon® Plain Nonfat Yogurt (2 oz.)	
Fat	None
Calories	28
Cholesterol	less than 2mg
Calcium	108mg
Protein	3g

You won't be able to tell by how they look. Or taste.

Because a baked potato topped with creamy Dannon® Plain Nonfat Yogurt is just as soul-satisfyingly delicious as one topped with sour cream.

But look at the bottom line

The Healthy Way To Eat.

and see how much better Dannon Plain is for you.

Dannon Plain Nonfat Yogurt not only has no fat and 70% less calories, but more calcium and protein, too.

It's amazing how different they really look now, isn't it?

Figure 3-5. An advertisement attempting to attract users from another product category
Courtesy of Dannon Yogurt, Inc.

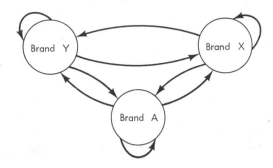

Figure 3-6.   Brand switching among existing customers

Increasing Usage

It is also possible to increase the usage of existing customers in the product class. In essence, the goal would be to reduce the time between purchases. Figure 3-8 shows a typical distribution of interpurchase times among existing customers. The effort would involve sliding the area under the curve to the left. Several approaches are available. Product use could be expanded by inducing people to use the product more frequently, or a new use application could be suggested. For example, Scotch tape could be used for decorative as well as conventional purposes, or the use of aspirin to fight second heart attacks might be suggested as a new application. It may be possible to get existing customers to use the product in the familiar way but more frequently. Here the aim would usually be to do more than just induce an extra purchase; we would want to actually change long-term behavioral patterns so that the increased usage, at least for some customers, would continue over time. The value of advertising will then be represented by the increased usage. If the increased usage extends over a long time period, it will obviously be of greater value. As before, however, the value must be balanced against the cost involved.

Behavioral or Action Objectives

An analysis of market dynamics can lead to behavioral measures that by themselves can provide the basis for operational objectives. If the advertising's target is new customers, the goal may be to get new customers to try a brand for the first time. The results would be measured by the number of new customers attracted. Such an estimate could be obtained from a consumer panel or by a count of a cents-off coupon if that were a part of the advertising effort. The number of new triers, of course, is quite different from short-run sales. The quantity of sales in the short run represented by new customers is usually minuscule and will be swamped by the behavioral patterns of regular customers (segment E).

The use of behavioral measures as objectives will be explored in detail in Chapter 10. They are often appropriate in retailing (store traffic measures), direct marketing, and sales promotion and in lead generation for salespeople. An example of an ad trying to generate leads is the Allied Van Lines ad in Figure 3-9. Clearly, the hope is that people who are about to move will be interested in the free booklet and will call the toll-free

Figure 3-7.   Maintaining brand loyalty
Courtesy of Campbell Soup Company.

telephone number, thus identifying themselves as prospects for a sales call. Usually, however, it is useful to analyze also the communication and decision process relevant in a
causal sense to the desired behavior and to identify intervening variables on which to base

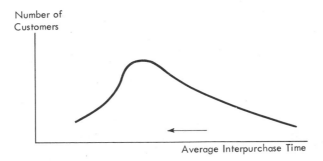

Figure 3-8.   Interpurchase time of existing customers

objectives. Of course, some situations could dictate the joint use of intervening and behavioral objectives.

ADVERTISING RESPONSE—VARiABLES INTERVENING BETWEEN ADVERTISING AND ACTION

Usually advertising is not well suited to directly precipitate action. Rather, it is better at conducting some communication, association, or persuasion task that will hopefully result in the desired action being precipitated. A communication results in the audience members learning something new or gaining an improved understanding or memory of some fact; for example, Jell-O comes in a low-calorie form. Associations link a brand to concepts such as types of people, use situations, or feelings; for example, driving a Pontiac creates an exciting feeling. Persuasion involves creating or changing an attitude toward an object; for example, I rather like that brand.

The identification and selection of the best advertising response variable upon which to base objectives is extremely difficult. There are countless numbers of advertising response variables to consider, as was discussed in the section on the persuasion/communication process in Chapter 2 and as will be discussed further in Chapter 5. Further, our understanding of both the given contexts and the communication and persuasion process is always incomplete. Nevertheless, there is still great payoff to proceed in this direction.

To identify and use advertising response variables, the key questions to be addressed are

1. What communication, association, or persuasion task will be likely to precipitate the desired action?
2. How can this task best be conceptualized and measured?

In asking the first question, there is a set of intervening variables that are frequently useful. They include brand awareness, brand comprehension, brand image or personality, brand attitude, the perception that an important reference group values that brand, and the association of desired feelings with a brand or use experience.

A moving story that has a great beginning, a snappy delivery, and a happy ending.

The story starts with a free copy of Allied's book—*"A Guide To Moving In The '90s."* This fact-filled reference contains everything from packing tips to parental advice from child psychologists.

For your free copy, call 1-800-367-MOVE.

The story builds to a move with prompt, reliable service from Allied, the van line that has moved more people over the years than any other. And it closes with the perfect ending—a happy home. To get your free moving guide, and the name of your nearest Allied agent, call 1-800-367-MOVE. **ALLIED**

© 1991 Allied Van Lines, Inc.

Figure 3-9. An advertisement aimed at attracting sales inquiries Used with permission of Allied Van Lines, Inc.

Brand Awareness

A basic communication task in which advertising excels is to create awareness. Awareness can be particularly needed when the goal is to stimulate a trial purchase perhaps of a new brand. The model is shown as Model A in Table 3-1. Advertising creates awareness in the new brand and the awareness will create the trial purchase after which the brand is on its own to gain acceptance. The awareness measure could be based upon a telephone survey where people are asked whether they have heard of the new brand and perhaps whether they know what type of product is involved (Yes, I've heard of Island Spice, it is a new tea). The percentage answering correctly would be the awareness measure. Different measures of awareness are possible: top-of-mind awareness (first brand mentioned, without any prompting), other unaided mention, or aided awareness.

Awareness may also be an advertising response measure that could be instrumental at generating loyalty such as postulated in Model B in Table 3-1. Some low-involvement products like gum, soap, or beer are purchased without much thought or consideration. The choice is often based upon which brand is most familiar. One role of advertising is to get a brand to be more prominent in people's mind so that it is the choice in those no-thought choices. The goal in such situations could be to improve top-of-mind awareness, since this should indicate maximum familiarity.

Brand Comprehension

Another communication task for which advertising is well suited is to communicate facts about the brand, in particular about its attributes. Thus, it may be pivotal to communicate that the brand tastes fresher than competitors or that it rides better. Model C in Table 3-1 shows a new brand context in which trial purchase is not only dependent upon brand awareness but also learning about a key brand attribute. The brand perception on that attribute could be measured by asking respondents whether they agree or disagree that the brand has that attribute:

Agree Strongly +3 +2 +1   0   −1 −2 −3 Disagree Strongly

In Model D in Table 3-1, the behavioral goal is to increase usage. The brand comprehension intervening variable is to communicate knowledge of a new application. Such a campaign was run by Arm & Hammer baking soda in 1972 who wanted to get people to use the product to deodorize refrigerators.[2] The percentage of households that reported having used the product in this application went from 1 percent to 57 percent in just 14 months. Later campaigns suggested its use as a sink, freezer, and cat-litter deodorizer.

In an industrial context, a goal might be to get organizations to purchase the advertised product. However, a realistic appraisal might indicate that a personal selling effort will play the key role in precipitating the decision. The role of advertising might then be to support the sales force by creating inquiries or by communicating information about the company as suggested by Models E and F in Table 3-1. McGraw-Hill's advertisement, shown in Figure 3-10, dramatically illustrates the role that advertising can play in supporting the sales effort. It is useful to note that communication is not expected to play any

TABLE 3-1. Intervening and Behavioral Variables

Model	Advertising variable	Intervening variables	Behavioral variables
A	Advertising	Brand Awareness	Trial Purchase
B	Advertising	Brand Awareness	Loyalty
C	Advertising	Brand Awareness → Knowledge of Brand Attributes	Trial Purchase
D	Advertising	Knowledge of New Application	Increase Usage
E	Advertising		Sales Leads
F	Advertising	Knowledge About Company	Sales Via Personal Selling
G	Advertising	Associate Brand with User Type	Loyalty
H	Advertising	Brand Attitude	Loyalty
I	Advertising	Associate Feelings with Brand Use	Loyalty
J	Advertising	Brand Awareness → Knowledge of Brand Attributes → Brand Attitude	Trial Purchase
K	Advertising	Knowledge of Brand Attributes / Brand Attitude	Trial Purchase

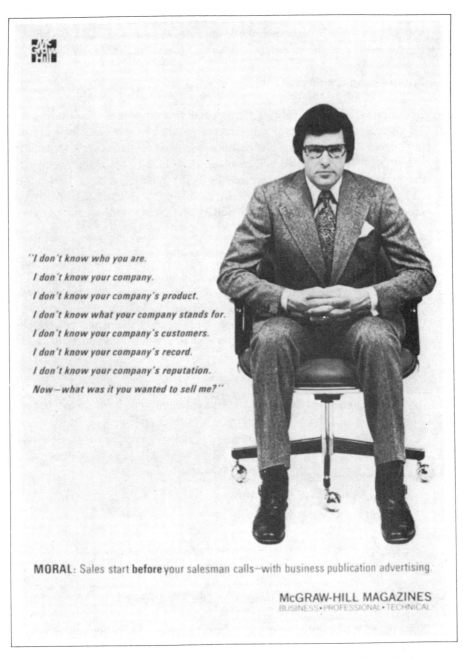

Figure 3-10.   Advertising's role in supporting the personal selling effort
Courtesy of McGraw-Hill Publications Company.

significant direct role in precipitating purchase decisions. Thus, it would not be reasonable to measure its impact in terms of purchase decisions. Rather, it is linked causally with the reception that the salesperson receives, particularly on early visits.

Brand Image and Personality

Brand image and personality refer especially to types of associations that the brand develops with a type of person or even another product. Thus, Charlie perfume, illustrated in Chapter 4 (Figure 4-2), is a perfume designed around a very specific type of female life-style. It is represented as Model G in Table 3-1. Macintosh computers compete in the personal computer marketplace by being positioned as a "friendlier" computer. Chapter 8 will explore in more detail the nature of a brand personality objective and a procedure for generating image objective alternatives and selecting among them.

Brand Attitude

A brand attitude represents the like-dislike feeling toward a brand. Model H in Table 3-1 shows a case where loyalty is predicated upon increasing the attitude toward the object.

Attitude can be measured in a variety of ways, as will be discussed in Chapter 6. One approach is to base it upon people's brand comprehension, perceptions of the brand with respect to specific attributes and characteristics. Another is to tap the like-dislike dimensions as with this scale:

$$\text{Dislike} \quad -3 \; -2 \; -1 \quad 0 \quad +1 \; +2 \; +3 \quad \text{Like}$$

Still another, to base it upon behavioral intentions, is closer to a behavioral measure:

- I will definitely buy this brand
- I will probably buy this brand
- I might buy this brand
- I doubt that I will buy this brand
- I will not buy this brand

Chapter 6 will cover attitudes and their use in advertising objectives in detail. It will also include the role that brand comprehension has in creating and changing attitudes.

Associating Feelings with Brands or Use Experiences

Sometimes the advertising objective can be to create feelings of warmth, energy, fun, anticipation, fear, or concern and associate those feelings with the brand and the use experience. Model I in Table 3-1 could represent a gum brand which is attempting to associate feelings of togetherness and happiness with its use.

There are well-developed models, concepts, and measures that guide our use of image and attitude objectives. In contrast, the role of feelings is much less mature and far less is known about how they work or even if they do work. It is likely that feelings influence both image and attitude, but it is not clear how the process occurs. Chapter 7 will present some emerging ideas about the feeling response to advertising. It suggests that in addition to measuring how audience members feel when being exposed to a commercial it might be useful to measure how they liked the commercial and their impressions of their use experience with the brand. The concept is that if feeling advertising (at least positive feeling advertising) is effective, it will probably result in advertising that is liked and should impact upon the use experience.

More Complex Models and Multiple Objectives

In many contexts, there are two or more advertising responses that are needed for a desired behavior to occur. For example, Model J in Table 3-1 shows a trial purchase model that suggested that awareness can lead to trial purchase directly or through the creation of attribute knowledge and brand attitude. There are thus two routes to precipitating trial. Model K shows another multiple construct model, one in which there is no sequence implied. Two tasks are required but need not precede the other.

When the advertising campaign can focus upon a single, well-defined objective, the communication task is made easier. When several objectives are introduced, there is always the danger that the campaign will become a compromise that will be ineffective with respect to all objectives. Copywriting wisdom suggests that simplicity in ad advertisement is vital: an ad that tries to say too much loses focus and becomes ineffective (we will discuss principles of good copywriting in Chapter 13).

In addition, research has shown that advertising which tries to maximize effectiveness with regard to one objective very often fails to be effective on other objectives. For instance, an advertisement that is very successful in attracting attention (for example, by creating anxiety or fear) may fail to persuade (because people may get defensive in the face of such anxiety). As another example, an advertisement using a famous spokesperson may get a lot of people to pay attention, but fewer copy points may get communicated because people who watch the ad may pay more attention to (and get distracted by) the spokesperson, thus paying less attention to the message content of the ad. This aspect of advertising response has been named the ''compensation principle'' by the psychologist William McGuire, who implies that single advertisements must therefore not aim at more than one objective, and that different and complementary advertisements must be created (as part of a total campaign) if there is more than one objective.[3]

Thus, when it is appropriate and necessary to deal with multiple objectives, these multiple objectives could require more than one advertising message, although such a need may not be determined until after the creative process has begun.

Multiple objectives could involve more than one target audience. For example, a computer company might need to gain awareness among one segment and to communicate the existence of a new product to another. Or there might be two communication tasks for the same target segment. For example, an industrial chemical company might need to generate sales leads for its salespeople and to establish an image of a solid company of

Figure 3-11. An advertisement with multiple objectives
Courtesy of Rensfield Importers, Ltd.

substance. The advertisement shown in Figure 3-11 has multiple objectives, according to William D. Tyler, an *Advertising Age* columnist.[4] It was designed both to create brand-name registration and to position the brand along several dimensions. With respect to positioning, it stresses the English origin, emphasizes a dryness theme, and at the same time makes it seem fun to drink.

A distinction should be made between multiple objectives and multiple measures of the same objective. A reminder advertising campaign might be measured by short-term sales and by top-of-mind awareness using unaided recall techniques. Involved are two measures of the impact of the advertising upon immediate purchase of the product, rather than two objectives.

SPECIFYING THE TARGET SEGMENT

A basic question in the objective-setting process is the identity of the target segment. To whom is the advertising to be addressed? The target audience can be defined in many ways, and Chapter 4 provides a detailed discussion of segmentation and segmentation variables. The process of objective setting is intimately connected with that of selecting a target segment and may involve subsegments that are relevant to the communication task. For example, in the case of marketing a product line to small banks, it might be appropriate to communicate cost savings for a computer model to bank presidents, software reliability to bank administrative personnel, and to ignore loan officers. Although the general marketing strategy would include all professionals in small banks, the advertising objectives could appropriately refine this group into subgroups.

The behavioral measures discussed in this chapter such as usage and loyalty can also be used to define target segments. A target thus could be the heavy user, the nonuser, the loyal user of our brand, or the group loyal to another brand. In Chapter 4, benefit segmentation will be explored where a target segment is defined by the benefits sought from a product. For example, a target segment might be those who are particularly concerned with the cost of operating a computer, whereas another segment might be interested primarily in the computer's speed.

The advertising response measures just presented can be particularly useful segmentation variables in the advertising context. Thus, segments can often be identified that are unaware of the brand, do not know or are not convinced that it has a key attribute, or have not yet developed a positive attitude. One or more of these segments can then be selected as the primary target. Such a segmentation choice can make the advertising more effective since a campaign designed to create awareness will tend to be very different from one designed to communicate a product attribute.

DAGMAR

The approach to setting advertising objectives just outlined will be expanded upon in the next seven chapters and in the balance of the book. Research findings, constructs, and measurement tools will be developed that will serve to make the approach effective and operational. In this section of this chapter, the historical foundations for our approach to setting advertising objectives will be presented. It provides a rationale and basis for the introduction of advertising response measures in advertising objectives and for the concept of measuring such objectives over time.

There are several reasons for this diversion. First, the historical roots of the approach are not only interesting but provide a deeper understanding of thrust and scope. Second, they provide suggestions on implementation that are still useful and valid.

In 1961, Russell H. Colley wrote a book under the sponsorship of the Association of National Advertisers called *Defining Advertising Goals for Measured Advertising Results.*[5] The book introduced what has become known as the DAGMAR approach to advertising planning and included a precise method for selecting and quantifying goals and for using those goals to measure performance. The performance measurement feature had great appeal to managers of the 1960s, who were frustrated by the available methods for controlling advertising efforts and impatient with embryonic methods of developing sales-response models.

The DAGMAR approach can be summarized in its succinct statement defining an advertising goal. An advertising goal is a specific communication task, to be accomplished among a defined audience, in a given period of time. Note that a communication task is involved as opposed to a marketing task and that the goal is specific, involving an unambiguously defined task, among a defined audience, in a given time period.

A COMMUNICATION TASK

An advertising objective involves a communication task, something that advertising, by itself, can reasonably hope to accomplish. It is recognized that advertising is mass, paid communication that is intended to create awareness, impart information, develop attitudes, or induce action.

In DAGMAR, the communication task is based on a specific model of the communication process, as illustrated in Figure 3-12. The model suggests that there is a series of mental steps through which a brand or objects must climb to gain acceptance. An in-

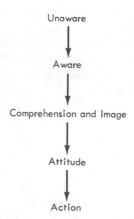

Figure 3-12.   A hierarchy of effects model of the communication process

dividual starts at some point by being unaware of a brand's presence in the market. The initial task of the brand is to gain awareness—to advance one step up the hierarchy.

The second step of brand comprehension involves the audience member learning something about the brand. What are its specific characteristics and appeals, including associated imagery and feelings? In what way does it differ from its competitors? Whom is it supposed to benefit? The third step is the attitude (or conviction) step and intervenes between comprehension and final action. The action phase involves some overt move on the part of the buyer like trying a brand for the first time, visiting a showroom, or requesting information.

A communication model like the DAGMAR model with the implication that the audience member will sequentially pass through a set of steps is termed a "hierarchy-of-effects" model. A host of hierarchy models have been proposed. The AIDA model, developed in the 1920s, suggested that an effective personal sales presentation should attract Attention, gain Interest, create a Desire, and precipitate Action. The new adopter hierarchy model, conceived by rural sociologists, postulated five stages: awareness, interest, evaluation, trial, and adoption.

Another hierarchy model is particularly interesting because of its close ties with social psychological theory. Developed by Robert Lavidge and Gary Steiner,[6] it includes six stages: awareness, knowledge, liking, preference, conviction, and purchase. They divided this hierarchy into the three components corresponding to a social psychologist's concept of an attitude system. The first stage, consisting of the awareness and knowledge levels, is comparable to the cognitive or knowledge component of attitude. The affective component of an attitude, the like-dislike aspect, is represented in the Lavidge and Steiner hierarchy by the liking and preference levels. The remaining attitude component is the conative component, the action or motivation element, represented by the conviction and purchase levels, the final two levels in the hierarchy.

A Specific Task

We have mentioned that DAGMAR emphasizes the communication task of advertising as contrasted to the marketing objectives of the firm. The second important concept of DAGMAR is that the advertising goal be specific. It should be a written, measurable task involving a starting point, a defined audience, and a fixed time period.

Measurable. DAGMAR needs to be made specific when actual goals are formulated. When brand comprehension is involved, for example, it is necessary to indicate exactly what appeal or image is to be communicated. Furthermore, the specification should include a description of the measurement procedure. If a high-protein cereal were trying to gain brand comprehension, managers could well decide to promote its protein content. However, merely mentioning its protein content is inadequate and open to different interpretations. Is the cereal to be perceived as one containing a full day's supply as a protection against illness or as one that supplies more energy than other cereals? If a survey includes the request, "Rank the following cereals as to protein content," then brand comprehension could be quantified to mean the percentage who rated it first.

Benchmark.   President Lincoln has been quoted as saying, "If we could first know where we are and whither we are tending, we could better judge what to do and how to do it."[7] A basic aspect of establishing a goal and selecting a campaign to reach it is to know the starting conditions. Without a benchmark, it is most difficult to determine the optimal goal. The selection of an awareness-oriented goal might be a mistake if awareness is already high. Without a benchmark measure, such a circumstance could not be ascertained quantitatively. In addition, benchmarks can suggest how a certain goal can best be reached. For example, it would be useful to know whether the existing image needs to be changed, reinforced, diffused, or sharpened. A benchmark is also a prerequisite to the ultimate measurement of results, an essential part of any planning program and of DAGMAR in particular. Despite the obvious value of having benchmarks before goals are set, this is often not done. In fact, the key to DAGMAR is probably the generation of well-conceived benchmarks before advertising goals are determined. With such measures, the rest of the approach flows rather naturally.

The Target.   A key tenet of DAGMAR was that the target audience be well defined. If the goal was to increase awareness, for example, it was essential to know the target audience precisely. Perhaps the goal was to increase awareness among the heavy user segment from 25 percent to 60 percent in a certain time period. The benchmark measure could not be developed without a specification of the target segment. Further, the campaign execution will normally depend on the identity of the target segment. The heavy user group will likely respond differently from a segment defined by a life-style profile.

Time Period.   The objective should involve a particular time period, such as six months or one year. With a time period specified, a survey to generate a set of measures can be planned and anticipated. All parties involved will understand that the results will be available for evaluating the campaign, which could lead to a contraction, expansion, or change in the current effort. The length of the time period must fit into various constraints involving the planning cycle of both a company and an agency. However, the appropriate time necessary to generate the kind of cognitive response desired should also be considered.

Written.   Finally, goals should be committed to paper. Under the discipline of writing clearly, basic shortcomings and misunderstandings become exposed, and it becomes easy to determine whether the goal contains the crucial aspects of the DAGMAR approach.

Suppose that the product of interest were an economy-priced bourbon. It has a bad quality image despite the fact that blind taste tests indicated that it does not have any real quality problems. An objective might be developed with respect to a scale ranging from -5 to $+5$ (inadequate taste to adequate taste). An admissible objective would be to increase the percentage of male bourbon drinkers in the United States who give a non-negative rating on the scale from 5 to 25 percent in a 12-month period. Notice that this objective is measurable and has a starting point, a definite audience, and a fixed time period.

The DAGMAR Checklist

An aid to those implementing the DAGMAR approach is a checklist of promotional tasks, partially reproduced as Table 3-2. The suggestion was to rate each of the promotional tasks in terms of its relative importance in the context of the product situation involved. The intent was to stimulate ideas or decision alternatives, often the most difficult and crucial part of the decision process.

TABLE 3-2.   Partial Checklist of Promotional Tasks[a]

To what extent does the advertising aim at closing an immediate sale?

1. Perform the complete selling function (take the product through all the necessary steps toward a sale).
2. Close sales to prospects already partly sold through past advertising efforts ("ask for the order" or "clincher" advertising).
3. Announce a special reason for "buying now" (price, premium, etc.).
4. *Remind* people to buy.
5. Tie in with some special buying event.
6. Stimulate impulse sales.

Does the advertising aim at near-term sales by moving the prospect, step by step, closer to a sale (so that when confronted with a buying situation, the customer will ask for, reach for, or accept the advertised brand)?

7. Create awareness of existence of the product or brand.
8. Create *brand image* or favorable emotional disposition toward the brand.
9. Implant information or attitude regarding benefits and superior features of brand.
10. Combat or offset competitive claims.
11. Correct false impressions, misinformation, and other obstacles to sales.
12. Build familiarity and easy recognition of package or trademark.

Does the advertising aim at building a long-range consumer franchise?

13. Build confidence in company and brand, which is expected to pay off in years to come.
14. Build consumer demand that places company in stronger position in relation to its distribution (not at the "mercy of the marketplace").
15. Place advertiser in position to select preferred distributors and dealers.
16. Secure universal distribution.
17. Establish a "reputation platform" for launching new brands or product lines.
18. Establish brand recognition and acceptance that will enable the company to open up new markets (geographic, price, age, sex).

How important are supplementary benefits of end-use advertising?

19. Aid salespeople in opening new accounts.
20. Aid salespeople in getting larger orders from wholesalers and retailers.
21. Aid salespeople in getting preferred display space.
22. Give salespeople an entree.
23. Build morale of company sales force.
24. Impress the trade.

[a]The complete list included 52 items.

Source: Russell H. Colley, *Defining Advertising Goals for Measured Advertising Results* (New York: Association of National Advertisers, 1961), pp. 61–68.

Following are two examples of the DAGMAR approach as presented in Colley's book. It is left to the reader to examine these examples critically to see if they satisfy the requirements of the approach as it has been presented here.

Overseas Airline Service[8]—A DAGMAR Case Study

The company is one of the smaller of several dozen airlines competing for American overseas airline passengers. It was recognized at the outset that it was impossible to compete with the giant airlines in advertising volume. The small budget would not permit the size of space, frequency, and media breadth used by the major airlines.

The copy and media strategy decided upon was, therefore, to concentrate on a particular segment of the audience, with a highly distinctive copy and art approach beamed at this particular audience.

Audience: experienced, sophisticated world travelers.

Message: the image of an airline that caters to a distinctive, discriminating, travel-wise audience.

Experience and judgment indicated that selling to the seasoned traveler was wise strategy. Not only does he or she make a more frequent customer, but his or her advice is sought and habits are emulated by the "first trippers."

Art and copy, in a highly distinctive style, were directed at attracting the attention and interest of the more experienced and sophisticated world travelers. In fact, a new name was coined and used extensively in the advertising to refer to such a person (TRAVOIR-FAIRE). Instead of featuring the more commonplace tourist attractions in the countries served, the advertising featured off-the-beaten-path scenes and unusual objects of art and interest. Whereas mass-appeal airlines were featuring hardware (make and speed of their jet service), advertising of the subject airline treated the make and speed of the airliner in a subtle manner and emphasized instead distinctive items of decor, comfort, cuisine, and service.

In addition to the usual reports of opinion on advertising effectiveness that come through inquiries and comments made to ticket and travel agents, the company conducted an inexpensive attitude survey. Travel agents in selected cities furnished names and addresses of overseas travelers (two or more trips). Mail questionnaires were sent out periodically to a representative sample of several hundred such persons. Questions were directed toward determining the following information:

Awareness: What airlines can you name that offer all-jet service to _____?

Image: Which of these airlines would you rate as outstanding on the following? (A checklist of characteristics and features was included.)

Preference: On your next overseas trip, which of these airlines would you seriously consider? Why?

An unusually high return of questionnaires was received because of the offer of a free booklet of high interest to international travelers. Survey costs were small (several hundred dollars for each semiannual survey).

The results shown in the accompanying table indicate a steadily rising awareness, a growing image as portrayed in the advertising, and an increase in preference. This was ample indication that advertising had succeeded in conveying the intended message to the selected audience.

Survey Results (Percent)

	Before advertising campaign	End of six month	End of one year
Awareness (have heard of company	38	46	52
Image (luxury all-jet overseas service)	9	17	24
Preference (would seriously consider for next trip)	13	15	21

Electrical Appliances[9]—A DAGMAR Case Study

The following case example concerns electrical appliances but serves to illustrate other consumer durables such as automobiles or furniture.

The market is 26 million housewives who are logical prospects. A logical prospect is defined as an owner of an appliance three years old or more, plus new households formed by marriage and new home construction.

Marketing Objective. Get sales action now, sell carloads of appliances this season, thus reducing substantial dealer and manufacturer inventories.

Advertising Objective. Induce immediate action. The brand name and product advantages are already well known through consistent and effective advertising.

Advertising's task, at this particular stage, is to persuade housewives to visit dealers' showrooms and see a demonstration. A special ice cube tray is offered as an added inducement.

Specific Advertising Goal. To persuade 400,000 homemakers to visit 10,000 dealers in four weeks, an average of 40 prospects who will physically cross the threshold of each dealer's showroom.

Results were measured in several different dimensions. The media: sponsorship of special audience telecasts. The results: two telecasts drew a combined audience of 84 million people. Approximately 18 percent, or 15 million people, could play back the commercial messages. Nearly half a million took immediate action by walking into a dealer's showroom and purchasing the special offer. Advertising accomplished its assigned task by inducing consumers to visit the dealer's showroom. It is true that dealers sold a large volume of appliances during the special promotion. But advertising cannot claim all the credit since it was only one factor in the consummation of the sale. However, further research indicated that 44 percent of the people who bought a refrigerator gave advertising as the major factor in choice of brand.

Challenges to DAGMAR

DAGMAR had enormous visibility and influence. It really changed the way that advertising objectives were created and the way that advertising results were measured. It introduced the concept of communication objectives like awareness, comprehension, image, and attitude. The point was made that such goals are more appropriate for advertising than is some measure like sales which can have multiple causes. In introducing communication objectives, behavioral science constructs and models such as attitude models were drawn upon. DAGMAR also focused attention upon measurement encouraging people to create objectives so specific and operational that they can be measured. In doing so, it provided the potential to improve the communication between the creative teams and the advertising clients.

A measure of the significance of an idea is the degree of both theoretical and empirical controversy that it precipitates. By this measure DAGMAR has been most significant. There have been six different kinds of challenges to DAGMAR.

Sales Goal.   First, some purists believe that only a sales measure is relevant. As pointed out by Michael Halbert, one of the pioneering group at Du Pont engaged in the use of experimental-design approaches to measure advertising effect,[10]

> When a study using one of the goals just mentioned [e.g., increase awareness] is published and reported at a meeting, I sometimes get the unsocial urge to question the author with, "So what?" If he has shown that advertising does, in fact, increase brand name awareness or favorable attitude toward the company, on what grounds does this indicate a justifiable use of the company's funds? The answer usually given is that more people will buy a product if they are aware of it or if they have a favorable attitude. But why leave this critical piece of inference out of the design of the original research?

For example, if awareness does not affect sales, why bother to measure it? If it does have a close relationship, why not measure sales directly? This argument has gained strength in recent years since it is now possible to measure advertising effects on short-term sales for packaged goods with great precision through controlled experiments utilizing scanner data panels (see Chapter 16). However, as mentioned before, even these tests cannot typically yield unambiguous estimates of the long-term effects of advertising. Thus the debate is inconclusive, and a more refined model of the communication process than is now available must eventually evolve.

Practicability.   A second objection focuses on the many implementation difficulties inherent in the DAGMAR approach. In particular, the checklist falls short of providing sufficient details to implement the approach. As Leo Bogart has observed, Colley provides broad outlines much like the dragonfly that, after showing a hippopotamus the relationship between wing movement and flying, was asked exactly how to do it and replied, "I'll give you the broad idea and you work out the details."[11] A level in the hierarchy to be attacked must be selected, and a campaign to influence those at that level must be developed. Neither of these tasks is easy.

Measurement Problems.   The third problem is measurement. What should we really measure when we speak of attitude, awareness, or brand comprehension? Substantial conceptual and measurement problems underlie all these constructs.

Noise in the System.   A fourth problem is noise that exists in the hierarchy model, just as it does in the other, more simple, response models involving immediate sales. We have argued that there are many causal factors other than advertising that determine sales. In a more complex model, it can be argued that there are many causal factors besides advertising that determine awareness. For example, variables such as competitive promotion or unplanned publicity can affect an awareness campaign.

Inhibiting the Great Idea.   The "great creative idea" is a dream or hope of many advertisers (see discussion in Chapter 13). DAGMAR is basically a rational, planned approach that, among other things, provides guidance to creative people. The problem is that if it does in fact have any influence on their work, it must also necessarily inhibit their efforts. When the creative approach of copywriters and art directors is inhibited, there is less likelihood that they will come up with a great idea and an increased probability of a pedestrian advertising campaign resulting. Of course, there might also be a lesser probability of a spectacularly ineffective advertising campaign.

Anthony Morgan, an agency research director, argues that the hierarchy model, which he terms the "HEAR-UNDERSTAND-DO" model, inhibits great advertising by emphasizing tests of recall, communication, and persuasion.[12] He gives two examples. First, a campaign with all music and warm human visuals which everyone loved failed to meet the "company standard" for the day-after recall test (where on the day after ad exposure viewers are asked to recall specific copy points—discussed in Chapter 14). A potentially great campaign was clearly being evaluated by the wrong criteria. A more appropriate model for this campaign might have been "SENSE-FEEL-RELATE." Chapter 7 will expand on this concept.

The second example is the Campbell's Soup "Soup Is Good Food" campaign created to arrest a ten-year decline in per capita consumption of Campbell's Red & White line of soups. The campaign objectives were to communicate news, to change the perception of soup, and to increase consumption. The first commercials received the lowest persuasion scores (from a test measuring the impact of commercial exposure on attitudes and intentions) that any Campbell's commercial had ever scored. However, the campaign, which stimulated three years of sales increases, was designed not to have much initial impact but to withstand enormous repetitions and to work over time. The testing was simply inappropriate. The implication is that it can be dangerous to rely on testing based on the hierarchical model (or any other single conceptualization). Rather, conceptual and research flexibility needs to be employed.

Hierarchy Model of Communication Effect.   The sixth type of argument against the DAGMAR approach attacks the basic hierarchy model which postulates a set of sequential steps of awareness, comprehension, and attitude leading to action. The counterargument is that other models may hold in various contexts and that it is naive to apply the DAG-MAR hierarchy models in all situations. For example, action can precede attitude formation and even comprehension with an impulse purchase of a low-involvement product. At this point there is general agreement that, indeed, the appropriate model will depend upon the situation and a key problem in many contexts is in fact to determine what that model is. We discuss such alternative models and their situational applicability in Chapter 5. However, the basic thrust of DAGMAR—the use of advertising response measures as the basis of objectives and the focus on measurement—does not depend upon the DAGMAR hierarchy model, so this issue is not really that crucial as it may have once appeared.

We now turn to implementation of the DAGMAR approach, using two applied examples.

Applied Example One: The Leo Burnett Program (CAPP)

CAPP, an acronym for continuous advertising planning program, was developed by the Leo Burnett advertising agency. As reported by John Maloney,[13] one of its architects, it is based on still another hierarchy-of-effect model consisting of unawareness, awareness, acceptance, preference, brand bought last, and brand satisfaction. Termed "the consumer demand profile," it is shown graphically in Figure 3-13.

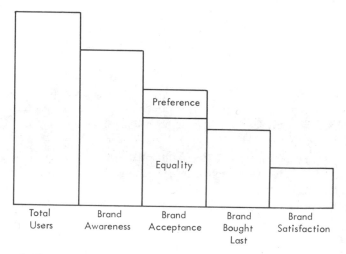

Figure 3-13.   Consumer demand profile

Source: John C. Maloney, "Attitude Measurement and Formation," paper presented at the Test Market Design and Measurement Workshop, American Marketing Association. Chicago, April 21, 1966.

Here, the acceptance level implies that the brand is acceptable to an individual; it meets his or her minimum requirements. Brand preference indicates the percentage of total product-class users who rate the brand, on a four-point scale, higher than any other brand. A unique element of the CAPP hierarchy is brand satisfaction, which is meant to reflect the performance of the brand after purchase and repeat buying.

A cross-sectional sample of 1,000 households, interviewed on a monthly basis, provided the data base. Information was obtained from each household on their media habits and their location on the CAPP hierarchy with respect to the brands of interest. Monthly data provide a sensitive indicator of the response to the advertising campaign. Clearly, such time-series information has much greater and more timely interpretative power than measures restricted to immediately before and immediately after a campaign. If a substantial change is to be generated in a hierarchy measure, progress should be observed along the way and an appropriate campaign developed accordingly.

Which Hierarchy Level?   How can knowledge of the CAPP hierarchy profile and its trends be helpful in determining what level to attack? Maloney suggested an examination of the hierarchy patterns. The adjacent levels in the hierarchy were of particular interest. For example, if there were a small number of people who were aware of the brand (relative to the number of total users), then a worthwhile target could be to increase awareness. If a substantial number of people had accepted the brand, but only a few preferred it, perhaps it would be necessary to sharpen up the brand image in some respect. On the other hand, if there were a high degree of acceptance but a very low level of brand bought last, then it might become necessary to stimulate a trial purchase. If brand satisfaction is low compared to brand bought last, then perhaps there is a basic problem with the brand itself, and some very specific questions should be asked about its capacity to satisfy customer wants and needs.

Essentially, the proposal is to consider the ratio of the size of adjacent levels, for example, the number of those who bought the brand last divided by the number who indicated brand satisfaction. A good level to consider as an objective is one for which this ratio involving the next lower level is high. This decision rule reflects the fact that it is usually worthwhile to concentrate on large segments and ignore smaller ones. It identifies that segment that contains large numbers of potential movers.

Naturally, it would be desirable to refine this decision rule by providing numerical guidelines. To do so, the profile histories associated with other brands in the product class would have to be considered to provide a frame of reference. The ultimate goal should be to expand the decision rule into a decision model that would make Maloney's suggestion explicit. Such a model will be developed, but in the context of our second applied example.

Applied Example Two: The General Motors Approach

Another major application of DAGMAR was the General Motors approach, as reported by Gail Smith.[14] Although General Motors reportedly does not use this approach currently,[15] believing that the effects of advertising and other marketing elements (such as word of mouth, dealer experience, news reports) are impossible to disentangle for even these intermediate nonsales effects, it nonetheless serves as an excellent example of the kind of analysis that DAGMAR makes possible.

· The data base for this effort consisted of six matched, cross-sectional surveys taken in September, October, December, January, March, and June. In the automobile industry, the impact of advertising effort is much more important in the fall than in the summer; therefore, the measurement schedule was adjusted accordingly. Seven types of information, shown in Table 3-3, were obtained in each survey. They included a hierarchy measure, product image, message registration, market behavior, product inventory, demographics, and media consumption.

The hierarchy used by General Motors consisted of awareness, "buying class," "consideration class," and first choice. A brand is in a respondent's buying class if she or he considers it similar to or competitive with the brands she or he would actively consider when entering the market. Consideration class consists of those brands the respondent will favorably consider the next time he or she enters the market. Both of these measures were obtained through open-ended questions. The first choice is the one brand the respondent would select if a choice were made at the time the questionnaire was administered.

TABLE 3-3. General Content of the Questionnaire Used to Establish Advertising Goals for General Motors Products

---

  I. Preference levels by brand, by series of brand
    Awareness
    "Buying class"
    "Consideration class"
  II. Product image
  III. Message registration
    Specific product attributes
    Slogans
    Story line
  IV. Market behavior
    Shopping behavior, dealer visits
    Purchases
    Intentions
  V. Product inventory
    Content and condition
  VI. Demographics
  VII. Media consumption
    Television: by hours per week, by selected programs
    Magazines: by hours per week, by selected magazines
    Radio: by hours per week, by time slot
    Newspapers: by hours per week, by type

Source: Gail Smith, "How GM Measures Ad Effectiveness," in Keith K. Cox, ed., *Readings in Market Research* (New York: Appleton-Century-Crofts, 1967), p. 172.

The image section consisted of 35 semantic differential questions measuring such dimensions as styling, prestige, and trade-in value. The message registration section measured the impact of the advertising. Did the slogans and the product attributes that were part of the advertising message get through to the audience? This information, in conjunction with the media consumption data, is, of course, interesting in itself. It provides the possibility of measuring the relative message impact of the various media. The market behavior section includes shopping behavior, purchases, and intentions. These kinds of constructs represent the ultimate payoff, and we shall attempt to use them to quantify the decision about which level to attack. The product inventory and demographic sections provided information that permits cross-classification on the data, a basic approach to evaluating segmentation strategies. For example, the answers from young owners of foreign cars might be compared with responses from young owners of American cars.

Which Hierarchy Level?   The existence of such cross-sectional information provides a firm basis for the DAGMAR approach. However, to provide sensitive measures of the economic value of goal accomplishment, it is desirable to measure the same respondent at several points in time. Accordingly, General Motors questioned a subsample of the respondents in each survey 12 months later. One purpose was to obtain a measure of the accuracy of answers regarding planned shopping behavior, dealer visits, and so forth. Table 3-4 summarizes such information for a car, here called Watusi, which was developed by General Motors for the youth market.

The first column of Table 3-4 shows the sample proportion in each hierarchy level. The second indicates the probability that the respondent will visit a dealer. The third, the probability of a Watusi purchase, potentially provides the basis for an economic judgment about which level in the hierarchy would be the most profitable to attack. The table indicates that, if a respondent gave Watusi as a first choice, his or her probability of buying would be 0.56, whereas if the Watusi was only in the consideration class, the purchase probability would be 0.22. Thus, if someone who moves up to the "first-choice"

TABLE 3-4.   Value of Preference Levels in Terms of Probability and Dealer Visitation and Purchase

Hierarchy level		Preference level proportion	Probability will visit Watusi dealer	Probability will buy Watusi
5	Watusi first choice	0.05	0.840	0.560
4	Watusi in consideration class	0.07	0.620	0.220
3	Watusi in buying class	0.08	0.400	0.090
2	Aware of Watusi	0.14	0.240	0.050
1	Not aware of Watusi	0.66	0.015	0.004
	Total	1.00		

Source: Gail Smith, "How GM Measures Ad Effectiveness," in Keith K. Cox, ed., *Readings in Market Research* (New York: Appleton-Century-Crofts, 1967), p. 175.

hierarchy level behaves like those already there, the latter's purchase probability would increase by

$$0.56 - 0.22 = 0.34$$

To determine the relative value of a campaign directed at those in the consideration class hierarchy level, it would also be necessary to weigh (1) the number of people in the consideration class hierarchy level and (2) the cost and effectiveness of an advertising campaign designed to move them to the first-choice hierarchy level.

Moving People up the Hierarchy.   How can advertising go about moving people from one hierarchy level to another? This problem will be addressed in later chapters of the book. However, it is useful to consider here the General Motors approach, which was based upon a 35-question semantic differential. Brand image profiles for all people on each level were obtained and an average secured for each level. Table 3-5 shows such average profiles for those in the consideration class and the buying class. These average profiles are then compared and significant differences between them are noted.

In Table 3-5, the largest difference is the image dimension labeled "trade-in value." Thus, it seems reasonable to work on this particular dimension to move the image of those in the buying class toward the image of those in the consideration class. The assumption is that, if an image can be so changed for an individual, he or she will change classes so that the new image will match the average image of "his or her class." Perhaps this is an extreme assumption. It places undue stress on the average. Nevertheless, this approach does have appeal.

TABLE 3-5.   **Ratings of Watusi, by Item, by Those Considering Watusi to Be in Their Buying Class (on scale of 1–100)**

	But will not give it favorable consideration	*But will give it favorable consideration*	*Difference*
Smooth riding	88	91	3
Styling	76	89	13
Overall comfort	81	87	6
Handling	83	86	3
Spacious interior	85	85	0
Luxurious interior	79	85	6
Quality of workmanship	80	83	3
Advanced engineering	77	83	6
Prestige	73	82	9
Value for the money	76	79	3
Trade-in value	59	77	18
Cost of upkeep and maintenance	63	67	4
Gas economy	58	58	0

Source: Gail Smith, "How GM Measures Ad Effectiveness," in Keith K. Cox, ed., *Readings in Market Research* (New York: Appleton-Century-Crofts, 1967), p. 176.

To implement these hypothetical conclusions properly, it is necessary to reach those in the level of interest, in this case, the buying class. The survey information reported in Table 3-3 includes a media-consumption section. Using these data, it may be possible to identify media vehicles that will be effective in reaching those in the buying class. Furthermore, it may be possible to reach those in that class who have a low impression of the trade-in value of the Watusi automobile. Thus, to the extent that vehicles can be so identified, the cost of changing the image of the average profile is minimized.

SUMMARY

Operational objectives provide criteria for decision making, standards against which to evaluate performance, and serve as a communication tool. Short-run sales usually do not provide the basis for operational objectives for two reasons: (1) advertising is usually only one of many factors influencing sales, and (2) the impact of advertising often occurs primarily over the long run.

The development of more operational objectives involves three considerations. First, the behavioral decisions or actions that advertising is attempting to influence need to be analyzed. The relevant behavior could be visiting a retailer, trying a new brand, increasing usage levels, maintaining existing brand loyalties, or donating money to a charity. Second, the communication and decision process that precedes and influences that behavior should be examined. This process will usually involve constructs like awareness, image, or attitude. Third, the specification of the target segment needs to be specified. Segment defining variables that are often useful include usage, benefits sought, awareness level, brand perceptions, and life-style.

This approach to setting objectives is a refinement and extension of an approach developed over a decade ago and known as DAGMAR. DAGMAR defines an advertising goal as a specific communication task to be accomplished among a defined audience in a given time period. Thus, a communication task is involved, as opposed to a marketing task, based on a hierarchy model of the communication process involving awareness, comprehension, attitude, and action. The goal is specific, with a definite measure, a starting point, a defined audience, and a fixed time period.

By introducing behavioral science theory into advertising management, DAGMAR provides the framework for the development of more operational objectives. However, it has been challenged through the years on several fronts. Some critics believe that the only appropriate measure of advertising is sales. Another objection is that it is difficult to select a hierarchy level on which to base objectives and to know how to move people up the hierarchy. Others believe that the approach is limited by measurement problems and noise in the system. By providing guidance to operating people, DAGMAR is said to inhibit the development of "the great idea."

Another criticism is that a single hierarchy model of the communication process is not appropriate, and that different hierarchies may be relevant in different kinds of situations. A crucial question in many advertising campaigns therefore is to determine which intervening variable is most important in leading to sales in different situations, and consequently needs to be the focus of the campaign. Here, research conducted over the last thirty years on "how advertising works" needs to be examined (see Chapter 5). In addition, the advertiser also needs to determine those hierarchy levels that have not yet been reached by large numbers of potential customers. An extension of this approach is to not only consider the size of the segment, but the difficulty, and therefore cost, of moving them up the hierarchy, as well as the likelihood of their eventually making the desired decision (e.g., to buy an automobile) once they have moved up.

DISCUSSION QUESTIONS

1. What are operational objectives? Consider various organizations. By research or by speculation, determine their objectives. Are they operational? Is profit maximization an operational business objective? Is sales maximization an operational advertising objective? Under what circumstances might it be?

2. Evaluate the judgment of a brand manager of Budweiser beer who decides that the goal of his advertising should be to remind people of the brand.

3. Why might advertising have an impact many years after it appears?

4. Distinguish between a communication objective and a marketing objective.

5. What is the difference between brand image or personality, brand comprehension, and brand attitude?

6. How would you go about selecting which advertising response variable on which to base an advertising objective?

7. If awareness does not affect sales, why bother to measure it? If it does have a close relationship to sales, why not measure sales directly? Comment.

8. What is the "great idea" concept? Identify some campaigns that would qualify. Attempt to specify a set of DAGMAR objectives that might apply. Is DAGMAR inconsistent with the hope of obtaining a truly brilliant creative advertising campaign?

9. Consider the CAPP data of Figure 3-13. Suppose that brand acceptance was 50 percent but brand preference was only 3 percent. What would be your diagnosis if you were a brand manager for a cereal? For an appliance? What if the brand awareness were 90 percent but brand acceptance were only 30 percent?

10. In the Watusi example, it was suggested that the "trade-in value" would be a good appeal to use. What were the assumptions that underlie that conclusion? Given Table 3-5, under what conditions would it be worthwhile to focus on the "spacious interior"?

11. Two case studies were presented in the chapter, Overseas Airline Service and Electrical Appliances. Two more are presented with the appendix, Regional Brand of Beer and Cranberries. For each of the four consider the following questions:
   a. Were the principles of DAGMAR followed to the letter?
   b. What objectives would you establish for the upcoming period?

NOTES

1. D. G. Clarke, "Econometric Measurement of the Duration of Advertising Effect on Sales," *Journal of Marketing Research,* 13, November 1986, pp. 345–357.

2. Jack J. Honomichl, "The Ongoing Saga of 'Mother Baking Soda,' " *Advertising Age,* September 20, 1982, pp. M2–M3.

3. William J. McGuire, "An Information Processing Model of Advertising Effectiveness," in H. L. Davis and A. J. Silk (eds.), *Behavioral and Management Science in Marketing* (New York: Ronald Press, 1978), pp. 156–180.

4. William D. Tyler, "Amazing, But It's True: Print Ads Are Getting More, Not Less, Gutzy," *Advertising Age,* March 5, 1973, p. 35.

5. Russell H. Colley, *Defining Advertising Goals for Measured Advertising Results* (New York: Association of National Advertisers, 1961).

6. Robert J. Lavidge and Gary A. Steiner, "A Model for Predictive Measurements of Advertising Effectiveness," *Journal of Marketing,* 25, October 1961, pp. 59–62.

7. Colley, *Defining Advertising Goals,* p. 31.

8. Ibid., p. 83.

9. Ibid., p. 73.

10. Michael Halbert, "What Do We Buy with an Advertising Dollar?" Speech presented at the Ninth Annual Seminar in Marketing Management, Miami University, Oxford, Ohio, May 1961.

11. Leo Bogart, *Strategy in Advertising* (New York: Harcourt Brace Jovanovich, 1967).

12. Anthony L. Morgan, "Who's Killing the Great Advertising Campaigns of America?" *Journal of Advertising Research,* 24, December 1984/January 1985, pp. 33–37.

13. John C. Maloney, "Attitude Measurement and Formation," paper presented at the Test Market Design and Measurement Workshop, American Marketing Association, Chicago, April 21, 1966.

14. Gail Smith, "How GM Measures Ad Effectiveness," in Keith K. Cox, ed., *Readings in Market Research* (New York: Appleton-Century-Crofts, 1967).

15. Andy Hardy, "GM's New Philosophy for Developing and Assessing Effective Advertising," Paper presented at a Conference of the Marketing Science Institute, June 8, 1988.

APPENDIX: ADDITIONAL CASE STUDIES

Regional Brand of Beer

The subject brand of beer has been the largest-selling brand in its headquarters market for generations. The company has gradually expanded distribution into contiguous markets and now distributes in over a dozen states. Company policy: avoid entering a new market until ready to go all out on advertising and distribution. The first year in a new market advertising expense, as a percentage of sales, will run three or four times the normal expenditure in an established market. It may take two or three years to reach the break-even point.

When first entering a new market, brand awareness is low. It is necessary to match or outspend the largest-selling brand in order to capture a share of the consumer's attention and gradually woo him or her to try the brand. Management believes that anyone who is not prepared to enter competitive combat, quantitatively and qualitatively, is wasting money trying to open up new markets in this industry.

Advertising objective: deep and incessant exposure. The goal is to establish an 80 percent level of brand identity among moderate to heavy beer drinkers in the market area within six months and to maintain that level thereafter. Through a series of simple unaided and aided recall tests, consumers are asked to identify various brands of beer sold and advertised in the market area. Experience in past market introductions has shown that the brand has always succeeded in getting a firm foothold in a market where an 80 percent brand awareness level has been established. Once the brand name is established through "investment" advertising, expenditures as a percentage of the sales dollar return to a normal level.

Cranberries

A hypothetical trade association is made up of growers of cranberries, including many small producers who cannot afford to advertise individually. Consumption of cranberries is highly seasonal, traditionally during the Thanksgiving and Christmas seasons. A poor season, because of weather or other conditions, threatens to wipe out many producers who depend on this single crop for their livelihood. Land is unsuitable for crop diversification. Hence, the salvation of many growers lies in better marketing. Broad marketing objectives are (1) to increase consumption of cranberries and (2) to diversify use of cranberries so that marketing activities are not crowded into one short season.

Marketing Strategy.   Develop new uses of product and create consumer demand through advertising, publicity, and promotion. The first step was to engage food technologists and home economists to develop delectable new recipes. Result: an exciting new product, cranberry bread, was developed and tested.

Advertising Goals.   To spread the word among homemakers that cranberry bread is delicious, easy to bake, and a culinary accomplishment that will bring praise to the cook by all who taste it. Specifically, these one-year goals were set:

> *Awareness (have heard about cranberry bread): 50 percent of market*
> *Favorable attitude (would like to bake it): 25 percent of market*
> *Action (have baked it): 10 percent of market*

Since advertising funds of cranberry growers were very limited, it was necessary to get participation and tie-in advertising of others who would benefit, such as flour millers and nut growers. With advertising as the pivotal force, retailers were willing to devote display space, food editors treated the new item editorially, and manufacturers of flour and other products were persuaded to include recipes on packages.

Proof of advertising performance was needed to convince all the cooperating groups of the success of the initial effort and of the advantages of continued support. The sales volume of cranberries was not, by itself, a suitable index of advertising effectiveness. The entire crop is always disposed of, if necessary, at distress prices. Furthermore, price received is not a reliable index since abundance of crops is governed by weather and other factors. Hence, measurement of the effectiveness of advertising alone was needed. Measurement was accomplished through a simple consumer panel survey to determine the percentage of homemakers who had heard about, wanted to try, or had actually baked the product. Results clearly indicated success of the first year's campaign and the desirability of continued promotional efforts, with emphasis on converting those who know about the product to repetitive users.

4

SEGMENTATION AND POSITIONING

Before you look at advertising, review the strategy . . . your target audience, your consumer benefit, or promise, and the support for that promise. . . . The results of your advertising depend less on how your advertising is written than on how your product or service is positioned—how you want the consumer to think about it. . . . Just as in war, the strategy is half the battle. The other half is the advertising itself.

Kenneth Roman and Jane Maas, heads of two
ad agencies, in _How to Advertise_

In the previous chapter we discussed factors to be considered in deciding what effect an advertising campaign must have on the target consumer—whether the communications objectives should be to increase brand awareness among them, or lead to more favorable brand attitudes, and so on. The other, equally important, aspect of objective setting is deciding who the target consumers should be for the advertising campaign. The present chapter examines this target-selection decision and considers the two most important concepts involved, segmentation and positioning.

Deciding which consumers the advertising campaign should be aimed at is a critical outcome of the situation analysis process, detailed in Chapter 2. It involves considerations of market size and trends, the process of consumer decision making, the benefits consumers seek from the product category, how consumers perceive the different brands in the category, and so on. Based on this analysis, the advertising decision maker has to decide which groups of consumers, or market segments, are most likely to be responsive to the competitive strengths of the brand being advertised. Since the competitive strengths of the brand can depend on how the brand is advertised, this identification of high-potential market segments is usually accompanied by the process of deciding exactly which aspect of the brand should dominate the advertising. What image or overall perception of the brand should consumers be left with, and what "position" must the brand occupy in their minds?

We discuss market segmentation first, followed by positioning strategy.

SEGMENTATION STRATEGY

The term "market segmentation" was not coined until the latter part of the 1950s. Since then, however, it has had a major impact on marketing and advertising theory and practice. It is based on the rather trivial observation that all potential customers are not identical and that a firm should therefore either develop different marketing programs for different subgroups of the population or develop one program tailored to just a single subgroup. The fact that consumers differ and a single marketing program directed to all of them is not always the best strategy may seem rather obvious. Yet it is the essence of market segmentation that has the potential to improve dramatically the management of a wide variety of organizations.

Market segmentation strategy involves the development and pursuit of marketing programs directed at subgroups of the population that an organization or firm could potentially serve. A variety of marketing tools can be utilized to implement a segmentation strategy. Products and services can be developed and positioned for particular segments of the population. Distribution channels can be selected to reach certain groups. A pricing strategy can be designed to attract particular types of buyers. An advertising program can be created to appeal to certain types of consumers. Although the emphasis in this book is on the advertising plan, a segmentation strategy is not limited to any one element of the marketing program.

In some situations, the marketing program may involve subsegments. A strategic program may require a particular segmentation scheme. In implementing the accompanying advertising campaign, a more detailed breakdown of the market may be required. Suppose that an organization has decided to focus on the clothing needs of the style-conscious upper class and has selected retail outlets and product lines that will attract members of this group. In developing the advertising plan, it may be useful to divide this upper-class segment further on the basis of age, thus creating two subsegments—the young, upper-class woman and those who are older—each of which will tend to be exposed to different media and will be attracted by different appeals.

An example of the use of subsegments can also be drawn from the area of industrial marketing, which deals with the problems of marketing to organizations. Suppose that a new, small computer for use by small firms was to be developed and marketed. The market could be divided into banks, food stores, and other business categories. Assume that it was decided to develop one marketing program especially for small banks and a second program for individual food retailers. This would be a market-segmentation strategy. As the program directed at the banks evolved, it might be useful to develop subsegments: the decision makers in the bank might be divided into the officers and the data processing personnel. Thus, two advertising campaigns would accompany the direct-sales programs.

The one directed at the officers might explain the economic advantages of the new computer and would run in magazines that bank presidents tend to read. The other would be more specialized in content and would explain the technical aspects and potential advantages of the computer to the data processing people. Such a campaign would appear in magazines favored by data processing managers.

Concentration Versus Differentiation Strategy

There are two different types of segmentation strategies. The first is the strategy of *concentration* in which the organization focuses on only one subgroup and develops a marketing program directed to it. The second is the strategy of *differentiation* in which two or more population subgroups are identified and marketing programs are developed for each. If segmentation is not employed and a single marketing program is developed and applied to all groups, the resulting marketing strategy is termed *undifferentiation* or *aggregation*.

If a strategy of concentration is pursued and a very large segment is the target, the approach is similar to one of undifferentiation in that an effort is made to reach a broad market. Such a strategy is enticing. Marketing decision makers often attempt to determine who the frequent users of the product are and then use that information to identify the target segment for a strategy of concentration. The problem is that competitors follow the same logic. They, too, have identified the segment with the "large" potential and are directing their efforts at it. As a result, the attractive segment might have several brands fighting for it, whereas there might be a smaller segment that no brand is attempting to serve. This phenomenon is very common and is called the majority fallacy.[1] The segment with the biggest potential is not always the most profitable, once the costs of fighting many competitors is considered! It may be much more profitable to attempt to gain a small segment heretofore ignored, even if it represents only 5 percent of the market, than to fight ten other brands for a share of a large segment that represents 70 percent of the market. It is obviously costly to do direct battle with large established competitors in a broadly based market segment.

A concentration strategy focusing on a smaller segment is particularly useful to a small firm that enters a market dominated by several larger ones. This is sometimes called a *niche* strategy. It may, in fact, be suicidal for the small company to compete with the larger ones for the large segment. However, if the small firm will concede the business represented by the large segment and discipline itself to direct its effort to a small segment with specialized needs, it may do very well. Furthermore, assuming that the smaller segment cannot really support two firms, the probability of losing the market to a competitor may then be rather small, since potential competitors will tend to avoid making an effort to secure a footing in this segment.

There are many examples of a concentration strategy. Midas Muffler does not attempt to satisfy the general service needs of car owners but concentrates instead on just servicing mufflers, a small part of total service needs. Successful computer companies, like Cray or Tandem, have not tried to attack IBM head-on: they have concentrated on specific segments (large-size research applications and transaction processing, respectively). A boat manufacturer may specialize in one particular type of boat oriented to only a small segment of the entire boat market.

Under a strategy of differentiation, an organization does not restrict its efforts to a single segment but rather develops several marketing programs, each tailored to individual segments. These programs could differ with respect to the product lines. Perhaps the classic case of a differentiated marketing program involving product lines is the General Motors organization. Early in the company's life, General Motors decided to develop a prestige product line (Cadillacs), an economy line (Chevrolets), and several others to fill the gap between the two. The company thus covered the whole market but divided it into segments and developed a line for each segment. A differentiated segmentation strategy could, however, involve just the advertising campaign. The advertising could emphasize one brand attribute to one segment and a different brand advantage to another. Thus, a bicycle manufacturer might stress the recreational uses of its bicycle in the United States and its transportation value in Europe, where it is more frequently used for that purpose.

Segmentation is not always the optimal approach. It may be that a single product and appeal will be equally effective for everyone. Naturally, this type of strategy requires substantial resources. The Coca-Cola Company could be considered to be pursuing an undifferentiated marketing segmentation strategy with Coca-Cola. The product name, package, and advertising are designed to appeal to virtually everyone, as Figure 4-1 illustrates. It could be argued, however, that the Coca-Cola Company too has moved away from a pure strategy of undifferentiation, with Diet Coke, different flavors (e.g., Cherry Coke, New Coke or Coke II), and caffeine-free versions. Such a move is partly a natural evolution. As a product class gains maturity, consumer needs often become more specialized and a segmentation strategy is a natural response of manufacturers to these needs.

Developing a Segmentation Strategy

The development of a segmentation strategy can take place in two ways, described in the paragraphs that follow. In each, the objective is to identify a group of consumers that (1) are not being served well presently by competition, and are therefore likely to try our brand; (2) are large enough, or growing in size; and (3) are most likely to respond positively to the benefits offered by our brand.

In the first approach to segmentation, one can attempt to segment a market on an *a priori* basis, assuming that differences must exist among, for example, older versus younger consumers, or heavy versus light users. Here, the basis on which the market might be segmented is determined before any data on the marketplace are actually examined. The data are then analyzed one variable at a time; for example, we might seek to "profile" male buyers versus female buyers, or consumers in different age groups, or heavy buyers of the product category versus medium and light buyers, or buyers who live in New York versus those who live in California.

A related strategy of a priori segmentation is to identify which subgroups in the population are growing most rapidly (for example, the number of dual-income couples and single-parent households is expected to grow rapidly in the 1990s) and then aim at

Figure 4-1.   An advertisement directed at a wide audience
Courtesy of The Coca-Cola Co.

them.[2] The logic here is that since these segments are only now becoming large, they are probably not being served adequately by our competitors at the moment and represent an untapped opportunity.

Some bases for a priori segmentation are discussed shortly, before we discuss the second kind of segmentation, called *empirical segmentation*. In this second approach, the segments are created directly on the basis of the differences in the benefits they seek or the life-styles they pursue, and demographic differences are then sought across these segments.

Age. A very basic but useful a priori demographic segmenting variable is age. People often seek different features or benefits depending upon their age (and, relatedly, their family life-cycle stage). Consequently, people in different age groups often differ in which brands they prefer within a product category, and it is sometimes possible to target particular brands at particular age groups. In making such targeting decisions, it pays to also know which age group in the population is likely to show significant growth. As one example, the 45- to 54-year-old age category is expected to grow rapidly between 1990 and the year 2000, as the 77 million "baby boomers" (those born between 1946 and 1964) move into that age category. It is useful to learn as much as possible about prospective target segments. What kinds of products and services will your target age group want to buy, what kinds of features will they seek, what kinds of advertising appeals and personalities will they be most responsive to? Such information is often collected through customized market research surveys, as well as through syndicated data sources (two of which are discussed later).

Income. Another useful a priori demographic variable is income. Not surprisingly, higher-income households tend to be less price sensitive, placing a higher value on buying higher-quality merchandise. Because of the growth in dual income households, there has been a dramatic growth in the proportion of total spending in the economy coming from such households, implying that the market for high-end products and services should increase substantially. While two-earner couples were only 29 percent of all married couples in 1960, by 1990 they formed 52 percent, and this is expected to rise to 57 percent by the year 2000. By one estimate, the number of households of 35- to 50-year-olds earning more than $50,000 per annum will triple between 1990 and 2000.

Geographic Location. Geographic location can often provide the basis for an effective a priori segmentation strategy. A firm with modest resources can dominate, if it so chooses, a small geographic area. Its distribution within the limited area can be intense. Local media such as newspapers or spot television can be employed, and it is possible to buy space in regional editions of major national magazines. The classic example of a concentration strategy is the local or regional organization that restricts itself geographically and attempts to tailor its marketing program to the needs of the people in that area. A local brewery or potato chip marketer may compete with national brands, but only in a limited geographic area. In response, national marketers (such as Frito-Lay) are increasingly developing specific advertising and marketing programs for specific regions of the country, often using a regionalized marketing organization. This helps the companies develop programs better tailored to regional differences: in snack foods, for instance, Frito-Lay found it faced competition from local tortilla products in the western United States, from pretzel manufacturers in the East, and from popcorn in Boston.[3]

Many advertisers often target markets geographically after developing indices for the per capita consumption of their brands in each market region, relative to the national average. For example, if their sales in Pittsburgh are two ounces per capita per year, while the national average is one ounce per capita per year, then the index (called brand development index, or BDI) is 200. A similar index is created for consumption of the product category overall, for all brands combined. This index is called the category development index, or CDI. It is then possible to examine a market's BDI and CDI and decide how much advertising attention needs to be given to each market. For instance, a market with a high CDI but low BDI would be a high-opportunity market, calling for high advertising spending, while a low-CDI but high-BDI market probably cannot be developed much further and should only receive maintenance-level budgets.

In recent years it has become increasingly possible to learn something about your target consumers simply by knowing the postal zip code they live in. Census-based demographic data on households, as well as life-style data (collected through warranty registration cards) and automobile registration data have been analyzed by various companies to yield "average profiles" for households in different segments, or groups, of zip codes. (These data are actually analyzed by finer classifications called census block groups, and the groups are called clusters.) In these analysis schemes, zip codes are placed into a common cluster if they have similar profiles on these variables, even if they are geographically far apart. Thus a zip code of an affluent suburb of Chicago might be classified as belonging to the same cluster as the zip code of an affluent town in Long Island, New York, because they are very similar to each in terms of their scores on these variables. An advertiser can examine these scores of each zip-based cluster and identify which ones are most likely to respond to an advertising or direct marketing effort. Direct marketing is discussed in Chapter 10.

Usage.   A natural and powerful a priori segmentation variable is product-class usage. Who are the heavy users of the product or service? In many product categories, the heavy users (who are usually 20 to 30 percent of the users) account for almost 70 to 80 percent of the volume consumed: this is sometimes called the "80:20" rule. It is obviously extremely valuable for a brand to have most of its users from the heavy user category, for that should lead to a disproportionately higher share of units sold.

One segmentation scheme might thus involve heavy users, light users, and nonusers. This particular segmentation scheme is likely to be useful wherever the focus is on building up the market. Each person is classified according to usage, and a program is developed to increase the usage level. The segments defined by usage usually require quite different marketing programs. So a program tailored to one of these segments can generate a substantially greater response than would a marketing program common to all segments. Of course, designing and implementing several marketing programs is costlier than developing one, but the resulting market response will often be significant enough to make it worthwhile.

How does one identify the demographics of these usage segments? One standard method is to use a syndicated data source such as the Simmons *Selected Markets and the Media Reaching Them*, from Simmons Market Research Bureau, or similar data from Mediamark Research, Inc. (MRI). Both these data services interview many thousands of consumers every year on the quantity of their consumption of hundreds of products and services, and the extent to which they buy the different brands available. These consumers are then classified as heavy, medium, or light users of each category and each major brand, based on certain cutoff levels (for example, someone who reports consuming more than 300 cans of soft drinks a year might be classified as a heavy user). The demographic and geographic profiles of these usage segments are then provided in tables, as are media data, using index numbers relative to the national average. One can scan the column of index numbers and find out if, for example, heavy users of ready-to-eat cereals tend to come disproportionately from certain age or income groups, or certain geographical regions. A sample page from a Simmons volume is provided in Table 4-1.

Brand Loyalty.   When a brand such as Tide is competing in a well-defined product class such as detergents, it is useful to consider brand loyalty as a basis for a priori segmentation. Loyalty data are also available from Simmons or similar services, or from customized research. The users of Tide can then be divided into those who are loyal buyers of the brand and those who are not. The nonloyal buyer tends to buy several brands, selecting, for example, the least expensive or the most convenient at the moment. Here, the objective is to increase the proportion of this user's detergent purchases that are Tide. This can be done either by giving coupons in or on the pack, good on the next purchase (see Chapter 10 on consumer sales promotions), or by creating advertising that serves to reinforce the loyalty of such purchasers.[4]

Similarly, nonusers of Tide can be divided into those who are loyal to other brands and those who buy several other brands. It is usually not easy to increase usage by turning nonloyal buyers into loyal buyers, since this tendency toward brand loyalty, with respect to a certain product class, has likely become ingrained over many years. The highest potential lies with the nonusers. The nonuser who is not loyal to another brand needs to be enticed to try the brand and thus to expand the *evoked set,* the group of brands he or she buys, to include the brand of interest. A special in-store display or a cents-off coupon might accomplish this task.

Buyers who are loyal to another brand will be very difficult and very costly to attract to a trial purchase. However, once attracted, there is an excellent chance of their becoming loyal buyers of the brand, since their tendency toward loyalty is not likely to change. Obviously, however, a special display or a cents-off coupon is unlikely to attract the buyer who is loyal to another brand. He or she must be presented with a solid reason to change. If such a reason does exist, there is still the problem of communication, as the loyal buyer of one brand is not seeking information and, in fact, tends to avoid advertising for other brands. Thus, there is a trade-off. On the one hand, the loyal buyer of another brand is an appealing prospect because if converted she or he will generate sales dividends for several years. On the other hand, the loyal buyer is difficult and costly to attract.

Attitudes and Benefits.   Attitudes and preferences and many related psychological constructs such as motivations, perceptions, beliefs, product benefits, and so on, can also be used to segment markets through the second, empirical segmentation approach. Variation

TABLE 4-1. Portions of Cold Breakfast Cereal: Usage in Last 7 Days (Female Homemakers)

	Total U.S. '000	ALL USERS A '000	B % Down	C Across %	D Index	HEAVY USERS TEN OR MORE A '000	B % Down	C Across %	D Index	MEDIUM USERS FIVE – NINE A '000	B % Down	C Across %	D Index	LIGHT USERS FOUR OR LESS A '000	B % Down	C Across %	D Index
Total Female Homemakers	86361	75496	100.0	87.4	100	21818	100.0	25.3	100	30219	100.0	35.0	100	23458	100.0	27.2	100
18 – 24	7911	6803	9.0	86.0	98	1650	7.6	20.9	83	2732	9.0	34.5	99	2421	10.2	30.6	113
25 – 34	20745	18318	24.3	88.3	101	6164	28.3	29.7	118	6930	22.9	33.4	95	5224	22.3	25.2	93
35 – 44	17764	15797	20.9	88.9	102	5953	27.3	33.5	133	5562	18.4	31.3	89	4282	18.3	24.1	89
45 – 54	12326	10630	14.1	86.2	99	3044	14.0	24.7	98	4318	14.3	35.0	100	3268	13.9	26.5	98
55 – 64	10847	9545	12.6	88.0	101	2081	9.5	19.2	76	4014	13.3	37.0	106	3451	14.7	31.8	117
65 or Older	16765	14402	19.1	85.9	98	2927	13.4	17.5	69	6663	22.0	39.7	114	4812	20.5	28.7	106
18 – 34	28656	25121	33.3	87.7	100	7814	35.8	27.3	108	9663	32.0	33.7	96	7645	32.6	26.7	98
18 – 49	53038	46487	61.6	87.6	100	15297	70.1	28.8	114	17606	58.3	33.2	95	13585	57.9	25.6	94
25 – 54	50837	44746	59.3	88.0	101	15161	69.5	29.8	118	16810	55.6	33.1	94	12774	54.5	25.1	93
35 – 49	24383	21366	28.3	87.6	100	7483	34.3	30.7	121	7943	26.3	32.6	93	5940	25.3	24.4	90
50 or Older	33322	29008	38.4	87.1	100	6522	29.9	19.6	77	12613	41.7	37.9	106	9873	42.1	29.6	109
Graduated college	14461	12652	16.8	87.5	100	4117	18.9	28.5	113	4393	14.5	30.4	87	4142	17.7	28.6	105
Attended college	15754	13704	18.3	87.0	100	3853	17.7	24.5	97	5461	18.1	34.7	99	4389	18.7	27.9	103
Graduated high school	36201	31843	42.2	88.0	101	9734	44.6	26.9	106	12931	42.8	35.7	102	9178	39.1	25.4	93
Did not graduate high school	19944	17297	22.9	86.7	99	4115	18.9	20.6	82	7434	24.6	37.3	107	5749	24.5	28.8	106
Employed	49122	42748	56.6	87.0	100	12767	58.5	26.0	103	16586	54.9	33.8	96	13396	57.1	27.3	100
Employed full-time	41357	35974	47.7	87.0	100	10162	46.6	24.6	97	14055	46.5	34.0	97	11756	50.1	28.4	105
Employed part-time	7765	6775	9.0	87.3	100	2605	11.9	33.5	133	2531	8.4	32.6	93	1639	7.0	21.1	78
Not employed	37238	32747	43.4	87.9	101	9051	41.5	24.3	96	13634	45.1	36.6	105	10062	42.9	27.0	99
Professional/Manager	13838	12127	16.1	87.6	100	3919	18.0	28.3	112	4278	14.2	30.9	88	3930	16.8	28.4	105
Tech/Clerical/Sales	22113	19271	25.5	87.1	100	5750	26.4	26.0	103	7502	24.8	33.9	97	6019	25.7	27.2	100
Precision/Craft	1208	1064	1.4	88.1	101	**264	1.2	21.9	87	*544	1.8	45.0	129	**256	1.1	21.2	78
Other employed	11963	10287	13.6	86.0	98	2835	13.0	23.7	94	4262	14.1	35.6	102	3191	13.6	26.7	98
Single	11628	9637	12.8	82.9	95	1911	8.8	16.4	65	3816	12.6	32.8	94	3910	16.7	33.6	124
Married	53109	47310	62.7	89.1	102	15906	72.9	29.9	119	18815	62.3	35.4	101	12589	53.7	23.7	87
Divorced/Separated/Widowed	21624	18549	24.6	85.8	98	4002	18.3	18.5	73	7588	25.1	35.1	100	6959	29.7	32.2	118
Parents	32364	29575	39.2	91.4	105	12491	57.3	38.6	153	10267	34.0	31.7	91	6817	29.1	21.1	78
White	74071	65082	86.2	87.9	101	19504	89.4	26.3	104	25495	84.4	34.4	98	20082	85.6	27.1	100
Black	10120	8539	11.3	84.4	97	1905	8.7	18.8	75	3899	12.9	38.5	110	2735	11.7	27.0	99
Other	2170	1875	2.5	86.4	99	*409	1.9	18.8	75	825	2.7	38.0	109	*641	2.7	29.5	109
Northeast–census	18325	16065	21.3	87.7	100	4059	18.6	22.2	88	7039	23.3	38.4	110	4967	21.2	27.1	100
Midwest	21483	19206	25.4	89.4	102	6844	31.4	31.9	126	6851	22.7	31.9	91	5511	23.5	25.7	94
South	29926	25776	34.1	86.1	99	6903	31.6	23.1	91	10279	34.0	34.3	98	8595	36.6	28.7	106
West	16626	14448	19.1	86.9	99	4012	18.4	24.1	96	6051	20.0	36.4	104	4386	18.7	26.4	97
Northeast–Mktg.	18809	16536	21.9	87.9	101	4228	19.4	22.5	89	7192	23.8	38.2	109	5116	21.8	27.2	100
East Central	12604	11075	14.7	87.9	101	3453	15.8	27.4	108	3906	12.9	31.0	89	3717	15.8	29.5	109
West Central	14706	13293	17.6	90.4	103	4894	22.4	33.3	132	4835	16.0	32.9	94	3565	15.2	24.2	89
South	25698	22096	29.3	86.0	98	5772	26.5	22.5	89	8939	29.6	34.8	99	7385	31.5	28.7	106
Pacific	14543	12495	16.6	85.9	98	3472	15.9	23.9	94	5348	17.7	36.8	105	3675	15.7	25.3	93

County size A	35301	40.2	85.9	98	9057	41.5	25.7	102	12548	41.5	35.5	102	8708	37.1	24.7	91
County size B	25652	29.9	87.9	101	6219	28.5	24.2	96	8766	29.0	34.2	98	7559	32.2	29.5	106
County size C	13413	15.8	89.1	103	3398	15.6	25.3	100	4791	15.9	35.7	102	3761	16.0	28.0	103
County size D	11994	14.2	89.1	102	3144	14.4	26.2	104	4114	13.6	34.3	98	3430	14.6	28.6	105
Metro Central City	27494	31.7	87.0	100	6244	28.6	22.7	90	10152	33.6	36.9	106	7532	32.1	27.4	101
Metro Suburban	39058	44.8	86.7	99	10644	48.9	27.3	108	13049	43.2	33.4	95	10134	43.2	25.9	96
Non Metro	19809	23.5	89.5	102	4910	22.5	24.8	98	7018	23.2	35.4	101	5792	24.7	29.2	108
Top 5 ADI's	19248	22.2	86.9	99	4565	20.9	23.7	94	7038	23.3	36.6	104	5124	21.8	26.6	98
Top 10 ADI's	26751	30.6	86.3	99	6390	29.3	23.9	95	9814	32.5	36.7	105	6882	29.3	25.7	95
Top 20 ADI's	39079	44.6	85.7	98	9717	44.5	24.9	98	13879	45.9	35.5	101	9892	42.2	25.3	93
Hshld inc. $60,000 or more	12765	14.8	87.3	100	4088	18.7	32.0	127	3906	12.9	30.6	87	3145	13.4	24.6	91
$50,000 or more	19492	22.4	86.9	99	5913	27.1	30.3	120	6352	21.0	32.6	93	4663	19.9	23.9	88
$40,000 or more	28802	33.4	87.5	100	8362	38.3	29.0	115	9615	31.8	33.4	95	7224	30.8	25.1	92
$30,000 or more	41434	48.1	87.6	100	12433	57.0	30.0	119	13748	45.5	33.2	95	10104	43.1	24.4	90
$30,000 – $39,999	12633	14.7	87.7	100	4071	18.7	32.2	128	4132	13.7	32.7	93	2879	12.3	22.8	84
20,000 – $29,999	14613	17.1	88.5	101	3764	17.3	25.8	102	5210	17.2	35.7	102	3959	16.9	27.1	100
$10,000 – $19,000	16772	19.5	87.6	100	3084	14.1	18.4	73	6403	21.2	38.2	109	5201	22.2	31.0	114
Under $10,000	13542	15.4	85.5	98	2537	11.6	18.7	74	4859	16.1	35.9	103	4194	17.9	31.0	114
Household of 1 person	13686	14.7	81.1	93	1110	5.1	8.1	32	4640	15.4	33.9	97	5351	22.8	39.1	144
2 people	29863	33.9	85.6	98	4942	22.7	16.5	66	11319	37.5	37.9	108	9311	39.7	31.2	115
3 or 4 people	32539	39.0	90.4	103	10738	49.2	33.0	131	11275	37.3	34.7	99	7401	31.6	22.7	84
5 or more people	10273	12.5	91.6	105	5029	23.0	49.0	194	2985	9.9	29.1	83	1394	5.9	13.6	50
No child in hshld	51214	57.3	84.5	97	8509	39.0	16.6	66	18731	62.0	36.6	105	16043	68.4	31.3	115
Child(ren) under 2 yrs	7771	9.5	92.5	106	2696	12.4	34.7	137	2343	7.8	30.2	86	2148	9.2	27.6	102
2 – 5 years	12431	15.2	92.3	106	5245	24.0	42.2	167	3969	13.1	31.9	91	2264	9.7	18.2	67
6 – 11 years	16564	20.1	91.8	105	7166	32.8	43.3	171	5299	17.5	32.0	91	2748	11.7	16.6	61
12 – 17 years	14864	18.0	91.4	105	5676	26.0	38.2	151	4901	16.2	33.0	94	3005	12.8	20.2	74
Residence owned	58684	68.6	88.3	101	15854	72.7	27.0	107	20477	67.8	34.9	100	15460	65.9	26.3	97
Value: $70,000 or more	29899	35.2	88.8	102	8883	40.7	29.7	118	10121	33.5	33.9	97	7561	32.2	25.3	93
Value: Under $70,000	28785	33.4	87.6	100	6971	32.0	24.2	96	10356	34.3	36.0	103	7900	33.7	27.4	101

*Projection relatively unstable because of sample base—use with caution

**Number of cases too small for reliability—shown for consistency only

Source: This report is the copyrighted property of Simmons Market Research Bureau, Inc. and is distributed pursuant to contract on a limited and confidential basis. Any reproduction, publication, disclosure, distribution or sale of this report in whole or whole part is strictly prohibited. © 1990 by Simmons Market Research Bureau, Inc. All rights reserved. Used with permission.

in evaluative beliefs, for example, can be used to identify groups of buyers who perceive brands in different ways. Also, the fact that buyers will tend to place different degrees of importance on the benefits typically obtained from that type of product or service leads logically to the fact that they represent different segments to which specific brands and advertising appeals can be directed.

The basic idea of segmenting on the basis of important attributes has been termed benefit segmentation by Russell Haley.[5] He illustrates the perspective by an analysis of the toothpaste market. Four segments are hypothesized, as shown in Table 4-2. The first is the Sensory segment, which values flavor and the appearance of the package. This segment tends to be represented by children characterized by high self-involvement and hedonistic life-style. Colgate and Stripe do well in this segment (Aim should, too, as should all gels). This segment should have high importance weights on flavor and appearance and tend to prefer brands whose product and advertising strategies have emphasized these dimensions.

The second segment, termed the Sociables, contains those who are interested in the brightness of their teeth. They are largely young people in their teens or early twenties who lead active lives and are very social. They have a relatively large percentage of smokers in their midst. Macleans, Plus White, and Ultra Brite are big sellers in this segment.

The benefit sought by the third segment is that of decay prevention. A high proportion of this segment has large families who tend to be heavy toothpaste users. In general, they have a conservative life-style and show concern for health and dental hygiene. Crest is disproportionately favored by this segment, which is termed the Worriers.

The fourth segment, the Independent segment, is made up of people oriented toward price and value. It tends to include men who are heavy toothpaste users. They probably are concerned with obtaining good value in all their purchases and tend to be attracted to whatever brand is on sale.

The value of benefit segmentation for advertising is seen by considering the different advertising approaches that will be appropriate for each segment. The copy should probably be light for the Sociable or Sensory segments but more serious for the others. The setting could also be adjusted; the focus should probably be on the product for the Sensory group, on a social situation for the Sociable segment, and perhaps on a laboratory demonstration for the Independent segment. Similarly, the media to be used can be selected with the particular target segment in mind. Television might be more appropriate for the Sociables and the Sensory segment, where there is less need to communicate hard information. A serious rational argument, possibly supported by clinical evidence, might appeal to the Independent group, assuming that such an argument can demonstrate value. A long, print advertisement, therefore, might be appropriate for this segment.

Haley has speculated on the possibility of generalizing benefit segmentation across product categories. Some of the following, he suggests, may appear as market segments across almost all product and service categories, although there is no guarantee that they will, and it is the purpose of the analysis to discover them:

1. The Status Seeker: a group that is very much concerned with the prestige of the brand purchased.

TABLE 4-2. Toothpaste Market Segment Description

Characteristics	Sensory segment	Sociables	Worriers	Independent segment
Principal benefit sought	Flavor, product appearance	Brightness of teeth	Decay prevention	Price
Demographic strengths	Children	Teens, young people	Large families	Men
Special behavioral characteristics	Users of spearmint-flavored toothpaste	Smokers	Heavy users	Heavy users
Brands disproportionately favored	Colgate, Stripe	Macleans, Plus White, Ultra Brite	Crest	Brand on sale
Personality characteristics	High self-involvement	High sociability	High health	High autonomy
Life-style characteristics	Hedonistic	Active	Conservative	Value-oriented

Source: Adapted from Russell I. Haley, "Benefit Segmentation: A Decision-Oriented Research Tool," *Journal of Marketing,* 32, July 1968, p. 33.

2. The Swinger: a group that tries to be modern and up to date in all of its activities. Brand choices reflect this orientation.

3. The Conservative: a group that prefers to stick to large successful companies and popular brands.

4. The Rational Person: a group that looks for benefits such as economy, value, durability, and so forth.

5. The Inner-Directed Person: a group that is especially concerned with self-concept. Members consider themselves to have a sense of humor, to be independent, and/or honest.

6. The Hedonist: a group that is concerned primarily with sensory benefits.[6]

As another example of benefit segmentation, the NPD Research Company identified four segments of food and beverage consumers in 1989 through an analysis of data: the traditional taste group, who liked butter, sweets, fried foods, and fast foods; the health maintainers, who place a premium on health, nutrition, and dieting considerations; the busy urbanites, who value convenience and eating out; and the moderates, who flip around a lot.[7]

Earlier, we mentioned that there were two broad approaches to segmentation, one of which we called "a priori." Note that benefit segmentation is an example of the second kind, called "empirical segmentation." While a priori segmentation begins by picking a variable such as income or frequency of usage, and then checks if people at different levels of these segmenting variables also differ in terms of the benefits they seek or the brands they buy in the product category, empirical segmentation works the other way around. In benefit segmentation, for instance, we begin by asking people what benefits they seek in the product category; we then group them into segments based on the similarity of the benefits they seek (often using a multivariate statistical technique called cluster analysis), and we then see what makes these segments (created only on the basis of benefit importance ratings) different, in terms of demographics, and so on. It is important, in generating market segments through such cluster analysis, to make sure that the segments that emerge from the data are reliable and valid—robust—through conducting the appropriate statistical tests.[8]

Life-style and culture segments are also usually created through this second, empirical approach: we group people into clusters based on their similarity of personalities, opinions, activities, interests, and so on, and then see how these life-style segments differ on demographics and brand usage.

Life-style.   A person's pattern of interests, opinions, and activities combine to represent his or her life-style. A knowledge of life-style can provide a very rich and meaningful picture of a person. It can indicate whether the person is interested in outdoor sports, shopping, culture, or reading. It can include information concerning attitudes and personality traits. Life-style also can be used to define a segment empirically; this is often called "psychographic" (as opposed to demographic) segmentation.

Life-style is particularly useful as a segmentation variable in categories where the user's self-image is important, such as fragrance; we therefore discuss it in some detail in Chapter 8. As an example of life-style segmentation in fragrances, Revlon's Charlie cosmetic line was targeted at a life-style segment profiled as follows:

- Is irreverent and unpretentious.
- Doesn't mind being a little outrageous or flamboyant.
- Breaks all the rules.
- Has her integrity based on her own standards.
- Can be tough; believes rules are secondary.
- Is a pacesetter, not a follower.
- Is very relaxed about sex.
- Is bored with typical fragrance advertising.
- Mixes Gucci and blue jeans; insists on individual taste, individual judgment.
- Has a sense of self and sense of commitment.

Figure 4-2 shows a Charlie advertisement.

Culture.   Cultural segmentation is particularly important when multinational firms attempt to develop a segmentation strategy with the world as a market. Given the increasing importance of global marketing (see Chapter 1), and the need to gain economies of scale in marketing expenditures, firms often try to develop common advertising themes or executions for countries that have similar cultural attitudes and values. Differences across cultures can affect product acceptance and advertising campaigns, and there are many ''war stories'' of ad campaigns which worked fine in some countries but were disasters in others where they were inappropriately extended, because certain cultural nuances were missed. Again, countries are often based into cultural segments on the basis of an empirical segmentation strategy, using techniques such as cluster analysis.

Reaching Target Segments

There are two ways by which markets can be reached: controlled coverage and customer self-selection.[9]

In the controlled-coverage approach, the objective is to reach desired target segments and to avoid reaching those who are not in the target segments. Suppose that a segment is defined as ''better golfers,'' and it is determined that they usually read *Golf Digest*. Suppose, further, that there are few readers of *Golf Digest* who are not in the target segment. Then an advertising campaign in *Golf Digest* would be an efficient way to communicate with the target segment. Another way might be to use direct marketing techniques to mail a message to people who are subscribers of *Golf Digest*, renting their names from the magazine or a list broker (see Chapter 10). As will be discussed in Chapter 10, many companies are now creating immense computerized data bases on their actual

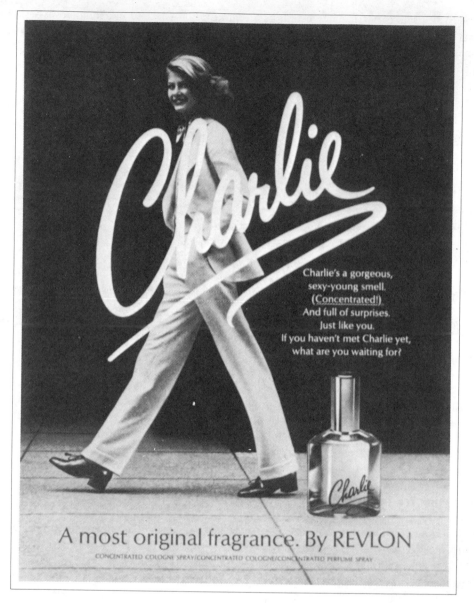

Figure 4-2.   A campaign directed at a defined life-style
Courtesy of Revlon.

and potential customers, enabling extremely targeted direct marketing communications. This technique is often called ''data-based marketing.''

Customer self-selection is an alternative approach. Here the advertising program is directed to a mass audience of which the target segment may be only a small part. Those in the target segment are attracted to the marketing effort since it is tailored to them. Those not in the target group will probably avoid exposure, not because the program is unavailable to them, but because they either consciously or unconsciously choose to avoid it. For example, although ski equipment has a rather narrow appeal, a firm may run an advertisement about it in a mass circulation magazine. The target segment, all skiers, will be attracted to the advertisement if it is well done, but nonskiers will probably not be tempted to read it.

POSITIONING STRATEGIES

Just as segmentation involves the decision to aim at a certain group of customers but not others, our next concept—positioning—involves a decision to stress certain aspects of our brand, and not others. The key idea in positioning strategy is that the consumer must have a clear idea of what your brand stands for in the product category, and that a brand cannot be sharply and distinctly positioned if it tries to be everything to everyone. Such positioning is achieved mostly through a brand's marketing communications, though its distribution, pricing, packaging, and actual product features also can play major roles. It is often said that positioning is not what you do to the product, but what you do to the consumer's mind, through various communications. The strategic objective must be to have segmentation and positioning strategies that fit together: a brand must be positioned in a way that is maximally effective in attracting the desired target segment.

A brand's position is the set of associations the consumer has with the brand. These may cover physical attributes, or life-style, or use occasion, or user image, or stores that carry it. A brand's position develops over years, through advertising and publicity and word of mouth and usage experience, and can be sharp or diffuse, depending on the consistency of that brand's advertising over the years.

A brand's position in a consumer's mind is a relative concept, in that it refers to a comparative assessment by the consumer of how this brand is similar to or different from the other brands that compete with it. Think of every consumer as having a mental map of the product category. The location of your brand in that map, relative to that of your competitors, is your position, and the locations of all the brands in that map are determined by the associations that the consumer makes with each brand. If all this sounds rather abstract, several examples are provided here which should clarify the concept.

A positioning strategy is vital to provide focus to the development of an advertising campaign. The strategy can be conceived and implemented in a variety of ways that derive from the attributes, competition, specific applications, the types of consumers involved, or the characteristics of the product class. Each represents a different approach to developing a positioning strategy, even though all of them have the ultimate objective of either developing or reinforcing a particular image for the brand in the mind of the audience. Seven approaches to positioning strategy will be presented: (1) using product characteristics or customer benefits, (2) the price-quality approach, (3) the use or applications approach, (4) the product-user approach, (5) the product-class approach, (6) the cultural symbol approach, and (7) the competitor approach.

Using Product Characteristics or Customer Benefits

Probably the most-used positioning strategy is to associate an object with a product characteristic or customer benefit. Imported automobiles illustrate the variety of product characteristics that can be employed and their power in image creation. Honda and Toyota have emphasized economy and reliability and have become the leaders in the number of units sold. Volvo has stressed safety and durability, showing commercials of "crash tests" and telling of the long average life of its cars. BMW attempts to put forth an image of performance in terms of handling and engineering efficiency. The tag line used by BMW is "the ultimate driving machine." BMW advertisements show the cars demonstrating their performance capabilities at a German racetrack.

Sometimes a new product can be positioned with respect to a product characteristic that competitors have ignored. Brands of paper towels had emphasized absorbency until Viva was successfully introduced stressing durability. Viva demonstrations showed its product's durability and supported the claim that Viva "keeps on working."

Sometimes a product will attempt to position itself along two or more product characteristics simultaneously. In the toothpaste market, Crest became the leader decades ago by positioning itself as a cavity fighter, a position that was established by an endorsement by the American Dental Association. Since then, Crest has enjoyed a market share of up to 40 percent. However, several other successful entries have positioned themselves along two product characteristics. Aim, introduced as a good-tasting, cavity fighter, achieved a share of more than 10 percent. More recently, Aqua-fresh was introduced by Beecham as a gel paste that offers both cavity-fighting and breath-freshening benefits. Aqua-fresh advertisements showed people arguing whether to buy a breath-freshener or cavity-fighting dentifrice. Of course, the solution was Aqua-fresh. Sometimes different models of a product may be positioned toward different segments by highlighting different attributes: the two Timex watches in Figure 4-3 are an example.

It is always tempting to try to position along several product characteristics as it is frustrating to have some good product characteristics that are not communicated. However, advertising objectives that involve too many product characteristics can be most difficult to implement. The result can often be a fuzzy, confused image, which usually hurts a brand.

Myers and Shocker[10] have made a distinction between physical characteristics, pseudophysical characteristics, and benefits, all of which can be used in positioning. Physical characteristics are the most objective and can be measured on some physical scale such as temperature, color intensity, sweetness, thickness, distance, dollars, acidity, saltiness, strength of fragrance, weight, and so on. Pseudophysical characteristics, in contrast, reflect physical properties that are not easily measured. Examples are spiciness, smokey taste, tartness, type of fragrance (smells like a . . .), greasiness, creaminess, and shininess. Benefits refer to advantages that promote the well-being of the consumer or user. Ginger ale can be positioned as a product that "quenches thirst." Thirst quenching is a benefit and provides the basis for this type of positioning strategy. Other examples are the following: does not harm the skin, satisfies hunger, is easy to combine with other ingredients, stimulates, is convenient, and so on.

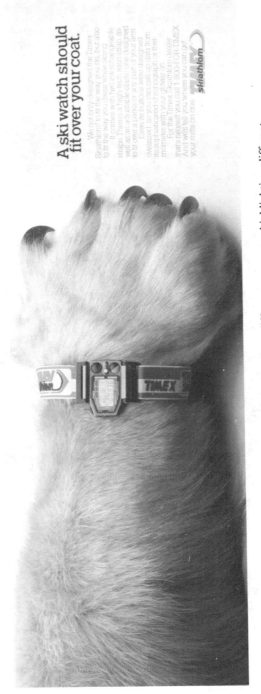

Figure 4-3. Two advertisements aimed at different segments, highlighting different attributes

Reprint permission granted by Timex Corporation.

Figure 4-3. (Continued)

Positioning by Price and Quality

The price-quality product characteristic is so useful and pervasive that it is appropriate to consider it separately. In many product categories, there exist brands that deliberately attempt to offer more in terms of service, features, or performance. Manufacturers of such brands charge more, partly to cover higher costs and partly to help communicate the fact that they are of higher quality. Conversely, in the same product class there are usually other brands that appeal on the basis of price, although they might also try to be perceived as having comparable or at least adequate quality. In many product categories, the price-quality issue is so important that it needs to be considered in any positioning decision.

For example, in general merchandise stores, the department stores are at the top end. Neiman-Marcus, Bloomingdale's, and Saks Fifth Avenue are near the top followed by Macy's, Robinson's, Bullock's, Rich's, Filene's, Dayton's, Hudson's, and so on. Stores like Sears, Montgomery Ward, and J. C. Penney are positioned below the department stores, but above the discount stores like K Mart and Walmart. It is usually very difficult to compete successfully using both quality and price: Sears is just one advertiser that has faced the very tricky positioning task of retaining the image of low price while communicating a quality message. There is always the risk that the quality message will blunt the basic "low-price" position or that people will infer that if the prices are low the quality must be low, too.

Positioning by Use or Application

Another way to communicate an image is to associate the product with a use or application. Campbell's Soup for many years positioned itself as a lunchtime product and used noontime radio extensively. The AT&T Telephone Company associated long-distance calling with communicating with loved ones in its "Reach out and touch someone" campaign.

Products can, of course, have multiple positioning strategies, although increasing the number involves obvious difficulties and risks. Often a positioning-by-use strategy represents a second or third position for the brand, a position that deliberately attempts to expand the brand's market. Thus, Gatorade, a summer beverage for athletes who need to replace body fluids, has attempted to develop a positioning strategy for the winter months. The concept is to use Gatorade when flu attacks and the doctor says to drink plenty of fluids. Similarly, Quaker Oats has attempted to position its product as a natural whole-grain ingredient for recipes in addition to its breakfast food niche. Arm & Hammer baking soda has successfully positioned its product as an odor-destroying agent in refrigerators as the storyboard shown in Figure 4-4 illustrates.

Positioning by Product User

Another positioning approach is to associate a product with a user or a class of users. Thus, many cosmetic companies have used a model or personality to position their product. Brut fragrance, for example, has used Joe Namath. The use of a life-style profile by

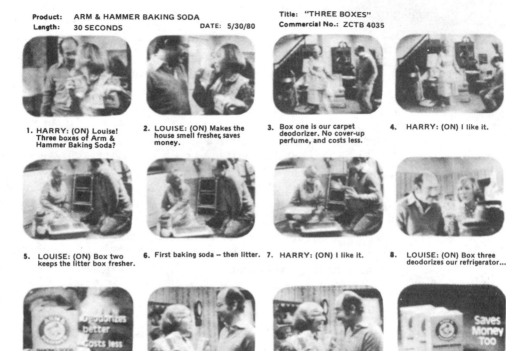

Product: ARM & HAMMER BAKING SODA
Length: 30 SECONDS   **DATE:** 5/30/80

Title: "THREE BOXES"
Commercial No.: ZCTB 4035

1. HARRY: (ON) Louise! Three boxes of Arm & Hammer Baking Soda?

2. LOUISE: (ON) Makes the house smell fresher, saves money.

3. Box one is our carpet deodorizer. No cover-up perfume, and costs less.

4. HARRY: (ON) I like it.

5. LOUISE: (ON) Box two keeps the litter box fresher.

6. First baking soda -- then litter.

7. HARRY: (ON) I like it.

8. LOUISE: (ON) Box three deodorizes our refrigerator...

9. (VO) better than the new gadgets and costs less.

10. (ON) Three boxes make the house fresher -- and save money.

11. HARRY: (ON) I like it. I like it. BOTH: (ON) I like it.

12. ANNCR: (VO) Arm & Hammer Baking Soda.

Figure 4-4. Positioning by application

Photographs courtesy of Arm & Hammer Division, Church & Dwight Co., Inc.

the Charlie line was noted earlier in this chapter. Makers of casual clothing like jeans have introduced "designer labels" such as Calvin Klein or Jordache to develop a fashion image. The expectation is that the model or personality will influence the product's image by reflecting the characteristics and image of the model or personality communicated as a product user.

Johnson & Johnson repositioned its shampoo from one used for babies to one used by people who wash their hair frequently and therefore need a mild shampoo. This repositioning resulted in a market share that moved from 3 percent to 14 percent for Johnson & Johnson.

In 1970, Miller High Life was the "champagne of bottled beers" and had an image of a beer suitable for women to drink. In fact, it was purchased primarily by upper-class socioeconomic groups.[11] Philip Morris then purchased Miller and moved the product out of the champagne bucket into the lunch bucket, repositioning it as a beer for the blue-collar working man who is the heavy beer drinker. The long-running campaign showed working men reaching the end of a hard day, designated as "Miller time," relaxing with a Miller beer. This campaign, which ran virtually unchanged for about 15 years, was extremely successful, though Miller's market share has since then dropped considerably.

Miller's Lite beer, introduced in 1975, used a similar positioning strategy. It was positioned as a beer for the heavy beer drinker (called "Six Pack Joe" in the industry), who wants to drink a lot but dislikes that filled-up feeling. Thus, Miller's used convincing beer-drinking personalities such as Dick Butkus and Mickey Spillane to communicate the fact that this beer was not as filling. In contrast, previous efforts by others to introduce low-calorie beers were dismal failures, partly because they emphasized the low-calorie aspect. One even claimed its beer had fewer calories than skim milk, and another featured a trim light beer personality. Of course, not every beer needs to go after the heavy users: some other light beers, such as Coors Light, have in fact tried to attract single women, depicting a very different kind of user than that shown in most beer advertising (see Figure 4-5).

Positioning by Product Class

Some products need to make critical positioning decisions that involve product-class associations. For example, Maxim freeze-dried coffee needed to position itself with respect to regular and instant coffee. Some margarines position themselves with respect to butter. Dried milk makers came out with instant breakfast positioned as a breakfast substitute and a virtually identical product positioned as a dietary meal substitute. The toilet soap Dove positioned itself apart from the soap category as a cleansing cream product, for women with dry skin.

The soft drink 7-Up was for a long time positioned as a beverage that had a "fresh clean taste" that was "thirst quenching." However, research uncovered the fact that most people did not regard 7-Up as a soft drink, but rather as a mixer beverage, and that this tended to attract only light soft drink users. The positioning strategy was then developed to position 7-Up as a "mainline" soft drink, as a logical alternative to the "colas" but with a better taste. The successful "Uncola" campaign was the result.

Positioning by Cultural Symbols

Many advertisers use deeply entrenched cultural symbols to differentiate their brands from competitors. The essential task is to identify something that is very meaningful to people that other competitors are not using and associate the brand with that symbol. The Wells Fargo Bank, for example, uses a stagecoach pulled by a team of horses and very nostalgic background music to position itself as the bank that opened up the West. Advertising is filled with examples of this kind of positioning strategy. Marlboro cigarettes chose the American cowboy as the central focus to help differentiate its brand from competitors and developed the Marlboro Man. The Green Giant symbol was so successful that the packing company involved was renamed the Green Giant Company. Pillsbury's "doughboy" and dozens of other examples illustrate this type of positioning strategy.

Figure 4-5. Positioning beer at light users: Coors Light
Courtesy of Coors Brewing Company.

Positioning by Competitor

In most positioning strategies, an explicit or implicit frame of reference is one or more competitors. In some cases the reference competitor(s) can be the dominant aspect of the positioning strategy. It is useful to consider positioning with respect to a competitor for two reasons. First, the competitor may have a firm, well-crystallized image developed over many years. The competitor's image can be used as a bridge to help communicate another image referenced to it. If someone wants to know where a particular address is, it is easier to say it is next to the Bank of America building than to describe the various streets to take to get there. Second, sometimes it is not important how good customers think you are; it is just important that they believe you are better than (or perhaps as good as) a given competitor.

Perhaps the most famous positioning strategy of this type was the Avis "We're only number 2. We try harder." campaign. The message was that the Hertz company was so big that they did not need to work hard. The strategy was to position Avis with Hertz as major car rental options, and therefore to position Avis away from National, which at the time was a close third to Avis. See Figure 4-6 for a classic ad from the Avis campaign.

Positioning with respect to a competitor can be an excellent way to create a position with respect to a product characteristic, especially price and quality. Thus, products that are difficult to evaluate, like liquor products, will often use an established competitor to help the positioning task. For example Sabroso, a coffee liqueur, positioned itself with the established brand, Kahlua, with respect to quality and also with respect to the type of liqueur. Its print advertisement showed the two bottles side by side and used the head, "Two great imported coffee liqueurs. One with a great price."

Positioning with respect to a competitor can be accomplished by comparative advertising, advertising in which a competitor is explicitly named and compared on one or more product characteristics. Subaru has recently used this approach to position some of their cars as being comparable in safety to Volvo, which has consistently stressed its safety qualities and is thus closely identified with safety. As Figure 4-7 illustrates, by comparing Subaru to a competitor that has a well-defined safety image, like a Volvo, the communication task becomes easier for Subaru.

DETERMINING THE POSITIONING STRATEGY

What should be our positioning strategy? The identification and selection of a positioning strategy can be difficult and complex. However, it becomes more manageable if it is supported by marketing research and decomposed into a six-step process.

1. Identify the competitors.
2. Determine how the competitors are perceived and evaluated.
3. Determine the competitors' positions.
4. Analyze the customers.
5. Select the position.
6. Monitor the position.

Avis is only No.2 in rent a cars. So why go with us?

We try harder.
(When you're not the biggest, you have to.)
We just can't afford dirty ash-trays. Or half-empty gas tanks. Or worn wipers. Or unwashed cars. Or low tires. Or anything less than seat–adjusters that adjust. Heaters that heat. Defrosters that defrost.

Obviously, the thing we try hardest for is just to be nice. To start you out right with a new car, like a lively, super-torque Ford, and a pleasant smile. To know, say, where you get a good pastrami sandwich in Duluth.
Why?
Because we can't afford to take you for granted.
Go with us next time.
The line at our counter is shorter.

Figure 4-6. Positioning by competitor: Avis Rent-a-Car
Courtesy of Avis, Inc.

Volvo Has Built A Reputation For Surviving Accidents. Subaru Has Built A Reputation For Avoiding Them.

The Volvo 240 has done a fine job of surviving accidents. And we, at Subaru, have always admired that.

So we gave the new Subaru Legacy unibody construction like the Volvo 240.

But at Subaru, we think there's something even better than surviving accidents. And that's not getting into them in the first place.

So unlike the 240, the Subaru Legacy offers an optional anti-lock braking system (ABS). A feature that pumps your brakes automatically for maximum maneuverability and gives you much greater steering control during heavy braking.

Unlike the 240, the Subaru Legacy

is available with full-time four wheel drive. A more civilized form of four wheel drive giving you greater traction on smooth high speed highways as well as on washboard dirt roads.

And unlike most cars in the world, the Subaru Legacy comes with both four wheel disc brakes and independent suspension.

At Subaru, we know that even cars not involved in accidents can eventually come apart. So every Subaru is put together to stay together through conditions which drive other cars into the ground. Of course, we can't guarantee how long every one of our cars will last. But we do know 93% of all Subaru cars registered in America

since 1979 are still on the road.*

And the new Subaru Legacy may even surpass that record for durability. A Subaru Legacy has broken the FIA World Speed/Endurance record by running 19 days at an average speed of 138.8 mph for more than 62,000 miles.**

So you see, it wasn't just accidents the Subaru Legacy was designed to avoid. But junk yards as well.

*R.L. Polk & Co. Statistics, July 1, 1988. **Validated by the Federation Internationale De L'Automobile.

Subaru® Legacy™

We Built Our Reputation By Building A Better Car.

Figure 4-7. Positioning by competitor: Subaru cars

Courtesy of Subaru of America, Inc.

In each of these steps one can employ marketing research techniques to provide needed information. Sometimes the marketing research approach provides a conceptualization that can be helpful even if the research is not conducted.

The first four steps or exercises provide a useful background. The final steps address the evaluation and measurement follow-up. Each step will be discussed in turn.

Identify the Competitors

A first step is to identify the competition. This step is not as simple as it might seem. Pepsi might define its competitors as follows:

1. Other cola drinks
2. Nondiet soft drinks
3. All soft drinks
4. Nonalcoholic beverages
5. All beverages except water

In most cases, there will be a primary group of competitors and one or more secondary competitors, and it will be useful to identify both categories. Thus, Coke will compete primarily with other colas, but other nondiet soft drinks and diet colas could be important as secondary competitors. As another example, the flower delivery service Teleflora will compete primarily with other flower delivery services such as FTD, but also secondarily with other gifts such as boxed chocolates. Such secondary competition is of special concern to brands that are market leaders in their categories, for they are the ones that need to be most considered with issues of category ("primary") demand.

A knowledge of various ways to identify such groupings will be of conceptual as well as practical value. One approach is to determine from buyers of a product which other products they considered. For example, a sample of cola drinkers might be asked what other beverages they might have consumed instead. Or the respondent could be asked what brand would have been purchased had that particular cola brand been out of stock. The resulting analysis will identify the primary and secondary groups of competitive products. Instead of customers, retailers or buyers knowledgeable about customers could provide the information.

Another approach is the development of associations of products with use situations.[12] A respondent might be asked to keep a diary or to recall the use contexts for Pepsi. One might be with an afternoon snack. The respondent could then be asked to name all the beverages that would be appropriate to drink with an afternoon snack. For each beverage so identified, the respondent could be asked to identify appropriate use contexts so that the list of use contexts was more complete. This process would continue for perhaps 20 or 30 respondents until a large list of use contexts and beverages resulted. Another group of respondents would then be asked to make a judgment, perhaps on a seven-point scale, as to how appropriate each beverage would be for each use situation. Then groups of beverages could be clustered based upon their similarity of appropriate use situations. Thus, if Pepsi was regarded as appropriate with snacks, it would compete primarily with other beverages regarded as appropriate for snack occasions. If it was not regarded as appropriate for use with meals, it would be less competitive with beverages deemed more appropriate for meals.

These two approaches suggest a conceptual basis for identifying competitors even when marketing research is not employed. The concept of alternatives from which customers choose and the concept of appropriateness to a use context can be used to understand the competitive environment. A management team or a group of experts, such as retailers or buyers who have an understanding of the customer, could employ one or both of these conceptual bases to identify competitive groupings.

Determine How the Competitors Are Perceived and Evaluated

To determine how competitor products are perceived, it is necessary to choose an appropriate set of product attributes for the comparison. The term ''attributes'' includes not only product characteristics and customer benefits, but also product associations such as product uses or product users. Thus for beer, a relevant ''attribute'' could be the association of a brand with outdoor picnics as opposed to a nice restaurant. Another could be the association with athletes.

In any product category there are usually a host of attribute possibilities. Further, some can be difficult to specify. Consider the taste attribute of beer. Taste testers in a Consumer Union study considered the taste attribute but also the related attributes of smell, strength, and fullness. However, the strength of a beer is probably related to both its taste and its aroma characteristics, and perhaps also to its alcoholic content. Likewise, the notion of fullness is highly interrelated with the other attributes. Fullness can refer to the degree to which the drinker is left with a ''full feeling'' after consuming beer, to the visual color and texture of the product, and to a wide variety of other possible attributes.

The task is to identify potentially relevant attributes, to remove redundancies from the list, and then to select those that are most useful and relevant in describing brand images.

One approach to the generation of an attribute list is the *Kelly repertory grid*. The respondent is first given a deck of cards containing brand names from which all unfamiliar brands are culled. Three cards are then selected randomly from those remaining. The respondent is asked to identify the two brands that are most similar and to describe why those two brands are similar to each other and different from the third. The respondent is then asked to rate the remaining brands on the basis of the attributes thus identified. This procedure is repeated several times for each respondent. As a variant, respondents could be asked to select a preference between two brands and then asked why one brand was selected over the other.

Such a technique will often generate a rather long list of attributes, sometimes as many as several hundred and usually well over 40. The next step is to remove the redundancy from the list. In most cases there will be a set of words or phrases that will essentially mean the same thing. Such redundancies can be identified using logic and judgment.

Another approach is to remove redundancy through a statistical technique called factor analysis.[13] Respondents are asked to rate each of the objects with respect to each attribute. For example, they might be asked to rate Budweiser on a seven-point scale as to the degree it is full bodied. Correlations between attributes are then calculated, and factor analysis essentially groups the attributes on the basis of those correlations.

After a list of nonredundant attributes is obtained, the next task is to select those that are the most meaningful and important to the customer's image of the competitive objects. The selected attributes should be those that are important and relevant to the customer in making distinctions between brands and in making purchasing decisions. One study found that the relevant attribute list for toothpaste was considered to include prevention of decay, taste, whitening capability, color and attractiveness of the product and its packaging, and price.[14] Chapter 6 will discuss several approaches for selecting the most useful and meaningful attributes.

Determine the Competitors' Positions

Another useful exercise is to determine how competitors (including our own entry) are positioned. The primary focus of interest is how they are positioned with respect to the relevant attributes. What is the customer's image of the various competitors? We are also interested in how they are positioned with respect to each other. Which competitors are perceived as similar and which as different? Such judgments can be made subjectively. However, it is also possible to use research to help answer such questions empirically. Such research is termed *multidimensional scaling* because its goal is to scale objects on several dimensions (or attributes). Multidimensional scaling can be based upon either attribute data or nonattribute data. Approaches based on attribute data will be considered first.

Attribute-Based Multidimensional Scaling. The most direct way to determine images is simply to ask a sample of the target segment to scale the various objects on the attribute dimensions. One approach is to use a seven-point agree-or-disagree scale. For example, the respondent could be asked to express his or her agreement or disagreement with statements regarding the Ford Escort: With respect to its class I would consider the Ford Escort to be

    Sporty
    Roomy
    Economical
    Good handling

Alternatively, perceptions of a brand's users or use contexts could be used to determine the brand image: I would expect the typical Escort owner to be

    Older
    Wealthy
    Independent
    Intelligent

The Escort is most appropriate for

> Short neighborhood trips
> Commuting
> Cross-country trips

Another approach, the *semantic differential,* was used by Mindak to obtain the image of three beer brands.[15] The resulting profiles are shown in Figure 4-8. Notice that the image is not only obtained with respect to nine product attributes but also with respect to ten customer characteristics. Several observations emerge. Brand X is especially strong on the refreshing dimensions. Brand Z is weak across the board. The consumer profiles are really similar, which, in this case, was regarded as good news for the makers of brand X, who deliberately tried to appeal to a broad segment.

Nonattribute-Based Multidimensional Scaling.   Attribute-based approaches have several conceptual disadvantages. A complete, valid, and relevant attribute list is not easy to generate. Furthermore, an object may be perceived or evaluated as a total whole that is not really decomposable in terms of attributes. These disadvantages lead us to the use of nonattribute data, such as similarity data.

Similarity measures simply reflect the perceived similarity of two objects in the eyes of the respondents. For example, each respondent may be asked to rate the degree of similarity of each pair of objects. Thus, the respondent does not have an attribute list that implicitly suggests criteria to be included or excluded. The result, when averaged over all respondents, is a similarity rating for each object pair. A multidimensional scaling program then attempts to locate objects in a two- or three- (or more if necessary) dimensional space. Such a space is again termed a perceptual map. The program attempts to construct the perceptual map such that the two objects with the highest similarity are separated by the shortest distance, the object pair with the second highest similarity is separated by the second shortest distance, and so on. Of course, the programs will rarely be able to accomplish this goal, but many different perceptual maps are tried to get as close as possible.

A study of car images several years ago used 50 owners of Granada and 50 nonowners.[16] Between-object similarities were obtained for six cars and an "ideal car." The resulting perceptual map is shown in Figure 4-9. At the time of the study, Granada was attempting to position itself with Mercedes-Benz. Clearly, with respect to the sample used in this pilot study, that attempt was not very successful. Note that there was an effort to compare the perceptions of Granada owners with that of nonowners, as perceptions often differ considerably between such groups. In this case, however, they were very similar. Granada owners did have a tendency to position the Granada farther from a Nova than the nonowners.

The disadvantage of the similarity-based approach is that the interpretation of the dimensions does not have the attributes as a guide. Thus, in Figure 4-9 one horizontal axis might be determined "prestige" and the other horizontal axis "size," but there are no attributes on which to base these judgments. Attribute data can be collected separately

CONSUMER PROFILE

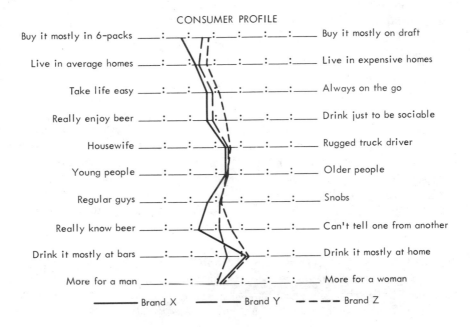

COMPANY IMAGE

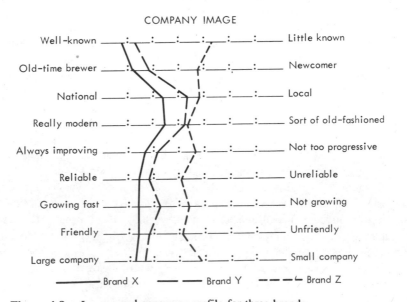

Figure 4-8. Images and consumer profile for three brands

Source: W. A. Mindak, "Fitting the Semantic Differential to the Marketing Problem," *Journal of Marketing*, 25, April 1961, pp. 31–32. Published by American Marketing Association.

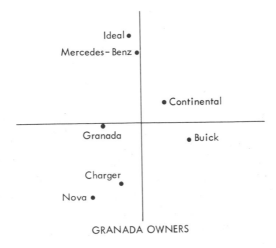

GRANADA OWNERS

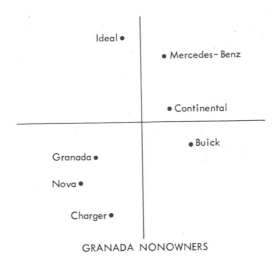

GRANADA NONOWNERS

Figure 4-9.   Similarity-based perceptual map

Source: Robert E. Wilkes, ''Product Positioning by Multidimensional Scaling,'' *Journal of Advertising Research*, 17, August 1977, p. 16.

and correlated with the dimensions found in Figure 4-9, but it would be a distinctly separate analysis. The underlying perceptual map, of course, would still be based upon the similarity data. In addition to the use of similarity data, methods have recently been developed that can extract positioning maps from purchase data of members of longitudinal purchase panels, based on the patterns of brand switching for individual households. These are not discussed here, and the interested reader is referred to marketing research texts and journals for more information.[17]

Analyzing the Customers

The ultimate positioning decision specifies where in the perceptual map the brand should be positioned. Making that decision obviously requires knowing which areas in the map will be attractive to the customers. In most cases, customers will differ markedly as to the area in the perceptual map they prefer even if their perceptions of brands are similar. Thus, the task is usually to identify segments or clusters of customers based on their preferred locations in the perceptual maps. The decision will then involve selecting the segment or segments as well as the target position.

One approach to segmentation is to identify which attributes or customer benefits are most important and then identify groups of customers who value similar attributes or benefits. In Chapter 6, methods to identify important attributes or benefits will be discussed. Another approach uses the concept of an "ideal object." An ideal object, also discussed in Chapter 6, is an object the customer would prefer over all others, including objects that can be conceptualized but do not actually exist.[18] It is a combination of all the customer's preferred attribute levels. Customers who have similar ideal objects will form relevant segments.

It is often important to consider customers' preference for attributes in the context for the use context.[19] Preferences may be very sensitive to use context. In one study focus groups (structured discussions involving 8 to 10 people) and judgment were used to identify nine relevant use contexts for coffee:[20]

1. To start the day
2. Between meals
3. Between meals with others
4. With lunch
5. With supper
6. Dinner with guests
7. In the evening
8. To keep awake in the evening
9. On weekends

In this study, there were differences across use occasion (Hill Brothers had a 7 percent share of breakfast use but only a 1.5 percent share of the remainder of the day). The major differences were found between A.M. coffee drinkers and P.M. coffee drinkers.

MAKING THE POSITIONING DECISION

The four steps or exercises just discussed should be conducted prior to making the actual positioning decision, as the results will nearly always contribute to the decision. The exercises can be done subjectively by the involved managers if necessary. Although marketing research will be more definitive, if research is not feasible or justifiable, the process should still be pursued. However, even with that background, it is still not possible to generate a cookbook solution to the positioning question. However, some guidelines or checkpoints can be offered.

1. *An economic analysis should guide the decision.*   As was noted in Chapter 3, the success of any objective basically depends on two factors: the potential market size times the penetration probability. Unless both of these factors are favorable, success will be unlikely.

The market segment size should be worthwhile. If customers are to be attracted from other brands, those brands should have a large enough market share to justify the effort. If new buyers are to be attracted to the product class, a reasonable assessment should be made of the potential size of that growth area. If a new attribute is to be the basis for a campaign, a reasonable-sized segment should be interested. A survey of 1,250 consumers indicated that the initial thrust of 7-Up into the noncaffeine soft drink market (which stimulated the introduction of noncaffeine colas) did tap a sizable segment. A total of 28 percent said that it makes a great deal of difference to them if their soft drink had caffeine.[21] In the same survey over 40 percent mentioned 7-Up when asked which noncaffeine soft drink first comes to mind.

The penetration probability indicates that there needs to be a competitive weakness to attack or a competitive advantage to exploit to generate a reasonable market penetration probability. An established brand will always find that the penetration probability will be higher among existing customers. The implication is that segments containing existing customers should be given high priority.

2. *Positioning usually implies a segmentation commitment.*   Positioning usually means that an overt decision is being made to ignore parts of the market and to concentrate only on certain segments. Such an approach requires commitment and discipline, because it is not easy to turn your back on potential buyers. Yet the effect of generating a distinct, meaningful position is to focus on the target segments and not be constrained by the reaction of other segments.

There is always the possibility of deciding to engage in a strategy of undifferentiation—that of attempting to reach all segments. In that case, it might be reasonable to consider deliberately generating a "diffuse image," an image that will mean different things to different people. Such an approach is risky and difficult to implement and usually would only be used by a large brand with a very strong market position. The implementation could involve projecting a range of advantages while avoiding being identified with any one. Alternatively, there could be a conscious effort to avoid being explicit about any particular feature. Pictures of bottles of Coca-Cola superimposed with the words "It's the real thing," or Budweiser's claim that "Bud is the king of beers," or "Somebody still cares about quality" illustrate these strategies.

It is possible to "oversegment" the market, and aim at too specialized a market. Some recent research shows that communicating several differentiating features for a brand in one ad (rather than few, spread over several ads), can lead to the perception of the brand being so different from the others in the category that it is seen as a "subtype," as being almost in a different product category than the "reference" category. This can have the advantage of clarity, and consumers are more likely to remember the brand's distinguishing features, but the possible disadvantage is that consumers might not know how to think of this brand (since they may think that what they know about the product category does not apply to this brand). In a complex product category, where it might be important to benefit from the consumer's prior knowledge of the category, such "over-segmentation" might thus hurt the highly differentiated brand.[22]

3. *If the advertising is working, stick with it.* An advertiser will often get tired of a positioning strategy and the advertising used to implement it and will consider making a change. However, the personality or image of a brand, like that of a person, evolves over many years, and the value of consistency through time cannot be overestimated. Some of the very successful, big-budget campaigns have run for 10, 20, or even 30 years. Larry Light, while the executive vice president of BBDO, a major New York advertising agency, said that the "biggest mistake marketers make is to change the personality of their advertising year after year. They end up with a schizophrenic personality at worst, or no personality at best."[23] Burger King, for example, which had five different advertising campaigns in the five years from 1985 to 1990, has been accused of weakening its positioning in the marketplace by this too-rapid change.[24]

4. *Don't try to be something you are not.* It is tempting but naïve, and usually fatal, to decide on a positioning strategy that exploits a market need or opportunity but assumes that your product is something it is not. Before positioning a product, it is important to conduct blind taste tests, in-home or in-office use tests to make sure that the product can deliver what it promises and that it is compatible with a proposed image.

Consider Hamburger Helper, introduced in 1970 as an add-to-meat product that would generate a good-tasting, economical, skillet dinner. It did well during the early 1970s when meat prices were high, but in the mid-1970s, homemakers switched back to more exotic, expensive foods. Reacting to the resulting drop in sales, a decision was made to make Hamburger Helper more exotic by positioning it as a base for casseroles. However, the product—at least in the consumers' minds—could not deliver. The consumers continued to view it as an economical, reliable convenience food; furthermore, they felt that they did not need help in making casseroles.

5. *Consider symbols.* A symbol or set of symbols can have strong associations that should be considered when making positioning decisions. Symbols like the Marlboro Man or the Jolly Green Giant can help implement a campaign, of course, but there can be existing symbols already developed by the brand or organization that can be used. Their availability can affect the positioning decision. For example, Wells Fargo bank has used the Wells Fargo stagecoach with all its associations for many years. The role of symbols in creating a brand personality is discussed further in Chapter 8.

A positioning objective, like any advertising objective, should be operational, in that it should be measurable. To evaluate the advertising and to generate diagnostic information about future advertising strategies, it is necessary to monitor the position over time. A variety of techniques can be employed to make this measurement; typically, test ads are shown to one group of consumers, but not to another, and differences in their positioning maps are then compared. Techniques have also been developed which can relate changes in brand purchasing histories, obtained from households that are members of longitudinal panels, to the advertising and other marketing mix elements aimed at those household panel members.[25] These methods allow managers to test different ad executions to see which ones are most likely to succeed in repositioning brands in desired directions on positioning maps, and subsequently to track changes in brand positioning over time.

SUMMARY

A key aspect of advertising objectives is to identify the target market segments. A concentration strategy involves the selection of a single segment while a differentiation strategy will have several segments, perhaps each having a separate advertising goal. Among the ways to identify segments that might be worthwhile and attractive is by describing them by age, income, geographic location, product usage, or brand loyalty. Segments can also be created by grouping customer in segments that want the same product benefits or share the same life-style or culture.

There are a variety of positioning strategies available to the advertiser. An object can be positioned as follows:

1. By product characteristics or customer benefit (Crest is a cavity fighter)
2. By price and quality (Sears is a ''value'' store)
3. By use or application (Gatorade is for flu attacks)
4. By product user (Miller is for the blue-collar, heavy beer drinker)
5. By product class (7-Up is a soft drink like the colas, not a mixer)
6. By cultural symbol (the Marlboro cowboy)
7. By competitor (Avis positions itself with Hertz)

Four steps should precede the selection of a positioning strategy. In the first, an effort should be made to identify the competitors. In the second step, the attributes used to perceive and evaluate competitors are determined. The third step involves the determination of the position of the various competitors. One approach is to scale the competitors on the various identified attributes. The fourth step involves customer analysis. What segmentation variables seem most relevant? What about benefit segmentation?

The positioning decision should involve an economic analysis of the potential target segments and the probability of affecting their behavior with advertising. Other suggestions include realizing that positioning involves a segmentation commitment, sticking to a strategy that is working, being sure that the product matches the positioning strategy, and consideration of available symbols that may contribute to image formation. Finally, consider the evaluation stage, where the position is monitored.

DISCUSSION QUESTIONS

1. Some argue that usage is the most useful segmentation variable. Others believe that the benefit provided by the product or service is the most useful. Still others will refute both statements. What is your position? Why?

2. Distinguish between controlled coverage and customer self-selection. Which approach would likely be most effective for the manufacturer of an expensive sports car?

3. Develop segmentation strategies for the following:
   (a) Wristwatch company
   (b) Manufacturer of electronic calculators
   (c) College
   (d) Police department
   (e) Pleasure-boat company
   (f) Large retail hardware store
   (g) Church
   (h) Hair spray

4. Select six television and ten print advertisements. How are the products positioned?

5. Can you expand the list of seven positioning strategies mentioned in the text?

6. Obtain two examples of each of the positioning strategies discussed in the chapter.

7. Consider the following beer brands: Lowenbrau, Miller Lite, Miller Genuine Draft, Coors, Coors Light, Bud, Bud Light, Michelob Dry, Schlitz Malt, Heineken, and Beck's.
   (a) In each case, write down what you think is the image the general public holds of that brand. Confine your answers to a few statements or phrases.
   (b) Generate an attribute list for beer, using the Kelly repertory grid approach. Revise your answer to part (a).
   (c) Identify the competitors of the listed brands of beer by asking consumers or potential consumers of that object what they would select if that object were not available.
   (d) Determine the use situations relevant to beer, and for three use situations list other products that might be appropriate.

8. Consider all possible pairs of the following brands of soft drinks: 7-Up, Pepsi, Diet 7-Up, Diet Pepsi, Coke, Orange Crush, Diet Coke, your ideal brand.
   (a) Rank order the brand pairs in terms of their similarity. Was the task a reasonable one? Are you comfortable with all your rankings?
   (b) Pick several sets of three brands, identify the two most similar brands in the set, and explain why you regard them as the most similar. Using the Kelly repertory grid technique, generate a list of attributes relevant to this product class. Scale each of the attributes in terms of how important they are to you in your choice of a soft drink.
   (c) How would you say each of these brands is "positioned"?

9. What would be the characteristics of an ideal brand of toothpaste for you? How might the concept of an ideal brand be related to benefit segmentation? What brand did you buy last? Why? How would your ideal brand differ from this brand?

10. Suppose Anheuser-Busch is interested in entering the soft drink market. They have developed a new drink called Chelsea, which is a carbonated apple juice drink containing 0.5 percent alcohol. It is packaged in a glass bottle partially wrapped in foil, like some of the labels used on premium beers. What are the positioning alternatives open to Chelsea? How would you go about selecting the optimal one?

NOTES

1. See Alfred A. Kuehn and Ralph L. Day, "Strategy of Product Quality," *Harvard Business Review*, 40, November/December 1962, pp. 100–110.

2. Most of the demographic figures mentioned here come from different issues of *American Demographics* magazine, which the interested advertising planner is urged to follow.

3. "Frito-Lay Packs $90m Ad Punch," *Advertising Age*, December 18, 1989, p. 18.

4. A. S. C. Ehrenberg, "Repetitive Advertising and the Consumer," *Journal of Advertising Research*, April 1974.

5. Russell I. Haley, "Benefit Segmentation: A Decision-Oriented Research Tool," *Journal of Marketing*, 32, July 1968, pp. 30–35.

6. Ibid., p. 3s. For a follow-up study, see R. I. Haley, "Beyond Benefit Segmentation," *Journal of Advertising Research*, 11, August 1971, pp. 3–8.

7. "Research Finds Fickle Consumers," *Advertising Age*, June 26, 1989, p. 31.

8. Russell I. Haley and Philip J. Weingarden, "Running Reliable Attitude Segmentation Studies," *Journal of Advertising Research*, December 1986/January 1987, pp. 51–55.

9. These concepts are developed in the context of a normative mathematical model in Ronald E. Frank, William F. Massy, and Yoram Wind, *Market Segmentation* (Englewood Cliffs, N. J.: Prentice Hall, 1972), especially in Chapter 8.

10. James H. Myers and Allan D. Shocker, "Toward a Taxonomy of Product Attributes," Working paper (Los Angeles: University of Southern California, June 1978), p. 3.

11. "Miller's Fast Growth Upsets the Beer Industry," *Business Week*, November 8, 1976.

12. George S. Day, Allan D. Shocker, and Rajendra K. Srivastava, "Customer-Oriented Approaches to Identifying Product Markets," *Journal of Marketing*, 43, Fall 1979, pp. 8–19.

13. David A. Aaker and George S. Day, *Marketing Research* (New York: John Wiley, 1989).

14. Russell J. Haley, "Benefit Segmentation: A Decision Oriented Research Tool," *Journal of Marketing*, July 1968, pp. 30–35.

15. W. A. Mindak, "Fitting the Semantic Differential to the Marketing Problem," *Journal of Marketing*, 25, April 1961, pp. 28–33.

16. Robert E. Wilkes, "Product Positioning by Multidimensional Scaling," *Journal of Advertising Research*, 17, August 1977, pp. 15–18.

17. See, for example, Steven M. Shugan, "Estimating Brand Positioning Maps Using Supermarket Scanning Data," *Journal of Marketing Research*, 24 (1), 1987, pp. 1–18.

18. In Figure 4-7, an ideal point is shown as a point on the map. However, if an attribute-based multidimensional scaling was involved and a scale such as "inexpensive to buy—expensive to buy" were employed, the respondent would prefer to be as far to the right as possible. In that case the "ideal point" would actually appear in the perceptual map as an ideal direction or vector instead of as a point.

19. Rajendra K. Srivastava, Robert P. Leone, and Allan D. Shocker, "Market Structure Analysis: Hierarchical Clustering of Products Based on Substitution in Use," *Journal of Marketing*, 45, Summer 1981, pp. 38–48.

20. Glen L. Urban, Philip L. Johnson, and John R. Hauser, "Testing Competitive Market Structures," *Marketing Science*, 3, Spring 1984, pp. 83–112.

21. Joseph M. Winski, "No Caffeine Choice: 7-Up," *Advertising Age*, May 30, 1983, p. 3.

22. Mita Sujan and James R. Bettman, "The Effects of Brand Positioning Strategies on Consumers' Brand and Category Perceptions: Some Insights from Schema Research" *Journal of Consumer Research*, 26, November 1989, pp. 454–467.

23. "Style Is Substance for Ad Success: Light," *Advertising Age*, August 27, 1979, p. 3.

24. "Burger King Is Hungry—For the Right Ad Campaign," *Business Week*, March 16, 1987, p. 82.

25. William R. Dillon, Teresa Domzal, and Thomas J. Madden, "Evaluating Alternative Product Positioning Strategies," *Journal of Advertising Research*, August/September 1986, pp. 29–35; Russell S. Winer and William L. Moore, "Evaluating the Effects of Marketing-Mix Variables on Brand Positioning," *Journal of Advertising Research*, February/March 1989, pp. 39–45.

CASES FOR PART II

DIAGNOSTIC CASE*

The following data have been collected in five samples.

Measure	Case 1	Case 2	Case 3	Case 4	Case 5
Brand awareness	30%	80%	80%	80%	80%
Favorable attitude toward brand	25	25	45	45	10
Purchased brand once	23	23	23	35	35
Repeat purchase	20	20	20	30	8

In case 1, 30 percent of all respondents were aware of the brand being examined. Twenty-five percent indicated that they had a favorable attitude toward the brand. All of these people were ones who were aware of the brand. Twenty-three percent of all respondents purchased the brand, and all of these were from among those who were favorable toward it. Finally 20 percent purchased the brand more than once.

For each of the five cases described, identify the problem, if any, and indicate your course of action to remedy the problem.

*Source: Professor Brian Sternthal, J. L. Kellogg Graduate School of Management, Northwestern University. Reproduced by permission.

SUZUKI SAMURAI*

In June 1985, Leonard Pearlstein, president and CEO of keye/donna/pearlstein advertising agency, and his colleagues were finalizing the presentation that they would make the next day to Douglas Mazza, vice president and general manager of American Suzuki Motor Corporation (ASMC). Pearlstein's agency was competing with a half-dozen other advertising firms to represent Suzuki's new entrant in the U.S. automobile market, the Suzuki Samurai. Mazza had asked each agency the question: "How do you feel this vehicle should be positioned?" He had given keye/donna/pearlstein eight days to prepare an answer.

Company Background

Suzuki Loom Works, a privately owned loom manufacturing company, was founded in 1909 in Hamamatsu, Japan, by Michio Suzuki. In 1952, the company began manufacturing and marketing a 2-cycle, 36 cubic centimeter (cc) motorcycle, which became so popular that in 1954 the company introduced a second motorcycle and changed its name to Suzuki Motor Company, Ltd. (Suzuki).

During the late 1950s, lightweight vehicle sales boomed in Japan. Suzuki's motorcycle business grew, and in 1959 it introduced a lightweight van. The van's success encouraged Suzuki to develop lightweight cars and trucks. In 1961, it introduced its first production car, the "Suzulight," the first Japanese car with a 2-stroke engine.

In 1964 Suzuki began exporting motorcycles to the United States, where it established a wholly owned subsidiary, U.S. Suzuki Motor Company, Ltd., to serve as the exclusive importer and distributor of Suzuki motorcycles. Suzuki quickly established itself as a major brand in the U.S. motorcycle industry.

By 1965, Suzuki's product line included motorcycles, automobiles, motorized wheelchairs, outboard motors, general-purpose engines, generators, water pumps, and prefabricated houses. The company concentrated, however, on producing and marketing lightweight vehicles. Until 1979, Suzuki cars and trucks were sold only in Japan, where they were popular as economical transportation. In 1979 Suzuki automobiles were introduced into foreign markets, and by 1984 they were available in over 100 countries and Hawaii.

In 1983, General Motors (GM) purchased 5 percent of Suzuki and helped the company develop a subcompact car for the U.S. market. The car, named the Chevrolet Sprint, was introduced on the West Coast in mid-1984 and was sold exclusively by Chevrolet dealers. The Sprint was Suzuki's first entry into the continental U.S. automobile market. The Sprint was subject to Japan's "voluntary" restraint agreement (VRA) on car shipments to the United States. The VRA, in place since 1981, limited the number of cars that each Japanese automobile manufacturer could ship to the United States in a given year. In

*Copyright © 1988 by the President and Fellows of Harvard College

Harvard Business School case 9-589-028

This case was prepared by Tammy Bunn Hiller under the direction of Professor John A. Quelch as the basis for class discussion rather than to illustrate either effective or ineffective handling of an administrative situation. Reprinted by permission of the Harvard Business School.

1984, Suzuki's total VRA quota of 17,000 cars went to GM as Sprints. GM quickly sold out its allotment even though Sprint's distribution was limited to its West Coast dealers.

American Suzuki Motor Corporation (ASMC)

GM's success with Sprint showed Suzuki that a market existed for its cars in the continental United States. Suzuki, which called itself "the always something different company," planned to introduce several unique vehicles into the U.S. market over time. Suzuki had no guarantee, however, that GM would be willing to market the vehicles. Therefore, Suzuki decided to established its own presence in the U.S. automobile industry.

Japan's VRA quotas made it impossible for Suzuki to export any cars other than the Sprint to the United States in the foreseeable future. Consequently, in 1985, Suzuki and GM began negotiations with the Canadian government to build a plant in Ontario that could produce approximately 200,000 subcompact cars per year. Suzuki management expected the plant to be on-line by early 1989, and the company could then begin selling cars in the United States under its own name.

Market forces, however, made Suzuki loath to wait until 1989. In 1984, Japanese imports achieved a record 17.7 percent share of U.S. new car and truck sales. Based on first quarter sales, industry experts predicted that Japanese imports would command a 19.2 percent share of the U.S. market in 1985. Total U.S. automobile sales were expected to grow by 10 percent in 1985, and this rapid growth made dealers optimistic and willing to invest money in new car lines, especially Japanese brands.

In addition, two other car companies, Hyundai Motor Company of South Korea and Zavodi Crvena Zastava (Yugo) of Yugoslavia, were expected to enter the U.S. car market in 1986. Suzuki managers believed that brand clutter might limit their success if they waited until 1989 to introduce the Suzuki name into the continental United States.

Suzuki management was convinced that the time was right to enter the continental United States and that Suzuki had the right product to do so, the SJ413. Its forerunner, the SJ410, was a mini 4-wheel-drive off-road vehicle with a 1,000 cc engine that Suzuki had introduced in 1960. By 1985, the SJ410 was sold in 102 countries and Hawaii. In 1985, Suzuki introduced the SJ413, an upgraded model that featured a 1,324 cc engine and was designed with the U.S. market specifically in mind. The SJ413 was more powerful and more comfortable than the SJ410. The upsizing of Suzuki's vehicle, combined with the downsizing of U.S. consumer automobile preferences, made the SJ413 a viable continental U.S. product.

If the SJ413 was imported without a back seat, the U.S. government classified it as a truck, for customs purposes. Trucks were not subject to Japanese VRA quotas; instead, they were subject to a 25 percent tariff versus a 2.5 percent tariff on cars. The tariff was high, but Suzuki management believed that it was worth paying.

On May 10, 1985, Suzuki hired Douglas Mazza to organize and head its new subsidiary, ASMC. Mazza was charged with developing a Suzuki dealer network to begin selling the SJ413 by November 1985. He was also responsible for creating the marketing plan for the SJ413, which would be named the Suzuki Samurai in the United States, as it was in Canada. Suzuki planned to market two versions of the Samurai in the United States, a convertible and a hardtop.

Samurai Dealer Network.   Mazza's goal was to establish ASMC as a major car company in the United States. To achieve this goal, he believed that he had to convince prospective dealers to build separate showrooms for the Samurai. If ASMC allowed a dealer merely to display the vehicle in an existing showroom, the dealer would invest little in the Samurai, monetarily or emotionally, and probably would sell only a few Samurais each month. Low Samurai sales per dealer and lack of facility and management commitment could jeopardize Suzuki's plan to introduce other cars into the United States, starting in 1989.

Therefore, Mazza drafted a dealer agreement that required prospective Samurai dealers to build an exclusive sales facility for the Samurai. The facility had to include a showroom, sales offices, and a customer waiting and accessory display area. Service and parts could share a facility with a dealer's other car lines, but a minimum of two service stalls had to be dedicated to Suzuki and operated by Suzuki-trained mechanics. Furthermore, Suzuki dealerships had to display required signs outside the sales office and in the service stalls. A minimum of three salespeople, two service technicians, one general manager, and one general office clerk had to be dedicated to the Suzuki dealership.

The prospectus also explained that, as the product line grew, dealer requirements would expand to include a full, exclusive facility complete with attached parts and service. This upfront expansion plan was a first in the industry and was based on the belief that quick dealer profitability would be key to success—as a dealer's sales opportunities grew, so too would the financial commitment and overhead.

ASMC's planned suggested retail price for the Samurai was $5,995. The planned dealer invoice price was $5,095, only 7.5 percent higher than ASMC's own landed cost for the vehicle. Mazza estimated that each dealership would need to sell approximately 30 Samurais per month to cover its monthly operating costs plus the finance charges on its initial investment.

To attract good dealers, Mazza knew that he must make the opportunity match the investment requirements. He therefore planned to limit the number of Samurai dealers so that ASMC could guarantee a minimum supply of 37 units per month to each one. Thus each dealership could earn a profit every month if it sold its total allotment. Suzuki had set Mazza the goal of selling 6,000 Samurais in the first six months of U.S. distribution, but Mazza and his new management team convinced the Japanese management that the U.S. opportunity was far greater. Suzuki raised its commitment to ASMC to 10,500 vehicles for the same time period. Consequently, Mazza decided to limit his initial dealer network to no more than 47 dealers. This small network implied rolling out the Samurai in only two or three states in November 1985. Mazza chose to introduce the Samurai into California, the nation's largest automobile market, and Florida and Georgia, where Japanese import sales were higher than the U.S. average.

Before Mazza could enlist dealers, he had to decide how to position the Samurai to consumers. The position he chose would help define the vehicle's target market, which, in turn, would influence ASMC's preferred dealer locations. By combining car registration data and census information, the concentration of owners of imported vehicles or owners of sport utility vehicles, for example, could be pinpointed by zip code. Dealerships could be selected with trading areas that encompassed zip codes with high concentrations of households that fell into Suzuki's target market.

Samurai Positioning

The keye/donna/pearlstein advertising agency had no experience in developing campaigns for automobiles. This appealed to Mazza, because he believed that a fresh approach was needed for his company's new product. After accepting Mazza's offer to compete for the Samurai account, Pearlstein and his associates quickly scanned automobile advertising of other manufacturers. They concluded that industry practice was to position vehicles according to their physical characteristics as, for example, subcompact cars versus compact cars versus luxury sedans. Most advertising was feature/benefit or price oriented. A typical ad noted that a vehicle was of a specific type and emphasized differentiating features and/or superior value for the money.

If they followed industry practice, Pearlstein's group had three options for positioning the Samurai based on its physical characteristics—as a compact sport utility vehicle, as a compact pickup truck, or as a subcompact car.

Exhibit 1 shows pictures of the Samurai. The most obvious position for the Samurai was as a sport utility vehicle. It looked like a "mini-Jeep," had 4-wheel-drive capability, and was designed to drive well off-road. Such a position would be consistent with the Samurai's heritage and its positioning in the 102 countries where the SJ410 and SJ413 were sold. Foreign owners praised the Samurai's reliability, ability to go places where larger utility vehicles could not, and ease of repair.

The Samurai's size and price distinguished it from all other sport utility vehicles sold in the United States in 1985. The Samurai was smaller and lighter than the other vehicles, and its $5,995 suggested retail price was well below the other vehicles' $10,000 to $13,000 price range.

Pearlstein believed that if the Samurai were positioned as a sport utility vehicle, it should be advertised as a "tough little cheap Jeep." Advertising copy would show the Samurai in off-road wilderness situations, squeezing through places where bigger sport utility vehicles could not go. Ads would also emphasize that the Samurai cost only half the price of an average Jeep.

Pearlstein was unsure, however, whether a compact sport utility positioning could generate the sales volume that Mazza envisioned for the Samurai. The market for sport utility vehicles was relatively small. As Exhibit 2 shows, total 1984 compact sport utility vehicles sales in the United States were less than 3 percent of total automobile industry sales. Mazza's goal was to build annual U.S. Samurai sales to 30,000 units within two years of the vehicle's introduction. To achieve this objective, annual Samurai sales would have to exceed the combined 1984 sales of all imported compact sport utility vehicles.

The second option, positioning the Samurai as a compact pickup truck, would tap a market that was two and one-half times the size of that for compact sport utility vehicles. Moreover, Japanese import trucks sold well in the United States, accounting for 54

EXHIBIT 1 Samurai Convertible and Hardtop

Convertible

Hardtop

EXHIBIT 2   U.S. Automobile Industry Unit Sales

Make	1984 unit sales	Projected 1985 unit sales
Compact Sport Utility Vehicles		
Suzuki SJ410 (Hawaii)	2,124	2,500
Mitsubishi Montero	2,690	2,800
Toyota 4Runner	9,181	19,300
Toyota Landcruiser	4,170	4,400
Isuzu Trooper	6,935	25,400
Total Japanese import	25,100	54,400
Ford Bronco II		
GM Chevrolet S10 Blazer/GMC S15	98,446	104,500
Jimmy	175,177	225,500
Jeep/CJ/YJ series	41,627	40,100
Jeep Cherokee/Wagoneer	84,352	113,900
Total domestic	399,710	483,700
Total compact sport utility	424,810	538,100
Compact Pickup Trucks		
Mitsubishi P/U	11,102	21,900
Toyota P/U	144,675	171,500
Nissan P/U	140,864	188,700
Mazda P/U	115,303	114,600
Isuzu P/U	32,372	46,200
Total Japanese import P/U 2WD	444,316	542,900
Jeep Comanche P/U	0	3,800
Ford Ranger P/U	173,959	185,800
Chevy/GMC S10/S15 P/U	181,692	200,200
Dodge Ram 50 P/U	37,356	56,100
Total domestic P/U 2WD	393,007	445,900
Total compact P/U truck 2WD	837,323	988,800
Mitsubishi P/U 4 × 4	2,156	1,900
Toyota P/U 4 × 4	81,904	101,400
Nissan P/U 4 × 4	51,082	65,400
Isuzu P/U 4 × 4	3,537	4,900
Total Japanese import P/U 4 × 4	138,679	173,600
Jeep Comanche 4 × 4	0	4,800
Ford Ranger 4 × 4	48,110	56,400
Chevy/GMC S10/S15 4 × 4	47,409	51,200
Dodge Ram 50 P/U 4 × 4	12,499	12,500
Total domestic P/U 4 × 4	108,018	124,900
Total compact P/U truck 4 × 4	246,697	298,500
Total Japanese import P/U 2WD and 4 × 4	582,995	716,500
Total domestic P/U 2WD and 4 × 4	501,025	570,800
Total compact P/U 2WD and 4 × 4	1,084,020	1,287,300

EXHIBIT 2   U.S. Automobile Industry Unit Sales (continued)

Make	1984 unit sales	Projected 1985 unit sales
Subcompact Cars		
Toyota Starlet	781	0
Toyota Tercel	107,185	95,400
Toyota Corolla	156,249	173,900
Nissan Sentra	194,092	225,700
Nissan Pulsar	39,470	51,400
Mitsubishi Mirage	2,354	12,400
Honda Civic	173,561	196,800
Mazda 323/GLC	43,641	60,000
Isuzu I-Mark	4,822	13,000
Total Japanese import	722,427	828,600
Volkswagen Rabbit/Golf	85,153	71,300
Chevrolet Spectrum	1,646	51,700
Chevrolet Sprint	9,464	29,700
Dodge/Plymouth Colt	82,402	96,100
Total domestic	944,668	1,112,900
Total subcompact	1,752,248	2,016,095
Total car and truck		
Total Japanese car	1,846,398	2,139,500
Total Japanese truck	664,813	849,800
Total Japanese car and truck	2,511,211	2,989,300
Total industry car	10,128,318	10,888,600
Total industry truck	4,048,998	4,675,200
Total industry car and truck	14,177,316	15,563,800

Note: Sums of individual vehicle makes do not always equal total since only the top-selling makes are listed.

Source: R. L. Polk & Company market report.

percent of total 1984 compact pickup truck sales. The Samurai could be used as a truck when purchased without a back seat or when its back seat was folded up. Therefore, positioning it as a truck seemed feasible.

ASMC set the Samurai's suggested retail price at $5,995 in order to price it comparably with Japanese import compact pickup trucks, which had a high level of U.S. consumer acceptance. Therefore, in Pearlstein's view, if advertised as a truck, the Samurai's price would not be emphasized but mentioned only to indicate parity with other truck prices. Advertising copy would probably be serious, practical, and male targeted and designed to portray the Samurai as a tough truck.

The third option, to position the Samurai as a subcompact car, would open up the largest of the three possible markets. Although the Suzuki SJ413 was not positioned as a car in Europe, a trend was developing in which professionals, especially doctors and lawyers, drove their SJ413s to their offices in the city and left their Mercedes at home. Similarly, in the United States, especially in California, sport utility vehicles were sometimes driven in town, although none had hitherto been positioned as a car.

The Samurai boasted an average 28 miles per gallon in combined city and highway driving, was priced lower than many subcompact cars, and offered more versatility. Therefore, it could reasonably be considered by those who were shopping for an economy car. If positioned against subcompact cars, Pearlstein believed that Samurai advertising copy should emphasize the vehicle's looks. The message to consumer would be "Why buy a Toyota Tercel or a Nissan Sentra when, for the same amount of money, you can buy a much cuter vehicle, the Samurai?" However, the vehicle might not meet consumers' expectations if it was positioned as a car. Because the Samurai was built on a truck platform, its ride was stiffer and less comfortable than even the least expensive subcompact.

Market Research.   Pearlstein defined positioning as "the unique way we want prospects to think about a product." Before choosing a position for the Samurai, he asked Don Popielarz, director of research and planning, to conduct research in order to gain a thorough understanding of not only the attributes that prospective buyers ascribed to the Samurai versus other vehicles but also the profile and characteristics of potential buyers. This information would help Pearlstein decide how to position the vehicle. Then his team could develop advertising copy and choose the media that would be most efficient in delivering the Samurai's message to its consumer target.

Popielarz started by reviewing the latest research available from outside sources. A demographic segmentation study conducted by J. D. Power and Associates divided new car buyers into demographic segments based on the size/style of the car that was purchased. The "basic small-car" segment included cars such as the Chevrolet Sprint, Ford Escort, Honda Civic, Toyota Tercel, and Mazda 323. Most (54 percent) of the car purchasers in this segment were men, but only 43 percent of the principal drivers were male. The median age of the buyers was 38. The average domestic car buyer was 41, while the average import car buyer was 36. Sixty percent of the car buyers were married; over one-third had executive/professional/technical careers, and 43 percent were college graduates. The median household size was 2.69 people, and the median household income was $34,240.

From a survey conducted by *Newsweek* for use by pickup truck and sport utility vehicle manufacturers, Popielarz learned how consumers perceived sport utility vehicles versus pickup trucks. Consumers were asked to rate 29 vehicle features of domestic and imported pickup trucks and sport utility vehicles. The features were aggregated into seven factors that were then plotted on two-dimension perceptual maps. The seven factors were everyday driving, off-road/snow driving, passenger comfort, quality/durability, styling, capacity, and gas mileage. Exhibit 3 lists the vehicle features that made up each of the seven factors. Exhibits 4–7 show four maps that summarize consumers' perceptions of pickup trucks versus sport utility vehicles on the seven factors.

After reviewing research from outside sources, Popielarz studied a survey that Suzuki had recently conducted in Canada, where it sold approximately 4,000 Samurais in

EXHIBIT 3 *Newsweek* **Study: Factors and the Features That Constitute Them**

Factor	Feature
Everyday driving	For highway driving
	Acceleration power
	Riding comfort
	Ease of handling
	Quietness
	Maneuverability in traffic
	For long-distance vacations
	Safety features
	Seating comfort
	Towing capacity
Passenger comfort	Passenger seating capacity as a family vehicle
	Interior roominess for long-distance vacations
	Seating comfort
	Level of luxury
	Riding comfort
Quality/durability	Quality of workmanship
	Durability/reliability
	Quality of materials
	Tough, rugged
Styling	Interior styling
	Exterior styling
	Design of instrument panel
	Level of luxury
	Ground clearance
Off-road/snow driving	Off-road capability for driving in snow
	Ground clearance
	Fun to drive
	Tough, rugged
Capacity	Ability to carry large items
	Cargo capacity
	Towing capacity
Gas mileage	Gas mileage/fuel economy

1984. Suzuki randomly surveyed 374 Canadian Samurai owners. The majority (75 percent) of the Samurai buyers were male, and 62 percent were between the ages of 18 and 34. The average age of the buyers was 33. The most frequently mentioned occupation was skilled tradesperson (32 percent). Only 21 percent were college graduates, and only 1 percent were currently students. Fifty-one percent of the buyers lived in two-person households, and the average household income was $43,800.

When asked "When you hear the name Suzuki, what do you think of," 40 percent of the Samurai owners responded "motorcycle." Other answers included 4 × 4/4-wheel drive (23 percent), Jeep (16 percent), Japanese product/efficiency (14 percent), quality/

EXHIBIT 4 **Perceptual Map from *Newsweek* Study: Off-road/Snow Driving Versus Everyday Driving**

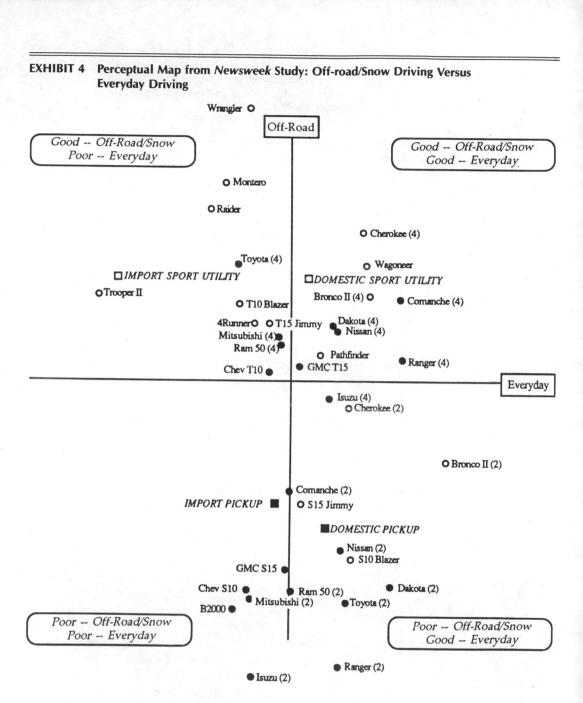

Wrangler ○

Off-Road

| Good -- Off-Road/Snow |
| Poor -- Everyday |

| Good -- Off-Road/Snow |
| Good -- Everyday |

○ Montero

○ Raider

○ Cherokee (4)

● Toyota (4)

○ Wagoneer

□ *IMPORT SPORT UTILITY*

□ *DOMESTIC SPORT UTILITY*

○ Trooper II

○ T10 Blazer

Bronco II (4) ○

● Comanche (4)

4Runner ○ ○ T15 Jimmy

Dakota (4) ●

Mitsubishi (4) ●

● Nissan (4)

Ram 50 (4) ●

○ Pathfinder

● Ranger (4)

Chev T10 ●

● GMC T15

Everyday

● Isuzu (4)

○ Cherokee (2)

○ Bronco II (2)

● Comanche (2)

IMPORT PICKUP ■

○ S15 Jimmy

■ *DOMESTIC PICKUP*

● Nissan (2)

○ S10 Blazer

GMC S15 ●

Chev S10 ●

● Ram 50 (2)

● Dakota (2)

B2000 ●

● Mitsubishi (2)

● Toyota (2)

| Poor -- Off-Road/Snow |
| Poor -- Everyday |

| Poor -- Off-Road/Snow |
| Good -- Everyday |

● Ranger (2)

● Isuzu (2)

● Perceptions of *specific* brands/models of *pickup trucks*
○ Perceptions of *specific* brands/models of *sport utility vehicles*
■ Perceptions of the *category of pickup trucks*
□ Perceptions of the *category of sport utility vehicles*

EXHIBIT 5 **Perceptual Map from *Newsweek* Study: Passenger Comfort Versus Styling**

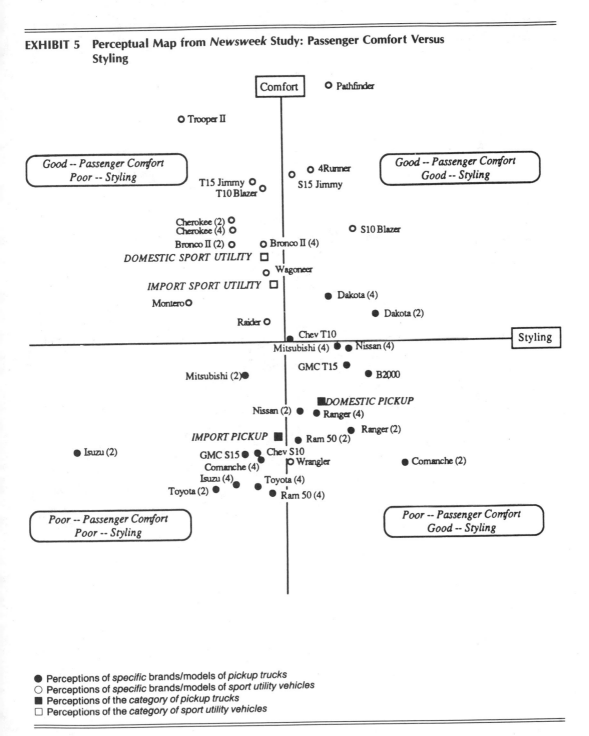

● Perceptions of *specific* brands/models of *pickup trucks*
○ Perceptions of *specific* brands/models of *sport utility vehicles*
■ Perceptions of the *category of pickup trucks*
□ Perceptions of the *category of sport utility vehicles*

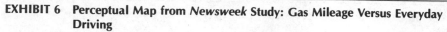

EXHIBIT 6 Perceptual Map from *Newsweek* Study: Gas Mileage Versus Everyday Driving

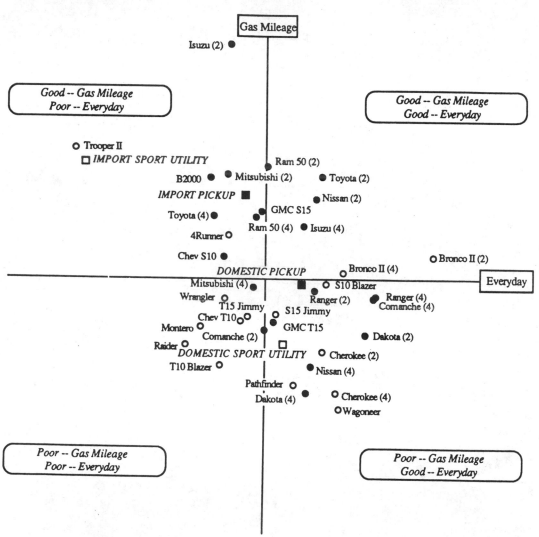

● Perceptions of *specific* brands/models of *pickup trucks*
○ Perceptions of *specific* brands/models of *sport utility vehicles*
■ Perceptions of the *category of pickup trucks*
□ Perceptions of the *category of sport utility vehicles*

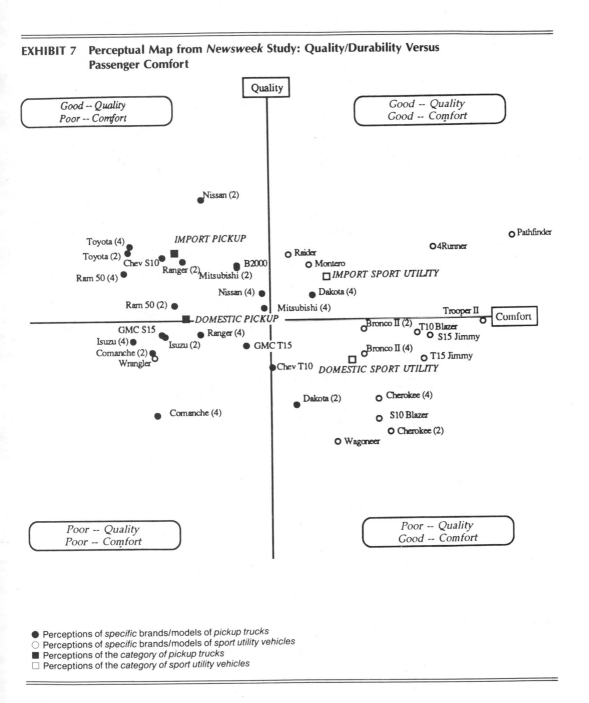

● Perceptions of *specific* brands/models of *pickup trucks*
○ Perceptions of *specific* brands/models of *sport utility vehicles*
■ Perceptions of the *category of pickup trucks*
□ Perceptions of the *category of sport utility vehicles*

well made (11 percent), dependable/reliable (10 percent), versatility/work/play/goes anywhere (10 percent), small (9 percent), pleasure vehicle/fun (8 percent), my car (7 percent), and economical (6 percent). When the owners were asked to describe the Samurai using only one word or phrase, the word most often mentioned was "fun." Exhibit 8 lists all the words that were volunteered by five or more owners.

As Exhibit 9 shows, design/appearance was mentioned most frequently by owners as their main reason for purchasing the Samurai. When asked "Before making your purchase, what other automobiles did you consider?" 29 percent mentioned various models of Jeep. Other vehicles mentioned included Ford Bronco and Ranger (24 percent), GMC Chevrolet Jimmy (7 percent), GM Chevrolet 5-10 Blazer (8 percent), Toyota 4 × 4 pickup truck and Landcruiser (12 percent), and Nissan 4 × 4 pickup truck (4 percent). No other model was mentioned by as many as 4 percent of the respondents. When asked why they selected the Samurai over the "first alternative" vehicle, the overwhelming response was economy/value (59 percent) followed by design/appearance (29 percent).

Popielarz was unsure how to interpret the data from the Canadian study, given climatic and cultural differences between the United States and Canada. Furthermore, the Samurai was positioned as a rugged utility vehicle in Canada, where it was priced higher than was planned in the United States. In Canada, the Samurai was priced similarly to the least expensive sport utility vehicles and substantially higher than both light trucks and subcompact cars.

EXHIBIT 8   Canadian Samurai Buyer Survey: Suzuki Samurai One Word/Phrase Description

Word/Phrase mentioned	Number of mentions
Fun	41
Jeep	15
Great	13
Goes anywhere	11
Good	11
Economical	10
Practical	9
Reliable	8
All-terrain	7
Fantastic	7
Pleasure	7
Tough	7
Four/wheel drive	6
Four-by-four	5
Sporty	5
Versatile	5

Note: Samurai buyers were asked, "If you had to describe the Suzuki Samurai using only one word or phrase, what would you say about it?"

**EXHIBIT 9   Canadian Samurai Buyer Survey: Reasons
for Purchasing Samurai**

Main reason for purchasing	Percent mentioning
Design/appearance (net)	64%
4 × 4/4-wheel drive/jeep	39
Appearance/good-looking/sporty looking	22
Convertible	19
Size/small compact	8
Economy value (net)	55
Economy/economical	18
Good mileage/fuel savings	18
Cost/reasonable price	18
Inexpensive/low price	10
Performance (net)	51
Traction/can go anywhere	19
All-season vehicle/functional	17
Fun/fun to drive	11
Ease of driving/handling/parking	7
Reliable/service (net)	19
Dependable/reliable	13
Quality/well made/good	7
Need for jeep/second vehicle	8
Suits my life-style needs/I like it	5

Note: Samurai buyers were asked, "What are your main reasons for
purchasing this vehicle?"

Fortunately, there was one continental U.S. market where Suzuki SJ410s were being sold, albeit unauthorized by Suzuki. In Florida, a "gray market" existed for Suzuki SJ410s. Since 1984, approximately 3,000 had been sold there by dealers who imported them from other Suzuki markets, including Puerto Rico, Guam, the U.S. Virgin Islands, and Panama.

Popielarz and Tim O'Mara, one of the agency's account supervisors, decided to conduct face-to-face interviews with five sales managers and sales representatives at three Florida dealerships that sold SJ410s. They asked the salespeople four questions. The first question was "Who is the buyer?" The dealers said the SJ410 buyer was young, on average, between 18 and 30 years old, often single, often a first-time car buyer, and often a student. Young women seemed to like the vehicle, and many sales involved fathers buying SJ410s for their children. Additionally, there was an important secondary buyer group comprising people over 30, both single and married, who bought the Suzuki to use as a third or fourth vehicle.

The second question, "What does the buyer see as competition?" elicited a unanimous response from the dealers. There was no direct competition. Indirect competition included 4-wheel drive vehicles, small cars, and convertibles. The SJ410 was less expensive than other convertibles and 4-wheel drive vehicles, however, and was more "fun and [had more] style than small cars."

"Why does the buyer want this vehicle?" was the third question the dealers addressed. The "most fun for the dollars" was usually mentioned. As one sales manager stated, "I don't see too many people driving down the road in Chevettes and having a blast." Other replies included convertible top; versatility, utility; gas mileage; durability; cute and unique; handles in rain, snow, and off-road; and great for fishing, camping, and skiing.

The final question, "How are they selling?" prompted smiles from the salespeople, who typically responded, "People were just lining up to get them. Just couldn't get enough of them in." The SJ410s sold for an average price of $8,500 at the three dealerships.

One of the dealerships, King Motors in Fort Lauderdale, routinely surveyed its automobile buyers. The dealership had surveys completed by 150 recent Suzuki SJ410 buyers, which it allowed Popielarz and O'Mara to study. The vehicle buyer filled out the questionnaire; however, in many instances, the buyer was not the ultimate driver. Information on age was incomplete, but of those who gave their age, 56 percent of the buyers were between 18 and 30; the rest were over 30. One-third of the purchasers were women.

Exhibit 10 tabulates the King Motors survey responses. The majority of buyers learned about the Suzuki through word of mouth or seeing it when driving by the dealership. Most buyers came to King Motors planning to buy the Suzuki rather than the AMC Jeep line, which was also sold there. Fewer than half of the buyers considered buying another vehicle, but when other automobiles were considered, they included both new and used Jeeps, small imported cars, and large used American convertibles.

Four-wheel drive was not the principal feature generating interest in the Suzuki. Only 45 percent of the men and 32 percent of the women surveyed said that it was an important factor in their purchase decision. The attributes that buyers rated as most important were price and the fact that it was a convertible model.

Popielarz knew that the Florida buyers who participated in the survey might not be typical of the kinds of people who would buy the Samurai once it was introduced nationwide. He did believe, however, that the survey results gave clues about who the early adopters were likely to be.

After interviewing the Florida dealers, Popielarz and O'Mara conducted focus group interviews in California with a group of women aged 25 to 33, a group of men aged 18 to 24, and another group of men aged 25 to 35. All of the participants were actively shopping for a new vehicle that was either a sport utility vehicle, a subcompact car, or an imported pickup truck. All had visited at least one dealer showroom within the previous two months.

During the sessions, focus group members viewed pictures of both the convertible and hardtop Samurais that would be sold in the United States, pictures of a variety of people who might drive the Samurai, a five-minute videotape showing the Samurai in action, and pictures of several vehicles with which the Samurai might compete. Respon-

EXHIBIT 10   King Motors' Suzuki SJ410 Buyer Survey

	Total	Total men	Total women
Where heard about Suzuki			
Word of mouth	39%	41%	42%
Dealer location	33	36	22
Ft. Lauderdale newspaper	19	17	24
Radio	6	5	7
Pompano Shopper	2	1	5
Came to dealer to see			
Suzuki	77	75	77
AMC jeep	17	21	14
Encore	1	0	2
Alliance	0	0	0
Wagoneer	0	0	0
Other	5	4	7
Considered other vehicle			
Yes	41	42	37
No	59	58	63
Considered AMC Jeep first			
Yes	27	30	25
No	73	70	75
Important purchase factors			
Price	89	72	80
Convertible	62	59	66
Gas mileage	47	46	45
4-wheel drive	41	45	32
Size of vehicle	37	37	41
Color	24	26	18
Driving and handling	21	22	16
Other	7	9	5

dents reacted favorably to the Samurai's appearance, describing it as "cute," "neat," and "fun." The Samurai's size invoked mixed reactions. Some believed its size would add to its drivability and maneuverability; they said it looked easy to drive around town and in the country. For others, especially those with children or pets, the small size was a drawback. Also, those who planned rugged off-road use said the Samurai was too small.

Group members who needed occasional 4-wheel drive capability readily accepted the Samurai as a viable alternative to other 4-wheel drive vehicles. Those people who did not need the 4-wheel drive feature said that it did not reduce their acceptance of the vehicle.

Some people said that the Samurai was exactly what they were looking for in a vehicle. They saw it as a symbol of their independence to do something different and their practicality to drive a versatile vehicle. Interest in the Samurai among focus group members appeared to be linked more to attitude than to age. When asked to choose potential Samurai buyers from the pictures that were shown to them, the interviewees chose the younger, more active people.

Most of the interviewees recognized the Suzuki name and associated it with motorcycles or the attributes of Japanese automobile manufacturers, that is, higher quality and better engineering than the domestic competition. Their price expectations were between $8,000 and $12,000, significantly higher than the planned $5,995 price tag. They were quite knowledgeable, however, about the prices of the competitive vehicles discussed. When told the Samurai's actual price, most people expressed surprise and pleasure. A few expressed suspicion about the vehicle's quality at that price.

Conclusions.   Popielarz and O'Mara reviewed the market research findings with Pearlstein and Spike Bragg, the agency's executive vice president. They concluded that any young or young-at-heart person considering the purchase of a small car, small truck, or sport utility vehicle was a prospect for the Samurai. Suzuki should, therefore, avoid positioning the Samurai as a specific type of vehicle so as not to exclude large groups of potential buyers.

Furthermore, they reasoned that Suzuki should not "overdefine" the vehicle. The Samurai appeared to represent different things to different people. Therefore, Suzuki should try to develop a position with broad enough appeal to attract a wide range of consumers so that each person could define the Samurai in his or her own way and rationalize the purchase decision in his or her own terms. Moreover, the ad agency thought that if each consumer was allowed to personally define the Samurai, this would lead to greater congruence between the vehicle's promise and its delivery than if Suzuki tried to tell consumers what the Samurai was.

Bragg suggested that the Samurai be positioned as "the alternative to small-car boredom." He reasoned that sport utility buyers could be attracted to the Samurai just by looking at the vehicle but that small-car buyers would need to be told that the Samurai was a fun alternative to dull automobiles. Furthermore, he believed that many purchasers of small trucks were buying them to use as cars because compact import pickup trucks were less expensive than import subcompact cars and offered more versatility. An "alternative to small-car boredom" positioning could, therefore, attract buyers from all three vehicle segments.

Pearlstein liked Bragg's idea but expanded on it. He thought that the Samurai should be positioned as the "antidote to traditional transportation." It was important that the Samurai not be labeled as any type of vehicle. No ads should refer to it as a car, truck, or sport utility vehicle.

Final Preparations for Presentation to Mazza

Pearlstein and his associates had to present their positioning recommendation to Mazza the following day. Although Mazza had not asked to be shown any creative execution of the position, the four men had developed copy that they believed would help to explain the "antidote-to-traditional-transportation" position that they had chosen. Exhibits 11 through 16 show examples of their proposed advertising copy.

EXHIBIT 11 "End of Dull" Proposed Print Ad

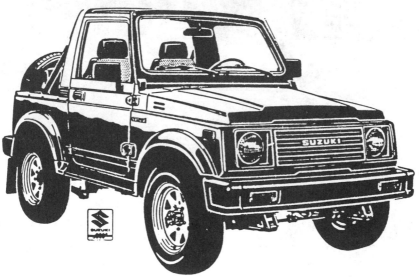

The end of dull. The start of Suzuki.

Introducing the Suzuki Samurai.™ The end of dull, point and steer, econo-box driving. The start of 4x4 versatility in a new compact size all its own, convertible or hard top. With a nifty 1.3 liter, SOHC, 4-cylinder engine, 5-speed stick, and room for four. The price? Low. The place? Where there's never a dull moment. Your Suzuki automotive dealer. See him for a Samurai test drive today.

EXHIBIT 12 "Dull Barrier" Proposed Print Ad

Stop suffering the heartbreak of econo-box boredom. Get quick relief where there's never a dull moment. Your Suzuki auto dealer.

Take one test drive in a Suzuki Samurai™ and you, too, will break the dull barrier. The Samurai handles differently than an ordinary passenger car. Avoid sharp turns and abrupt maneuvers, and always wear your seat belt. For specific details, read your owner's manual.

SUZUKI SAMURAI BREAKS THE DULL BARRIER

(DEALER NAME)

EXHIBIT 14   Copy for Proposed Television Ad

Setting:	A road leading from awesome mountains.
Atmosphere:	Dawn. Mysterious electrical storm flashes over the mountains. Something is about to happen. Something strange or wondrous.
What happens:	We see headlights approaching camera. From the dramatic music and overblown announcer, whatever's coming must be magnificent. Then the little Suzuki drives by at casual speed. People inside wave to camera, giggle, car drives out of frame. Camera does double take, then watches the car drive away.
(Dramatic music begins)	
Voiceover:	"Prepare for the most extraordinary event of your lifetime . . ."
(Music builds)	
	"An event that will forever alter the course of mankind and womankind . . ."
(Music builds)	
	"The next major turning point in the history of all civilization."
(Music crescendos, then stops)	
(Beep, beep)	
People in the car:	"Hi!"
(Music continues)	
	"Introducing the new Suzuki Samurai 4 × 4
Voiceover:	
(Fades)	The beginning of the universe was dull in comparison. . . . The discovery of fire pales in significance."
(Live announcer dealer tag)	

Mazza had told Pearlstein that he planned to spend $2.5 million on advertising and promotion during the first six months after the Samurai's introduction. For 1985, estimated Jeep advertising was $40 million for the American market. Industry experts expected total 1985 car, truck, and sport utility vehicle advertising expenditures in the United States to approximate $4.25 billion. Traditionally, automobile manufacturers spent between $200 and $400 per vehicle on advertising and up to an additional $500 per vehicle on incentives such as rebates and extended warranties.

Pearlstein and his group had to recommend how the Samurai's advertising budget should be spent. A typical automobile manufacturer spent 77 percent of its advertising dollars on television ads, 10 percent on radio commercials to add frequency to the television schedule, 10 percent on print ads, and 3 percent on highway billboards. The print ads were run in both general interest magazines and enthusiast magazines—depending on the vehicle's positioning as a car, truck, or sport utility vehicle. Pearlstein addressed his colleagues:

> If we are to win the ASMC account, tomorrow we must sell our Samurai positioning strategy to Mazza. To sell it to him, we must be convinced that it is the best positioning for the Samurai. Let's now discuss the pros and cons of the "unposition" we are proposing versus the

EXHIBIT 15   Storyboard for Proposed "Dull Barrier" Television Ad

EXHIBIT 16   Storyboard for Proposed "Amusement Park" Television Ad

three options we originally considered. We must be able to back up our positioning recommendation with sound market research data. We must address any risks associated with our recommended positioning. Finally, we must develop a recommendation on how to spend the $2.5 million six-month advertising budget. We should discuss how our budget allocation recommendations would vary according to the positioning strategy chosen.

5

HOW ADVERTISING WORKS: SOME RESEARCH RESULTS

"Because you see," says Bloom, "for an advertisement you must have repetition. That's the whole secret."

from *Ulysses*, by James Joyce

This part of the book moves on to considerations of message strategy: What kind of communication effect should the ad attempt to achieve? As outlined in Figure 2-3 of Chapter 2, advertising can work on consumers in various ways, and the mechanism—or "route" of effect—sought in any particular situation needs to be clearly specified and understood before an ad can actually be created. Should the element influenced by advertising be changes in attitudes, or awareness, or brand personality, or the social norms concerning the brand, or the feelings associated with it? Or should it simply be the inducement of some kind of action? Should certain kinds of thoughts be evoked in the consumer's mind? And once we have established what we are trying to accomplish, what is the best way to go about doing it?

Questions like these can be answered better once we have an understanding of how advertising "works." Because of the visibility of advertising, and because it touches all our lives, everyone has a pet theory of how advertising has its (supposedly strong and pernicious) effects. It is said that every person is an expert in two fields—the field he or she is really an expert in, and in advertising. However, while our common sense and intuition may indeed be accurate, they may also be wrong, and so it is useful to review what scientific research has revealed—or suggests—about how advertising really works. Such research results can help us challenge and reassess the validity of the many myths and pieces of conventional wisdom that populate the advertising business and guide us to better advertising decision making.

Such research-based insights can change our very basic understanding of how consumers process advertising. For example, while discussing objective setting earlier in Chapter 3, we relied primarily on a single hierarchy-of-response model, in which awareness preceded attitudes, which in turn led to buying action. Taken literally, this hierarchy would suggest that advertisers should always first create advertising to increase awareness, follow up with a campaign to change attitudes, and subsequently aim to induce trial action. Is this always true? If not, what implications might it have for how we design ads?

As we indicated in Chapter 3, the choice of which objective to set for one's advertising campaigns is, in fact, not as simple as the DAGMAR hierarchy implies, and different hierarchies might indeed be relevant in different situations. A tremendous amount of research exists on which hierarchy level should be the target of advertising for what kinds of brands and consumer segments and marketing situations, and it is clearly in the advertiser's interest to become familiar with this research so that the choice of advertising objective can be made in a more informed manner.

In this chapter, therefore, we discuss what research has to tell us about what kind of effect an ad should try to create, in what kind of situation. To do this, we review several streams of research that bear on the question of how advertising "works," discussing these research results in the order of their historical development. The following chapters in the book discuss more specific guidance on *how* ads can be used to change attitudes, create awareness, associate feelings with the brand, and so on. Before we get to that, however, we need to understand *when* each of these "target variables" becomes more important. The objective in reviewing these different "research streams" is to create such understanding.

RESEARCH STREAM ONE: FOCUS ON EXPOSURE, SALIENCE, AND FAMILIARITY

Some ads have very low information content and yet seem to be effective at affecting attitudes, particularly with repetition (as James Joyce aptly observed in the opening quote for this chapter). Why? Some answers will be provided in Chapter 16, when repetition is discussed. However, one explanation considered here is that repeated exposure to an advertised brand can, by itself, create a liking for it.

The most extreme and controversial version of this *"mere exposure effect"* was initially offered in the late 1960s by a prominent psychologist, Zajonc, who hypothesized that preference is created simply from repeated exposure, with no associated cognitive activity.[1] In one study, for example, Kunst-Wilson and Zajonc presented subjects with a series of polygons, at different levels of repetition.[2] They then exposed the subjects to pairs of polygons, asking which one they had seen previously and which one was new, and which they preferred. The previously exposed polygons were preferred even though there was no recognition above chance levels as to which they had seen previously.

This implies that the exposure effect occurred at some preconscious level, and not simply because subjects preferred those polygons they thought they had seen earlier. Other evidence also suggests that such preconscious information processing does occur, confirming that people do process incoming information at an unconscious "preattentive" level before they decide if it is worth paying attention to. Research has shown that aspects of advertisements (such as whether they are dominated by pictures or text) can make us like or dislike these advertisements through effects at this "preattentive" level, without our being aware of these effects.[3]

Clearly, one must be careful in jumping from research on polygons to making decisions about advertising processing, because advertisements (unlike polygons) contain meaningful information and can therefore be cognitively processed. Nevertheless, these studies suggest that advertising repetition may in some situations itself lead to preference, even if consumers don't absorb information on product benefits. It is therefore clear that keeping brand awareness at a high level should often be considered as a possible advertising objective.

Such "brand salience" is especially important when the advertising is aimed not so much at getting new customers, but at making existing customers buy a particular brand even more frequently, by increasing the proportion of times they select this brand instead of other brands in the category. In such cases the advertising serves mostly to reinforce (rather than create) brand preference, and one way of reinforcing it is to keep the advertised brand "top of mind," through frequent repetition.[4]

A related view of the exposure effect suggests that repeated exposure creates a conscious sense of *familiarity* with the brand, which then causes liking. The concept here is that familiar, known objects are evaluated more highly than are unknown objects with associated uncertainty. Perhaps uncertainty creates a tension, which is undesirable. Or familiarity may create positive feelings of comfort, security, ownership, or intimacy. As the advertising researcher Krugman has pointed out, a product is often preferred not because it is indeed better but because of "the pleasure of its recognition . . . sheer familiarity."[5] Certainly most of us have experienced such a phenomenon with a poem, a song, a food, or a brand name with which we are familiar. Liking can emerge as the object becomes more familiar. One study, conducted by Obermiller, used random melodies and found that liking was related to repetition for those melodies that had become familiar (the subject thought that he or she had heard it before) but not for those melodies that were not familiar.[6]

This familiarity model would explain why people develop positive attitudes toward brands and advertisements that are recognizable, even if these people cannot provide any facts about the brands. Although the "familiarity model," like the "mere exposure model," does not involve any in-depth cognitive activity, there is evidence proving that people can actually perceive objects faster if they are familiar with them, a phenomenon called "perceptual fluency." Such perceptual fluency is believed to lead to the feeling of familiarity people experience when they encounter these previously repeated objects.[7] Again, this evidence suggests that creating such familiarity, through awareness-building advertising (as well as extensive distribution, etc.) should be an important advertising objective in situations when consumers are unlikely to extract much meaningful, "hard" information from advertisements.

RESEARCH STREAM TWO: LOW-INVOLVEMENT LEARNING

In the DAGMAR hierarchy discussed in Chapter 3, comprehension of advertising content leads to attitude change. An alternative view is Krugman's classic model of television advertising, *low-involvement learning,* first offered in 1965.[8] Krugman, who at that time was an advertising manager with General Electric, observed that when products are advertised on television, consumers have little opportunity to think deeply about them, because TV ads cannot be slowed down or stopped to be viewed at the consumer's pace. In contrast, a consumer can linger over and return to a print ad that he or she likes, thus relating more cognitively to the ad. If people don't learn much information from TV ads, then just how do TV ads have their effect?

In a study comparing consumer thoughts in response to TV ads versus print ads, Krugman found fewer responses linking the ad to a person's own life for the TV ads. Krugman observed, however, that despite their apparent inability to communicate much, information, TV ads nonetheless did appear to increase brand preference, after repetition. He reasoned that perhaps repeated TV ads led to a gradual perceptual change in the consumer about what the brand represented. Thus, a brand might be considered primarily "reliable" instead of being primarily "modern." The brand may be seen as just as modern as before and no more reliable. However, repeated exposure to an advertising message can alter the viewer's frame of reference and now give reliability the primary role in organizing the concept of the brand.

This subtle change in cognitive structure provides the potential to see a brand differently and can trigger a behavioral event such as an in-store purchase of the brand. This act of buying, or trial, event can then subsequently generate an attitude change or adjustment that is more consistent with the shift in perceptual structure. Thus, in low-involvement situations, product adoption can be characterized in Krugman's terms as occurring through gradual shifts in perceptual structure, aided by repetitive advertising in a low-involvement medium such as television, activated by behavioral choice situations, and followed at some time by a change in attitude.

Further work on such low-involvement learning was reported by Ray and colleagues, in a series of repetition studies done at Stanford in the early 1970s.[9] In essence, they argued that when the products involved were of low risk and low interest (and thus of low involvement) to the consumer, and when the ads involved were television ads, advertising did not lead to an information-based attitude change, which then led to trial. Instead, the ads appeared to lead to trial simply because of greater top-of-mind awareness; this trial then led to attitude change. In short, in low-involvement situations the sequence of advertising effects was not

cognitive (product features) → attitudinal → behavorial (which they called
the "high-involvement" hierarchy, and resembles the DAGMAR hierarchy),

but instead cognitive (awareness) → behavioral → attitudinal.

In recent years, substantial additional research has been done on the concept of involvement and its importance in determining the way in which advertising shapes consumer attitudes and behaviors. While some researchers now equate involvement with the amount of attention paid to the brand information in the advertisement, others measure it by the extent to which the message is personally relevant to the consumer, or the degree to which the consumer's thoughts, while viewing the ad, concern the brand instead of the way the ad is made.[10] Regardless of these conceptual differences, there is substantial agreement that the degree to which the consumer is "involved" is of critical importance in determining which part of the advertisement will shape the consumer's final attitude toward the brand. Later in this chapter we discuss one such view, the "elaboration likelihood model."

It is also commonly agreed that consumers are more highly involved when they consider the message content more relevant (high motivation), when they have the knowledge and experience to think about that message content (high ability), and when the environment in which that message content is presented does not interfere with such thinking (high opportunity).[11]

Involvement is not, of course, the only variable that determines the extent to which the consumer will process the message attribute information in the ad: there are many others, including the kind of benefit the consumer is seeking from the product category. When the benefit is primarily sensory or image/ego enhancement, for example, the advertising might need to focus more on evoking the right kinds of emotions or imagery, rather than providing factual message content.[12] We discuss these situations in Chapters 7, 8, and 9.

For advertising managers seeking to make decisions about objectives, the overall implication of this research on involvement is that when advertisers are in a high-involvement situation, with the consumer seeking rational or problem-solving benefits, the advertisers ought to have as their objectives the communication of product benefits, through message content, for only that can lead to the attitude change necessary for behavioral effects. Low-involvement situations, however, should lead to the targeting of greater awareness as a primary objective, rather than the communication of attitude-enhancing arguments about why the brand is better.

RESEARCH STREAM THREE: CENTRAL VERSUS PERIPHERAL ROUTES TO PERSUASION AND THE ELABORATION LIKELIHOOD MODEL

In the preceding section on involvement we said that considerable research has highlighted the crucial role played by involvement, in determining which aspect of the ad has the biggest effect on consumer preference for the brand. One model of advertising that focuses on the role of such involvement is the *elaboration likelihood model*, or ELM.

According to the ELM, developed by psychologists Petty and Cacioppo, a basic dimension of information processing and attitude change is the depth or amount of information processing. At one extreme, the consumer can consciously and diligently consider the information provided in the ad, in forming attitudes toward the advertised brand. Here, attitudes are changed or formed by careful consideration, thinking, and integration of information relevant to the product or object of the advertising. Using our previous terminology, the consumer is highly involved in processing the advertisement. This type of persuasion process is termed the "central route" to attitude change.[13]

In contrast, there also exists what Petty and Cacioppo term the "peripheral route" to attitude change. In the peripheral route, attitudes are formed and changed without active thinking about the brand's attributes and its pros and cons. Rather, the persuasive impact occurs by associating the brand with positive or negative aspects or executional cues in the ad that really are (or should not be) central to the worth of the brand. For example, rather than expressly considering the strength of the arguments presented in an advertisement, an audience member may use cognitive "shortcuts" and accept the conclusion that the brand is superior because

- There were numerous arguments offered, even if they were not really strong and logical.
- The endorser seemed to be an expert, or was attractive and likable.
- The consumer liked the way the ad was made, the music in it, and so on.

Conversely, a conclusion may be rejected not because of the logic of the argument but because of some surrounding cues. For example,

- The position advocated may have been too extreme.
- The endorser may have been suspect.
- The magazine in which the ad appears was not respected.

Attitudes resulting from central processing should be relatively strong and enduring, resistant to change, and predict behavior better than attitudes framed by the peripheral route. Such an observation makes sense particularly if the extreme cases are considered. If a person reaches a conclusion after conscious thought and deliberation, that conclusion should be firmer than if he or she merely based attitudes on peripheral cues.

Obviously, an advertiser setting objectives needs to predict whether, in a given context, the central route is feasible—whether audience members will exert the effort involved to "deeply" process an advertisement with strong arguments. If this is unlikely, and the consumer is more likely to form attitudes peripherally, then the advertiser is better off creating an ad with likable or credible spokespeople, rather than relying on strong, logical arguments.

Which Route?

Petty and Cacioppo have proposed the framework in Figure 5-1, which predicts when the audience member will cognitively "elaborate" and follow the central route. Two factors identified in the ELM model as significant are an audience member's motivation to process information, and ability to process information (note that their definition of "ability" also includes what we called "opportunity" earlier). Consumers are most likely to process centrally when both motivation and ability are high; when either is low, peripheral processing is more likely. These motivation and ability factors are now discussed in greater detail.

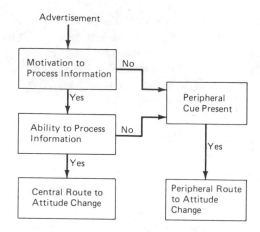

Figure 5-1.   The ELM model of attitude change

Motivation to Process Information

Central processing requires first the motivation to process information, because information processing requires effort. Unless there is some reason to expend the energy or pay the price, the "hard" information in the ad will not be processed. Such effort will not be expended unless the consumer is involved with the product and associated purchase decision, and unless the information in the advertisement is both relevant and important. For an advertisement to be relevant, the consumer should, at a minimum, be a user or potential user of the product. A confirmed user of drip coffee will be unlikely to want to process information about instant coffee. There may also be situational factors: the choice of a wine for a special occasion, or a gift, will be more important than if a routine use occasion was involved.

Ability (and Opportunity) to Process Information

In addition to being motivated to process information centrally, the consumer must also have the ability and capacity to process information. There is no point in attempting to communicate information or make an argument that the target audience simply cannot process without a level of effort that is unacceptably high. For example, someone not familiar with the vocabulary and refinements of stereo systems or high-end personal computers may lack the knowledge and experience to process a highly technical presentation of such equipment. Further, someone listening to a short radio ad, in a cluttered and distracting listening environment, may simply not have the opportunity to think about what is being said.

An ELM Experiment

A print ad for disposable razors was used to illustrate and test the ELM model.[14] Respondents were shown a booklet of ten ads. A high-motivation half of these respondents were told that they would be able to select a brand of razor as a gift and that the product would soon be available in their geographical area. The low-motivation half were told they would select a free toothpaste and that the products in the booklet were being tested in another area. Half of each group were shown ads with strong arguments such as "in direct comparison tests, the Edge blade gave twice as many close shaves as its nearest competitor." The other half received weak arguments such as "designed with the bathroom in mind." Finally, the endorser was either a celebrity (a professional athlete) or an "average" citizen of Bakersfield, California.

Figure 5-2 summarizes the results. The ELM model would predict that the celebrity status of the product endorsers would have a greater impact on product attitudes under low- rather than high-motivation conditions because, being a peripheral cue, it would be used more in the former situation. In fact, the famous endorser did enhance attitude impact only under the low-motivation condition, where the peripheral route would be employed. Further, the impact of a strong argument was considerably more in the high-motivation condition, where central processing would tend to occur, than in the low-motivation condition of peripheral processing.

The ELM model is a useful conceptualization of attitude change, but it is not perfect. For example, if the product is one involving sensory or pleasure benefits (such as a shampoo), audience members may process cues such as endorser attractiveness centrally rather than peripherally. Remember also that processing does not have to be either central or peripheral in mutual exclusion, but could consist of a blend of both.

From the advertising planning point of view, however, the key implication of this research stream is that the motivation and ability of the target audience are key criteria in objective setting. If motivation and ability are both high, and central processing is most likely, it makes sense to try to focus on changing attitudes, through strong "reasons why" the brand is better. But if either motivation or ability are low, and peripheral processing is more likely, the objective should be to create a likable feeling for the brand through the choice of the spokesperson and/or executional elements, rather than through the strength and quality of the arguments about the brand.

Another related stream of research, which we discuss more fully in Chapter 7, has examined the effects on brand attitudes of a consumer's liking for the ad itself (called attitude toward the ad). This overall attitude toward the ad is based on many aspects, but the consumer's feelings toward the way the ad was put together—peripheral aspects such as the endorser, music, and so on—are presumed to be a major component. Once again, some research (but not all) suggests that this "peripherally based" attitude toward the ad also plays a more important role in shaping brand attitudes in low-involvement conditions, which is similar to the ELM's basic prediction.[15]

RESEARCH STREAM FOUR: THE COGNITIVE RESPONSE MODEL AND THE RELATIONSHIP BETWEEN RECALL AND PERSUASION

Research streams two and three have established that in low-involvement situations it may be more appropriate to create ads that raise awareness and change brand attitudes through

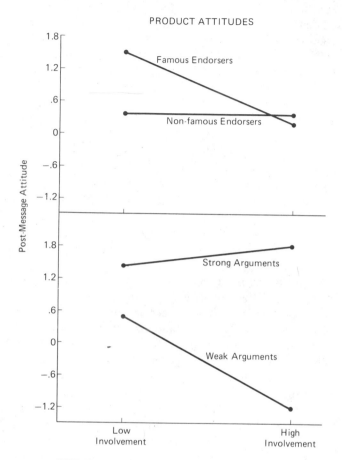

NOTE: Top panel shows interactive effect of involvement and endorser status on attitudes toward Edge razors. Bottom panel shows interactive effect of involvement and argument quality on attitudes toward Edge razors.

Figure 5-2.   Product attitudes

Source: Richard E. Petty, John T. Cacioppo, and David Schumann, "Central and Peripheral Routes to Advertising Effectiveness: The Moderating Role of Involvement," *Journal of Consumer Research*, 10, September 1983, p. 142. Published by The University of Chicago.

executional liking and credibility and that in high-involvement situations it may be better for ads to provide strong "reasons why" the brand is superior. Ways to accomplish the former strategy can be thought of intuitively—using attractive or credible endorsers, creating likable advertising, and so on. But exactly how do we get strong "reasons why" advertising to change attitudes in the high involvement, central route?

It is natural to assume that when advertisements change consumer attitudes in such high-involvement, central processing situations it is because consumers learn the content of the advertisement, and that this learning then leads to changes in attitude toward the brand. If this were true, then advertisers should attempt to design ads that maximize this consumer learning of message content. It would also make sense to test the effectiveness of these advertisements by measuring how much of their content was actually learned by consumers exposed to them, by asking consumers what they remembered from the ad.

Research in the late 1960s and early 1970s showed, however, that there was only a weak relationship between what a consumer could recall about the content of a message and that consumer's attitude toward the brand in the message.[16] Instead, what appeared to be really important in determining attitudes was the nature of the thoughts that went through the consumer's head as the ad was shown, as the consumer evaluated the incoming information in the context of past knowledge and attitudes. These thoughts that the consumer has when viewing an ad are called *cognitive responses*.

Research into cognitive response usually involves asking audience members during the ad exposure or just after it to write down all the thoughts that occurred to him or her during the exposure. A variety of types of cognitive responses are potentially relevant in such analysis. A *counterargument* (CA) occurs when the audience member argues against the message argument presented by the ad. There are several different types of CAs. A person could disagree with the logic or content of the ad ("I don't believe the clothes are whiter"). The conclusion might be questioned ("My existing brand of soap is perfectly adequate"). A cognitive response that attacks the source or execution style in some way, or the context or situation depicted in the ad, rather than the message argument itself, is termed *execution derogation*. Examples of these might be "He had to be paid a lot to say that" or "I don't believe that a housewife would say such a thing; it's phony."

A *support argument* (SA) is a cognitive response that affirms the argument made by the ad ("I could use a product that could provide whiter clothes"). It similarly could take several forms. It could involve an affirmation of the logic or the conclusion of the ad. If the positive thought concerns the execution style or quality, or the spokesperson, rather than the message being communicated, it is called *execution bolstering* ("This is a really clever ad.")

Obviously, the impact on attitude of cognitive responses will depend on the nature of the cognitive responses evoked by the ad. The basic prediction is that the number of support arguments will be positively associated with changes in beliefs, attitudes, and behavioral intentions and that the number of counterarguments will be negatively correlated. This model prediction has been generally (although not always) supported in dozens of studies in advertising and psychology, especially in high-involvement situations.[17]

In situations where consumers watching the ad are not particularly interested in deciding whether or not they like the brand (because they are not highly involved), their later attitudes about the brand are more significantly influenced by the execution-related responses they have (source bolstering and derogation responses) than by support or counterarguments about the message content of the ad. Thus, it seems safe to conclude that when trying to create or change attitudes, especially in high-involvement situations, it is desirable to stimulate SAs and minimize CAs.

It also seems safe to conclude that when measuring the effectiveness of an ad, one must look not only at what was learned from the ad, but, more important, exactly what the consumer was thinking when he or she saw the ad.

How SAs and CAs Can Be Controlled

We said earlier that to create favorable attitudes we need our ads to raise the number of SAs and reduce the number of CAs. The research to date has provided some clues as to what can affect the amount, and ratio, of the SAs and CAs that consumers have when processing ads.[18]

The *total number* of cognitive responses (SAs + CAs) evoked by an ad determine whether the ad is being processed centrally or peripherally. A smaller number of total cognitive responses means the brand is not really being thought about very much and that attitudes are being shaped peripherally. Factors that influence this total number of cognitive responses include

- *Ad Medium.* The more control the consumer has over the pace of presentation, the more SAs and CAs are generated. For example, print ads can lead to more cognitive responses than faster-paced TV or radio ads. Thus broadcast media are more likely to lead to peripherally created attitudes.
- *Involvement or motivation.* Consumers more interested and involved with the content of the ad (e.g., the product category itself) will generate more total cognitive responses and form attitudes centrally.
- *The knowledge level of the subjects.* More knowledgeable people will be able to generate more SAs and CAs than less knowledgeable people, and will form attitudes centrally.
- *Distraction.* If either the environment for the ad, or something in the ad itself, distracts the consumer, fewer SAs and CAs are produced, reducing central processing.
- *Emotion.* If the ad evokes a positive emotion that puts the consumer in a good mood, the consumer is often less willing to spend the energy thinking about the ad content and thus generates fewer total cognitive responses and forms attitudes peripherally rather than centrally.
- *Need for cognition.* Some individuals are simply more interested in thinking about things (i.e., they have a higher "need for cognition"), and they usually generate more SAs and CAs. Thus their attitudes are more centrally based.

Several factors have also been found that shape the *nature* (positive versus negative) of the cognitive response being generated:

- *Repetition.* Studies have found that the number of CAs fall and then rise with repetition, while SAs do the reverse. As a result, the net positive balance (SAs minus CAs) is often highest at intermediate levels of repetition levels—so that this repetition level is where attitudes are usually at their highest level.
- *Discrepancy from the previously held position or belief.* If the currently held position or belief matches the communication, SAs are likely, but as the discrepancy increases, so will the number of CAs. So don't expect to have a hostile audience won over easily.

- *Strength of argument.* If the argument being made by the ad has some logic and strength to it, SAs are generated; if it is a weak argument, CAs are generated. Implication: Unless you have a strong message, discourage central processing!
- *Nature of emotion being felt.* If people are put in a positive mood, either by the ad or by something else while they process the ad, they are more likely to generate SAs and less likely to generate CAs. If you don't have a strong message, create an ad that puts people in a good mood while you tell them your story.

Obviously, it is in an advertiser's interest to increase the number of SAs generated, especially when advertising to an hostile audience. Thus when advertising to people who have a negative prior attitude about the brand, it may help to use distraction, or to create positive moods, because these might help reduce the number of CAs produced.

It was stated that recall of message content does not have a very strong relationship to persuasion, overall. This general conclusion must be qualified by several factors. Recall does indeed relate to persuasion (and thus is an appropriate advertising objective) when the consumer is in a low-involvement situation and is therefore not evaluating the brand at the time the advertisement is seen (because the consumer does not see the need for such an on-the-spot evaluation). Consequently, when such a low-involvement consumer eventually needs to pick a brand (later in time), he or she has to search in memory for facts to use in that choice decision—and brands that they can recall more about stand a better chance of being selected. This fits in quite nicely with what we reviewed in the very first research stream discussed. Here, too, what matters is not the sheer amount of material that can be recalled about the brand, but rather what the recalled material implies about the brand's quality, and whether it is believable.[19]

Another way to think about whether or not recall should be an advertising objective is to remember that recall is a necessary but not sufficient condition for persuasion. That is, if someone does not remember the ad, they cannot possibly remember what was in it and are unlikely to develop a preference for the advertised brand. Recall of the ad is necessary for comprehension of ad content, and comprehension of ad content is necessary for persuasion—but such persuasion also requires, in addition to recall and comprehension, message content that sets the brand apart from competition, thus leading to SAs and on to preference.[20]

This, of course, is what the DAGMAR hierarchy model we discussed earlier has long maintained: awareness is necessary for comprehension, and comprehension for persuasion, but awareness by itself is not sufficient to create persuasion (though awareness may be especially crucial in low-involvement situations). At least in high-involvement situations, the ad must not only create awareness and recall, but must also have message content that the consumer reacts favorably to, by generating favorable cognitive responses.

SUMMARY

Four research streams on "how advertising works" were reviewed. The first dealt with the effects of ad exposure and ad-created brand familiarity. The most extreme version of the "mere exposure" effect hypothesizes that liking can be created simply from exposure with no cognitive activity at all. Such a phenomenon has been demonstrated for nonsense syllables and could provide insights as to how repetition affects the impact of advertising. The "familiar model" suggests that people like objects with which they are familiar and that advertising leads to such familiarity.

Second, "low-involvement learning" research postulates that television advertising, operating under low involvement and perceptual defenses, creates changes in perceptual structure that can trigger a behavioral act, which in turn affects attitude. Related research develops this "low-involvement" hierarchy (behavior change preceding real attitude change) for certain types of products, and contrasts it with the high-involvement DAGMAR hierarchy reviewed earlier (in which behavior follows attitude change).

The third stream of research covered the "elaboration likelihood model." Here, the central route to persuasion describes an active, conscious, in-depth processing of information and adjustment of attitudes. In the peripheral route, in contrast, peripheral cues such as the credibility of the source influence attitudes with little active thinking about the object. The central route will be employed only when the audience member is motivated to process information and has the ability to do so. For motivation to be present, the audience member needs to be involved with the product, and the information in the ad needs to be relevant and important. A problem is to determine exactly what will be processed as a peripheral cue and exactly how it will affect attitudes.

Finally, in high-involvement situations, during or just after being exposed to a communication the audience can engage in cognitive responses such as counterarguing or support arguing. In the cognitive response model this activity is assumed to affect attitudes. By this model advertising can increase its effectiveness by encouraging support arguing and by inhibiting counterarguing.

In sum, these research streams suggest that when consumers are highly involved in a purchase, and are knowledgeable about the product category, they are likely to carefully process ad claims about the brand, and use their reactions to these claims (called "cognitive responses") to determine their brand attitudes. This was called the "central route" to forming and changing attitudes. When consumers lack the motivation and ability to process such brand information, however, their attitudes toward the brand are based more on their liking of the ad's "peripheral" aspects, such as the endorser or music, or on their ability to recall the brand name and their sense of familiarity with the brand.

It is therefore crucial, in deciding which intermediate variable to target in an ad, to consider carefully the nature of the consumer's motivation and ability.

DISCUSSION QUESTIONS

1. In proposing that liking can occur without any cognitive activity, Zajonc suggests that the acquisition of tastes for very hot spices in Mexico (spices that others would dislike intensely) need not involve any rational decision or cognitive activity but might involve parental reinforcement, social conformity pressures, identification with a group machismo, and so on. Do you agree that no cognitive activity is involved in the development of such tastes?

2. Subliminal advertising is that in which a message such as "Drink Coke" is flashed during a movie so fast that it is not visible but still influences behavior. Such stimuli have been shown to activate drives such as hunger, but the consensus among advertisers is that it simply does not work in the advertising context. Relate subliminal advertising to the exposure effect.

3. Do people first form beliefs and then attitudes, or the reverse? Do people change attitudes before changing behavior?

4. What other types of cognitive responses are there besides support and counter-arguments? How could they be useful in predicting and managing response to advertising?

5. Why might the number of CAs start high, then recede, and then increase with repetition? What else might you predict about cognitive response over repetition?

6. Contrast the central and the peripheral routes to persuasion. Categorize the other approaches covered in the chapter as to whether they follow the central or peripheral route.

7. Bring in a print ad that provides an example of a peripheral cue and another with an example of a central cue.

8. Provide an example of a case when a reader of a print ad would not be motivated to process information and an example when a reader would not be able to process the information in the ad.

9. Under what circumstances is the "standard" (DAGMAR) hierarchy model most likely to hold? When will awareness precede and contribute to brand comprehension? When will brand comprehension precede and contribute to attitude? When will attitude change cause behavioral change? In particular, consider various product classes, various usage histories, and various decision processes.

10. When is maximizing advertising recall a valid advertising objective? When is maximizing the likability of the advertising itself (through the use of a likable endorser, likable music, or humor) most appropriate? When are these two strategies *not* appropriate?

NOTES

1. R. B. Zajonc, "Attitudinal Effects of Mere Exposure," *Journal of Personality and Social Psychology Monograph*, 9 (2, Part 2), 1968, pp. 1–28; R. B. Zajonc, "Feeling and Thinking: Preferences Need No Inferences," *American Psychologist*, 35, 1980, pp. 151–175; and R. B. Zajonc and H. Markus, "Affective and Cognitive Factors in Preferences," *Journal of Consumer Research*, 9, September 1982, pp. 123–131.

2. William R. Kunst-Wilson and Robert B. Zajonc, "Affective Discrimination of Stimuli That Can Not Be Recognized," *Science*, 207, February 1980, pp. 557–558.

3. Chris Janiszewski, "Preconscious Processing Effects: The Independence of Attitude Formation and Conscious Thought," *Journal of Consumer Research*, 15, September 1988, pp. 199–209.

4. A. S. C. Ehrenberg, "Repetitive Advertising and the Consumer," *Journal of Advertising Research*, April 1974.

5. H. E. Krugman, "The Learning of Consumer Likes, Preferences and Choices," in F. M. Bass, C. W. King, and E. A. Pessemier (eds.), *Applications of the Sciences in Marketing Management* (New York: John Wiley, 1968).

6. Carl Obermiller, "Varieties of Mere Exposure: The Effects of Processing Style and Repetition on Affective Response," *Journal of Consumer Research,* 12, June 1985, pp. 17–31.

7. Larry Jacoby, "Perceptual Enhancement: Persistent Effects of an Experience," *Journal of Experimental Psychology: Learning, Memory and Cognition,* 9, 1983, March, pp. 21–38.

8. Herbert E. Krugman, "The Impact of Television Advertising: Learning Without Involvement," *Public Opinion Quarterly,* 29, 1965, p. 353.

9. Michael L. Ray et al., "Marketing Communication and the Hierarchy of Effects," in P. Clarke (ed.), *New Models for Communications Research* (Beverly Hills, CA: Sage Publications, 1973).

10. See, for example, Rajeev Batra and Michael L. Ray, "Operationalizing Involvement as Depth and Quality of Message Response," in R. P. Bagozzi and Alice M. Tybout, eds., *Advances in Consumer Research,* Vol. 10, (Ann Arbor, MI: Association for Consumer Research, 1983), pp. 309–313, Meryl Paula Gardner, Andrew A. Mitchell, and J. Edward Russo, "Low Involvement Strategies for Processing Advertisements," *Journal of Advertising,* 14 (2), 1985, pp. 4–13; Anthony G. Greenwald and Clark Leavitt, "Audience Involvement in Advertising: Four Levels," *Journal of Consumer Research,* 11 (June), 1984, pp. 581–592; Andrew A. Mitchell, "The Dimensions of Advertising Involvement," in Kent Monroe, ed., *Advances in Consumer Research,* Vol. 7, (Ann Arbor, MI: Association for Consumer Research, 1981), pp. 25–30; Judith Lynne Zaichkowsky, "Measuring the Involvement Construct," *Journal of Consumer Research,* 12 (3), 1985, pp. 341–352.

11. Rajeev Batra and Michael L. Ray, "How Advertising Works at Contact," in L. F. Alwitt and A. A. Mitchell, eds., *Psychological Processes and Advertising Effects* (Hillsdale, N. J.: Erlbaum, 1985), pp. 13–44; Deborah J. MacInnis and Bernard J. Jaworski, "Information Processing from Advertisements: Toward an Integrative Framework," *Journal of Marketing,* 53 (October), 1989, pp. 1–23.

12. See, for example, Deborah J. MacInnis and Bernard J. Jaworski, "Information Processing from Advertisements: Toward an Integrative Framework," *Journal of Marketing,* 53 (October), 1989, pp. 1–23; Richard Vaughn, "How Advertising Works: A Planning Model Revisited," *Journal of Advertising Research,* February/March 1986, pp. 57–66.

13. See Richard E. Petty and John T. Cacioppo, "Central and Peripheral Routes to Persuasion: Application to Advertising," in Larry Percy and Arch Woodside, eds., *Advertising and Consumer Psychology* (Lexington, MA: Lexington Books, 1983), pp. 3–23; and Richard E. Petty, John T. Cacioppo, and David Schumann, "Central and Peripheral Routes to Advertising Effectiveness: The Moderating Role of Involvement," *Journal of Consumer Research,* 10, September 1983, pp. 135–146.

14. Petty, Cacioppo, and Schumann, "Central and Peripheral Routes to Advertising Effectiveness."

15. Cornelia Dröge, "Shaping the Route to Attitude Change: Central Versus Peripheral Processing Through Comparative Versus Noncomparative Advertising," *Journal of Marketing Research,* 26 (May), 1989, pp. 193–204; see also Pamela M. Homer, "The Mediating Role of Attitude Toward the Ad: Some Additional Evidence," *Journal of Marketing Research,* 27 (February), 1990, pp. 78–86.

16. Anthony G. Greenwald, "Cognitive Learning, Cognitive Responses to Persuasion, and Attitude Change," in A. G. Greenwald et al., eds., *Psychological Foundations of Attitudes,* (New York: Academic Press, 1968), pp. 147–170; Peter L. Wright, "The Cognitive Responses Mediating the Acceptance of Advertising," *Journal of Marketing Research,* 10 (February), 1973, pp. 53–62.

17. See a review by Peter Wright, "Message-Evoked Thoughts: Persuasion Research Using Thought Verbalizations," *Journal of Consumer Research,* 7, September 1980, pp. 151–175. See also Manoj Hastak and Jerry C. Olson, "Assessing the Role of Brand-Related Cognitive Responses as Mediators of Communication Effects on Cognitive Structure," *Journal of Consumer Research,* 15 (March), 1989, pp. 444–456.

18. Ibid., pp. 166–171; Richard E. Petty and John T. Cacioppo, *Communication and Persuasion* (New York: Springer, 1986); Rajeev Batra and Douglas M. Stayman (1990), "The Role of Mood in Advertising Effectiveness," *Journal of Consumer Research,* 17 (September), pp. 203–214.

19. Amitava Chattopadhyay and Joseph W. Alba, ''The Situational Importance of Recall and Inference in Consumer Decision-Making,'' *Journal of Consumer Research,* 15 (June), 1988, pp. 1–12.
20. David W. Stewart, ''The Moderating Role of Recall, Comprehension, and Brand Differentiation on the Persuasiveness of Television Advertising,'' *Journal of Advertising Research,* April/May 1986, pp. 43–46.

6

CHANGING
BENEFIT-BASED ATTITUDES

Said a tiger to a lion as they drank beside a pool, "Tell me, why do you
roar like a fool?"
   "That's not foolish," replied the lion with a twinkle in his eyes.
"They call me king of all the beasts because I advertise."
   A rabbit heard them talking and ran home like a streak. He
thought he would try the lion's plan, but his roar was a squeak. A fox
came to investigate—and had his lunch in the woods.
   The moral: When you advertise, be sure you've got the goods!

                                                              Fable

Once the target market for an advertising campaign has been identified, and communication and positioning objectives set, the advertising manager needs to make decisions
about the content of the advertising message, or what we call *message strategy*. For example, what should be the basic thrust or message of the TV commercials or magazine
ads that will make up the ad campaign for the brand in question?

   Here—based in part upon the kinds of research reviewed in the last chapter—the
manager must decide if the message needs to focus on communicating product benefits
(and, if so, exactly what benefits), developing or reinforcing a brand image or personality
(and, if so, what specific personality), evoking and associating specific feelings and emotions with the brand, making the brand appear fashionable by creating social and group
influences, or creating buying action. These topics are covered in the five remaining
chapters that constitute Part III of this book.

   This chapter focuses on the question of which benefits need to be communicated, in
order to change consumer attitudes toward the brand. Until we provide a better definition
later in this chapter, a product benefit can be thought of as a positive payoff to the consumer from a certain product attribute, and we will use the terms "attribute" and
"benefit" interchangeably. In general, advertisers want to accent the positive and focus
advertising on those attributes which are perceived as advantages of the product (either in

an absolute "good-for-you" sense, or relative to competitor products). Sometimes it is advantageous to focus part of the advertising message on negative attributes of your product. Refutational advertising (Volkswagen is a "lemon") employs this technique. The point is that to analyze the question of which *benefits* to communicate, we really need to know which *attributes* are considered in making the brand-choice decision, and which of them are most important in the targeted product-market situation.

Also, in order to know whether a particular positioning strategy will really work, we need to know whether the product attributes and images are linked to overall attitudes in the consumer's mind. Do his or her perceptions, feelings, and beliefs about the attributes of a brand really influence the decision process? All these are questions about attitude and market structure.

The attitude concept we refer to is one of the most important ideas in advertising management. The basic argument is that consumers' purchases are governed by their attitudes toward product alternatives and that advertisers can do something to affect those attitudes. The attitude concept really encompasses a system of interrelated subconcepts and the relations among them. The chapter therefore begins with a brief overview of the attitude construct and various approaches to measuring attitude. This is followed by a section on how to identify the important attributes and benefits in a given product-market situation. Then some well-known models of attitude are presented, and some of the things to look out for in using the models are noted. The use of the attitude construct for segmentation and market planning rounds out the chapter.

ATTITUDE COMPONENTS AND MEASUREMENT

Attitude is a central concept to the entire field of social psychology, and theories and methods associated with its explanation and measurement have largely evolved from the work of social psychologists and psychometricians. Gordon W. Allport, for example, has stated that "Attitude is probably the most distinctive and indispensable concept in American social psychology. No other term appears more frequently in experimental and theoretical literature."[1]

The most widely held view of the structure of an attitude is that it is made up of three closely interrelated components: cognitive (awareness, comprehension, knowledge), affective (evaluation, liking, preference), and conative (action tendencies such as intentions, trial, or purchase). Attention is usually focused on the middle (affective) component, assessing the degree of positive or negative feelings for an object. The underlying assumption is that this overall liking component is based on the cognitive component (beliefs and knowledge about the brand) and then leads to the intention to try (or lack of it).[2] In other words, we buy something because we like it, and we like it because we cognitively evaluate its benefits to us as good.

There have recently been arguments that people often develop overall attitudinal liking for objects without first cognitively evaluating them as good, with such overall attitudes being based purely on emotions and feelings rather than some rational, cognitive belief- or benefit-based evaluation.[3] This might be especially true in situations where consumers lack the interest or knowledge (motivation and ability) to really think about the merits of competing brands: the kind of "low-elaboration likelihood" situation we discussed in Chapter 5. We will discuss such feeling-based attitudes in Chapter 7, when we focus on creating feelings through advertising.

For the moment, let us suppose that we are in the kind of high-involvement situation where consumers actually base their overall attitudes toward competing brands on the basis of an evaluation (either thorough, or more casual) of the benefits offered by these different brands. In such situations, we must know how to measure overall attitude and to understand the basis on which it is formed, in order to develop an advertising campaign that strives to increase the favorability of attitudes toward our brand.

Attitude can be measured directly by asking a respondent to indicate whether he or she likes or dislikes a brand or by attempting a direct assessment of the degree of like or dislike on a positive-negative scale. While this is useful, it does not give us "diagnostics": it does not tell us *why* a brand is liked or disliked. To get this information, we can rely on the attitude models that assume that this overall liking is based on a cognitive evaluation of underlying attributes or benefits of the brand, and get consumer ratings of the brand on those underlying aspects. For example, a consumer could be asked to judge a brand on the basis of several attributes or characteristics according to whether it was positive or negative on each, and the mean of her or his scores taken as the attitude measure. Such measures are called *multiattribute evaluations of the brand* because they are based on the evaluation of attributes that are assumed to underlie the directly measured overall attitude.

Direct Measures of Overall Attitude

The simplest way to measure overall attitude toward an object (brand, store, product class, or whatever) is to ask a respondent whether he or she likes or dislikes it. There are no explicit attribute criteria given on which the evaluation is made. Respondents are simply asked to answer "yes" or "no," and the responses are used to determine the brand attitude.

If interest centers on attempting to capture the degree of attitude, the question can be put in the form of a scale. For example, a respondent could be asked to express how much she or he liked a brand on a scale ranging from "very much" (1) to "very little" (7). Other terms could be used, such as "excellent-poor" or "good-bad." George S. Day,[4] a Wharton professor, for example, suggested the seven-point scale shown in Figure 6-1 as being particularly appropriate for durable products. He points out how parts of the scale might be used to identify segments, and whether or not it is likely to be considered if a purchase situation developed.

Another approach is to provide an explicit reference to a comparison stimulus or stimuli [for example, another brand(s) or company(ies)]. Subjects can be asked to rank objects in the order of their preferences for them. An attitude for an object would then be the ranking it received. The attitude for a respondent group might be the percentage that ranked the object first or among the first three. By adding a scale such as "How much do

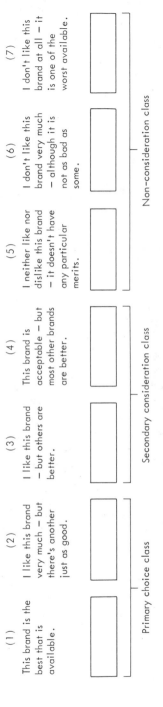

Figure 6-1. A relative rating scale for brand attitudes

Source: George S. Day, *Buyer Attitudes and Brand Choice Behavior* (New York: Columbia University Press, 1970), p. 160.

you prefer brand A over brand B?'' the relative distance between brands in terms of over-all attitude might be determined. A variation of this technique is called *paired compari-sons*. Respondents make their judgments concerning the brand by considering pairs presented two at a time.

An important question is whether attitudes are related to brand choice and market behavior. Obviously, of course, the attitudes have to be measured in the way that is most specifically relevant to the behavior being predicted.[5] Even if measured correctly, positive attitudes toward a brand will not always result in purchase behavior. A person can have a positive attitude for a brand and yet not be willing or able to buy it. Many teenagers have strong positive attitudes for a Porsche, but few are likely to be purchasers. Further-more, situational events at the time of purchase and/or ''impulsive'' behavior can throw off short-run sales predictions made on the basis of attitude measures taken some time previous to the purchase occasion. As a third example, a consumer may end up buying a brand even if he or she does not have a favorable attitude, if the consumer feels that other people such as experts or a peer group like it, recommend it, or will be im-pressed by it. (These kinds of group norm effects are discussed in Chapter 9.) However, if these types of cases are basically exceptions and are not dominant in the market or segment of interest, a strong relationship between attitude and purchase behavior should emerge.

Achenbaum[6] has demonstrated that attitude and usage levels are associated in sev-eral consumer product categories. Figure 6-2 shows the attitude-usage relationship for a brand of cigarettes, deodorant, gasoline, laxative, and a dental product. The data are based on impressive sample sizes usually involving over 1,000 respondents. For each of the four brands, the percentage using the brand is strongly related to the attitude toward it. For the dental product, the attitude profiles of current users are compared with those of former users. Current users tend to have positive attitudes, whereas former users tend to have negative attitudes. Although not shown in Figure 6-2, Achenbaum reports the ten-dency for a third category of individuals—those who have never tried the brand—to have mainly neutral attitudes.[7]

According to some recent research, the relationship between attitudes and purchase behaviors gets stronger as the consumer gets more ''direct'' information about the brand (such as that obtained through actual trial): the consumer then feels more certain and confident about the attitude, and is more likely to use it in making purchase decisions.[8] Information about a brand obtained through advertising is relatively less ''direct.'' Re-peated advertising exposure, however, can increase how much information the consumer has about the brand, which can increase the confidence with which attitudes are held and thus increase their impact on behavior.[9]

OVERALL ATTITUDE AS AN OBJECTIVE

Why is the attitude construct so important in advertising? A simple answer is that millions of dollars of advertising and great financial risks ultimately depend on what happens to attitude. Brand attitude is the pillar on which the sales and profit fortunes of a giant cor-

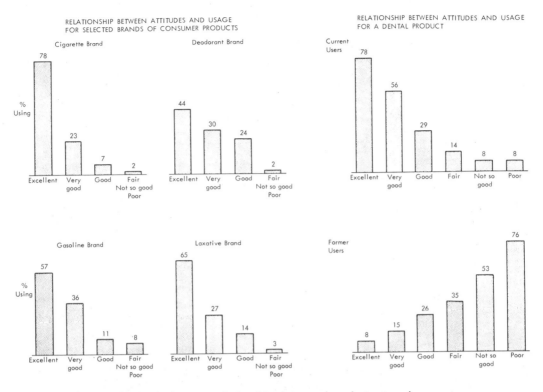

Figure 6-2. Attitude-usage relationships in several product categories

Source: Reprinted from Alvin A. Achenbaum, "Knowledge Is a Thing Called Measurement," in Lee Adler and Irving Crespi, eds., *Attitude Research at Sea* (1966), p. 113, published by American Marketing Association.

poration rest. Consider the stakes involved in the Coca-Cola Company's decision to change the taste of Coke in early 1985 in its battles with Pepsi, in an attempt to improve teenagers' attitudes toward Coke.

Attitudes are used for objective setting, strategic decision making, and evaluating performance in advertising. A range of attitudes can be identified for a brand that has been on the market for a short period. Figure 6-3 suggests that seven attitude segments might be identified for the brand, ranging from segment 1, holding strong negative attitudes, through segment 4, holding neither positive nor negative attitudes, to segment 7, holding strong positive attitudes. The tails of the distribution represent attitude extremes. The majority fall in the middle segments, holding slight tendencies in either direction or no *predisposition* one way or another with respect to the brand. These segments represent alternative targets for an advertising campaign.

Segment 7 might represent a small group of relatively heavy users who have become satisfied with the brand and are strongly loyal to it. Attitude in this case could be a measure of brand loyalty. We would expect this group to express strong positive feelings to back up their behavior and purchasing patterns.

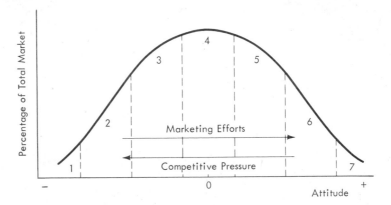

Figure 6-3. Attitude segments for a hypothetical brand

Segment 4, on the other hand, could hold no attitude for our brand for at least two reasons. First, it represents people who do not yet know that our brand exists. They have not learned of it from our advertising, from friends, or by any chance use experience. Such people have not yet entered the *awareness* stage (this is the situation for new brands). Second, some people in this segment could be aware of the brand but be so un-involved in purchasing with respect to the product class that no meaningful direction of predisposition exists. They could purchase it on one occasion but just as easily choose another brand on another occasion. Another representation of such consumers is to say that they see no meaningful differences in the brand choices available: their choice process is essentially random with respect to this product class, although it may not be with re-spect to others.

Segment 1 represents a small group of buyers who probably confine their purchases to other competitive brands in the class, and reject ours. In other words, our brand is not in their *consideration class* or *evoked set* of alternatives from which they make a choice, even though they are aware of it. Their negative attitudes could be based on a host of reasons, many of which are sustained by our competitors.

In any of these situations, an argument can be made for continuing to engage in advertising to sustain or change attitudes for two fundamental reasons. First, attitudes de-cay over time, and go below the threshold needed for active consideration. Just as a good friend can be forgotten when not around, so a good brand can be forgotten unless effort is expended to keep its name before the public. The rate of decay and the number of in-sertions necessary to sustain the threshold level are questions to be examined later, in Chapter 17. The second reason is that in most market situations competitors are con-stantly attempting to create favorable attitudes for their brands at the expense of our own. In terms of Figure 6-3, there is in effect a constant force operating in the opposite direc-tion to our marketing efforts, as shown by the opposing arrow, a force that attempts to pull our customers away.

IMPORTANCE OF ATTRIBUTES

Although an advertiser can glean much useful information from knowing the market's attitude for his or her brand, it is equally or more important to know what lies behind those attitudes. Basically, what are the strengths and weaknesses of the brand and what are the important criteria or attributes on which decision making is based? Particularly significant is the identification of the one or the few attributes used by consumers to choose between brands that are relatively similar or, as some would say, "functionally equivalent."

In most cases, copy development will focus on one or a few attributes. Competition for the consumer's attention is usually so intense that it is only possible to get one or a few ideas across, and it thus becomes crucial to identify the attribute (or the few attributes) that are most important in consumer decision making. Should a toothpaste manufacturer, for example, focus on decay prevention, bright teeth, fresh breath, or perhaps the taste of the product? Would a university be better off stressing the international reputation of its faculty, the physical environment in which it resides, or some exceptional aspect of its teaching or research programs?

Many of the questions reviewed in the last chapter concerning which positioning strategy to adopt can be reduced to "which attribute(s) is most important in a given purchasing or choice situation?" More precisely, these questions are ones of identifying the attributes that are most important in attitude formation and change and ultimately in the purchase-choice decision itself. Every product, service, or choice situation has associated with it a set of attributes on which the choices are made. In the case of choosing between Coke and Pepsi, for example, taste is likely to be very important.

Attributes can be examined at different levels. Myers and Shocker[10] have made a distinction between physical characteristics, pseudophysical characteristics, and benefits, all of which can be used in positioning and attribute selection. Physical characteristics are the most objective and can be measured on some physical scale such as temperature, color intensity, sweetness, thickness, distance, dollars, acidity, saltiness, strength of fragrance, weight, and so on. Pseudophysical characteristics, in contrast, reflect physical properties which are not easily measured. Examples are spiciness, smokey taste, tartness, type of fragrance (smells like a . . .), greasiness, creaminess, and shininess. Benefits refer to advantages that promote the well-being of the consumer or user. Psychological benefits can usually be classified at the benefits or pseudophysical level.

Another useful way of distinguishing between the different levels of attributes is through the *means-end chain model*.[11] This model focuses on the connection between product attributes, consumer consequences, and personal values, through a process called "laddering":

product attributes → consumer consequences → personal values

In this model, values represent the desired end states. They can have an external orientation ("feeling important" or "feeling accepted"), or they can relate to how one views oneself (''self-esteem,'' ''happiness,'' ''security,'' ''neatness,'' ''accomplish-ment''). Product attributes and consumer consequences represent the means that can be used to achieve the desired ends. Product attributes include measurable physical charac-teristics such as ''miles per gallon'' or ''cooking speed'' and subjective characteristics such as ''tastes good,'' ''strong flavor,'' or ''stylish.'' Consumer consequences are any result occurring to the consumer. Consequences can be functional (''saves money'' or ''don't have to wash your hair every day'') or can affect self-perceptions (''having more friends,'' ''having fun,'' or ''being more attractive'').

The means-end chain model suggests that it is the associational network involving attributes, consequences, and values that really represent needs to be understood in de-veloping message content. Effective advertising should thus address all levels and not just be concerned with the product attributes. The major positive consumer consequences should be communicated verbally or visually, and the value level should provide the driv-ing force behind the advertising.

One approach to eliciting a means-end chain can be illustrated using an airline example.[12] The process begins with a repertory grid exercise in which consumers are asked to state how two airlines out of a set of three are similar and how they differ. Sup-pose the attribute ''has wide-bodied aircraft'' emerges from this exercise. Consumers are then asked why an attribute such as ''wide bodies'' is preferred. One response might be ''physical comfort.'' The consumer is then asked why ''physical comfort'' is desired. The answer could be to ''get more done.'' Another ''why'' question yields a value, ''feel bet-ter about self.'' Similarly, the ''ground service'' attribute leads to ''save time,'' ''reduce tension,'' ''in control,'' and ''feeling secure.''

A campaign based on the ground service attribute would then address the conse-quences (''save time,'' ''reduce tension,'' and ''in control'') and value (''feeling secure'') dimensions. A mother needing personal service might be presented traveling with children. The theme is being ''in control;'' being able to cope with the situation. The result is a feeling of security. The creative group will, of course, have knowledge of the total means-end structures as they develop the campaign. An example of a hypothetical means-ends chain for the airline category is presented in Figure 6-4. An ad that illustrates the means-ends distinction is that for Sharp's nonalcoholic beer in Figure 6-5: here the ''means'' is nonalcoholic beer, but the ''end'' is ''keeping your edge'' for the next bowling game.

What is fundamental is that there is an important or salient set of attributes or benefits for every choice situation, and the identification of this set is the advertiser's first task. The size of the set is likely to vary with the complexity of the product and the im-portance of the decision involved. Because of limits on human information processing, it is unlikely that over seven attributes are used in most decision making. In other terms, people tend to compare alternatives using a relatively small set of characteristics, at-tributes, or benefits as the basis for comparison.

An important attribute is one that is considered an important benefit toward the sat-isfaction of needs and wants that the product is to fulfill. Obviously, some attributes within the target set will be more important than others. However, an attribute may be important, but buyers may perceive all brands to be virtually identical with respect to that attribute and thus the attribute does not affect decision making. A buyer, for example,

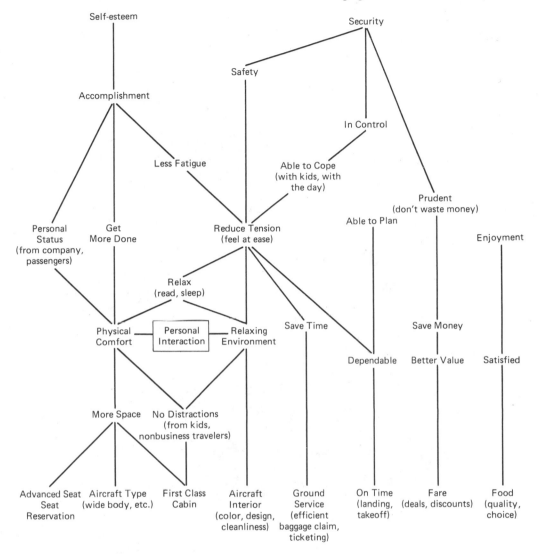

Figure 6-4. Means-ends chain for airline industry

Source: Thomas S. Reynolds and Jonathan Gutman, "Advertising Is Image Management," *Journal of Advertising Research*, 25, February/March 1984, p. 34. © 1984 by the Advertising Research Foundation.

may consider power steering to be an important and essential requirement in the next car purchase, but if all the cars being considered at the time the decision is made have power steering, this feature could really not be considered a cause of the final choice. Airline safety is another example. Safety may be the most important airline characteristic, but all major airlines are perceived to be equally safe (or unsafe). Attributes on which product offerings are perceived to differ and which are considered important are called *determinant attributes* because they will often be determinant in final choice decisions. Thus, the

Figure 6-5. An advertisement showing the brand as a means to an end
Courtesy of Miller Brewing Company.

identification of important attributes is a necessary step, but the advertiser should be sensitive to the possibility that an important attribute may not be determinant. We will return below to the issue of identifying those attributes that are determinant and have "leverage."

IDENTIFYING IMPORTANT ATTRIBUTES

A great many methods, approaches, and techniques have been developed to identify and determine the relative importance of the set of attributes on which brands are perceived and evaluated. In some cases, the relevant set of attributes will be known from past experience with the product category or past research with similar brands. In others, the first task will be to conduct research designed to reveal the attribute set itself. Once this set has been found, other procedures for developing specific measures or importance weights on each attribute can be used.

Suppose an advertiser faces a situation in which very little is known about how buyers choose among alternatives. How can the relevant attribute set be identified? Procedures such as the Kelly repertory grid[13] and factor analysis, reviewed in Chapter 4, can be used. Jacoby and others[14] developed an extension of the repertory grid that uses an information display board. Analysis procedures have been developed that allow the ordering of the attributes identified in this way on the basis of their importance.[15]

Once the set of attributes has been identified, the problem of identifying which of them are more or less important can be addressed. In particular, the advertiser needs a specific measure of the importance of each attribute in the set. Various forms of attribute rating and ranking instruments can be used to obtain judgments about the attributes themselves. Also, methods called *conjoint analysis,* which give respondents levels of each attribute to consider, are employed. Examples of these various approaches are presented in the next sections.

Rating, Ranking, and Conjoint Analysis

Attributes or benefits, rather than brands or objects, can be the focus of research, and procedures similar to those used for measuring overall attitude given earlier applied to measure their importance. The most straightforward ranking approach is simply to ask consumers to rank a list of attributes in order of importance. This is much like voting data in political elections, and the attributes that receive the most "votes" are considered to be the most important.

The most straightforward rating method, which has the advantage of ease of understanding and administration, is to present the attributes as a list with a very important–very unimportant scale alongside each. The consumer simply checks the appropriate scale position in each case according to how important the particular attribute is in the purchase decision. A modification of this procedure is to use a Likert scale. In this case, statements such as "It would be very important for me to know whether the next tire I purchased was steel-belted or nylon-belted" are developed. The respondents are asked to record the degree to which they agree or disagree with each such statement.

The direct rating and ranking methods, particularly those which ask in a straight-forward way the degree of importance of each attribute, are comparatively inexpensive and easy to administer. The argument is that, if some attributes are included that are un-important, this will simply show up in the final data analysis. A problem, of course, is that consumers are prone to want "everything" and tend to reflect these desires by rating everything as important. Most products are in effect trade-offs of desirable attributes, and the direct methods tend not to uncover these trade-offs. What the advertiser really wants to know is the degree to which consumers are willing to trade off one desirable feature in favor of another.

Another problem with the direct methods is that they do not specify what really is meant by "more" or "less" of an attribute. The respondent is presented with the attribute only, and not levels of the attribute. Much interest has thus been generated in methods designed to recover importance weights from data generated by presenting respondents with combinations of attribute levels. As a group, these procedures are known as conjoint analysis or conjoint measurement. The goal of conjoint analysis is to derive importance weights of the attributes and attribute levels; this is similar to that of the ranking-rating methods, but the procedures differ in how the data are collected and analyzed. In all ver-sions of the technique, the consumer is asked to make trade-offs between various at-tributes, all of which may be seen as desirable.

Figure 6-6 gives an example of a stimulus card used in conjoint analysis for a study of automobile tires in which five attributes—brand, tread life, sidewall, price, and type

I. Trade-Off Approach

	TREAD LIFE		
BRAND	30,000 Miles	40,000 Miles	50,000 Miles
Goodyear	8	4	1*
Goodrich	12	9	5
Michelin	11	7	3
Brand X	10	6	2

1* Denotes best-liked combination

II. Full-Profile Approach

Brand: Brand X
Tread Life: 50,000 Miles
Sidewall: White on Black
Price: $55
Type of Belt: Steel Belted Radial

Respondent Rating?

7

Least Liked								Most Liked
1	2	3	4	5	6	7	8	9

Scale Board

Figure 6-6.   Examples of stimulus cards used in trade-off and full-profile ap-proaches of conjoint analysis

Source: Patrick J. Robinson, "Applications of Conjoint Analysis to Pricing Problems," in David B. Montgomery and Dick R. Wittink, eds., *Market Measurement and Analysis* (Cambridge, MA: Marketing Science Institute, 1980), p. 185.

of belting—were involved. Various computer analysis routines can be used to derive importance weights from the data collected. Figure 6-7 shows that in this study, for example, respondents valued long tread wear (80,000 miles) and low price ($40) very highly in comparison with whether sidewalls were a particular color or even the tire brand. Also, as can be seen, whether the tire is steel-belted or fiberglass appears to make a significant difference. Respondents value steel-belted much more than fiberglass.

The overall importance of each attribute can also be derived from such data. Figure 6-8 shows the results in this study. As can be seen, price and tread life are the most important attributes in the set of five attributes tested, whereas type of belt, brand, and sidewalls follow in that order.

A significant advantage of conjoint measurement is that new combinations of attributes, and hence judgments about the relative attractiveness of new "products" can be derived from the data. By knowing how important each level of an attribute is, the researcher can combine various levels and derive the overall value of the new combination.

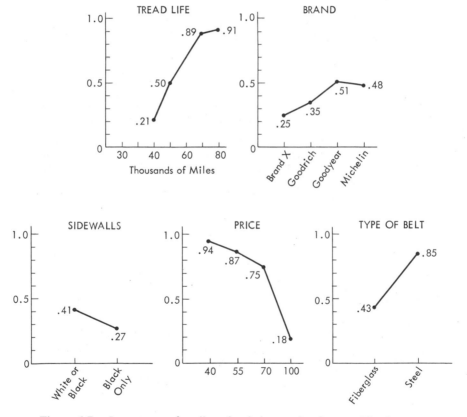

Figure 6-7. Importance of attribute levels in a study of automobile tires

Source: Patrick J. Robinson, "Applications of Conjoint Analysis," in David B. Montgomery and Dick R. Wittink, eds., *Market Measurement and Analysis* (Cambridge, MA: Marketing Science Institute, 1980), p. 186.

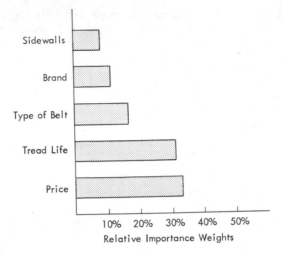

Figure 6-8. Overall attribute importance in the automobile tires study

Source: Patrick J. Robinson, "Applications of Conjoint Analysis," in David B. Montgomery and Dick R. Wittink, eds., *Market Measurement and Analysis* (Cambridge, MA: Marketing Science Institute, 1980), p. 186.

Ranking, rating, and conjoint analysis procedures are most useful for deriving importance weights on a set of attributes as well as providing the advertiser with many additional insights into feasible brand and product combinations. Whether such attributes do in fact determine attitudes and ultimate brand purchases is the subject of the next section.

Leverage and Determinant Attributes

Are the attributes identified by consumers as important really the ones that affect their attitudes and brand choices? This is the question of research in the area of leverage and determinant attributes. We want to know whether the attributes derived in any of the ways just described really make a difference when it comes to overall brand attitudes, preferences, and choices.

An attribute that has high leverage is one that has a high degree of influence on overall attitude. Its influence may derive from its importance to individuals in their attitude structure, the attribute weight. However, its influence may not be totally reflected by the importance weight. It is not unlikely that one attribute affects another in a cognitive structure. Thus, a communication that affects perception or belief along one attribute might have a significant indirect effect on other attributes and thus on the attitude structure. For example, an attribute like styling may have high leverage not only because the consumer values it highly (and by itself) with respect to a product class, but also because it may affect evaluations on other attributes like performance and convenience. Thus a change in brand perception on the styling dimension may affect perception with respect to performance and convenience, and therefore have a stronger influence on attitude than might at first be suspected. If styling is, for some reason, the foundation for performance and convenience, a change in either of the latter may not have a similar effect on styling.[16]

One approach to measuring leverage might be to measure the strength of the cognitive link between one attribute and others. An attribute that is independent and not "connected" to other attributes might be considered to have no influence beyond that represented by its importance weights. Another attribute that seemed closely intertwined with other attributes (tends to have strong cognitive association) might have more leverage than is reflected by its importance weights. Research is needed to operationally define cognitive links and how they can be measured.

Another more direct approach to measuring leverage might be to alter systematically the perception of a brand on a dimension and observe the change on the overall attitude scale. Attributes that had the greatest impact on overall attitude would be those with the highest leverage. Yet another approach is to obtain evaluative beliefs on a set of attributes and correlate these with brand attitude scores or buying intentions. The attributes with the highest correlations are considered to have the highest amount of leverage and are called determinant attributes.

Myers and Alpert[17] examined correlations of five attributes of a snack mix with a measure of overall attitude and buying intention. The new snack food was placed in 200 homes in the Los Angeles area, and homemakers were asked to serve it to families and friends. After serving, they were asked to rate the snack food in terms of color, appearance, taste, strength of flavor, and spiciness. Overall opinion (attitude) and buying intention measures were also obtained. The correlations (a number between -1 and $+1$ that indicates the degree of association) between these scales are given in Table 6-1. Of the five product attributes, taste has a much higher positive correlation with buying intention. Not only was taste by far the best predictor of buying intention, but it was a better predictor than overall attitude. Taste is obviously important in judging a snack food, but it may not be a useful criterion for distinguishing one brand of snack food from another.[18]

The Grey Advertising Agency has applied a similar conceptual approach by using different data collection and analysis procedures in well over 20 studies of attitudes and product usage over an eight-year period. Its studies have involved relatively large (over 1,000 subjects) well-developed samples and explicit consideration of object (brand) dif-

TABLE 6-1.   Correlation Matrix of Product Ratings for Snack Mix

	1	2	3	4	5	6	7
1. Overall opinion		0.325	0.209	0.782	−0.324	−0.313	0.609
2. Color			0.498	0.308	−0.045	−0.099	0.189
3. Appearance				0.260	0.006	−0.133	0.036
4. Taste					−0.172	−0.161	0.617
5. Strength of flavor						0.759	−0.092
6. Spiciness							−0.084
7. Buying intention							

Source: James H. Myers, "Finding Determinant Buying Attitudes," *Journal of Advertising Research*, 10, December 1970, p. 11. © 1970 by the Advertising Research Foundation.

ferences, and thus have an impressive credibility. The procedure essentially begins with developing a large attribute list for the product class. For example, 40 attributes were used in a study of women's hosiery, and as many as 130 in a study of general merchandise stores. Importance weights are obtained for each attribute. The attribute list is then reduced via factor analysis to a smaller set of relevant dimensions that account for most of the variance in the data. Evaluative belief ratings are then obtained for brands in the product class with respect to this set of dimensions: each brand is rated on how adequate it is on each dimension. Respondents are also asked to express their overall feelings for each brand along a poor-to-excellent scale. The final data input is thus a set of dimension and overall attitude ratings of each brand by each respondent. Brands are selected two at a time from the brand set, differences in dimension and overall ratings are calculated, and the correlation of these difference scores between dimensions and overall attitude is examined. Subsequent dimensions are then put through a similar analysis. Those dimensions that correlate most highly with overall attitude are considered to be those with the highest leverage.

Achenbaum,[19] in describing the Grey approach, points out that it has in many practical situations provided information useful for product development and packaging, as well as advertising. In general, it is a diagnostic tool for understanding why particular attitude states exist. He provides an interesting summary of general findings from many replications of the procedure:

1. No one set of specific attributes is universally applicable to all products. Each product category has its own unique set of factors by which people evaluate the desirability of the product. They range in number from 5 to 18—the mean being 10.

2. In every case studied, the product either provided more than one functional benefit or the functional benefit was multidimensional.

3. Nonfunctional benefits came up in every case, many of which rarely showed up when using traditional questioning techniques.

4. Certain factors, like safety, although relevant, rarely had competitive leverage among the major brands rated. Presumably most consumers consider the major brands to be safe to use although this may not be the case with some of the less well-known brands.

5. Attitude factors that count with people did not always reveal themselves in terms of specific benefits. Often, some product attribute takes on such importance or provides so many diverse benefits that it is considered intrinsically desirable in itself, for example, menthol in a cigarette or whether a shampoo is a cream or a liquid.

6. Some benefits were more likely to be stated in terms of the way the product performed than the specific benefits it provided. For example, people talked about the ease of opening, carrying, or storing a paper product, rather than the benefit of convenience, although all three performance qualities are concerned with convenience.

7. Although considerable variation was found among products, on the basis of one or two specific attempts to replicate the procedure using the same product category, there is considerable stability in results by time and location and by groups of consumers.[20]

The question of the connection between attributes (or benefits) and attitudes is further complicated by the fact that not just importance weights but also beliefs about a particular brand or object should be taken into account. A consumer, for example, may feel that the attribute miles per gallon is very important, but that a Volvo gets very poor miles per gallon. A negative attitude for Volvo, in this case, would not result from a lack of importance of the attribute, but rather from the consumer's perception (belief) that this car did not possess the right amount of it.

Multiattribute attitude models therefore bring together the belief and importance-weight components. Also, as we will see, they draw attention to the fact that in most choice situations not only are multiattributes involved, but also multiobjects.

MULTIATTRIBUTE ATTITUDE MODELS

There are dozens of models and theories about the connection between perception and preference or attributes and attitudes. In economics, for example, a long tradition of utility theory and associated models exists that essentially deals with this question. In social psychology, they are often referred to as evaluative belief models of cognitive structure to emphasize that attitudes are the product of both evaluations of the attributes and beliefs about how much of the attributes are possessed by the attitude object, as present in the consumer's cognitive understanding of the product category and brand. Paralleling the development of evaluative belief models and procedures has been a class of models that depend on deriving the attitude measure from a knowledge of the consumer's *ideal point*. Brands or objects that are closest to the ideal point in a positioning (multidimensional scaling) map are considered most preferred, and those farthest away, least preferred. The focus is first on locating the ideal point, and then deriving attitudes for each object as a function of the distance from this point.

In this section, the basic principles underlying each of these model classes are presented and assessed. An impressively large amount of research has been done to test their validity. Much of it has to do with the basic question of whether attributes, beliefs, and perceptions are related to attitudes and subsequent behavior.

Evaluative Belief Models of Cognitive Structure

A cognitive structure model assumes that a person forms an attitude toward an object by developing beliefs about that object and then combining those beliefs into a general overall attitude toward the object. The most commonly used cognitive structure model in advertising is the evaluative belief model, where the attitude is the sum of the evaluative beliefs about how well each brand scores on each attribute, weighted by the importance of that attribute:

$$A_o = \Sigma w_d a_{od}$$

where A_o = attitude of an individual or segment toward object o

a_{od} = evaluation of an individual or segment toward object o with respect to attribute or dimension d, the evaluative belief

w_d = measure of the relative importance or weight of attribute d to the individual or segment

Suppose that A_o represents the attitude for a particular model of automobile, a Ford Escort, for example, and three characteristics—size, miles per gallon, and price—are most important to a particular segment. A study of the segment revealed the following set of weights and evaluative beliefs:

$$\begin{aligned} A_o &= w_1 a_{01} + w_2 a_{02} + w_3 a_{03} \\ &= 2(-2) + 5(+1) + 3(+1) \\ &= +4 \end{aligned}$$

How could advertising improve the attitude toward the Escort? There are three routes. The first is to change the weights. Advertising might attempt to decrease the importance of the size factor, for example, either by explicitly downplaying it or by ignoring it altogether and emphasizing good gas mileage instead. Second, the segment could be enticed to include new attributes, such as reliability, in their appraisal. Third, their evaluative beliefs could be altered by advertising. For example, a comparative advertisement could show that the Escort gets better mileage than its nearest competitors, and at the same time, costs less.

Model Assumptions

The model includes several explicit assumptions that may not always hold. For example, it assumes that there are a limited number of known attributes with known weights. In some circumstances, a consumer may not be aware of all the attributes used. A consumer, for example, may rationalize the purchase of a small sporty convertible on the basis of gas mileage, but actually buy it on a subconscious drive to lead an exciting life. Further, the model assumes that the weighted evaluative beliefs are added when there could be interactions present. A person may want some combination of attributes and will not value the object highly unless the desired set of attributes is included.

Another assumption is that a person first obtains belief information and then uses that information to alter attitudes. However, the process could actually work the opposite way. In one clever study, the psychologists Nisbett and Wilson had subjects observe an interview with a person with a European accent.[21] For one group the person spoke in an agreeable and enthusiastic manner, while for another group, the same person appeared autocratic and distrustful. The students then rated the person's likability and three other attributes that were the same for both groups: physical appearance, mannerism, and accent. Subjects in the "warm" condition found these attributes attractive, whereas subjects in the "cold" condition found them irritating. Further, subjects in both conditions were certain that their liking of the teacher did not influence the attribute ratings, but rather, the reverse was true.

Other Attitude Models

There are dozens of other attitude models that are elaborations of the basic evaluative belief model. Some, such as *ideal-point models*, rely on different approaches to data collection and an assumption that a particular combination of levels on each attribute can be found that represents a person's or total market's "ideal" combination. These models involve perceptual mapping and multidimensional scaling procedures reviewed in Chapter 4.[22] Given the importance of attitude in advertising and marketing, a great deal of research attention has been given to testing various models and evaluating their performance and reliability and validity.[23]

Noncompensatory Models

The evaluative belief models wc have discussed are examples of "compensatory" models. A low rating on one dimension can be compensated for by a high rating on another dimension. There are also a set of "noncompensatory" models that might be better in certain situations. Three such models are the conjunctive, disjunctive, and lexicographic.

The conjunctive model emphasizes low ratings on the various attributes. An object will be deemed acceptable if it meets a minimum standard (a minimum attribute level) on each attribute. This process has been shown to operate in supermarket buying decisions. In one study,[24] new grocery products were considered for stocking by buyers only if they rated at least average in quality, company reputation, sales representation, and category volume and were less than 110 percent of the cost of the closest substitute. If they failed to meet any of these criteria, they were excluded. Similarly, one can imagine that a student buying a personal computer might have minimum requirements in terms of memory, chip speed, and so on. An advertiser must, in such situations, ensure that the ad's content does not make any "errors of omission" and present information about all the key attributes.

The disjunctive model stresses high ratings. It regards objects as positive only when they have been rated outstanding on one or more of the relevant attributes. For instance, ready-to-eat breakfast cereals have many attributes (such as taste, nutritional content, etc.), but there may be some eaters of such cereals who care most about the cereal not getting soggy in milk. Thus a cereal advertiser advertising to them needs to ensure that advertising focuses on the "stays crispy" benefit. The lexicographic model assumes that an individual will evaluate the brand on the most salient attribute. If two or more brands "tie" on this attribute, the evaluation will shift to the second most salient attribute. The process will continue until a brand is selected.

Research shows that some of these noncompensatory models (e.g., the lexicographic one) are often used when the consumer is not really very involved, or is under time pressure to make a choice, so that choosing the very best brand is not the prime concern, just a brand that "is good enough." It is also quite possible that an individual in some contexts may use more than one model. He or she could, for example, use a conjunctive model to determine a set of brands to consider and then use a compensatory model to make the final decision. Clearly, the existence of such multimodel decision processes makes model evaluation more difficult.

Category Evaluation Models

The implicit assumption of cognitive structure models is that products are made up of discrete attributes and the decision makers combine these attributes to form an overall product attitude. A very different approach is "category-based evaluation" based on the premise that people often divide the world into categories. In evaluating a new stimulus, it is placed into a category, and the attitude toward that category is retrieved from memory and applied to the stimulus. Reactions toward an individual can result from matching up that individual to a person category and applying the established attitudes toward that category.

For the category-based evaluation approach to operate, consumers develop a set of expectations about the product category. This expectation can be represented by either a typical example of the category, a "prototype," or by a good example of the category, an "exemplar."[25] To implement an advertising strategy based on the category-based model, the advertising should focus on positioning the brand with respect to some category exemplar. There would be no effort to communicate explicitly at the attribute level. One example is the humorous advertising for Parkay margarine which has a voice coming out of a box saying "butter." The advertising serves to position margarine with butter.

Another good example are the ads for the Yugo, the boxy Yugoslavian car that was introduced into the U.S. market at a base price under $5,000. The goal was to communicate that it was not only small and inexpensive but also dependable and reliable. The solution was to associate it with the Volkswagen Beetle. A TV commercial opened with a Beetle sitting in a white one-car garage with a voice-over saying: "The beloved Beetle. Once the lowest-priced car in America. Dependable. Basic transportation. But homely. And then it went away. Leaving an emptiness in the hearts of America." A Yugo print ad is shown in Figure 6-9.

SEGMENTATION USING ATTITUDE STRUCTURE

When the attitude is specified for a group rather than an individual, the attribute values are themselves averaged over those in the group. In such averaging, an implicit assumption is that the group is not excessively heterogeneous so that this average is representative of the total group, rather than only a small portion. As suggested in the section in Chapter 4 on segmentation, it is unlikely that all attributes are equally important to all people. In fact, it is much more likely that while consumer perceptions of how well the different brands perform on the different attributes are similar across consumers, their ratings of the relative importance of different attributes in brand selection will likely be

Introducing the same old idea.

Every generation or so, some smart people figure out how to make basic transportation at an affordable price. First came the Model T, a basic, affordable idea that put millions behind the wheel.

But then, over the years, bigger and more expensive became the norm. Until the Beetle brought things back to reality. Unfortunately the Beetle went away, leaving nothing in its place.

Until the Yugo.

The Yugo gives you dependable, front-wheel drive transportation, imported from Europe, for only $3990. On one hand, the Yugo is very basic. But on the other, it's not. There's an overhead cam engine, 4-wheel independent suspension, rack and pinion steering, and lots more.

Every generation, some smart people figure out how to make basic transportation at an affordable price. For all the other smart people who want to buy it.

YUGO, $3990.

THE ROAD BACK TO SANITY

$3990, MFR'S SUGG. RETAIL PRICE FOR YUGO GV. EXCLUDING TAX, TITLE, DEALER PREP. AND TRANSPORTATION.

Figure 6-9.   Positioning a brand with respect to a category

Courtesy of Yugo-America.

different. Thus while all consumers may agree that the Honda Civic car is very good in terms of fuel economy, and that Volvos are very highly rated on safety, these consumers will probably differ in the relative importance they place on fuel economy or safety in their choice of a car.

It is therefore usually inadvisable simply to look at the average importance ratings for attributes in any market. Instead, these differences across consumers in the importance placed on different product category attributes should be used to create segments for advertising campaigns and marketing strategy. In Chapter 4, for instance, we saw an example of benefit segmentation, where toothpaste users were placed into segments of the sensory consumers (highly valuing the attributes of flavor and appearance), sociables (highly valuing the brightness benefit), worriers (highly valuing decay prevention), and so on. The typical way to create these segments, as we discussed, was to collect research data from individual consumers on their attribute importance ratings, then to use cluster analysis techniques to create benefit segments, and then to compare ("profile") the different segments in terms of their demographics, brand preferences, and media habits, so that only appropriate segments could be targeted, and messages created just for them.

Another example should illustrate this process (see Table 6-2 for some "made-up" data to illustrate the example). Suppose you were the advertising manager for AT&T's residential long-distance service telephone program. It is possible that research might show that AT&T was widely perceived as being the higher-quality telephone service, with better reliability, better customer service, and better operator assistance than its competitors (such as MCI). On the other hand, MCI might be rated higher on price (i.e., perceived as the lower-priced service). These perceptions might be pretty much the same for all consumers. However, consumers might differ in the importance placed on these attributes. One segment might want simply the lower-priced service, placing a greater weight on the price attribute than on quality, customer service, and operator assistance (let us call this the "price segment"). A second segment might place higher ratings on quality, customer service, and operator assistance, and lower value on cheaper prices (the "quality segment").

TABLE 6-2. Possible Analysis of Attitude Segments for Long-Distance Telephone Residential Market

Attribute	"Price segment"			"Quality segment"		
	Importance weight[a]	RATINGS OF[b] AT&T	MCI	Importance weight[a]	RATINGS OF[b] AT&T	MCI
Reliability	3.4	6.3	5.5	5.9	6.4	5.3
Customer service	4.6	6.5	5.1	6.3	6.7	4.9
Operator assistance	4.4	6.2	4.6	5.8	6.5	4.5
Price	6.2	5.5	6.5	4.6	5.7	6.2

[a]7 = most important, 1 = least important.
[b]7 = rated better, 1 = rated worse.

If this is what the research data showed, then it would make sense for AT&T to target the quality segment, *because this segment places greater value on the attributes that AT&T is strong on*, so that AT&T is at a greater competitive advantage in this segment. (Conversely, MCI might decide that it makes more sense to target the price segment.) Research would show who the quality segment is (for example, older and more affluent consumers, heavy readers of business magazines), and so AT&T could then develop advertisements for them demonstrating AT&T's superiority on these quality attributes, and place them in appropriate media.

In the longer run, however, AT&T might also try to convert the price segment, by aiming campaigns at them that AT&T is not in fact more expensive in price (trying to change brand attribute adequacy perceptions), or by trying to convince them that they ought to place a greater weight on quality than on price (thus increasing consumer importance weights for an attribute that AT&T is competitively strong on). Conversely, MCI might in the longer run try to convert the quality segment by showing it was as good (or better) on quality as AT&T, or by increasing the importance weight on price.

As a different strategy, of course, AT&T (as the market leader, with close to 70 percent of the market), might try to increase total primary demand for residential long-distance phone calls. As discussed in Chapter 3, this strategy makes more sense for the market leader than for a small-share brand.

SUMMARY

Once the target market has been identified and communication and positioning objectives set, decisions must be made about the content of the advertising message. This is called message strategy. Should the message focus on communicating product benefits, on developing/reinforcing brand image or personality, on evoking specific feelings and emotions, or on developing group associations? This chapter has focused on the benefits question. Benefits are the characteristics or attributes of a product that consumers perceive positively. In order to decide which and how many of them to focus on in an advertising campaign, we must understand attitude structure and processes of attitude formation and change. Attitude is a central concept in social psychology and has become, perhaps, the most significant focus of study in the fields of advertising management and consumer behavior. The most well-accepted view is that attitude is made up of three interrelated components called cognitive, affective, and conative. There are numerous approaches to attitude measurement, but they can be broadly classified into those that involve direct overall measures and those that involve derived multiattribute measures.

Direct measures involve questioning or observations of respondent behavior in which no explicit attribute criterion concerning the product is provided. Derived measures, on the other hand, rely on deriving overall attitude from a combination of subject response to attributes of the product. Attitude models generally refer to models which use attributes and derived measures to determine attitude. Such models provide useful diagnostic information, not generated in the direct case.

A market can be segmented on the basis of varying degrees of attitude—positive, neutral, and negative—held by customers or potential customers of a brand. Advertising objectives can then be cast in attitude terms with respect to specific segments or the market as a whole. In general, the two broad classes of objectives from this viewpoint are to attempt changes in the market from some negative or neutral to some positive position, or to sustain and to maintain a positive attitude and avoid attitude decay. Competition in this context is a force attempting to shift attitudes in the opposite direction.

Although knowing the overall market attitude for his or her brand is very useful for the advertiser, it is equally significant to identify the reasons for the attitude. In other terms, the advertiser needs to know what attributes, beliefs, and benefits are most important in the product-market situation, and in particular which of them are determinant in brand choice. The means-end chain model is useful in explaining the links between product attributes, consumer consequences, and personal values. Identifying the relevant set of attributes is crucial to the analysis. Several procedures for doing this have been developed. Specific importance weights on each attribute can be derived by rating, ranking, and conjoint analysis methods. Leverage and determinant attribute research show how attributes that appear to have the greatest leverage in affecting an attitude structure or are most closely related to brand choice and behavior can be identified.

Attributes, benefits, and beliefs and their relation to overall attitudes have been formally studied in the context of evaluative belief attitude models. It is possible to focus on the two central constructs of an attitude model, evaluative beliefs and importance weights, and perform a segmentation analysis useful for diagnostic purposes. Each construct provides a criterion for classifying consumers into different market segments that have important strategy implications.

DISCUSSION QUESTIONS

1. Discuss the strategy implications of a bimodal (two-humped) distribution of brand attitude rather than the distribution shown in Figure 6-3.

2. Day recommends the following seven-point scale for obtaining direct measures of brand attitude:
   (1) This brand is the best that is available.
   (2) I like this brand very much, but there's another just as good.
   (3) I like this brand, but other brands are better.
   (4) This brand is acceptable, but most other brands are better.
   (5) I neither like nor dislike this brand—it doesn't have any particular merits.
   (6) I don't like this brand very much, although it is not as bad as some.
   (7) I don't like this brand at all—it is one of the worst available.

   Administer this scale to 20 to 30 friends using five to ten brands in an appropriate product class. What are the shapes of the resulting distributions? What explanation could you offer for the shapes?

3. Discuss ways in which you could assess the strength (sometimes called the "valence") of an attitude. Is it true that a highly valenced attitude is always more stable than a weak one?

4. Compare and contrast the several methods used for identifying important attributes.

5. What fundamental assumption about belief-attitude relations underlies the "leverage" approaches to assessing the relative worth of alternative attributes? Why might an attribute be regarded as important but have low leverage? How might leverage be determined?

6. Explain the concepts of benefit, belief, attribute, and cognition.

7. Use the means-end chain model to explain the associational network that needs to be understood in developing message content for buying
   (a) an automobile
   (b) an expensive wristwatch
   (c) shampoo

8. Collect data on attribute beliefs and weights for a MacIntosh personal computer. Explain the alternative strategies Apple could use to advertise the Mac based on these data.

9. Suppose other research showed that personal computers were usually purchased based on "noncompensatory" evaluations. What does noncompensatory mean in this context. Be specific and give examples. How would this affect message strategy for the Mac?

10. Assume the following information is available to you concerning the locations of four cereal brands on the two benefits of sweetness and crunchiness:

Brand	Sweetness	Crunchiness
A	2	−3
B	−1	2
C	4	5
D	3	2

Calculate the segment's attitude for each brand using the benefits information only. Rank the brands on this basis. Suppose that the importance weight for sweetness was found to be 0.80 and for crunchiness, 0.20. Recalculate attitude for each brand using the weighted belief model in the chapter. How would this change the rankings? Now suppose attitudes were formed using a conjunctive model in which the minimal desired sweetness level was 2. How would this change the rankings? What about a disjunctive model where only crunchiness mattered? Assume that you are the manager of brand B. Discuss the implications of these results for product and advertising strategy.

11. Think of a product category that you can meaningfully relate to, perhaps something you have contemplated buying but have not gotten around to. What comes to mind

first as you contemplate the purchase, the attributes and benefits you would like to have satisfied, or the brands that are available to satisfy them? Will all people tend to follow this processing sequence? If so, why? If not, why not?

12. Write down the attributes that are meaningful to you and assign importance weights to each for jogging shoes or sneakers. Compare your results with two or three friends doing the same exercise. What problems occur in developing "importance weights" in this fashion?

NOTES

1. Gordon W. Allport, "Attitudes," in C. Murchison, ed., *Handbook of Social Psychology* (Worcester, MA: Clark University Press, 1935). Reprinted in Martin Fishbein, ed., *Readings in Attitude Theory and Measurement* (New York: John Wiley, 1967), p. 3.

2. Martin Fishbein and Icek Ajzen, *Belief, Attitude, Intention and Behavior: An Introduction to Theory and Research* (Reading, MA: Addison-Wesley, 1975).

3. Robert B. Zajonc, "Feeling and Thinking: Preferences Lead to Inferences," *American Psychologist,* 35, 1980, pp. 151–175.

4. George S. Day, *Buyer Attitudes and Brand Choice Behavior* (New York: Free Press, 1970), p. 160.

5. Izek Ajzen and Martin Fishbein, "Attitude Behavior Relations: A Theoretical Analysis and Review of Empirical Research," *Psychological Bulletin,* 84 (5), 1977, pp. 888–918.

6. Alvin A. Achenbaum, "Knowledge Is a Thing Called Measurement," in Lee Adler and Irving Crespi, eds., *Attitude Research at Sea* (Chicago: American Marketing Association, 1966), p. 126.

7. Ibid., p. 114.

8. Russell H. Fazio and Mark P. Zanna, "On the Predictive Validity of Attitudes: The Roles of Direct Experience and Confidence," *Journal of Personality,* 46 (2), 1978, pp. 228–243; and Robert E. Smith and William R. Swinyard (1983), "Attitude-Behavior Consistency: The Impact of Product Trial vs. Advertising," *Journal of Marketing Research,* 20 (3), pp. 257–267.

9. Ida E. Berger and Andrew Mitchell, "The Effect of Advertising on Attitude Accessibility, Attitude Confidence and the Attitude-Behavior Relationship," *Journal of Consumer Research,* 16 (December), 1989, pp. 269–279.

10. James H. Myers and Allan D. Shocker, "Toward a Taxonomy of Product Attributes," Working paper (Los Angeles: University of Southern California, June 1978), p. 3.

11. Thomas J. Reynolds and Jonathan Gutman, "Advertising Is Image Management," *Journal of Advertising Research,* 25, February/March 1984, pp. 29–37; and Jonathan Gutman, "A Means-End Chain Model Based on Consumer Categorization Processes," *Journal of Marketing,* 46, Spring 1982, pp. 60–73. See also S. Young and B. Feigin, "Using the Benefit Chain for Improved Strategy Formulation," *Journal of Marketing,* 39, July 1975, pp. 72–74.

12. Reynolds and Gutman, "Advertising Is Image Management," p. 32.

13. W. A. K. Frost and R. L. Braine, "The Application of the Repertory Grid Technique to Problems in Market Research," *Commentary,* 9, July 1967, pp. 161–175; and G. A. Kelly, *Psychology of Personal Constructs,* Vols. I and II (New York: W. W. Norton, 1955).

14. Jacob Jacoby, George J. Szybillo, and J. Busato-Schach, "Information-Acquisition Behavior in Brand Choice Situations," *Journal of Consumer Research,* 3, March 1977, pp. 209–216.

15. John A. Quelch, "Behavioral Measurement of the Relative Importance of Product Attributes: Process Methodology and Pilot Application," Working paper 180R (London, Canada: School of Business Administration, University of Western Ontario, 1978).

16. John G. Myers and Francesco M. Nicosia, "Cognitive Structures, Latent Class Models, and the Leverage Index," Paper presented at the Annual Meetings of the American Association for Public Opinion Research, Western Division, Santa Barbara, California, May 1968.

17. James H. Myers and Mark I. Alpert, "Determinant Buying Attitudes: Meaning and Measurement," *Journal of Marketing,* 32, October 1968, pp. 13–20.

18. Mark I. Alpert, "Identification of Determinant Attitudes: A Comparison of Methods," *Journal of Marketing Research,* 8, May 1971, pp. 184–191.

19. Achenbaum, "Knowledge Is a Thing Called Measurement."

20. Ibid., pp. 123–124.

21. Richard E. Nisbett and Timothy D. Wilson, "Telling More than We Can Know: Verbal Reports on Mental Processes," *Psychological Review,* 84, May 1977, pp. 231–259.

22. For some classic papers on the foundations of the work in advertising, see Ledyard R. Tucker, "Intra-individual and Inter-individual Multidimensionality," in H. Gulliksen and S. Messick, eds., *Psychological Scaling: Theory and Applications* (New York: John Wiley, 1960); C. H. Coombs, "Psychological Scaling Without a Unit of Measurement," *Psychological Review,* 57, 1950, pp. 148–158; and J. F. Bennett and W. L. Hays, "Multidimensional Unfolding: Determining the Dimensionality of Ranked Preference Data," *Psychometrika,* 25, 1960, pp. 27–43.

23. Many of the evaluation issues are reviewed in William L. Wilkie and Edgar A. Pessemier, "Issues in Marketing's Use of Multi-attribute Attitude Models," *Journal of Market Research,* 10, November 1973, pp. 428–441.

24. David B. Montgomery, "New Product Distribution—An Analysis of Supermarket Buyer Decisions," *Journal of Marketing Research,* 12, August 1975, pp. 255–264.

25. Eleanor Rosch and Barbara B. Lloyd, *Cognition and Categorization* (Hillsdale, NJ: Erlbaum, 1978).

7

ASSOCIATING FEELINGS WITH THE BRAND

Advertising that works is advertising that makes somebody feel something. . . . All advertising has some emotion. Some advertising is all emotion.

Hal Riney, creative director,
Hal Riney & Associates

In Chapter 6, our discussion of message strategy focused on the thinking or cognitive response to advertising. The consumer processed information which potentially could change beliefs, attitudes, and behavior. This response often involves a logical, rational, thinking process. As a result of the advertising, the audience member often learns relevant facts about the brand. Thus, the audience learns that a toothpaste cleans better or that Pepsi won a taste test. Advertising that attempts predominately to communicate or inform and thus activate the thinking process is termed "thinking" advertising.

Advertising can also work by creating feelings that can ultimately influence attitudes and behavior. Thus, a commercial could portray active teenagers playing volleyball at the beach and enjoying 7-Up. A feeling of energy, vitality, fun, and belonging could be created that gets associated with the brand and thereby affects brand attitudes and behavior. In this chapter the focus turns to the feeling side of advertising. Since these feeling responses usually are considered positive (liked) or negative (disliked), they are also termed affective responses. In this chapter we shall spend most time discussing positive feeling responses, since those are the kind that advertisers most often want to associate with their brands.

"Feeling" advertising is used here to describe advertising for which audience feeling response is of primary importance, and usually (but not always) little or no information content is involved. It usually is very much execution focused, as opposed to message focused, and relies on the establishment of a feeling, emotion, or mood and the association of this feeling, emotion, or mood with the brand. The association of such a feeling with the brand has been labeled a process of "emotional bonding" by some advertising

agencies. Feeling advertising is also termed execution focused, emotional, end-benefit oriented, mood, experiential, or associational advertising. Some of these feelings lead to brand imagery and personality, which we discuss in the next chapter.

It should be clear that all commercials, even the most logical and informative, can develop feeling or affective responses. Similarly, some argue that even the most emotional commercials, seemingly without information content, can evoke some type of thinking and cognitive activity. Thus, there is a spectrum between pure "feeling" and pure "thinking" advertising according to the relative importance of the thinking response as opposed to the affective or feeling response. *Thinking response* refers to any thinking activity about the advertisement or brand, usually with the potential to change beliefs.

In fact, the Marschalk Company believes that an effective advertisement should communicate at both the rational and emotional levels, using what they term the "emotional hard sell."[1] The idea is that it is necessary to arouse an emotional response, but the advertising needs that rational hook—the tangible end benefits that the product will fulfill.

MODELING THE FEELING RESPONSE TO ADVERTISING

In Chapter 6 we have discussed a variety of models and approaches that were most relevant to understanding the thinking response to advertising. Most of these models are relatively well developed and accepted. In contrast, remarkably little is known about the feeling or affective response to advertising and how it works. Models of feeling advertising are just beginning to emerge.

Emerging models of feeling or affective response tend to introduce one or more of four constructs. The first are the feelings that are engendered by the advertisement, feelings such as warmth, excitement, fear, and amusement. The second is the attitude toward the advertisement, the degree to which an audience member likes or enjoys the advertisement. The third is the transformation of the use experience, where attributes that may be intangible are effectively added to the brand. The fourth is the process, usually considered the classical conditioning process, by which the feelings, the attitude toward the advertisement, or the transformed use experience get associated with the brand.

Figure 7-1 provides one model of how feeling or affective response works.[2] The advertisement exposure can first have a thinking response, which usually involves factual learning, discussed at length in Chapter 6. The second (simultaneously felt) response is the affective response, the feelings that are created or aroused by the advertising. Feelings can be positive, such as feeling warm, cheerful, happy, energetic, active, or giving. Or they could be negative, such as feeling afraid, depressed, guilty, anxious, or irritated. Feelings are not as extreme or pronounced as emotions, although they have been described as mild emotions, and we will sometimes use the two terms interchangeably.

Feelings are shown in Figure 7-1 as having four possible types of impact.

First, they can affect the amount and nature of the thinking response. Positive feelings may promote positive thoughts, because people in good moods want to stay in good moods, and thus evaluate brand attribute arguments more positively than they otherwise

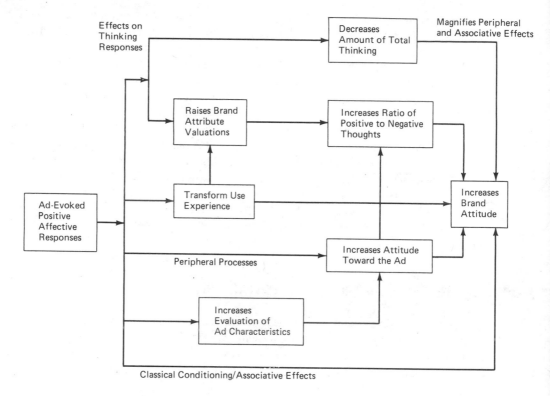

Figure 7-1.   A model of the feeling response to advertising

would, leading to an increase in the ratio of support to counterarguments. In addition, however, people in good moods also think fewer total thoughts than they otherwise would, because thinking is effortful and can reduce their good mood. While the relative increase in the ratio of support to counterarguments serves to increase brand attitudes, the decrease in the number of total thoughts can serve to make brand attitudes based more on peripheral cues and attitude to the ad (discussed shortly), than on central message arguments. We can see that the effects of feeling responses on thinking responses are really quite complex.

Second, feelings can also work by "transforming" the use experience. The theory is as follows. After many exposures to a McDonald's commercial (to pick one example) showing a happy, family scene, a family's felt experience at McDonald's will actually be different because of the exposure to the advertising. The advertising exposures make their visit to McDonald's feel warmer and happier than it would otherwise be. Their McDonald's experience is transformed into one more closely matching that shown in the advertising. This transformation has the effect of adding a "warm and happy" attribute to an assessment of McDonald's, and thus creating a "new belief" about McDonald's. This raises brand attitudes toward McDonald's.

Third, Figure 7-1 shows that feelings can also work by creating a positive attitude toward the advertisement (1) directly, through the kinds of "peripheral" mechanisms discussed in Chapter 5 and (2) indirectly, through increasing the favorability of evaluation of the ad's characteristics. For example, ads for Kodak film are usually extremely warm commercials. These warm feelings themselves lead to a liking for these ads, but they additionally lead to a more favorable assessment of the way the ad was made (its executional characteristics). Thus the Kodak ads tend to be well liked for both these reasons. The model suggests that this attitude toward the advertisement then becomes directly associated with or transferred to the brand.

As mentioned earlier, the reduction in cognitive elaboration (amount of thinking) by positive feelings accentuates the effect of attitude to the ad on brand attitudes. In addition to this "direct" effect, a favorable attitude to the ad can also increase brand attitudes "indirectly" by making ad-evoked thoughts about the brand more positive than they would otherwise have been.

The fourth and final way in which these ad-evoked feelings can become directly associated with the brand is through processes such as classical conditioning or other associative mechanisms. The result of this association could be an effect on the brand attitude or brand choice or both. The feelings of warmth that the audience experienced when being exposed to the Kodak commercials could, over time and with multiple exposures, become associated with Kodak film, and this association could directly affect the attitude toward the brand and purchase behavior. This impact would occur simply because of the association formed between the feeling and the brand through many repetitions.

We need to point out here that the ad-evoked feelings, the attitude toward the advertisement, and the use transformation can themselves be affected by the thinking activity—the arrow of effect doesn't simply flow from feelings and ad attitude to thinking, but also from thinking to feelings and ad attitude. For example, prior cognitive beliefs (for example, that it is offensive to advertise hemorrhoid products on television) could influence an attitude toward an advertisement (for example, a hemorrhoid advertisement). Also, an advertisement could be liked because it is informative, even when it essentially generates no feelings at all. We will discuss this aspect of liking for an ad later on.

The Association Process

Note the important role that the associative processes play in the model. In particular, the positive feelings or positive attitudes toward the advertisement or the transformed use experience created by the advertisement need to be associated with the brand. Advertising history is full of examples of campaigns that have been extremely entertaining and well liked but had no impact in part because the ads did not get associated with the brand. Audience viewers could recall much of the ad but not the brand advertised. The association is enhanced when the brand is made the hero of the ad, and when some kind of unique link is suggested between the brand and the feeling.

A very successful Dr Pepper campaign, for example, had people search for an unusual and exciting ("out of the ordinary") drink option.[3] The main character would voice dissatisfaction with ordinary drinks. There would be a certain anger and tension even though the total setting was bizarre and the commercial as a whole was humorous. The solution, as illustrated in Figure 7-2, was Dr Pepper. The brand was an integral

Figure 7-2. The brand as hero—Sugar Free Dr Pepper
Courtesy of Dr Pepper Company.

part of the ad, the hero. It would be impossible to recall the ad without recalling its hero, Dr Pepper.

Theory and research from psychology can provide insights into how this association is created. One such theory, the exposure effect, was discussed in Chapter 5. In the balance of this chapter the various components of the Figure 7-1 model will be explored. A discussion of how advertising can transform the use experience will be followed by a section on the attitude toward the advertisement. Classical conditioning will be discussed next in this chapter. The focus will then turn to specific types of feelings (such as humor, warmth, and fear), discussing what they are, how and when they should be targeted, and so on. Conditions under which feelings will emerge or be enhanced, and conditions under which "emotional advertising" is most appropriate, will then be explored.

ADVERTISING THAT TRANSFORMS THE USE EXPERIENCE

Transformational advertising, a concept associated with Dr. William Wells of DDB Needham, involves developing associations with the brand or brand use such that the experience of using the brand is transformed or changed into something quite different.[4] Puto and Wells note that transformational advertising contains the following characteristics:[5]

1. It must make the experience of using the product richer, warmer, more exciting, and/or more enjoyable than that obtained solely from an objective description of the advertised brand.
2. It must connect the experience of the advertisement so tightly with the experience of using the brand that consumers cannot remember the brand without recalling the experience generated by the advertisement.

How Transformational Advertising Works

There are several theoretical explanations as to how transformational advertising might work. One is that the feeling engendered during the commercial gets transferred to the use experience. The audience understands and relates so closely with the actors in the advertisement that the experience portrayed corresponds to actually having the experience. The key, then, would be for the commercial to be empathetic, believable, and meaningful, perhaps reminding the audience of experiences they have had in their lives. Thus, when the use occasion occurs, the experience and associated feeling are simply repeated. The use experience then makes the feeling experience stimulated by the next commercial exposure even stronger.

Another explanation is that the audience perceives the strong feeling response from the actors toward the use of the brand.[6] Over time, and with repetition, the audience will eventually associate the feeling response to the brand just as the actors did. In essence, through repetitions of the advertising and use experience, the vicarious experience becomes a real experience.

A third explanation is based on the generalized emotion concept of Clynes.[7] Transformational advertising may facilitate the recall of past experiences associated with the feeling engendered by the advertising. The recall is effortless and the focus is on drawing on similar feelings from past experiences rather than the recall of the actual experiences. Further, the audience may create new fantasies that will then be associated with the feeling. They may, in effect, embellish the scene in the commercial to make it more relevant to them. Puto and Wells note that this fantasy creation is illustrated by the Marlboro Country advertising, where "viewers were free to overlay their own feelings and fantasies onto the scene, and these feelings and fantasies then become permanently associated with the experience of smoking the advertised brand of cigarette."[8]

Wells has suggested that a successful transformational advertising campaign must be able to make and maintain the necessary associations, and it must put forth a positive campaign that rings true and seems authentic, even if it is not literally true.[9]

Creating and Maintaining Associations

Transformational advertising involves two types of associations. Creating and maintaining both are crucial to its success. The first are the associations of feelings with the use experience. It may be desired to associate with the use experience feelings (the use of Grandma's Cookies generates "motherly" feelings) or the type of user (active, stylish people wear Levi's jeans). A Löwenbrau beer campaign, for example, may try to associate warm feelings and relaxed camaraderie with the Löwenbrau use experience. The second is the association between the use experience that has to be created and the brand.

To achieve these associations, it is necessary to

- Have a substantial media budget
- Maintain consistency over time
- Closely connect the brand with the advertising

Adequate Budget.   Informational advertising can sometimes work with a single exposure. However, transformational feeling advertising requires heavy repetition to build the associations. The link between the advertiser and the use experience requires constant reinforcement. If Marlboro were to stop advertising, someone else could occupy Marlboro Country. Thus, a media budget and schedule delivering frequent exposure are necessary. Further, advertising testing must also adjust to the reality that the advertising impact is based on many exposures. Thus, single-exposure tests will probably understate the impact and may actually have little relevance in the evaluation of a commercial's ultimate performance in a transformational campaign.

Consistency.   To obtain and retain the desired associations, transformational advertising must be consistent over time. The thrust of the campaign cannot be allowed to change frequently. It might be desirable or even necessary to be consistent for decades. That does not mean that the advertising needs to be repetitive (variations on a theme, rather than the same identical execution, could be used). It simply means that it needs to be cohesive, supporting the same associations.

Links to the Brand.   The advertising needs to connect the use experience that is being created to the brand so tightly that people cannot recall one without thinking of the other. What will be ineffective is to establish the right use experience but not the association with the brand. Wells notes that a series of soap ads used the lines[10]

- "New blouse?" "No, new bleach"
- "New dress?" "No, new bleach"
- "New shirt?" "No, new bleach"

Almost everyone remembered the line but almost no one remembered the advertiser.

Prescriptions for Transformational Advertising

Effective transformational advertising should be positive. It should make the experience richer, warmer, and more enjoyable. An implication is that transformational advertising may be inappropriate for some products. It will be difficult to turn scrubbing the floor, cleaning the oven, or taking a laxative into fun, upbeat experience. However, transformational advertising has been used to mitigate an unpleasant experience. For example, some of the transformational airline advertising has probably helped some face the anxieties of flying.

Conversely, there are some situations when transformational advertising is more likely to work. Hoch and Ha have suggested and shown that advertising is more capable of influencing consumers' perceptions about the quality of products, and by implication the nature of their usage experiences, when these consumers are less able to make quality judgments for themselves (situations that they label "ambiguous").[11] For instance, if I walk into a fast-food establishment that is clearly and unambiguously filthy, it will be more difficult for advertising to transform that into a warm and enjoyable experience. Transformational advertising is more likely to work when a consumer cannot make quality judgments for himself or herself and needs advertising to help interpret the product or use experience, because the situation is open to multiple interpretations. This is more likely in service situations, situations when sensory experiences are involved (fragrances, liquor, food, etc.), and when consumer expertise and knowledge are minimal.

Transformational advertising must also ring true. It will not be effective if it is disconfirmed by real-life experiences with the product. No amount of "ride the friendly rails" would transform the experience of riding dirtier sections of the New York subway. This does not mean that the ad must be *literally* true; most people watching an ad for Keebler don't believe in elves, but they do accept that elves would behave as depicted in those ads, if elves did in fact exist. This property of "ringing true" (even if not literally true) has been called "verisimilitude" and is discussed further later in this chapter.

ATTITUDE TOWARD THE ADVERTISEMENT

Perhaps the simplest explanation of how a feeling advertisement works is that people like it or dislike it *as an ad*, and this attitude gets transformed to or associated with the brand in the ad. There is thus the potential for a direct causal link between the attitude toward an advertisement and attitude and behavior toward a brand. As noted in Figure 7-1, feelings engendered by an ad can create or influence an attitude toward the ad directly, as well as indirectly, through assessments of the quality of the ad's executional characteristics. In fact, some researchers believe that attitude to the ad really has two different components: an affective one, reflecting the direct effect of the feelings evoked by the ad, and a second more cognitive one, reflecting how well made and useful the ad is considered to be.[12]

Mitchell and Olson demonstrated that the attitude toward an ad provided an impact over and above any ability of the ad to communicate attribute information.[13] They created four print ads for facial tissue, one with an explicit softness claim, another with a picture of a kitten, a third with a sunset picture, and a fourth with an abstract painting. Subjects were exposed to each ad either two, four, six, or eight times in a single setting. A significant amount of the brand attitude created could be explained by beliefs as to the tissue's softness, absorbency, and other attributes. However, a substantial additional amount of the brand attitude was caused by the attitude toward the ad. This shows that it is important, in understanding how an ad ultimately affects brand attitude, to see what kind of attitude people develop toward the ad itself. If the feelings that the ad creates are positive, and if the way the ad is made is evaluated favorably, then the ad should elicit a favorable attitude toward itself.

A considerable amount of research has been conducted on the mechanisms through which the thoughts and feelings evoked by an ad lead to a favorable attitude to the ad, and how (and under what conditions) the attitude to the ad leads to favorable brand attitudes. According to researchers MacKenzie, Lutz, and Belch, attitude to the ad is influenced by the cognitions (thoughts and feelings) that the ad viewer has about the ad; this ad attitude then affects brand attitudes, which then affects the intention to buy or not buy the brand. In addition, however, the attitude toward the ad also affects the viewer's cognitions that relate to the brand, which of course also affect attitude to the brand. In other words, attitude toward the ad affects attitude toward the brand both directly, and indirectly (through shaping brand cognitions).[14] If we like an ad we are predisposed to being less critical about what the ad is saying about the brand. This is similar to the top portion of Figure 7-1, where we said that positive feelings evoked by an ad can lead to more positive (and fewer negative) thoughts about the brand.

Researchers have also tested if the attitude to the ad has a greater effect on brand attitudes under low-involvement conditions. Intuitively, just as the elaboration likelihood model (ELM) suggests a greater effect of peripheral cues on brand attitudes under low-involvement conditions, one would expect a greater effect of attitude to the ad on brand attitudes under low-involvement conditions (since the feelings that play a major role in shaping attitude to the ad are clearly peripheral in nature). Yet the research on this question has not always shown this relationship; it seems instead that attitude to the ad is often a contributor to brand attitudes under both high- and low-involvement conditions.[15] Why this is so is not totally clear, but it seems that the different components of attitude to the ad (evaluation of the pleasure from it, and its usefulness), taken together, require *both* central and peripheral processing, so that it becomes an important variable under both high- and low-involvement conditions.[16] In other words, while the feelings that we are focusing on in this chapter are a major contributor to the attitude to the ad, they are not the only factors leading to it: a more cognitive, "central," appraisal of how useful the ad is, how informative it is, and how well made it is also plays a major role.

Factors Leading to High Attitudes Toward the Ad

The preceding sentence suggests we should spend some time discussing exactly what factors lead to an ad toward which consumers develop a favorable attitude. It is not enough to simply look at the net attitude toward the ad; we need to understand how it is created. According to a recent model,[17] the attitude to the ad is influenced by the feelings evoked by the ad and the mood of the ad viewer, the ad viewer's attitude toward all ads in general, his or her attitude toward this advertiser in general, his or her perceptions of the executional characteristics of the ad, and his or her perceptions of the credibility and believability of the ad. While the first three are relatively more "peripheral" (being mostly involuntary and automatic reactions), the last two are relatively more "central," in that they require the ad recipient to process cognitively the content of the ad. This model supports the idea that the attitude to the ad has both "peripheral" and "central" influences, though exactly which of these influences is most important would itself vary with the consumer's involvement with the message in the ad, the ad's own distinctiveness in its execution, and so on.

In the model just described, one factor shaping attitude to the ad is the nature of the execution. Different ads can lead to the same overall level of attitude to the ad by following very different executional strategies. For example, three equally liked commercials (i.e., having the same levels of attitude to the ad), one using slapstick humor, another employing serious informative copy, and a third with warm, sentimental copy, may impact the consumer in completely different ways, as could two equally disliked commercials, one that is considered boring and the other irritating.

There has been little research attempting to determine what it is that makes some commercials liked and how the liking level is affected by repetition. One study by Aaker and Bruzzone did explore the copy characteristics that distinguished irritating commercials.[18] They located 18 pairs of commercials for the same product (10 had a common brand and 5 had common copy) with significantly different irritation levels. They found that the ads with higher irritation levels tended to portray an unbelievable situation, a "putdown" person, a threatened relationship, graphic physical discomfort, tension, an unattractive or unsympathetic character, a suggestive scene, poor casting, or a sensitive product with a product-focused message. Irritation levels were lowered when the commercial included or conveyed a happy mood, a warm mood, a credible spokesman, humor, or useful information.

Of interest was the level of irritation that crept in when a person was "put down" or an important relationship such as that of a mother and daughter or a wife and husband was threatened. For example, in one Head and Shoulders commercial, a wife, who is positioned as a hair expert, smiles as she tells her husband about his dandruff problem and about Head and Shoulders. In contrast, in the companion commercial that had virtually identical copy, a husband is serious when voicing the key line, ''I've got something to tell you.'' In this case, the wife seemed much more vulnerable and threatened. Apparently, it was irritating to see the husband being so judgmental about the woman's appearance and perhaps even her acceptability.

Recall Effects of the Attitude Toward an Advertisement

A positive attitude toward an advertisement, in addition to creating higher levels of attitude to the brand, can also affect advertising impact in a variety of other ways, such as improving the recall of the advertised material.[19] Remember from Chapter 5 that recall and attitudes are different goals, achieved through different information processing mechanisms. A well-liked ad, not surprisingly, is also remembered longer (though some standard recall copy tests actually show feeling ads doing poorer on recall measures than they should, a point discussed later in our copy-testing chapter). Interestingly, there is an argument that even disliked commercials can be effective in terms of recall and that, in fact, it is much better to be disliked than to be ignored. That is, both liked and disliked ads are supposed to be better on recall than are neutral ads.

There is no shortage of anecdotal evidence that irritating commercials have been effective. The classic example is the strong Rosser Reeves campaigns of past decades featuring his Unique Selling Propositions for Anacin, in which a hammer hitting a head was shown again and again and again. There are two explanations as to why a disliked ad can be effective in leading to brand preference via creating high recall.[20] First, in some contexts, attention to the ad, and processing of the information in it, could be increased without the negative feeling reaction being transferred to the product. Second, brand familiarity is created which, particularly for low-involvement products that are bought on the basis of awareness rather than attitudes, may lead to increased brand choice. This is most likely to be effective if, over time, the negative ad becomes disassociated from the brand (termed the ''sleeper effect''). Thus, the impact of the ad-created negative feelings on the attitude to the brand declines over time, while the brand's awareness and familiarity remain high.

THE ROLE OF CLASSICAL CONDITIONING

One explanation as to how feeling advertising works draws on the theory of classical conditioning, which is based on Pavlov's work in the 1920s. Pavlov exposed a neutral stimulus, a metronome, termed a conditioned stimulus (CS), to a hungry dog. The conditioned stimulus was followed by another stimulus, the unconditioned stimulus (US), namely, food. The food automatically evoked a response, called the unconditioned response (UR), namely, salivation. As a result of the pairing of the two stimuli, the metronome (CS) and the food (US), the dog eventually salivated even when only the metronome stimulus was present, a response which is called the conditioned response (CR)—the dog became conditioned to it. Diagrammatically,

UNCONDITIONED STIMULUS (US)→UNCONDITIONED RESPONSE (UR)
Food   Salivation
Commercial   Positive attitude or feelings

CONDITIONED STIMULUS (CS) ——→ CONDITIONED RESPONSE (CR)
Metronome   Salivation
Brand or brand use   Positive attitude or feelings

Notice that there is no reinforcement present. The conditioned response does not occur because the subject has been rewarded or reinforced. It is simply due to the fact that the conditioned and unconditioned stimuli are related systematically in time (i.e., one always follows, precedes, or occurs simultaneously with the other), and the two thus became associated. In our context, there is a commercial with actors and a scene that represents the unconditioned stimulus. The positive attitude toward the ad or the positive feelings are the unconditioned response. The idea is to pair the brand or use of the brand, which is the neutral or conditioned stimulus, with the commercial content, the unconditioned stimuli. The goal is to have the unconditioned response become the conditioned response, that is, the brand or use of the brand should precipitate the same positive attitude or feelings that the commercial did.

The classical conditioning theory has rarely been applied to affect (liking) in humans. Thus, there is a good deal of controversy as to whether it can be used to explain the use of advertising, particularly feeling advertising, to create positive attitudes. Three influential studies addressing this very point are described in the paragraphs that follow.

Three Conditioning Experiments

In a pioneering experiment, Gorn showed that background music (UC) could be associated with a colored pen (CS).[21] Two hundred students heard music played while watching a slide containing a print ad with little information for an inexpensive pen costing 49 cents. Half the group heard a known "liked" one-minute segment of music from a popular musical. The ad showed a beige pen for half of this group and a light blue pen for the other half. The other half heard classical Indian music, known to be disliked by these students. All subjects later were invited to select one of the two colored pens. A total of 79 percent picked the color associated with the liked music. When asked why, 62 percent said they had a reason. Most said they had a color preference and no one mentioned the music. While Gorn's study suggests that conditioning processes do work in advertising, with just one exposure, two subsequent studies failed to get results similar to Gorn's, and it is not really clear whether Gorn's results were actually due to conditioning, or to some other processes.[22]

Another study, by Bierley et al., exposed 100 subjects to four sets of three colored arbitrary geometric stimuli.[23] In the first two sets, red stimuli were always followed by well-liked music, and yellow was never followed by this music. In the second set the colors were changed. In the third, continuous music was in the background, and in the fourth, no music was present. The preference for a stimulus was higher when it predicted music than when it did not for both colors.

Finally, Kroeber-Riel paired a model brand name with emotion-loaded pictures in slide advertisements.[24] The pictures conveyed emotional events concerned with eroticism, social happiness, and exotic landscapes. A day after the conditioning the name alone aroused significant emotional reactions. Importantly, the conditioning worked only after 30 five-second exposures (20 was inadequate), and only if the stronger of two emotional scenes was used.

Some Relevant Classical Conditioning Findings

There has been an enormous amount of classical conditioning research conducted over the past five decades, and many of the findings have relevance to advertising. Research has consistently shown that for conditioning effects to emerge, you need (1) multiple exposures; (2) the CS consistently preceding the US in time, so that the consumer becomes aware that the two are associated—that one follows the other; (3) a CS and a US that somehow "fit" or "belong" together; (4) CSs that are novel and unfamiliar, such as brands that are new; and (5) USs that are biologically or symbolically salient (i.e., they "stand out").[25] Typically, conditioning effects cannot emerge with single exposures, or if the US is an already familiar stimulus (such as a well-known piece of music, unless the music is being used in a very novel way or a different context).

In addition, consider the following relevant phenomena:

1. *Acquisition.* The strength of the conditioned response increases as a function of the number of pairings of the US and the CS. However, each pairing results in a smaller increase in strength than the previous one until, after many pairings, the strength of the CR does not increase meaningfully. Thus, advertisers should plan to use enough repetitions to create the necessary associations. The speed of acquisition of the CR will depend on the salience of the US—how interesting and important it is to the audience. Therefore, it is important to involve strong US (the advertisement should make an impact), and CS (the brand or its use) needs to be prominent and strongly linked to the US.

2. *Extinction.* Classical conditioned behavior will disappear if the relationship between the US and the CS is broken because, for example, a new advertising campaign does not maintain the same US. Suppose that a jingle (US) which generates a positive, upbeat feeling (UR) has been associated with a soft drink (CS). If the soft drink advertising is presented without the jingle, the CR will also disappear. Note that extinction is different from forgetting. The jingle may still be recalled, but the association will not be there.

3. *Generalization.* Generalization occurs when a new conditioned stimulus (CS_2) resembles the original conditioned stimulus (CS_1) and thus generates the same con-

ditioned response. The color preferences generated in the Bierley et al. experiment generalized to colored shapes different from those used in the experiment. Thus, product extensions such as new varieties of a breakfast cereal might be presented in such a way as to create generalization.

The discrimination/generalization phenomenon is particularly important when competitive advertising is considered. There is always the possibility that your brand could be generalized to a competitive brand, a development that could have a positive as well as a negative impact. For example, COMPAQ makes a computer compatible with the IBM PC. It may be very helpful for COMPAQ to have generalization occur. They could then actually benefit from IBM's advertising.

FEELINGS EXPERIENCED BY AUDIENCE MEMBERS

Undoubtedly, there are countless numbers of feelings and combinations of feelings that could potentially be precipitated by advertising. The fact is that we not only know little about how such feelings affect the persuasion process, but we do not even really know which feelings are the most relevant. There do exist many lists of feelings, emotions, and moods that may be helpful.

The psychologist Plutchik, for example, developed a list of 40 emotion words, including[26]

Defiant	Adventurous	Disgusted
Surprised	Inquisitive	Expectant
Enthusiastic	Affectionate	Curious
Receptive	Shy	Hopeless
Unhappy	Perplexed	Hesitant
Afraid	Bewildered	Annoyed
Hesitant	Sad	Cheerful
Joyful	Elated	Hostile

Any of these could be important to a given advertisement. Sadness would be aroused by a commercial showing an older woman reflecting on the loss of a mate or by an advertisement attempting to gain support for resources for a famine stricken country such as Ethiopia by portraying an undernourished child. Enthusiasm and joy might be created by commercials showing people playing volleyball at a beach with upbeat, active music in the background. A political ad might try to raise hostility toward the opponent.

Some ads can create a feeling of confidence, others can create feelings of elegance. A perfume ad showed a sophisticated woman preparing for a ball. A BMW ad showed a stylish, elegant woman slowly entering a car. Both ads surely engendered feelings of elegance, style, and class for some audience members. The Travelers ad in Figure 7-3 shows yet another feeling, that of serenity. A quiet, warm day out in the country is the feeling

Figure 7-3. Evoking a feeling of serenity: Travelers Insurance
Courtesy of the Travelers Corporation.

evoked by the L. L. Bean ad in Figure 7-4. Clearly, many of the feelings evoked by ads are not technically called emotions; some theorists call them "quasi-emotions" that may be of interest in these respective product categories.

There has by now been substantial research on the different types of feelings that can be and are created in advertising, and on how different kinds of ad content can lead to different kinds of feelings.[27] Batra and Holbrook, for instance, have identified 20 different types of distinct feelings that ads can create and have shown how to measure them validly and reliably. Based on such research, some advertising agencies consciously decide which kinds of feelings they need to create in particular situations and then design ads that have appropriate content and executional elements (such as the type of music, visual editing, and celebrity used). The ads can then be copytested to see if the targeted feelings are indeed being created, and if feelings that are not sought are inadvertently emerging.

Among the feelings that have been studied in the advertising context in some depth are warmth, humor, and fear.

Warmth in Advertising

When audiences are asked to describe advertisements, one dimension that is used can be interpreted as perceived warmth. The Aaker and Bruzzone study found a warmth dimension associated with commercials that utilized sentimental/family/kids/friends–feelings/feel good about yourself creative approaches.[28] Wells et al. included adjectives such as gentle, tender, soothing, serene, and lovely into a dimension they termed sensuousness.[29] Schlinger found an "empathy factor" associated with commercials involving affectionate couples, warm relationships, mother-child interactions, attractive products, vacation settings, or appealing characters such as Pillsbury's soft and cuddly doughboy.[30]

The warmth construct emerging from these dissimilar studies, although certainly complex, has some consistent characteristics and associations. It has been defined by Aaker, Stayman, and Hagerty to be "a positive, mild, transitory emotion involving physiological response and precipitated by experiencing directly or vicariously a love, family or friendship relationship."[31] A detached expression of love or friendship without concurrent involvement and physiological arousal would not generate warmth. On the other hand, a relationship experience in which the involvement, depth of feeling, and physiological arousal were extremely high would be too intense to be warm. Warmth is thus positioned as moderate in terms of involvement, depth of feeling, and physiological arousal. It is short term in duration—capable of being created or changed in seconds or minutes rather than hours or days.

A notable aspect of the definition is the suggestion that the direct or vicarious experience of a love, family, or friendship relationship is involved. Thus, it follows in the tradition of Charles Darwin, who did pioneering work on emotions in humans and animals, and many modern psychologists who view emotions in a social context. Averill, for example, defines emotions as transitory social roles.[32] Thus, a social object such as a person or persons, animal, organization (for example, fraternity, team, or club), or institution (for example, country) will usually be involved. Further, this social object will

When I was growing up, you rode a
10-speed, took long road trips,
and pedaled furiously all day. Now,
it's more relaxed. The kids and I
take it slow, poking around these old
dirt roads. It's real quiet and
the air smells fresh and clean. We've
even snuck up on a deer now and
then. Plus, it's nice to get out and do
something special with my children.
Just the three of us.

L. L. Bean.
For the outdoors inside each of us.

For 78 years, L. L. Bean has offered durable, practical products for men and women who love the outdoors.
Our catalog includes active and casual apparel, footwear, equipment and accessories.
All fully guaranteed and honestly priced. If you'd like a copy, please call 1-800-543-9089 anytime.

© L. L. Bean, 1990

Figure 7-4. Evoking feelings of outdoors, "with nature" relaxation: L. L. Bean
Courtesy of L. L. Bean.

usually be linked to another social object in a relationship that involves emotions such as love, pride, acceptance, joy, sentimentality, tenderness, or happiness.

In the advertising context, warmth can be experienced vicariously when one or more characters in a commercial are experiencing warmth. For example, a happy dinner scene in a Löwenbräu commercial between a proud father and a son who just passed his bar exam shows feelings of warmth in both characters. The viewer could become involved enough to share the emotional experience vicariously with one or perhaps both. An advertisement could also involve a relationship between the audience member and a character in the commercial. The commercial character might be the object of pride or love. For example, an audience member might be proud of an elderly person seen accomplishing a difficult task or an athlete winning an Olympic gold medal. Finally, a viewer might be reminded of a prior warm experience by a commercial and be stimulated to relive it. For example, a Christmas scene could recall warm family moments.

A Warmth Experiment.   One series of experiments concluded the following about the warmth construct:[33]

1. A "warmth monitor," where respondents continuously recorded their felt warmth by moving a pencil down a paper that was scaled from "emotional, moist eyes" to "warmhearted, tender" to "neutral" to "absence of warmth," was used to show that commercials are capable of altering felt warmth levels substantially with even the first portion of a 30-second commercial.
2. Warmth was accompanied by physiological arousal. The warm level was correlated (the correlation averaged 0.67 across six warm commercials) with galvanic skin response (GSR), one of the commonly used measures of physiological arousal.
3. Warm commercials were clearly more effective in terms of postexposure measures such as liking of the ad, copy recall, and purchase intention when they followed a humorous or irritating commercial rather than another warm commercial, even when the humorous commercial was equally well liked. The probable explanation from adaption theory is that a warm commercial will appear warmer when the audience becomes used to the warmth level of a very different type of commercial.
4. A strong relationship between warmth levels and the change in warmth throughout the commercial and the postexposure commercial impact was found, which suggests that warmth does indeed contribute to a commercial's impact.

Humor

As noted previously, humor appeals—because of the feelings of amusement and pleasure they evoke—can potentially affect information processing in a variety of ways such as attracting attention, improving memory of the brand name, creating a good mood, and distracting the audience from counterarguing. In recent years, as the amount of advertising clutter has increased dramatically, the ability of humorous ads to gain attention has become even more valuable. Advertising testing results have confirmed that humorous ads have higher recall.[34]

The concern here is with the feeling that accompanies humor in advertising and the associated laughter. In terms of the foregoing list, it probably involves feelings such as surgency, energy, cheer, joy, and happiness. The potential exists, of course, for the feelings engendered by this humor to become associated with the brand, thereby affecting the attitude toward the brand and perhaps its image/beliefs as well. Clearly, a humor-based appeal is complex and much is yet to be learned about it.

Of course, even a casual observer of humor in advertising will note that there are very different types. For example, some humorous advertising is very warm, such as a charming old couple teasing one another. Other humor efforts are very sophisticated and clever, such as a series in which James Garner bantered with Mariette Hartley about Polaroid. Then there is the heavy slapstick commercials such as those for Dorito Corn Chips, in which characters are knocked over by the sound of a loud crunch. Consider also the boisterous, silly commercials for Miller Lite Beer. Humor can be created through the use of puns, understatement, jokes, ludicrous executional elements, satire, irony, and so on. Clearly, each of these approaches will involve different sets of feelings.

One of the difficulties in working with humor is that what strikes one person as humorous, another will simply consider silly and irritating. Thus, it is particularly important with humor to have a good concept of the target audience. Further, the tendency for humor to irritate undoubtedly will increase with repetition. Since feeling advertising requires repetition to build associations, the tendency for some to become irritated is enhanced. The use of many executions for the same campaign will reduce the problem but it still will remain. A third problem is that humor is often very successful in attracting attention to and creating liking for the ad, but can hurt the comprehension of the main intended copy point—though, if communicated, that copy point may be accepted more easily (perhaps because the humor distracts the consumer from generating counterarguments). It has also been found that the use of humor can enhance the appeal of an endorser who has to make an otherwise dull appeal.[35]

The use of humor is definitely culture-bound: tastes for different kinds of humor vary over cultures, and the acceptability of humor as an advertising creative approach also varies. British ads, for instance, use more humor than do U.S. ads,[36] and British humor does not always play well in the United States. A U.S. campaign for Kronenbourg beer which used a heavy dose of British humor was disliked by the managers of the French parent firm.[37] The campaign would have been killed had it not been so successful. Sales increased 22.5 percent during the year, while sales for total imported beers were up only 14 percent. One radio spot (featuring John Cleese of the Monty Python group) described the brew's slogan "better, not bitter" as the "current No. 1 advertising disaster" and that the beer is a "terrific beer that doesn't taste as if it had a dead rat in it."[38] Later spots begged the audience to try the beer, as "it is the leading bottle of beer in the whole of Europe—it's not going to kill you."[39]

Fear Appeals

Fear or anxiety, a very different type of feeling than warmth or humor, has been used in a variety of contexts.[40] The most obvious are those involving a product designed to protect a person from loss of property (automobile or home insurance) or health (life insurance or antismoking campaigns). Advertising for seat belts and against smoking have both focused on the fear of losing one's life. There are also more subtle fears associated with social and psychological motivations—the loss of friends, status, or job or a sense of failure to be a good parent or homemaker. Such fears are relevant to personal-care products (mouthwash, toothpaste) and homemaking products (foods and appliances).

Fear appeals engender the emotional response of fear as well as related feelings such as fright, disgust, and discomfort. However, one well-accepted theory of fear appeals, the "parallel response model" of the psychologist Leventhal, suggests that a cognitive response, the belief that harm is likely to occur, is evoked in addition to the emotional response.[41] Both responses need to be considered in attempting to predict the reaction of audience members. The preferred audience reaction is to comply with the communication and change attitudes or behavior accordingly. The alternative is to engage in defensive processes such as to deny vulnerability, counterargue, become irritated at something in the ad, or ignore it.

For the preferred "comply" reaction to occur, the fear needs to be at just the right level. If it is too low, the emotional response will not be forthcoming and the ad will not be successful at creating attention and interest in the basic problem. If it is too high, the audience member will attempt to activate some defense mechanism to avoid facing the problem. Clearly, the level will be sensitive to the target audience. Strong fear appeals for campaigns such as antismoking should probably be directed at teens who do not now smoke. If they were directed at smokers already concerned, a strong appeal may result in an avoidance strategy. For low-involvement products such as mouthwash, the problem may be to generate a strong enough appeal to break through the perceptual filter.

Equally important to the fear level is to provide an acceptable solution to the problem, one that the audience member feels that he or she is capable of pursuing. Without some reassurance that the solution is feasible, the audience member will tend to "turn off" the message. Thus, there needs to be a cognitive element. According to a recent view called "protection motivation theory," a fear needs four elements to be successful: the ad must convince the target that (1) the depicted threat is very likely, (2) that it will have severe consequences, (3) that the advocated behavioral change or action will lead to a removal of the threat, and (4) that the target consumer can in fact carry out the advocated behavior.[42] For example, an antidrug ad aimed at teenagers must show that drug consumption will very likely lead to addiction; that such addiction will create severe biological, financial, and social consequences, possibly even death; that it is possible to not take drugs, even when faced with peer pressure; and that the target consumer has that capability to fight peer pressure.

WHAT AFFECTS THE INTENSITY OF FEELINGS?

The intensity of feelings or emotions precipitated by the advertising will depend on many factors. Although research is still preliminary, it seems likely that an advertisement attempting to generate an emotional response should be believable and engender empathy.[43]

Believability.   If a person is to share an emotional experience vicariously or to be stimulated to relive a prior emotional experience, it may be necessary for there to be literal believability. If the scene is not realistic, if it could not happen in real life, it will be more difficult to generate a meaningful emotional response.

For any emotional response to occur, it seems evident that the advertisement must have verisimilitude—the appearance of truth or the depiction of realism, as in the theater or literature. The scene may not be literally true, but the commercial generates a willing suspension of disbelief. It has a ring of truth—if paper towels could speak, they would speak that way. There is no distracting thought that the scene is phony, contrived, or silly. For example, the introduction of a mouthwash solution to a social situation might be so contrived as to disrupt the verisimilitude and prevent the desired emotion from emerging. Thus, believability can act as a block to and/or an enhancer of an emotional response.

Empathy.   If empathy is high and thus the understanding of another's situation is deeper, the emotional response should be more likely and more intense. Empathy will tend to be higher if the characters in the commercial are similar to the audience member and the settings are familiar. It will also tend to be higher when the audience member has had an experience identical or similar to that shown in the advertisement. The expectation is that a prior experience should make it easier to experience another's feelings vicariously. If a viewer has experienced the exultation of winning a tennis championship, he or she may be more likely to share vicariously the emotions of a commercial character who is clearly experiencing such emotions.

It has been suggested that one way to increase the amount of consumer empathy (and also the amount of verisimilitude, discussed earlier), is to make an advertisement that uses a "drama" form, that depicts a situation and draws in the viewer into the action it portrays (contrasted with the more usual "lecture" form, which makes straightforward arguments about why the brand is better). A good drama has both a plot and distinct characters. When a drama is successful, the audience becomes "lost" in the story and experiences the concerns and feelings of the characters.[44] A drama's appeal is processed empathically; it succeeds if the viewer is in fact pulled into the story.

WHEN ARE FEELINGS MORE IMPORTANT?

The role of feelings in advertising is most obvious for commercials that contain little or no product information for which feelings obviously play an important role. Ray and Batra have suggested that attitudes toward a brand have two components, an evaluative component that is influenced by beliefs about the brand and a brand-specific "liking" component that cannot be explained by knowledge about beliefs.[45] This "liking" component is presumed to be based on the attitude toward the ad as well as by exposure effects. The relative importance or "percentage contribution" of "liking" will be high when the amount of brand attribute information and associated processing effort are low. This suggests that feelings are probably more important in shaping brand attitudes in low-involvement situations. Consistent with this view, humor—as one example of feeling appeals—has not tended to be appropriate for high-involvement situations. Federal Express Corporation dropped its lighthearted, humorous campaigns in favor of more serious, technology-based arguments (such as spare jets and backup computers, used to increase reliability), when competition intensified in the overnight package delivery business intensified in 1989.[46] The use of the Peanuts characters by Met Life (see Figure 7-5) to create a warm, likable feeling for the insurance company (and its agents) did not succeed in communicating its unique products and performance record.[47] Alka-Selzer's famous and well liked "I can't believe I ate the whole thing" humor ads did not stop the brand from losing sales when consumers decided they wanted antacid products with different formulations.[48]

However, involvement is only part of the story. According to the Foote, Cone & Belding (FCB) advertising agency, product categories (and different segments of product categories) can be classified into four categories, based on whether they are high or low in involvement and on whether they are "thinking" or "feeling" products. Thus "feeling" products can be either high involvement (as in the case of cosmetics, jewelry, and fashion clothing) or low involvement (e.g., beer, cigarettes, and candy). On the thinking products side, high-involvement products are illustrated by big-ticket items such as cars, appliances, and insurance, while low-involvement products are represented by paper towels, household cleaners, and gasoline. (See Figure 7-6.) This "grid" has been extensively researched by FCB in many countries, and the firm recommends that feeling advertising is most appropriate for products and services that fall on the feeling side of the grid.

It should not be assumed that feelings are always inappropriate in commercials that are informative, stressing product attributes. For example, one commercial was classified as very informative because its thrust was to communicate the effectiveness of a mosquito repellant. The commercial recruited a person to test the product by placing an arm in a container of mosquitoes. The shock and horror of the participant was extremely emotional, and this emotion unquestionably affected the commercial's impact.

SUMMARY

In addition to communicating information, advertising can generate feelings such as warmth, happiness, and fear. Such feelings can become associated with the brand and can influence attitudes and behavior toward the brand in four ways.

First, ads that put people in positive moods can increase the number of positive thoughts about the brand, and reduce the number of negative thoughts. This can raise brand attitudes. People in positive ad-induced moods also tend to do less thinking about the intrinsic quality of the brand and tend to form brand attitudes based more on ad likability (the "peripheral" route of attitude formation).

Second, "transformational" advertising transforms the use experience by associating feelings with it. It makes the experience richer, warmer, more exciting, and/or more enjoyable. For transformational advertising to work, it must be positive and ring true and the associations (between the feelings and the use experience and between the brand and the use experience) must be created and maintained with heavy repetition.

Figure 7-5. Creating a warm, likable feeling: MetLife

Courtesy of Metropolitan Life Insurance Company and United Feature Syndicate, Inc.

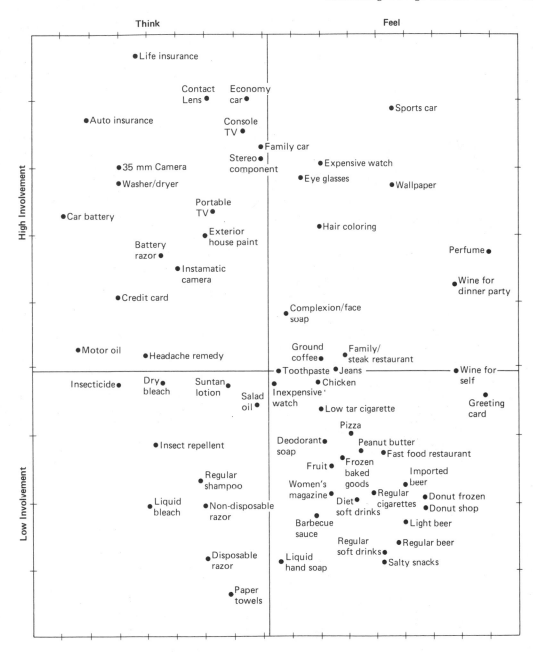

Figure 7-6. FCB grid for 60 products

Source: Modified from Ratchford, *Journal of Advertising Research*, August/September 1987, p. 31.
© 1987 by the Advertising Research Foundation.

Third, research has shown that a positive attitude toward the advertisement itself can affect the brand over and above any communication effect. Ads can be liked for one (or both) of two basic reasons: they are enjoyable, and they are informative and useful. When a feeling-based ad leads to a more positive attitude toward the ad, it can lead to more positive brand attitudes, and also to more positive thoughts about brand attributes.

Fourth, classical conditioning provides another way in which feeling responses become associated with the brand. The feeling response (UR) is associated with the commercial (US). The commercial is then associated with the brand (CS). Finally, exposure to the brand even without the commercial stimulates the same feeling response (CR). The strength of the association between the feeling and the brand or brand use will depend on several factors, such as the number of repetitions, the time since the last exposure, and how closely the brand is linked to the commercial.

There are many feelings and combinations of feelings that have potential relevance to advertising, including warmth, humor, and fear. Warmth has been shown to be very volatile, changing in a matter of seconds, yet capable of stimulating a physiological response (as measured by GSR). It is precipitated by experiencing directly or vicariously a love, family, or friendship relationship. A fear appeal in a context such as insurance advertising creates an emotional response and also a cognitive awareness of a problem. The ad should attempt to generate the optimal level of emotional response and provide a feasible solution to the problem. With humor, care is needed to ensure that some people are not irritated instead of entertained, especially over repetition.

Regardless of the specific type of feeling being evoked, advertisers have to be careful to make the evoked feeling "ring true." It must also be used in situations where it is more effective, such as the appropriateness of the product category's character ("thinking" versus "feeling" benefits), and the stage of the product life cycle (with mature brands, now less involving to consumers, being the most appropriate).

DISCUSSION QUESTIONS

1. Identify a feeling television commercial or print advertisement. Analyze exactly how it works. What feelings might be engendered by it? How will those feelings help the brand? Did the ad do well in creating an association between the brand and the feelings? How would you change the ad?

2. Analyze Figure 7-1. How would you change the model? What characteristics of the ad will affect the feeling response? To what extent is it important to have cognitive empathy—that is, the audience understanding the characters or literal believability?

3. What characteristics of the audience will be relevant in predicting the feeling response of the ad? What characteristics of the context in which the exposure is embedded will affect the emotional response?

4. Using an example of an actual commercial, explain to a friend how classical conditioning works.

5. What implications for advertising do you see for the three classical conditioning experiments that were reported? What problems do you see in applying them to the "real" world? Do the first two indicate that you do not need many repetitions?

6. What are some ads that you liked? Why? What makes an ad well liked?

7. Under what circumstances will an ad be effective even if it is disliked?

8. What is transformational advertising? How does it work? What are some examples? When should it be used? "If Marlboro ever left Marlboro Country (stopped the Marlboro Country campaign), someone else could move right in." Comment.

9. A transformational ad must "ring true." Must it have literal believability? You should not use transformation advertising for avoidance products such as oven cleaners. Do you agree?

10. What is warmth in advertising? Must a social relationship be involved? Can a sunset generate a feeling of warmth? Give some examples of warm advertising. How did the "warmth" help? Would a warm ad be more effective if it followed a humorous ad, a warm ad, or an irritating ad? Why? What would you predict would be the response to a warm ad over repetition?

11. How does humor work in advertising? Give some examples. What about fear? What other feelings can you identify as being present in advertising?

12. The chapter talks of believability, both literal and "verisimilitude." What is verisimilitude? Give some examples from current advertising. In your example, what emotional response is likely?

13. Classify products such as cars, jewelry, cigarettes, food, candy, house furnishings, and motorcycles as to whether they should use thinking or feeling advertising. Within each class divide them into high- and low-involvement products.

14. There is a saying in the advertising business, "When you have nothing to say, sing it," meaning that feeling-based advertising is most appropriate for brands that have no real point of difference over the competition. Does the research reviewed in this chapter support this saying?

NOTES

1. Stuart J. Agres, "Cognitive and Emotional Elements in Persuasion and Advertising," Working paper, The Marschalk Company, undated.

2. For tests of portions of this model, see Rajeev Batra and Michael L. Ray, "Affective Responses Mediating Acceptance of Advertising," *Journal of Consumer Research*, 13, 1986, pp. 234–249; Morris Holbrook and Rajeev Batra, "Assessing the Role of Emotions as Mediators of Consumer Responses to Advertising," *Journal of Consumer Research*, 14, December 1987, pp. 404–419; Marian Chapman Burke and Julie A. Edell, "The Impact of Feelings on Ad-Based Affect and Cognition," *Journal of Marketing Research*, 26, February 1989, pp. 69–83; Rajeev Batra and Douglas M. Stayman, "The Role of Mood in Advertising Effectiveness," *Journal of Consumer Research*, 17, September 1990, pp. 203–214; and Scott MacKenzie, Richard Lutz, and George Belch, "The Role of Attitude Toward the Ad as a Mediator of Advertising Effectiveness: A Test of Competing Explanations," *Journal of Marketing Research*, 23, May 1986, pp. 130–43.

3. Sid Hecker, "The Reality of Fantasy," Paper presented at the American Marketing Winter Conference, Phoenix, Arizona, 1985.

4. William D. Wells, "How Advertising Works," Unpublished paper, 1980, and Christopher P. Puto and William D. Wells, "Informational and Transformational Advertising: The Differential Effects of Time," in Thomas C. Kinnear, ed., *Advances in Consumer Research*, Vol. 11 (Ann Arbor, MI: Association for Consumer Research, 1983), pp. 638–643.

5. Ibid., p. 638.

6. Richard E. Petty and John T. Cacioppo, *Attitudes and Persuasion: Classic and Contemporary Approaches* (Dubuque, IA: Wm C. Brown, 1981).

7. Manfred Clynes, "The Communication of Emotion: Theory of Sentics," in Robert Plutchik and Henry Kellerman, eds., *Emotion: Theory, Research, and Experience* (New York: Academic Press, 1980), pp. 271–301.

8. Puto and Wells, 1984, "Informational and Transformational Advertising," p. 639.

9. Wells, "How Advertising Works."

10. Ibid.

11. Steven J. Hoch and Young-Won Ha, "Consumer Learning and the Ambiguity of Product Experience," *Journal of Consumer Research*, 13, October 1986, pp. 221–233.

12. Terence A. Shimp, "Attitude Toward the Ad as a Mediator of Consumer Brand Choice," *Journal of Advertising*, 10 (2), 1981, pp. 9–15, and Thomas A. Madden, Chris T. Allen, and Jacqueline L. Twible, "Attitude Toward the Ad: An Assessment of Diverse Measurement Indices Under Different Processing 'Sets,' " *Journal of Marketing Research*, 28, August 1988, pp. 242–252.

13. Andrew A. Mitchell and Jerry C. Olson, "Are Product Attribute Beliefs the Only Mediator of Advertising Effects on Brand Attitude?" *Journal of Marketing Research*, 18, August 1982, pp. 318–332. See also Meryl Paula Gardner, "Does Attitude Toward the Ad Affect Brand Attitude Under a Brand Evaluation 'Set'?" *Journal of Marketing Research*, 22, May 1985, pp. 192–198, and Richard J. Lutz, Scott B. MacKenzie, and George Belch, "Attitude Toward the Ad as a Mediator of Advertising Effectiveness: Determinants and Consequences," in Richard Bagozzi and Alice Tybout, eds., *Advances in Consumer Research*, Vol. 10 (Ann Arbor, MI: Association for Consumer Research, 1983), pp. 532–539.

14. Scott MacKenzie, Richard Lutz, and George Belch, "The Role of Attitude Toward the Ad as a Mediator of Advertising Effectiveness: A Test of Competing Explanations," *Journal of Marketing Research*, 23, May 1986, pp. 130–143.

15. For a review, see Pamela M. Homer, "The Mediating Role of Attitude Toward the Ad: Some Additional Evidence," *Journal of Marketing Research*, 27, Feburary 1990, pp. 78–85.

16. Scott B. MacKenzie and Richard J. Lutz, "An Empirical Examination of the Structural Antecedents of Attitude Toward the Ad in an Advertising Pretesting Context," *Journal of Marketing*, 53, April 1989, pp. 48–65.

17. Ibid.

18. David A. Aaker and Donald E. Bruzzone, "What Causes Irritation in Television Advertising?" *Journal of Marketing*, Summer 1985, 45, pp. 47–57.

19. Michael L. Ray and Rajeev Batra, "Emotion and Persuasion in Advertising: What We Do and Don't Know About Affect," in Richard P. Bagozzi and Alice M. Tybout, eds., *Advances in Consumer Research*, Vol. 10 (Ann Arbor, MI: Association for Consumer Research, 1983), pp. 543–547.

20. Alvin J. Silk and Terrence G. Vavra, "The Influence of Advertising's Affective Qualities on Consumer Responses," in G. D. Hughes and M. L. Ray, eds., *Consumer Information Processing* (Chapel Hill: University of North Carolina Press, 1974), pp. 157–186.

21. Gerald J. Gorn, "The Effects of Music in Advertising on Choice Behavior: A Classical Conditioning Approach," *Journal of Marketing*, 1, Winter 1982, pp. 94–101.

22. Chris T. Allen and Thomas J. Madden, "A Closer Look at Classical Conditioning," *Journal of Consumer Research*, 12, December 1985, pp. 301–315, and James J. Kellaris and Anthony D. Cox, "The Effects of

Background Music in Advertising: A Reassessment,'' *Journal of Consumer Research*, 16, June 1989, pp. 113–118.

23. Calvin Bierley, Frances K. McSweeney, and Renee Vannieuwkerk, ''Classical Conditioning of Preferences for Stimuli,'' *Journal of Consumer Research*, 12, December 1985, pp. 316–323.

24. Werner Kroeber-Riel, ''Emotional Product Differentiation by Classical Conditioning,'' in Thomas C. Kinnear, ed., *Advances in Consumer Research*, Vol. 11 (Ann Arbor, MI: Association for Consumer Research, 1983), pp. 538–543.

25. Terence A. Shimp, ''Neo-Pavlovian Conditioning and Its Implications for Consumer Theory and Research,'' in T. S. Robertson and H. H. Kassarjian, eds., *Handbook of Consumer Theory and Research*, 1991.

26. Robert Plutchik, ''A General Psychoevolutionary Theory of Emotion,'' in Robert Plutchik and Henry Kellerman, eds., *Emotion: Theory, Research, and Experience* (New York: Academic Press, 1980), p. 18.

27. Rajeev Batra and Morris B. Holbrook, ''Developing a Typology of Affective Responses to Advertising,'' *Psychology and Marketing*, 7, Spring 1990, pp. 11–25; Marian C. Burke and Julie A. Edell, ''The Impact of Feelings on Ad-Based Affect and Cognition,'' *Journal of Marketing Research*, 26, February 1989, pp. 69–83; and Morris B. Holbrook and Rajeev Batra, ''Assessing the Role of Emotions as Mediators of Consumer Responses to Advertising,'' *Journal of Consumer Research*, 14, December 1987, pp. 404–420.

28. David A. Aaker and Donald E. Bruzzone, ''Viewer Perceptions of Prime-Time Television Advertising,'' *Journal of Advertising Research*, October 1981, pp. 15–23.

29. William D. Wells, Clark Leavitt, and Maureen McConville, ''A Reaction Profile for TV Commercials,'' *Journal of Advertising Research*, December 1971, pp. 11–15.

30. Mary Jane Schlinger, ''A Profile of Responses to Commercials,'' *Journal of Advertising Research*, 19 (2), 1979, pp. 37–46.

31. David A. Aaker, Douglas M. Stayman, and Michael R. Hagerty, ''Warmth in Advertising: Measurement, Impact, and Sequence Effects,'' *Journal of Consumer Research*, 12, March 1986, pp. 365–381.

32. James R. Averrill, ''A Constructivist View of Emotion,'' in Robert Plutchik and Henry Kellerman, eds., *Emotion: Theory, Research, and Experience* (New York: Academic Press, 1980), p. 305, and ''The Communication of Emotion,'' Clynes, p. 276.

33. Aaker, Stayman, and Hagerty, ''Warmth in Advertising.''

34. *The New York Times*, August 19, 1990, p. F5.

35. For a review of the relevant literature on humor, see Brian Sternthal and C. Samuel Craig, ''Humor in Advertising,'' *Journal of Marketing*, 37, October 1973, pp. 12–18, from which much of this discussion is taken.

36. Marc G. Weinberger and Harlan E. Spotts, ''Humor in U.S. vs. U.K. Commercials: A Comparison,'' *Journal of Advertising*, 18 (2), 1989, pp. 39–44.

37. ''Dry Humor Is Building a Thirst for Kronenbourg,'' *Business Week*, March 11, 1985, p. 120.

38. Ibid.

39. Ibid.

40. Michael L. Ray and William L. Wilkie, ''Fear: The Potential of an Appeal Neglected by Marketing,'' *Journal of Marketing*, 32, January 1970, pp. 54–62.

41. T. John Rosen, Nathaniel S. Terry, and Howard Leventhal, ''The Role of Esteem and Coping in Response to a Threat Communication,'' *Journal of Research in Personality*, 16, Spring 1983, pp. 90–110.

42. Ronald W. Rogers, ''Cognitive and Physiological Processes in Fear Appeals and Attitude Change: A Revised Theory of Protection Motivation,'' in J. Cacioppo and R. Petty, eds., *Social Psychophysiology* (New York: Guilford, 1983).

43. David A. Aaker and Douglas M. Stayman, ''What Mediates the Emotional Response to Advertising? The Case of Warmth,'' in Pat Caferata and Alice Tybout, eds., *Proceedings of the 1985 Advertising and Consumer Psychology Conference*, Chicago, 1986.

44. John Deighton, Daniel Romer, and Josh McQueen, "Using Drama to Persuade," *Journal of Consumer Re-serach,* 16, December 1989, pp. 335–343.

45. Michael L. Ray and Rajeev Batra, "Emotion and Persuasion in Advertising: What We Do and Don't Know About Affect," in Richard P. Bagozzi and Alice M. Tybout, eds., *Advances in Consumer Research,* Vol. 10 (Ann Arbor, MI: Association for Consumer Research, 1983), pp. 543–547.

46. *Advertising Age,* August 7, 1989, p. 58.

47. *Adweek's Marketing Week,* November 13, 1989, pp. 2–3.

48. *The New York Times,* January 26, 1990, Business section.

8

DEVELOPING
BRAND PERSONALITY

Modern goods are recognized as essentially psychological things which are symbolic of personal attributes and goals and of social patterns and strivings . . . all commercial objects have a symbolic character, and making a purchase involves an assessment — implicit or explicit — of this symbolism, to decide whether or not it fits.

Sidney Levy, in *Symbols for Sale*

We hold that every advertisement must be considered as a contribution to the complex symbol which is the brand image, as part of the long term investment in the reputation of the brand.

David Ogilvy, in *Confessions of an Advertising Man*

Thus far, we have discussed how advertising can make consumers more favorable to the brand by communicating information regarding product attributes or benefits (Chapter 6) or by associating certain highly valued feelings with the brand (Chapter 7). There is another way in which advertising can make brands more desirable to the consumer: the development of a "personality" for the brand. As will become clearer shortly, the task of creating a brand image often needs to move beyond attributes or feelings, to include the ultimate consequences of product use and the relationship of product use to people's life-styles, needs, and values. A positioning strategy that focuses only on attributes or feelings can be shallow and less effective than one that is based on a richer knowledge of the customer.

This chapter is divided into four major sections. First, we discuss the meaning of brand personality, and what it implies. Second, we discuss reasons why it matters, both to the consumer and to the marketer. Third, we discuss the types of advertising situations when brand personality is more likely to be important in consumer brand selection decisions. In the final section we discuss how brand personality can be created or enhanced through advertising—how it can be researched, targeted, and executed.

THE BRAND PERSONALITY

Joseph Plummer, former research director of Young & Rubicam, indicates that there are three components to a brand image: attributes, consequences, and brand personality.[1] It is perhaps more inclusive to think of a brand's image as encompassing *all* the associations that a consumer has for that brand: all the thoughts, feelings, and imagery that are mentally linked to that brand in the consumer's memory. Thus McDonald's could be linked to a character such as Ronald McDonald, an image of a "typical user" as being a young teenager or a small child (rather than a middle-aged adult), a feeling of having fun, a product characteristic such as service, a symbol such as the golden arches, a life-style such as harried and being into "junk food," an object such as a car, or an activity such as going to a movie theater next to McDonald's.

In previous chapters we have discussed at length how advertising can influence some of these associations: those with attributes or benefits (Chapter 6) and those with feelings (Chapter 7). Here we will turn to those associations within the overall brand image that are typically called "brand personality," which include (but are not limited to) associations with particular characters, symbols, endorsers, life-styles, and types of users. In the McDonald's instance, the brand personality might encompass Ronald McDonald, golden arches, fast-food consumption, and teenagers having fun. Together, such brand personality associations create a composite image of a brand that is not very different from the image that we have of other people: they make us think of a brand as if it were a person. Just as a person will have certain characteristics that define his or her personality, so can a brand.

When we think of a person, what do we think of? First, of course, there are the obvious demographic descriptors: gender (male or female), age (young or old), and income or social class (poor, middle class, or rich). Similarly, a brand can often be thought of as masculine or feminine, modern or old-fashioned, and everyday blue collar or elegantly upper class.[2] Such a characterization is often made not just of particular brands but of certain product categories or segments of them: thus wine could be thought of as more upper class than beer, regardless of the specific wine in question (though there will, of course, be gradations among wines themselves on this dimension). In thinking about the personalities of retail stores, for instance, one is quite likely to find the differences in perceived social class as being dominating: a Saks Fifth Avenue or Neiman-Marcus, for instance, has a markedly more upscale store personality than a Walmart or K Mart. Apart from the quality and high prices of the merchandise, such a store personality is also created through layout and architecture, symbols and colors used in advertising and design elements, and the quality and character of the sales personnel.[3]

Brand personality, just like human personality, goes beyond demographic descriptors, however. People typically characterize each other on hundreds of personality trait adjectives. Thus we may describe someone as being warm, stupid, mean-spirited, aggressive, and so on. Psychologists who have studied personality descriptions typically subscribe to a "trait" approach to studying and measuring human personality and believe that every person can be calibrated on the extent to which he or she possesses certain traits (such as being aggressive, warm, etc.). This approach is widely attributed to the psychologists Gordon Allport, H. J. Eysenck, and Raymond Cattell, who developed it from the late 1930s to the early 1960s. While people could potentially be measured on infinite trait adjectives, personality researchers have reduced the various adjectives to five basic underlying dimensions or factors:

1. Extraversion/introversion (example adjectives: adventurous-cautious, sociable-reclusive)
2. Agreeableness (examples: good-natured-irritable; gentle-headstrong)
3. Conscientiousness (examples: responsible-undependable; tidy-careless)
4. Emotional stability (composed-excitable; calm-anxious)
5. Culture (artistically-sensitive-insensitive; intellectual-unreflective; refined-crude; imaginative-simple)[4]

Similarly, a brand could be characterized as adventurous, headstrong, undependable, excitable, and somewhat crude. As will be elaborated on shortly, a brand could acquire such a personality profile through advertising-created associations with certain types of users (the kinds of people depicted as using it) or the kinds of people used to endorse it in the advertising. Of course, other sources of such associations might be more important than advertising, including direct observations of typical users, culturally ingrained stereotypes, word-of-mouth, and news media reports or publicity. Indeed, these avenues should be considered in tandem with advertising as ways of developing or enhancing brand personalities (developing group or peer norms are discussed in the next chapter).

In addition to being characterized on these personality traits, brand personalities—like human personalities—imply associated feelings. Thus, just as we can think of someone (or some brand) as being adventurous and excitable, we are likely also to associate with this person (or brand) feelings of surgency, excitement, or fun (for example, Pepsi). Alternatively, the act of buying or consuming some other brand might carry with it associated feelings of security and calmness (such as eating Ritz Crackers) or back-slapping folksiness (such as Bartles and Jaymes wine coolers). Eating Pepperidge Farm cookies, or drinking Campbell's soup, are likely to evoke warm, ''homey'' feelings, due to years of consistent advertising using such imagery.

Further, a brand's personality also creates an association of that brand with certain important life values. A ''value'' has been defined by Rokeach as a ''centrally held, enduring belief which guides actions and judgments across specific situations and beyond immediate goals to more ultimate end-states of existence.''[5] Examples of values are the pursuit of an exciting life, the search for self-respect, the need to be intellectual, the desire for self-expression, and so on.[6] Individuals differ in the extent to which they hold different values as being central to their lives: while one person may highly value the pursuit of fun and excitement, another may be more concerned with self-expression or security. A brand that acquires a distinctive personality may get strongly associated with a certain value, and strongly attract people who attach great importance to that value. For example, Pontiac cars have positioned themselves as ''building excitement,'' and are likely to attract that value segment. The value preferences of a key target segment ought to be researched and used in the development of a personality for a brand: if young adults who drink beer rank ''fun and excitement'' as their highest value, then the development of a ''party animal'' brand personality for Bud Light beer (using the celebrated spokesanimal Spuds MacKenzie) seems a logical advertising strategy.

Finally, what often matters more than the specific personality attributed to a brand is the question of whether a brand has any clear personality at all. A brand that over the years acquires a distinctive, well-known personality becomes like an ''old friend;'' consumers feel familiar and comfortable with it, it offers a sense of security and reassurance, and most consumers would rather pick it up rather than a newer brand from which they feel more psychologically distant. One of the reasons that market-leading brands tend to stay that way (for example, Tide detergent) is that they acquire this ''good friend'' personality. However, such a personality can also become a liability, if the brand slowly becomes perceived as being old fashioned and out of step with the times, and consumers (at least a sizable segment of them) begin to prefer a more contemporary, new-and-different brand. It becomes vital in such situations to ''contemporize'' and ''freshen'' the brand personality over the years.

For example, research on Betty Crocker, conducted in the late 1970s involving more than 3,000 women, found that in general, Betty Crocker was viewed as a company that is

Honest and dependable
Friendly and concerned about consumers
A specialist in baked goods

but

Out of date
Old and traditional
A manufacturer of ''old standby'' products
Not particularly contemporary or innovative

The conclusion was that the Betty Crocker image needed to be strengthened to become more modern and innovative and less old and stodgy.[7] As a result of such research, the depicted face of Betty Crocker, the fictional advice-giving spokeswoman for General Mills, has been changed seven times since the first portrait was painted in 1936.[8] Figure 8-1 shows how Betty Crocker looked in 1936, 1955, 1965, 1968, 1972, 1980, and 1986.

This concept of brand personality, of a ''brand as a person,'' is used by various advertising agencies and marketing client companies. It has proved especially valuable in studies of corporate image.[9] Using this concept, Young & Rubicam developed a campaign for a Swedish insurance company which markets a low-involvement, avoidance product. A series of humorous commercials shows that most accidents could happen to anyone and actually are humorous and not really that tragic if looked at with the right perspective. The advertising created a personality of a firm that is approachable, warm, and most of

Figure 8-1. Updating a brand's personality: Betty Crocker
Used with the permission of General Mills, Inc.

all, human. Through other Y&R campaigns, Dr Pepper made great sales progress during the 1970s by creating a personality of being original, fun, offbeat, and underdog.

WHY IS BRAND PERSONALITY IMPORTANT?

This question can be answered from two perspectives: that of the advertiser and that of the consumer.

For the advertiser, the development and reinforcement of a personality for a brand serves to differentiate the brand from competition. At a time when many brands are at or near parity in terms of technology (or are perceived to be so by consumers), the only difference between brands is often the personality that is associated with them. By creating a favorable and liked brand personality, a marketer can set his brand apart, which often enables the marketer to gain market share and/or to charge a higher price (or, at minimum, to avoid losing share to competitive brands that charge lower prices or run frequent consumer or trade promotions). Further, a brand personality is often unique and nonpreemptible: while competitors can match your brand's features and price, they usually cannot duplicate your brand personality (and, if they try to do so, they may simply end up giving your brand free advertising).

There are other, longer-term, advantages to building a distinctive brand personality. If advertising is not simply to be a short-term expense, but a longer-term investment, a brand's advertising should not merely lead to immediate sales but should also lead to the long-term enhancement of the brand's "equity" or "goodwill." Companies that create advertising which enhance such brand equity treat the value of a brand (or brand name) as an asset, much like a bank deposit. Advertising that creates or reinforces a brand's personality serves to increase the asset value of that brand; advertising that lacks such character serves to depreciate this asset value.

Why care about this hard-to-quantify asset value? There are several reasons. First, a brand—like other assets—can be bought or sold. Much of the growth of the consumer product giant corporations in the 1980s was achieved by a strategy of acquiring valuable brand names from other companies, often at huge prices that vastly exceeded the valuation of the plants and machinery (the so-called "hard assets") that went with these transactions. As examples, think of the acquisitions by Philip Morris of General Foods and Kraft, by Procter & Gamble of Richardson-Vicks, and by Unilever of Chesebrough-Pond's. In these transactions, the price paid was two or three times the book value of the physical assets, presumably because of the nonquantified value of the brand names acquired in the transaction. Second, a brand's asset value can command such high prices because of what it gives the company that owns it: access to a distribution network, with shelf facings in the stores; high consumer awareness and loyalty, leading to a stream of repurchases (and therefore income) in the years to come; and economies in terms of marketing expenses, especially in the costs of launching new brands. "Line extensions" bearing an already known brand name do not require the huge budgets otherwise required to launch a new brand name.

Brand personality is important to the consumer for a rather different set of reasons. Knowingly or unknowingly, consumers regard their possessions as part of themselves; people acquire or reinforce their sense of self, their identities, in part through the goods they buy and what these material goods symbolize, both to themselves and to others they come into contact with and care about. What is "me" depends, in part, on what is "mine"; we define who we are not only by our physical bodies and our occupations, but also by our possessions (such as the watch we wear). That is why a loss of material possessions—such as in a robbery or a natural disaster—leaves us feeling as if a "part of us" is gone. Of course, the extent to which we "invest our selves" in products and brands varies: more, for example, in automobiles and clothing, less (perhaps) in the brand of paper towel we buy.[10]

It is also plausible to suggest that as traditional institutions in society—such as the family, and religion—decline in importance, more and more individuals in society define their self-worth in terms of material possessions and their symbolic associations, their "social value." Further, in such an "outer-directed" society our sense of belonging to peer and other groups can depend significantly on a sense (and display) of shared brand ownership. We use our possessions not only to define ourselves as individuals, but also to define which groups we belong to—and do not belong to.

As part of this "self-defining" process, consumers select those brands that have a brand personality that is congruent with their own self-concept. That is, a consumer who does not think of himself as "flashy" is likely to feel uncomfortable in a car that is extremely attention grabbing and different from the norm; there is a lack of congruency in such a situation.[11] In one study, it was found that automobile consumers sought out cars whose product image was similar to their own image, on various personality attributes (such as exciting/dull).[12] Importantly, there is some evidence that the type of congruency that is important in such brand choice is not that between a brand's personality and a consumer's actual personality but rather that between a brand's personality and a consumer's "ideal" or "aspirational" personality, though the evidence on this is not unequivocal.[13]

WHEN IS BRAND PERSONALITY MORE IMPORTANT?

It was mentioned earlier that, to the extent that consumers select brands because of the congruity between their self-image and the brand's personality, this "self-definition" rationale would be stronger in some product categories than in others.

Specifically, we said that consumers are more likely to "invest their sense of self" in product categories such as automobiles and clothing than in paper towels. As would make sense intuitively, researchers have argued that such image congruence is of greater importance in those situations where the product is "socially conspicuous," which certainly characterizes automobiles and clothing.[14] This makes sense because our sense of self is supposed to grow out of the reactions of significant others; the symbolic aspects of brand and product choice should thus matter more when others can see us choose or use them. Put another way, brand personality should be a more important determinant of brand choice in situations where the "social signaling value" of that brand or product category is greater. This also applies when different consumption occasions for the same product are involved: drinking a beer at home by oneself is not socially conspicuous, but drinking a beer at home in front of guests—and drinking beer in a bar—are certainly more "socially conspicuous" situations, where self-definition and brand personality become more important.

Another factor contributing to this "signaling value," in addition to social conspicuousness, is the relative scarcity of the product category—luxury goods, being relatively more scarce, tell people more about the user's affluence and/or taste than do products that are more commonly available. A fur coat would not be as socially symbolic if everyone in sight were wearing one.

A third factor that research has shown as relevant is the extent to which the good is "ambiguous" regarding its inherent quality level.[15] If a consumer is not enough of an expert in a product or service category to clearly determine for himself or herself that the brand is of superior quality, then the consumer is more likely to rely on the image created through advertising to make that determination (and is more likely to believe what the advertising says). Brand personality is more likely to sway consumer purchases in such instances. Thus, "ambiguous" purchasing occasions may arise in the purchase of high-tech products, sensory (food, drink, fragrance) products, and consumer service situations. Brand personality (sometimes created through the "transformational advertising" discussed in the last chapter) is more likely to be important in such situations.

Finally, while we have only discussed differences in *product categories* until now, it has also been found that certain types of *individuals* are also more susceptible to brand personality symbolism. These are individuals who are always more conscious of how they appear to other people, how they are being evaluated by others, and who are constantly "modifying" their own personalities to appear more likable to others. Psychologists call such people "high self-monitors" and have shown that such people are more sensitive to imagery advertising appeals than are "low self-monitors."[16]

IMPLEMENTING A BRAND PERSONALITY STRATEGY

There are three steps to implementing a brand personality strategy through advertising: researching the symbolic associations that currently exist with the product category and competitive brands, deciding which brand personality is going to be of greatest value with the target consumer segment, and executing the desired brand personality strategy (creating, enhancing, or modifying the brand's personality). These are discussed in the paragraphs that follow.

Researching Brand Personality

There are various ways to learn about the brand personalities that consumers associate with the different brands in a product category, as well as with the product category itself. Some are more direct and quantitative, while others are more indirect and qualitative.

Among the quantitative techniques available, perhaps the simplest is to have consumers rate a brand, and/or users of that brand, on various personality adjectives. Thus a consumer might rate Pepsi, and/or a user of Pepsi, as being relatively high on scales for the adjectives of being competitive, aggressive, and so on. Different brands in a product category could then be "profiled" (compared) on these personality adjective scales.

In one study conducted by Young & Rubicam, respondents were asked to indicate which of a set of 50 personality-related words and phrases they would use to describe each of a set of brands.[17] A total of 39 percent said that Holiday Inn was "cheerful," whereas only 6 percent said that Bird's Eye was "cheerful." Holiday Inn was also described as friendly, ordinary, practical, modern, reliable, and honest, while Oil of Olay was described as gentle, sophisticated, mature, exotic, mysterious, and down-to-earth.

While easy to do, this method of using scales and adjectives suffers from at least two disadvantages: the list of specific personality scales used might be incomplete (or some of them might be irrelevant), and consumers may be unable or unwilling to give their true opinions about a brand's personality through such "direct" elicitation techniques. The qualitative, projective techniques which we will discuss next attempt to get over this second limitation. The hope is that they will be more able to get at some of these "unconscious" (or difficult-to-articulate) personality perceptions that a consumer may have about a brand. For example, if a reason for buying designer jeans is that consumers feel more socially accepted when they wear them because others wear them too, this is less likely to emerge in direct methods—where a logical, functional rationalization may be provided instead—but may well appear in these qualitative methods.

One way to obtain qualitative insight into the personality associations with the typical users of the product is to use "photo sorts." Consumers are given photographs of individuals, asked to pick which ones they think use particular brands, and then asked to describe these individuals. In a twist on this technique, conducted when instant coffee was somewhat new, two groups of consumers were shown a seven-item shopping list. For one group of consumers Maxwell House drip grind coffee appeared while Nescafé instant coffee was on the companion list. Consumers were asked to describe the type of housewife who would use each type of list. The profiles of the two women were very different. The instant coffee buyer was perceived as being lazy, a bad homemaker, and slovenly, whereas the woman buying the drip grind coffee was industrious, a good homemaker, and orderly.[18]

Another of these qualitative methods is the use of free associations: the subject is given a stimulus word (such as the brand name or advertising slogan) and then asked to provide the first set of words that come to mind. For example, Bell Telephone found that its slogan "The system is the solution" triggered negative "big brother is watching you" reactions among some people. Such a test for McDonald's yielded strong associations with Big Macs, golden arches, Ronald McDonald, everywhere, familiar, greasy, clean, cheap, kids, and so on. Since such free association tasks can yield a huge number of associations, consumers can be then asked (for each key association) how well it fits the brand (on a scale of "fits extremely well" to "fits not well at all").

A variant of word association is sentence completion. The respondent is asked to complete a partial sentence: "People like the Mazda Miata because . . . ," or "Burger

King is . . . ," and so on. Again, the respondent is encouraged to respond with the first thought that comes to mind.[19]

Another approach is to have consumers interpret a scene presented visually in which the product or brand is playing a role. For example, a consumer could be given one of two scenes: a break after a day hike on the mountains or a small evening barbecue with close friends. In each, the beer served was either Coors or Löwenbräu. Consumers were asked to project themselves into the scene and indicate on a five-point scale the extent to which they feel "warm," "friendly," "healthy," and "wholesome." The study was designed to test whether the advertising of Coors and Löwenbräu had established associations with the use context—Coors with hiking, wholesome, and health and Löwenbräu with a barbecue-type setting, friends, and warmth. The results showed that Coors was evaluated higher in the mountain setting and Löwenbräu in the barbecue setting, as expected, but that the other associations were not sensitive to the setting. Coors, for example, in the hiking context was higher on the "warm" and "friendly" dimensions as well as on "healthy" and "wholesome."[20]

Other projective techniques are also used. Ernest Dichter, the father of motivational research, routinely used a "psychodrama" technique where he asked people to act out a product. "You are Ivory soap. How old are you? Are you masculine or feminine? What type of personality do you have? What magazines do you read?"[21] McCann-Erickson has respondents draw figures of typical brand users.[22] In one case, they asked 50 people to draw figures of two brands of cake mix, Pillsbury and Duncan Hines. Pillsbury users were consistently portrayed as apron-clad, grandmotherly types. In contrast, Duncan Hines' purchasers were shown as slender, contemporary women.

Finally, another frequently used qualitative approach is to ask consumers to relate brands to other kinds of objects such as animals, cars, people, magazines, trees, movies, or books. For example, if this brand was a car, what type of car might it be? In one study, Young & Rubicam found that Oil of Olay was associated with mink, France, secretary, silk, swimming, and *Vogue* magazine. Kentucky Fried Chicken, in contrast, was associated with Puerto Rico, a zebra (recall the stripes on a KFC bucket!), a housewife dressed in denim, camping, and *TV Guide*. Clearly, the result of such techniques is a rich description of the product that suggests associations to develop and ones to avoid.

Targeting a Brand Personality

The personality scale ratings or associations obtained through the methods just described can next be compared to the target consumer's ratings of his or her own personality, both actual and aspired-to, and inferences can be drawn on which aspects of a brand's personality need to be reinforced or changed through advertising. Clearly, this process of selecting a "target" brand personality requires a good sense of judgment, for one must choose a personality that corresponds to the "ideal" personality for a brand in that category, given the relevant use-setting and context, keeping in mind the personality strengths and weaknesses of competitive brands. It also goes without saying that the targeted personality must be consistent with the functional or psychological benefit that the brand is promising: if a bank is advertising good service, the personality must obviously be one of friendly, but efficient, service.

In this judgmental process it is often useful first to identify the demographics of the target segment: are they women, or teenagers, or blue-collar men? One can then use research (and commonsense observation) to see what life values and personality traits the target segment is likely to aspire to. For instance, research has shown that women are more likely than men to identify warm relationships with others and a sense of belonging as their most important value, while men are more likely to value a sense of accomplishment and fun-enjoyment-excitement.[23] Fun-enjoyment-excitement are also typically valued more by younger consumers, while security as a value increases with age.[24]

Various typologies of consumers exist that use personalities, values, life-styles and attitudes as variables, among them VALS and the more recent VALS 2, values and life-styles typologies created by SRI, Inc.[25] In its first version, VALS focused on the distinction between inner-directed consumers, driven by their convictions, passions, and need for self-expression, and outer-directed consumers, driven by their responses to signals from other people. Using this distinction, it grouped people into nine categories (called Survivors, Sustainers, Belongers, Emulators, Achievers, I-Am-Me's, Experientials, Societally Conscious, and Integrateds). VALS 2 uses the additional classifying dimension of the "resources" people have (education, income, etc.) to create eight categories (called Fulfilleds, Believers, Achievers, Strivers, Experiencers, Makers, Strugglers, and Actualizers). (See Figure 8-2.) Again, one can typically (through custom or syndicated research) profile one's target segment in terms of such a typology and then try to develop a brand personality that will appeal most to the target segment. For example, Merrill Lynch tried to create a personality of being aggressive and independent in its financial recommendations ("a breed apart") to try to appeal to the target segment that did above-average stock trading, who research showed tended to be independent-minded "Achievers."[26]

In doing this targeting it is extremely important to be aware of social trends—how certain values become more or less important with time—and aware of how brands can

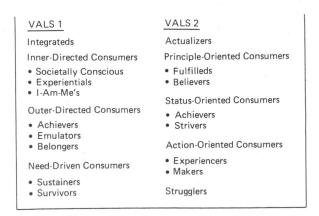

Figure 8-2.   The VALS 1 and VALS 2 values and life-styles typologies

Source: *Advertising Age*, February 13, 1989, p. 24. Copyright by Crain Communications, Inc. All rights reserved. Used with permission.

acquire personalities that seem contemporary to one generation but old fashioned and inappropriate to later, succeeding, generations. For instance, Cadillac's luxury image is very appealing to a cohort of older Americans, but appears somehow less interesting and less exciting to a generation of younger (but also affluent) consumers, who would rather spend their luxury dollars buying BMWs. It is extremely important that advertisers track, over time, both the imagery that surrounds their brands as well as the possibly changing appeal of that imagery.

Executing a Brand Personality Strategy

Once a brand personality has been researched and targeted, advertising must be developed that creates, reinforces, or changes that target personality. While the following discussion is limited to the role of advertising in such brand personality development, it is extremely important to note that every element of the marketing and communication mix plays a role—especially packaging, pricing, sales promotions, and distribution. Further, the extent to which a brand personality gets successfully created depends significantly on the extent to which these different forces operate synergistically. Expensive-looking advertising is not going to work if the product is priced at $1.99 and is distributed through every cheap neighborhood store.

Key advertising elements that contribute to a brand's personality are the following:

Endorser.   The choice of an endorser is often crucial, because the personality of the endorser can get transferred to the brand with enough repetition. For example, Bill Cosby has done much to give Jell-O its warm personality, while Bruce Willis contributed substantially to the "party animal" image of Seagram wine coolers. David Ogilvy created a very strong image for Hathaway shirts by using a spokesperson wearing an eye patch (Figure 8-3). Nike athletic shoes has gained tremendous personality definition by its use of basketball star Michael Jordan. The endorser need not be real, or even human: the Marlboro cowboys, or the spokesdog Spuds MacKenzie, who gave Bud Light beer the fun-loving personality that made it so appealing to its young male target segment—ages 25–34 (Figure 8-4). Where the characters are not real, the casting becomes vital: the people chosen to play a role need to be "exactly right."

User Imagery.   The kind of brand user portrayed in the ad can also be very important. The American Express card creates a very specific user image, for instance, in its photographic portrait campaign featuring celebrity cardholders (Figure 8-5), as does Dewar's Scotch whisky with its profiles of successful (but not necessarily well-known) drinkers. *Rolling Stone* magazine recently tried to change the perception of who its readers were by its depiction of "perceived" versus "real" readers (Figure 8-6). Again, the portrayed users can be fictional, as in the case of Calvin Klein jeans or fragrances.

Executional Elements.   Elements such as the choice (in broadcast ads) of music, visual direction, pace and nature of editing, color schemes used, and (in print ads) of color, layout, and typography can all contribute substantially to a brand's personality. Some

The man in the Hathaway shirt

AMERICAN MEN are beginning to realize that it is ridiculous to buy good suits and then spoil the effect by wearing an ordinary, mass-produced shirt. Hence the growing popularity of HATHAWAY shirts, which are in a class by themselves.

HATHAWAY shirts *wear* infinitely longer—a matter of years. They make you look younger and more distinguished, because of the subtle way HATHAWAY cut collars. The whole shirt is tailored more *generously,* and is therefore more *comfortable.* The tails are longer, and stay in your trousers. The buttons are mother-of-pearl. Even the stitching has an ante-bellum elegance about it.

Above all, HATHAWAY make their shirts of remarkable *fabrics,* collected from the four corners of the earth—Viyella and Aertex from England, woolen taffeta from Scotland, Sea Island cotton from the West Indies, hand-woven madras from India, broadcloth from Manchester, linen batiste from Paris, hand-blocked silks from England, exclusive cottons from the best weavers in America. You will get a great deal of quiet satisfaction out of wearing shirts which are in such impeccable taste.

HATHAWAY shirts are made by a small company of dedicated craftsmen in the little town of Waterville, Maine. They have been at it, man and boy, for one hundred and fifteen years.

At better stores everywhere, or write C. F. HATHAWAY, Waterville, Maine, for the name of your nearest store. In New York, telephone MU 9-4157. Prices from $5.50 to $25.00.

Figure 8-3. Brand personality via a sophisticated, mysterious endorser: Hathaway shirts
Courtesy of C. F. Hathaway, Inc.

Figure 8-4. Brand personality via a "party animal": Spuds MacKenzie for Bud Light beer

Courtesy of Anheuser-Busch, Inc.

campaigns that have used the choice of executional elements to convey a personality of intelligence and wit include the recent print campaign for Absolut vodka (Figure 8-7) and the TV campaigns for Honda cars (Figure 8-8).

A very useful executional element is the use of an idiosyncratic brand symbol, such as McDonald's golden arches, Merrill Lynch's bull, or Prudential Bache's rock. If your brand doesn't have such a symbol, consider creating one, to give it identity and personality. Examples here include the Jolly Green Giant, Charlie the Tuna, the Keebler elves, and so on.

Consistency. In addition to the *content* of the advertising, one other basic advertising principle is very important in executing a brand personality strategy. It is the principle of predictability and consistency. Just as in any positioning strategy, a brand personality can only develop successfully if the important symbolic aspects of the brand—such as those just described—remain consistent over time. Brands that change these elements risk diluting their personalities, or end up having no brand personality at all. Finally, decisions about other marketing elements—especially pricing, promotions, and distribution—must always support and reinforce a brand's basic personality, not reduce its character.

Ella Fitzgerald. Cardmember since 1961.

Membership has its privileges.℠

Don't leave home without it.
Call 1-800-THE CARD to apply.

Figure 8-5. Brand personality via upscale user imagery: American Express
Courtesy of American Express.

Perception.

Figure 8-6. Brand personality via depiction of ''actual'' users: *Rolling Stone* magazine

Reality.

To a new generation of Rolling Stone readers, pigs live on farms. You'll find the cops living in Beverly Hills or on Hill Street, now heralded instead of hated. If you're looking for an 18 to 34 year old market that is taking active part instead of active protest, you'll have a riot in the pages of Rolling Stone.

Figure 8-7. Brand personality via intelligent, witty ads: Absolut Vodka
Courtesy of Carillon Importers, Ltd.

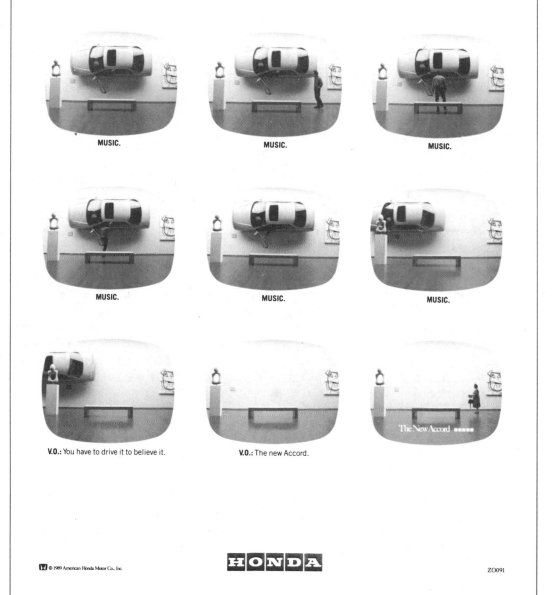

Figure 8-8. Brand personality via intelligent, witty ads: Honda cars
Courtesy of Honda of America, Inc.

SUMMARY

Just as people have individual personalities, brands too can develop personalities—if the advertising for these brands identifies and develops a consistent image that is reinforced over time. Through such a personality, brands can be seen as young or old, masculine or feminine, aggressive or introverted, or sophisticated or blue collar and in a variety of different ways. Just as with people, the brands we know can come to symbolize certain important life values and certain associated emotional characteristics.

Brand personalities matter because consumers are attracted to brands that possess personalities they themselves identify with, or seek. Consumers often use their choice of brands to tell themselves, and other people they care about, what kinds of individuals they really are (or want to be seen as). To the companies that market these brands, a brand with a strong brand personality represents brand equity that can be capitalized on in marketing efforts (such as launching brand extensions much more economically than would otherwise be the case), and also represents brand goodwill that has intrinsic financial value.

While a brand personality can always add a defining character to a brand, it is especially important in leading to sales and market share in product categories that are expensive, purchased or consumed in socially conspicuous situations, and help a consumer calibrate product quality in otherwise "ambiguous" situations. Certain people, called high self-monitors, are especially swayed by a brand's personality.

Implementing a brand personality situation first calls for defining the target consumer segment and understanding what kind of brand personality to which they are most likely to be responsive, and how they currently rate different brands on different personality characteristics. A variety of quantitative and qualitative techniques can be used at this stage. Once a target personality has been defined for the brand, the appropriate personality can be created through the choice of an endorser or spokescharacter, portrayal of matching user life-styles and imagery, the use of appropriate executional elements and actors, and so on. It is important that the personality sought be maintained both over time and over different elements of the communication and marketing mix.

DISCUSSION QUESTIONS

1. Select ten brands with which you are familiar, and describe the brand personality you think each has. Then analyze just how the advertising and other marketing mix elements for these brands have contributed to the development of a brand personality.

2. List five product or service categories where you think consumers select brands based in large measure on their brand personality. Then think through what, if anything, these categories have in common, and relate your thoughts to the research presented in the chapter on when brand personality becomes more important.

3. Select any one product or service category, and analyze the brand personality of the different competitors in it. Identify the specific elements of the advertising that have

contributed to the development of this personality over time. For brands where you fail to find a clear or distinct brand personality, ask yourself why none has developed thus far.

4. Suppose you were a new entrant into the market you analyzed in question 3. How might you select a "target" brand personality for your new brand?

5. How might you create advertising to develop that brand personality?

6. Discuss the pros and cons of the different research techniques used to study the brand personalities of competing brands. Select one that you prefer, and explain why.

7. Identify a target segment of consumers that you have some interest marketing to, and discuss the kinds of brand personalities they might be most responsive to.

8. Certain brand personality "dimensions" were listed in the chapter, based on the research of trait personality psychologists. Expand this list to a more comprehensive one that is more applicable in marketing contexts, using your intuition and observations about brand marketing strategies.

9. What is meant by an "ambiguous" product category? Why is this concept important in planning and working with a brand's personality?

10. In addition to advertising, what other elements of the communication and marketing mix can contribute to a brand's personality? Discuss three cases where a brand appears to have successfully integrated these elements in developing and enhancing a brand personality, and three cases where it has not.

11. Can you think of brands where the brand personality appeals to one age cohort or generation, but not to another? Does this matter to these brands' long-term sales potentials? If it is a problem, why did it emerge? What can be done now to eliminate this problem?

NOTES

1. Joseph T. Plummer, "Brand Personality: A Strategic Concept for Multinational Advertising," Paper presented to the AMA 1985 Winter Marketing Educators Conference, Phoenix, Arizona, February 1985.

2. Sidney J. Levy, "Symbols for Sale," *Harvard Business Review*, July/August 1959, pp. 117–124.

3. Pierre Martineau, "The Personality of the Retail Store," *Harvard Business Review*, January/February 1958, pp. 47–55.

4. For a fuller discussion, see Walter Mischel, *Introduction to Personality* (New York: Holt, Rinehart and Winston, 1986), on which this discussion is based.

5. Donald E. Vinson, Jerome E. Scott, and Lawrence M. Lamont, "The Role of Values in Marketing and Consumer Behavior," *Journal of Marketing*, April 1977, 44–50.

6. Sharon E. Beatty, Lynn R. Kahle, Pamela Homer, and Shekhar Misra, "Alternative Measurement Approaches to Consumer Values: The List of Values and the Rokeach Value Survey," *Psychology and Marketing*, 2 (3), 1985, pp. 181–200.

7. Keith Reinhard, "How We Make Advertising," Paper presented to the Federal Trade Commission, May 11, 1979, pp. 22–25.

8. Hal Morgan, *Symbols of America* (New York: Penguin Books, 1987), p. 126.

9. Aaron Spector, "Basic Dimensions of Corporate Image," *Journal of Marketing*, 25 (6), October 1961, pp. 47–51.

10. For a wonderful exposition of this concept, see Russell W. Belk, "Possessions and the Extended Self," *Journal of Consumer Research*, 15 (2), September 1988, pp. 139–168.

11. M. Joseph Sirgy, "Self-concept in Consumer Behavior: A Critical Review," *Journal of Consumer Research*, 9, December 1982, pp. 287–300.

12. A. E. Birdwell, "A Study of Influence of Image Congruency on Consumer Choice," *Journal of Business*, 41, January 1968, pp. 76–88.

13. Sirgy, "Self-concept in Consumer Behavior," p. 288.

14. Ibid., p. 295.

15. John Deighton, "The Interaction of Advertising and Evidence," *Journal of Consumer Research*, 11, December 1984, pp. 763–770, and Stephen J. Hoch and Young-Won Ha, "Consumer Learning: Advertising and the Ambiguity of Product Experience," *Journal of Consumer Research*, 13, September 1986, pp. 221–233.

16. Mark Snyder and Kenneth G. DeBono, "Appeals to Image and Claims about Quality," *Journal of Personality and Social Psychology*, 49 (3), 1985, pp. 586–597.

17. Joseph T. Plummer, "How Personality Makes a Difference," *Journal of Advertising Research*, 24, December 1984/January 1985, pp. 27–31.

18. Mason Haire, "Projective Techniques in Marketing Research," *Journal of Marketing*, April 1950, pp. 649–656.

19. Joseph S. Newman, *Motivation Research and Marketing Management* (Boston: Harvard University Press, 1957), p. 143.

20. David A. Aaker and Douglas M. Stayman, "Implementing the Concept of Transformational Advertising," *Psychology and Marketing*, forthcoming.

21. Rena Bartos, "Ernest Dichter: Motive Interpreter," *Journal of Advertising Research*, February/March 1986, pp. 15–20.

22. Annetta Miller and Dody Tsiantar, "Psyching out Consumers," *Newsweek*, February 27, 1989, pp. 46–47.

23. Lynn R. Kahle, ed., *Social Values and Social Change: Adaptation to Life in America* (New York, Praeger, 1983), p. 75.

24. Ibid, pp. 82–91. See also Lynn R. Kahle, Basil Poulos, and Ajay Sukhdial, "Changes in Social Values in the United States During the Past Decade," *Journal of Advertising Research*, February/March 1988, pp. 35–44.

25. Arnold Mitchell, *The Nine American Lifestyles* (New York: Macmillan, 1983), and *Advertising Age*, February 13, 1989, p. 24. For a review of earlier research on psychographics, see William D. Wells, "Psychographics: A Critical Review," *Journal of Marketing Research*, 12, May 1975, pp. 196–213.

26. *Advertising Age*, November 9, 1981, p. 82.

9

CREATING SOCIAL NORMS

What we shall call opinion leadership, if we may call it leadership at
all, is leadership at its simplest. . . . It is not leadership on the high level
of a Churchill, nor of a local politico, nor even a social elite. It is quite
the opposite extreme; it is almost invisible, certainly inconspicuous
form of leadership at the person-to-person level of ordinary, intimate,
informal, everyday contact.

Katz and Lazarsfeld, 1955

In addition to changing brand attitudes, associating feelings with the brand, and creating
a brand personality, advertising can also associate the brand with certain social or other
groups (called "reference groups") that the consumer values highly. This section focuses
on such reference group factors, particularly on the interplay between advertising and
such personal influence. Personal influence refers to the influence on brand choice and
purchasing that flows from a consumer's friends and associates, or from the people that
the consumer considers to be experts in a product category. Some of this influence can
occur through the processes of "word-of-mouth advertising" and "diffusion," and these
are also discussed in this chapter.

Lessig and Park define a reference group as actual or imaginary institutions, individuals or groups having significant relevance on the target individual's evaluations, as-
pirations, or behavior.[1] Such reference groups could be those (1) used as standards of
comparison for self-appraisal (the "Joneses" we try to keep up with), (2) those considered to be informative experts, or (3) those used as a source of norms, standards, and
attitudes. They need not be the groups in which the individual participates, although they
sometimes are, but can be large social groupings—social class, ethnic group, subculture,
and so on—that the individual is a member of, aspires to being a member of, or otherwise
exerts influence on the individual.

The important feature of the reference group concept is that an individual does not
have to be a member of the group for the influence to occur. Thus, a student's behaviors
and life-style can be heavily determined by emulation of the people in a group to which
he or she aspires to belong. An occasional jogger (a so-called "weekend athlete") might
aspire to belong to a group of serious athletes and might place tremendous weight on the

fact that a Michael Jordan or a Bo Jackson endorses Nike running shoes. The key point is that the relationship between the target individual and the reference group should be motivationally and psychologically significant.[2]

Various studies have demonstrated that such reference groups do in fact have an impact on consumer behavior. Fishbein has extended the basic evaluative belief attitude models reviewed in Chapter 6 to include an explicit measure of this type of personal influence, referred to as the *subjective norms* associated with the choice object.[3] In this "extended behavioral intention model," total behavioral intentions toward buying a brand can be thought of as based on both the target consumer's own attitude toward buying it as well as a "subjective norm." The consumer's *own* attitude is based on an assessment of the consumer's importance ratings of the attributes of the product, weighted by the consumer's perception of the extent to which the brand adequately possesses those attributes (as discussed in Chapter 6). In a similar fashion, the *subjective norm* is expected to be based on the consumer's beliefs about what the reference group is expected to like, weighted by the consumer's motivation to comply with that perceived expectation from the reference group. Ryan has shown that while this formulation is theoretically elegant there are several difficulties in applying it in practice.[4]

NATURE OF REFERENCE GROUP INFLUENCES ON BRAND CHOICE

One way to think of different kinds of reference group influence is to make a distinction between influences that are (1) external and explicit and (2) internal and implicit. By external we mean the likelihood that decision making involves explicit social interactions such as a situation in which two or more people (for example, a husband, wife, and children) are involved. The consumer might search out friends and neighbors in the decision-making process or otherwise refer to the product in the course of conversations and social interactions. An industrial buyer might seek advice or information from associates. This is often called *word-of-mouth* advertising to distinguish this kind of communication from *mass communication* advertising.

Internal personal influence refers to the likelihood that decision making is affected by mental processes that involve people or groups. Thus, for example, many products are purchased as gifts for someone else where no interaction takes place with the intended recipient. Others are purchased primarily for their symbolic role. They may symbolize a particular social class position or status. Still others, particularly in the clothing and fashion industry, are heavily influenced by the decision maker's judgment of "what other people might think" or "how I will look to the Joneses" and so on. Many products are purchased so as to be "first with the latest thing." In all these instances, personal influence is operating but may involve little or no explicit social interaction or specific conversation between the consumer and someone else.

Another key distinction often made by researchers is that between reference group influence that is (1) informational and (2) normative.[5] Informational reference group effects pertains to situations in which low-knowledge consumers seek information from other people—friends, or salespeople, or media personalities—that they consider experts in the product category. Our discussion of the expertise and credibility of endorsers in Chapter 12 pertains to such situations. The second kind of influence, normative influence, refers to situations where consumers identify with a group to enhance their self-image and ego or comply with a group's norms to gain rewards or to avoid punishments.

Why do reference groups have such influence, informative or normative? There are several explanations. For one, individual consumers are placed in various social roles throughout their lives.[6] Some of these roles are ones we voluntarily seek out and acquire (e.g., that of a successful businessperson); others are ascribed to us by society (e.g., age and sex roles). When consumers "play" a role, they use consumer goods to symbolize that role and to perform adequately in it. For example, someone playing the role of an athlete has to own (and show others that he/she owns) the right sports equipment, a gourmet cook has to own a food processor, a "hip" teenager may have to have purple-colored punky hair, and a new parent may proudly display a "child in car" bumper sticker on the family car. Since we are not all brought up knowing how to perform these roles, we look to others—to reference groups, actual or depicted in media—to learn how that role is played. When we are uncertain about what to do in a social situation, we turn to others for guidance. Media stereotypes, direct contact and instruction, and advertising are all important here, and advertising can use this influence to link the brand in question to the successful performance of a certain role. For instance, Nike can imply in its ads that a serious athlete always wears Nike running shoes. As consumers actually acquire that role, they are likely to deviate from the media-depicted stereotype and modify it in ways that individualize themselves. Further, not all consumers accept the stereotypic role description to begin with, so advertising needs to use role depiction with care (for example, sex roles for men and women are changing rapidly in our times, and depicting what the "right" role is for women in society is obviously fraught with considerable danger).

A second explanation for the importance of reference groups in our social lives is that we are members of several different groups (political, religious, ethnic, occupational, etc.), and we use consumer goods to help us define what groups we belong to and differentiate ourselves from the groups we don't belong to. This group influence may owe its power to the fact that if we don't do what the group does it may reject us (for example, a "nerdy" appearance may lead to rejection from a "hip" teenage group). Alternatively, it may be because we identify deeply with the group (for example, a consumer may drive an imported car because he identifies strongly with the "smart and sophisticated" crowd). Finally, the influence may simply be internalized and subconscious, to the extent that the group's values become considered "personal" values—for example, a strongly proenvironmental shopper may not even consider himself part of a proenvironmental group, though those values in essence define what that group is.

Whatever the nature of the influence, the essential point is that every group has its norms or standards and values, and the kinds of consumer goods and services that group members do and do not buy form a key part of these norms (for example, the kinds of clothes we wear, the types of food we buy, the liquor we drink). These norms are communicated within the group through role models—members of the group who have greater than average influence either because they are seen as experts, or because they are seen as powerful or especially attractive, or because they are very similar to the average group member. What advertising can do is to communicate that purchase and consumption of the consumer good or service being advertised is an integral part of the norms of a group that the target consumer seeks to belong to and to communicate this through an explicit or implicit endorsement from (or association with) a role model. For example, in the soft drink industry, susceptible teenagers—who are target consumers because they are the "heavy users"—are told that to "belong" with other teenagers they should drink Pepsi or Coke (as the case may be), and this message is communicated by showing Michael Jackson drinking Pepsi, George Michael drinking Coke, and so on.

FACTORS INFLUENCING THE DEGREE OF GROUP INFLUENCE

It is well known that the degree to which such social influence processes operate is affected by the nature of the product, service, or idea in question, as well as the characteristics of the consumer and of the decision-making process. An advertiser considering the use of advertising to create social or group influence needs to evaluate the extent to which these factors increase the role of social and group influences in a particular situation.

Individual Differences in Susceptibility

Consumers differ with respect to the extent of their susceptibility to social and group influence.[7] Some people are simply more "persuadable" than others, more extroverted, more likely to engage in social interactions, and more affected in their decisions by the opinions of friends, neighbors, role models, and so on. This heterogeneity can be found within any particular market target. Research by Bearden, Netemeyer, and Teel has shown that there is a difference between susceptibility to "informational" reference group influence and that to "normative" influence. It has been found by Park and Lessig[8] that younger consumers are more susceptible to reference group influence. This could be because they tend to have lower product category knowledge (and thus reduced self-confidence in brand choice), or have more social contacts and greater social visibility, or are undergoing more intense identity-seeking and socialization processes.

Decision-Making Unit

The purchase of a package of gum, a breath mint, or numerous other types of consumer products, particularly in the "impulse" category, is predominantly an individual-oriented decision. The decision-making unit (DMU) tends to be one individual, and such purchases are unlikely to involve a group decision. In contrast, many major family purchase decisions, such as that of a home or an automobile or a vacation spot, are group decisions. Such family decision making obviously involves personal influence, and the advertiser should make a determination of the existing and potential uses of the product in the consumption system of the family and the likely relative influence of various family members. Does the wife tend to carry most weight in choosing a brand for this product? The husband? Are children likely to be a significant influence? Similarly, a large number of industrial product decisions are group decisions, in which the person who finally uses it is usually not the one who places the order or even the one who influences or finally approves the decision. At least two, and often several, people will be involved, and it is a better understanding of this group decision-making process that advertisers in these product categories must acquire.

An implicit personal influence process takes place in many other purchase decisions. Many purchases that appear to be made for the self are in fact being made with some other individual or reference group in mind. Thus, the homemaker, for example, in buying provisions for the household, is often more concerned with what others in the household will want, use, and eat than with his or her own personal consumption. The distinction between the "consumer" and the "customer" in each situation must be clearly understood. The consumer of men's socks is in the majority of cases men. The customer for men's socks, however, is often a woman. All products given as gifts fall into this category, and it is of fundamental importance to assess the nature of the thing being advertised from this viewpoint.

Nature of the Product Category

Are there certain kinds of product categories where reference group influence is likely to be stronger? Although there are no definitive conclusions, researchers have found that personal influence will be more likely to operate in situations where large rather than small amounts of money are involved, when the decision *is riskier*, when the product is not easily testable, and when the consumer is more *involved* in the choice.[9] Thus, consumers are likely to seek out and acquire information of all kinds, including the advice and opinion of friends, family, and experts, where the financial and emotional investment is high. Where risk and high involvement are present, personal influence will also be likely to occur at the decision and postdecision stages of the process. Thus a salesperson plays a more important role with some products than with others, and the opinion of friends may be actively sought out after the decision has been made. These conditions are most likely for products such as large appliances, television sets, home computers, automobiles, and furniture.

Another key attribute of product categories high in reference group influence is that they are generally "socially conspicuous." The product must be conspicuous in the most obvious sense that it can be seen and identified by others, and it must be conspicuous in the sense of standing out and being noticed. No matter how visible a product is, if virtually everyone owns it, it is not conspicuous in the second sense. Thus such conspicuousness has two aspects: relative scarcity (such as the purchase of luxury goods) and public visibility, where ownership or consumption can be seen by others.[10] Such product categories, where the reference group can see what the consumer has bought or is consuming, are sometimes nicknamed "badge products" or "wardrobe products," for obvious reasons. Examples are clothing, footwear, automobiles, watches, and jewelry.

Nature of the Consumption or Purchasing Situation

The *situation* for which the purchase is made is another factor that has been intensively studied and shown to affect product attitudes and choice. Personal influence is often the major distinguishing characteristic between one situation and the next. Purchasing beer or wine to drink by oneself can differ from purchasing these products for an important social occasion (as in a bar or in a party at home with guests). Clearly, one's sensitivity to what the reference group feels is likely to be much greater in the second situation. The advertiser must appreciate that his or her product may be locked into a particular situational use for which personal influence will operate to a greater or lesser degree.

INFORMATIONAL INFLUENCE: WORD-OF-MOUTH AND DIFFUSION PROCESSES

Chapter 12 later in this book will explore the ways in which endorsers can serve as credible experts in convincing consumers that an advertised brand is worth buying, which is one way in which reference groups can have an informational influence. Another way in which informational influences operate is through the operation of "word-of-mouth" processes, in which a potential consumer relies on the opinion of another to decide on brand adoption; adoption through such mechanisms is part of what has been called the "diffusion" process. Diffusion and personal influence are important topics for an advertiser for several reasons.[11] First, great advertising campaigns and many apparently worthwhile products have floundered because of a failure to stimulate diffusion and word-of-mouth communication to support the product or service advertised. Some campaigns, on the other hand, have achieved great success, primarily because of the word-of-mouth communication that they stimulated. Second, there are significant reasons why, in many product categories, the relative influence of face-to-face communications greatly surpasses the influence of advertising in stimulating or determining brand choice. Third, segmentation strategies must take into account the fact that a target segment may have an important influence on the attitudes and behaviors of other groups not included within it. Next, we discuss several characteristics that increase the likelihood of success of word-of-mouth communications.

Motivational Characteristics

What motivates people to talk to others about a product or ad campaign? Dichter[12] argued that for talking to take place, there must exist some material interest: there must be satisfaction or reward associated with the behavior. In other words, a speaker will choose products, listeners, and words that are most likely to serve basic needs and goals. In a study of product talking and listening behavior, he found that talking motivations tended to fall into four categories, each associated with various kinds of involvement.

The first is *product involvement*. People have a tendency to want to talk about distinctly pleasurable or unpleasurable things. Talk can serve to relive the pleasure the speaker has obtained and dissipate the excitement aroused by the use of a product or the experience of having shopped for and purchased it. Talk can confirm ownership of it for the speaker in many subtle ways.

The second is *self-involvement*. The speaker essentially seeks confirmation of the wisdom of the decision from his or her peers and as a way to reduce dissonance. Self-confirmation behavior is engaged in to gain attention, show connoisseurship, and enhance feelings of being first with something, having inside information, suggesting status, spreading the gospel, seeking confirmation of one's own judgment, and asserting superiority. The point is that a product or advertising object can be the central focus of conversations engaged in for these kinds of goals and motivations.

The third is *other involvement* in which the major motivation is the need and intent to help other persons and share with and enjoy the benefits of the product. Products can serve to express sentiments of neighborliness, care, friendship, and love. The fourth motivation for speaking about products is called *message involvement* and derives from the nature of advertising itself. Advertising, for many reasons, can stimulate word-of-mouth communications and often itself becomes the focus of such conversations.

Characteristics of the Innovation

In the case of new products or, more generally, *innovations,* five concepts[13] are important in determining the extent to which the innovations get talked about and, ultimately, adopted:

1. *Relative advantage (RA)*:   the degree to which the new product is perceived as superior to the one it replaces or to existing products with which it will compete.

2. *Compatibility (CO)*:   the degree of consistency between the current set of alternatives used by the consumer to satisfy needs and the new product.

3. *Complexity (CM)*:   the degree of difficulty the consumer has in understanding or using the product.

4. *Divisibility (DV)*:   the degree to which the new product or samples of it can be tried out with a minimum of financial or time investment. Can the consumer easily reverse the decision in the sense of choosing not to adopt the product without at the same time losing or risking a great deal?

5. *Communicability (CN)*:   how difficult is it to communicate information about the new product?

All these factors will affect the degree to which information about the new product is passed along and the extent of word-of-mouth advertising that takes place. RA, CO, DV, and CN are essentially supportive factors in the diffusion and personal influence process, whereas CM will tend to retard the process.

A recent extension of these ideas is to consider the risk and habit factors associated with an innovation.[14] The basic argument is that reception of a new product will hinge on the degree of risk associated with its purchase and the prior entrenchment of consumer purchase habits in the product class.

Opinion Leadership

Who are the kinds of people who have the most impact on others in such informational and word-of-mouth processes? The concept of the opinion leader is relevant here, and it has been a central focus for much empirical research in sociology and marketing.[15] It is interesting to recall that Katz and Lazarsfeld first defined the concept as "leadership at its simplest," "almost invisible," at the "person-to-person level of ordinary, intimate, informal, everyday contact."[16]

In their pioneering study, four types of opinion leaders were identified: marketing, fashion, movie, and public affairs leaders. Marketing opinion leaders were found to be married women with comparatively large families, gregarious, and not concentrated at any particular social-status level. In contrast to the influence of immediate family members (for example, husband and child), the authors stressed the importance of extrafamilial influence in many consumer product situations.

Since the publication of this study, a great deal of other research attention has been devoted to the concept of opinion leadership, both in marketing and in other disciplines. Myers,[17] for example, found in the case of the adoption of new frozen-food products, in which the new products were given to "positive" and "negative" opinion leaders, that group opinions toward the new products tended to follow those of the opinion leader in both positive and negative cases.

One of the first questions that needs to be asked is whether opinion leadership is a general or a specific phenomenon. It is not at all clear that an opinion leader in one product class (e.g., fashionable clothes) also tends to be an opinion leader in another (e.g., personal computer equipment). From an advertiser's viewpoint, another important question is the degree to which opinion leaders are differentially responsive to advertising appeals. Without the establishment of this fact, many of the basic postulates of a two-step flow of mass communications break down. It is ultimately a question of the connection, or lack of connection, between the formal mass media channel and the informal channels of interpersonal communication and influence. Do individuals play different roles in introducing advertising communications into a social network?

In an important book on the subject, Rogers[18] argued that at the time of introduction of an innovation, the population can be divided into five groups (segments) made up of *innovators, opinion leaders, early majority, late majority,* and *laggards.* He further argued that the distribution of these groups approximated a normal curve: the early and late majority groups would tend to be much larger than those at the tails, innovators and laggards. Second, he redefined the process of diffusion and adoption as involving five stages: *awareness, interest, evaluation, trial,* and *adoption.* The argument is that all people go through this process on the way to adoption (or rejection) of an innovation. Mass media and impersonal sources of influence tend to be most important at the early stages of awareness and interest, and word-of-mouth and personal influence tend to be most important in the later stages of evaluation, trial, and adoption.

Researchers have focused attention on the degree to which the five types of market segments exist during new product introductions. The results are mixed and depend heavily on the nature of the new product and the competitive and other conditions at the time of entry. The concept of "innovator" has received particular attention. It is useful to consider the innovator concept for several reasons. First, it can be a useful segmentation variable. An advertiser may want to reach an innovator if a new product is involved simply because innovators may represent the most attractive segment, especially at the onset. Second, an innovator may, by example, influence others. Noninnovators tend to wait until innovators have acted. Therefore, it is reasonable to look first at the innovator segment. Finally, much research has gone into describing innovators in marketing. Since there is evidence of an overlap between innovators and opinion leaders, this research should also be relevant to those who would attempt to identify opinion leaders.

Motivations for Listening to Opinion Leaders

Thus far we have talked about the nature of the people who are at the sending end of the word-of-mouth communications. But what about the listeners—who are they more likely to be? Motivations for listening also require that the listener receive some satisfaction or reward from the interaction. Dichter[19] found two conditions particularly important: (1) that the person who recommends something is interested in the listener and his or her well-being and (2) that the speaker's experience with and knowledge about the product are convincing. Obviously, basic questions of the trust the listener-receiver has in the speaker-sender are involved and the credibility of the source of the communications. Seven kinds of sources were found to be particularly important and potentially successful in their influence attempts: commercial authorities, celebrities, connoisseurs, sharers of interest, intimates, people of goodwill, and bearers of tangible evidence. A discussion of the dimensions of source credibility will be found in Chapter 12.

Implementing an Informational Influence Strategy

If informational influence is desired, the most straightforward strategy implication is that the advertiser can attempt to single out the crucial innovator and opinion leadership segments and target promotion and advertising messages to them, using the appropriate credible sources as endorsers. This strategy has not been followed as often as it might seem. Because of the costs of attempting to identify innovators in many product or market situations and the inherent spillover effects of mass media like television, it is often more efficient to segment on the basis of other criteria such as age, income, education, and so on.

There are, however, many ways in which advertising can be designed so as to appeal to innovators and/or otherwise enhance the diffusion and personal influence process. It is possible to directly *simulate* personal influence in the content of the advertisement itself. This is effectively used in "slice-of-life" advertising, which shows a group of people discussing the product. Normally, one of the individuals takes the role of spokesperson for the product and demonstrates or persuades the other or others to use it. Robertson[20] has argued that the advertiser can essentially seek to "simulate," "stimulate," "monitor," or "retard" personal influence. Concerning simulation, for example, advertising can be used as a replacement for personal influence. An advertising message can show people similar to the viewer who are buying and using the product and, in this sense, act as a "personal influence."

Advertisements can stimulate either information giving or information receiving. The giver of information is most likely to be a recent purchaser. He or she is likely to be in dissonance, and advertising information or direct-mail programs should supply information that can readily be passed along to others. A seeker of information is most likely to be someone considering a purchase. Advertising here should encourage themes like "Ask the man who owns one" to stimulate personal influence. A good example is the advertisement for Advil pain reliever shown in Figure 9-1.

Media can also be chosen to encourage or, in one way or another, take advantage of the flow of personal influence. In some cases, it may be appropriate to single out opinion leaders and, through selective magazines or journals (for example, *Engineering News, Golf Digest*) or through direct-mail campaigns, appeal to them directly. This type of strategy is particularly appropriate in industrial marketing. Direct mail possibly can make the communication more personal and give the recipient a feeling that she or he is part of a select group.

A wide variety of other sales and promotional devices have been used to stimulate word-of-mouth activity and to take advantage of personal influence.[21] Block parties are often used to promote china and silverware sales. In-store demonstrations give the consumer an opportunity to use the product without buying it. House-to-house sampling puts the product physically into the hands of both leaders and nonleaders and can result in source- or recipient-initiated conversations about it. The Ford Motor Company used a number of programs in introducing the Mustang. Disc jockeys, college newspaper editors, and airline stewardesses were loaned Mustangs on the theory that they were likely to influence other people. Upon evaluation, the airline stewardess program was felt to have been unsuccessful since stewardesses were not looked upon as a source of information about automobiles. The other programs were considered successful. Automobile companies, in general, attempt to stimulate adoption and interpersonal information flows through the medium of rental cars. It is a way in which the consumer or potential consumer has the opportunity to use the product without actually purchasing it.

NORMATIVE INFLUENCE: HOW ADS CAN GIVE BRANDS CULTURAL MEANING

As discussed earlier in this chapter, reference groups can influence consumers not only through the provision of information perceived to be "expert," but also through the provision of norms—standards, values, attitudes, and the like—that are influential with those who belong to, aspire to, or identify with this reference group. As with informational influence, this normative influence of reference groups is also stronger in some situations, and is particularly important and relevant with new products. In many cases, the mere fact that the product is new and other people do not yet have it is the crucial motivation for buying. New products that are significant breakthroughs at the time of

Why more and more muscle ache sufferers are switching to Advil.®

"I was given Advil and it works...It's helped my aches and pains...It's never upset my stomach."—*Derek Green*

Maybe you exercised harder than usual. Maybe you lifted something you shouldn't have. Maybe you just slept in an awkward position.

Well, whatever you did, you're paying for it with muscle aches. Just like these muscle ache sufferers, but they know what to do about it, and so should you.

Take Advil.

These people switched to Advil because it makes their muscle aches go away. They find that one Advil is just as effective as two regular aspirin or two regular-strength Tylenol. Not only that, Advil works just as well on headache, backache, and minor arthritis pain.

Yet as strong as Advil is, it doesn't upset the stomach the way aspirin sometimes can.

1899 1955 TODAY

So don't let those muscle aches make you miserable.

Learn from the experience of others like you. Switch to Advil.

advanced medicine for pain

ADVANCED MEDICINE FOR·PAIN.™
from Whitehall Laboratories

Advil contains a non-prescription strength of ibuprofen. Appearance of the brown Advil tablet and caplet is a trademark of Whitehall. © 1991 Whitehall Laboratories, N.Y., N.Y.

"Advil has always worked for me, and my doctor recommended it, so I can't go wrong."
—*Yvonne Barber*

"After a workout sometimes...I hurt all over. I take Advil and that takes the pain away. I can move freely."—*Scott Redford*

Figure 9-1. Stimulating personal influence: Advil
Courtesy of Whitehall Laboratories.

their introduction such as television sets, hand-held calculators, home computers, CD players, and so on, are particularly likely to be affected by normative influence.

However, even established products and brands vary in the degree to which normative influence operates, and this variation is due (as discussed earlier in the chapter) to differences in social visibility and conspicuousness. Staples such as salt, sugar, and pepper are not likely to be affected, whereas clothing items, particularly in the area of fashion, will be. Radios are socially very important among teenagers. Furniture and automobiles serve important social as well as functional needs and are much affected by normative influence. It might be argued that whenever the nature of the perceived risk in a product category is primarily functional, a high level of such perceived risk is accompanied by high informational interpersonal influence. In contrast, if the perceived risk is high in a social sense—when there exists uncertainty about how the consumer should act or dress or consume in a socially visible way—the nature of the reference group is likely to be normative.

While the preceding discussion may give the idea that normative reference group influence applies mainly to considerations of socially visible status, this is far from the case. We are talking here not merely of status but of every aspect of what a consumer thinks of as his or her "true self."[22] Perhaps the more inclusive way to conceptualize what is going on here is to think of the *cultural* aspects of the product or brand.

Culture has been defined by the consumer anthropologist Grant McCracken as the "lens" through which all phenomena are seen. It determines how these phenomena will be apprehended and assimilated. Culture is also the "blueprint" of human activity. It determines the coordinates of social activity and productive activity, specifying the behaviors and objects that issue from both. As a lens, culture determines how the world is seen. As a blueprint, it determines how the world will be fashioned by human effort. In short, culture constitutes the world by supplying it with meaning.[23]

According to McCracken, this "meaning" can be characterized in terms of two concepts: cultural categories and cultural principles. Cultural categories are the distinctions with which a culture divides up the world, for example, the distinction between leisure and work time or the distinctions of class, status, gender, age, and occupation. These distinctions are made concrete, among other things, through material objects. Food and clothing, for instance, can be used to set apart different levels of class and status, or gender and age. The kind of food and clothing that is considered acceptable for one may not be considered acceptable for another, and these differences in acceptability help define these different levels or classes of class and status, or gender and age. Cultural principles are the ideas with which this category creation is performed. For example, the clothing differences that are used to show the discrimination between men and women, or between high social classes and low, may do so by communicating the supposed "delicacy" of women and the supposed "strength" of men, the "refinement" of a high social class and the "vulgarity" of a lower one. "Goods are both the creations and the creators of this culturally constituted world," according to McCracken. The science of studying the kinds of cultural symbolism and signs implicit in goods is called semiotics.

Where does advertising come into all this? Well, advertising can be used to "transfer" a particular kind of cultural meaning from the outside world to a brand. Later, when the consumer buys the brand, that same meaning is then transferred from the brand to the consumer, through possession, and so on.

How is meaning transferred to a brand? An ad can bring together the brand and some other widely accepted symbol of a particular kind of cultural meaning, in such a way that the ad's viewer or reader sees an essential similarity between the two, so that that particular kind of cultural meaning now becomes a part of the brand. The cultural meaning that is desired to be communicated to the brand (e.g., gender, age, social class, ethnicity), for instance, may be currently associated (in people's minds) with certain kinds of people, places, activities, objects, times of day, and so on, and the ad may cleverly associate them with the brand, using the appropriate tone, pace, camera direction, voice-overs, and so on.

For example, a detergent ad that shows the backyard of a suburban country home, in a weekend afternoon in the summer, with a barbecue going on, then cuts to a family member embracing a small daughter—whose clothes have just been washed by that detergent—while the mother watches with pride, can be interpreted as taking the "family warmth" meaning of the embrace and transferring it to the product, so that when a mother buys and uses it she feels more like a warm, caring mother.[24] Or think of the transference of masculinity from the cultural symbol of the lone cowboy out on the range in sunset, to Marlboro cigarettes, and how that masculinity is then felt by every smoker of Marlboro.

From an advertising planning perspective, the planner needs to think about what kind of cultural meaning currently exists for the product category and the brand, then think about what kind of competitively unique cultural meaning is sought for the brand, and then finally think about how that desired cultural meaning can be linked to it. Is the product or brand used already, or to be used, as a symbol of social-class position, aspiration, or mobility? Should all social classes or genders or age groups use the product (for example, Coca-Cola) or should its use be largely confined to one social category? Is the product bound to a particular ethnic group such as kosher foods, or does the ethnic background of the consumer play little or no role? Does or should ownership signify membership in a particular subculture, such as teenage punkers (which may exclude it from the more general market)? Finally, the family *life cycle* should be considered.[25] Is the product suitable to the "empty nest" family, the young couple just starting out, or some other stage of the family life?

SUMMARY

Advertising can take advantage of reference group effects by associating the brand with certain social or reference groups. The important point about reference group effects is that the individual does not have to be a member of the group for influence to occur. In other words, the influence can occur either internally (implicitly) or externally (explicitly), and in the internal case explicit social interaction need not necessarily take place. Another key distinction is between informational influence and normative influence. Informational refers to situations in which consumers who don't know much about the product seek information from friends, salespeople, or media personalities. Normative influence refers to situations where consumers identify with a group to enhance self-image and ego, or comply with a group's norms to gain rewards or avoid punishments.

The major factors that influence the degree of group influence are (1) individual differences in susceptibility, (2) the type of the decision-making unit, (3) the nature of the product category, and (4) the kind of consumption or purchasing situation involved.

Word-of-mouth and diffusion are informational influence processes in which a potential consumer relies on the opinion of others to decide on trying and/or adopting the product. Great advertising campaigns and many otherwise worthwhile products have floundered because of a failure to stimulate diffusion and word-of-mouth communication. And the reverse is true. Some campaigns have achieved great success because of the effectiveness of diffusion and word-of-mouth. The major factors which determine the rate of diffusion and determine the success or failure of word-of-mouth are motivational characteristics of the audience (including involvement in the product being advertised, self-involvement, and other-involvement) and characteristics of the product or "innovation."

Opinion leadership is very important in understanding adoption processes. The basic idea is that certain individuals, called opinion leaders, serve to influence the attitudes and behaviors (such as buying or not buying) of others around them. The concept has been elaborated and the process of diffusion and adoption extended in many ways such as in studies of the motivations for listening to opinion leaders. From a strategies perspective, the advertiser can simulate, stimulate, monitor, or retard reference group influence.

Advertising can give brands cultural meaning through normative influence. Although products take on meaning in the absence of advertising, advertising can create, reinforce, and extend such meanings in a wide variety of ways. McCracken states that meaning can be characterized by either cultural categories or cultural principles. Cultural categories are made concrete through material objects such as food and clothing. Cultural principles are the ideas with which the category creation is performed, for example, clothing differences to distinguish men and women. Advertising can be used to transfer a particular kind of cultural meaning to a brand. The advertising planner needs to think about what kinds of cultural meaning currently exists for the product category and brand, and about how a desired cultural meaning can be linked to it.

DISCUSSION QUESTIONS

1. Identify a "reference group" to which you relate or have related in the past. Trace the situations and instances in which you have been influenced by it and whether the influence was implicit or explicit.

2. What is the difference between informative and normative reference group influence? Which is likely to play a greater role in brand choice?

3. Analyze your own motivations for sending and receiving information regarding purchasing behavior and television commercials. Compare these with the ideas of Dichter given in the chapter.

4. Design an advertisement specifically directed to stimulate a diffusion process. What are its characteristics? Why did you choose particular elements and components?

5. Find a case example of a successful and unsuccessful new product introduction. Analyze the advertising campaigns in each case from the viewpoint of the concepts and ideas given in the chapter.

6. There are five characteristics of a new product that determine adoption rate. What are they? Evaluate a new brand of laptop computer from this perspective.

7. Identify the "opinion leaders" in your class. What are their characteristics? What, if any, influence might they have on buying behavior of other class members?

NOTES

1. V. Parker Lessig and C. Whan Park, "Promotional Perspectives of Reference Group Influence: Advertising Implications," *Journal of Advertising,* 7, 1978, pp. 41–47.

2. For an excellent review of the literature on reference group effects, see William O. Bearden and Michael J. Etzel, "Reference Group Influence on Product and Brand Purchase Decisions," *Journal of Consumer Research,* 9, September 1982, pp. 183–194.

3. Martin Fishbein, "Attitude and the Prediction of Behavior," in Martin Fishbein, ed., *Readings in Attitude Theory and Measurement* (New York: John Wiley, 1967), pp. 477–492.

4. Michael J. Ryan, "Behavioral Intention Formation: The Interdependency of Attitudinal and Social Influence Variables," *Journal of Consumer Research,* 9, December 1982, pp. 263–278.

5. William O. Bearden, Richard G. Netemeyer, and Jesse E. Teel, "Measurement of Consumer Susceptibility to Interpersonal Influence," *Journal of Consumer Research,* 15, March 1989, pp. 473–481.

6. Robert B. Settle and Pamela L. Alreck, *Why They Buy* (New York: John Wiley, 1989), Chapter 7.

7. Bearden, Netemeyer, and Teel, "Measurement of Consumer Susceptibility to Interpersonal Influence."

8. C. Whan Park and Parker V. Lessig, "Students and Housewives: Differences in Susceptibility to Reference Group Influence," *Journal of Consumer Research,* 4, September 1977, pp. 102–110.

9. Thomas S. Robertson, *Innovative Behavior and Communication* (New York: Holt, Rinehart and Winston, 1971).

10. Bearden and Etzel, "Reference Group Influence on Product and Brand Purchase Decisions."

11. For recent articles on diffusion research and opinion leadership, see Hubert Gatigon and Thomas S. Richardson, "A Propositional Inventory of New Diffusion Research," *Journal of Consumer Research,* 11, March 1985, pp. 849–867, and Dorothy Leonard-Barton, "Experts as Negative Opinion Leaders in Diffusion of a Technological Innovation," *Journal of Consumer Research,* 11, March 1985, pp. 914–926.

12. Ernest Dichter, "How Word-of-Mouth Advertising Works," *Harvard Business Review,* 44, November/December 1966, pp. 147–166.

13. Everett M. Rogers, *Diffusion of Innovations* (New York: Free Press, 1962).

14. Jagdish N. Sheth, "Psychology of Innovation Resistance: The Less Developed Concept (LDC) in Diffusion Research," Working paper No. 622, College of Commerce and Business Administration, University of Illinois, Urbana, October 1979.

15. The earliest and best known follow-up studies to Katz and Lazarsfeld's *Personal Influence* (see note 16) were done on physician drug adoptions. See Herbert Menzel and Elihu Katz, "Social Relations and Innovation in the Medical Profession: The Epidemiology of a New Drug," *Public Opinion Quarterly,* 19, Winter 1956, pp. 337–352. For a fully developed treatment of the two-step flow model, see Elihu Katz, "The Two-Step Flow of Communication: An Up-to-Date Report on an Hypothesis," *Public Opinion Quarterly,* 21, Spring 1957, pp. 61–78.

16. Elihu Katz and Paul F. Lazarsfeld, *Personal Influence* (New York: Free Press, 1955), p. 138.

17. John G. Myers, "Patterns of Interpersonal Influence in the Adoptions of New Products," in Raymond M. Hass, ed., *Proceedings of the American Marketing Association* (Chicago: American Marketing Association, 1966), pp. 750–757.

18. Rogers, *Diffusion of Innovations.*

19. Dichter, "How Word-of-Mouth Advertising Works."

20. Robertson, *Innovative Behavior and Communication,* pp. 210–223.

21. Mancuso, for example, reports on a study in which high school students selected for their opinion leadership potential were given the new product (a new rock and roll record) and encouraged to use and develop positive opinions for the record among fellow classmates. See Joseph R. Mancuso, "Why Not Create Opinion Leaders for New Product Introductions?" *Journal of Marketing,* 33, July 1969, pp. 20–25.

22. Russell W. Belk, "Possessions and the Extended Self," *Journal of Consumer Research,* 15, September 1988, pp. 139–168.

23. Grant McCracken, *Culture and Consumption* (Bloomington: Indiana University Press, 1988), Chapter 5.

24. Grant McCracken, "Advertising from a Cultural Point of View: One Approach to the Gain Ad," Paper presented at the Annual Conference of the Association for Consumer Research, New York, September 1990.

25. William D. Wells and G. Gubar, "Life Cycle Concept in Marketing Research," *Journal of Marketing Research,* 3, November 1966, pp. 355–363.

10

PRECIPITATING ACTION

I belong to the school which holds that a good advertisement is one which sells the product *without drawing attention to itself*. It should rivet the reader's attention to the product. Instead of saying, "What a clever advertisement," the reader says, "I never knew *that* before. I must try this product."

It is the professional duty of the advertising agent to conceal his artifice. When Aeschines spoke, they said, "How well he speaks." But when Demosthenes spoke, they said, "Let us march against Philip." I'm for Demosthenes.

David Ogilvy, in *Confessions of an Advertising Man*

Advertising is a communication tool, and in most cases it is advantageous to set objectives and measure results in terms of intervening variables like brand awareness, brand image, or attitude. However, these communication tasks are ultimately expected to create a behavioral response to the marketplace. This behavior could be a first purchase of a brand, a visit to a retailer's showroom, or simply the act of continuing to buy the brand. Without the ultimate behavioral response, advertising can become simply good or bad entertainment.

Previous chapters have discussed the link between communication goals and behavior. In this chapter the focus is on behavior itself. It is useful to examine behavior in more detail because it provides additional insight into the nature of the link between communication goals and behavior and because there are circumstances in which behavioral measures are appropriate measures on which to base objectives. These situations will tend to have two characteristics. First, advertising will be the primary cause of immediate sales or share. The sales or share will not be affected to any substantial extent by any other types of marketing variables, nor will they be meaningfully affected by external events or actions that can be identified. Second, there will tend to be little carryover effect. Sales will be generated primarily by current advertising. Past advertising will have little relevance to the buying decision, and current advertising will have relatively little impact on future sales. Discussions follow of situations that have these characteristics to a greater or lesser extent.

It is also important to discuss these situations from another perspective. Early in this book, in Chapter 2, we mentioned that advertising has various strengths and weaknesses, and that it thus has a certain role within the company's total communications and marketing programs. One of advertising's weaknesses is its frequent failure to induce immediate action. Very often advertising can create high awareness and favorable attitudes, but it cannot create the final "push" needed to get the inquiry, trial, or sale. When such a situation appears, a marketer must use one of the other tools available. In this chapter, we discuss some of these tools: direct marketing, retail and co-op advertising, reminder advertising, inquiry-generating business-to-business advertising, and sales promotions. Using the sales force to close a sale is another element, but for a discussion of that we defer to books on sales force management.

Measuring Action/Intentions Effects

In gauging the success of action-oriented advertising, a variable often used as a good substitute for a direct behavioral measure is to ask a consumer her or his intentions with respect to brand purchase. Thus, people could be asked, on a zero- to seven-point scale, their likelihood of trying a brand or using it in a new context. The use of intentions measures is especially important in copy testing when it is often inconvenient to obtain direct measures of behavior.

The use of such purchase intention measures to predict actual purchase behavior is not without its problems. Research has shown that the correspondence between stated intentions and actual behavior is lower when the consumer actually is uncertain about the characteristics of the brand, does not really like the brand, when the brand is not easily affordable, when others are consulted or involved in the actual decision, when there is a long information search process (as with expensive durables), and when the brand is not widely available. In such (and certain other) situations, it may be advisable to "adjust" the stated intentions measures to get a more accurate reading on likely sales effects, using certain "weighting" schemes that researchers have developed.[1]

DIRECT MARKETING

The clearest example of a situation where advertising relates closely enough to sales to warrant specific behavioral objectives is in direct marketing efforts, where direct solicitations (through the mail, the phone, or other means) try to make a sale without being overly concerned with establishing the firm's name or drawing on a previously established name. In this case, factors like store location, shelf display, and other marketing variables are not involved. The direct marketing advertisement could be assumed to be the principal force in precipitating a purchase decision. Furthermore, there would be no carryover effect, assuming that the impact of that one exposure does not induce purchasing on future occasions. In this instance an advertising objective based on a sales measure becomes highly appropriate and operational. Decisions regarding copy and audience can indeed be made using short-term sales as a criterion. Furthermore, the results can be measured and compared against the objective.

Figure 10-1 shows an advertisement from a very successful mail-order campaign. Although the advertisement is not a one-time effort but part of a continuing campaign, its primary goal is intended to precipitate immediate response and its effectiveness can properly be measured by this response.

Direct marketing advertising has long been recognized as being perhaps the only area in advertising in which immediate sales are a reliable indication of advertising performance. As a result, advertising professionals look to the experience of mail-order advertisers to learn what works and what doesn't. In 1923 Claude Hopkins, one of the great creative people in advertising, wrote a book called *Scientific Advertising* in which he made this point. In his words,

> The severest test of an advertising man is in selling goods by mail. But that is a school from which he must graduate before he can hope for success. There cost and result are immediately apparent. False theories melt away like snowflakes in the sun. The advertising is profitable or it is not, clearly on the face of returns. Figures which do not lie tell one at once the merits of an ad.
>
> This puts men on their mettle. All guesswork is eliminated. Every mistake is conspicuous. One quickly loses his conceit by learning how often his judgment errs—often nine times in ten.
>
> There one learns that advertising must be done on a scientific basis to have any fair chance at success. And he learns how every wasted dollar adds to the cost of results. Here he is taught efficiency and economy under a master who can't be fooled. Then, and only then, is he apt to apply the same principles and keys to all advertising. . . . A study of mail order advertising reveals many things worth learning. . . . Study those ads with respect. There is proved advertising, not theoretical. It will not deceive you. The lessons it teaches are principles which wise men apply to all advertising.[2]

Direct marketing actually has two key advantages that differentiate it from regular, mass, advertising: the ability to target specific, individual consumers (not just demographically described segments) and the just-mentioned ability to directly measure response. It is these two features that have led to the tremendous growth in direct marketing over the past decade. In fact, more and more traditional "mass market" advertisers have taken to combining direct marketing efforts with their regular advertising efforts. For example, a magazine advertisement for an automobile may feature a coupon inviting the reader to write in for a free copy of a book that will help him make a better automobile buying decision. The coupon collects not just the reader's name, address, and telephone number, but also information on his present car, and how soon he expects to buy his next car. This information is then entered into a computer data base, and this data base is subsequently utilized to target certain individuals for further mailings or telemarketing efforts. Every response (or nonresponse), which can be directly tracked and attributed to a specific mailing piece or phone call, is entered into this data base, and the cycle of targeting and measuring response continues.

Figure 10-1. A successful mail-order advertisement
Courtesy of Book-of-the-Month Club, Inc.

Because of the high cost of personal sales calls, companies also often use direct marketing in after-market sales (e.g., selling copier supplies to people who bought copiers, and whose names and addresses and phone numbers are now in a data base), and in generating sales inquiries that can then be followed-up by telephone and personal sales calls. The use of data bases also allows companies to use direct market to target mailings of coupons and samples to only high-opportunity individuals and households. The traditional users of direct marketing have always been the magazines and newspapers (who use it to sell subscriptions), the marketers of insurance-by-mail, the record and book clubs (in what are called the "negative option continuity programs," where you get sent something every few weeks till you say no), and of course the catalog retailers (such as Sears, Land's End, etc.).

The targeting ability of direct marketing can be greatly enhanced by a systematic development of the direct marketer's data base. Someone who knows your address, and thus your postal zip code, can obtain information from data base companies about various characteristics (such as the median income, average age, etc.), of the zip code in which you live, based on the average for the geodemographic "cluster" in which you live (such clusters were discussed in Chapter 4). This information is then used to assess whether you are a likely prospect for a particular product, on the assumption that your individual profile is similar to the average data available for your zip code. The "average profile" of people living in Donnelley's "ClusterPLUS" 47 clusters are provided in Figure 10-2; every household can be classified into one of these clusters based on its zip code. In addition, data are also available that apply to you as an individual: life-style (hobby and activity) information supplied by you on product warranty registration cards can be purchased, as can driving licence and automobile registration data (in most states). These data are used by companies to decide who to mail, and who not to mail, thus, it is hoped, boosting response rates to a particular mailing.[3]

Typically, the direct marketing companies compute response on a "response rates per thousand mailings" basis, transformed to CPO (cost per order). They can tell which mailing you responded to by using code numbers (called key codes) on the response coupons, where a particular key code uniquely identifies a mailing package. Companies continually test different mailing packages to see which ones pull best.

Response rates—which can be very low, often just 1 to 2 percent of the people mailed—are a function of many factors. First, of course, there is the product being offered, at a certain price and payment term, and with or without a premium or free gift. Second, there are the quality and responsiveness of the names in the mailing lists that the direct marketer is renting, through a list broker or list compiler (perhaps paying a hundred dollars for every thousand names mailed). Third, of course, is the quality of the creative message: the letter, the brochure, the envelope, and so on.

This is where the psychology of inducing action becomes important. Think about the state of mind of a consumer opening a direct-mail solicitation. He or she has doubts about the quality of the product, since it cannot physically be inspected. There is no salesperson to answer questions and overcome objections. And there is the very human tendency to postpone things: even if the consumer feels vaguely interested, there will typically be a reaction of "I'll get around to this later, not now."

What good direct marketing copywriters have discovered—and this is the wisdom that even "general" advertisers can benefit from—is that direct-mail copy that gets action tries hard to (1) use testimonials and guarantees to develop confidence; (2) use as

Figure 10-2. Demographic characteristics of selected ClusterPLUS℠ neighborhood clusters

Cluster code

01	Highest SESI, highest income, prime real estate areas, highest education level, professionally employed, low mobility, homeowners, children in private schools
02	Very high household income, new homes and condominiums, prime real estate areas, highly mobile, high education level, professionally employed, homeowners, families with children
03	High income, high home values, new homes, highly mobile, younger, high education level, professionally employed, homeowners, married couples, high incidence of children, larger families
04	High income, high home values, high education level, professionally employed, married couples, larger families, highest incidence of teenagers, homeowners, homes built in 60's
05	High income, high home values, high education level, professionally employed, low mobility, homeowners, homes built in 50's and 60's
06	Highest incidence of children, large families, new homes, highly mobile, younger, married couples, above average income and education, homeowners
07	Apartments and condominiums, high rent, above average income, high education level, professionally employed, mobile, singles, few children, urban areas
08	Above average income, above average education, older, fewer children, white collar workers
09	Above average income, average education, households with two or more workers, homes built in 60's and 70's
10	High education level, average income, professionally employed, younger, mobile, apartment dwellers, above average rents
11	Above average income, average education, families with children, high incidence of teenagers, homeowners, homes built in 60's, small towns
12	Highly mobile, young, working couples, young children, new homes, above average income and education, white collar workers
13	Older, fewer children, above average income, average education, white collar workers, homeowners, homes built in 50's, very low mobility, small towns
14	Retirees, condominiums and apartments, few children, above average income and education, professionally employed, high home values and rents, urban areas
15	Older, very low mobility, fewer children, above average income and education, white collar workers, old housing, urban areas
16	Working couples, very low mobility, above average income, average education, homeowners, homes built in 50's, urban areas
17	Very young, below average income, high education level, professionally employed, highly mobile, singles, few children, apartment dwellers, high rent areas
18	High incidence of children, larger families, above average income, average education, working couples, homeowners

Source: Donnelley Marketing Information Services.

much information as is necessary in the letter to clarify doubts, overcome objections, and increase the reader's level of desire for the product; (3) make it easy for the consumer to take action, by having easy-to-use response cards or toll-free telephone numbers; (4) "involve" the reader, through devices such as peel-off stamps and scratch-off numbers; and (5) impel urgency about the need for immediate response, by saying that the offer or free premium is good "for a limited time," expires by a certain date, and so on. In direct marketing, as in all marketing, the key barrier to getting consumers to act is sheer inertia, and ads that target such inertia directly are most likely to obtain action.

RETAIL ADVERTISING

Another example of a situation that comes close to meeting the two criteria when action objectives are appropriate is the advertising of retailers. Although shopping trips are influenced by a host of variables, there are situations in which advertising can have an important and immediate impact on store traffic and sales. David Ogilvy, in fact, has pointed out that, next to direct-mail advertising, the

> most valuable source of information as to what makes some techniques succeed and others fail is the experience of department stores. "The day after they run an advertisement they can count the sales it has produced. That is why I am so attentive to the advertising practices of Sears, Roebuck, who are the most knowing of all retailers."[4]

What are the advertising practices of successful retailers? The best retail advertisements are those that provide the consumer with a lot of specific information, so that the consumer can see immediately that he or she must indeed visit the store. It is not enough, therefore, to say (for example) that the shirts on sale are available in various colors and sizes; it is much more action-inducing to list the exact colors, sizes, and prices. Any piece of missing information could hinder action. It is also important to create a sense of immediate availability and urgency, by stressing that this availability (and these prices) are "for a limited time only."

While there is probably little carryover effect of advertising of a specific storewide sale, retail advertisers are very particular that every retail ad fit and enhance the specific long-term image of the store. Every ad from Bloomingdale's, Lord & Taylor, Bergdorf's, and so on is carefully tuned to the particular character—the "look and feel"—that the store has carefully developed over the years.

For durable products, such as large appliances and automobiles, an appropriate behavioral objective for advertising might be to entice customers to visit a dealer's showroom. For large-ticket consumer items, the final phases of the selling process are usually best handled by a person-to-person sales effort, with advertising used appropriately to draw people to the showroom. In such situations, "traffic-building" advertising becomes key, and (once again) the advertising must try to create a strong sense of desire, curiosity, and urgency to get the reader or viewer to make that store visit.

With any behavioral measure, it is important, for purposes of budgeting and performance evaluation, to estimate the value of the behavioral action. Thus, the value of a visit to an automobile showroom should be estimated. What percentage of those visiting a showroom eventually buy an automobile? Is this percentage different for those attracted by the advertising?

Similarly, retailers and shopping centers often have as the primary objective of advertising the generation of store traffic. Thus, a count of shoppers (or a surrogate measure such as cars entering the parking lot) might be a better measure of advertising than daily sales. One study attempted to evaluate the impact of a small sales catalog mailed directly to more than 290,000 residents of a metropolitan area.[5] The catalog contained 210 items, emphasized price, and was sent by a chain of seven large discount department stores. In-store interviews of 1,400 shoppers were conducted to determine the impact of the catalog. Of the total sample,

- 66.5 percent received the catalog.
- 57.8 percent read the catalog.
- 28.6 percent were in the store to buy something advertised in the catalog.
- 24.9 percent bought something read about in the catalog.

Such data fall short of providing the number attracted to the stores by the advertising, because it is not known how many of the 57.8 percent who read the catalog might have come to the chain store that day anyway. One approach would be to ask the respondents when they last shopped at the chain and to compare their answers to those obtained from a second, control sample. The increase in shopping frequency would allow an estimate of the extra shoppers generated by the advertising.

COOPERATIVE ADVERTISING

A closely related situation to retail advertising is cooperative advertising, in which a manufacturer offers retailers an advertising program for the latter to run.[6] The program may include suggested advertising formats, materials to be used to create actual advertisements, and money to pay a portion (often, half) of the cost. It also often includes requests or requirements that the retailer stock certain merchandise quantities and perhaps use certain displays. By some estimates, almost one-half of retail advertising is some form of co-op advertising. There are three types of co-op advertising: vertical (when an "upstream" manufacturer pays for a "downstream" retailer's ads), horizontal (when local dealers in a geographical area pool money, as in automobiles or fast-food chains), and ingredient producer co-op (when the producer of an ingredient, such as Nutrasweet, pays part of an ad run by the "user" product, such as Diet Coke).

The intent of cooperative advertising, in part, is often to stimulate short-term sales. The advertising is well suited to this task because it is usually specific as to the product, the place at which it can be purchased, and the price. However, co-op advertising also has other longer-term objectives: namely, to reinforce the brand image of the original manufacturer or service provider and to maintain the manufacturing company's leverage with the retail trade. The former implies that the manufacturer needs to monitor and control co-op advertising content carefully, to ensure that it is consistent with the national ad campaign. The latter is especially important because retail store buyers and salespeople often favor products that come with large allowances, to the extent that a product not having the expected co-op amount can find itself losing distribution.

Given these pressures from the retail trade (and from one's own sales force) to maintain and even increase co-op advertising allowances, a marketer is often tempted to allocate more money into co-op at the expense of national advertising. In deciding how much money to allocate to co-op, the marketer needs to determine if his product will really benefit from being associated with a store's image. Such benefits are typically higher for the case of fashion goods, hi-fi stereo equipment, and so on, which are expensive and image-driven products where consumers seek retail information and endorsements; these benefits are lower for inexpensive, frequently purchased products (such as toothpaste or shampoo) where the consumer does not seek retail advice. The key question is: What are the relative roles of national advertising and store advertising in influencing consumer brand choice processes?

In addition to looking at consumer decision processes, the advertising planner must also be concerned with the need to acquire or expand distribution; a high need typically compels higher co-op allowances. Further, legal and administrative requirements must be met. For example, co-op allowances have to be offered on an "equally available to all" basis, unless it can be demonstrated that certain stores (to whom proportionately higher allowances are being offered) will lead to a greater gain in new customers to the manufacturer.[7] A co-op program is likely to yield greater benefits to the manufacturing company if the program is tightly monitored (e.g., limited to certain slow-moving sizes of products rather than all sizes).

REMINDER ADVERTISING

Sometimes the primary role of advertising is to act as a reminder to buy and use the brand. The brand may be established and have a relatively solid, stable image. Reminder advertising then serves to stimulate immediate purchase and/or use to counter the inroads of competition. A good example is the Budweiser advertisement shown in Figure 10-3. Because the primary impact of advertising is thus immediate and because other factors such as distribution and price are likely to be fairly stable, sales or market share become appropriate measures of advertising.

Reminder advertising can work in several ways. First, it can enhance the top-of-mind awareness of the brand, thus increasing the probability that the brand gets included on the shopping list or gets purchased as an impulse item. A media plan that aims to enhance or maintain top-of-mind awareness through reminder ads might utilize shorter ads (such as 15-second commercials) with a high level of frequency or use media such as outdoor billboards or transit that are suited to such reminder advertising. In addition, it is

Figure 10-3. A reminder advertisement
Courtesy of Anheuser-Busch, Inc.

often useful in such situations to use items of "specialty advertising," useful products given free to consumers that have the manufacturer's name and related information on them. Specialty advertising items go beyond the usual calendars, ball-point pens, coasters and Rolodex cards to all kinds of creative, high-quality products (such as a refrigerator magnet for Domino's Pizza that reminds a hungry but time-starved consumer which phone number to call for quick, home-delivered pizza). Manufactured by "supplier" companies, such specialty advertising items are not usually dealt with by traditional advertising agencies but by organizations called specialty distributors or specialty advertising agencies.[8]

Second, in addition to maintaining top-of-mind awareness for a particular brand, reminder advertising can also increase the motivation for the use of the product class as a whole. In this context the advertising may tend to simply increase the purchase and use of the product class and thus work to the advantage of the leading brand. Thus, reminder advertising for Royal Crown Cola may tend to increase purchases of other colas to the advantage of Coke and Pepsi. Similarly, Campbell's Soup is the soup brand that is in the best position to conduct reminder advertising.

INDUSTRIAL MARKETING: SALES LEADS

Industrial ("business-to-business") marketing is similar to the marketing of durables in that advertising can rarely be expected to make the sales. Rather, a salesperson is usually required to supply information and to handle the details of the transaction. Advertising, in this case, can provide the engineer or buyers with the opportunity to express interest in the product by returning a card which is a request for additional information. These inquiries or leads are then typically "qualified" by a telemarketing callback to determine if an in-person sales call is necessary and cost effective. Often this telemarketing call can itself lead to a sale. Once "qualified," the salesperson then follows up these leads by calling on the prospect, discussing his or her requirements, and trying to "close" the sale. Thus, for industrial advertising, a useful objective is to generate such inquiries or leads. Figure 10-4 shows a rather dramatic industrial advertisement for Savin copiers. The reader can get specific information by calling the toll-free number in the ad.

SOCIAL DEMARKETING

Some marketing programs, especially in the social marketing field, are designed to get people to use less of a product or to discontinue the use of a product completely. In such cases, a behavioral measure will often be a useful basis for a primary or secondary advertising objective. For example, advertising campaigns have been developed that included such behavioral objectives as encouraging people

- To stop smoking or drug abuse
- To reduce the temperature level in homes in the winter
- To reduce the use of the automobile
- To reduce the use of bridges and highways during rush hours
- To refrain from driving while drinking

Such "social" action objectives are often very difficult to achieve, because the consumer is not offered any immediate reward (indeed, the advocated behavior often reduces pleasure), and because the target behavior is reinforced by a complex of other social forces (for example, peer pressure). An excellent discussion of the problems faced by such advertising can be found in an article by Rothschild.[9]

SALES PROMOTIONS

Sales promotions are of two broad types: consumer promotions, such as coupons, sampling, premiums, and sweepstakes, and trade promotions, such as allowances for featuring the product in retail advertising, display and merchandising allowances, and the like. They are used to get consumers to try or repurchase the brand, and to get the retail trade

The original Savin 750

THIS COPIER OUTLASTED 52 VPs, 14 SR VPs, 4 CFOs, AND ONE S.O.B.

Ah yes, the ever-changing faces at the office. Some with titles they're not even aware of. But nobody ever talks behind a Savin copier's back. They're so dependable they've been known to last twenty years. Perhaps the only reason you'd replace your old Savin copier is to get your hands on the full range capability of a new one. Take the new Savin 9710. It has all the features you

© 1991 Savin Corporation

need in this don't-give-me-any-problems-I-have-to-have-it-now-or-the-S.O.B.-will-fire-me business world. Like high speed and high volume performance, with a 3700-sheet paper capacity. Seven

The new Savin 9710

preset enlargement/reduction modes, automatic copying from unburst computer forms, simple guidance display, and a Job Card System that makes those tedious copying jobs duck soup. So here are two suggestions. Pray that the S.O.B. doesn't resurface at your next job. And call Savin today at 1-800-52-SAVIN.

WE MIND YOUR BUSINESS.

Figure 10-4. An industrial ad seeking inquiries and leads
Courtesy of Savin Corporation.

302

to carry and "push" the brand. While this is a book about advertising management, and while sales promotions is a distinct area of research and management—with its own textbooks[10]—it is necessary for us to spend some time discussing sales promotions. There are three reasons for doing so.

First, sales promotions are a key element in inducing trial or repurchase in many communications programs in which advertising creates awareness and favorable attitudes, but fails to spur action. Thus it is important to understand the complementary roles of advertising and sales promotions in order to conduct situation analyses properly and to set communication, advertising, and sales promotions goals.

Second, according to a 1989 survey of promotional practices in 70 leading companies, sales promotions take up about 66 percent of marketing expenditures (about 27 percent on consumer promotions, 40 percent on trade promotions), while advertising takes up about 33 percent.[11] The share of the marketing dollar spent on promotions has risen rapidly in recent years, in part due to the growing power of ever-larger retail chains, which now have access to accurate checkout scanner data on which brands are moving fast off the retail shelves, and which are not. Clearly, since advertising expenditures take place in this total promotional context and not in isolation, it is essential that the advertising manager have a good understanding of sales promotions as well. While the implementation details of sales promotions and advertising are handled by different individuals in most marketing organizations, brand managers usually are responsible for both areas.

Finally, advertising and sales promotions operate together in their impact on the consumer. When designed and run in tandem, they yield powerful synergies that magnify their individual effects. For example, a coupon offer in a Sunday newspaper free-standing insert (FSI) can have a higher redemption rate if theme ads for that brand are run concurrently. On the other hand, if advertising and sales promotion efforts are designed and run in isolation, they can lead to effects that hurt each other—poorly designed promotions, in particular, can quickly erode the long-term image of the brand that advertising has worked hard to build up over several years. This longer-term "brand equity dilution" effect of promotions is probably greater for brands in highly involving image and "feeling" products, where promotions might "cheapen" a brand's image, rather than for brands in product categories where choices are based on "economic," price-minimizing criteria.[12]

It is therefore essential that the advertising manager understand the need for this interaction between advertising and sales promotions. The thrust of this section thus will be to explore this interaction. Before we do that, however, we will briefly describe several different types of sales promotion, stressing those aspects that relate in some way to the advertising program.

Consumer promotions are designed to offer consumers an incentive (such as a lower price or a free or low-cost premium or gift) to try a brand for the first time, to switch back to it, or to repurchase it. Coupons are perhaps the most frequently used consumer promotion—over 263 billion coupons were distributed in the United States through print media in 1989, with a face value of about $115 billion—but only about 4 percent, or $4.5 billion worth, were redeemed.[13] Though over 75 percent of all coupons are currently distributed through newspaper FSIs,[14] coupons distributed through direct mail are more targeted than are those distributed through print media (newspapers and magazines), and thus have much higher redemption rates (about 9 to 10 percent in direct mail versus about 2 to 3 percent in newspapers). While coupons that are in or on the pack are specifically designed to build repeat purchase and loyalty, those that are carried in other products consumed by a similar target market (such as coupons for a baby shampoo carried in a diaper product) are designed to attract new customers. These latter coupons are called ''cross-ruff'' coupons. Coupons (or cash checks) are often offered as straight price ''rebates'' for durable products, such as cars or appliances, and are sometimes offered as ''refunds,'' mailed to consumers who send in proof of purchase.

The important thing in couponing, from an advertising perspective, is to design the coupon ad in such a way that it builds off of, and reinforces, the positioning and key benefits developed in theme advertising, rather than having a different theme (or no theme at all, other than the price incentive). Similarly, a rebate offer might be creatively designed to play off a brand strength—for instance, an offer to pay for a car's gas consumption or maintenance expenses in its first year might better highlight the car's gas economy or repair record than a simple rebate check.

This synergy can work the other way as well: coupons or other promotional offers can be used to increase the effectiveness of an ad, by increasing readership. Apple Computer supported the introduction of its Macintosh with a ''Test Drive a Macintosh'' promotion, which allowed customers to leave computer showrooms with $2,400 worth of equipment.[15] The budget was $10 million, of which $8 million went to advertising and the rest supported such activities as in-store displays and carrying the inventory costs. Around 200,000 Macintoshes were test driven, at a cost of only $5 each.

Giving people free samples or trial packs (door to door, at street corners, in stores, or through the mail) is another promotional technique and is an excellent (but expensive) way to get trial. Figure 10-5 shows an ad for Lipton's new teas that asks consumers to write in for trial tea bags. It is often appropriate to do such sampling for new brands, after running an introductory flight of ads to build awareness and favorable attitudes (so that consumers who receive the free sample already know about it and are predisposed to try it). It may often be more cost effective to do such sampling than to run additional advertising for such new brands, after that introductory advertising. When feasible, the advertising could feature an in-store coupon for a free trial pack or a toll-free phone number to call for one.

Price packs (packs that offer a lower than usual price, or greater than usual quantity) are another kind of consumer promotion that can both attract switching and reinforce loyalty. Here again, it may be more supportive of the brand's advertised image to offer ''extra'' product volume than to simply lower price. For some products (such as tea, coffee, detergents, etc.), it may be possible to offer the ''extra'' volume in a special container (such as a glass carafe, or plastic dispensing unit) that reinforces some aspect of the brand's image.

The same kind of thinking can be used to select premiums that are offered to consumers (these are ''free'' products that are provided in the pack or mailed if multiple proofs of purchase are sent in, either at no cost or at below-retail prices. If the latter, they

Figure 10-5. Sampling via trial packs: Lipton Teas

Courtesy of Thomas J. Lipton Company.

are called self-liquidating premiums, because the company recovers its out-of-pocket costs). An intelligently selected premium can be used to reinforce a brand image: Mueslix cereal from Kellogg, from instance, which built its initial advertising campaign around a European heritage, offered consumers a packet of European currency notes if they sent in the required number of proofs of purchase. In-pack premiums (such as toy characters in children's cereals) can also be designed to build a brand's image.

Sweepstakes are another kind of consumer promotion, and these offer the greatest potential to reinforce a brand's advertising platform. McDonald's, for instance, ran a sweepstakes promotion at the same time that its ads were featuring a "McDonald's menu song" in which consumers had to play a plastic record to find out if they had won—with the record featuring the same menu song. Benson & Hedges cigarettes, around the time it launched a 100mm-length version, ran a sweepstakes in which consumers had to pick which one of a hundred minicontests they wanted to enter, in which each of these minicontests had as their prize 100 units of something (such as 100 pints of ice cream).

The key thought in the foregoing discussion on consumer promotions is that promotions often hurt a brand's image by cheapening it but that this is not necessary if the promotion is designed with a view to working with and strengthening the brand's advertised image. A similar logic applies to trade promotions. These are financial incentives given to the trade to buy in larger quantities, to move merchandise from the warehouse onto the retail shelf, to display the brand in end-aisle displays, to feature the brand in local retailer advertising (such as on "best food days" such as Wednesdays or Thursdays), including offering retailer coupons, and so on. (Co-operative advertising was discussed earlier in this chapter.) These trade promotions often have the objective of "buying" retail shelf space and getting additional retailer "push" by loading the retailer with extra inventory or of giving the retailer a temporarily lower price in the hope that some of the price cut is passed on to the consumer.

There is emerging consensus that these trade promotions also have the potential to erode a brand's franchise and image. They do this by reducing the amount spent on advertising, and in increasing the extent to which the consumers buy the brand in the supermarket because it is "on deal" that week, rather than because of its advertised image. This leads to an increase in the perception that the brand is a commodity, or parity product, rather than something with unique added values (the subject of Chapters 6 through 9). Here, again, the smart advertiser must strive to "focus" these trade deals on advertising-enhancing activities (such as thematically linked displays or thematically consistent retailer advertising). In the longer run, of course, only an advertiser with a strong brand consumer franchise—built up through consistent advertising—will have the market clout to withstand retailer pressure to provide higher and higher trade allowances. Strong brands with demonstrated "sell-through" (advertising-induced consumer demand) will not have to give as much to the retailer (though the trade will often "push" stronger brands of their own accord) and will thus end up as more profitable brands.

Thus far we have discussed the interaction between advertising and promotions mainly in terms of the *content* of both. Another form of interaction pertains to their *timing:* consumers are more likely to notice the advertising for a brand and the promotions for it if both are run concurrently rather than in separate time periods. Such a coordinated campaign is more likely to break through the clutter. This is likely to enhance the effectiveness of both the advertising campaign (through higher readership or viewership) and of the promotional program (through greater coupon redemption or in-store sales from special displays).

SUMMARY

When there is a strong link between advertising and sales or market share, and carryover effects are small, it can be appropriate to use immediate sales or share as a basis for setting advertising objectives and measuring performance. Such a situation often exists in direct marketing campaigns, retailer advertising (including co-op advertising), reminder advertising, business-to-business advertising intended to generate sales leads, sales promotions, and some "social demarketing" campaigns.

Even when carryover effects are substantial, it can be useful to have immediate sales or shares as part of a dual objective. Other behavioral measures can also be appropriate in some situations. A durable goods manufacturer may wish to precipitate visits to a showroom. An industrial advertiser may want to generate leads for his or her salespeople. A demarketing campaign may want to reduce driving. For copy-testing purposes, the behavior response could be estimated by some form of intention measure.

Direct marketing is one communications approach that aims to evoke action. Its distinctive features are the ability to target small segments of consumers, to measure response to different offers, and to build customer data bases. Direct marketing ads try to get consumers to respond immediately by building confidence, providing information, making it easy to order, involving consumers in the order process, and creating a sense of urgency to battle inertia.

Retail ads aim both to build the store's image and to create immediate sales, through building store traffic. They do this by giving the consumer a large amount of information on prices, locations, and the exact nature of the products being sold, and by creating a sense of urgency about the sale. Co-op ads, paid for by both the retailer and the manufacturer, are another important form of retail advertising. The important decision for a client in the case of co-op advertising is deciding how much money should be spent on it, and how its effectiveness can be maximized.

Reminder advertising seeks to maintain high top-of-mind awareness, through high frequency and other visibility-enhancing means. Industrial ads seek to generate leads and inquiries that can then be followed up through sales calls. Social demarketing efforts seek to change behaviors, in socially beneficial ways.

Sales promotions can be designed to create trial purchases, to stimulate short-term sales, to enhance purchase volume or brand loyalty, or to affect the brand image. Consumer promotional devices include coupons, samples, price packs, premiums, and sweepstakes. Trade promotions attempt to obtain or maintain shelf space, build retail inventory, get retail "push," and lower retail prices. More money is spent on sales promotions than on advertising, and it is essential that sales promotion efforts be coordinated with advertising efforts, to maximize the effectiveness of each and to ensure that the sales promotions do not dilute the long-term image of the brand.

DISCUSSION QUESTIONS

1. Suppose that you are the advertising manager of a large department store who had been asked by the president to establish a system to measure the effectiveness of advertising. How would you go about developing such a system? What measures would you use? How would you test the advertisements before they run to determine if they will be effective?

2. What types of behavioral measures might the following consider using as the basis for advertising objectives? How would they go about determining which to select? How would they formulate the objective: establishing the number and nature of behavioral responses?
   a. Cereal company
   b. Pest-control company
   c. Oil company
   d. Farm equipment manufacturer
   e. Large bank
   f. *Time* magazine
   g. Computer company

3. Provide examples of current advertising campaigns that seem to be directed at generating behavioral response. Are they attempting to communicate information and/or change attitudes or are they concerned solely with behavior? Write a reasonable objective for each campaign that is operational. How would you measure results against that objective?

4. Consider the American Airlines frequent flyer program, a free sample program for a new soap, a 25 percent off price offered to retailers by a cereal brand, and two promotions that recently affected your purchasing. What were the objectives of these promotions? What role does advertising play in these promotions? What impact will these promotions have in the long-term? How would you measure that impact?

5. Compare the advantages and disadvantages of the different consumer promotions techniques with respect to alternative objectives of (a) getting trial from new consumers, (b) "holding" (retaining) present customers, and (c) building brand image.

6. Examine a direct-mail promotional piece you (or somebody you know) has recently received. Look at every element of the package, and discuss its role in promoting consumer action.

7. Select an ad (or public service announcement) that has recently been attempting to change a consumer behavior, and discuss its strengths and weaknesses. Why is it usu-

ally so difficult for such messages to succeed in such objectives? How could such messages be better designed?

8. Select two retailers' ads, from different product categories, that you have recently seen, and discuss their strengths and weaknesses with respect to (a) building store image and (b) increasing sales in the short term. If you were a manufacturer being pressured to increase co-op advertising allowances in these two cases, in which one is it more beneficial to you to do so? Why?

9. Identify a sales promotion that has recently been run that you think works to enhance the brand image, and one that serves to hurt brand image. Justify your selections.

NOTES

1. Linda F. Jamieson and Frank M. Bass, ''Adjusting Stated Intentions Measures to Predict Trial Purchase of New Products: A Comparison of Models and Methods,'' *Journal of Marketing Research*, 26, August 1989, pp. 336–345.

2. Claude C. Hopkins, *My Life in Advertising/Scientific Advertising* (Chicago: Crain Books, 1966), pp. 229–230.

3. For information on data-based direct marketing, consult *The New Direct Marketing: How to Implement a Profit-Driven Database Marketing Strategy*, by David Shepard Associates, Inc. (Homewood, IL: Dow Jones-Irwin, 1990). For more general information on direct marketing, see Robert Stone, *Successful Direct Marketing Methods*, 4th ed. (National Textbook Company, NTC Business Books, Lincolnwood, IL, 1988).

4. David Ogilvy, *Confessions of an Advertising Man* (New York: Atheneum, 1964), p. 92.

5. Danny N. Bellenger and Jack R. Pingry, ''Direct-Mail Advertising for Retail Stores,'' *Journal of Advertising Research*, 17, June 1977, pp. 35–39.

6. Robert F. Young, ''Cooperative Advertising, Its Uses and Effectiveness: Some Preliminary Hypotheses,'' Marketing Science Institute Working Paper, 1979.

7. Isadore Barmash, ''FTC Plans Rule Change on Co-op Ads,'' *The New York Times*, February 21, 1989.

8. For details, see George L. Herpel and Steve Slack, *Specialty Advertising: New Dimensions in Creative Marketing*, published by the Specialty Advertising Association International, Irving, Texas.

9. Michael L. Rothschild, ''Marketing Communications in Nonbusiness Situations, or Why It's So Hard to Sell Brotherhood Like You Sell Soap,'' *Journal of Marketing*, 43, Spring 1979, pp. 11–20.

10. See, for example, Robert C. Blattberg and Scott A. Neslin, *Sales Promotions: Concepts, Methods, and Strategies* (Englewood Cliffs, NJ: Prentice Hall, 1990); John A. Quelch, *Sales Promotion Management* (Englewood Cliffs, NJ: Prentice Hall, 1989); Don E. Schultz and William A. Robinson, *Sales Promotion Management* (Chicago: Crain Books, 1982); John C. Totten and Martin P. Block, *Analyzing Sales Promotions: Text and Cases* (Chicago: Commerce Communications, 1987); and Stanley M. Ulanoff, ed., *Handbook of Sales Promotion* (New York: McGraw-Hill, 1985).

11. *Adweek*'s Promote, February 5, 1990, p. P4.

12. Blattberg and Neslin, *Sales Promotions*, p. 474.

13. *Advertising Age*, May 21, 1990, p. 45.

14. *Advertising Age*, April 3, 1989, p. 38.

15. William A. Robinson and Kevin Brown, ''Best Promotions of 1984: Back to Basics,'' *Advertising Age*, March 11, 1985, p. 42.

CASES FOR PART III

SEVEN-UP*

The 7-Up soft drink was introduced under the name of Bib-Label Lithiated Lemon-Lime Soda in 1929, two weeks prior to the stock market crash. It was promoted as a product "for home and hospital use." Consumers used the product primarily as a mixer and as a cure for hangovers. Demand for the product was modest during the 1930s, primarily because 7-Up faced competition from about 600 other lemon-flavored soft drinks.

In 1942, the Chicago office of J. Walter Thompson was hired as the agency for 7-Up. At that time the name was changed to 7-Up. Sales for 7-Up showed impressive growth over the next two decades, and Seven-Up emerged as the third largest producer of soft drinks behind Coca-Cola and Pepsi.

In the 1960s, sales of the soft drink category grew dramatically. The post–World War II baby boom had caused a significant increase in the 14- to 24-year old age category, and this category comprised a disproportionate number of the heavy users of soft drinks. However, as Exhibit 1 shows, Seven-Up failed to keep up with industry growth. For example, while industry dollar sales grew 8 percent between 1964 and 1965, Seven-Up experienced no growth in sales. Seven-Up also lagged the industry in 1966 and 1967. Part of the problem appeared to be the introduction of lemon-lime–flavored drinks by competitors. Coca-Cola introduced Sprite and Fresca, PepsiCo marketed Teem, Royal Crown promoted Upper-10, and Canada Dry introduced Wink. Seven-Up management also was concerned that 7-Up was being viewed by consumers as a mixer. This was a concern because the demand for mixers was much smaller than the demand for soft drinks.

EXHIBIT 1   Percentage Change in Dollar Sales from Previous Years

	1965	1966	1967
Industry	8	13	11
7-Up	0	6	4

To determine how 7-Up might compete effectively, the Seven-Up Company and J. Walter Thompson conducted research. One question posed to consumers involved naming all the soft drinks they could think of. People named Coke, Pepsi, RC, Tab, Diet

*Source: Professor Brian Sternthal, J. L. Kellogg Graduate School of Management, Northwestern University. Reproduced by permission.

Rite. 7-Up was mentioned infrequently. Yet when people were later asked what 7-Up was, almost all respondents knew it was a soft drink. Apparently, people knew what 7-Up was, but had little top-of-mind awareness of the brand when cued with the stimulus soft drink.

Research was also conducted to determine the characteristics people associated with Coke, Pepsi, and 7-Up. People were presented with an attribute and asked whether or not each brand had that attribute. The percentage of those respondents who believed Coke, Pepsi and 7-Up had the attribute inquired about is shown in Exhibit 2.

On the basis of this information, a decision had to be made regarding how to promote 7-Up. One possibility was to emphasize attributes such as 7-Up's value in mixing and for indigestion. This approach would capitalize on the fact that consumers believed 7-Up had these attributes. Another possibility was to stress those attributes consumers associated with Coke and Pepsi, but not 7-Up. This strategy seemed appealing because it would place 7-Up in the mainstream with other soft drinks. Whether one of these strategies or some other one was chosen, it was important that recognition be made of the fact that Seven-Up had relatively limited resources. Coca-Cola was spending about $30 million to advertise this brand, PepsiCo was spending about $20 million, and Seven-Up was allocating approximately $12 million to advertising.

EXHIBIT 2   Consumer's Perception of Soft Drink Brand Attributes

Attribute	% INDICATING BRAND HAS ATTRIBUTE		
	7-Up	Coke	Pepsi
Good for mixing	66	18	4
Good for indigestion	60	17	8
Thirst quenching	60	20	28
Good tasting	58	62	59
Good for snacks	39	62	61
Good for meals	32	47	44
For active, vital people	38	60	66
A drink my friends like	30	55	53
A good buy	28	38	50

CANADA PACKERS: TENDERFLAKE*

In December 1979, Mr. Brian Burton, brand manager for Canada Packers' Tenderflake lard was writing the annual marketing plan for the fiscal year ending in March 1981. He had been assigned to Tenderflake one year earlier, and his first action had been to initiate a basic attitude and usage study on Tenderflake and its competitors. With these data in hand, Mr. Burton was considering possible changes in brand strategy.

*K. G. Hardy et al., *Canadian Marketing: Cases and Concepts* (Boston: Allyn & Bacon, Inc., 1978).

Background

Canada Packers Limited was incorporated in 1927 as a meat-packing company. The company had diversified into a wide variety of products, one of which was Tenderflake lard. Lard is a pork by-product produced by every major meat-packing company in Canada because it offers an opportunity to utilize raw materials fully.

Until 1970, Canada Packer's lard had been distributed in the same manner as the company's meat products. Canada Packers had divided the country into five regions, each of which had been serviced by a separate and autonomous plant. Each plant manager had set prices for his products and had operated a sales force that called on grocery stores in that region. The company had not advertised lard extensively because personal service and low price had been considered the important factors in selling to food wholesalers and supermarkets.

In 1969 top management at Canada Packers had felt that the company's packaged-goods lines were not reaching their profit potential under this decentralized approach. In 1970, they established the Grocery Products Division, and by 1973, this division marketed the company's lines of shortening, margarine, lard, canned meats, cheese, soap, pet food, peanut butter, and salted nuts. Each product had been assigned to a brand manager whose responsibility was to develop strategy and monitor the performance of the brand.

Tenderflake Brand History

Tenderflake lard had never been advertised, but it benefited from the high awareness and reputation of the Tenderflake name, the Maple Leaf family brand name, and the Canada Packers corporate name. Tenderflake lard had achieved sales of 25 million pounds in fiscal 1979, which represented 65 percent of the total lard market. This dominant share had been achieved by Canada Packers' aggressive pricing, which few competitors could match. As a result the brand had generated pretax profits of only 1 cent a pound in fiscal 1978, 1.6 cents a pound in fiscal 1979, and would be fortunate to break even in fiscal 1980.

Tenderflake was distributed across Canada by the 65-person Grocery Products sales force. Each salesperson had a territory that included large and medium-sized grocery outlets and a few wholesalers who serviced the very small grocery stores. Chain retail outlets took a markup of 16 percent on their selling price. In 1979 a standard co-op advertising program was offered to retail outlets whereby Canada Packers put 1 percent of the invoice value of a customer's purchase into a fund used for advertising. Standard volume discounts amounted to another 1 percent variable cost for the brand.

The Market

Mr. Burton knew that shortening and lard were used interchangeably. Company executives estimated that 84 million pounds of lard and shortening would be sold in fiscal 1981. The combined sales of lard and shortening had been declining at about 2 percent per year.

Of the 84 million pounds of lard and shortening to be sold to consumers in fiscal 1981, approximately 60 percent would be shortening. Crisco would sell 55 percent of the shortening poundage, and Tenderflake would sell 65 percent of the lard poundage.

Shortening is white and odorless because it is made from vegetable oil or from a mixture of animal and vegetable fat. Tenderflake is white and odorless (which is not true of all lards) because Canada Packers employed a superior refining process that completely removed all odor and color from the lard. Regardless of color or odor, lard tends to produce a flakier pie crust than shortening because lard creates more layers of pastry, and most experts agreed that lard is easier to use. Major industrial consumers in the quality pastry area specified lard regardless of price.

The price of shortening appeared to influence the sales of lard. Mr. Burton had noted that whenever the price of lard was less than 7 cents below the price per pound of shortening, consumers tended to switch from lard to shortening. Retail prices of lard and shortening had traditionally fluctuated with the price of raw materials. Only Crisco had maintained stable prices and growth in sales and profits despite the general market decline. The prices of competitive products as of December 1979 were as shown in Exhibit 1.

Competition

Crisco shortening was marketed by Procter & Gamble, and it was the only major advertised brand of lard or shortening. Mr. Burton estimated that Procter & Gamble spent approximately $550,000 per year in advertising Crisco. Campaigns had stressed that Crisco was all vegetable, that the product was dependable, and that it was desirable for deep frying and pastry making. Crisco was promoted by the Procter & Gamble sales force, which sold a wide line of paper, food, and soap products to grocery outlets and a few wholesalers. Procter & Gamble's only trade incentive on Crisco was a co-op advertising plan that paid 18 cents on every 36-pound case. Crisco followed a premium price strategy

EXHIBIT 1	Prices of Competitive Products, December 1979
	Retail price per pound
Lards	
Tenderflake	$0.45
Burns	0.44
Schneider	0.44
Swifts	0.45
Shortenings	
Crisco	0.56
Average of cheaper shortenings	0.50
Average of all shortenings	0.53

that appeared to produce a profit of 8 cents per pound on the product. Exhibit 2 shows the estimated cost structures of Crisco and Tenderflake as of December 1979.

Crisco and Tenderflake both were packaged in 1-pound and 3-pound containers. Approximately 5 percent of Tenderflake's sales came from the 3-pound container, the majority of these coming from western Canada, while 39 percent of Crisco's sale came from the 3-pound size. Mr. Burton believed that Crisco had higher sales on the 3-pound size because it was priced at a lower cost per pound than the 1-pound size. Because of the low margins and higher per pound packaging cost on the larger size, Canada Packers sold the 3-pound size at a slight premium to the 1-pound package, and Mr. Burton believed that the higher price was responsible for the low proportion of sales in the 3-pound size.

EXHIBIT 2   Estimated Cost Structure of Crisco and Tenderflake

	Crisco per pound	Tenderflake per pound
Retail price	$0.56	$0.45
Less: Retail margin	0.09	0.07
Factory price	0.47	0.38
Cost of good sold	0.31	0.31
Gross margin	0.16	0.07
Expenses (including sales force, general administration, freight, distribution, trade allowances, co-op advertising, and volume discounts, but excluding media advertising)	0.06	0.06
Media advertising	0.02	
Profit	0.08	0.01

Consumers

Mr. Burton's first action as brand manager of Tenderflake had been to commission a consumer study to determine the usage of lard and competing products, a profile of the consumer, and the consumer's attitude toward lard and its competition. A well-known market research company had conducted interviews with a representative sample of 1,647 women across Canada, and this research had been the basis of the "Fats and Oils Study,"[1] that Mr. Burton had received in March 1979.

Women were asked about the time of year when they baked, and this led to the development of the baking seasonality index.

Spring	132
Summer	100
Fall	161
Winter	196

---

[1]Lard, shortening, cooking oil, butter, and margarine are defined as fats and oils.

The report indicated that lard and shortening were used mainly for baking. Lard was used primarily for pastries, while shortening was used more for cakes and cookies. Exhibit 3 shows how consumers use various fats and oils; Exhibit 4 gives specific data on lard and shortening users.

The attitude toward the product itself seemed to be largely rooted in the usage role of lard and the tradition of passing this role from one generation to the next. Exhibit 5 shows the data on consumer perceptions of lard as a specific product, perceptions of brands, and reasons for using or not using lard.

Crisco and Tenderflake showed uniform strength across the country, but smaller brands of lard and shortening demonstrated some regional strength (Exhibit 6).

In addition to the fats and oils study, Mr. Burton had employed a commercial research firm to conduct several focused group interviews in order to obtain "soft" or qualitative data on Tenderflake and its competitors. Typically, 10 to 15 women gathered and talked freely about baking and oil products under the leadership of a skilled psychologist. Little attempt was made to generalize from these interviews because the samples were small and were not selected randomly. However, the technique produced ideas for marketing strategy and could be verified by the fats and oils study.

EXHIBIT 3   Consumer Use of Fats and Oils[a] (percent)

	Salad cooking oil	Butter	Margarine	Shortening	Lard
Pan frying	43	6	21	13	13
Deep-fat frying	24	1	2	14	11
Salad dressing	25	—	—	—	—
Baking cakes	8	8	20	24	4
Baking cookies	3	10	24	27	13
Baking pastries	1	2	3	49	62
Spreading	—	84	53	—	—
Total ever used	90	89	85	78	58

Users of Lard and Shortening by Application (percent)

			DUAL USERS	
Total (1,565)[b]	Lard only (287)	Shortening Only (609)	Use of Lard (669)	Use of shortening (669)
Pastries	60.6	49.0	61.9	28.0
Cakes	4.9	14.6	4.0	23.1
Cookies	15.0	15.9	12.6	26.0
Pan frying	11.5	10.1	10.6	10.7
Deep-fat frying	8.0	10.3	12.3	11.9

[a]Tables may not sum to 100% because of multiple mentions.

[b]Number of women responding.

EXHIBIT 4 Average Pounds of Lard and Shortening Used per Week

		REGION				
	Total users	Maritimes	Quebec	Ontario	Prairies	British Columbia
Lard	0.42	0.45	0.65	0.35	0.42	0.25
Shortening	0.49	0.91	0.60	0.40	0.32	0.37

	LANGUAGE	
	French Quebec	Remainder of Canada
Lard	0.70	0.37
Shortening	0.62	0.45

	CITY SIZE			
	500,000 and over	100,000–499,999	10,000–99,999	Under 10,000
Lard	0.35	0.35	0.40	0.52
Shortening	0.35	0.45	0.47	0.64

	FAMILY SIZE		
	2	3–4	5 and over
Lard	0.35	0.34	0.57
Shortening	0.33	0.44	0.70

	INCOME			
	Under $4,000	$4,000–6,999	$7,000–9,999	$10,000 and over
Lard	0.57	0.52	0.35	0.27
Shortening	0.59	0.59	0.44	0.36

	AGE			
	Under 35	35–44	45–54	55 and over
Lard	0.42	0.44	0.39	0.43
Shortening	0.51	0.58	0.45	0.41

	HEAVINESS OF USE					
	Total users	Heavy	Heavy medium	Medium light	Light	Non-respondents
Lard						
Users	(956)[a]	(174)	(206)	(209)	(354)	(13)
Usage per week (lb)	0.42	1.41	0.40	0.25	0.05	
Percent consumption	100%	62%	21%	13%	4%	
Shortening						
Users	(1,278)[a]	(300)	(271)	(295)	(364)	(48)
Usage per week (lb)		1–2	1½	1	1	

[a]Number of women responding.

EXHIBIT 5   Perceptions of Brands of Lard[a] (percent)

		Total users (956)
All brands are equally good		55
One brand is better		42
Tenderflake/Maple Leaf	21	
Burns	3	
Schneider	3	
Crisco[a]	8	
Miscellaneous	7	

Volunteered Reasons for Preferring a Particular Brand of Lard (percent)

	Crisco (79)	Tenderflake/ Maple Leaf (199)	Burns (32)
Baking end benefits			
Flaky/better pastry dough	32	34	38
Excellent for pies/cookies/doughnuts	13	13	6
Good/better tasting/baked product	11	13	3
Product benefits			
Easier to handle/blend	14	11	3
Less greasy/not greasy	11	6	—
Better texture	5	11	9
Smells better	4	5	3
Other reasons			
Good result	20	18	34
Always used it	5	18	9
Cheap	4	6	3
Miscellaneous	18	20	22

Perceptions of Lard and Shortening by Users (percent)

Perceived product performance	Lard users said	Shortening users said
Best for pie shells		
Lard	62	25
Shortening	30	68
No difference	8	7
Total	100	100
Produces flakiest pastry		
Lard	54	24
Shortening	38	69
No difference	8	7
Total	100	100
Best for frying		
Lard	38	20
Shortening	35	60
No difference	27	20
Total	100	100

Perceptions of Lard and Shortening by Users (percent) (continued)

Perceived product performance	Lard users said	Shortening users said
Cheapest		
Lard	74	62
Shortening	6	14
No difference	20	24
Total	100	100
Most tolerant		
Lard	31	9
Shortening	46	71
No difference	23	20
Total	100	100

Volunteered Reasons for Not Using Lard (percent)

	Total Nonusers (691)
Prefer other product	
Prefer/use shortening/Crisco	26
Prefer/use oil/margarine/butter	12
Health reasons	
Too much fat/animal fat	12
Not good for heart/liver	11
Difficult for digestion/too heavy	6
Too greasy	6
Do not eat fried things/grease	2
Dislike product	
Do not like taste	7
Do not like it	6
Other reasons	
Never tried it	9
Don't see need for it	4
Don't get good results	2
Miscellaneous responses	12

[a]Tables may not add to 100% because of multiple mentions.

The focused group interviews suggested that flakiness and fear of failure were the key areas of consumer concern. For pastries, lard was perceived as a better product than shortening among lard users, and Tenderflake seemed to have a premium-quality image. Among women who used only shortening, there was a strong perception that lard was an oily, cheaper product.

Attack by Crisco

Early in 1979 Crisco aired the television advertisement shown in Exhibit 7. The commercial clearly attacked lard's major product advantage, and Mr. Burton felt that Tender-

EXHIBIT 6   Brand of Shortening Bought Last[a] (percent)

		REGION				
Brand	Total (1,278)	Maritimes (122)	Quebec (345)	Ontario (487)	Prairies (193)	British Columbia (131)
Crisco	52	38	64	47	42	64
Fluffo	12	24	1	15	19	7
Domestic	8	10	9	7	6	6
Others	8	20	2	6	13	11
Don't remember	20	8	24	25	20	12

Brand of Lard Last Bought

Brand	Total (859)	Maritimes (48)	Quebec (176)	Ontario (308)	Prairies (235)	British Columbia (92)
Tenderflake	52	69	49	60	51	36
Burns	13	2	2	7	23	30
Swift	7	—	5	5	6	22
Schneider	5	—	1	12	1	—
Crisco	11	4	39	3	4	2
Miscellaneous	18	27	22	14	23	7

[a]Tables may not add to 100% because of multiple mentions or rounding.

flake, as the major lard producer, might lose market share to Crisco. He saw this as the same type of approach directed at lard that Procter & Gamble had used previously to pull Crisco ahead of the cheaper shortenings. By December 1979, Mr. Burton had developed several options, and he was about to take action.

Options

Mr. Burton saw an opportunity to raise the price of Tenderflake and to begin advertising. The reasoning was that advertising could help to ensure the stability of Tenderflake volume while improving the gross margin in order to cover advertising and profit. Further decisions would be to define target audiences, brand positioning, and copy strategy for Tenderflake. Mr. Burton thought that the fats and oils study suggested a number of opportunities. In Mr. Burton's judgment an advertising budget of $350,000 probably would receive management approval provided it was well conceived and promised a financial payout.

The sales manager had pointed out that the chain store buyers saw the main competition as other lards and that raising the price of Tenderflake would permit cheaper lards to erode Tenderflake's market share. He strongly advised that Tenderflake maintain its price position with other lards rather than "chasing after Crisco."

EXHIBIT 7   Crisco TV Advertisement

Product:	Crisco	
Length:	30 seconds	
Monitored:	Toronto	
	December 1978	
Frame 1:	Scene:	*Young man and woman in kitchen*
	Woman 1:	John, you never have seconds of my pie.
	Man:	Marie, this pie crust is so flaky.
Frame 2:	Scene:	*Close-up of Crisco can on table.*
	Woman 1:	OK, Marie, how'd you make your pie crust?
	Woman 2:	With Crisco.
	Woman 1:	But isn't lard cheaper?
Frame 3:	Scene:	*Close-up of ingredients being blended in a bowl. Crisco can in background.*
	Woman 2:	Maybe . . . but Crisco's worth the difference. It's softer than lard, so blending's easier.
Frame 4:	Scene:	*Close-up of ingredients being blended in a bowl. Crisco can in background.*
	Woman 2:	Even the bottom crust has such delicate flakes they blow away.
Frame 5:	Scene:	*Two women talking in the kitchen*
	Woman 2:	And Crisco's one hundred percent pure vegetable
	Man:	Mmmm . . . really flaky
Frame 6:	Scene:	*Woman 1 and man in another kitchen*
	Woman 1:	Seconds, John?
	Man:	Mmmm.
	Announcer:	Use all-vegetable Crisco instead of lard. You'll think it's worth the difference.

The most difficult task would be to estimate the probable results of whatever marketing strategy Mr. Burton chose. However, senior marketing managers at Canada Packers would expect the annual marketing plan for Tenderflake to show sales and profit projections for the next five years.

11

ATTENTION
AND COMMUNICATION

I advise you to include the brand name in your headline. If you don't,
80 percent of the readers (who don't read your body copy) will never
know what product you are advertising. If you are advertising a kind of
product only bought by a small group of people, put a word in your
headline that will flag them down, such as asthma, bedwetters, women
over 35.

David Ogilvy

The advertiser must provide vivid incentives if he is to gain the favorable attention of a person whose senses have been dulled by fatigue
or relaxation.

Darrell Lucas and Steuart Britt, *Advertising
Psychology and Research*

There are two important prerequisites for a successful advertising message. First, an individual must be exposed to it and pay some attention to it. As the hierarchics-of-effect
model (discussed in Chapters 3 and 5) pointed out, gaining a consumer's attention is usually the first step in creating effective advertising. Getting such attention is rarely enough
by itself, but an ad that fails to get attention is unlikely to achieve anything else. One
might say that getting (and holding) a consumer's attention is a necessary but not sufficient condition in creating effective advertising. In the second step, a consumer who does
pay attention to an ad must interpret it in the way the advertiser intended it to be interpreted. The communication must not be misinterpreted or miscomprehended; if this does
happen, the ad is unlikely to lead to the kind of attitude change that the advertiser seeks.

Each of these steps of attention and interpretation represents, in some sense, a
perceptual barrier through which many advertisements fail to pass. Some advertisements are not successful at stimulating sense organs in the recipient to a minimal threshold level of interest or awareness. Other advertisements have their meaning distorted by
the recipient in such a way that the effect of the advertisement is quite different from what
the advertiser intended.

Perception has been defined as "the process by which an individual maintains contact with his environment"[1] and elsewhere as "the process whereby an individual receives stimuli through the various senses and interprets them."[2] Stimuli here can refer to sets of advertisements, to a single advertisement, or to a portion of an advertisement. The process, as conceptualized in Figure 11-1, includes two stages—attention and interpretation. Both play a role in helping an individual cope with the infinite quantity of accessible stimuli, a quantity that would be impossible to process. The first stage is the attention filter. Getting a consumer's attention is not easy. An individual, overtly or accidentally, avoids exposure to stimuli. Researchers have attempted to measure the number of advertisements that each consumer is potentially exposed to every day, and these estimates range from at least several hundred to a couple of thousand.[3] The advertising environment is truly "cluttered"; most major magazines, for example, have almost one-half of their pages carrying advertisements, the other half carrying editorial matter. Amid all this advertising "noise," it is not easy to create an ad that stands out enough to get noticed, processed, and remembered. As one might expect, research by Burke and Srull does show that consumer memory for a particular brand's ad does get hurt—less brand information is remembered—if the consumer sees that ad in the midst of competitive advertising, and especially if the consumer is not processing the ad with a view to possible purchase.[4]

The situation is made worse in the broadcast media, especially television. Viewers have always had the freedom to do other things while a program is being shown, including leaving the room mentally or physically, but the use of remote control devices has made channel-switching endemic. Television advertisers today have to cope with the phenomena of *zapping* (switching across programs using a remote control device) and *zipping* (fast-forwarding through ads when viewing prerecorded programs on a videocassette recorder).

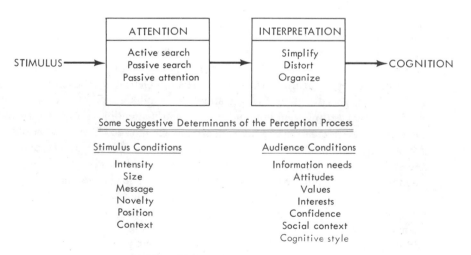

Figure 11-1.   The perception process

The second stage in perception is the interpretation process. An individual organizes the stimulus content into his or her own models of reality, models that may be very different from those of other individuals or of the sender. In doing so, the person often simplifies, distorts, organizes, and even "creates" stimuli.[5] The output of this process is a cognitive awareness and interpretation of the stimulus—a cognition.

Given this background on the perceptual process, it is clearly helpful to develop some understanding of the psychological processes that come to play when the consumer decides which ads to pay attention to. In the balance of the chapter we will consider, in turn, attention and interpretation.

ATTENTION

Attention can be viewed as an information filter—a screening mechanism that controls the quantity and nature of information any individual receives. The fact is that there are an infinite number of stimuli to which an individual could be exposed and an infinite variety of parts or components of a stimulus to which he or she might attend. Clearly, it is possible for an individual to absorb only a small fraction of the available stimuli.

The attention filter operates at various levels of effort and consciousness. At one extreme is the process of *active search* wherein a receiver actually seeks information. He or she might solicit opinions of friends or search through magazines not normally read. Another level could be termed *passive search*. A receiver searches for information only from sources to which he or she is exposed during the normal course of events. The final level might be called *passive attention*. Here a receiver has little immediate need for the information and makes no conscious effort to obtain it, but some information may nevertheless enter the system.

At all three levels it is appropriate to discuss why a person obtains information. There are, of course, as many reasons as there are situations and individuals. However, it is instructive to examine four general motives for attending to informative stimuli. A first motive is to obtain information that will have a high level of utility for a person. In an advertising context, an individual will obtain product information that will help make better purchase decisions. Second, people may be motivated to expose themselves to information that supports their opinions—supportive exposure—and to avoid "discrepant" information. Third, there is a desire to be exposed to information that stimulates. Finally, people are motivated to find stimuli that are interesting to them. These motives will be examined in turn.

Information of Practical Value

It might seem more than slightly redundant to mention that advertising does, in fact, inform and that people do use such information in making decisions. Although advertising practitioners and behavioral scientists search for subtle and often-disguised explanations for why some advertisements register and others do not, it is too easy to overlook the obvious and principal role of advertising as a mechanism for informing. Indeed, psychologists cite studies that demonstrate that people do expose themselves to information that has practical value to them. By now, the reader should not require such evidence. Clearly, there is a practical need for product information, and effective advertisements tend to fulfill this need.

The Shell Company advertisement shown in Figure 11-2 is an example of an advertisement that offers to the reader some practical information, the availability of one of its "answer series" booklets. A measure of the success of the campaign was the fact that 600 million of these booklets were distributed during the first three years of the campaign. Clearly, the offered information was regarded as useful. Incidentally, the Shell campaign was effective in affecting the Shell image. One image scale concerned people's perception of Shell as a company that provides useful information for consumers.[6] Shell went from 31 in January 1977 to 43 in May 1978, while its closest competitor fell from 26 to 12 in the same period.

Many advertising copywriters have noted that in their experience many of the advertisements that do well in attracting attention (as evidenced, for example, by coupon returns) have headlines that promise free, useful information. A very successful headline format, for instance, is "How to . . . ," used in the context of the problem that the consumer is trying to solve with the purchase of this particular product. A consumer in the market for a refrigerator, for example, will very likely notice and read an advertisement that offers, in the headline, information on "How to select the best refrigerator for your needs."[7]

Burnkrant applies a general theory of motivation that the behavioral tendency to process information is based upon three factors.[8] The first is the need for information about some topic. Obviously, audience members will have more information need for some products than others. For example, products that are costly, complex, or somewhat unknown because they are new or for some other reason will have associated with them an information need. The second is the expectancy that processing a particular stimulus will lead to relevant information exposure. It would be scaled as a probability. The third would be a measure of the value of the message as a source of relevant information. It is measured in terms of the goodness or badness of the message as an information source. This structure provides an approach to determine the extent to which a person might be motivated to process information.

Long Copy.   An advertisement with short copy can be informative. A new brand or model in an established product class with strikingly different features may require no copy at all. However, in many situations a truly informative advertisement requires rather long copy (see our discussion of direct marketing copy in Chapter 10). The use of long copy and, consequently, the development of advertising with high informative content is inhibited by a widely accepted "rule" of the advertising business. This rule stipulates that copy must be short and punchy to be read. The concept is that readers will turn away from formidable lengthy copy.

Although such a rule may indeed apply for some products in some situations, it is by no means universally true. If a reader has a real use for the information and the in-

Figure 11-2. An advertisement offering practical information
Courtesy of Shell.

formation is well packaged, she or he can be induced to read long copy. Furthermore, it is often a small sacrifice to lose readership among those who do not need the information and thus are not motivated to read it. David Ogilvy makes the case for long copy, illustrating his point by his own print advertising.

How long should your copy be? It depends on the product. If you are advertising chewing gum, there isn't much to tell, so make your copy short. If, on the other hand, you are advertising a product which has a great many different qualities to recommend it, write long copy: the more you tell, the more you sell.

There is a universal belief in lay circles that people won't read long copy. Nothing could be farther from the truth. Claude Hopkins (a great copywriter in the first part of the century) once wrote five pages of solid text for Schlitz beer. In a few months, Schlitz moved up from fifth place to first. I once wrote a page of solid text for Good Luck Margarine, with most gratifying results.

Research shows that readership falls off rapidly up to 50 words of copy, but drops very little between 50 and 500 words. In my first Rolls-Royce advertisement I used 719 words—piling up one fascinating fact on another. In the last paragraph I wrote, "People who feel diffident about driving a Rolls-Royce can buy a Bentley." Judging from the number of motorists who picked up the word "diffident" and bandied it about, I concluded that the advertisement was thoroughly read. In the next one I used 1,400 words.

In my first advertisement for Puerto Rico's Operation Bootstrap, I used 961 words. Fourteen thousand readers clipped the coupon from this advertisement and scores of them later established factories in Puerto Rico. . . . We have even been able to get people to read long copy about gasoline. One of our Shell advertisements contained 617 words, and 22 percent of male readers read more than half of them.[9]

Active Search. There are situations in which buyers will not obtain adequate information for decision making from sources to which they are normally exposed. In such cases they may actively seek out information from advertising in special interest magazines, by soliciting opinions from others, or by reading technical reports. Active search generates exposures that are extremely important because of the salience of the information to the receiver. Such exposures will be more likely to affect product knowledge and attitude structure than those not associated with effort. Furthermore the receiver is apt to be close to a purchase and the chances of forgetting the message are therefore lower. Active search is more likely to occur when risk and uncertainty are high—with major purchases, products involving relatively high involvement, and products that are new. The need for information will be highest for new products and lowest for brands with which a buyer is very familiar. As buyers develop brand loyalty, for example, their need for product information will be reduced. Evans found that automobile buyers who repurchased the same make are less likely to shop than are those who switched from one make to another.[10] The active search for information is likely to be highest among those consumers who already have some knowledge and expertise about the product category—prior knowledge facilitates comprehension of additional information. Those with lesser knowledge may seek less "hard" information, process it less analytically, and rely more on friends and salespeople for advice.[11]

Future Reference.   A purchase need not necessarily be imminent for a person to collect product information. It is reasonable to acquire such information for future use, using processes we have described as passive search or passive attention. It costs time and effort to engage in active search, but such costs can be avoided or reduced if an individual keeps informed about a product class. For example, young men or women may keep informed about motorcycles, to prepare themselves for the time when they make a purchase. Of course, there will likely be other motivations as well. Howard and Sheth mention the need ''to be a well-informed buyer in fulfilling a social role, in maintaining a social position. One is valued according to how much one knows with regard to the availability and value of products.''[12]

Information That Supports: The Consistency Theories

A natural and intuitively appealing hypothesis is that people have a psychological preference for supportive information. It follows that they therefore tend to avoid nonsupportive or discrepant information. This latter tendency is illustrated by a line attributed to comedian Dick Gregory: ''I have been reading so much about cigarettes and cancer that I quit reading.'' The term *selective exposure* has been applied to these twin drives.

Selective exposure can be explained by the consistency theories, such as dissonance theory, which suggest that people have a cognitive drive to develop consistent cognitions and behaviors about objects. Dissonance theory predicts that cognitive dissonance, the existence of conflicting cognitive elements, is discomforting and that people will try to reduce it. One mechanism for reducing dissonance is selective exposure—to obtain supportive information and to avoid discrepant information.

Efforts to confirm the selective exposure hypothesis in psychology have not been definitive. In part, this has been due to the difficulty of disentangling selective exposure from the other motives to process information, particularly information utility and interest factors. However, the evidence in contexts more relevant to advertising is much more positive.

Ehrlich and other psychologists showed recent car buyers eight envelopes allegedly containing advertisements for different makes of cars. Over 80 percent of the respondents chose the advertisements for their own cars—advertisements that would presumably be supportive.[13] Engel interviewed two matched samples, one of which had purchased a new Chevrolet (a later replication used Volkswagens) a short time before (from one day to two weeks). New car owners seemed to have greater recall and interest in Chevrolet advertising.[14] Mills found that, after controlling for differences in product desirability, a positive interest for advertisements of chosen products existed although there was no negative interest in advertisements for rejected products.[15] Using sophisticated statistical techniques on awareness data from a study of repeated magazine ads, Batra and Vanhonacker found evidence that ad awareness was higher for those who already seemed to have higher brand attitudes.[16]

Involuntary Exposure.   Selective exposure should tend to increase when an individual's position is threatened by involuntary exposure to nonsupportive information. Consider a person who has a stable attitude and is loyal to one or several automobile models. Suppose that he or she is told of a rumored government report suggesting that one of the models he or she prefers has a characteristic that makes it tend to develop transmission difficulties. The person might then be sensitive to information that would support his or her position—that the model is actually quite reliable. An advertiser might therefore stand ready to respond immediately to any negative information his or her customers are likely to receive. Such a campaign would capitalize on selectivity and could be very effective. Its target would be existing customers, even loyal buyers, instead of those not now buying the brand.

Combating Selective Exposure.   How does an advertiser combat selective exposure—be it overt or de facto? He or she can use rewards, contests, or premiums to get people to read the material. Users of direct-mail advertisements have had great success with using contests to break through the selective-exposure barrier. An alternative is to not even try to reach certain segments directly, but to try to do it indirectly by a two-step flow of information, that is, reach opinion leaders and rely on word of mouth to reach others (see Chapter 9).

Information That Stimulates: The Complexity Theories

There is a set of theories termed complexity theories that consistently makes predictions inconsistent with the consistency theories. The most dramatic position among the complexity theorists is held by Maddi, who puts forth his variety theory as follows:

> Its essence is that novelty, unexpectedness, change, and complexity are pursued because they are inherently satisfying. The definition of novelty and unexpectedness must stress the difference between existing cognitive content and current or future perceptions, and hence, the experience of variety is very likely to also be the experience of inconsistency.[17]

Maddi's theory rests on the very reasonable assumption that people get bored and are motivated to reduce that boredom by seeking stimuli that are novel, unusual, and different. People are curious about the world around them, and this curiosity will influence exposure patterns. In particular, they may be motivated to seek out information that does not support their positions. A similar position is advocated by Berlyne,[18] who suggests that stimuli attract attention because of their *physical* properties (such as brightness, color, and size) and their *collative* properties (such as complexity, novelty, motion, etc.).

The complexity theories have empirical support of their own.[19] Studies of exploratory behavior have found that when a new element is introduced into the environment, individuals will attempt to learn about it. In that respect, the use of the journalistic sense for what is news and how it can be dramatized can be useful to copywriters. David Ogilvy suggested as much when he advised copywriters to inject news into their headlines. He wrote that "the two most powerful words you can use in a headline are free and new. You can seldom use free but you can always use new—if you try hard enough."[20] Other studies have indicated that variety in the form of small degrees of novelty and unexpectedness is pleasurable, whereas completely predictable events become boring. It certainly seems obvious that advertising should avoid being predictable, especially in situations wherein selectivity can easily operate to screen out advertisements. Another empirical conclusion is that variety is not only pursued and enjoyed, but is actually necessary to normal living.

It is useful to consider the stimulus itself and search for generalizations relating descriptors of the stimuli, such as size and shape, to attention. If, as Berlyne argues, stimuli attract attention because of their physical and collative properties, what stimulus characteristics will attract attention?

Stimulus Conditions.   Many stimulus characteristics contribute to the ability of an advertisement to attract attention.

The size and intensity of a stimulus will often influence attention. Advertisement readership will increase with advertisement size, although not linearly. Research using Starch measures of advertising readership (discussed in Chapter 14) has found that readership scores of full-page ads using four colors are about 85 percent higher than are scores of half-page ads using four colors.[21]

A "loud" stimulus will be more likely to be perceived than one of less intensity. Color presentations will usually attract more attention than will those in black and white. Starch concludes that the use of four colors generates about 50 percent more readership than black and white for one-page and two-page ads. Position can also influence attention. The left side of the page and the upper half get slightly more readership because of people's reading habits. Starch has concluded that ads on the back of a magazine will attract about 65 percent more readers than those toward the middle. Ads on the inside front and back covers will attract about 30 percent more readers.

Research has also highlighted the attention-getting properties of "vivid" information—information that is concrete rather than abstract, imagery provoking, emotionally interesting, containing a great deal of detail and specificity about objects, actions, outcomes, and situational context. It has been suggested that advertising phrased in concrete, detailed, and specific terms will attract more attention (and be more influential in shaping product quality judgments) than will copy phrased in abstract and general terms.[22] It is important, however, for the message itself to be vivid, not simply the presentation of it, and for the consumer to process the information in terms of its imagery: vivid but irrelevant information may get initial attention but may not get processed and have no impact on subsequent attitudes.[23]

Several studies have also investigated the impact of an ad's "collative" properties on the amount of attention given to them. Holbrook and Lehmann found that ads rated as surprising, incongruous, or funny were more likely to have been read,[24] and Morrison and Dainoff found that the visual complexity of magazine ads was positively related to the time that readers spent looking at these ads.[25]

Adaptation-Level Theory.   Helson has developed an adaptation-level theory that is relevant to this discussion.[26] He suggests that it is not only the focal stimuli that determine perception, but also the contextual stimuli (background) and residual stimuli (past experience). The individual learns to associate a stimulus set with a reference point or adaptation level. Attention is then created when an object deviates markedly from that level. For example, if a person has a hand in hot water for a period of time, the hand will adapt to that temperature and other water will be perceived relative to it. Thus, a dish of warm water could be perceived as cold, relative to an individual's adaptation level.

In an advertising context, a humorous advertisement may attract attention if it is surrounded by more conventional copy approaches. However, if many humorous advertisements are involved, the ability of one of them to attract attention would be reduced. The residual stimuli, the culmination of past experience, also contribute to the establishment of a reference point. If past experience has suggested that most comparable advertising avoided humor in its copy, then one using humor may attract attention even if it is not unusual in its present context.

Helson studied the adaptation-level construct in various contexts—among them, light intensity, colors, and lifting tasks. He found empirically that a weighted average of the logarithm of the various stimuli—focal, contextual, and residual—provided a reliable predictor for the adaptation level. The inclusion of the logarithm suggests that a very intense stimulus may not dominate the adaptation level to the exclusion of the others. Helson indicated that adaptation levels can be found for such stimulus properties as beauty, prestige, significance, quality, and affective value.

Weber's Law. A logical question is how different do the stimuli have to be from the adaptation level to be perceived as different. One answer is in the form of a law, termed *Weber's law*, after a nineteenth-century researcher. Weber's law suggests that

$$\frac{\Delta I}{I} = K$$

where ΔI = smallest increase in stimulus intensity that will be perceived as
          different from the existing intensity (or adaptation level)
I = existing stimulus intensity (or adaptation level)
K = constant that varies across senses

The law states that the degree to which a stimulus will be regarded as different will depend not on the absolute stimulus change but on the percentage of change from some point of reference. Furthermore, the percentage of change that is detectable will depend on the sense. Considerable effort has been devoted to determining K for the various senses. It was established, for example, that K for pitch is much lower than K for taste. Obviously, K will vary substantially over individuals and with the exact nature of the stimuli involved.

These concepts suggest that advertisements that are sufficiently different from an audience's adaptation level and expectations will attract attention. Within an advertisement, the illustration or copy may similarly stand out from the balance of the advertisement if it is sufficiently unusual or unexpected.

A Reconciliation. How does one reconcile consistency and complexity theories, two intuitively plausible but conflicting positions? One approach is to assume that tendencies toward consistency and variety both exist. The one that will dominate will depend on the personality and the situation involved.[27] Assume that there is a level of activation at which an individual is comfortable and effective. When the activation level is lower than desired, the individual will pursue variety to increase it. When it is high, she or he will be motivated to reduce stimulation and seek harmony such as is predicted by consistency theories. Obviously, there will be differences across people in terms of the optimal activation level. The situation will also determine behavior. If a high level of activation is required for optimal task performance, variety seeking will emerge. Thus, if a person is embarking on a major purchase, he or she may require a variety of information; if it is a routine purchase, such a drive will not tend to emerge. McGuire indicates that this reconciliation of the two theories is quite reasonable and suggests a nonmonotonic relationship between psychological tension and cognitive variety. He concludes that he "would readily agree with Maddi that the organism probably likes a little bit, but not too much novelty and surprise, with this optimal point shifting predictably with personal and situational characteristics."[28]

Information That Interests

People tend to notice information that is interesting to them. In turn, they are interested in subjects with which they are involved. They are essentially interested in themselves and in various extensions of themselves. Katz summarizes and interprets some relevant empirical findings:

> Apart from the quest for support and for utility, mere interest would seem to be an important factor in selectivity. The desire to see one's self-reflection is part of this. So is the desire to keep watch over things in which one has invested one's ego. Thus moviegoers identify with screen stars of similar age and sex: one reads in the newspaper about an event in which one personally participated; one reads advertisements for the product one purchased; political partisans immerse themselves in political communications regardless of its source; smokers choose to read material supporting the smoking-lung cancer relationship no less than material disclaiming the relationship, and much more avidly than nonsmokers; after one has been introduced to a celebrity, one notices (or "follows") his name in print even more frequently.[29]

The relationship of interest to attention can be seen by noting the difference in advertisement readership across product classes. A study in the early 1950s of nearly 8,000 one-page advertisements in *Post* and *Life* was conducted by Starch, a service that regularly reports advertising readership. It revealed that automobile advertisement readership by men, according to one of their measures, was five times as high as that for women's clothes and about twice as high as for toilet goods, insurance, and building materials. For women, the highest categories were motion pictures and women's clothing, which had twice the readership of advertisements for travel and men's clothing and four times that for liquor and machinery.[30]

Haley offers several case studies to support his opinion that people are more apt to look at and remember things in which they are interested than things in which they are not.[31] He further hypothesized that people are interested in information concerning benefits that they feel are important in a product. He thus applies benefit segmentation to the task of penetrating the attention barrier. In one on-air television test the interest in the benefit offered in the commercial was measured for each of five segments, as was the attention level achieved by the commercial. The results showed a nice relationship between interest and attention:

Segment	Interest	Attention
1	17	43
2	12	35
3	12	23
4	10	25
5	8	27

In another study reported by Haley, the target segment was preoccupied with their children's welfare. A child-oriented test advertisement received an attention level over five times that of each of the five other advertisements.

A most effective approach for gaining attention would be to run an advertisement about the person or persons to whom it is directed, mentioning him by name and discussing his activities. Max Hart (of Hart, Schaffner & Marx) reportedly scoffed at his advertising manager, George L. Dyer, when the latter offered to bet him $10 that he could compose a newspaper page of solid type that Hart would read word for word. Dyer said, "I don't have to write a line of it to prove my point. I'll only tell you the headline: THIS PAGE IS ALL ABOUT MAX HART."[32]

Such an approach is usually impossible (except in direct marketing mail pieces, where the letter and envelope can often be "personalized" by laser printing the recipient's name), but advertisements can be developed with which people can readily identify. For instance, an insurance company ran a series of advertisements in which agents were presented in a most personal way. Their hobbies and life-styles were discussed in a manner that made it easy for readers to identify with them. Such advertisements, of course, were sure to have an enormous impact on the company's agents, who could easily picture themselves in them. A firm's own employees or its retailers are often an important audience, even if not the primary one.

Another approach is to present a communication involving topical issues—those in which the audience is likely to be heavily involved. Thus, in the late 1980s and early 1990s many companies began tying their advertising appeals to various aspects of the highly topical issues of ecology and recycling. As long as the copy is handled properly, the resulting association will very likely be positive. Naturally, the advertising must guard against irritating the reader by gaining his attention through false pretenses.

Attraction Versus Communication.   An advertiser should be concerned not to attract attention in a manner that diverts interest from the important points of the message. In particular, it is not useful to attract an individual with a highly interesting subject if the brand

and its message get lost in the process. For example, sexually attractive models tend to generate high interest among some audience segments, but they can also divert a reader from the message. Steadman showed 60 male respondents 12 photographs, 6 of which were neutral (a house, a landscape, and so on) and 6 that were photographs of females in various stages of undress. Below each picture was printed a well-advertised brand name. The brand was randomly assigned to the photographs, and the set of advertisements was left with the participant for 24 hours. At the end of that time, the brand names were removed and the subjects were asked to recall them. Brand recall for the sexually oriented photographs was higher than for the others, but not significantly so. However, when the recall test was repeated seven days later, the nonsexual "advertisements" had 61 percent recall (of 360 data points) and the sexual advertisements had only 49 percent—a considerable difference. The effect was even more pronounced for those who disapproved of sexual illustrations in advertising.[33] Thus, it appears that a portion of the advertisement can dominate a reader's perception to the detriment of the communication impact if that portion that dominates is not related to the advertisement objective.

The deleterious effects of such distracting executional elements were also highlighted in a recent study of the copy-test scores of 750 television commercials by ASI Market Research, Inc.[34] This analysis showed, first, that certain camera and sound techniques that detract from clarity of communication—such as camera techniques that interfere with clear framing, logical flow, and smoothness of motion, or sound effects and music that make it difficult for the words of the copy to be clearly heard—decrease attention to the ad. Second, the extent to which the viewer links the ad to the brand name, in memory, is dependent on how early and how often the brand name is mentioned. It seems clear that when an ad is being scripted, priority must be given to communicating the brand name and the key copy points, and attention-getting executional elements must not be allowed to interfere with the consumer's ability to pay attention to, understand, and remember these vital brand-related elements.

Combating Zapping, Zipping, and Clutter

Only a few years ago the major concern of television advertisers was to inhibit viewers from leaving the room during the commercials. Now there is a much more serious problem—commercials can get zapped without leaving the room.[35] A viewer can turn off the sound or change channels with a remote control tuner (zapping) or run fast-forward on a prerecorded program (zipping). Households with remote controls for their TV sets zap ads 60 percent more than do those without remotes—and such remotes are now in almost 50 percent of all U.S. TV homes, and there are more of them every day.[36] According to proprietary studies by Information Resources, Inc. (IRI), zapping tends to be higher for the first ad in a commercial break, and higher among more media-savvy younger consumers, especially those who are higher income and male. As for zipping, consumers playing back prerecorded programs on their videocassette recorders tend to zip through ads over 60 percent of the time.[37]

A related problem is the difficulty of gaining attention in the face of the increase in advertising clutter. The number of network commercials jumped from 1,856 per week in

1967 to 4,566 per week in 1983. This gain was caused by the dramatic increase in the use of 30-second commercials and the increase in the time allocated to commercials. The increasing use of 15-second commercials in recent years—they now form almost 40 percent of all network TV ads[38]—should only make the matter worse. Research by Webb and Ray has clearly shown that higher levels of clutter hurt the performance of individual ads—the more the clutter, the lower are average levels of ad recall, for instance.[39] For an average commercial, another study showed the following drop in the correct brand recall of the last commercial seen between 1965 and 1981:

Year	Percent
1965	18
1974	12
1981	7

An approach to combating zipping, zapping, and clutter is to create commercials that are so interesting that viewers will prefer to watch them rather than zap or zip them.[40] Research shows that zapping tends to occur most strongly during the first five seconds of a commercial, so that it is crucial to sustain the consumer's interest during these first few seconds. In sustaining the viewer's interest, advertisers can make use of all the principles that we have just discussed—offer information that is useful, create ads that are complex and interesting, create ads that "fit" with prior expectations and attitudes, and so on. In making such ads, the "interesting" and "novel" elements appear to be more important than the "useful information" aspects, at least for casual, low-involvement viewers. Indeed, a recent study by Olney, Holbrook, and Batra found that viewers' tendency to zip and zap commercials was reduced to the extent they found the commercials pleasurable—but increased for ads that were simply useful and utilitarian.[41] A study by the McCann-Erickson agency also found that zapping was reduced for ads that were more entertaining.[42] Having said that, it must also be pointed out that getting and gaining attention is not everything: the executional elements that are used for these purposes must not detract and distract from the real, eventual purpose of the ad, such as changing attitudes.

Ideally, viewers would look for or wait for commercials to come on. Pepsi spent $2 million on a set of Michael Jackson commercials in an effort to make them especially interesting. Several firms have tried creating movie-quality epics. Wrangler sportswear, for example, created a 45-second commercial costing over $1 million featuring a young couple out of movies such as *Raiders of the Lost Ark* or *Romancing the Stone* who survive one crisis after another. After taking a huge emerald from an idol, they escape by swinging on vines over a deep chasm as the voice-over solemnly intones, "Out here people need a Wrangler style . . . because no matter what they're doing, they want to look their best. Anytime, anywhere." Data General illustrated tomorrow's technology by simulating a catapult and a medieval battle staged complete with 150 extras and an authentic medieval setting.

Perhaps the most spectacular commercial of recent times was a spot for the Apple Macintosh computer. Called ''1984,'' it aired only once during the Super Bowl. A young woman is shown throwing a sledgehammer through a giant TV screen featuring Big Brother. The tag line was: ''Apple computer will introduce Macintosh and you'll see why 1984 won't be like *1984*.'' The ad was enormously successful at generating interest in the computer. Apple's ''Lemmings'' commercial, aired at the 1985 Super Bowl, however, was less successful.[43] Other advertisers combat zipping by developing commercials that use visual elements (such as brand logos) that will be visible even if the viewer is fast-forwarding through the ad. In the print medium, several advertisers have tried to fight clutter by using devices as varied as three-dimensional pop-ups to musical microchips in their magazine ads. These ads can cost millions of dollars apiece, but they do succeed in getting nearly 100 percent readership.[44] Whether this translates into attitudinal or sales effects, of course, is another matter altogether.

INTERPRETATION

We turn now to our second perceptual step, the interpretation of stimuli. The tenets of Gestalt psychology are useful in understanding this psychological process.[45]

During the nineteenth century, psychologists attempted to analyze consciousness by breaking it down into its most fundamental components, elementary sensations and associations. One of the pioneers of Gestalt psychology, Max Wertheimer, challenged this approach. He pointed out that when a light in one place is turned off and another nearby is turned on, movement is perceived to occur, an illusion often used in outdoor advertising. He termed this phenomenon the *phi phenomenon,* and it served to stimulate the study of the perceptual process from a different orientation. It demonstrated that an analysis of elementary associations—several lights going on and off—would be a futile way to understand what is perceived, that is, movement. The Gestalt view is that it is necessary to consider the organized whole, the system of elementary events, since the whole has a meaning distinct from its individual parts. The German word *gestalt* is roughly translated into configuration, or whole, or pattern.

Two other researchers, Kohler and Koffka, shared with Wertheimer the early development of this orientation. They enunciated two principles. The first is the concept of the organized whole, or gestalt. Stimuli are perceived not as a set of elements, but as a whole. When a person looks at a landscape, she or he does not see many blades of grass, several trees, white clouds, and a stream, but, rather, a field or total configuration. This total has a meaning of its own that is not necessarily deducible from its individual components. The second concept is that an individual has a cognitive drive toward an orderly cognitive configuration or psychological field. An individual desires to make the psychological field as good as possible. A good field or gestalt is simple, familiar, regular, meaningful, consistent, and complete. The modern consistency theories, such as dissonance theory, so useful in attitude research, are outgrowths of this second tenet, which was developed in the study of the perceptual process.

In the following section, the first and basic principle of Gestalt psychology will be discussed and illustrated in an advertising context. The emergence of the organized whole from a limited set of stimuli is demonstrated by a set of classic experiments. The importance of interrelationships among stimuli is brought out. An implication of the Gestalt view is that a brand must be considered as an organized whole and not simply as the sum of independent attributes. Another is that the context is important. After these implications are considered, we turn to the concept of a cognitive drive toward a ''good'' Gestalt and to some determinants of perceptual organization.

The Organized Whole

S. E. Asch conducted a classic set of experiments, reported in 1946, that demonstrated how individuals form organized wholes and the importance of interactions among component parts.[46] A group was read a list of personal characteristics and asked to write a brief impression of the person described by the list. The list contained seven attributes: intelligent, skillful, industrious, warm, determined, practical, and cautious. A second group, with the same instructions, was read the same list except that the word ''warm'' was replaced by the word ''cold.'' The difference in the two groups' perceptions was striking. The warm person was perceived to be happier, better natured, more sociable, more altruistic, more humorous, and more imaginative. Further experiments indicated that when polite versus blunt was used instead of warm versus cold, the differences became relatively minor. Also, Asch determined that the first few terms established a context in which later terms were evaluated. Perception was affected by the order in which the terms were presented.

Asch generated several conclusions from these experiments. Even when the stimuli are incomplete, people seem to strive to form a complete impression of a person or object. Thus, advertising copy does not necessarily have to tell the whole story; an individual will naturally fill in the gaps. The studies indicated that stimuli are seen in interaction. The intelligence of a warm person is perceived differently from that of a cold person. Because of such interaction effects, the total impact of an advertising campaign needs to be considered. An appeal or an advertisement that may prove effective by itself may not be effective in the context of the whole campaign. Furthermore, the studies suggested that some attributes (warm-cold) are more central to the conceptual process than others (polite-blunt). Finally, the experiments indicated that the first few traits formed a set or context within which others are interpreted. Thus, an advertiser should be very concerned with first impressions. Generating trial with a big giveaway program may project a sleazy image from which a brand may never recover.

Mason Haire, in the late 1940s, used the basic Asch methodology with a shopping list as the stimuli set and 100 housewives as the sample. Half the sample was shown a shopping list that included an instant coffee. The other half was shown an identical list, except that a regular coffee was substituted for the instant. The instant coffee housewife was described as lazy, a poor planner, and even by some as a spendthrift and a bad wife. The regular coffee housewife, on the other hand, was described quite favorably. The study helped to explain the early resistance to instant coffee even among those who could not distinguish instant from regular in a blind taste test.[47] A later replication of Haire's experiment found that the negative image of the instant coffee user had been replaced by one of a busy woman, not necessarily a bad wife.[48] Furthermore, the differences between the two diminished considerably, although the regular coffee user was still regarded as being somewhat thriftier. The increased acceptance of convenience foods, in an era of women working outside the home, probably had much to do with the altered image.

Principles of Perceptual Organization

An important tenet of Gestalt psychology is that there is a cognitive drive to obtain a good Gestalt or configuration, one that is simple, familiar, regular, meaningful, consistent, and complete. The human mind is not above making minor or even major distortions of the stimuli to accomplish this purpose. The following principles are related to this cognitive drive.

Closure.   If we see a symbol that would be a square except that a small segment of one side is missing, our minds will fill in this gap and a square will be perceived. This process is called *closure*. In the Asch experiment, in which rather strong perceptions in individuals were obtained from a short list of attributes, closure was occurring. A detailed picture of an individual emerged from a sketchy list of cues.

An advertiser can use the closure process to make a campaign more efficient. A 60-second commercial can, for example, be run several times so that the content has been learned by a worthwhile percentage of the target audience. To combat forgetting, a shorter spot—maybe only 5 or 10 seconds long—could be used. Or, a radio campaign could be used to supplement a television campaign. Research by Edell and Keller has shown that a viewer of the short TV spot, or a listener of the radio spot, will tend to visualize the omitted material.[49] Thus, the material contained in the 60-second commercial will have been transmitted in a much shorter time. Furthermore, the risk of boring the viewer with repeated showings is reduced.

Another use of the closure concept is leaving a well-known jingle uncompleted. Those exposed will have a strong cognitive drive to effect closure by mentally completing the jingle. For example, Salem cigarettes mounted a campaign in which they presented "You can take Salem out of the country but you can't . . . " The audience then had to provide the familiar ending "take the country out of Salem." The Hathaway shirt advertisements showing the man in a dress shirt and eye patch ran without any mention of Hathaway. Again, the audience was expected via the closure process to insert the manufacturer's name. The ad for J&B scotch whisky in Figure 11-3 invites the reader to use closure to fill in the brand's initials. Activating the closure process in this manner can get the reader involved, even to the extent of stimulating effort on his or her part. Such involvement often enhances learning. Research by Kardes and others has shown that forcing consumers to make their own inferences from an ad (rather than having the ad itself

Figure 11-3. Seeking closure: J&B Scotch whisky
Copyright by The Paddington Corporation. Reprinted by permission.

drawing that conclusion explicitly) leads to consumer attitudes that are more accessible from memory, and more stable over time, because such inferences require cognitive effort.[50] Such inference-based accessible attitudes should then be more likely to have an impact on behavior.

Closely related to closure is the process of interpreting an ambiguous stimulus. Again, the interesting part of the process is the participant's involvement. The hope is that ambiguity will stimulate sufficient interest to sustain the cognitive activity necessary to "figure it out." There are several ways in which an advertisement can be made "ambiguous." Consider, for example, an advertisement made up of three principal elements—a picture, some written material, and the brand name. Ambiguity can be introduced into any of these components (and may be a way to highlight or emphasize a component) or into the relationship among components. The picture, for example, could be made ambiguous by leaving out parts of it or using some form of abstract art. The written material could contain innuendo or indirect meanings. For example, "Does she or doesn't she?" and "I'm Sylvia—fly me to Miami" contain other associations besides those of hair coloring and air travel. Even the brand or company name could be made relatively or completely "ambiguous," as in the Hathaway shirt example. The object of ambiguity can be to tease an individual's curiosity, to draw attention to the advertisement, to initiate consideration and thinking, or to motivate an individual to learn.

There are, of course, dangers in making an advertisement itself or any component thereof too ambiguous. Many examples of "bad advertising" illustrate this point. The blonde model sitting on the drill press in an industrial trade magazine is typical. There is so much discrepancy between what is communicated by the two objects— the model and the drill press—that the viewer may more likely be "turned off" than "turned on."

Assimilation-Contrast.   Another principle of perceptual psychology is called assimilation-contrast. Cognitively, an individual will seek to maximize or minimize the differences among stimuli. Assimilation and contrast operate in cases where stimuli are neither very similar nor very different. In these cases, an individual will tend to perceive them as being "more" similar than they really are (assimilation) or to exaggerate the differences (contrast) cognitively. Both tendencies are related to the cognitive drive to simplify stimuli. There is a certain simplicity in the perception of two identical stimuli or in two contrasting stimuli that does not exist in two stimuli that are only somewhat distinct. The perception process is made easier if one can eliminate the shades of gray.

An advertiser can take advantage of the assimilation principle in many ways. It provides a rationale for family or umbrella brands like Kellogg's, Betty Crocker, or Westinghouse. The hope is that buyers will tend to generalize their past experiences with the brand to a new product (a cereal, a cake mix, or a dishwasher) carrying the brand name. This tendency to assimilate a new product into a family brand will be enhanced by the use of advertising styles that have come to be associated with the family brand. The assimilation principle can also be used to advantage by a relatively small advertiser who might seek to associate himself by using a similar name, for example, with a large well-regarded competitor. The Avis car advertisement "We're number 2 . . . we try harder" (in Chapter 4) was, at least initially, probably effective largely because the campaign seemed to associate Avis with Hertz.

Assimilation can also work to an advertiser's disadvantage. Thus, a new product variation may be perceived as the same as the old one unless efforts are made to guard against this reaction. Also, advertisements for similar products, like menthol cigarettes, that tend to use similar appeals run the danger of being assimilated. As a result, a smaller brand may not get much mileage out of its advertising since the audience may not distinguish it from its more widely known competitor. In such situations it is sometimes necessary to use dramatic means as UPS Overnight Delivery Service does in Figure 11-4, trying to distinguish itself from its more widely known rival, Federal Express.

Miscomprehension of Advertising

If consumers can "naturally" misinterpret communications through the drive for closure and through such assimilation-contrast processes, then it could be argued that some of the advertising accused of being deliberately deceptive (see Chapter 18) is not intended to be so, but gets misinterpreted "naturally." To see what proportion of televised and written communications were miscomprehended, the Educational Foundation of the American Association of Advertising Agencies conducted two studies a few years ago. The first covered television communications, and was conducted in 1979. Sixty 30-second televised communications—including ads, public service communications, and editorial content—were tested for miscomprehension among nearly 2700 consumers.[51] The study found that somewhere between 28 and 30 percent of the communications (ads or other content) were miscomprehended, as measured by a particular series of true/false questions. While this percentage should not be accepted uncritically, since it comes from one study using one particular research method, it does show the wide extent to which consumers can read unintended meanings into communications.

The second study was conducted a few years later and covered print (magazine) ads and editorial content.[52] Some 1,350 consumers were asked questions about 54 full-page magazine ads and another 54 editorial pages. This time, roughly 20 percent of the material was miscomprehended, with another 15 percent being not understood (the consumers said they "didn't know" when asked about 15 percent of the information). In both studies, miscomprehension was higher among older, less educated consumers. Taken together, these studies clearly point to the importance of creating ads that not only get attention, but also communicate clearly and unambiguously the key copy points that are intended to be gotten across.

SUMMARY

A successful advertising message must, first of all, be able to attract attention. The ad that fails to get attention is unlikely to achieve anything else. It must also be interpreted in the way that the advertiser intended. Perception is the process of attending to and interpreting stimuli. The first stage is the attention filter, and the second is the interpretation process.

Figure 11-4. Fighting assimilation: UPS Overnight Delivery

Courtesy of United Parcel Service of America, Inc.

Each exists as a potential perceptual barrier through which an advertisement must pass if it is to influence the viewer, listener, or reader. Getting attention is not easy, particularly in television where viewers can do other things while a program is showing. Zipping (fast-forwarding through ads when viewing prerecorded programs on a videocassette recorder) and zapping (switching across programs using a remote control device) have made the problem of getting and holding viewer attention particularly difficult. Zipping and zapping can be reduced by creating commercials that are very interesting or entertaining. The perception process includes both attention and interpretation and is influenced by stimulus characteristics such as copy size, intensity, and message, and by audience variables such as needs, attitudes, values, and interests.

To understand the attention filter, it is instructive to determine why people attend to advertisements. One motivation is to secure information that has practical value to them in making decisions. In some circumstances people will engage in active search for information. A second motivation is selective exposure, obtaining information that supports attitudes or purchase decisions and avoiding nonsupportive information. A third motivation is to obtain variety and combat boredom. Adaptation-level theory postulates that individuals learn to associate a stimulus with a reference point or adaptation level. Attention is created when an object differs significantly from what it is supposed to be like. Weber's law addresses the question of how different a stimulus has to be from the adaptation level to be perceived as different. Finally, people are attracted to advertisements that are interesting.

Two concepts from Gestalt psychology help us to understand the interpretation process. The first is that stimuli are perceived as a whole. What is important in an advertisement interpretation is the total impression that it leaves. The second is that an individual has a cognitive drive toward an orderly cognitive configuration. Closure is an example of the cognitive drive toward a familiar, regular, and meaningful configuration. If a subject realizes that something is missing from a picture, his or her mind will add it. Assimilation-contrast, another example of this cognitive drive, is used by the audience member to remove ambiguity from a stimulus. A host of audience conditions can influence interpretation, among them needs, values, brand preferences, social situation, cognitive styles, and cognitive needs. Studies of miscomprehension in advertising have shown that from 20 percent to 30 percent of ads and other content are misinterpreted. It is vital that ads are created not only to gain attention, but also to communicate key copy points clearly and unambiguously and minimize miscomprehension.

DISCUSSION QUESTIONS

1. For each of the following products, indicate under what circumstances, if any, an audience member would engage in active search, passive search, or passive attention.
   (a) Automobiles
   (b) Toothpaste
   (c) Sugar
   (d) Cement mixers

    (e) Business forms

    (f) Greeting cards

    (g) Computers

2. Under what conditions are people likely to read long copy?

3. Consider five advertisements you have read recently. Why did you read them? What was your motivation? Does your motivation fit into one of the four categories listed in the chapter? Should other categories be added?

4. In one study it was found that recent car purchasers tended to read advertisements for the brand they bought. How do you explain this finding? Are there explanations in addition to those of consistency theory?

5. Pick out a print and a television advertisement that you feel is informative and one of each that you feel is not informative and explain your choices. Do you feel that television advertising in general is informative?

6. What are the factors that determine when a person will seek consistency and when a person will seek complexity? Suppose that you are advertising toothpaste and have identified one segment in one category and another segment in the other. How do you decide upon which segment to focus? How would the advertising campaigns for the two segments differ?

7. How should a copy team go about balancing the need to attract attention and gain advertisement readership with the need to generate a certain kind of impact? Be specific. What procedures should be followed? Can these procedures be embedded in a formal decision model?

8. What is adaptation-level theory in the advertising context? How could one measure the environment of the advertisement quantitatively?

9. How have advertisers attempted to minimize zipping and zapping? Which, in your opinion, is the more serious of the two problems? Estimate the economic impact of zapping for a brand of coffee with an annual advertising budget of $52 million.

10. Recall advertisements that use the concept of closure. Were they, in your opinion, more effective because of it? Why? What is the difference between closure and contrast?

11. Give an example of an advertisement that will motivate assimilation for some and that will activate a contrast mechanism for others.

12. What is meant by the "collative" property of an ad? What effect might it have on attention and interpretation?

NOTES

1. James J. Gibson, "Perception as a Function of Stimulation," in Sigmund Koch, ed., *Psychology: A Study of a Science* (New York: McGraw-Hill, 1959), p. 457.

2. David T. Kollat, Roger D. Blackwell, and James F. Engel, *Research in Consumer Behavior* (New York: Holt, Rinehart and Winston, 1970), p. 48.

3. Steuart H. Britt, Stephen C. Adams, and Allan S. Miller, "How Many Advertising Exposures per Day?" *Journal of Advertising Research*, 12, December 1972, pp. 3–9.

4. Raymond R. Burke and Thomas K. Srull, "Competitive Interference and Consumer Memory for Advertising," *Journal of Consumer Research*, 15, June 1988, pp. 55–68.

5. By creation, we refer in part to the closure process, which will be discussed later in this chapter.

6. David A. Aaker, "Developing Corporate Consumer Information Programs," *Business Horizons*, October 1981.

7. John Caples, *Making Advertising Pay* (New York: Dover Publications, 1966), and *Tested Advertising Methods* (Englewood Cliffs, NJ: Prentice Hall, 1974).

8. Robert E. Burnkrant, "A Motivational Model of Information Processing Intensity," *Journal of Consumer Research*, 3, June 1976, pp. 21–30.

9. David Ogilvy, *Confessions of an Advertising Man* (New York: Atheneum, 1964), pp. 108–110.

10. Franklin B. Evans, "Psychological and Objective Factors in the Prediction of Brand Choice: Ford Versus Chevrolet," *Journal of Business*, 32, October 1959, p. 363.

11. Joseph W. Alba and J. Wesley Hutchinson, "Dimensions of Consumer Expertise," *Journal of Consumer Research*, 1987, 13, March 1987, pp. 418–419.

12. John A. Howard and Jagdish N. Sheth, *The Theory of Buyer Behavior* (New York: John Wiley, 1969), pp. 164–165.

13. D. Ehrlich et al., "Post-decision Exposure to Relevant Information," *Journal of Abnormal and Social Psychology*, 54, 1957, pp. 98–102.

14. J. F. Engel, "Are Automobile Purchasers Dissonant Consumers?" *Journal of Marketing*, 27, 1963, pp. 55–58.

15. Judson Mills, "Avoidance of Dissonant Information," *Journal of Personality and Social Psychology*, 2, 1965, pp. 589–593.

16. Rajeev Batra and Wilfried R. Vanhonacker, "Falsifying Laboratory Results Through Field Tests: A Time-Series Methodology and Some Results," *Journal of Business Research*, 16, 1988, pp. 281–300.

17. Salvatore R. Maddi, "The Pursuit of Consistency and Variety," in R. P. Abelson et al., eds., *Theories of Cognitive Consistency* (Chicago: Rand McNally, 1968).

18. Daniel E. Berlyne, *Conflict, Arousal, and Curiosity* (New York: McGraw-Hill, 1960).

19. A wide variety of relevant studies are reported in D. W. Fiske and S. R. Maddi, eds., *Functions of Varied Experience* (Homewood, IL.: Dorsey Press, 1961).

20. Ogilvy, *Confessions of an Advertising Man*, p. 105.

21. These and subsequent Starch results are taken from Daniel Starch, *Measuring Advertising Readership and Results* (New York: McGraw-Hill, 1966).

22. Scott B. MacKenzie, "The Role of Attention in Mediating the Effect of Advertising on Attribute Importance," *Journal of Consumer Research*, 13, September 1986, pp. 174–195.

23. Ann L. McGill and Punam Anand, "The Effect of Vivid Attributes on the Evaluation of Alternatives: The Role of Differential Attention and Cognitive Elaboration," *Journal of Consumer Research*, 16, September 1989, pp. 188–196.

24. Morris B. Holbrook and Donald R. Lehmann, "Form Versus Content in Predicting Starch Scores," *Journal of Advertising Research*, 20, August 1980, pp. 53–62.

25. Bruce J. Morrison and Marvin J. Dainoff, "Advertisement Complexity and Looking Time," *Journal of Marketing Research*, 9, November 1972, pp. 396–400.

26. H. Helson, "Adaption Level Theory," in *Psychology: A Study of a Science: 1, Sensory Perception and Physiological Formulations* (New York: McGraw-Hill, 1959).

27. Developed in Fiske and Maddi, *Functions of Varied Experience*.

28. William J. McGuire, "Résumé and Response from the Consistency Theory Viewpoint," in Abelson et al., *Theories of Cognitive Consistency*, p. 259.

29. Elihu Katz, "On Reopening the Question of Selectivity in Exposure to Mass Communications," in Abelson et al., *Theories of Cognitive Consistency,* p. 793.

30. Starch, *Measuring Advertising Readership and Results,* p. 89.

31. Russell I. Haley, "Beyond Benefit Segmentation," *Journal of Advertising Research,* 4, November, 1971, pp. 3–8.

32. This anecdote was reported by Ogilvy, *Confessions of an Advertising Man,* p. 6.

33. Major Steadman, "How Sexy Illustrations Affect Brand Recall," *Journal of Advertising Research,* 9, March 1969, pp. 15–19.

34. David Walker and Michael F. von Gonten, "Explaining Related Recall Outcomes: New Answers from a Better Model," *Journal of Advertising Research,* June/July 1989, pp. 11–21.

35. Felix Kessler, "In Search of Zap-Proof Commercials," *Fortune,* January 21, 1985, pp. 68–70.

36. Barry M. Kaplan, "Zapping—The Real Issue Is Communication," *Journal of Advertising Research,* April/May 1985.

37. *Advertising Age,* October 26, 1986.

38. *Advertising Age,* November 13, 1989, p. 16.

39. Peter H. Webb and Michael L. Ray, "Effects of TV Clutter," *Journal of Advertising Research,* 19, June 1979, pp. 7–12.

40. Mark Lacter, "TV Commercial Industry Fights Back," *San Francisco Chronicle,* February 11, 1983, p. 59.

41. T. J. Olney, Morris Holbrook, and Rajeev Batra, "Consumer Responses to Advertising: The Effects of Ad Content, Emotions, and Attitude on Viewing Time," *Journal of Consumer Research,* March 1991.

42. John McSherry, "The Current Scope of Channel Switching," *Marketing and Media Decisions,* June 1985.

43. Joseph M. Winski, "Apple Fails to Register," *Advertising Age,* January 28, 1985, pp. 1, 98.

44. *Business Week,* November 23, 1987, p. 38.

45. For an excellent introduction to Gestalt and other theories in social psychology, see Morton Deutsch and Robert M. Krauss, *Theories in Social Psychology* (New York: Basic Books, 1965).

46. S. E. Asch, "Forming Impressions of Personality," *Journal of Abnormal and Social Psychology,* 41, 1946, pp. 258–290.

47. Mason Haire, "Projective Techniques in Marketing Research," *Journal of Marketing,* 14, April 1950, pp. 649–656.

48. Frederick E. Webster, Jr., and Frederick Von Pechman, "A Replication of the 'Shopping List' Study," *Journal of Marketing,* 34, April 1970, pp. 61–65.

49. Julie A. Edell and Kevin L. Keller, "The Information Processing of Coordinated Media Campaigns," *Journal of Marketing Research,* 26, May 1989, pp. 149–163.

50. Frank Kardes, "Spontaneous Inference Processes in Advertising: The Effects of Conclusion Omission and Involvement on Persuasion," *Journal of Consumer Research,* 15, September 1988, pp. 225–233.

51. Jacob Jacoby and Wayne D. Hoyer, "Viewer Miscomprehension of Televised Communication: Selected Findings," *Journal of Marketing,* 46 (4), 1982, pp. 12–26.

52. Jacob Jacoby and Wayne D. Hoyer, "The Comprehension/Miscomprehension of Print Communication: Selected Findings," *Journal of Consumer Research,* 15 (4), 1989, pp. 434–443.

12

CREATIVE APPROACHES

We despise no source that can pay us a pleasing attention.

Mark Twain

Good advertising is a dialogue with people that lets them bring something to the communication process.

Lee Clow, creative director, Chiat/Day/Mojo

After an advertiser decides on the content of an ad—the "what to say" decision—the task of creating the ad itself is usually handed-off to the creative people at the ad agency. Before these writers and art directors proceed to conceptualizing and creating the ad, however, it is usually a good idea to give some thought to the broad framework within which the ad should be created: What kind of appeal should the ad utilize? For instance, should the ad attempt a competitive comparison (a "rational") approach? Or should it use some type of emotional appeal, such as fear, or humor? Should it use an endorser, and if so, what kind of endorser—an expert, or a likable celebrity?

One way to think about different message executions is that the ad can focus on either *ethos*, *pathos*, or *logos*. Messages that are designed to focus a receiver's attention on the source are said to appeal to ethos. An alternative is to concentrate on generating emotional reactions such as a pleasant mood, bolstering the ego, or appealing to a person's dreams, wishes, and fantasies. This approach essentially emphasizes pathos. Finally, a receiver's attention can be directed mainly to the claim being made. The appeal is to logic and to the receiver's capacity to think and reason logically. This approach is often referred to as appealing to logos or logic.

While decisions of this sort are not always part of the advertising planning process at either the client or the agency (because of a desire not to limit the flexibility of the creatives, or because of ignorance), the ad creation process could undoubtedly benefit from the accumulated knowledge on when each of these creative approaches is most appropriate, and how each can be implemented most effectively. This chapter will thus present some material on various creative approaches (such as the use of endorsers, or of fear), focusing both on *when* each approach is most appropriate, as well as *how* it is best implemented. We will discuss, in turn, the use of comparative and refutational advertising, of emotional advertising (such as fear, or humor), and of endorsers.

RATIONAL CREATIVE APPROACHES

Comparative Advertising

Comparative advertising is a form of advertising in which two or more specifically named or recognizable brands of the same product class are compared and the comparison is made in terms of one or more specific product attributes.[1] It is interesting that prior to about 1970, comparative advertising was illegal and could not be used. It is now perfectly legal, however, and is used quite widely, especially where objective comparisons can be made between brands (e.g., the Ford Taurus advertising that it has more features for the money than competing brands, as in Figure 12-1). A 1988 provision of the Trademark Revision Act has clarified what can and cannot be said in comparative ads—survey or other research used to back up a comparative claim has to be used very fairly and carefully; claims cannot be misleading or deceptive.[2] One estimate is that as of 1977, from 7 to 25 percent of all advertising in major media was comparative advertising.[3] Another example of a comparative ad is the one for the AT&T PRO WATS℠ in Figure 12-2.

Is a comparative advertisement more effective than a noncomparative one? Much research has focused on this question, and the evidence on greater effectiveness is often equivocal.[4] Consumer advocates and the Federal Trade Commission, which legalized comparative advertising in the 1970s, have argued that the increased (and more "distinctive") information should be beneficial to consumers and increase the chances for better decision making. Some researchers have, however, found that comparative advertising can lead to greater consumer confusion (creating awareness and preference for the competing brand), especially if the ad is being run on TV or radio, where more confusion is likely. Further, people may consider a comparative ad offensive, less credible, and less informative (especially if they happen to like the brand being shown in a negative light). Some studies have shown that comparative advertising appears to stimulate more elaboration and counterarguing.[5]

Recent studies shed some light on under what conditions comparative advertising might be the better way to go. Sujan and Dekleva have found that comparative ads gain in relative effectiveness when aimed at more expert consumers, and when they make comparisons with specific, well-known brands (rather than types of brands), because the comparative ad can be interpreted more richly under these conditions.[6] Swinyard[7] argues that the relative effectiveness of comparative advertising relates to the degree of counterarguing it evokes and whether the message is "one sided" or "two sided." A message is one sided if it presents only positive arguments or attributes; and two sided if some qualifications (usually about relatively minor attributes) are presented. Figure 12-3 shows some of the results of an experimental field study in which consumers were exposed to comparative and noncomparative versions of retail advertising.

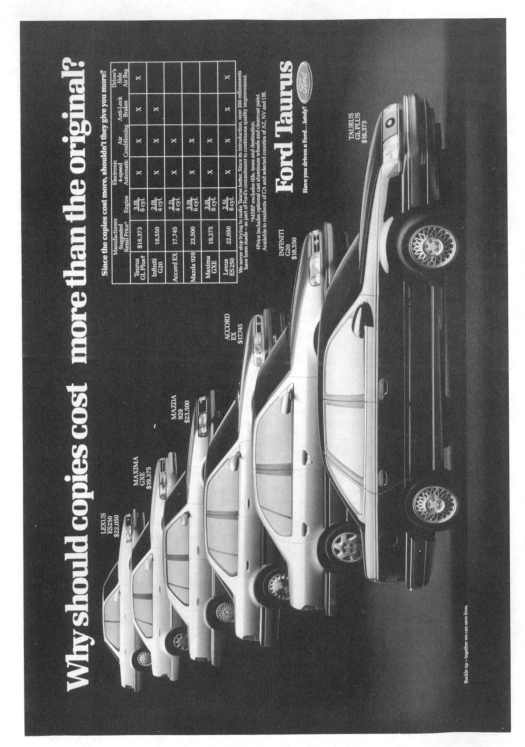

Figure 12-1. A consumer-oriented comparative ad: Ford Taurus Courtesy of Ford Motor Company.

Here's why over 29,000 customers returned to AT&T *PRO*^{SM} WATS in less than 90 days.

	AT&T *PRO*^{SM} WATS	MCI® PRISM PLUS^{SM}	US SPRINT® DIAL 1 WATS
Local,* intrastate, interstate, international calls on same line	YES	YES	YES
No special lines or installation	YES	YES	YES
Discounts 24 hours a day	YES	YES	YES
Free call detail	YES	YES	YES
Discounted rates	YES	YES	YES
Credit card discounts on every out-of-state direct-dialed call	YES	NO	NO
Fastest call set up time	YES	NO	NO
Highest call completion rates	YES	NO	NO
Highest error-free data connections	YES	NO	NO
Largest reach of international countries	YES	NO	NO
Most reliable network	YES	NO	NO

We wouldn't make this guaranteed offer if AT&T PRO WATS wasn't the best value.

If your business spends $120 a month or more on long distance, and you think AT&T *PRO* WATS is for you, call us.

1. We'll pay the sign-up fee.
2. We'll pay any switchover charges.
3. If you're replacing your dedicated access service, we'll pay up to $150 toward the installation of a regular business line for every dedicated line you switch.

4. We guarantee you'll be satisfied not only with our price, but also with our quality and service. Or you have up to 90 days to change your mind. And we'll pay any charges to switch you back to your old carrier.

P.S. If your business spends $5,000 a month or more on long distance, you should also call us. And take advantage of our special AT&T MEGACOM® WATS Promotion and Service Guarantee. Which can save you even more.

Time runs out on August 10, 1989.
Call us now: 1 800 222-0400, Ext. 42.

For information about resident services and pricing plans, call 1 800 225-7466, Ext. 8146.

AT&T The right choice.

Figure 12-2. A business-to-business comparative ad: AT&T PRO^{SM} WATS service
Courtesy of AT&T, Inc.

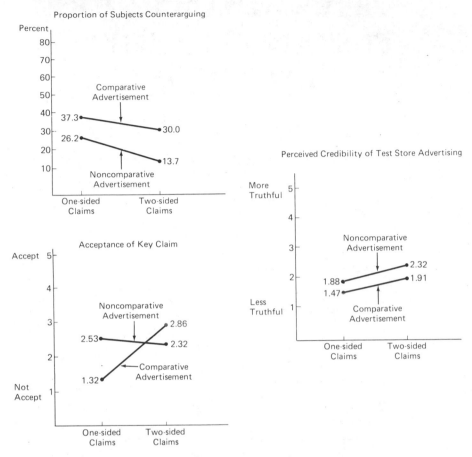

Figure 12-3. Interactions between comparative advertising and copy claims

Source: William R. Swinyard, "The Interaction Between Comparative Advertising and Copy Claim Variation," *Journal of Marketing Research,* 18, May 1981, pp. 175–186. Published by the American Marketing Association.

As can be seen in the upper left panel, the comparative version resulted in a higher percentage of people who engaged in counterarguing than the noncomparative version. Counterarguing declines however in the case of two-sided comparative claims, and relatively more counterarguing occurs if only one-sided claims are presented. The center panel shows that comparative ads were also perceived as less truthful, and also that the claims were perceived as less truthful. The final panel shows an interesting interaction effect. Acceptance of the key claim increases dramatically when two sides are presented in the comparative advertisement rather than just one side. The nature of the claim does not, on the other hand, appear to have a significant effect in the noncomparative case. Other research has also shown the general superiority of two-sided appeals, especially with more educated audiences, with those initially opposed to the brand making the claims, and on attitudes rather than purchase intentions.

Gorn and Weinberg[8] point out that although many research studies appear to show that comparative advertising is no more effective than noncomparative advertising, advertisers are making increasing use of comparative advertising. The risks of using comparative advertising are that the competitive brand is explicitly exposed, and the audience may not believe the comparative claims. A leading brand might therefore *not* want to engage in comparative advertising, whereas a challenger brand might gain from associating itself with the leader. As one senior marketing executive puts it, "Comparative ads are good when you're new, but when you're the standard, it just gives a lot of free publicity to your competitors."[9]

Gorn and Weinberg conducted an interesting experiment to see if a challenger brand gains by using comparative advertising. The study involved exposing students to comparative and noncomparative versions of ads for brands of toothpaste, cigarettes, and golf balls. One condition was exposure of the challenger ads with the leader ad versus exposure to the challenger ad without the leader present. As expected, it was found that comparative ads evoked more counterarguing. Also, it was found that a relatively greater degree of counterarguing occurred when the leader ad was absent than when it was present. Table 12-1 shows a count of the number of counter, support, and other types of arguments and responses in each condition.

TABLE 12-1. Cognitive Responses to Challenger Ad: Number and Percentage of Cognitive Responses by Experimental Condition[a]

| | NONCOMPARATIVE | | | | COMPARATIVE | | | |
| | Leader absent | | Leader present | | Leader absent | | Leader present | |
	No.	%	No.	%	No.	%	No.	%
Specific counter	9	15	2	4	7	18	6	13
General counter	7	12	1	2	4	10	1	2
Source derogation	7	12	11	19	10	25	10	22
Negative responses	23	39	14	25	21	52	17	37
Specific support	4	7	4	7	2	5	6	13
General support	2	3	2	4	1	2	2	4
Source enhancement	8	14	13	23	0	0	2	4
Positive responses	14	24	19	33	3	8	10	22
Other responses	16	27	21	37	13	32	12	26
Blank	6	10	3	5	3	8	7	15
Total responses	59		57		40		46	
Total respondents	41		39		29		32	

[a]Percent totals may not add up due to rounding.

Source: Gerald J. Gorn and Charles B. Weinberg, "The Impact of Comparative Advertising on Perception and Attitude: Some Positive Findings," *Journal of Consumer Research*, 11, September 1984, pp. 719–727. Published by The University of Chicago.

Although counterarguments were greater for comparative ads, comparative advertising was found to be much more effective than noncomparative in increasing perceived *similarity* of the challenger and leader brands. This was particularly true in the leader-present condition. This study thus lends support to the idea that comparative advertising by new brands or challenger brands makes sense as an excellent positioning tool. For example, the Subaru ad in Figure 4-9 (see Chapter 4), in which Subaru claims a safety record as good as Volvo's, will clearly help to position Subaru as a "safety car," in the same league as Volvo. Research by Johnson and Horne shows that comparative ads promote the consumer perception that the brands being compared are similar to each other in a positioning sense, and should be especially useful to low-share brands or new market entries.[10] Obviously, the attributes chosen as the basis for comparison should be chosen with care, and the claims made should be believable (legally, they should be capable of being supported by research evidence). There is, nevertheless, always the basic trade-off to be made between the risks of stimulating more counterarguing and careful scrutiny versus the benefits of associating with a leading brand and gaining instant recognition.

Another relevant issue is whether conclusions and arguments should be spelled out explicitly in a comparative advertisement or whether the receiver should be left to draw his or her own conclusions about the superiority of the brand sponsoring the comparison. It is often advantageous to leave something out of a message: the closure principle discussed in Chapter 11 comes in here. Leaving something out can stimulate curiosity and motivation to seek additional information about the brand and lead to a consumer-generated belief that is relatively more powerful than a belief created by an explicit statement in the ad. This would argue for not making explicit claims of the sponsoring brand's superiority. However, there is some risk in assuming that a receiver will "draw his own conclusions." Research suggests that conclusions should be stated explicitly when there is a significant chance that the audience will not be motivated to draw their own conclusions, or when there are real risks of having them draw the wrong conclusions.

"Inoculative Advertising": Building Resistant Attitudes

Can a person be made to resist attempts by competitors or outside influences to change his or her attitudes? A great deal of advertising activity is associated with this goal of "defensive" marketing. Given that we have developed favorable patronage—have a good share of market, for example—how can it be sustained? In attitude theory terms, how can we induce those currently loyal to our brand to remain loyal?

A consumer can be made more resistant to competitive appeals either by attempting to make a brand offering more attractive or by attempting to train the consumer to withstand the persuasive efforts of competitors. From the first viewpoint, for example, one strategy would be to anchor beliefs about the brand to other beliefs that the consumer values highly. The brand might be shown to be significant in maintaining one's self-esteem or in otherwise enhancing the ego in various ways. The alternative, of attempting to train a consumer to withstand competitive attacks, has been the subject of some empirical work in marketing. The diffusion of advertising messages can be thought of as similar to the diffusion of germs in the spread of a disease through a population. If individuals are given weakened doses of the germs, they can build defenses to withstand the more potent ones, and thus be made resistant to the disease when exposed to it. The medical or biological analogy is, of course, the notion of inoculating an individual with a weakened dosage, and for this reason it has been called the "inoculation approach."[11]

The biological analogy is a good one. Disease resistance can be enhanced by pre-exposing a person to a weakened dose of the attacking material that is strong enough to stimulate his or her defenses, but not strong enough to overcome them.

It has been demonstrated that preexposure to weakened forms of counterargument (arguments counter to the position or object being defended) is more effective in building up resistance to strong subsequent attacks than is prior presentation of supportive arguments. Bither and his colleagues tested the proposition that "a portion of the sub-population exposed to an immunization message designed to induce resistance to persuasion will show less change in belief level following an attack on the belief than will those subjects who were not exposed to the immunization prior to the attack."[12] The belief chosen was that there would be little or no censorship of movies. Support for the immunization argument in this experiment was provided by "high-prestige" sources. High-prestige sources seemed capable of immunizing subjects by a sequence of counter-arguments followed by refuting arguments. Other research has also shown that a refutational appeal (discussed shortly) provides a greater resistance to attack than a standard supportive appeal.

A 1990 ad campaign utilizing this inoculation approach was that of AT&T's, warning consumers not to switch to a rival long-distance telephone service on the basis of a telemarketing call promising big savings in monthly phone bills. One newspaper ad said: "Another long distance company might be calling soon. They'll tell how you can save big over AT&T. With quality better than AT&T. How you have nothing to lose by switching now. But you do. If you don't get their pitch in writing. Because there are lots of things they may *not* tell you . . . Don't get taken in by big claims. Get the facts." As a result of this hard-hitting campaign AT&T was able to hold on to a 67 percent market share of the residential long-distance market, despite enormous marketing expenditures by MCI in its largely unsuccessful attempt to gain share from AT&T.

Refutational Advertising

Another term closely related to inoculation is "refutation." It refers to the process of explicitly or implicitly stating competitive appeals (or consumer beliefs) and then refuting them, instead of dealing exclusively with brand benefits. Ray[13] has shown that, although advertising only the advantages of a brand may appear to be more effective in the usual before-after commercial test situation, these test situations do not take into account the longer-run impact of advertising nor the competitive environment in which most advertisements are read. Refutational advertisements may be superior when these two elements are taken into account.

Consider the benefits of regular toothbrushing. The positive benefits of brighter teeth, less decay, better health, and so on could be stressed. This is often referred to as the supportive approach to advertising. If competitive claims are taken into account, a competitive claim might be mentioned and then refuted. For example, the charge that too frequent toothbrushing pits the teeth could be refuted by evidence that this is not true. This is the refutational approach. Hertz and Avis advertising are examples of both refutational and supportive advertising. Hertz for many years used a supportive approach, emphasizing the many benefits of renting a Hertz car. Avis, on the other hand, refuted the implicit claim that "No. 1 equals the best" by suggesting that "No. 2 tries harder." Another example of a refutational automotive ad is the one for Nissan in Figure 12-4, in which they try to refute the perception that Honda and Toyota are the better quality Japanese imports.

In the headache remedy area, Bayer refutes the claim that various products are stronger or better than aspirin as follows: "Does buffering it, squaring it, squeezing it, fizzing it, flavoring it, flattening it, gumming it or adding to it improve aspirin?"

Perhaps the classic case of refutational advertising is Volkswagen. Like any small car, the main counterclaim is small size. VW meets this claim squarely: "So if you're 7'1'' tall like Wilt Chamberlain, our car is not for you. But maybe you're a mere 6'7''." Or, "Anybody for half a station wagon?" As Ray states,

> although refutational messages are superior to supportive in almost all studies of inducing resistance to persuasion, it was found in one study that people are more interested in reading supportive than refutational essays or articles . . . in order for a refutational ad to be read and to be effective, the headline should include some supportive aspects and should not be ambiguous and possibly threatening.[14]

He cites three reasons why refutational messages appear to work:

1. They are more stimulating than supportive messages. They underline conflict and get people concerned about an area. This motivating factor alone can be quite effective, since refutational defenses can work even if they deal with claims other than those that appear in subsequent attacks.
2. They refute counterclaims and thus make the competitive attacks appear less credible when they appear. This refutation is probably quite satisfying. Statements of counterclaims can arouse dissonance or imbalance. The refutation can restore balance.
3. Refutational messages do contain some supportive information, even though less than supportive messages.[15]

Other research by Kamins and Assael has also shown that refutational ads lead consumers to generate more support-arguments, and fewer source derogations (see Chapter 5) than ads with only supportive information.[16] Like all social psychological laboratory-oriented research findings, there is the question of whether the principles of refutation developed in laboratory situations are appropriate to field advertising situations. Ray mentions, for example, that, unlike most designs involving laboratory experiments on the effects of refutational messages, when respondents are given the choice of what they can read (for example, in actual field situations), the advantage of refutation is muted. One

Re-Orient your thinking.

1989 J.D. POWER INITIAL QUALITY SURVEY (ASIAN IMPORTS)

Rank	Name
1.	Nissan
2.	Honda
3.	Toyota
4.	Acura
5.	

If you think Honda or Toyota is at the top of the list of the most trouble-free Asian imports sold in America, maybe you should think again.

According to the 1989 J.D. Power and Associates Initial Quality Survey, Nissan® rated higher than both of them. And every other Asian import. As well as every domestic nameplate. And all but two of the European imports.

The results were obtained by asking owners to report the number of problems encountered during the first 90 days of ownership. The nameplate with the fewest problems per 100 cars is considered the most trouble-free. Among Asian imports that nameplate is Nissan.

Here's something else to consider. Among individual car models, the Nissan Maxima® had the fewest problems, making it the most trouble-free car sold in America. And that includes such prestigious stalwarts as the Mercedes-Benz S-Class, the BMW 325 and the Porsche 911.

This kind of owner satisfaction is tremendously satisfying for us.

And something for you to keep in mind when thinking about your next car.

NISSAN

Built for the Human Race.

Figure 12-4. A refutational ad: Nissan cars

Courtesy of Nissan.

disadvantage of refutational messages is that they provide a viewer with information about a competitor's product and thus might enhance rather than defend against competitive alternatives. It is, nevertheless, a preferred approach to market situations in which the goal of an advertiser is to build resistance to attitude change and defend against competitive attack.

As mentioned earlier, a refutational approach can be useful not only against a competitive claim but also against a prior consumer belief that is negative. The famous ad for Life cereal that featured the little boy called Mikey is an example of refutational advertising. Here, the challenge was to convince mothers that their kids would actually like Life cereal, despite the fact that it was a "healthy" cereal. The TV spot showed two other boys watch Mikey eat Life cereal, betting that he wouldn't like it—and then watching with amazement when he ate it up. As another application, if a certain segment of American consumers believe that Japanese cars are superior on quality, an ad by an American auto manufacturer aimed at this segment might be more successful in credibly communicating the actually high quality of American cars by first acknowledging this belief about poor quality and then refuting it with evidence (instead of making no reference to that prior belief about lower quality).

A refutational ad in such a situation might gain even more credibility if it was two sided—conceding that quality in prior years was in fact poor, but then going on to argue that it has since improved substantially. An example of this creative approach is an ad run by the USAir airline in August 1990 in *The Wall Street Journal*, talking about the on-time arrival record of its flights. The ad spanned two bottom half-pages, starting with the headline "It was the worst of times" and ending with "It was the best of times." Under the first headline was a panel of on-time performance statistics from January 1990, showing USAir in sixth place among major airlines. Four other monthly panels followed, showing USAir in second place, followed by the last panel for June 1990 showing that USAir was now number 1. The headline at the bottom of the second page said it all: "USAir now leads the six largest U.S. airlines in on-time arrivals. My, how times have changed."

EMOTIONAL CREATIVE APPROACHES

The creative approaches discussed thus far are "rational" in the sense that they rely for their persuasive power on arguments, or reasons, about brand attributes. For instance, a comparative approach attempts to show, based on reasons, why the sponsoring brand is superior to competition. There is of course the whole category of creative approaches that rely on emotions or feelings for their effectiveness, such as the attempted evocation of warmth and affection, or urgency and excitement, or the use of humor, or of fear. Since Chapter 7 was devoted completely to the role of feeling responses to advertising, we will not repeat that material here. Instead, we will only mention once again that emotion-evoking creative approaches are most suitable when the product category is one where, typically, consumers buy the product because of a "feeling" benefit—either the low-involvement "small pleasures" of candy or soda pop or the highly involving feelings associated with fragrances, sports cars, and jewelry. Emotion-evoking creative approaches do not appear to be very successful in "high-involvement, thinking" situations (see Chapter 7 for a fuller discussion).

USING AN ENDORSER

An endorser is a "source" of the information in the ad. Source factors play an important role in persuasive communication. Research on source factors and their influence on persuasion has a long history in social psychology and mass communication and can provide some insight into this aspect of copy information and how it works. How the receiver perceives this person can affect the persuasive impact of the advertisement. All such perceptions are usually referred to as the *credibility* of the source, and it is on this aspect of mass communication information that much basic research focuses.

However, the "source" in advertising is not just the spokesperson: the credibility of other components of copy information must also be considered. In advertising, the idea of the "source" of the message is complicated because many types of sources can be involved within any particular advertisement or commercial. For example, it has been shown that the credibility of the manufacturer of the product or, in general, the sponsor of the advertising is a factor that affects persuasive impact. And it is easy to appreciate that the product itself (the object of the advertising) can be considered by receivers to have higher or lower amounts of "credibility." Another factor on which source credibility comes into play is the vehicle in which the advertisement appears. Different magazines, for example, have been shown to have different credibility ratings.

To complicate matters further, not only are there multiple source components of advertising on which credibility judgments can be assessed, but source credibility itself is a complicated multidimensional construct. On what criteria can the credibility of a particular advertising component be judged? As we shall see, any particular component can be considered highly credible on one dimension of credibility and have low credibility on another dimension.

A Model of Source Factors in Advertising

Figure 12-5 shows various factors of source on which research has focused and about which creative copy decisions must be made. The central idea is the *credibility of a source component*. Research on source credibility can be divided into (1) studies concerned with the impact of credibility on social influence and (2) research on the underlying dimensions of credibility.[17] In the former, a general conclusion is that the more credible the source, the more persuasive he or she is likely to be. In the latter, attention focuses on how an audience judges the credibility of the source. The three dimensions of trustworthiness, expertise, and likability were most often used in early research.

More recently, researchers have recognized that some judgments about a source concern a cognitive dimension and others an affective dimension. The cognitive dimension includes judgments about the power, prestige, competence (expertise) of the source,

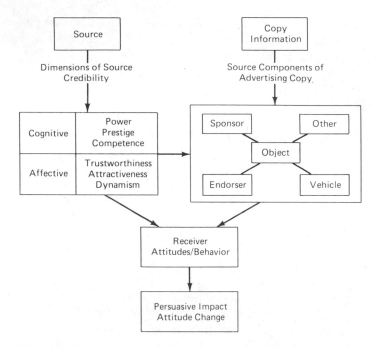

Figure 12-5. A model of the source dimensions of copy information

and the affective judgments about trustworthiness, attractiveness, and dynamism.[18] Other constructs, such as unbiasedness, similarity (between the source and receiver), and physical attractiveness, have also been the focus of research. All such constructs are considered to be dimensions on which the credibility of a source component can be measured. A source can be high on one dimension and low on another. Consider the competence and unbiasedness dimensions. A doctor could be regarded as very competent (an expert) in recommending a drug product, but he or she would have less persuasive influence if listeners or viewers considered the recommendations to be biased by money payments given the doctor for making the commercial. Similarly, many politicians, although regarded as expert in their field, are also considered biased in their viewpoints.

Shown to the right in Figure 12-5 are various source components of advertising copy. At the center is the object of the advertising. This can be a brand, product, service, idea, political candidate, corporation, and so on. The *credibility* of the object of the advertising is often crucial to understanding source effects. For example, Zanot and Maddox[19] studied the credibility of the Mark Eden Developer and Bustline Contouring course among groups of college and noncollege women. The questions were phrased in terms of the company's advertisements, such as "Do you think the Mark Eden ads are honest?" As might be expected, a large majority of female respondents (from 79 to 94 percent) judged the ads to be dishonest, in poor taste, and unbelievable. Although credibility judgments of noncollege women were slightly higher, both groups were very skeptical of claims being made for this particular service.

The *sponsor* is another source component of advertising copy about which credibility judgments are made. A famous study by Levitt,[20] for example, tested whether the effects of salespeople representing a prestigious company (Monsanto Chemical), a medium-credible company (Denver Chemical), and an anonymous company had a differential impact on purchasing agents. It was found that the better the company's reputation, the better were the salespeople's chances of getting a first hearing for a new product and early adoption of the product. Company source effect declined, however, with the riskiness of the decision. For high-risk decisions, the nature of the sales presentation and other factors were more important than the "source effect."

A third source component is called the *endorser.* The endorser in an advertisement is the person, celebrity, spokesman, announcer, and so on, who endorses or who demonstrates the product. Not all advertisements have an endorser as a copy component, but many of them do. Most of the work on source credibility in advertising has focused on this component, and we shall discuss findings and implications later.

A fourth is the *vehicle.* This source component has also been shown to have an impact and is called the vehicle source effect. The same advertisement appearing in *Ladies Home Journal,* for example, can have a different impact than if it appeared in *Playboy* magazine. We will discuss this source component further in later chapters dealing with media decisions, but you should recognize here that it is also an important source factor in advertising.

The next part of the model recognizes the importance of existing receiver attitudes and behavior in understanding source effects. How the receiver perceives a particular source component is crucial. Sources that are highly credible to some audiences (for example, teenagers) will be less credible to others (for example, adults).

Finally, the last part of the model suggests that a source effect can be analyzed in terms of its persuasive impact on the receiver-audience. Such effects can be identified as changes in beliefs about the object, changes in the affect (feelings) for the object, or changes in the intentions to purchase, use or behave (vote) toward the object in some way. Obviously, behavior itself (purchasing, voting, information search, and so on) can also be used in assessing several source credibility impacts.

Consistency Theories

The effects of a source on the attitudes toward the advertised brand can be understood using consistency theories of attitude. This important group of attitude-change theories rests on the assumption that attitude change results by exploiting a person's drive for consistency among the facts associated with an object. For example, an audience member may have a negative opinion about a brand but a positive opinion about a person who is endorsing the brand in an advertisement. This inconsistency should create a tension and a drive to reduce that tension.

There are three obvious routes to the reduction of tension in this context. First, it can be assumed that the endorser is not really enthusiastic about the brand. Second, the positive opinion of the endorser can be altered to one less positive. Third, the attitude toward the brand can be changed to one more positive. If the advertising can select an endorser for which audiences have strong positive attitudes and link the endorser strongly to the brand, there will be a tendency to engage in brand-attitude change. To maximize the likelihood of attitude change, it's useful for the source not only to be well liked but also relevant and credible with respect to the product class involved. Otherwise, the audience member can resolve the inconsistency by observing that the endorser's opinion about the product is not relevant because the endorser is not knowledgeable about the product or that the endorser's experience will not apply to others.

Consistency theory can also work with respect to the evaluative beliefs a person holds about a brand. Suppose that research has shown that taste is the most important attribute in selecting catsup. However, communicating good taste is difficult. One solution is to focus on other evaluative beliefs about the catsup brand, the attractiveness or convenience of the package, the freshness of the ingredients, or even the public spirit of the firm. The logic would be that if positive evaluative beliefs can be developed for several attributes, the drive for consistency will help encourage the consumer to develop positive evaluative beliefs on attributes such as taste that are not mentioned in the advertising. In fact, research has shown that there is a tendency for evaluative beliefs to be consistently negative or consistently positive (this is sometimes called the "halo effect").

There are several types of consistency theories, including balance theory (which emphasizes the role of an endorser), congruity theory (which predicts the size of attitude change knowing the strengths of existing attitudes and the size of the advocated change), and dissonance theory (which considers the drive to make attitudes consistent with behavior). They all focus attention on tension created by cognitive inconsistency that can be resolved by changing beliefs and attitudes.

In the Jell-O campaign, for example, in which Bill Cosby is shown with little children expounding the benefits of Jell-O, the congruity theory explanation is that people who like Cosby may shift their liking for Jell-O because the Jell-O–Cosby link is so strong and positive. Of course, the reverse is true for people who do not like Cosby. The theory offers predictions of the overall attitude effect for conditions such as dislike Cosby–like Jell-O, like Cosby–dislike Jell-O, and so on. However, the proposition that highly credible sources (Cosby) will always lead to an increase in positive attitude for the object (Jell-O) must be qualified somewhat. The theory predicts that although a low-credible product should gain from the association with a high-credible source, the source will tend to lose some credibility from the association as well. The predictions of relative gains and losses of each component are functions of the initial credibility positions of each before the association occurs.

Conditions under which the basic proposition that "high-credible sources lead to higher persuasion" breaks down have been the focus of some studies.[21] There are situations where a low-credible source is about *equal* in effectiveness to a high-credible source. Even more interesting are those situations where a low-credible source is *more* effective than a high one.

Low-credible sources are about equal in effectiveness to high-credible sources where

1. The message is incongruous with the source's best interests or the source justifies the position advocated with unfamiliar arguments.
2. The audience is highly authoritarian or highly involved in the product.
3. The message is in some way threatening.

There are at least two situations in which it might be preferable to choose a low-credible source over a high one. In other words, a low-credible source can be *more* effective. First, it has been found that when receivers feel their behavior is being controlled, negative reactions—such as "this endorser must have been paid to say this"—can be increased if the source is highly credible. According to psychological theories of *attribution*,[22] we are more likely to believe that another person really believes what he says if we cannot easily find another reason (such as financial inducements) why he might have said what he did. That is why so-called "hidden camera" ads that show ordinary people saying nice things about the advertised brand can often be very effective—since the ordinary "people on the street" are not being paid to say what they are saying, they must believe it. The second case occurs in situations where receivers have a strong initial positive attitude about the brand or product. Such people tend to generate more support arguments during exposure if the source has low credibility rather than high. The reason is that they are more highly motivated to assure themselves that the position with which they agree is the right one, when the endorser is of low credibility rather than high credibility.

The choice of a source to be included in an advertisement must therefore be done very carefully. If the strategy is to try to increase positive attitudes, high-credible sources should be used. However, if the strategy is to induce behavior such as product trial directly, it is possible that using a highly credible source can undermine the formation of positive attitudes and reduce the incidence of repeat purchases and brand loyalty.

Source Credibility Research

In terms of the Figure 12-5 model, this section presents a brief review of some research on source credibility which focuses on the endorser component. Interest in this area has increased because of the costs in copy creation and production of using celebrities as endorsers. Michael Jackson is reported to have received $5.5 million in 1984, and Madonna $5.0 million in 1989, for appearing in Pepsi's commercials.[23] Experts and typical consumers who are not celebrities are also widely used as endorsers, but there are costs associated with using these elements as well. Testimonial advertising is representative of this kind of advertising and is widely used by all kinds of advertisers in all kinds of media. Why is the endorser strategy so popular, and what does research show about the relative value of using high- versus low-credibility sources?

Research has been reported that shows testimonials enhance readership scores.[24] Testimonials have also been shown to increase awareness and induce positive attitude change toward a company and its products.[25] Ads featuring endorsers well known for certain personality characteristics might also "rub off" these personality characteristics on the brand's own personality. For instance, Coca-Cola hoped that ads featuring George Michael might improve Coke's image as being "young" and "modern."[26] In general, the more credible a source, the more persuasive that source is likely to be. It has also been found that celebrities can be overused and may lose their effectiveness if they serve as endorsers for too many products.[27] Other research shows that the effectiveness of an endorser is related to the type of product being endorsed. There must be a reasonable match between the celebrity chosen and the product being advertised. In an experiment comparing the impact of using an expert rather than a typical consumer or celebrity in advertising a low-priced but fairly technical product (electronic calculator), it was found that the expert was more effective than either a typical consumer or a celebrity. In contrast, celebrities are often more effective in situations where the product has a high element of psychological and "social" risk (e.g., costume jewelry). Good reviews of the source credibility literature are available.[28]

A source can be used to attract attention even if there is high risk of the perceived credibility of the source being low. The reason is called the *sleeper effect*. The sleeper effect refers to the case where the persuasive impact of a message actually increases rather than decreases over time. Advertisers would, of course, like to have this happen in airing any particular commercial or in showing a print advertisement. One theory of why persuasive impact increases is that at the time of viewing or reading, some cue, such as the source, is negative or "discounting," and with the passage of time, the association of this negative cue with the message breaks down. The result is an increase in the overall impact of the message over time. Another explanation focuses on the information that is available at the time of exposure. This theory emphasizes the cognitive *elaboration* idea discussed in Chapter 5. If elaboration can be focused on the message rather than the cue, and these elaborations are more "support arguments" than they are "counterarguments," persuasion increases with time because the discounting cues are again lost or suppressed. Although the idea is intuitively appealing, there are surprisingly few studies that have demonstrated the presence of a "sleeper effect," even though dozens of experiments have been done on the subject.[29]

Creating Source-Oriented Advertising

There are four primary endorser types from which a copy writer must choose in selecting an endorser for situations like this one: (1) a celebrity, (2) an expert, (3) a typical satisfied customer, and (4) an announcer. Using a celebrity has the advantage of the publicity and attention-getting power of the celebrity virtually regardless of the product type. Large segments of the audience can instantly recognize and identify with the famous person, and the attraction and goodwill associated with the celebrity can be transferred to the product. Local celebrities or actors and actresses who are not so well known can often be used in local or regional market situations to good effect. On the negative side, this type of copy strategy will often be the most expensive and risky. Celebrities not only cost a lot, but are hard to get, and if they are already being used by other advertisers, they may be losing credibility at the time they are chosen. Research by Kamins suggests that the credibility of celebrity endorsers can be raised if they say things that are not only in favor of the brand but also a few things that are mildly critical of it—that is, a two-sided ad with a celebrity endorser works better than a one-sided ad with a celebrity endorser.[30] Also, as noted earlier, in cases where the audience is already very supportive of the product, the highly credible source can result in less persuasive impact than one which has lesser power and prestige. There is also the very real danger that while the consumer may find the ad with the celebrity entertaining, very little benefit may actually accrue to the brand being advertised.

An expert is likely to be the best choice where the product is technical or consumers need to be reassured that the product is safe to consume. An expert can allay fears in the audience concerning the product whether those fears arise from not knowing how something works, concern about side effects, concern about fulfilling a role such as father, mother, housewife, and so on, or health-related concerns about product use. Doctors, dentists, lawyers, engineers, and other kinds of experts can be chosen and at considerably less cost than a national celebrity. Of course, celebrities can also be experts in some situations—a celebrity like TV talk-show host Oprah Winfrey was also an "expert" when she announced to the world in 1988 that she had lost 67 pounds when using a weight-loss product called Optifast (she had been visibly overweight before). As a result of her endorsement, sales of diet products soared in the following two years.[31]

A typical satisfied consumer is often the best choice, particularly where it can be anticipated that there will be strong audience identification with the role involved, the person is "like" many members of the audience, and attributes of sincerity and trustworthiness are likely to come through. To maximize the naturalness of the situation, it is often useful to use a hidden camera and capture the consumer's real-world reactions to using the product in a situation with which the audience can identify. The choice might be a child rather than an adult, or an animal, such as an enthusiastic dog for a dog food commercial.

The national or local "talk show" in television, and a great deal of local radio advertising, typifies the choice of the announcer format. Johnny Carson and Ed McMahon (or local radio disk jockeys) are classic examples of using an announcer spokesperson as the essential source component. The choice in this case is really determined by the availability of the show and the particular announcer associated with that show. The actual copy generation process is often less expensive because only the script and, in television, some simple props must be provided. This does not imply that the media buy will be less expensive, but the trade-off is really deciding to put more money into the media buy than into copy production. The addition of props or ways to have the announcer do more than simply sit behind a desk and talk about the product can often enhance the persuasive impact considerably.

Three dimensions of source credibility are particularly important in advertising. These are discussed next.

Prestige.   Prestige derives from past achievements, reputation, wealth, political power, and the visibility of a person in some reference group—from a circle of friends to a nationally prominent reference group such as movie stars or athletic heros. A research firm, Marketing Evaluations, annually determines a familiarity and evaluative rating of top male and female personalities based on a mail questionnaire survey of television viewers. The basic rating is obtained by dividing the number who rated the personality as "one of my favorites" by those who indicated that they were "totally familiar" with the personality.

Similarity.   The source, instead of being admired or envied, could be effective by being liked and by having the audience member strongly identify with it. A source that is presented as being similar to the audience member in terms of attitudes, opinions, activities, background, social status, or life-style could achieve both liking and identification. There are many situations in which people will tend to like people with whom they have things in common. At the extreme, an audience member would like to see himself or herself in a commercial. The next best thing could be to see someone like him or herself. In addition, it should be easier to establish empathy and identification with sources that exhibit some similarity. Obviously, in most circumstances, prestige versus similarity present two very distinct alternatives.

Physical Attractiveness.   The research on physical attractiveness tends to show that "what is beautiful is good." All other things being equal, the stronger the physical attraction of the source, the greater the liking will be, and the stronger will be the persuasive impact. One study showed that attractive female models resulted in greater intention to buy perfume among males than when unattractive models were used. However, when the product was coffee, endorsement by the unattractive models led to a greater intention to buy. Significant attention has been given to the sexuality dimension. Although research suggests that sexually appealing sources are generally more persuasive, extreme or exotic poses can distract. Advertisements using nude models, for example, have been shown to be significantly less appealing than those where the model is clothed seductively.

Like the design of any advertising, source-oriented advertising needs to attend to the *compatibility of components* at the creation and design stage. This is perhaps the premier lesson of source credibility research. Such advertising should strive for impact while remaining believable and combining elements that lead to a persuasive and realistic impression in the minds of the audience. Also, like any advertising, the decision as to which of thousands of alternative elements to choose should largely be governed by copy research. In other words, source-oriented copy should be tested for its impact using representative samples of an audience to whom it will be directed. Because of the complexity of advertising copy, it can never really be known how consumers will react until they are exposed to the copy itself (or at least the central ideas involved).

One of the key aspects that should be copytested when an advertisement uses endorsers is whether the endorser's presence, while possibly raising awareness of the ad and/or brand, is also detracting from communication of the main copy points. Research shows that this often does happen: an ad with an endorser, compared to an ad without one, often has higher awareness but communicates less about the brand's characteristics or advantages. This typically happens because the endorser's presence *distracts* the consumer from the main message in the ad about the brand. Since distraction effects are often of interest in advertising, we turn now to discussing them more thoroughly. As we shall see shortly, distraction of an audience—created through an endorser, or by other means—can actually be of benefit to the advertiser in some situations.

DISTRACTION EFFECTS

Probably the most useful research finding supported by numerous studies is that distraction (e.g., from elements of the ad execution such as endorsers or music) can affect the number of support arguments and counterarguments evoked by an ad (discussed in Chapter 5). In some situations this can enhance persuasion: negatively predisposed audience members who would otherwise have generated counterarguments can be distracted from counterarguing, so that the communication will be more effective. For example, in a study by Festinger and Maccoby, a strong persuasive tape-recorded message opposing fraternities was more effective at changing attitudes among fraternity men when a silent film on modern painting was shown rather than pictures of fraternity scenes.[32] Other studies using distracting tasks, such as monitoring flashing lights while listening to an audio message, have also usually found that distraction can enhance attitude change in such circumstances. In general, distractor tasks that involve cognitive activity result in more distraction than do tasks that simply provide visual distraction or manual skills.

An advertiser interested in using distraction to break down resistance to her or his arguments is faced with the delicate task of devising something that will interfere with counterarguing but not, at the same time, interfere with the reception or learning of the message. This is a formidable task that must take into consideration all aspects of the communication and the audience. As Gardner explains, the critical question in defining distraction seems to be whether the process of counterarguing is interfered with. If attitude change *is* more apt to be induced due to interference with counterargument, then this is defined as distraction. Based on this definition, distraction takes on many dimensions. If an element in the communication is designed to add support to the message—that is, mood music or artwork—this cannot be defined as distraction because it does not interfere with the counterarguing process; what is support in one communication could be distraction in another due to products, audiences, channels of communication, or a host of unique factors.[33]

A good example of the use of distractors in trying to communicate with a hostile audience is a campaign developed by the Standard Oil Company of California for its Chevron brand.[34] At the time, many consumers were very hostile to oil companies generally; the oil company image as a good corporate citizen was considerably tarnished. One of the first campaigns involved on-the-scene stories, showing tankers being built, explorations, and other activities. Although reasonably successful, the company subsequently developed a whimsical campaign around the theme "We're running out of dinosaurs" to encourage energy conservation. The campaign not only proved effective in educating consumers about the energy situation, but most important, resulted in a significant shift in favorable attitudes for Standard Oil.

SUMMARY

Before ads are handed off to the advertising agency and actual creative work begins, it is important to consider the broad framework and creative approaches open to copywriters and art directors. This chapter reviews several "rational" and "emotional" approaches and some of the research that has been done on each. According to the Greeks, all persuasive messages emphasize ethos (the source of the message), pathos (moods and emotions), or logos (logic and rational support arguments).

The chapter is organized around a discussion of the rational approaches such as comparative advertising, inoculative advertising, and refutational approaches, emotional approaches, using endorsers and the ethos–source-oriented approaches, and the use of distraction in advertising. Comparative advertising is advertising in which two or more specifically named brands of the same product are compared in terms of one or more attributes. It is now widely used even though it was illegal prior to 1970. The research on comparative advertising presents a mixed picture of it being more or less effective than noncomparative advertising depending on counterarguing and other information processing mechanisms which come into play. From a strategic viewpoint, comparative advertising is more appropriate for follower brands than for leader brands.

Inoculative advertising utilizes the principles of inoculation in medicine. The objective is to inoculate the audience with small doses of the offending campaign (competitor arguments) so that when the full campaign hits they will be less susceptible and "resistant" to those arguments. It has been demonstrated that preexposure to weakened forms of counterargument is more effective in building resistance than prior presentation of supportive arguments. AT&T's famous campaign to counter MCI inroads is a good example.

Refutational advertising involves explicitly stating competitive claims and then refuting them. It is often contrasted to supportive advertising which focuses on a one-sided presentation of brand benefits only. The original Volkswagen's Beatle campaign is a well-known example of the refutational approach. USAir's "Best of times, Worst of times," campaign is a more recent example.

There is a whole category of approaches that rely on emotions or feelings and pathos as the essential ingredient. Attempts to evoke feelings of warmth, affection, urgency, and excitement do not necessarily have to include rational arguments or explicit claims based on specific benefits such as good gas mileage or fast acceleration in the case of cars. Emotion-evoking approaches are most suitable when the product category is one where buying is based on a "feeling" benefit—either the low-involvement small pleasures of candy or soda pop or the highly involving feelings associated with products like perfume, sports cars, or jewelry.

Endorsers are often used in testimonial advertising and are examples of source-oriented approaches. There are many types of sources in advertising and a model of source factors shows the range of source components and the cognitive and affective ways in which the credibility of any of the components can be assessed. Consistency theories encompass a range of theories of attitude change (balance, dissonance, and congruity) that explain endorser and source effects. Research on source credibility has shown that in some cases a low-credible source can be more effective than a high-credible source. In advertising, three dimensions of course credibility—prestige, similarity, and physical attractiveness—are particularly important. A final approach is called distraction and involves trying to distract the audience from counterarguing during the viewing or listening process. The Chevron dinosaur campaign, "We're running out of dinosaurs," designed to divert and dissipate some of the audience hostility against oil companies during the energy crisis, is an example.

DISCUSSION QUESTIONS

1. Bring to class three examples of broadcast or print advertising that illustrate the ethos, pathos, and logos approaches.

2. Using examples of comparative and noncomparative advertisement for the same product category, explain in your own words why or why not you think one is more effective than the other. Consider a modification of the comparative ad that includes more/fewer explicit attribute comparisons and discuss why the changes would increase (or decrease) effectiveness. Be specific in specifying the criteria you use to evaluate effectiveness.

3. Discuss the desirability of using a doctor instead of a dentist as an endorser in a toothpaste commercial. Assume that the same advertising objectives and the same type of target audience are involved in each case.

4. Choose two testimonial advertisements. Assess their relative persuasiveness using the source factors model given in the chapter.

5. Develop an advertisement for Coors Light beer that is based on the refutational approach (relative to Bud Light, for example). Discuss the degree to which it would be likely to build resistant attitudes among current Coors drinkers versus the degree to which it might attract new drinkers to the brand.

6. What exactly is distraction in advertising? What is its purpose? What provided the distraction in the Chevron advertisements? Provide other examples of distraction in advertising.

7. Develop a consistency model of attitude change that would predict the changed attitude toward Jell-O knowing the existing attitude on a -5 (strongly dislike) to zero (neutral) to $+5$ (strongly like) scale; the existing attitude toward Cosby as the source, also on a -5 to $+5$ scale; and the link between the source and the brand on a 0 (weak link) to $+5$ (strong link) scale.

8. What is cognitive tension? Recall an instance in which you experienced it. How would you measure cognitive tension?

9. Explain why refutational advertising works, and discuss situations in which it would be more (and less) effective.

10. What criteria would you use in choosing an endorser for a new line extension in the "chip" market (potato or corn chips)? Discuss the importance of each in your evaluation of potential candidates and how you would make the final decision.

NOTES

1. William L. Wilkie and Paul Farris, "Comparison Advertising: Problems and Potential," *Journal of Marketing*, 39, October 1975, pp. 7–15.

2. *Adweek's Marketing Week*, June 12, 1989, p. 17.

3. Gordon H. C. McDougall, "Comparative Advertising: Consumer Issues and Attitudes," in B. A. Greenberg and D. N. Bellenger, eds., *Contemporary Marketing Thought* (Chicago: American Marketing Association, 1977), pp. 286–291.

4. George E. Belch, "An Examination of Comparative and Noncomparative Television Commercials: The Effects of Claim Variation and Repetition on Cognitive Response and Message Acceptance," *Journal of Marketing Research*, 18, August 1981, pp. 333–349.

5. For recent work in the marketing area, see Albert J. Della Bitta, Kent B. Monroe, and John M. McGinnis, "Consumer Perceptions of Comparative Price Advertisements," *Journal of Marketing Research*, 18, November 1981, pp. 416–427; Michael Etgar and Stephen A. Goodwin, "One-Sided Versus Two-Sided Comparative Message Appeals for New Brand Introductions," *Journal of Consumer Research*, 8, March 1982, pp. 460–465; Z. S. Demirdjian, "Sales Effectiveness of Comparative Advertising: An Experimental Field Investigation," *Journal of Consumer Research*, 10, December 1983, pp. 362–364; and Roobina O. Tashchian and Mark E. Slama, "Involvement and the Effectiveness of Comparative Advertising," in J. H. Leigh and C. R. Martin, Jr., eds., *Current Issues and Research in Advertising 1984* (Ann Arbor: Graduate School of Business Administration, University of Michigan, 1984), pp. 79–92.

6. Mita Sujan and Christine Dekleva, "Product Categorization and Inference Making: Some Implications for Comparative Advertising," *Journal of Consumer Research*, 14, December 1987, pp. 372–378.

7. William R. Swinyard, "The Interaction Between Comparative Advertising and Copy Claim Variation," *Journal of Marketing Research*, 18, May 1981, pp. 175–186.

8. Gerald J. Gorn and Charles B. Weinberg, "The Impact of Comparative Advertising on Perception and Attitude: Some Positive Findings," *Journal of Consumer Research*, 11, September 1984, pp. 719–727.

9. "Creating a Mass Market for Wine," *Business Week*, March 15, 1982, pp. 102–118.

10. Michael D. Johnson and David A. Horne, "The Contrast Model of Similarity and Comparative Advertising," *Psychology and Marketing*, Fall 1988, pp. 211–232.

11. William J. McGuire, "The Nature of Attitude and Attitude Change," in G. Lindzey and E. Aronson, eds., *The Handbook of Social Psychology*, Vol. 3 (Reading, MA: Addison-Wesley, 1969), p. 263.

12. Stewart W. Bither, Ira J. Dolich, and Elaine B. Nell, "The Application of Attitude Immunization Techniques in Marketing," *Journal of Marketing Research*, 8, February 1971, pp. 56–61.

13. Michael L. Ray, "The Refutational Approach in Advertising," Paper presented to the Advertising Division, Association for Education in Journalism, Boulder, Colorado, 1967.

14. Ibid., p. 7.

15. Ibid., p. 8.

16. Michael A. Kamins and Henry Assael, "Two-Sided Versus One-Sided Appeals: A Cognitive Perspective on Argumentation, Source Derogation, and the Effect of Disconfirming Trial on Belief Change," *Journal of Marketing Research*, 24, February 1987, pp. 29–39.

17. Joanne M. Klebba and Lynette S. Unger, "The Impact of Negative and Positive Information on Source Credibility in Field Settings," in Richard P. Bagozzi and Alice M. Tybout, eds., *Advances in Consumer Research*, Vol. 10 (Ann Arbor, MI: Association for Consumer Research, 1982), pp. 11–16.

18. Galen R. Rarick, "Effects of Two Components of Communicator Prestige," unpublished doctoral dissertation, Stanford University, Stanford, California, 1963.

19. Eric J. Zanot and Lynda M. Maddox, "An Empirical Study of the Credibility of Bust Developer Advertisements Among Young Women," in James Leigh and Claude R. Martin, Jr., eds., *Current Issues and Research in Advertising 1978* (Ann Arbor: Graduate School of Business Administration, University of Michigan, 1978), pp. 53–62.

20. Theodore Levitt, *Industrial Purchasing Behavior* (Boston: Harvard University Graduate School of Business Administration, 1965).

21. Ruby Roy Dholakia and Brian Sternthal, "Highly Credible Sources: Persuasive Facilitators or Persuasive Liabilities?" *Journal of Consumer Research*, 3, March 1977, pp. 223–232. See also Brian Sternthal, Ruby Dholakia, and Clark Leavitt, "The Persuasive Effect of Source Credibility: Tests of Cognitive Response," *Journal of Consumer Research*, 4, March 1978, pp. 252–260.

22. See Edward E. Jones and Keith E. Davis, "From Acts to Dispositions," in Leonard Berkowitz, ed., *Advances in Experimental Social Psychology*, 2nd ed. (New York: Academic Press, 1965).

23. *The New York Times*, March 27, 1989, p. 30.

24. See W. Freeman, *The Big Name* (New York: Printer's Ink, 1957), and H. Rudolph, *Attention and Interest Factors in Advertising* (New York: Printer's Ink, 1947).

25. R. B. Fireworker and H. H. Friedman, "The Effects of Endorsements on Product Evaluation," *Decision Sciences*, 8, 1977, pp. 576–583, and Joseph M. Kamen et al., "What a Spokesman Does for a Sponsor," *Journal of Advertising Research*, 15, 1975, pp. 17–24.

26. *The New York Times*, p. 30.

27. John C. Mowen and Stephen W. Brown, "On Explaining and Predicting the Effectiveness of Celebrity Endorsers," in Kent B. Monroe, ed., *Advances in Consumer Research*, Vol. III (Ann Arbor, MI: Association for Consumer Research, 1981). For recent studies, see Lynn R. Kahle, "Physical Attractiveness of the Celebrity Endorser: A Social Adaption Perspective," *Journal of Consumer Research*, 11, March 1985, pp. 954–961, and John L. Swasy and James M. Munch, "Examining the Target Receiver Elaborations: Rhetorical Question Effects on Source Processing and Persuasion," *Journal of Consumer Research*, 11, March 1985, pp. 877–886.

28. See Hershey H. Friedman and Linda Friedman, "Endorser Effectiveness by Product Type," *Journal of Advertising Research*, 19, October 1979, pp. 63–71. For reviews of literature, see W. Benoy Joseph, "The Credibility of Physically Attractive Communicators: A Review," *Journal of Advertising*, 11, 1982, pp. 15–24, and Brian Sternthal, Lynn W. Phillips, and Ruby Dholakia, "The Persuasive Effect of Source Credibility: A Situational Analysis," *Public Opinion Quarterly*, 42, Fall 1978, pp. 285–314.

29. Darlene B. Hannah and Brian Sternthal, "Detecting and Explaining the Sleeper Effect," *Journal of Consumer Research*, 11, September 1984, pp. 632–642.

30. Michael A. Kamins, "Celebrity and Non-celebrity Advertising in a Two-Sided Context," *Journal of Advertising Research*, June/July 1989, pp. 34–42.

31. *Business Week*, April 16, 1990, p. 86.

32. L. Festinger and N. Maccoby, "On Resistance to Persuasive Communications," *Journal of Abnormal and Social Psychology*, 68, 1964, pp. 359–367.

33. David M. Gardner, "The Distraction Hypothesis in Marketing," *Journal of Marketing Research*, 10, December 1970, pp. 25–30.

34. Lewis C. Winters, "Should You Advertise to Hostile Audiences?" *Journal of Advertising Research*, 17, June 1977, pp. 7–15.

13

THE ART OF COPYWRITING

*"The cat sat on the mat" is not a story. "The cat sat on the dog's mat,"
now that's a story.*

Gerry Miller, creative director, Dentsu

Once the message strategy and the broad creative approach have been determined, it is time to create the actual advertising. Although much advertising, particularly local advertising, is created by someone at the client and media level without the inputs of an advertising agency, most national advertising involves an agency. It is the job of the creative department of the agency to generate alternative advertising ideas and ultimately to pick one or a few that will go forward into production. The creative department is made up of copywriters who have the main responsibility for creating the advertising and art directors who are expert at creating or otherwise introducing illustration and pictorial materials. These people are generally under the supervision of a creative director, and a team of such people is involved in developing the advertising to be used on any one campaign. An individual art director will, however, be the person responsible for generating the layout associated with a particular print advertisement or commercial storyboard. The creative team also must work closely with and coordinate its activities with the traffic department and a production supervisor. People in traffic work on scheduling the process and making sure that deadlines are met and that finished advertising reaches media at the times specified in the contract.

The creation stage encompasses the creative (idea generation) process, the generation of written copy (copywriting), artwork of various kinds (illustrating), and a preliminary or comprehensive version of the advertisement (layout). Obviously, client approval and supplier selection are also important activities that must be done before final production can begin. First, we consider the creative process.

THE CREATIVE PROCESS: COMING UP WITH AN IDEA

The creative process is concerned with taking the baldly-stated marketing proposition, usually derived from and couched in terms of marketing research and manufacturing specifications, and turning it into one or more creative ideas that clearly, powerfully, and persuasively convey to the consumer what the brand does for them and why it should matter to them. For example, the long-distance company U.S. Sprint wanted to communicate to consumers that its phone lines were made of fiber optics, which led to clearer communications. A noncreative marketing person might simply decide to run a commercial in which an announcer simply makes such an announcement, using a "talking head" format. It takes a creative person to come up with the creative idea that the fiber optic lines allow such clear communication that if a pin is dropped in New York it is heard to fall in Los Angeles when the sound is picked up by a microphone and communicated over U.S. Sprint phone lines. Or, as in another ad, that if a singer in a studio in Los Angeles sings a high note, that note can shatter a wine glass in New York if the sound is carried over U.S. Sprint's fiber optic phone lines. Or consider the choice of Bo Jackson—the multisport star athlete—to promote cross-training shoes from Nike. Or, finally, consider the idea to show the exhaustive coverage of the NYNEX Yellow Pages by finding unusual category subheadings and building a pun-filled story around each. A powerful, "big" idea can add immeasurably to the effectiveness of an ad campaign, and the presence or absence of such an idea must be the first thing you look for in evaluating a proposed ad campaign.

How do we come up with such ideas? The creative process has interested many different types of people for some time. One of the pioneers in studying creativity, Alex Osborn, was a founder of Batten, Barton, Durstine & Osborn, one of the largest agencies (now known as BBDO, and part of the Omnicom group). Osborn saw the creative process as starting with the following.[1]

1. Fact finding
   a. Problem definition: picking out and pointing up the problem
   b. Preparation: gathering and analyzing the pertinent data
2. Idea finding
   a. Idea production: thinking up tentative ideas as possible leads
   b. Idea development: selecting from resultant ideas, adding others, and reprocessing by means of modification, combination, and so on

The process begins with fact finding—picking out and identifying the problem and gathering and analyzing pertinent data. The raw material for ideas is information—information from all sources. Leo Burnett once said, "Curiosity about life in all of its aspects, I think, is still the secret of great creative people."[2] Of course, some information is more useful than others. In particular, the creative team should become immersed in as much factual information about the company, the product, competition, and the target audience (their language, needs, motivations, desires) as possible. Obviously, they should have access to the available consumer research. Sometimes it is worthwhile to get first-hand knowledge of the consumer. Claude Hopkins, whom we met in Chapter 1, would always go out and discuss products with housewives. One of the top agency executives today still makes it a point to visit supermarkets regularly and ask shoppers why they make certain shopping decisions. Leo Burnett believes in depth interviewing, "where I come realistically face to face with the people *I* am trying to sell. I try to get a picture in my mind of the kind of people they are—how they use this product, and what it is they don't often tell *you* in so many words—but what it is that actually motivates them to buy something or to interest them in something."[3] Focus group interviewing is another approach that tends to generate useful ideas and appropriate words and phrases for use in developing copy.

Fact finding should include a careful discussion of the advertising objectives. The objectives provide the point of departure for the creative process while, at the same time, constraining it. The creative team might properly challenge the constraints implied by the objectives, at least in the early stages of campaign development. In doing so they might open the way for worthwhile alternatives and provide their own input to formulating objectives. Some solutions to tough problems come only when the focus of the problem is broadened. Thus, the objective need not be viewed as a unilateral, rigid set of constraints, but rather as a flexible, dynamic guide that is the result of creativity as well as empirical research and managerial experience.

Fact finding should include a digestion and incubation time. The various facts need to be absorbed or "digested," and usually the best ideas emerge only after a period of incubation.

Idea generation, after the information has been digested, is the heart of the creative process. The key is to generate a large quantity of ideas—to avoid inhibiting the process. Evaluating a set of alternatives is a relatively trivial problem next to that of obtaining good alternatives to evaluate. It is somewhat ironic that in refining decision theory very sophisticated methods have been developed to choose among alternatives although we still have only the crudest notion of how to generate alternatives.

Osborn tells of a successful copywriter at BBDO who starts a job by clearing his mind and sitting down at a typewriter and simply writing everything that comes to mind.[4] He even includes silly, worthless phrases with the thought that they will block others if they are not included. In some cases, a piece of copy will be generated on the first try, but, more typically, hundreds of possible ideas will be created before several reasonable alternatives are generated. There are certain questions that, when posed, can suggest ideas (see Table 13-1). One of the most fertile is the suggestion to combine various concepts. There have been several systematic approaches proposed to aid the process. One such approach is termed HIT, or the heuristic ideation technique.[5] Several relevant dimensions of a problem area are identified. For a citrus drink we might consider the context in which it is used (snack, breakfast, or parties), the benefit it provides (nutrition, preparation ease, color), and the personalities who could endorse it (an athlete, a popular singer, a nutritionist). Then the total set of ideas is the set of all possible combinations of these concepts. Techniques similar to this one have been successful at stimulating new product ideas. One can readily see that products such as toaster waffles, breakfast milkshakes, canned whiskey sours, and aerosol hair sprays could have been conceived with such methods. In a similar vein, some agencies have developed computer-aided name generators. Various words or combinations of letters are systematically combined to provide alternative names for new products.

For some, idea generation comes easier in a group, where more information and associations are collectively available. The difficulty here is to overcome the inhibiting

TABLE 13-1.   Questions That Spur Ideas for New and Improved Products

Put to other uses?	New ways to use it? Other uses if modified?
Adapt?	What else is this like? What other ideas does this suggest? Does past offer parallel? What could I emulate?
Modify?	New twist? Changing meaning, color, motion, sound, odor, form, shape? Other changes?
Magnify?	What to add? More time? Greater frequency? Stronger? Higher? Longer? Thicker? Extra value? Plus ingredient? Duplicate? Multiply? Exaggerate?
Minify?	What to subtract? Smaller? Condensed? Miniature? Lower? Shorter? Lighter? Omit? Streamline? Split up? Understate?
Substitute?	Who else instead? What else instead? Other ingredients? Other material? Other process? Other power? Other place? Other approach? Other tone of voice?
Rearrange?	Interchange components? Other pattern? Other layout? Other sequence? Transpose cause and effect? Change pace? Change schedule?
Reverse?	Transpose positive and negative? How about opposites? Turn it backward? Turn it upside down? Reverse roles? Change shoes? Turn tables? Turn other cheek?
Combine?	How about a blend, an alloy, an assortment, an ensemble? Combine units? Combine purposes? Combine appeals? Combine ideas?

Source: Philip Kotler, *Marketing Management: Analysis, Planning and Control* (Englewood Cliffs, NJ: Prentice Hall, 1967), p. 247, adapted from Alex F. Osborn, *Applied Imagination*, 3rd rev. ed. (New York: Scribners, 1963), pp. 286–287.

aspects of group behavior. One technique to encourage the free flow of ideas is brainstorming.[6] Developed by Osborn and used regularly at BBDO, it features a group of six to ten people who focus on a problem. The cardinal rule is that criticism is prohibited. All evaluation is withheld until later. The wilder the idea that survives, the better, for it may stimulate a new association that will trigger a more useful idea. The participants are encouraged to build on ideas that appear, combining and improving them. The atmosphere is positive. The objective is quantity. Osborn reported that one such session generated 144 ideas on how to sell blankets.

A related technique, called *synectics,* was developed by William J. J. Gordon.[7] It differs from brainstorming in that it does not focus on a clearly specified problem. Rather, a discussion is stimulated around a general idea that is related to the ultimate specific problem. Instead of being concerned with marketing a citrus beverage, the group might discuss drinking. When a variety of ideas is exposed, the leader starts directing the discussion toward the specific problem. The sessions tend to last longer than the 60- or 90-minute brainstorming sessions, based on a belief that fatigue tends to remove inhibitions.

John Keil,[8] in a book on creativity, argues that there are several myths about creativity and creative people, none of which are really supported by the facts. Keil's six myths of creative people are as follows:

1. Creative people are sophisticated and worldly. They are cultured, well read, and snobbish.
2. Creative people are more intelligent than others.
3. Creative people are disorganized.
4. Creative people are witty and seldom boring.
5. Creative people are more involved with liquor and drugs than others are.
6. Drugs and alcohol stimulate creative thinking.

Like the social stereotypes of any profession, Keil essentially cautions against such stereotyping and argues that creative people have a wide variety of habits, styles, and values. There are boring creative people, as well as witty ones. The incidence of alcoholism and drug abuse in this profession appears no greater than in others such as law or medicine.

The creative process culminates in the specific activities of writing copy, illustrating, and layout. Each of these activities is briefly described in the next sections.

Copywriting

Copywriting, illustrating, and layout are different activities associated with the creative stage of advertising development and are usually done by different people who specialize in one or the other. Copywriting in print is the activity of actually putting words to paper, particularly those contained in the main body of the text (the main arguments and appeals used), but also including attendant bylines and headlines. In broadcast, the copywriter is in effect a "script" writer who develops the scenario or script to be used in a radio or television medium; writing a jingle, or the lyrics for music, may also be involved. Illustrating is usually the work of an artist in the case of television. Layout generally refers to the activity of bringing all the pieces together and, as will be seen, differs in the case of print and broadcast.

How does one write good copy? John Caples is a member of the Advertising Hall of Fame, and his wisdom is worth reading. He retired in 1981 after 54 years at Batten, Barton, Durstine & Osborn, the last 40 years as vice president. Caples was one of the giants contributing to the success of BBDO. A classic direct-mail advertisement created by Caples is shown in Figure 13-1. Caples states that the best ads are "written from the heart." "Write down every idea that comes into your head, every selling phrase, every key word. Write down the good ideas and the wild ideas. Don't try to edit your ideas at the start. Don't put a brake on your imagination."[9] In his book, he develops a checklist of important guidelines for copywriting:

1. Cash in on your personal experience.
2. Organize your experience.
3. Write from the heart.
4. Learn from the experience of others.
5. Talk with the manufacturer.

"Can he really play?" a girl whispered.
"Heavens no!" Arthur exclaimed. *"He
never played a note in his life."*

They Laughed When I Sat Down
At the Piano
But When I Started to Play!~

ARTHUR had just played "The Rosary." The room rang with applause. I decided that this would be a dramatic moment for me to make my debut. To the amazement of all my friends, I strode confidently over to the piano and sat down.

"Jack is up to his old tricks," somebody chuckled. The crowd laughed. They were all certain that I couldn't play a single note.

"Can he really play?" I heard a girl whisper to Arthur.

"Heavens, no!" Arthur exclaimed· "He never played a note in all his life. . . But just you watch him. This is going to be good."

I decided to make the most of the situation. With mock dignity I drew out a silk handkerchief and lightly dusted off the piano keys. Then I rose and gave the revolving piano stool a quarter of a turn, just as I had seen an imitator of Paderewski do in a vaudeville sketch.

"What do you think of his execution?" called a voice from the rear.

"We're in favor of it!" came back the answer, and the crowd rocked with laughter.

Then I Started to Play

Instantly a tense silence fell on the guests. The laughter died on their lips as if by magic. I played through the first few bars of Beethoven's immortal Moonlight Sonata. I heard gasps of amazement. My friends sat breathless—spellbound!

I played on and as I played I forgot the people around me. I forgot the hour, the place, the breathless listeners. The little world I lived in seemed to fade—seemed to grow dim—unreal. Only the music was real. Only the music and visions it brought me. Visions as beautiful and as changing as the wind blown clouds and drifting moonlight that long ago inspired the master composer. It seemed as if the master

musician himself were speaking to me—speaking through the medium of music—not in words but in chords. Not in sentences but in exquisite melodies!

A Complete Triumph!

As the last notes of the Moonlight Sonata died away, the room resounded with a sudden roar of applause. I found myself surrounded by excited faces. How my friends carried on! Men shook my hand—wildly congratulated me—pounded me on the back in their enthusiasm! Everybody was exclaiming with delight—plying me with rapid questions. . . . "Jack! Why didn't you tell us you could play like that!". . . "Where did you learn?"—"How long have you studied?"— "Who was your teacher!"

"I have never even *seen* my teacher," I replied. "And just a short while ago I couldn't play a note."·

"Quit your kidding," laughed Arthur, himself an accomplished pianist. "You've been studying for years. I can tell."

"I have been studying only a short while," I insisted. "I decided to keep it a secret so that I could surprise all you folks."

Then I told them the whole story.

"Have you ever heard of the U. S. School of Music?" I asked.

A few of my friends nodded. "That's a correspondence school, isn't it?" they exclaimed.

"Exactly," I replied. "They have a new simplified method that can teach you to play any instrument by mail in just a few months."

How I Learned to Play Without a Teacher

And then I explained how for years I had longed to play the piano.

"A few months ago," I continued, "I saw an interesting ad for the U. S. School of Music—a new method of learning to play which only cost a few cents a day! The ad told how a woman had mastered the piano in her spare time at home—and *without a teacher!* Best of all, the wonderful new method she used, required no laborious scales — no heartless exercises — no tiresome practising. It sounded so convincing that I filled out the coupon requesting the Free Demonstration Lesson.

"The free book arrived promptly and I started in that very night to study the Demonstration Lesson. I was amazed to see how easy it was to play this new way. Then I sent for the course.

"When the course arrived I found it was just as the ad said — as easy as A.B.C! And, as

the lessons continued they got easier and easier. Before I knew it I was playing all the pieces I liked best. Nothing stopped me. I could play ballads or classical numbers or jazz, all with equal ease! And I never did have any special talent for music!"

Play Any Instrument

You too, can now *teach yourself* to be an accomplished musician—right at home—in half the usual time. You can't go wrong with this simple new method which has already shown 350,000 people how to play their favorite instruments. Forget that old-fashioned idea that you need special "talent." Just read the list of instruments in the panel, decide which one you want to play and the U. S. School will do the rest. And bear in mind no matter which instrument you choose, the cost in each case will be the same—just a few cents a day. No matter whether you are a mere beginner or already a good performer, you will be interested in learning about this new and wonderful method.

Send for Our Free Booklet and Demonstration Lesson

Thousands of successful students never dreamed they possessed musical ability until it was revealed to them by a remarkable "Musical Ability Test" which we send entirely without cost with our interesting free booklet.

If you are in earnest about wanting to play your favorite instrument—if you really want to gain happiness and increase your popularity—send at once for the free booklet and Demonstration Lesson. No cost — no obligation. Right now we are making a Special offer to a limited number of new students. Sign and send the convenient coupon now — before it's too late to gain the benefits of this offer. Instruments supplied when needed, cash or credit. U. S. School of Music, 1631 Brunswick Bldg., New York City.

- - -

Pick Your Instrument

Piano	'Cello
Organ	Harmony and
Violin	Composition
Drums and	Sight Singing
Traps	Ukulele
Banjo	Guitar
Tenor	Hawaiian
Banjo	Steel Guitar
Mandolin	Harp
Clarinet	Cornet
Flute	Piccolo
Saxophone	Trombone
Voice and Speech Culture	
Automatic Finger Control	
Piano Accordion	

U. S. School of Music,
1631 Brunswick Bldg., New York City.

Please send me your free book, "Music Lessons in Your Own Home", with introduction by Dr. Frank Crane, Demonstration Lesson and particulars of your Special Offer. I am interested in the following course:

....

Have you above instrument? ....

Name..................................
(Please write plainly)

Address...............................

City...............State.............

Figure 13-1. A famous direct-mail advertisement of John Caples

Source: *Advertising Age*, August 1, 1983, p. M50.

6. Study the product.
7. Review previous advertising for the product.
8. Study competitors' ads.
9. Study testimonials from customers.
10. Solve the prospect's problem.
11. Put your subconscious mind to work.
12. "Ring the changes" on a successful idea.

Following these rules is good advice in creating copy. The idea of "ring the changes" is particularly useful and interesting. Once a successful idea has been found, it should be used repeatedly with variations on the central theme. For example, an insurance company found that ads featuring retirement annuities brought the most coupon replies. So all the ad headlines featured retirement. However, the appearance of the ads was varied by using different illustrations such as a man fishing . . . a couple sitting on the beach under a palm tree . . . an elderly couple embarking on a cruise ship. As Caples says,

> Once you have found a winning sales idea, don't change it. Your client may tire of it after a year or two. He sees all the ads from layout stage to proof stage to publication stage. Explain to him that when he is tired of the campaign, it is just beginning to take hold of the public.[10]

Copywriting obviously becomes more important in the case of long copy and less important in the case where few words are included. Copy should be only as long as necessary to complete the sales job—this means that long copy is often appropriate only for the highly interested reader (such as people contemplating car purchases).

While there are no (and should never be any) "rules" for what makes for good copy, it is worthwhile to become familiar with some generally accepted principles. Regardless of the specific ad medium, copy is usually more effective if it is simple, containing only one or two key ideas; contains a benefit or idea unique to the brand being advertised; is "extendible" (can lead to several variations in a campaign); flows naturally and smoothly from beginning to end; is specific, using facts and figures and believable details instead of generalities; frequently mentions the brand name and key consumer benefit; and concludes by linking back to its beginning, with a strong call to some kind of action. One overriding rule for developing copy is to keep the format simple, uncluttered, and straightforward. Whether in print or in broadcast, the tendency for including too much information or for complicating the television commercial with too many scene changes, or scenes that are not well integrated, should be avoided. This principle of simplicity extends to the language used as well. Like cluttered format, complicated language is unlikely to induce people to spend the time to "figure it out." The message should always be true to the product. Claims should be substantiable, and the style should not be radically altered over the life cycle of the product.

For print ads, one of the key elements is the headline, which must flag down the target reader and pull him or her into the body copy, offering a reward for reading on. This is best achieved by headlines that appeal to the reader's self-interest (e.g., by offering free, useful information), are newsy, offer new twists on familiar sayings, and/or evoke curiosity (e.g., by asking a quizlike question).[11] It helps if the brand name is mentioned in the headline itself. Since most people reading print ads never go beyond the headline, it is also extremely important that the headline and visual complement each other so well and "tell the story" so easily, that a reader who only looks at the headline and main visual can "get the message" without having to read a word of the body copy. An excellent example of an ad that has the headline and visual working together is shown in Figure 13-2, for Cheerfree detergent. "Story appeal" is another effective copy device, as can be seen in the Paco Rabanne ad in Figure 13-3.

Television scripts (which are discussed further shortly) must usually be written to take advantage of the visual nature of the medium, by using demonstrations, pack close-ups, and the like. Since TV ads are fleeting and cannot usually easily communicate much information, simplicity (and frequent and early mention of the brand name and key idea) are strongly recommended. For radio ads, a key principle usually is to write copy that "creates a picture in the mind's eye" of the listener—through the human voice, sound effects, humor, and music, the ad must pull the listener in from whatever is being done when the ad comes on, into an imagined situation. It is usually also important in radio to mention the brand name and the key selling benefit early and often. Short words and short sentences are usually easier to understand on the radio.

For outdoor ads, where the message must be communicated in a few seconds, the copy and visual (such as a large pack shot) must be extremely short, simple, strong, and obvious—there is no time for subtlety. Retail ads usually must contain specifics about the merchandise being offered (such as exact sizes, colors, and prices) in order to stimulate immediate buying action. Yet they must also be created in a manner consistent with (and must strive to reinforce) the image of the store. Since business-to-business ads are usually written to an audience seeking problem-solving or profit-improving information, they should usually be informative and offer specifics, serious (but not boring), and (ideally) offer case histories of how the advertised brand helped someone else in a similar situation. (See Figure 13-4 for an excellent example.) A coupon or phone number can be used to provide more detailed information and generate a lead for a subsequent sales call, either in person or via the telephone.

Illustrating

The activity of illustrating is of crucial importance for many consumer nondurable products where pictures or photographs are used to convey a central idea, and there is little or no need for long explanations or a recitation of copy points. Normally, an artist will be involved in selecting materials or will actually draw original pictures for the advertising. Artwork is equally if not more important than writing copy, particularly where the goals of the advertising are attention getting or building awareness. As in writing copy, pictorial materials should be developed that are tied into the self-interest and understanding of the audience, "tell a story" at a glance, are relevant to the product and copy theme, and accurate and plausible in the context of the selling message. Another popular rule is to include pictures of at least some or all of the product.

Figure 13-2. Headline and visual working together: Cheerfree

© The Procter & Gamble Company. Used with permission.

Figure 13-3. An ad with story appeal: Paco Rabanne

Figure 13-4. A business-to-business ''case history'' ad: Digital Courtesy of Digital Equipment Corporation.

Illustrating also involves decisions as to what "identification marks" to include. These fall into one of three categories: company or trade name, brand name, and trademarks. In family-branding strategy, the company name, such as Del Monte or Levi Strauss, will obviously play a major role. In other cases, the company name may not even be mentioned or deemphasized, as in many of the detergent brand advertisements of Proctor & Gamble. The decision regarding brand name will probably have been made prior to actual copywriting, but it may not. A great deal of time and research effort may be required to arrive at the right brand name. Trademarks, service marks, and certification marks like the *Good Housekeeping* seal of approval must also be considered for inclusion in the visual materials. Often a caricature or identifying symbol such as the Pillsbury doughboy, the Green Giant, or Mr. Peanut will be included, and decisions as to how they will be positioned will be required. The visual content, color, artwork, and identification mark decisions are a crucial aspect of print advertising, and choices will heavily determine the effectiveness of the final result.

The United States Trademark Association lists the following as desirable characteristics of a trademark: it is brief, easy to remember, easily readable and speakable, easily adapted to any media, suitable for export, and subtle; has no unpleasant connotations; and lends itself to pictorialization.

Though color ads are assumed to have more impact than black-and-white ads (which usually cost less money to run), Guest provided one of the few studies that examined the differential effect of color.[12] He asked respondents to evaluate companies after being exposed to advertisements. Half the respondents saw a color version of the advertisements and the other half saw a black-and-white version. The ones in color consistently did better across advertisements and years (the study was replicated three times), but the differences were small and usually not statistically significant. Guest concludes that "these studies do not support the contention that companies sponsoring colored advertisements receive a bonus of greater prestige as a consequence of color only."[13]

Many of the same kinds of decisions must be made with respect to the video portion of a television commercial. Here, however, the emphasis is on action and the dynamics of each scene. The director must take into account how one scene will blend into the next, how video materials will serve to enhance and reinforce the audio message, which will be mainly attention-getters, which will carry the copy points, and so on. Chapter 15 has a description of the production of an American Express commercial that illustrates many of these points. The task is further complicated in television by the addition of music or sound effects other than voice.

Layout

The layout activity involves bringing all the pieces together before the advertising is sent out for production. A layout can be in relatively unfinished form, a *preliminary* layout, or can be a very detailed specification of all aspects of the production requirements, a *comprehensive* layout. The decision as to how detailed the layout is to be will rest on the agency's trust in the supplier firms. Many agencies choose to send on only preliminary layouts to allow room for a significant amount of creativity in the production process.

Layout involves decisions as to how the various components of headline, illustration, copy, and identification marks are to be arranged and positioned on the page. The size of the advertisement will obviously have an effect on this decision. There are five considerations to take into account in developing print layout:

1. *Balance*:   the arrangement of elements to achieve a pleasing distribution or visual impression.
2. *Contrast*:   using different sizes, shapes, densities, and colors to enhance attention value and readability.
3. *Proportion*:   the relation of objects to the background in which they appear and to each other.
4. *Gaze-motion*:   the headline, illustration, copy, and identification marks in that order will usually provide the most logical sequence for gaze-motion (in some cases, however, it may be useful to alter this typical pattern).
5. *Unity*:   the qualities of balance, contrast, proportion, and gaze-motion should be combined to develop unity of thought, appearance, and design in the layout. Coupons, for example, should not be placed at the beginning of an advertisement unless the copy theme is built around the idea of clipping the coupon. Unity is best achieved by keeping the layout simple and uncluttered and to ease the reader's task in comprehending the advertisement. Simplicity can be carried forward in many instances by judicious use of "white space" in which most of a large part of the advertisement shows nothing.

Concerning layout, Stephen Baker, an art director, draws a distinction between "arranging elements on a page" and "visualizing an idea." He states

> The former is a designer's (or layout man's) feat; his innate sense of composition, balance, color is brought fully into play. On the other hand, presenting the clearest visual interpretation requires a strong desire to communicate with the audience, a flair for the dramatic, the ability to think in pictorial terms (usually referred to as "visual sense") and, probably most significant, a firm understanding of the advertiser's goal.[14]

The rules of balance, contrast, proportion, gaze-motion, and unity should be considered in a good layout.

The layout of a television commercial is the storyboard; various examples of storyboards have appeared in earlier chapters. Here, again, it can be generated in a relatively primitive form, in which only artist sketches and suggestive copy are included, or in a more comprehensive form that details more precisely what actors are to say, how scenes will blend in, and the precise location of identification marks, background music, special effects, and so on. The copy/art team creating a TV commercial will indicate the nature of the camera shots and camera movements, the level and type of music, and so on. Of course, much will change as the commercial is actually shot and then edited, by the director selected for the commercial (see Chapter 15).[15]

TYPES OF TELEVISION COMMERCIALS

Audio and visual elements can be combined to produce several types of television commercials, just as a story can be told in many different ways. Emphasis can be placed on the story itself, on the problem to be solved, on the central character such as in a testimonial, or on special human emotions or storytelling techniques such as satire, humor, fantasy, and so on. Book and Cary[16] provide a useful classification of the possible alternatives, based on the point of emphasis, focus, or style adopted. Each is referred to as a particular kind of commercial structure to emphasize that a commercial is other than an unrelated jumble of ideas and techniques. The 13 types of structure identified by them follow:

1. *Story line*:   a commercial that tells a story; a clear, step-by-step unfolding of a message that has a definite beginning, middle, and end.

2. *Problem-solution*:   presents the viewer with a problem to be solved and the sponsor's product as the solution to that problem. Probably the most widely used and generally accepted example of a TV commercial.

3. *Chronology*:   delivers the message through a series of related scenes, each one growing out of the one before. Facts and events are presented sequentially as they occurred.

4. *Special effects*:   no strong structural pattern; strives for and often achieves memorability through the use of some striking device, for example, an unusual musical sound or pictorial technique.

5. *Testimonial*:   also called "word-of-mouth" advertising; uses well-known figures or an unknown "man in the street" to provide product testimonials.

6. *Satire*:   a commercial that uses sophisticated wit to point out human foibles, generally produced in an exaggerated style; parodies on James Bond movies, *Bonnie and Clyde*, *Hair*, and the like.

7. *Spokesperson*:   the use of an on-camera announcer who basically "talks." Talk may be fast and hard sell or more personal, intimate sell.

8. *Demonstration*:   uses some physical apparatus to demonstrate a product's effectiveness. Analgesic, watch, and tire commercials employ this approach heavily.

9. *Suspense*:   somewhat similar to story-line or problem-solution structures, but the buildup of curiosity and suspense to the final resolution is given a heightened sense of drama.

10. *Slice-of-life*:   a variation on problem solution; begins with a person at the point of, and just before the discovery of, an answer to a problem. This approach is heavily used by detergent manufacturers.

11. *Analogy*:   offers an extraneous example, then attempts to relate it to the product message. Instead of delivering a message simply and directly, an analogy uses one

example to explain another by comparison or implication: "Just as vitamins tone up your body, our product tones up your car's engine."

12. *Fantasy*:   uses caricatures or special effects to create fantasy surrounding product and product use: Jolly Green Giant, White Knight, White Tornado, the washing machine that becomes ten feet tall.

13. *Personality*:   a technical variation of the spokesperson or announcer-on-camera, straight-sell structure. Relies on an actor or actress rather than an announcer to deliver the message. Uses a setting rather than the background of a studio. The actor plays a character who talks about the product, reacts to its use, or demonstrates its use or enjoyment directly to the camera.

These structures are, of course, not mutually exclusive, but rather serve to provide points of focus for analysis, copy production, and research. For example, in testimonials and, perhaps, in spokesperson and demonstration commercials, the credibility of source and/or the mode of presentation are likely to be most important. Customer reactions to source could receive special attention, utilizing the ideas on source credibility given earlier in Chapter 12. In story-line, problem-solution, and perhaps the chronology and analogy structures, focus would tend to center more on the type of argument (for example, one- versus two-sided or refutation) or the order of argument (primacy-recency, stating a conclusion) dimensions. A researcher would be particularly interested, for instance, in whether the problem conveyed and the solution presented in the commercial were perceived as such by a sample of potential customers. Each of these seven types of commercials also tends to be more factual in orientation.

The remaining six types all are more emotional in orientation and can be distinguished on the basis of whether the emotion-arousing capacity or the *characterization* being used relates to source or message. The personality and slice-of-life structures, for example, are likely to be more source oriented. The choice of the personality to be used or the characters who will play the role in the slice-of-life situation are emphasized. Source effects would also tend to be the point of focus, but specific attention might be devoted to the *attractiveness* component of source and whether the respondents tended to identify readily with the personality or characters involved. In this sense, the overriding concern with commercials of this type may be the emotions and interest aroused and what the consequences of that arousal process are.

The special effects, fantasy, satire, and suspense structures are all fundamentally emotional in orientation. Special effects, for example, might be used to arouse emotions with respect to fear, sex, or status. Attention here would not focus so much on the people in the advertisement as on the special effects—the type of humor used, whether a particular form of background music achieved the desired mood, whether the satire was indeed satirical, and so on. In other words, *message* rather than *source* would be the focus. Once again, however, the principal objective would be emotional arousal, and interest would center on whether the particular emotion was manifested in the test group (for example, laughter, anxiety) and what the consequences of the arousal process were for the object being advertised.

CREATIVE STYLES

As has already been suggested, creating advertising is a little like creating art. Two artists viewing the same scene may paint it quite differently, but both can produce high-quality paintings and "effective" products. In this portion of the chapter, several of the creative giants of advertising and examples of their work are presented. An important factor that tends to distinguish them is the nature of the product or market situation. As will be seen, however, there are points of emphasis and style that tend to characterize the approach and make it recognizable. Just as an art critic can distinguish a Picasso from a Monet, so an experienced copy director can distinguish the work of a David Ogilvy from that of a Leo Burnett. The styles of creative giants in advertising have, over time, become exaggerated to the point of caricature. Furthermore, right or wrong, their approaches become associated with a considerable amount of advertising of the agency with which they are associated. Thus, any description of their creative style may tend to be exaggerated. Such an exaggeration is useful for our purposes, however, because it helps to illustrate the diversity among creative teams in the advertising profession.

The first set of examples profiles the works of David Ogilvy, William Bernbach, Rosser Reeves, and Leo Burnett. These creative giants have had major impacts on advertising over the years, and it is useful to study their styles and classic examples of their work. This is followed by three copy directors who have achieved prominence and recognition in recent years: Philip Dusenberry, Lee Clow, and Hal Riney. Each has had a major impact on the creative output of the advertising agencies with which they are associated and, in many respects, represent the "state of the art" in advertising in the early 1990s.

DAVID OGILVY: THE BRAND IMAGE

David Ogilvy—who, now retired from the business, lives in a chateau in France—is most concerned with the brand image. Due in part to the nature of the products with which he works, this usually means that he is concerned with developing and retaining a prestige image. He argues that, in the long run, it pays to protect a favorable image even if some appealing short-run programs are sacrificed in the process. In his words,

> Every advertisement should be thought of as a contribution to the complex symbol which is the brand image. If you take that long view, a great many day-to-day problems solve themselves. . . . Most of the manufacturers who find it expedient to change the image of their brand want it changed upward. Often it has acquired a bargain-basement image, a useful asset in time of economic scarcity, but a grave embarrassment in boom days, when the majority of consumers are on their way up the social ladder. It isn't easy to perform a face-lifting operation on an old bargain-basement brand. In many cases it would be easier to start again, with a fresh new brand. . . . A steady diet of price-off promotions lowers the esteem in which the consumer holds the product; can anything which is always sold at a discount be desirable?[17]

Ogilvy goes on to say that the personality of the brand is particularly important if brands are similar:

> The greater the similarity between brands, the less part reason plays in brand selection. There isn't any significant difference between the various brands of whiskey, or cigarettes, or beer. They are all about the same. And so are the cake mixes and the detergents, and the margarines. The manufacturer who dedicates his advertising to building the most sharply defined personality for his brand will get the largest share of the market at the highest profit. By the same token, the manufacturers who will find themselves up the creek are those shortsighted opportunists who siphon off their advertising funds for promotions.[18]

When Ogilvy obtained the Puerto Rico account, he indicated that what was needed was to "substitute a lovely image of Puerto Rico for the squalid image which now exists in the minds of most mainlanders."[19]

One of the most distinctive aspects of many of Ogilvy's most well-known campaigns is the use of prestigious individuals to convey the desired image for the product. In two cases he actually used clients to represent their own products: Commander Whitehead for Schweppes Tonic and Helena Rubinstein for her line of cosmetics. One of the original advertisements for the Schweppes campaign is shown in Figure 13-5. Others he "created" or developed from individuals or ideas not explicitly part of the original company. One of the most successful was the campaign for Hathaway shirts in which a male character with an eye patch was featured. Ogilvy tells how the campaign evolved, for a product with an initial advertising budget of only $30,000.

> I concocted eighteen different ways to inject this magic ingredient of "story appeal." The eighteenth was the eye patch. At first we rejected it in favor of a more obvious idea, but on the way to the studio I ducked into a drugstore and bought an eye patch for $1.50. Exactly why it turned out to be so successful, I shall never know. It put Hathaway on the map after 116 years of relative obscurity. Seldom, if ever, has a national brand been created so fast, or at such low cost. . . . As the campaign developed, I showed the model in a series of situations in which I would have liked to find myself: conducting the New York Philharmonic at Carnegie Hall, playing the oboe, copying a Goya at the Metropolitan Museum, driving a tractor, fencing, sailing, buying a Renoir, and so forth.[20]

Ogilvy will, when possible, obtain testimonials from celebrities. Usually their fee will go to their favorite charity. Thus, Ogilvy has used Queen Elizabeth and Winston Churchill in "Come to Britain" advertisements and Mrs. Franklin Roosevelt saying that Good Luck margarine really tastes delicious. His agency, Ogilvy & Mather (now part of the WPP Group) continued this approach in the 1980s for American Express in a print campaign showing interesting photographs of famous celebrities who were card members, with no copy but for the line "Member since 19xx" (see Chapter 8). A campaign for the *Reader's Digest* featured many national figures explaining that they relied on such a magazine because of their busy schedules.

Ogilvy, in addition to being very creative, is also research oriented. He looks to the experiences of direct-mail advertisers and the various advertising readership services for

The man from Schweppes is here

MEET Commander Edward White-head, Schweppesman Extraordinary from London, England, where the House of Schweppes has been a great institution since 1794.

The Commander has come to these United States to make sure that every drop of Schweppes Quinine Water bottled over here has the original bittersweet flavor essential for an authentic Gin-and-Tonic.

He imports the original Schweppes elixir and the secret of Schweppes unique carbonation is securely locked in his brief case. "Schwepper-vescence," says the Commander, *"lasts the whole drink through."*

Schweppes Quinine Water makes your favorite drink a truly patrician potion—and Schweppes is now available at popular prices throughout Greater New York.

Figure 13-5. An early advertisement for Schweppes
Courtesy of Schweppes U.S.A. Limited.

possible generalizations. He also looks to his colleagues and competitors for insights. From these sources he puts forth various guides, rules, and commandments for the creation of advertising by his staff. The following are his 11 commandments for creating advertising campaigns.[21]

1. What you say is more important than how you say it. Two hundred years ago Dr. Johnson said, "Promise, large promise is the soul of an advertisement." When he auctioned off the contents of the Anchor Brewery he made the following promise: "We are not here to sell boilers and vats, but the potentiality of growing rich beyond the dreams of avarice."

2. Unless your campaign is built around a great idea, it will flop.

3. Give the facts. The consumer isn't a moron; she is your wife. You insult her intelligence if you assume that a mere slogan and a few vapid adjectives will persuade her to buy anything. She wants all the information you can give her.

4. You cannot bore people into buying. We make advertisements that people want to read. You can't save souls in an empty church.

5. Be well mannered, but don't clown.

6. Make your advertising contemporary.

7. Committees can criticize advertisements, but they cannot write them.

8. If you are lucky enough to write a good advertisement, repeat it until it stops pulling. Sterling Getchel's famous advertisement for Plymouth ("Look at All Three") appeared only once and was succeeded by a series of inferior variations which were quickly forgotten. But the Sherwin Cody School of English ran the same advertisement ("Do You Make These Mistakes in English?") for 42 years, changing only the typeface and the color of Mr. Cody's beard.

9. Never write an advertisement which you wouldn't want your own family to read. Good products can be sold by honest advertising. If you don't think the product is good, you have no business to be advertising it. If you tell lies, or weasel, you do your client a disservice, you increase your load of guilt, and you fan the flames of public resentment against the whole business of advertising.

10. The image and the brand: it is the total personality of a brand rather than any trivial product difference which decides its ultimate position in the market.

11. Don't be a copy cat. Nobody has ever built a brand by imitating somebody else's advertising. Imitation may be the "sincerest form of plagiarism," but it is also the mark of an inferior person.

WILLIAM BERNBACH: EXECUTION

Perhaps the most exciting agency in the 1960s and 1970s was the one William Bernbach established in 1949, Doyle Dane Bernbach (now, as DDB Needham, part of the Omnicom group). It has been enormously successful although apparently violating several well-established dictums of the advertising business. One of the most sacred laws in evaluating an advertisement is to determine if it really communicates a persuasive message or if it is merely clever or memorable. The primary job of an advertisement is to sell—to communicate a persuasive message. David Ogilvy's first rule for copywriters is "What you say is more important than how you say it." Bernbach replied that "execution can become content, it can be just as important as what you say . . . a sick guy can utter some words and nothing happens; a healthy vital guy says them and they rock the world."[22] In the Bernbach style, the execution dominates.

To say that Bernbach emphasized execution is, of course, a rather incomplete description of his style. What kind of execution? Although it is difficult to verbalize such an approach because it does not lend itself to rules, there are certain characteristics that can be identified. First, Bernbach did not talk down to an audience. An audience is respected. As Jerry Della Femina, a colorful advertising executive, put it, "Doyle Dane's advertisement has that feeling that the consumer is bright enough to understand what the advertising is saying, that the consumer isn't a lunkhead who has to be treated like a twelve year old."[23] The copy is honest. Puffery is avoided, as are clichés and heavy repetition. The advertising demands attention and has something to say. Second, the approach is clean and direct. Bernbach pointed out that "you must be as simple, and as swift and as penetrating as possible. . . . What you must do, by the most economical and creative means possible, is attract people and sell them."[24] Third, the advertisement should stand out from others. It should have its own character. In Bernbach's words,

> Why should anyone look at your ad? The reader doesn't buy his magazine or tune in his radio and TV to see and hear what you have to say. . . . What is the use of saying all the right things in the world if nobody is going to read them? And, believe me, nobody is going to read them if they are not said with freshness, originality and imagination . . . if they are not, if you will, different.[25]

Finally, the often-repeated rule that humor does not sell is ignored. Doyle Dane Bernbach frequently uses humor to gain attention and to provide a positive reward to an advertisement reader. Robert Fine, one of Bernbach's copywriters, said

> We recognize that an advertisement is an intrusion. People don't necessarily like advertisements, and avoid them if possible. Therefore, to do a good advertisement you're obligated, really, to reward the reader for his time and patience in allowing you to interrupt the editorial content, which is what he bought the magazine for in the first place. This is not defensive. It just takes into account the fact that an advertisement pushes its way uninvited into somebody's mind. So entertainment is sort of repayment.[26]

Doyle Dane Bernbach deemphasizes research, believing that it tends to generate advertisements too similar to those of competitors. The assumptions are that others are doing the same type of research, interpreting it the same way, and generating the same policy implications. In Bernbach's words,

> One of the disadvantages of doing everything mathematically, by research, is that after a while, everybody does it the same way. . . . If you take the attitude that once *you* have found

out what to say, your job is done, then what you're doing is saying it the same way as everybody is saying it, and you've lost your impact completely.[27]

One of Bernbach's first accounts in 1949 was Levy's bread, a relatively unknown New York bread. Bernbach developed radio spots that featured an unruly child asking his mother for "Wevy's Cimmanon Waison Bwead" and getting his pronunciation corrected. In addition, subway posters were used. One showed three slices of bread, one uneaten, one with a few bites gone, and the third with only the crust remaining. The copy read simply "New York Is Eating It Up! Levy's Real Jewish Rye." Without using a single product claim, Levy's bread reportedly became one of the best known brands in town.[28] An ad from the campaign appears in Figure 13-6.

Doyle Dane Bernbach also generated the now-classic Avis campaign (see Figure 4-8).[29] The "We're Number 2, We Try Harder" campaign was effective for various reasons. It dared to admit that a firm was indeed in second place. At the same time, it turned this fact to advantage by indicating that a customer could expect better because Number 2 would naturally tend to try harder. It was the perfect application of two-sided communication: state the opposing position first (Hertz is the largest), and then rebut it (we try

Figure 13-6. One of Bernbach's ads for Levy's bread
Courtesy of Best Foods, Inc.

harder). The campaign was supported by red "We Try Harder" buttons and by a real effort to improve the Avis service. The service was affected, in part, owing to the impact of the campaign on Avis employees. Ironically, despite the fact that the campaign was directed at the giant Hertz, the impact fell primarily on Avis's other competitors. When the campaign began, Avis and National were neck and neck and Hertz was ahead. The campaign made the rent-a-car industry seem to be a two-firm affair. As a result, National and the other competitors were damaged much more than Hertz. In fact, because primary demand was stimulated, Hertz probably benefited from the Avis advertisements. The campaign received an impetus when Hertz decided to reply directly. This reply, which was a controversial strategy, was perhaps the first time the top dog actually recognized a competitor publicly. The strategy was triggered in part by a need to boost the morale of Hertz employees. This whole situation is a good example of how advertising has an impact on employees, which usually is not considered in campaign planning.

It was the Volkswagen campaign that really established the Bernbach approach. As Jerry Della Femina said, "In the beginning there was Volkswagen."[30] It ushered in a decade of the hot, creative agencies that attempted to duplicate the Doyle Dane Bernbach success. The Volkswagen advertisements, like many Doyle Dane Bernbach advertisements, almost always had a large photograph of the product in a setting with a headline and copy below. The headline was usually provocative and tempted readers to continue to the copy. One advertisement showed steam coming out of a nonexistent radiator with the caption "Impossible." A headline under a picture of a flat tire read "Nobody's Perfect." Several advantages of the car were listed under the headline "Ugly is only skin-deep." The two real classics were the lines "Think Small" and "Lemon."

The Lemon advertisement was particularly noteworthy. (See Figure 13-7.) Many of the advertisements directly disparaged the product, an approach that was frowned on in many circles and never used to the extent it was in the Volkswagen campaign. Even for the Volkswagen campaign, Lemon was extreme and was approved by the Volkswagen management only after some tribulation. The copy went on to identify a defect caught by 1 of 3,389 inspectors and discussed the elaborate quality assurance program of the firm.

The campaign eventually moved into television. One of the early television advertisements was described as follows:

> The camera looks through the windshield of a car traveling on a dark, snowcovered country road. Heavy loads of fresh snow bend down pine and fir branches. No announcer's voice is heard; the only sound is that of an engine prosaically purring along. In shot after shot the headlights illuminate the falling snow ahead, piling up deeper on the winding, climbing, untracked road. Robert Frost's haunting lines about the woods on a snowy night are inevitably evoked. Curiosity and a measure of suspense are created: Who is driving and where? What errand has taken him out on such a night? Finally the headlights swing off by a large dark building and are switched off. A high door opens and a powerful snowplow rolls past as the announcer's voice begins, "Have you ever wondered how the man who drives the snowplow drives to the snowplow? This one drives a Volkswagen. So you can stop wondering."[31]

The Volkswagen advertising was particularly fresh when contrasted with the competition. Most Detroit advertising, for example, tended to use drawings rather than

Lemon.

This Volkswagen missed the boat.

The chrome strip on the glove compartment is blemished and must be replaced. Chances are you wouldn't have noticed it; Inspector Kurt Kroner did.

There are 3,389 men at our Wolfsburg factory with only one job: to inspect Volkswagens at each stage of production. (3000 Volkswagens are produced daily; there are more inspectors than cars.)

Every shock absorber is tested (spot checking won't do), every windshield is scanned. VWs have been rejected for surface scratches barely visible to the eye.

Final inspection is really something! VW inspectors run each car off the line onto the Funktionsprüfstand (car test stand), tote up 189 check points, gun ahead to the automatic brake stand, and say "no" to one VW out of fifty.

This preoccupation with details means the VW lasts longer and requires less maintenance, by and large, than other cars. (It also means a used VW depreciates less than any other car.)

We pluck the lemons; you get the plums.

Figure 13-7. A classic Volkswagen ad from Bernbach

Copyrighted by, and reproduced with the permission of, VW of America, Inc.

photographs so that the impression of elegance could be enhanced. Their copy tended to be rather predictable and bland. The Volkswagen use of photographs, which very realistically set forth the product in all its commonness, and its copy with a tendency to laugh at itself, had to be refreshing.

The campaign was by any measure a phenomenal success. Sales climbed impressively, even when the domestic compacts were introduced, and other foreign cars were severely hurt. The advertising undoubtedly contributed to sales performance. The advertisements were consistently well read, even on occasion substantially outscoring cover stories and editorial features.[32] They were talked about by the man in the street and won all sorts of creative awards in the profession. The Volkswagen story is a good illustration of the Bernbach approach to copywriting.

ROSSER REEVES: THE USP

Especially under the scrutiny of advertising critics, it is considerably easier to justify or explain advertising that is clever, tasteful, and entertaining than advertising that is not so described. In that regard, the approaches of Ogilvy or Bernbach are somewhat easier to defend than the style attributed to Rosser Reeves of the Ted Bates agency (now part of Backer Spielvogel Bates, itself part of the Saatchi group). Reeves did not, of course, try to produce advertising that is not tasteful, but he did make it clear that he wrote not for esthetic appeal but to create sales. He challenged the "artsy, craftsy crowd" by observing, "I'm not saying that charming, witty and warm copy won't sell. I'm just saying that I've seen thousands of charming, witty campaigns that didn't sell."[33]

His conception of the appropriate role of advertising is illustrated in the following questions he posed:

> Let's say you have $1,000,000 tied up in your little company and suddenly, for reasons unknown to you, your advertising isn't working and your sales are going down. And everything depends on it, your family's future depends on it, other people's families depend on it. And you walk in this office and talk to me, and you sit in that chair. Now, what do you want out of me? Fine writing? Do you want masterpieces? Do you want glowing things that can be framed by copywriters? Or do you want to see the . . . sales curve stop moving down and start moving up? What do you want?[34]

Reeves was particularly critical of approaches in which the copy is so clever that it distracts from the message. Reeves proposed that each product develop its own unique selling proposition (USP) and use whatever repetition is necessary to communicate the USP to the audience. There are three guidelines to the development of a USP. First, the proposition needs to involve a specific product benefit. Second, it must be unique, one that competing firms are not using. Third, it must sell. It therefore must be important enough to the consumer to influence the decision process. The most successful USPs such as "M&M candies melt in your mouth instead of your hand" result from identifying real inherent product advantages. The determination of a USP generally requires research on the product and on consumer use of the product. When a good USP is found, the development of the actual advertisement is a relatively easy process. Among Ted Bates' USPs are "Colgate cleans your breath as it cleans your teeth," "Viceroys have 20,000 filter traps," and "Better skin from Palmolive."

Reeves relied heavily on product research to support specific claims. This support often took the form of rather elaborate experiments. The research tended to be reliable in the sense that others, if they wished, could replicate it and generate similar conclusions. In one case, Ted Bates and Colgate spent $300,000 to prove that washing the face thoroughly (for a full minute) with Palmolive soap would improve the skin.[35] The concern over support of claims is, of course, a useful precaution to avoid FTC action. Reeves did not obtain the documentation only for legal purposes. The fact is that good research can be used to help make the claim more credible.

Once an effective USP is found, Reeves believed that it should be retained practically indefinitely. Such a philosophy requires vigorous defending, especially when a client gets tired of a campaign, which usually happens before the campaign even starts. One client asked Reeves, "You have seven hundred people in that office of yours, and you've been running the same advertisement for me for the last eleven years. What I want to know is, what are those seven hundred people supposed to be doing?" Reeves replied, "They're keeping your advertising department from changing your advertisement."[36] According to Reeves, Anacin spent over $85 million in a ten-year period on one advertising commercial. Reeves pointed out that the commercial "cost $8,200 to produce and it made more money than *Gone With the Wind*."[37] The psychological learning theories with their emphasis on habit formation via repetition provide some theoretical support for the use of heavy repetition in advertising.

The Reeves approach was undoubtedly successful. However, the approach is highly controversial. People object to the style and to the repetition. The use of a USP is particularly troublesome in political campaigns, when many feel that a more thorough discussion of issues is appropriate. In 1952 the Reeves approach was applied to the Eisenhower campaign.[38] Reeves made a set of 20-second spot commercials for Eisenhower. They all started with the statement "Eisenhower Answers the Nation." Then an ordinary citizen would ask a question such as, "What about the high cost of living?" Eisenhower would then reply. To the cost-of-living question, he said, "My wife, Mamie, worries about the same thing. I tell her its our job to change that on November fourth." Such advertisements may have been effective, but they created a storm of controversy about the nature of political advertising campaigns that exists to this day.

LEO BURNETT: THE COMMON TOUCH

The Leo Burnett agency differs from other larger agencies in that it is not located in New York but, rather, in Chicago. Perhaps partially because of that, it is associated with the common touch. Burnett often used plain ordinary people in his advertisements. The Schlitz campaign featured a neighborhood bartender. A Maytag advertisement showed a grandmother with 13 grandchildren and a vintage Maytag. In that respect he contrasts rather vividly with David Ogilvy. Burnett put it this way:

> As I have observed it, great advertising writing either in print or television, is always deceptively and disarmingly simple. It has the common touch without being or sounding patronizing. If you are writing about baloney, don't try to make it sound like Cornish hen, because that is the worst kind of baloney there is. Just make it darned good baloney.
>
> Not only is great copy "deceptively simple"—but so are great ideas. And if it takes a rationale to explain an ad or a commercial—then it's too complicated for that "dumb public" to understand.
>
> I'm afraid too many advertising people blame the public's inability to sort out commercial messages or advertisements in magazines on stupidity. What a lousy stupid attitude to have! I believe the public is unable to sort out messages, not just because of the sheer flood of messages assaulting it every day, but because of *sheer boredom!* If the public is bored today—then let's blame it on the fact that it is being handed boring messages created by bored advertising people. In a world where nobody seems to know what's going to happen next, the only thing to do to keep from going completely nuts from frustration is plain old-fashioned work! Having worked many, many years for peanuts and in obscurity, I think I know how a lot of writers feel today and I sympathize with them, but I also wonder if a lot of writers aren't downright spoiled.[39]

Burnett further described his orientation by indicating that the best copywriters have "a flair for expression, putting known and believable things into new relationships. . . . We [the Chicago school of advertising] try to be more straightforward without being flatfooted. We try to be warm without being mawkish."[40] The key words are warm and believable. The approach aims for believability with warmth.

In the spirit of providing a common touch, Burnett looks for the "inherent drama" of a product—the characteristic that made the manufacturer make it, that makes the people buy it. The objective is to capture the inherent drama and make it "arresting itself rather than relying upon tricks."[41] Burnett is impatient with a dull factual recitation or a cleverness with words or a "highfaluting rhapsody of plain bombast."[42] The preferable approach is to dig out the inherent drama and present it in a warm, realistic manner. The inherent drama is "often hard to find, but it is always there, and once found it is the most interesting and believable of all advertising appeals."[43]

The Green Giant Company has been with Burnett since the agency was established in 1935. One early advertisement illustrates the use of the inherent drama concept. Burnett wanted to communicate the fact that Green Giant peas were of good quality and fresh. He used a picture of a night harvest with the caption "Harvested in the Moonlight" and included an insert of the giant holding a pod of peas. As Burnett states, "It would have been easy to say, 'Packed Fresh' in the headline, but 'Harvested in the Moonlight' had both news value and romance, and connoted a special kind of care which was unusual to find in a can of peas."[44] A series of four advertisements that featured paintings by Norman Rockwell also were used in early campaigns. One showed a farm kitchen with a boy enjoying a platter of corn on the cob. Jerry Della Femina comments on the Green Giant campaign:

Burnett even tells people what a corny agency he has, but he's not corny. He is a very brilliant man. . . . That Jolly Green Giant is fantastic. He sells beans, corn, peas, everything. When you watch the Jolly Green Giant, you know it's fantasy and yet you buy the product. Do you know what Libby does? I don't. Most food advertising is like gone by the boards, you don't even see it. But the Jolly Green Giant, it's been automatic success when he's on the screen.[45]

The Pillsbury account arrived in 1945. One series of advertisements was termed the Pillsbury "big cake campaign." A large picture of a cake with several slices removed dominated the advertisements, another example of " inherent drama" letting an appetizing picture do the selling. The Marlboro campaign started in the mid-1950s. The Marlboro cowboy, the tattoo, the Marlboro Country approach is still going strong and is probably considered one of the classic campaigns. The country flavor and the use of the tattoo provided the common touch. Another early product that used the common touch was Kellogg's cereal. For example, in the campaign for Kellogg's corn flakes, the headline "the best to you each morning" was used in conjunction with an appealing human interest photo (see Figure 13-8).

In what follows, several creative directors who have achieved prominence in recent years are profiled, and some of their well-known agency styles are discussed. It is interesting and useful to compare and contrast them with David Ogilvy, William Bernbach, Rosser Reeves, and Leo Burnett. We will also provide some insights into their life-styles, their particular approaches to creating advertising, and the agencies with which they are associated.

PHILIP DUSENBERRY: ENTERTAINMENT AND EMOTION

Producing television commercials can be dangerous! During the shooting of a commercial for Pepsi-Cola in 1984, the central figure, the well-known rock star Michael Jackson, was injured when his hair caught on fire. Although obviously unplanned, it became a national news event. Philip Dusenberry, vice chairman and executive creative director of Batten, Barton, Durstine & Osborn, was the person responsible for development of this famous campaign. Another Dusenberry-BBDO effort was an 18-minute film of President Reagan shown at the Republican Convention in the summer of 1984 before the president's acceptance speech. The film showed people, all presumably Reagan supporters, getting married, eating ice cream cones, delivering newspapers, and generally feeling "proud to be an American." According to Dusenberry, too much mention of issues is simply "boring." The film was intended to appeal to the viewer's sense of pride and the needs for developing feelings of patriotism and loyalty. This film also became national news when the networks refused to air it. The criticism was that it did not address the issues and lacked balance.

Dusenberry advocates flexibility and "shunning of the familiar" as basic tenets for good creative strategy. "Don't get too happy too soon with the first idea that comes into your head." His style is one that tries to make heavy use of emotion and warmth, and to create commercials that are very entertaining, through the use of star endorsers and star commercial directors (such as Bob Giraldi, who directed the Pepsi commercials with

Figure 13-8. A Kellogg's Corn Flakes advertisement
Courtesy of the Kellogg Company.

Michael Jackson). He uses the latest cinematic techniques, including rapid cutting and eye-catching visual images, and tries out special effects worthy of Steven Spielberg or George Lucas. One Pepsi commercial, called "Archeology," won the top advertising prize at the International Film Festival at Cannes, the industry's most coveted award, and several others. It shows a twenty-third-century teacher leading a class through the ruins of a twentieth-century home. The class comes across a Coke bottle, and asks what it is. The puzzled teacher doesn't know, as the screen reveals the phrase "Pepsi, the choice of a new generation."[46] Most of his work focuses more on the people who use a product and on the benefits or enjoyments it brings than on the product itself. A characteristic of this style is to "elevate people above the product," and to use people in lively and engaging situations. In the Pepsi campaign, the emphasis is on "Pepsi people," for example. This approach is especially clear in his ads for General Electric, in which warm, homey images are used to say that "GE brings good things to life." This style does have its critics— some in the industry say his work relies too heavily on stars and does little to promote the attributes of the product it is supposed to sell.

Dusenberry has been described as a "rabid baseball fan" and one-time aspiring big league catcher. Among his many other accomplishments is a screenplay he wrote called *The Natural*. It met nothing but rejections before catching the eye of the actor-director Robert Redford. Redford directed and played a starring role in the film, which became a box office hit and a popular videocassette. As we will see, many of the creative giants in advertising have made similar impressive creative contributions outside the field of advertising. The son of a Brooklyn cab driver, Dusenberry left college early, and became a professional singer and then a disk jockey before becoming an advertising copywriter.

For many years, BBDO was considered a rather conservative agency and the Pepsi campaign emphasizing "Choice of a New Generation" was a significant break with traditional styles. As stated by one reviewer, "the long Coke versus Pepsi battle over which one could sing a better jingle or portray people having more fun at picnics finally came to an end, or at least entered a lull."[47] The attempt was to reach out to the younger generation in their own language, not just through a single campaign format. In addition to Michael Jackson, takeoffs on popular science fiction movies at the time, such as *E.T.* and *Close Encounters of the Third Kind,* were used. Much of this turnaround in style is attributed to Allen Rosenshine, BBDO's chairman, chief executive officer, and former creative director. According to Rosenshine,

> When parity products develop creative strategies, they all come out the same. Using line extensions and market segmentation to differentiate only adds to the problem. All aimed to be authoritative, assertive, competitive, and convincing about why one product was better than the other. For BBDO, it became clear that the way to go was to leave the rational sell behind. We are far more devoted now to the concept that advertising is a consumer experience with the brand. We are more sensitive too and careful that the experience is enjoyable, pleasant, human, warm and emotional, while no less relevant from the sales strategy viewpoint.[48]

LEE CLOW: IRREVERENCE

Clow has been identified as "the force behind some of the most remarkable U.S. ad campaigns of recent years."[49] Among his major accomplishments was a 60-second minimovie for Apple Computer's Macintosh, showing a club-wielding symbol of freedom smashing the 1984 Orwellian nightmare. Although aired only once, it generated enormous publicity. Although its successor, a commercial called "Lemmings," was not as successful, it nevertheless established an irreverent style that has become Apple's trademark in advertising. The creative genius behind these commercials was Lee Clow, executive vice president and creative director of Chiat/Day/Mojo, a Los Angeles–based agency.

Other major campaigns with which he has been associated are for products such as Nike brand sports apparel, PepsiCo's Pizza Hut, and Porsche automobiles. In one famous billboard campaign for Nike, he had unidentified Olympic hopefuls in striking poses, such as clearing hurdles at the track, displayed on massive outdoor billboards and the sides of buildings, with only the smallest mention of the sponsor, Nike. He has been described as having a unique ability to spot an idea and know if it will work. In discussing his creative style, Clow argues for the need to generate confidence and to take the lead in sticking to an idea.

> If you don't act sure of yourself, it's very easy for other people's faith in your product to get shaky. Apple's 1984 commercial, for example, was an idea that was very easy to get nervous about. If it seems that you have some misgivings or second thoughts about something, it's easy for people who are less tuned into creative communication to get nervous about it. Most ideas are a bit scary, and if an idea isn't scary, it's not an idea at all.[50]

The adopted son of an aerospace worker in the Los Angeles area, Clow is reported to lead a surprisingly traditional life and to be an avid television watcher. It is interesting that Clow attributes to DDB and Volkswagen advertising much of his inspiration for getting into advertising and has described this campaign as the "single greatest advertising work in the history of the business." Volkswagen advertising was launched during the so-called creative revolution of the 1960s, and Clow acknowledges creative artists such as the Beatles, Andy Warhol, and major events during the period, such as the assassinations of President Kennedy and Martin Luther King, Jr., and going to the moon, as having a major impact on his creative development. The fact that he works in advertising, the antithesis of many of the values espoused during this period, doesn't seem to bother him.

Although Clow reputedly does not actually draw many ads himself, he is a major force in developing the concepts on which many famous Chiat/Day campaigns are based. His style is designed to create impact, and he emphasizes the need for an honest dialogue with the consumer and respect for consumer intelligence.

> If you think you have a better mousetrap or car, or shirt, or whatever, you've got to tell people, and I don't think that has to be done with trickery, or insults, or by talking down to people. I think it can be an honest dialog with the consumer. Good advertising is a dialog

with people. . . . The smartest advertising is the advertising that communicates the best and respects the consumer's intelligence. It's advertising that lets them bring something to the communication process, as opposed to some of the more validly criticized work in our profession in which they try to grind the benefits of a soap or cake mix into a poor housewife's head by repeating it 37 times in 30 seconds.[51]

HAL RINEY: SMALL-TOWN WARMTH

You may not have heard of Hal Riney, but you have probably seen and chuckled at Frank Bartles and his none-too-talkative friend Ed Jaymes advertising their Bartles and Jaymes Premium Wine Cooler (actually made by the Gallo Winery) and "thanking you for your support." One of the most successful ad campaigns of the 1980s, the characters and the line were the brainchild of ad man Hal Riney, who now runs the San Francisco ad agency that bears his name. The process of creating these two folksy characters was actually quite serendipitous: they first decided to give the new wine cooler initials that could be used to order it in a bar (just like "J&B" Scotch), settled on B&J, then expanded these initials to the names of Bartles and Jaymes by looking at a phone book, and then began to dream up characters to go with these names. Initially, the characters selected were two down-on-their-heels Madeira (wine) merchants in London who had to get rid of their wine inventory, but these became two cattle farmers instead. Riney then procured the services of an old fraternity brother and fishing buddy to play the silent heavy, Ed, and an actual Oregon cattle farmer to be Frank.[52] The series (that ran to over 100 different spots) began with Frank explaining that, in order to start their wine cooler business, Ed had "taken out a second mortgage on his house and written to Harvard for his MBA." Since Ed had a balloon payment coming up on the mortgage, Frank asked people to start buying their wine cooler—and began thanking people for their support, which became the standard closing line. The campaign was so successful that it enabled the brand to jump from 40th to 1st place in wine cooler sales a few months after being launched in 1985, and even attracted a few checks from people who wanted to help Ed out with his balloon payment.

In addition to the Bartles and Jaymes wine cooler campaign, Riney's agency is also responsible for the Gallo Wines campaign in which the ads evoke familial love, cutting from moment to emotional moment, with cathedral-like music from Vangelis, with an "All the best" from Gallo. Another campaign is for Perrier, in which quick-cut scenes of children and nature reassure you that whatever had to happen to make Perrier just right did indeed happen. And, like Phil Dusenberry, Riney was part of Ronald Reagan's re-election ad campaign in 1984, showing warm scenes of small-town American life and coming up with the establishing line, "It's morning again in America." What all these campaigns share is a sentimental, emotional tone that pulls at the heartstrings, using a series of evocations, with mellow sequencing, soft voices, small-town realism, soft wit, and very often Hal Riney's own gravelly narration. Riney's agency also often eschews market research, often preferring to rely on its own intuition about what feels right in a particular situation.

Riney is known as a perfectionist, who makes complex ads that look like films—using quick cuts, overlapping dialogue, and other elements that attempt to create emotional nuance. Realistic casting and stage props are another element of his style—for a Henry Weinhard beer commercial, he remodeled an old log cabin, an hour-and-a-half from the nearest highway, into an 1882 saloon, instead of constructing it on a sound stage. (A Henry Weinhard beer storyboard is reproduced in Figure 13-9.) For a beer spot featuring Eskimo traders, he and director Joe Pytka traveled to the Arctic Circle to find faces that looked just right.[53] Such realism is considered crucial because it makes it easier to appeal to genuine human emotions. Riney made good use of such realism in his recent launch campaign for Saturn cars.

Riney grew up in semirural Oregon, son of a schoolteacher mother and an itinerant salesman father who left home when Riney was 6. He began working in advertising in San Francisco in the mid-1950s, at BBDO, then with a small agency called Botsford Ketchum, and then with Ogilvy & Mather. In 1976, he started his own agency, with the blessings of Ogilvy. His style, along with that of Chiat/Day in Los Angeles (discussed earlier) and Weiden and Kennedy in Portland, Oregon (which created the very successful "Bo knows" commercials featuring Bo Jackson, for Nike), has led to the emergence of a distinctly high-profile "West Coast" school of advertising that in recent years has emphasized the need to take creative risks in creating memorable and (often, but not always) sales-increasing advertising.

IS EXECUTION MORE IMPORTANT THAN CONTENT?

There are, of course, many other advertising agencies and many other creative approaches and styles that could be presented and discussed. Those reviewed in this chapter are, how ever, fairly representative of the range of creative output, at least in the leading agencies. Of course, there are dozens of other creative people associated with highly successful agencies and creative output that could have been reviewed as well.

One way to think of the range of creative styles is to think of a continuum from the "what you say is crucial" camp (such as Reeves's USP style) to the "how you say it is crucial" view (represented by the more freewheeling creative styles of Clow and Riney). To the extent this book is going to advocate a position on who is right, we would suggest that both are necessary—a message must be both on strategy in terms of "what" it is communicating *and* highly creative in "how" it communicates that message. Even though this chapter has focused on the importance of the creative process, we must point out that according to research by Stewart and Furse the single most important factor in an ad's impact on persuasion, recall, and message comprehension is the presence of a strong brand differentiating message—which is a content, not an executional variable.[54]

Thus the best advertising combines both meaningful content and brilliant creative execution. While the strategy part of the mixture is amenable to rigorous analysis (such as that developed in this book), the creative part is as much art and genius as it is science, which is what makes the advertising business rely so much on the talents of people like the ones just profiled.

"CHUCK WAGON"

:60 Commercial

COOK: Come and get it!
VO: Back when the West was young...

COWBOY: Where'd you have to send to to
get that saddle?
VO: Getting just about anything took a lot of
time and trouble.
2nd COWBOY: Mexico.

VO: Even a good beer was a rarity.
COOK: Anybody want a Henry's?

COWBOY: Henry's?
VO: In fact, to get the West's finest beer...
2nd COWBOY: Henry Weinhard's?

VO: Beer drinkers would sometimes
wait for months...
COOK: Just come into town.

VO: Because it would often have to come from
hundreds of miles away.
COWBOY: Where'd they have to send to
to get that beer?
2nd COWBOY: Oregon.

VO: But while it may seem unusual to have taken
so much time and trouble just for a better beer...
COOK: Now for supper...
VO: It really wasn't.
COOK: There's a few things that's not on the
regular menu...

VO: Even then, Westerners always tried to do
everything in a very special way.

COOK: In addition to the beef, we have a nice
loin of buffalo in a light cream sauce.

COOK: Our fresh fish tonight is
brook trout almondine.

COWBOY: Where'd they have to send to
to get that cook?
2nd COWBOY: Los Angeles.

COOK: There's roast antelope with a peach
brandy glaze, braised jack rabbit on fruit,
rattlesnake fritters with herbed tomatoes...

Figure 13-9. One of Hal Riney's campaigns: Henry Weinhard beer
Courtesy of Blitz Weinhard Brewing Company.

SUMMARY

The creative process concerns the translation of a marketing proposition into the verbal and visual devices that will communicate the essence of that proposition in ways that are attention getting and persuasive. Working in teams, copywriters and art directors try to come up with creative ideas that set their advertising apart from the clutter. Such idea generation is an extremely challenging task, and various techniques have been developed to facilitate the idea generation process. The best ideas are those that are "on strategy" as well as executionally very distinctive.

In evaluating proposed advertising, it is important to remember that the riskiest advertising is often that which takes no risks at all—playing it safe can mean advertising that is ineffective. Therefore, the "rules" of advertising copy should not be so venerated that they are never broken: the best ads are sometimes those that break all the rules. However, this does not mean that we should not learn from the experience of the great practitioners of the art, or from what copy-testing research can teach us. Such experience and research has taught us much about what makes for good ads in print, radio, television, outdoor, retail, and business-to-business, and some of this learning was reviewed in this chapter.

As in art, two or more creative people can look at the same problem and develop advertising that is quite different. These differences are differences in the creative style of the individual or agency. Even though different, the advertising and the campaigns that evolve can be "successful." For example, the styles of William Bernbach and Rosser Reeves are very different in terms of philosophy and execution, but each has been associated with highly successful advertising. Seven profiles of leading creative people in advertising and the agencies with which they are associated were presented and discussed. The first four, David Ogilvy, William Bernbach, Rosser Reeves, and Leo Burnett, are notable for setting the standards of creative style in the early 1950s and 1960s. The next three, Philip Dusenberry, Lee Clow, and Hal Riney, represent current leaders in an analogous set of currently leading advertising agencies.

Although descriptions of creative styles are difficult and tend to become exaggerated and stereotypical, it is nevertheless useful to compare and contrast them. In the more recent profiles, some additional information is provided on the background and other activities of the person, to provide insights into who creative people are and where they come from.

DISCUSSION QUESTIONS AND EXERCISES

1. Select two print ads aimed at consumers that have recently run (either in magazine ads or in newspapers), one of which you consider to be a "good" ad and one a "bad" ad. Then write a one-page assessment on each, justifying your assessment.
2. Repeat the exercise in question 1 for a pair of radio ads, a pair of television ads, a pair of retail ads, and a pair of business-to-business ads.

3. Take a marketing positioning statement, based on a situation analysis for a brand and product category that you may have worked on for some marketing project, and attempt to come up with five creative ideas that could be used in creating advertising for the selected brand.

4. Now select one of these creative ideas for further development, and create rough or mock ads (a print ad, a television storyboard, and a radio script) that build off that creative idea.

5. Ogilvy, Bernbach, Reeves, and Burnett are all creative giants in advertising who have retired or passed on. Compare and contrast their styles with those of Dusenberry, Clow, and Riney, who are current leaders in the field. Who is more like whom? Why?

6. The creative styles of Bernbach and Reeves are probably two ends of a continuum, yet both are associated with highly successful agencies and campaigns. One could conclude that creative style makes no difference. Do you agree or disagree? Why or why not?

7. Suppose that you were chairperson of a billion-dollar agency and were having to choose among three candidates for the position of creative director. Discuss the qualities you would look for in filling the position. What are the characteristics of a top-quality creative person?

NOTES

1. Alex F. Osborn, *Applied Imagination*, 3rd rev. ed. (New York: Scribners, 1963), p. 11.

2. Leo Burnett, "Keep Listening to That Wee, Small Voice," in *Communications of an Advertising Man*, copyright 1961 by Leo Burnett Company, Inc., from a speech given before the Chicago Copywriters Club, October 4, 1960, p. 160.

3. Denis Higgens, ed., *The Art of Writing Advertising* (Chicago: Crain Books, 1965), p. 43.

4. Alex F. Osborn, *Your Creative Power* (New York: Dell, 1948), p. 135.

5. Edward M. Tauber, "HIT: Heuristic Ideation Technique—A Systematic Procedure for New Product Search," *Journal of Marketing*, 36, January 1972, pp. 58–61.

6. Osborn, *Your Creative Power*, p. 294.

7. Discussed in Philip Kotler, *Marketing Management: Analysis, Planning, and Control* (Englewood Cliffs, NJ: Prentice Hall, 1967), p. 256.

8. John M. Keil, *The Creative Mystique: How to Manage It, Nurture It, and Make It Pay* (New York: John Wiley, 1985). See also, "Popular Myths About Creativity Debunked," *Advertising Age*, May 6, 1985, p. 48.

9. John Caples, *How to Make Your Advertising Make Money* (Englewood Cliffs, NJ: Prentice Hall, 1983).

10. John Caples, "A Dozen Ways to Develop Advertising Ideas," *Advertising Age*, November 14, 1983, pp. M4ff.

11. Richard F. Beltramini and Vincent J. Blasko, "An Analysis of Award-Winning Advertising Headlines," *Journal of Advertising Research*, April/May 1986, pp. 48–52.

12. Lester Guest, "Status Enhancement as a Function of Color in Advertising," *Journal of Advertising Research*, 6, June 1966, pp. 40–44.

13. Ibid., p. 44.

14. Stephen Baker, *Advertising Layout and Art Direction* (New York: McGraw-Hill, 1959), p. 3.

15. For an interesting book on the subject of making television commercials, see Michael J. Arlen, *Thirty Seconds* (New York: Farrar, Straus & Giroux, 1980).

16. Albert C. Book and Norman D. Cary, *The Television Commercial: Creativity and Craftsmanship* (New York: Decker Communication, 1970).

17. David Ogilvy, *Confessions of an Advertising Man* (New York: Atheneum, 1964), pp. 100–102.

18. Ibid., p. 102.

19. Ibid., p. 51.

20. Ibid., pp. 116–117.

21. Ibid., pp. 93–103.

22. Martin Mayer, *Madison Avenue, U.S.A.* (New York: Pocket Books, 1958), p. 64.

23. Jerry Della Femina, with Charles Spokin, ed., *From Those Wonderful Folks Who Gave You Pearl Harbor* (New York: Simon & Schuster, 1970), p. 29.

24. Higgens, *The Art of Writing Advertising*, pp. 117–118.

25. Mayer, *Madison Avenue, U.S.A.*, p. 66.

26. Frank Rowsome, Jr., *Think Small* (New York: Ballantine Books, 1970), p. 81.

27. Ibid., p. 12.

28. Mayer, *Madison Avenue, U.S.A.*, p. 65.

29. For an interpretation of this campaign from which these comments were drawn, see Femina, *From Those Wonderful Folks*, pp. 38–39.

30. Ibid., p. 26.

31. Rowsome, *Think Small*, p. 116.

32. Ibid., p. 117.

33. Higgens, *The Art of Writing Advertising*, p. 120.

34. Ibid., pp. 117–118.

35. Mayer, *Madison Avenue, U.S.A.*, pp. 59–61.

36. Ibid., p. 52.

37. Higgens, *The Art of Writing Advertising*, p. 124.

38. Described in Mayer, *Madison Avenue, U.S.A.*, p. 300.

39. Burnett, "Keep Listening to That Wee, Small Voice."

40. Higgens, *The Art of Writing Advertising*, p. 17.

41. Ibid., p. 44.

42. Burnett, "Keep Listening," p. 154.

43. Mayer, *Madison Avenue, U.S.A.*, p. 70.

44. Higgens, *The Art of Writing Advertising*, p. 45.

45. Femina, *From Those Wonderful Folks*, p. 141.

46. *The New York Times*, November 16, 1990, p. F29.

47. Stewart Alter, "Ad Age Honors BBDO as Agency of Year," *Advertising Age*, March 28, 1985, pp. 3ff.

48. Ibid., p. 4.

49. Jennifer Pendleton, "Bringing New Clow-T to Ads, Chiat's Unlikely Creative," *Advertising Age*, February 7, 1985, pp. 1 ff.

50. Ibid., p. 5.

51. Ibid.

52. *Insight* magazine, September 14, 1987, pp. 38–40.

53. *The New York Times Magazine*, December 14, 1986, pp. 52–74.

54. David W. Stewart and David F. Furse, *Effective Television Advertising: A Study of 1000 Commercials* (Lexington, MA: Lexington Books, 1986).

14

ADVERTISING COPY TESTING

Think of an ad not as what you put into it, but as what the consumer takes out of it.

Rosser Reeves, in *Reality in Advertising*
© 1961 by Alfred A. Knopf, Inc.

Will a proposed copy theme be effective at achieving advertising objectives? Does the set of advertisements that makes up an advertising campaign create the desired interest level and image? Will an individual advertisement attract the attention of the audience? Such questions are addressed in copy testing.

Copy testing is an important part of advertising management and also an interesting subject from the professional and scientific points of view. Professionally, there are now hundreds of companies that offer services having to do with assessing the effectiveness of print advertisements or broadcast commercials. A significant industry has evolved in the United States and increasingly in other countries made up of companies in the business of supplying this kind of service.[1] From the scientific viewpoint, advertising research reflects the applications of theories and methodologies that derive from psychology, sociology, and economics and, more specifically, from various branches of each of these disciplines.

The chapter begins with a section on copy-testing strategy. Four widely used criteria in copy testing and examples of related services are then presented and discussed. This is followed by a review of other tests. A final section is devoted to evaluating copy tests.

COPY-TESTING STRATEGY

There are three factors that have to be addressed in copy testing: (1) whether or not to test, (2) what and when to test, and (3) what criteria or test to use. Every advertising manager must consider these factors in the context of the overall advertising plan. Copy testing implies that funds will be allocated to *research* on consumer reactions to the advertising before the final campaign is launched.

The first decision is really whether or not to spend more money on research. It is interesting that in terms of total advertising volume, the usual decision is "no." Most local advertising is not tested, and there are many cases in national advertising where copy is used without formal copy testing of any kind. Not only are there money costs involved in testing, but there are time costs as well. Copy testing can mean weeks or months of delay in launching a campaign. On the other hand, if you are managing a new product entry involving a $20 million advertising budget, investing in copy testing makes sense. Relying solely on the judgments of a creative team, your own experience, or somebody's intuition is very risky when so much is at stake. What is needed is a test of how potential *consumers* will react, that is, copy testing.

Having said that, it should be pointed out that several "hot" creative agencies strongly believe that their creative product tends to be more fresh and original because they do not test their ads before running them. Many creative people in agencies (but certainly not all) hold a rather negative view of copy testing, viewing it as a report card, a policeman, something that only tells them what is working or not, but not why. Of course, total creative license (with no copy testing) has also been known to have led to ad campaigns that have "bombed" in the marketplace, so most creatives appreciate the "reality check" it provides. It is really important to select a copy-testing system that the creatives respect and believe in, and find useful, and it is important that ads not be created simply to score well on the copy-testing system being used, in a political, "gaming" fashion.

What and when to test? Copy testing can be done at (1) the beginning of the creative process, (2) the end of the creative process (at the layout stage), (3) the end of the production stage, and/or (4) after the campaign has been launched. In general, tests at the first three stages are called *pretests* and those at the final stage are called *posttests*.[2] Various types of tests can be used at any of the four stages and will differ by whether broadcast or print advertising is involved. Testing at the beginning of the creative process often involves qualitative research, such as focus group interviews to get reactions to copy ideas. At stage 2, rough mock-ups of the finished copy or, in television, partially complete commercials are tested because of the lower expenses involved (a fully produced commercial typically costs in excess of $150,000). While these rough ads (called "animatics" or "photomatics") are reasonably good predictors of final effectiveness, they must be used with caution in situations where the success of the ad will eventually depend substantially on the actual casting of characters, the actual/final editing of scenes, and so on. Stage 3 is often bypassed, particularly in cases where the advertising has been shown or aired several times and the new copy is not radically different. A basic issue is whether to develop and test just one version of the advertising, or whether two or more versions should be developed and tested. It is logical, but also expensive, to have alternatives to test. In general, it is more expensive to test at the third and fourth stages. When there is much at stake, when millions of dollars of media time and expensive creative and production effort are involved, a substantial investment in copy testing at all stages is easily justified.

What criteria or copy test should be used? Copy-testing services can be distinguished by the nature of the response variable used in the test. Although many other factors enter into the choice of a copy test, the criterion (dependent) variable is probably the most important thing on which to focus. What does a particular test measure? How accurate or valid are these measures? These are some of the considerations of copy-test strategy that must be addressed. The next section reviews four criteria widely used in copy testing and gives examples of copy-testing services based on them.

FOUR CRITERIA USED IN COPY TESTING

Why is one advertisement effective and another a dud? Much depends on the criteria used to measure effectiveness. The criteria will, of course, depend on the brand involved and its advertising objectives. There are four basic criteria or categories of response that are widely used in advertising research. The first is advertisement recognition. The second, used heavily in television, is recall of the commercial and its contents. The third is persuasion. How persuasive is a commercial, for example? Finally, the criterion of purchase behavior is used. In many cases, this is most important. Does the advertisement or the advertising campaign have an effect on purchase behavior?

Each criterion and the measures and service associated with them will be illustrated and discussed in what follows. Concerning the copy strategy question of which is used where, some will be seen to be more suitable for posttesting of running advertisements, and others for pretesting. Most can be adapted to either pre- or posttesting, however.

Recognition

Recognition refers to whether a respondent can recognize an advertisement as one he or she has seen before. An example of recognition testing is the Bruzzone Research Company (BRC) tests of television commercials. These tests are done by mail survey in which questionnaires, such as the one shown in Figure 14-1, are mailed to 1,000 households. The sample is drawn from a specially prepared mailing list of households that have either a registered automobile or a listed telephone number. Interest in the task and a dollar bill enclosed with the questionnaire usually generates a return sample of about 500. The recognition question is shown at the top. At the bottom is the brand association question, a critical dimension of most campaigns. On average, 60 percent will recognize a commercial, and 73 percent of these can correctly select the right brand from a list of three alternatives.[3] Test-retest correlations of 0.98 have been reported.

Communicus is another company that uses recognition measures for either television or radio commercial tests. In television, respondents are shown brief (ten-second) edited portions of the commercial, excluding advertiser identification. They are asked to indicate if they have seen or heard it before, to identify the advertiser, and to play back other identifying copy points. Some research has shown that there is a dropoff in the percentage of people who can identify a sponsor, falling from an average of 59 percent in 1974 to about 50 percent in 1980, perhaps because of increased clutter.[4]

The most widely known service in measuring print advertising recognition is Starch INRA Hooper. This service began in 1923. In a typical Starch test, respondents are taken through a magazine and, for each advertisement, asked if they saw it in the issue. Three

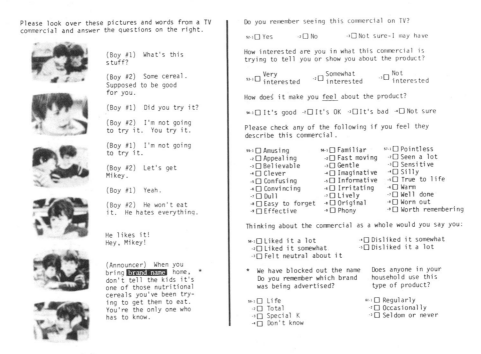

Please look over these pictures and words from a TV commercial and answer the questions on the right.

(Boy #1) What's this stuff?

(Boy #2) Some cereal. Supposed to be good for you.

(Boy #1) Did you try it?

(Boy #2) I'm not going to try it. You try it.

(Boy #1) I'm not going to try it.

(Boy #2) Let's get Mikey.

(Boy #1) Yeah.

(Boy #2) He won't eat it. He hates everything.

He likes it!
Hey, Mikey!

(Announcer) When you bring brand name home, * don't tell the kids it's one of those nutritional cereals you've been trying to get them to eat. You're the only one who has to know.

Do you remember seeing this commercial on TV?

52-1 ☐ Yes   -2 ☐ No   -3 ☐ Not sure-I may have

How interested are you in what this commercial is trying to tell you or show you about the product?

53-1 ☐ Very interested   -2 ☐ Somewhat interested   -3 ☐ Not interested

How does it make you feel about the product?

54-1 ☐ It's good -2 ☐ It's OK -3 ☐ It's bad -4 ☐ Not sure

Please check any of the following if you feel they describe this commercial.

55-1 ☐ Amusing	56-1 ☐ Familiar	57-1 ☐ Pointless
-2 ☐ Appealing	-2 ☐ Fast moving	-2 ☐ Seen a lot
-3 ☐ Believable	-3 ☐ Gentle	-3 ☐ Sensitive
-4 ☐ Clever	-4 ☐ Imaginative	-4 ☐ Silly
-5 ☐ Confusing	-5 ☐ Informative	-5 ☐ True to life
-6 ☐ Convincing	-6 ☐ Irritating	-6 ☐ Warm
-7 ☐ Dull	-7 ☐ Lively	-7 ☐ Well done
-8 ☐ Easy to forget	-8 ☐ Original	-8 ☐ Worn out
-9 ☐ Effective	-9 ☐ Phony	-9 ☐ Worth remembering

Thinking about the commercial as a whole would you say you:

58-1 ☐ Liked it a lot   -4 ☐ Disliked it somewhat
-2 ☐ Liked it somewhat   -5 ☐ Disliked it a lot
-3 ☐ Felt neutral about it

* We have blocked out the name Do you remember which brand was being advertised?

Does anyone in your household use this type of product?

59-1 ☐ Life   60-1 ☐ Regularly
-2 ☐ Total   -2 ☐ Occasionally
-3 ☐ Special K   -3 ☐ Seldom or never
-4 ☐ Don't know

Figure 14-1.   Advertising campaign effectiveness survey
Courtesy of Bruzzone Research Company.

measures are generated for each advertisement in the magazine called *noted, seen associated,* and *read most.* Each is a percentage derived as follows:

- *Noted*: the percentage of readers of the issue who remember having seen the advertisement
- *Seen associated*: the percentage who saw any part of the advertisement that clearly indicates the brand, service, or advertisement
- *Read most*: the percentage who read half or more of the copy

Studies using Starch data show that recognition depends on the product class, on the involvement of the segment in the product class, and on variables such as size, color, position, copy approach, and the nature of the magazine or media. Various reviews of these Starch (and similar) data are available.[5] Although Starch scores are highly reliable in a test-retest sense, there is concern about validity. The respondent can claim readership where none exists to please or impress the interviewer or because of confusion with prior advertising for the brand. Though this bias can be difficult to predict for a particular advertisement, researchers such as Singh and colleagues have suggested ways to adjust claimed recognition scores to obtain better estimates of actual recognition.[6]

Recognition is a necessary condition for effective advertising. If the advertisement cannot pass this minimal test, it probably will not be effective. In one study of inquiries received by an advertiser of electronic instrumentation, those with low Starch scores were also low in inquiries received. Tatham-Laird and Kudner, a Chicago agency, finds out which specific portions of a TV ad are effective in gaining recall by asking consumers if they recognize photographs of different frames (opening shot, closing shot, etc.) 15–20 minutes after they see the ad. Of course, high recognition does not guarantee effectiveness, but this agency has found a strong relationship between final overall recall and the nature of the opening and closing shots and the amount of product linkage built into the other shots of the ad.[7] There is also some evidence that "emotional" television ads, those that do not feature much verbalizable copy, are better measured for their attention-getting ability on tests of recognition rather than are tests of verbal recall (this issue is discussed further later in the chapter).

It should also be noted that high recognition scores are easier to achieve than are high recall scores, since recognition requires only a judgment about the stimulus and does not require as much retrieval of information from memory as is required by, say, an unaided recall task.[8] Thus recognition can be created by even partly attentive television viewing that does not lead to conscious recall. This may make visually oriented recognition scores a more suitable measure of memory than recall for short (15-second) television ads.[9] Finally, some researchers believe that recognition scores decline more slowly over time than recall scores do, though Singh, Rothschild, and Churchill have shown that a "forced-choice" recognition measure that is "tougher" than a usual yes/no measure does in fact decay over time and is a sensitive measure of the memory effect of a commercial.[10]

Recall

Recall refers to measures of the proportion of a sample audience that can recall an advertisement. There are two kinds of recall, *aided recall* and *unaided recall*. In aided recall, the respondent is prompted by showing a picture of the advertisement with the sponsor or brand name blanked out. In unaided recall, only the product or service name may be given. The best known recall method in television, interviewing viewers within 24 to 30 hours after the commercial is aired, is called the day-after-recall method.

Day-After-Recall.   The day-after-recall (DAR) measure of a television commercial, first used in the early 1940s by George Gallup, then with Young & Rubicam, is closely associated with Burke Marketing Research.[11] "How did the ad Burke out?" is a common question. The procedure is to telephone 150 to 300 program viewers 24 hours after a television commercial appears. (Some other companies use a different time period, such as 72 hours.) They are asked if they can recall any commercials the previous day in a product category (such as soap). If they cannot identify the brand correctly, they are then given the product category and brand and asked if they recalled the commercial. They are then asked for anything they can recall about the commercial, what was said, what was shown, and what the main idea was. DAR is the percentage of those in the commercial audience (who were watching the show before and after the commercial was shown) who recalled something specific about the commercial, such as the sales message, the story line, the plot, or some visual or audio element. This is called the "percent proven recall." A less tightly defined measure—of people who have seen something of the ad but maybe don't play back a very specific element—is called "percent related recall." These recall percentages for the ad being tested are always compared against the "norm"—the historical average for ads of similar length, from similar product categories, from similar (old/new) brands. The Burke DAR test also provides specific verbatims (transcripts) of what people remember of the ad and analyzes them for the nature of the main message that got communicated.

The DAR is an "on-air" test in that the commercial exposure occurs in a natural, realistic in-home setting. (Sometimes, to save money, the ad is aired on a local cable channel, and viewers are preinvited to watch the program on that channel.) It is well established and has developed extensive norms over the years. The average DAR is 24. One-fourth of all commercials score under 15 and one-fourth score over 31. It also provides diagnostic information about which elements of the commercial are having an impact and which are not. Gallup & Robinson and Mapes & Ross provide a similar measure for print media. They place a magazine with 150 regular readers of that magazine and ask that it be read in a normal manner. The next day readers are asked to describe ads for any brands of interest. Similar tests have also been developed for radio: consumers in a shopping mall fill out a questionnaire in a room while listening to the radio in the background (which plays the radio ad being tested). Twenty-four hours later they are called back on the telephone and asked questions about recall as well as diagnostic questions on what they like and why.

Recall measures have generated controversy over the years and, as a result, are not as influential as they once were. One concern is that they are an inappropriate measure of emotional commercials. Foote, Cone & Belding measured both masked recognition (where the brand name is blocked out) and DAR for three "feeling" commercials and three "thinking" commercials.[12] The DAR was much lower for the feeling commercials (19 versus 31) whereas the recognition scores were only marginally lower (32 versus 37). The conclusion was that recognition is a better measure of the ability of a feeling commercial's memorability than DAR, which requires the verbalization of the content.

A more basic concern with DAR is that it simply is not a valid measure of anything useful.[13] First, its reliability is suspect. Extremely low test-retest correlations (below 0.30) have been found when commercials from the same product class have been studied. Second, DAR scores are unduly affected by the liking and nature of the program. For example, DAR scores of commercials in new programs average 25 percent or more below commercials in other shows. Third, the scores vary markedly with the nature of the consumer being tested: if the consumer is a recent purchaser of the product category, scores are higher than if the purchaser is not really in the target market. Fourth, and most compelling, of eight relevant studies, seven found practically no association between recall and measures of persuasion. Neither is there evidence of a positive association between recall and sales. In contrast, there is substantial evidence linking persuasion measures with sales. Thus, copy-test interest has turned toward persuasion.

Persuasion

Forced-Exposure Brand-Preference Change.   Theater testing, pioneered by Horace Schwerin and Paul Lazarsfeld in the 1950s, is now done by McCollum/Spielman, ASI, and ARS.[14]

The McCollum/Spielman test uses a 450-person sample spread over four graphically dispersed locations.[15] The respondents are recruited by telephone to come to a central location to preview television programing. Seated in groups of 25 in front of television monitors, they respond to a set of demographic and brand/product usage questions that appear on the screen. The respondents view a half-hour variety program featuring four professional performers. In the midpoint, seven commercials, including four test commercials, are shown.

Performer A	Performer B	T 1	C	T 2	C	T 3	C	T 4	Performer C	Performer D

C = Constant Commercials   T = Test Commercial

After audience reactions to the program are obtained, an unaided brand-name recall question is asked that forms the basis of the clutter/awareness score (the percentage who recalled that the brand was advertised). The clutter/awareness (C/A) score for 30-second commercials averages 56 percent for established brands and 40 percent for new brands.[16] The four test commercials are then exposed a second time surrounded by program material:

Program Intro.	T 1	Program	T 2	Program	T 3	Program	T 4	Program

                                                        T = Test Commercial

An attitude shift (AS) measure is obtained. For frequently purchased package goods such as toiletries, the preexposure designation of brand purchased most often is compared with the postexposure brand selection in a market basket award situation. The respondents are asked to select brands they would like included if they were winners of a $25 basket of products. In product fields with multiple-brand usage, such as soft drinks, a constant sum measure (ten points to be allocated to brands proportional to how they are preferred) is employed before and after exposure. For durables and services, the pre- and postpreference is measured by determining

- The favorite brand
- The next preferred alternative

- Those brands that would not be considered
- Those brands that are neither preferred not rejected

An important element of the test is the use of two exposures. McCollum/Spielman and many advertisers argue that fewer than two exposures represents an artificial and invalid test of most advertising. It is especially important that "emotional" ads be tested in a multiple-exposure copy test, because (compared to "rational" ads) such ads "build" (gain in response) more slowly with repetition, and a single-exposure copy test would not accurately gauge the response they would get when frequently exposed in the marketplace.

Finally, diagnostic questions are asked. Some of the areas that are frequently explored include

- Comprehension of message/slogan
- Communication of secondary copy ideas
- Evaluation of demonstrations, spokesperson, message
- Perception of brand uniqueness/brand differentiation
- Irritating/confusing elements
- Viewer involvement

In a rare copy-test validity check, McCollum/Spielman asked advertisers of 412 campaigns (some campaigns consisted of several commercials) that were tested over a three-year period whether the brand had exceeded marketing objectives during the time that the campaign was being aired.[17] These advertising campaigns were then divided into four groups:

- High AS (attitude shift) and high A/C (awareness/communication)
- High AS and low A/C
- Low AS and high A/C
- Low AS and low A/C

The results are shown in Figure 14-2. Clearly, the AS persuasion measure was a good predictor of campaign success. The A/C recall measure, on the other hand, may have diagnostic value but it had little relationship to campaign success.

The ARS (Research Systems Corporation) approach is similar except that their proven recall measure is the percent of respondents that 72 hours later claim having seen the advertisement and can give some playback of it.[18]

ARS obtained a correlation of 0.78 with their proven recall measure and the unaided brand awareness level achieved by 24 new brands in test markets. Their pre-/postpersuasion measure had a correlation of 0.85 with the trial rate of 26 new brands in test markets. Further, the ARS persuasion score correctly predicted which of two commercials would achieve higher test market sales. ASI, which uses a central Los Angeles location, relies on a pre-/postmeasure of brand selection in a prize-drawing context.

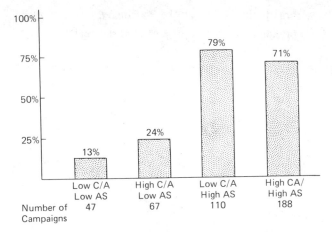

Figure 14-2. The percentage of campaigns exceeding marketing objectives by their performance in the McCollum/Spielman test

Source: Adapted from Peter R. Klein and Melvin Tainter, "Copy Research Validation: The Advertiser's Perspective," *Journal of Advertising Research,* 23, October/November 1983, pp. 9–18. Copyright © 1983 by the Advertising Research Foundation.

Reliability studies across 100 commercials in 15 product categories yielded test-retest reliability correlations of from 0.81 to 0.88. Fifteen hundred commercials per year are tested by ASI, so well developed and current norms are available.[19]

The Buy Test design of the Sherman Group does not involve a central location. The respondents are often recruited and exposed to advertising in shopping malls.[20] A series of unaided questions on advertisement and copy recall identify those in the "recall/understand" group. The advertising "involvement" group are those who had a favorable emotional response, who believed that the brand positioning fit the execution, and who felt that the advertisement was worth looking at (or reading). The "buying urgency" group is identified in part by intentions to buy, improved product opinion, and the motivation to tell someone something about it. A basic measure, the BUY score, is the percentage of those exposed who become part of all three groups. In 75 percent of 50 cases, the BUY score generated different outcomes from other persuasion measurements. In 20 test-retest contexts the average difference of the BUY score was within three percentage points.

On-Air Tests: Brand-Preference Change. In a Mapes & Ross test, commercials are aired in a preselected prime-time position on a UHF station in each of three major markets. Prior to the test, a sample of 200 viewers (150 if it is an all-male target audience) are contacted by phone and invited to participate in a survey and cash award drawing that requires viewing the test program. Respondents provide unaided brand-name awareness and are questioned about their brand preferences for a number of different product categories. The day following the commercial exposure, the respondents again answer brand preference as well as DAR questions. The key Mapes & Ross measure is pre and post brand-preference change.

A Mapes & Ross study involved 142 commercials from 55 product categories and 2,241 respondents who were recontacted two weeks after participating in a test. Among those who bought the product category, purchases of the test brand were 3.3 times higher among those who changed their preference than among those who did not change.[21]

The ASI Apex system differs from the Mapes & Ross approach in several important ways.[22] First, before exposure, brand preference is measured by determining the brand bought most often and the brand most likely to be bought next. Thus, people who both use the brand and plan to buy it next are distinguished from those who answer only one or none of those questions positively. The impact of sample composition with respect to brand usage is thus potentially controlled (although the test samples of size 200 are limiting in this respect). Second, the after-exposure brand-preference measure, based on the brand to be selected if the respondent won a drawing and the brands they would consider if their preferred brand were unavailable, differs from the before measure. The use of different before-after measures reduces the likelihood that the before measure will influence the after measure. Third, the results are compared to a control group of 600 who go through the complete procedure but do not see the test advertisements. Thus, the impact of the procedure itself on brand preference for a given product class can be determined.

Customized Measures of Communication/Attitude.   Standardized copy-test measures are useful because they come with norms sometimes based on thousands of past tests. Thus, the interpretation of the test becomes more meaningful. In fact, some copy-test services provide "adjusted" scores, where the executional impact of the particular ad execution being tested is separated from the impact of the product category itself, the newness of the brand itself, and so on. They point out that most—up to 80 percent—of an ad's score on recall and/or persuasion can be a function not of the ad itself but of these background variables. Thus it is clearly useful to use these standardized, "normed" tests. However, some objectives, particularly communication objectives, are necessarily unique to a brand and may require questions tailored to that brand. For example, Chevron ran a series of 12 print ads in 1980, such as the one shown in Figure 14-3, mostly telling people that Chevron made a lot less profit than people thought.[23] A posttest sample of 380 respondents were interviewed. Belief change was measured on the item "Chevron makes too much profit" for those aware of the advertising. The ads had a small effect, as those agreeing fell from 81 percent to 72 percent.

Interestingly, however, data from the same study showed that people seeing these print ads and the very positive "Energy Frontier" television campaign actually had less attitude change toward Chevron than did those seeing only the television ads. Thus, the print ads (20 percent of the budget) actually reduced the impact on the attitude toward the firm. Creating a positive attitude obviously had a positive impact on all belief dimensions. Calling attention to a source of irritation—oil company profits—tended to counteract the positive attitude change. The Chevron experience graphically illustrates the risk of measuring a part of a campaign in isolation.

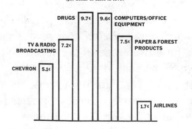

Figure 14-3.   A Chevron "profit" print advertisement
Courtesy of J. Walter Thompson USA.

Purchase Behavior

The fourth criterion is actual brand choice in an in-store, real-world setting. These tests focus on the effects of exposure to shifts in actual purchase behavior. Two well-known tests are those using coupons to stimulate purchasing and those involving split-cable testing.

Coupon-Stimulated Purchasing.   In the Tele-Research approach, 600 shoppers are intercepted in a shopping center location, usually in Los Angeles, and randomly assigned to test or control groups. The test group is exposed to five television or radio commercials or six print ads. Around 250 subjects in the test group complete a questionnaire on the commercial. Both groups are given a customer code number and packets of coupons, including one for the test brand, which can be redeemed in a nearby cooperating drugstore or supermarket. The selling effectiveness score is the ratio of purchases by viewer shoppers divided by the rate of purchases by control shoppers. Purchases are tracked by scanner data. Although the exposure context is highly artificial, the purchase choice is relatively realistic in that real money is spent in a real store.

Coupon Use or Inquiries: Split-Run Tests.   A somewhat different test is often used in the industrial marketing context, where ads are designed to generate inquiries (often via coupons) that, it is hoped, will eventually be converted into sales via sales calls. Here, it is often possible to conduct a "split-run" test, where two different versions of an ad are created and placed into one magazine print run in such a way that ad versions A and B are placed into random halves of the print run. Each ad has a coupon or other response device (such as a toll-free telephone number), and each ad has a unique code or "key" number to track which of those ads pulled each response that comes in. Once these logistics are in place, it is easy to test which one of the two ads being tested is the more effective in generating inquiries or leads.

Split-Cable Testing.   Split-cable testing by firms such as BehaviorScan will be described in detail in Chapter 16. A panel of around 3,000 households is recruited in test cities. An ID card presented by the panel member to the checkout stand, coupled with a computerized scanner system, allows the purchases of the member to be monitored. The in-store activity is also monitored. Further, panelists have a device connected to their TV set that allows BehaviorScan to monitor what channel is tuned and also to substitute one advertisement for another. Thus, panelists can be divided into matched groups and different advertising directed at each. In Chapter 16, the use of split-cable testing to conduct advertising weight tests will be discussed. Such split-cable facilities can and are also used to test one set of advertisements against another or to evaluate a host of options, such as the time of day or program in which the ad appears, the commercial length, or the bunching of exposures (versus an even distribution through time). These tests are very expensive, costing in the hundreds of thousands of dollars, and are typically not used to test one ad against another but rather two different creative strategies, each tested as a multi-exposure ad campaign lasting several months.

AT&T used the AdTel (Burke) split-cable system to test a new "Cost of Visit" campaign against the established "Reach Out" campaign.[24] Research had determined that a substantial "light-user" segment had a psychological "price barrier" to calling and over-estimated the cost, particularly at off-peak times.

The campaign objective was to communicate among the light users how inexpensive a 20-minute telephone visit can be and to stimulate usage during off-peak times. The "Cost of Visit" theme contained surprise (of the low cost), the appropriateness of a 20-minute visit, and the total cost of $3.33 (some believed that it would cost $20.00). One of the ads, "AT&T Long Lines Residence," is shown in Figure 14-4.

Two matched AdTel panel groups of 8,000 were created. During a 15-month period the two campaigns were aired, one to each group. Each household received three exposures per week (300 gross rating points per week). Compared to the "Reach Out" campaign, the "Cost of Visit" campaign increased calls during the deep discount period by 0.6 calls per week among all households and 1.5 calls per week among light-user households. Projections indicated that the campaign would generate $100 million in extra revenue during a five-year period.

Two additional analyses are of interest. During the six months after the test ended, usage fell off but not to the level prior to the test. However, it was clear that reinforcement advertising was needed. The "Cost of Visit" campaign changed two key attitudes more than the "Reach Out" campaign, the attitude toward the value of a long-distance call and the attitude about the rates.

Split-cable testing is the ultimate in testing validity, because it allows the advertiser to control experimentally for the effects of the other marketing mix elements and accurately measure the effect of advertising on short-term sales. However, as mentioned, it can cost from 20 to 50 times that of a forced exposure test ($100,000 to $200,000) and take six months to a year or more before the results are known. By that time, new brands or changing consumer preferences could make the results somewhat obsolete. Further, the sales results themselves, when viewed in isolation, offer no clue about the longer-term effect of the advertising on a brand's equity or goodwill. For these reasons, most firms use the split-cable testing far less than other alternatives.

OTHER DIAGNOSTIC TESTS

An entire category of advertising research methods is designed primarily not to test the impact of a total ad but to help creative people understand how the parts of the ad contribute to its impact. Which are the weaker parts of the ad, and how do they interact? Most of these approaches can be applied to mock-ups of proposed ads as well as finished ads.

Qualitative Research

Focus groups research is widely used at the front end of the development of an advertising campaign. In one study of the techniques used by 112 (out of 150 surveyed) of the top advertisers and agencies, focus groups were used 96 percent of the time to generate ideas for advertisements, and 60 percent of the time to test reactions to rough executions.[25]

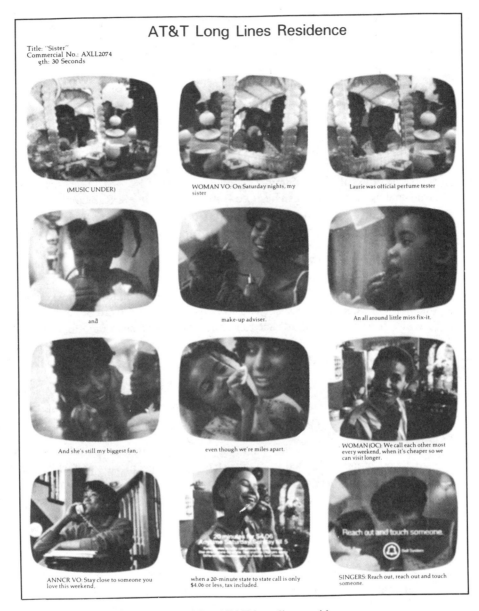

Figure 14-4.   AT&T long lines residence
Courtesy of AT&T Communications.

Audience Impressions of the Ad

Many copy tests add a set of open-ended questions to the procedures designed to tap the audience's impressions of what the ad was about, what ideas were presented, interest in the ideas, and so on. One goal is to detect potential misperceptions. Another is to uncover unintended associations that may have been created. If too many negative comments are elicited, there may be cause for concern. A Volkswagen commercial showing a Detroit auto worker driving a VW Rabbit because of its superior performance was killed because a substantial part of the audience disliked the company disloyalty portrayed.[26]

Adjective Checklists

The BRC mail questionnaire, shown in Figure 14-1, includes an adjective checklist that allows the advertiser to determine how warm, amusing, irritating, or informative the respondent thinks it to be. Similar checklists are used by ASI, Tele-Research, and other firms and agencies. The agencies Leo Burnett and Young & Rubicam use a similar phrase checklist extensively, often called a VRP (for viewer response profile). Several of their phrases tap an empathy dimension. "I can see myself doing that," "I can relate to that," and so on. Some believe that unless advertisements can achieve a degree of empathy, they will not perform well. Recently some advertising agencies (including Ayer and McCann-Erickson) have begun testing their ads using exhaustive batteries of possible emotional and feeling responses, to gauge whether their ads are evoking the targeted emotions and whether some undesirable negative emotions are being evoked by accident. Various sets of scales have been reported that can be used to gauge such emotional response.[27]

Physiological Measures

Several kinds of physiological instruments are used to observe reactions to advertisements.[28] In general, they attempt to capture changes in the nervous system or emotional arousal during the exposure sequence. The first two reviewed focus on eye movement.

Eye Camera.   This is a device that photographs eye movements, either by photographing a small spot of light reflected from the eye or by taking a motion picture of eye movement. A device used by Burke records the point on a print advertisement or package, where the eye focuses 60 times each second. Analysis can determine what the reader saw, what he or she "returned to," and what point was "fixed upon." In package research, a respondent can be asked to find a test brand placed on a shelf of competing packages.

Pupillometrics.   Pupillometrics deals with eye dilation. Eyes dilate when something interesting or pleasant is seen and constrict when confronted with unpleasant, distasteful, or uninteresting things. One interesting application is its use in screening new television programs.[29] Several related eye-movement devices are used, including the tachistoscope, blur meter, distance meter, illumination meter, and stereo rater.[30]

CONPAAD.   Conjugately programmed analysis of advertising (CONPAAD) has a respondent operate either a foot or hand device which controls the intensity of the audio and video channels of a television set. The viewer must exert effort to sustain the signals, which have been programmed to decay in a specific pattern. His or her effort to keep audio and video going is used as a measure of attention and interest in the advertising.[31]

Brain Waves.   Some companies test ads by means of the amount, nature, and distribution of the brain waves evoked. Consumers are placed into seats and have electrodes placed on different parts (front, back; left, right) of their scalps. As the ad is shown to them, the brain wave activity in various regions of their brains is recorded through electroencephalography (EEG). These measures cover various frequency ranges and are averaged over time and "normalized" for each individual being tested. Analysis of the frequency and amplitude of this activity can be interpreted to check the attention-getting power of different parts of the commercial, as well as of the ad as a whole.[32] The possible problems with such data, as with other physiological data (such as galvanic skin response, etc.) are (1) the contaminating effects of "artifacts" (irrelevant instrument or person-related factors that don't really measure the effectiveness of the ad) and (2) the somewhat difficult-to-interpret nature of the data (What does reduced or increased brain wave activity really mean in terms of cognitive processes, for example?).

Monitoring Commercial Response

A device used by respondents to register interest is part of ASI in-theater tests. It is a dial that can be turned up or down to indicate high or low interest. Data from the dial interest recorder are used to provide diagnostic information on what parts of the commercial were of high or low interest. Aaker, Stayman, and Hagerty have used a computer joystick to measure respondent reactions to feelings of warmth while viewing commercials. This procedure can also be used to monitor other feelings, such as irritation, humor, or liking.[33] MacLachlan and Myers have used the time it takes the respondent to make a choice between competing brands as a measure of the relative effectiveness of advertising. This is called "response latency" and has several other applications in advertising research.[34] Another potentially useful technique is called "facial action coding." By observing changes in facial expression during exposure, several kinds of emotional responses can be monitored.[35]

Market Facts has developed a system in which a respondent presses a button when something in the commercial strikes her or him as especially interesting or irritating. The respondent is then shown the commercial again and asked why the button was punched at each point. The result is a second-by-second understanding of audience reaction.

TRACKING STUDIES

When a campaign is running, its impact is often monitored via a tracking study. Periodic sampling of the target audience provides a time trend of measures of interest. The purpose is to evaluate and reassess the advertising campaign and perhaps also to understand why it is or is not working. Among the measures that are often tracked are advertisement awareness, awareness of elements of the advertisement, brand awareness, beliefs about brand attributes, brand image ratings, occasions of use, and brand preference. For durables such as cars, consumers are asked what brands they would consider buying on their next purchase, and what brand they are most likely to buy next. Of particular interest is knowing how the campaign is affecting the brand, as opposed to how the advertisement is communicating.

Figure 14-5 shows the tracking of an advertising campaign directed at children for a beverage product. Personal interviews were held with children from 6 to 12 years old. They were shown visual stimuli such as pictures of brand packaging or line drawings of advertising characters. The mostly open-ended questions were consistently coded over five years. The interest was in the "main character," who was the personification of the brand and playback of the "story" of the advertising, the main creative element.[36]

The successful campaign of year 1 was expanded with additional executions which apparently did not have comparable impact. The disappointing results of year 2 led to a fresh round of copy development aimed at making it more "modern" and "relevant" for kids. However, the decline continued in year 3. An analysis of verbatim playback suggested that the predictability of the main character's actions were too predictable and new ads were developed which placed it in a more heroic role, "rescuing" children in adventurous situations. In year 4 the main character measure turned up. For the next season, the campaign used situations from a child's real life to attempt to make the advertising more relevant. The result in year 5 was a dramatic increase in recall of the central creative element and an important increase in two other measures. The tracking program provided in this case actionable information over time, allowing the advertising to be adjusted around the same theme to become more effective.

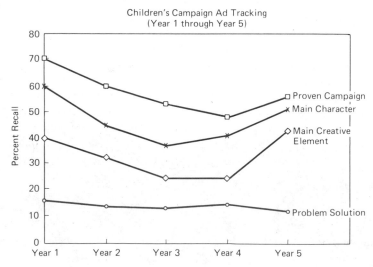

Figure 14-5.   Examples of ad tracking

Source: Reprinted from the *Journal of Advertising Research* © copyright 1985, by the Advertising Research Foundation.

The TEC Audit

The Eric Marder firm provides one approach to obtaining tracking data without doing customized studies.[37] They maintain a panel of 3,000 women from 1,000 areas. Each woman keeps a record of all television commercials she sees in the course of one randomly assigned day each month. Before watching television on her assigned day, she records her buying intention for each product category. On the assigned day she watches television normally except that she records the time, the channel, and the brand advertised from every ad she sees, and her buying intention immediately after exposure. The received messages (RMs) are defined as the total number of commercials recorded per 100 women. The persuasion rate (PR) is defined as the net percent of the RM that produces a shift in buying intention from some other brand to the advertised brand. Subscribers obtain quarterly reports of the RM and PR from all competing brands in the product class.

SELECTING COPY TESTS

A very wide range of copy-testing alternatives has been developed and is available to the advertiser. Beyond the question of whether to test copy at all lies the question of what particular test or tests should be used. The question has occupied the attention of professional and academic researchers since copy testing first began, and a great deal has been written on the subject. Much of the interest lies in assessing the validity and reliability of various types of tests. The subject is also important because considerable stakes are involved by research supplier companies who tend to offer a particular kind of testing service or rely on one testing method. The Advertising Research Foundation maintains a standing committee to monitor and encourage the development of new and better testing methods, and its annual conferences generally relate to questions of the strengths and limitations of particular methods or techniques.

The basic question in test selection is whether or not a test is valid and reliable. Does it really measure the effectiveness of advertising? More specifically, are the particular measures used in any one test true measures of the constructs involved? Is the test reliable and will it measure the same thing each time it is used? Can one test measure everything or are multitests required? These are some of the questions of copy-test selection.

Copy-Test Validity

The first problem in assessing copy-test validity is that, if the advertisement is to be tested with respect to a communication objective and a copy test evaluated in that context, there must exist an operational objective—a measurable and useful variable that represents the objective. As Chapter 3 indicated, the development of an operational objective is no simple task. In fact, researchers must often work with a vague or ill-defined set of objectives. Clarity in what is being sought from the ad—and therefore being tested in the copy test—is crucial. One measure cannot generally substitute for another: recall does not measure persuasion, and one must decide which of those is being sought for a particular ad.

Obviously, therefore, the validity of a particular copy test will depend on the advertising response that is desired. A campaign that is designed to gain awareness may not best be measured by a test that focuses on immediate behavioral response. A campaign that attempts to create an image or an association with a feeling such as warmth might require many repetitions and a subtle measurement method, perhaps asking some questions directed at the use experience. A single-exposure test with a coupon-redemption measure may not be appropriate at all. Thus, the usefulness of the various criteria used in testing needs to be evaluated in the context of the advertising objectives involved.

Once such objectives have been set, which copy-test measures are most valid for each objective? In a recent study conducted by the Advertising Research Foundation,[38] which involved six copy-testing measures, five pairs of packaged-goods commercials, and sales measures obtained over a year using split-cable testing, it was found that

- the best (most predictive of sales differences) copy-testing measure for persuasion was a simple poor-to-excellent rating of the brand, obtained after exposure.
- the best copy-testing measure for salience was the number of times the brand was mentioned first in unaided awareness for that category.
- the best copy-testing measure of communication was "other than to get you to buy the product, what was the main point of the commercial?"
- a big predictor of sales was an agree/disagree rating for the statement "this ad is one of the best I've seen recently."
- ads led to sales if they were rated high on either or both of "tells me a lot about how the product works" and "this advertising is funny or clever," but not if they rated high on "I find this ad artistic" or "this ad doesn't give any facts, it just creates an image."

Stewart has pointed out that the success or failure of a particular ad campaign can only be assessed completely if the measurements are conducted in a competitive context—and if measures are collected not only for the brand in question but also for competitive brands. Thus, though an ad may not show increases in favorable beliefs or overall attitudes for the target brand, it may show effects of leading to declines in the beliefs and attitudes for competitive brands—which will not show up in a copytest unless these competitive measures too are collected.[39]

The second issue here is that, given that a target population can be sensibly defined, the subjects in the test should be representative of the target population. Ideally, they should be selected randomly, and the sample size should be large enough so that the results are statistically valid. Of course, compromises must be made. It is often not feasible economically to obtain large random samples, especially if personal interviews are involved. The bias introduced by nonrespondents is a problem that is particularly crucial in some tests. People differ widely in their propensity to answer questions, to participate in laboratory experiments, to be subjects in physiological tests, and to be members of consumer panels. The danger is that those who refuse to participate may respond differently from those who do. In addition, mall intercept methods obviously access only mall shoppers, and cable-based tests miss those not connected to a cable. There is also a question as to whether one or even three or four cities can provide a representative sample. Consequently, the results may not represent the population for which the sample was drawn.

Third, and perhaps most significant, is the reaction of the respondents to the test environment and the measuring instruments. This reaction can distort the results. When a respondent is in a test situation, he or she tends to act differently. The main problem in any advertising study is the tendency of respondents to act as they should act (called reactive effect, role selection, the guinea pig effect, etc.). There is evidence that this problem is minor in a system such as BehaviorScan when the panel member becomes acclimated to the system. However, it is of greatest concern in systems which demand that the respondent give an attitude response. Is the respondent willing and able to respond accurately?

There are techniques to minimize the reactive effect. One is to divert respondents from the actual purpose of the experiment. Thus, a respondent may be told that she or he is evaluating television programs instead of their accompanying commercials. This technique, however, by no means eliminates all such bias. Furthermore, it has moral and ethical implications. How much deception should a respondent be subjected to without his or her consent? Another approach is to use, wherever possible, nonreactive measures. Thus, one might unobtrusively observe store traffic or sales. Direct-mail tests can usually be conducted with little reactive effect since a nonreactive response measure to the direct-mail advertisement is usually available.

A fourth issue is whether a rough mock-up or a finished ad is used. Several copy-test firms have reported high correlations with mock-up measures and finished copy measures. The seriousness of the problem will depend on the difference between the mock-up and the finished commercial and the impact of this difference on audience response. For example, it is very difficult to test humor in rough form.

A fifth issue is the frequency of response. To what extent can a copy test predict the response to a campaign that will involve dozens or even hundreds of exposures? Can a single exposure provide meaningful results, or should a minimum of two or three be used? Still another issue is the context in which the test advertisement is embedded. The use of a cluster of advertisements embedded in a program or magazine is the most realistic but adds complexity and is possibly confounding.

Finally, such approaches as the theater tests or mall intercept exposure contexts are termed forced exposure tests because the setting is artificial and the respondent is required to watch. The others, such as the BehaviorScan split-cable testing, are termed ''on-air'' tests because the exposure is a natural home setting in the context of watching a show. Approaches such as the ASI Apex method are on-air but the respondents realize they are in a test and are not watching a show they would watch at a time they would normally watch it. Thus, there is still concern that the exposure context may affect the results.

Thus, running through the validity considerations is a spectrum from artificial to natural. At one extreme would be forced exposure to a commercial mock-up with a paper-and-pencil response using a convenience mall intercept sample. At the other would be the BehaviorScan system, where the audience member realizes that he or she is in a panel but otherwise everything is completely natural, including multiple exposures over time.

These are some of the considerations that need to be taken into account in assessing test validity. Figure 14-6 provides an overview of some of the important ways in which copy tests can differ. Each dimension involves validity issues and trade-offs with cost.

Copy-Test Reliability

Copy-test selection must also take into account the reliability of a particular test. Will it measure the same thing each time it is used? Some work has also been done on this question. In a study by Clancy and Ostlund, for example, a second measure taken at a later time was developed for 106 on-air recall-tested commercials. The authors report reliability coefficients (the correlation of scores taken at one time with those taken at another time) of 0.67 and (when product category effects were removed) of 0.29.[40] These are comparatively low, and on this basis the authors challenge the reliability of on-air tests. Silk[41] has pointed out some of the dangers of using the test-retest approach to reliability assessment. It is important that test-retest conditions be equivalent. If, for example, consumers have been exposed to the advertising in different contexts between the two testing occasions or to competitive advertising, the testing conditions may not be equivalent, and a low correlation may not signify low reliability. Research by Hornik has even shown that the copytest scores can vary depending on the time of day—immediate recall is highest if the ad is tested at 9 A.M., because people are most alert at that time![42] It is indeed difficult to make straightforward assessments of copy-test reliability using the test-retest procedure because of such factors.

Other Considerations

Copy-test selection should take into account several other considerations concerning the nature of a particular test or supplier providing the test. In addition to reliability and validity, for example, Plummer[43] recommends that tests be assessed on five other criteria:

1. *Sensitivity.* The test should be able to discriminate between different commercials within brand groups.
2. *Independence of measures.* The different test measures should have little interrelationship across many testing experiences.
3. *Comprehensiveness.* It should provide, in addition to basic evaluative scores, some information that will indicate the reason for the levels of the evaluative scores.

The Advertisement Used

- Mock-Up
- Finished Advertisement

Frequency of Exposure

- Single exposure test
- Multiple exposure test

How It's Shown

- Isolated
- In a clutter
- In a program or magazine

Where the Exposure Occurs

- In a shopping center facility
- At home on TV
- At home through the mail
- In a theater

How Respondents are Obtained

- Prerecruited forced exposure
- Not prerecruited/natural exposure

Geographic Scope

- One city
- Several cities
- Nationwide

Alternative Measures of Persuasion

- Pre/post measures of attitudes or behavioral that is, pre/post attitude shifts
- Multiple measures that is, recall/involvement/buying commitment
- After only questions to measure persuasion that is, constant sum brand preference
- Test market sales measures that is, using scanner panels

Bases of Comparison and Evaluation

- Comparing test results to norms
- Using a control group

Figure 14-6.   Alternative methods of copy testing

4. *Relationships to other tests*.   It should provide similar results for the same stimuli tested by a similar but different measurement system.

5. *Acceptability*.   It must have some acceptance by those responsible for decisions in terms of a commitment to work with the test findings.

In choosing a supplier, obviously the reputation of the company, such as its service and delivery record, availability of norms, and stature in the industry, will be important. Things like geographic location and costs of the service relative to competitive offerings also come into play. There are suppliers in each of the three major categories of copy-testing research: laboratory tests, simulated natural environment tests, and market tests. In television, laboratory and simulated natural environment tests involve forced exposure, whereas market tests tend to be on-air recall tests. A study of advertiser and agency executive opinion on preferences between different versions of on-air and forced-exposure tests[44] revealed the most preferred to be single-exposure, multiple-market tests in the on-air case (rather than single exposure, single market; multiple exposure, single market; or multiple exposure, multiple market). In the forced-exposure case, in-theater and laboratory tests were preferred to mobile trailer and in-home forced-exposure tests. These data, of course, indicate overall general preference, and test choices should be made on the basis of the particular situation involved.

The choice of a copy test should be guided by the riskiness of the decision involved. To begin a major new campaign involving strategic departure is a high-risk decision that requires a total evaluation of all the constructs mentioned earlier. It is also important to assess whether the copy appears to antagonize respondents in any way. A total evaluation should also involve enough diagnostic information about consumer reactions to the execution so that the decision could be based on all the evaluative and diagnostic measures. It is possible to get high awareness but negative reactions. Total evaluation is not always economically practical or necessary. Extensions of existing campaigns are low-risk decisions requiring only *partial* evaluation. In particular evaluations, persuasiveness or attitude change will sometimes be the issue and attention will be of little concern. Sometimes clarity of communication will be the issue, and a subjective judgment of its persuasiveness will suffice. Sometimes the major concern will be focused on possible negatives in execution. In each case, the objectives of the copy test will differ.

In 1982, a coalition of 21 advertising agencies developed the following principles of copy testing, called PACT (positioning advertising copy testing), which summarizes much of what we have developed earlier in this chapter and introduces a few others:[45]

1. A good copy-testing system provides measurements which are relevant to the objectives of the advertising.

2. A good copy-testing system is one which requires agreement about how the results will be used in *advance* of each specific test.

3. A good copy-testing system provides *multiple* measures because single measurements are generally inadequate to assess the performance of an advertisement.

4. A good copy-testing system is based on a model of human response—the reception of a stimulus, the comprehension of the stimulus and the response to the stimulus.

5. A good copy-testing system allows for consideration of whether the advertising stimulus should be exposed more than once.

6. A good copy-testing system recognizes that the more finished a piece of copy is the more soundly it can be evaluated, requiring, as a minimum, that alternative executions be tested in the same degree of finish.

7. A good copy-testing system provides controls to avoid the biasing effects of the exposure context.

8. A good copy-testing system is one that takes into account basic considerations of sample definition.

9. A good copy-testing system is one that can demonstrate reliability and validity.

SUMMARY

During and after the creation and production process, the advertiser must decide whether to invest in copy-testing research and what kinds of tests to use. An industry of research supplier companies has evolved to supply copy-testing services. There are hundreds of methods used to test copy. Much advertising is placed without formal copy testing, particularly by local advertisers for whom the investment in advertising does not warrant the extra expense. Certain "creative" agencies also do not believe in pretesting commercials, arguing that it restricts the creativity of their work. Copy testing tends to be done mostly by large national advertisers where the risks and investments are high.

Copy testing can be done at the beginning of the creation process, at the end (layout) stage of the creation process, at the end of the production stage, and after the campaign is launched. Tests at the first three stages are called pretests, whereas those at the fourth stage are posttests. Numerous types of criteria and constructs are used to guide copy-testing research. Many tests are associated with attention, recognition, and recall constructs. The argument is that if these objectives are accomplished the advertising will at least achieve the essential steps in communication. The full array of constructs involved in the hierarchy of response model can, however, be used. In this case, several types of tests will be needed and expenses will increase accordingly.

Criteria used in copy testing can be usefully grouped into four types: recognition, recall, persuasion, and behavior. BRC uses mail questionnaires to measure television commercial recognition and brand-name association, Communicus for television, and Starch for print use personal interviews. Day-after-recall is widely used but controversial because of its inability to predict persuasion or behavior, especially for emotional appeals. Persuasion has been measured in forced exposure or on-air contexts, by change in brand preference after an exposure to an ad on a UHF station, by change in prize-list brand preference in a theater test, by comparison of the effect on brand preference with a non-exposed control group, by measures of advertising involvement and brand commitment, and by measures tailored to particular advertising objectives. Behavior measures include coupon-stimulated buying after a forced exposure to an ad, split-run tests of ad-generated inquiries, and scanner-based monitoring of panelists in a split-cable testing operation.

Diagnostic testing, to evaluate the advertisement content at all stages of the process, includes qualitative research, audience ad impressions, adjective checklists, checklists of emotions evoked by the ad, eye movement, and the monitoring of audience response during the commercial. Within the laboratory–physiological methods group, measuring devices such as the eye camera, polygraphs, tachistoscopes, pupillometers, brain wave measures, and computer-assisted effort measurement are the major alternatives. Recent developments in this area include response latency and face-coding methods. Simulated natural environment tests include those based on intercept research and mobile trailers, fixed-facility research, and in-home interviewing. Many of the recognition, rather than the recall, methods fit into this category. Services provided by ARS, ASI, Starch INRA Hooper, and Bruzzone Research are representative of these kinds of tests.

A tracking study provides measures of advertising impact over time by taking periodic (monthly, quarterly, or yearly) surveys of audience response. Awareness of the advertising or of specific claims or elements of the advertising is often included, but any measure relevant to the objectives can be used.

Given the vast array of alternative methods and commercial services for copy testing, the question becomes how to choose sensibly among them. The basic question is whether a particular test is valid and reliable. Three major factors must be considered with respect to validity. First, the test must measure what the campaign seeks to achieve. A test designed to measure one objective (e.g., recall) is different from one that aims to measure another objective (e.g., persuasion). Second, subjects in the test should be representative of the target population. Third, reactions of the subjects to the testing situation that might bias the results should be minimized. Copy-test validity concerns usually focus on the appropriateness of the response measure, the reactive (or guinea pig) effect of being in an experiment (especially when the exposure setting is not natural and when an attitude measure is required), the use of mock-ups, and the representativeness of the sample.

Generally, it has been found that no one test or method is sufficient to satisfy all the needs of copy research, but that tests designed to measure different constructs can indeed do so. Which tests are better, particularly whether recall or persuasion tests are better for testing television commercials, is a continuing debate in the industry. Test reliability must also be considered. Here, again, because of the difficulties of measuring reliability, there are no definitive answers. The norms developed by suppliers over years of testing remain the advertiser's best guide to this question.

Many other practical considerations about the supplier (reputation, service, location, costs, and so on) and the service or test (sensitivity, independence, comprehensiveness, relationships to other tests, and acceptability) should be included in the selection process. The overriding considerations in this decision are that the test or tests chosen should be governed by the objectives of the advertising, the amount of investment involved, and the extent to which there is little or no past experience on which to guide decision making in a particular product or market situation.

DISCUSSION QUESTIONS

1. Make a list of the factors you would consider in deciding whether to invest in copy-testing research at each of the four stages of testing given in the chapter.

2. Why measure recognition anyway? Why would it ever be of value to have an audience member recognize an ad when he or she could not recall it without being prompted and could not recall its content? Why not just measure recall?

3. Compare the BRC recognition method with the Communicus method. What are the relative strengths and weaknesses?

4. DAR is widely used. Why? Would you use it if you were the product manager for Löwenbräu? For American Express? Under what circumstances would you use it?

5. Review the validity problems inherent in the McCollum/Spielman theater testing approach. Compare these to
   (a) The Mapes & Ross method
   (b) The ASI Apex method
   (c) The Tele-Research approach
   (d) The BehaviorScan approach

6. Why conduct tracking studies? Why not just observe sales?

7. How will adjective checklists help a creative group? What about eye movement data?

8. Suppose that the advertising objective is to entice people to try a new brand. Predictive validity is whether recall predicts purchase, whether memorability predicts purchase, whether arousal and interest predict purchase, or whether attitudes predict purchase. From what has been reviewed in previous chapters, discuss the validity question at each of these levels.

9. The various methods of copy research are representative of the various methods of research in social science, particularly psychological and sociological research methods. Give an example in which the methods used by psychoanalytic (Freudian) or clinical psychologists, stimulus-response (behavior) psychologists, multidimensional scalers, attitude researchers, and sociologists are employed in copy research.

10. Laboratory methods are often criticized for their "artificiality" in copy-testing research. Are there any counterarguments? Discuss.

11. Discuss the advantages and disadvantages of an in-theater method compared to a market test and a recall method versus a recognition method.

12. Design an ideal test of copy effectiveness. Assuming the measures would be made in a natural environment, critically examine the difficulties involved.

NOTES

1. One estimate is that as much as $125 million is spent annually on copy testing. Robert Mayer of Young & Rubicam advertising agency suggests that there are "33,000 ways" to test advertising copy. Basal skin response, brain waves, eye movement, pupil dilation, physical effort, aided and unaided noting and recall, copy-point recall, visual and slogan recall, interest and attitude toward the advertisement, knowledge and attitude toward brand product attributes and benefits, buying intentions, coupon redemption, and simulated sales response are some of the measures used. Copy-testing designs include prepost or post-only studies, single versus multiple exposure, projectable versus nonprojectable samples, natural exposure versus forced exposure. Other alternatives include where the exposure should take place (in-home, in-theater, mobile trailer, shopping center intercept, fixed facility), whether the testing is done in groups (such as the family) or individually, and whether the exposure should attempt to simulate the natural setting by introducing distraction or competitive advertising.

2. Readers should refer to the materials in Chapter 15 on the creation and production process for a better understanding of where testing "fits in."

3. Donald E. Bruzzone, "The Case for Testing Commercials by Mail," Paper presented at the 25th Annual Conference of the Advertising Research Foundation, New York, October 23, 1979.

4. Lewis C. Winters, "Comparing Pretesting and Posttesting of Corporate Advertising," *Journal of Advertising Research,* 23, February/March 1983, pp. 25–32.

5. See, for example, Alan D. Fletcher and Paul R. Winn, "An Intermagazine Analysis of Factors in Advertising Readership," *Journalism Quarterly,* 51, Autumn 1974, pp. 425–30; Dominique M. Hanssens and Barton A. Weitz, "The Effectiveness of Industrial Print Advertisements Across Product Categories," *Journal of Marketing Research,* 17, August 1980, pp. 294–306; Donald W. Hendon, "How Mechanical Factors Affect Ad Perception," *Journal of Advertising Research,* 13, August 1973, pp. 39–45; Morris B. Holbrook and Donald R. Lehmann, "Form Versus Content in Predicting Starch Scores," *Journal of Advertising Research,* 20, August 1980, pp. 53–62; John R. Rossiter, "Predicting Starch Scores," *Journal of Advertising Research,* 21, October 1981, pp. 63–68; Lawrence C. Soley and Leonard N. Reid, "Predicting Industrial Ad Readership," *Industrial Marketing Management,* 12, 1983, pp. 201–206; Richard M. Sparkman, Jr., "Cost Effectiveness of Advertising," *International Journal of Advertising,* 4 (2), 1985, pp. 131–141; and Rafael Valiente, "Mechanical Correlates of Ad Recognition," *Journal of Advertising Research,* 13, June 1973, pp. 13–18.

6. Surendra N. Singh and Gilbert A. Churchill, Jr., "Response-bias-free Recognition Tests to Measure Advertising Effects," *Journal of Advertising Research,* June/July 1987, pp. 23–36.

7. Charles E. Young and Michael Robinson, "Guideline: Tracking The Commercial Viewer's Wandering Attention," *Journal of Advertising Research,* June/July 1987, pp. 15–22.

8. George M. Zinkhan, William Locander, and James H. Leigh, "Dimensional Relationships of Aided Recall and Recognition," *Journal of Advertising,* 15(1), 1986, pp. 38–46.

9. Herbert E. Krugman, "Low Recall and High Recognition of Advertising," *Journal of Advertising Research,* February/March 1986, pp. 79–86.

10. Surendra N. Singh, Michael L. Rothschild, and Gilbert A. Churchill, Jr., "Recognition Versus Recall as Measures of Television Commercial Forgetting," *Journal of Marketing Research,* 25, February 1988, pp. 72–80.

11. Benjamin Lipstein, "An Historical Perspective of Copy Research," *Journal of Advertising Research,* 24, December 1984, pp. 11–15.

12. Hubert A. Zielske, "Does Day-After-Recall Penalize 'Feeling' Ads?" *Journal of Advertising Research,* 22, February/March 1982, pp. 19–22.

13. Lawrence D. Gibson, "Not Recall," *Journal of Advertising Research,* 23, February/March 1983, pp. 39–46.

14. Lipstein, "An Historical Perspective."

15. AC-T Advertising Control for Television, undated publication of McCollum/Spielman Research.

16. Ibid.

17. Lipstein, "An Historical Perspective."

18. "Advertising Quality Deserves More Weight!" Research Systems Corporation, August 1983.

19. ASI Laboratory Methodology, ASI Market Research, Inc., New York, undated.

20. Milton Sherman, "The BUY Test," Paper presented to The Market Research Society, Manchester, England, May 20, 1982.

21. Descriptive material from Mapes & Ross.

22. APEX, ASI Market Research, Inc., New York, March 1984, p. 46.

23. Winters, "Comparing Pretesting and Posttesting," p. 28.

24. Alan P. Kuritsky, John D. C. Little, Alvin J. Silk, and Emily S. Bassman, "The Development, Testing, and Execution of a New Marketing Strategy at AT&T Long Lines," *Interfaces,* 12, December 1982, pp. 22–37.

25. Benjamin Lipstein and James P. Neelankavil, "Television Advertising Copy Research: A Critical Review of the State of the Art," *Journal of Advertising Research,* 24, April/May 1984, pp. 19–25.

26. "VW Has Some Clinkers Among Classics," *Advertising Age,* September 9, 1985, p. 48.

27. See, for example, Rajeev Batra and Morris Holbrook, "Developing a Typology of Affective Responses to Advertising: A Test of Validity and Reliability," *Psychology and Marketing,* 7(1), Spring 1990, pp. 11–25, and David M. Zeitlin and Richard A. Westwood, "Measuring Emotional Response," *Journal of Advertising Research,* October/November 1986, pp. 34–44.

28. For a review, see David W. Stewart, "Physiological Measurement of Advertising Effectiveness," *Psychology and Marketing,* 1, 1984, pp. 43–48.

29. Eckhard H. Hess, "Pupillometrics," in F. M. Bass, C. W King, and E. A. Pessemier, eds., *Applications of the Sciences in Marketing Management* (New York: John Wiley, 1968), pp. 431–453.

30. A variation introduced by Haug Associates of Los Angeles utilizes a modified portable tachistoscope device that is taken into the home and allows testing in the in-home environment. Respondents are shown the first few seconds of a commercial and asked if they know what it is and, if so, to reconstruct the copy points.

31. See, for example, Ogden R. Lindsley, "A Behavioral Measure of Television Viewing," *Journal of Advertising Research,* 2, September 1962, pp. 2–12, and Lewis C. Winters and Wallace H. Wallace, "On Operant Conditioning Techniques," *Journal of Advertising Research,* 5, October 1970, pp. 39–45. Associates for Research in Behavior in Philadelphia provides a copy-testing service based on CONPAAD.

32. Michael L. Rothschild, Yong J. Hyun, Byron Reeves, Esther Thorson, and Robert Goldstein, "Hemispherically Lateralized EEG as a Response to Television Commercials," *Journal of Consumer Research,* 15 (2), September 1988, pp. 185–198.

33. David A. Aaker, Douglas Stayman, and Michael Hagerty, "Warmth in Advertising," Working paper, University of California, Berkeley, 1985.

34. James M. MacLachlan and John G. Myers, "Using Response Latency to Identify Commercials That Motivate," *Journal of Advertising Research,* 23, October/November 1983, pp. 51–57. For a book on the subject, see James M. MacLachlan, *Response Latency: New Measure of Advertising* (New York: Advertising Research Foundation, 1977).

35. John G. Myers, "Response Latency and Facial Action Coding Research in Advertising," American Marketing Association Doctoral Consortium, University of Chicago, 1978. See also John L. Graham, "A New System for Measuring Nonverbal Responses to Marketing Appeals," American Marketing Association Proceedings, 1980.

36. Douglas F. Haley, "Advertising Tracking Studies: Packaged-Goods Case Histories," *Journal of Advertising Research,* 25, February/March 1985, pp. 45–50.

37. The TEC Audit, TEC Measures, Inc., New York.

38. Russell I. Haley, "The ARF Copy Research Validity Study: A Topline Report," Paper presented at the ARF 36th Annual Conference, April 1990, New York.

39. David W. Stewart, "Measures, Methods, and Models in Advertising Research," *Journal of Advertising Research,* June/July 1989, pp. 54–60.

40. Kevin J. Clancy and Lyman E. Ostlund, "Commercial Effectiveness Measures," *Journal of Advertising Research,* 16, February 1976, pp. 29–34. See also Derek Bloom, Andrea Jay, and Tony Twyman, "The Validity of Advertising Pretests," *Journal of Advertising Research,* 17, April 1977, pp. 7–16, and Richard P. Bagozzi and Alvin J. Silk, "Recall, Recognition, and the Measurement of Memory for Print Advertisements," *Marketing Science,* 2, Spring 1983, pp. 95–134.

41. Alvin J. Silk, "Test-Retest Correlations and the Reliability of Copy Testing," *Journal of Marketing Research,* 14, November 1977, pp. 476–486.

42. Jacob Hornik, "Diurnal Variation in Consumer Responses," *Journal of Consumer Research,* 14 (March) 1988, pp. 588–590.

43. Joseph T. Plummer, "Evaluating TV Commercial Tests, " *Journal of Advertising Research,* 12, October 1972, pp. 21–27.

44. Lyman E. Ostlund, Rakesh Sapra, and Kevin Clancy, "Copy Testing Methods and Measures Favored by Top Ad Agency and Advertising Executives," Working paper, Graduate School of Business, University of Arizona, 1978.

45. PACT Agencies, "Positioning Advertising Copy Testing," *Journal of Advertising,* 11 (3), pp. 3–29.

APPENDIX: NOTES ON FOUR COPY-TESTING SERVICES

BURKE MARKETING RESEARCH: DAY-AFTER-RECALL (DAR)

Methodology

- Prime-time spots are purchased in three markets. The spots are to be within a program (other than news) that does not have a low rating among the target audience.
- Using the telephone directory as a sampling base, 100 program viewers are called.
- They are asked if they can recall any commercials the previous day in a product category (like soap).
- If they cannot identify the brand correctly, they are then given the product category and brand and asked if they recalled the commercial.
- They are then asked for anything they can recall about the commercial, what was said, what was shown, and what the main idea was.
- All respondents are asked if they can recall specific incidents in the program that occurred just before and just after the commercial.
- DAR is the percent of those in the commercial audience who recalled something specific about the commercial, such as the sales message, the story line, the plot, or some visual or audio element. The commercial audience is all those who saw the

program and were not distracted or changing channels when the commercial was on or who correctly recalled the program segment that occurred just before and just after the commercial or who saw the commercial.

- Approximate cost: $4,600 plus media cost.
- Rough commercial testing is available for approximately $2,200 including media for female audiences and approximately $4,000 for male audiences including media costs. The approach is the same except that the respondents are recruited by calling them prior to the program and asking them to watch and evaluate a particular program. The program is a daytime show in a certain city (for men the program is an early afternoon Sunday program).

Discussion

Burke's DAR has two salient attributes. First it provides the commercial exposure in a natural, realistic in-home setting. Second, it is well established and has developed extensive norms over the years. The average DAR is 24. One-fourth of all commercials score under 15 and one-fourth score over 31.

MAPES & ROSS

Methodology

- Commercials are aired in a preselected prime-time position on a UHF or independent station in each of three major markets.
- Prior to the test, a sample of 200 viewers (150 if it is an all-male target audience) are contacted by telephone and invited to participate in a survey that requires viewing the test program (a drawing for three cash awards is an incentive). Appointments are set up to interview the respondents the day after the program is aired. Respondents are questioned about their brand preferences for a number of different product categories. Respondents provide brand names on an unaided basis.
- The day following the airing of the test program those who watched the program are asked on an unaided basis their brand preferences for a number of product categories.
- The respondents are then asked on an aided basis about the recall of six commercials that appeared within the program. Open-ended questions pertaining to what the commercial was about, what ideas were presented, interest in the ideas, and reactions to the commercial are asked of all respondents claiming recall.
- As an option, respondents can be asked to provide ratings on a ten-point scale on statements about the test brand or test commercial.
- Demographic and brand bought last questions complete the interview.
- Approximate cost per commercial: $3,500 plus air time of approximately $700.

Discussion

The key measure provided by Mapes & Ross is pre- and postbrand-preference change. A 1979 study by Mapes & Ross in which they related recall and brand-preference change to purchase behavior is instructive. They recontacted 2,241 respondents two weeks after they had participated in a standard Mapes & Ross test. A total of 142 commercials from 55 product categories were represented. They were questioned about their purchases in the two-week period. Among those who bought the product category, purchases of the test brand were 3.3 times higher among those who changed their preference than among those who did not change. Proven recallers exhibited somewhat higher brand buying levels than nonproven recallers. However, this higher buying level can be attributed in large measure to those within the proven recall group who also changed their preference toward the test brand. Those who did prove recall, but who did not change their preference toward the test brand, exhibited a purchase level only slightly higher than those who neither proved recall nor changed their preference. A total of 7,283 product category purchases were involved, 758 of which represented a switch to the test brand.

ASI MARKET RESEARCH, INC.

Methodology

- A sample of 410 respondents are recruited by telephone from shopping centers. Of this group, 250 are selected to match a standard audience profile, which may be augmented to reflect some target group specification.
- The respondents come to a Los Angeles theater, 200 seats of which are equipped with dial interest recorders that allow the respondents to continuously dial their interest in the material. The information from 150 seats that are active at any one time is monitored by a computer and presented graphically as continuous-line charts. Respondents who forget or refuse the dials are switched to "inactive" status.
- The audience completes a classification questionnaire and a preexposure brand preference measure presented in the form of a prize list.
- The audience is then exposed to a control cartoon, a television pilot, a control commercial, and a set of four noncompeting test commercials.
- If desired, ten respondents are pulled out of the audience and asked to participate in a group discussion.
- Respondents are apologetically told by a moderator that the prize list was incomplete—one product category was omitted—so they will have to complete a corrected sheet from which the drawing will be made.
- After viewing another control cartoon and an entertainment segment, the respondents are asked to write down brands and product categories of commercials to-

gether with anything they could remember seeing or hearing in them. Door prizes are then awarded.

- An option is to then reexpose the audience to the test commercials and to administer a customized questionnaire that can contain up to three open-ended questions.
- Among the outputs are interest and involvement in the commercial obtained from the dial interest recorders, communication recall achieved, the pre- and postbrand-preference measure, and optionally the diagnostic information from the discussion group and the refocus exposure questionnaire.
- Approximate cost: $3,025, plus $925 for the refocus exposure, plus $300 to $900 for the group discussion (depending on the length and depth).

Discussion

ASI checks the representativeness of each audience by measuring demographics, product usage patterns, television viewing patterns, audience reactions to control material, and preference changes obtained in a product category for which no commercials were run. If the audience is judged abnormal, it is discarded. Reliability studies across 100 commercials in 15 product categories yielded test-retest reliability correlations of from 0.81 to 0.88.

TELE-RESEARCH, INC.

Methodology

- Six hundred shoppers are intercepted in a shopping center location in Los Angeles (other markets are available at higher cost) and randomly assigned to test or control groups.
- A short brand usage and demographic interview is followed by exposure to five commercials (television or radio). One commercial is a control, and the others are noncompetitive test commercials. When print is used, six advertisements are used instead of five. The test group sees the test commercial and the control group does not.
- One hundred subjects in the test group complete a self-administered questionnaire, which includes questions on the main point, likes, dislikes, believability, influence on attitudes (increase versus decrease in interest in the brand), and an adjective checklist (clever, informative, silly, stale, and so on).
- Both groups are given packets of coupons, including one for the test brand, which can be redeemed in a nearby cooperating drugstore or supermarket.
- Selling effectiveness score is the ratio of purchases by viewer shoppers divided by the rate of purchases by control shoppers. A percentile ranking is obtained by comparing to category norms.

- Delayed telephone recall based upon 150 of the 200 viewers who did not participate in the postexposure questionnaire has an approximate additional cost of $2,000.
- Approximate cost: $3,000 per commercial.

Discussion

A prime selling point of Tele-Research is that it provides a behavioral response measure that is based on the highly realistic context of a shopper spending his or her own money in a real store. Some early 1960s research by Tele-Research is relevant. The studies compared day-after-recall scores with selling effectiveness scores for 300 commercials. Those commercials that had DAR scores in the lowest quartile tended to have low selling effectiveness scores. However, there was little correlation between DAR and selling effectiveness among the balance of the commercials. In the same study, the Tele-Research forced-exposure DAR was compared with that of the nonforced-exposure (in-home) DAR for 182 commercials. The correlation between the two was approximately 0.80, but the recall levels were much higher for the forced-exposure conditions.

There is a problem in applying the Tele-Research methodology directly to products like clothing. A clothing store familiar to the respondents may not be at the shopping center. More serious is the fact that the purchase cycle is relatively long and many of the respondents may not be in the market for clothing. One approach to adapt would be to offer subjects a $5-off coupon for an item of clothing and ask their first and second choice brand. They would then be told that all coupons for those brands not available are not available and be given $5 in cash instead.

15

PRODUCTION AND IMPLEMENTATION

Once upon a time I was riding on the top of a Fifth Avenue bus, when I heard a mythical housewife say to another, "Molly, my dear, I would have bought that new brand of toilet soap if only they hadn't set the body copy in ten point Garamond."
Don't you believe it.

David Ogilvy, in *Confessions of an Advertising Man*

In the previous chapters we have examined how an ad campaign gets planned and have discussed both the strategic and tactical aspects of that planning. Having decided what to say in the ad, and how to say it, the advertiser now has rough copy and art, or a storyboard, or a radio ad script. Perhaps this has been pretested in rough (or even finished) form, as discussed in Chapter 14. Now the ad is ready and approved. It is time to get the ad produced and sent out to the media to be "run": time to move on to actual implementation.

This chapter discusses two aspects of such implementation. First, we discuss the production process for an ad, both print and television. We then move on to a broader discussion of the relationship between the client and agency, looking at that relationship not only at the time of the production of the ad but throughout the advertising process. What do both the client and the agency need to do to maximize the mutual benefits from the relationship, and to get advertising that is both creative, on strategy, and leads to increased sales?

THE ADVERTISING PRODUCTION PROCESS

The production of advertising is a process involving many people, much time, and significant expenditures of money. Although the major components of this process can be described, it is very difficult to explain precisely how effective ads are actually created.

It is like asking an artist to explain how to create and produce a great painting. Although we might recognize greatness in the final output of the process, it is difficult to set up a creation and production system that will always guarantee such greatness. Behind any print advertisement or television commercial lie hundreds of decisions involving artistic and other judgments by teams of people inside and outside the agency.

Production decisions are important because all the investment on research and development for a new product or maintaining sales levels of an established product is at stake. A produced ad is the means through which advertising objectives are carried out and strategy is executed. All the attention to careful specification of objectives can be ruined by a poor finished ad. And producing ads is expensive. Creating, producing, and conducting the research done on one television commercial, for example, can involve hundreds of thousands of dollars. Although media costs will be even more expensive (on average, media costs represent about 85 percent of a total advertising budget), their success too ultimately depends on the nature of the finished ad.

This chapter reviews the ad production process. A general model is first presented which traces the various stages and activities involved in the overall process. The creation stage part of the model comes first; this is the part we discussed in Chapter 13, and it is only briefly reviewed here. This is followed by a review of activities at the production stage. Production differs according to whether copy is being produced for print media or for broadcast media. In print media, the important components concern typography and engraving, whereas in broadcast, casting, filming, and editing are of central importance.

What are the basic tasks involved in creating and producing an advertisement? Who does what at which stage? What are the important ways of generating ideas and carrying them forward into final production? What should an advertising manager know about the creation and production process?

A MODEL OF THE CREATION AND PRODUCTION PROCESS

Figure 15-1 presents a model of the creation and production process. Note that two basic stages are involved, *creation* and *production*. The distinction is somewhat artificial because creative activities can take place at any point throughout the entire process, but it is a convenient distinction for several reasons. First, the activities associated with the creation stage take place largely within the confines of the advertising agency. Those associated with production are usually done by outside suppliers to the agency. Second, creation activities are in many ways similar for either print or broadcast advertising. In most cases the generation of words (copywriting) and the generation of pictures (illustrating) are involved whether the end result is a print advertisement or a broadcast commercial. A preliminary print advertisement ready to be shipped out for production is called a *layout*. In the case of a prospective television commercial, the layout is called a *storyboard,* but the creative activities involved in the generation of each are in many ways similar. Finally, production activities by external suppliers do differ in significant respects for print production or broadcast production. Print production involves the graphic arts

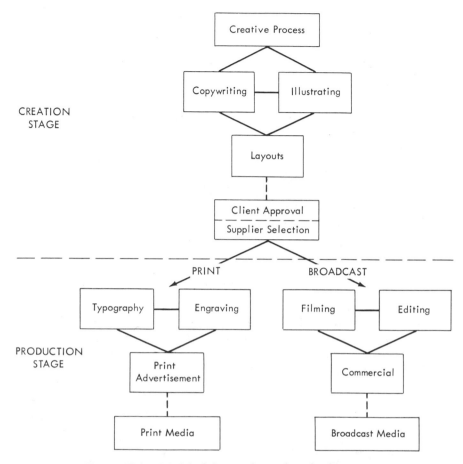

Figure 15-1. Model of the creation and production process

and specialists in typography, engraving, printing, and so on. Broadcast production, particularly in television, involves audiovisual studios, production houses, and the basic tasks of filming and editing, which are very similar to the production of a movie. In sum, different types of external suppliers are involved for print and broadcast at the production stage.

The important input to the generation of advertising is referred to as the *creative process* in the model. Much attention has been given to ways of improving this process and generating ideas. Following the generation of copy and a layout, discussed in Chapter 13, the creative director and the agency account executive will next seek the client's approval for the layout and the general nature of the advertising to be produced. Pretest copy research may be sought at this point (using the layout or rough stage, or alternative finished executions) to assist in the decision, following the procedures outlined in the previous chapter.

An important decision at the point of production is the selection of suppliers to actually produce the finished advertisements. These tasks are noted in the model as *client approval* and *supplier selection.*

Following production, the final print advertisements or broadcast commercials are distributed to the appropriate newspapers, magazines, radio, or broadcast stations (media) for printing and airing. This step completes the copy-decision aspects of advertising management insofar as the basic messages are created and produced. Posttest copy-testing research, the subject of Chapter 14, can then be done to see how well the ad actually does, perhaps through tracking studies.

Client Approval and Supplier Selection

Following the creation of the copy and layout, the creative director and account executive usually get client approval of the advertising prior to production. There is always the danger at this point that the client will evaluate it subjectively and get involved in the creative process. When that happens, the result is usually a creative effort that is compromised. Rather, the focus of discussion should be on the advertising objectives and the relationship of the proposed copy to those objectives. The client could, properly, discuss copy testing that has been considered or planned to demonstrate that the advertising will be effective in achieving those objectives.

Suppliers (typographers, engravers, and printers in the case of print and production houses; sound studios and many others in the case of broadcast) must be selected at this stage. In print, it is usual for an agency to have a group of suppliers that it has come to know and trust and for which print production activities are carried out. In broadcast, particularly television, it is more usual to "put the production out to bid." Often, this involves obtaining bids from three different production studios who will use the storyboard as a basis for bidding. Television commercials in this sense are like other supplies the corporation buys, and getting them produced is treated as a bidding process in much the same way.

PRODUCTION STAGE

Production of advertising generally involves a great number of external outside supplier firms and individuals. Although we have not stressed this component of the overall advertising system presented in Chapter 1, it is indeed interesting and represents a "fifth" level or institution that depends heavily on advertising. Print advertising production differs in significant respects from broadcast production, and we have stressed this fact in the Figure 15-1 model. In print, firms specialized in type and typesetting called typographers will be involved. Others specialized in graphic materials, engravers, may be necessary. Some large printers include these services as part of their offerings. The choice of whether to use specialists or one large printer is another decision facing the creative team.

Concerning broadcast, many other kinds of specialists are needed. These can include a producer, director, set designer, film editor, actors and actresses, composers, musicians, talent scouts, casting directors, music arrangers, camera crews, video and audio equipment supply companies, and many others. Many of these people freelance, and the process of producing a television commercial may require considerable effort in bringing a team together. Often production is channeled through a production house that will contain a sound studio and most of what is necessary to get the job done.

Production is a process that takes a considerable amount of time; from six to eight weeks can be involved. In what follows, we provide a brief sketch of the major activities involved in print and broadcast production. The advertising manager should not hope to become an expert in the graphic arts, but decision making can be enhanced once the basics are known.

Print Production

The most important components of print production deal with the art and science of typography and engraving. Each is a fast-evolving field that has been affected greatly in recent years by computerization.

Typography is done by a specialist in type and typesetting. What the advertiser needs to know is that there are thousands of different type styles and forms from which choices must be made for a specific print advertisement and many ways of composing type. Figure 15-2 provides an example of an ad using different type styles for dramatic effect. Typography is a complex field in itself that takes significant skill and experience to master. It should be appreciated that there is a range of alternatives from which to choose, and the creative director must be prepared to question and oversee those choices. Figure 15-3 gives some valuable lessons on typography from an article by David Ogilvy.

The second major activity in producing a print advertisement is *engraving*. Engraving basically deals with the generation and reproduction of pictures, photographs, and the visual elements of the advertisement. Photoengraving is the process using photography to create a printing surface. Through the photoengraving process, artwork (line charts, drawings, photographs) and paste-up of type can be transferred to a negative photochemically, and the image on the negative transferred to a metal plate for printing. Photoengraving is most commonly used to reproduce artwork, but is also used to reproduce combinations of illustration and type.

Actual printing of the advertisement involves yet another process and more alternatives. Printing can be done by letterpress, gravure, lithography, or silk screening. The first three are processes associated with basic ways of photoengraving. In each case, some type of plate or "mat" is developed from which copies are run.

Broadcast Production

In explaining the basic elements of broadcast production, we focus on television commercial production. Many of the elements of radio commercial production are analogous to the audio portion of television commercials and involve audiotapes rather than videotapes or films. Much radio commercial production is very uncomplicated, consisting of "live commercials" in which written copy is simply provided to a disk jockey or news commentator who reads the copy at the appropriate time slot (with appropriate emphasis, voice delivery, and so on).

Producing one television commercial can, on the other hand, involve 100 or more

Figure 15-2. Creative uses of typefaces: Celestial Seasonings
Courtesy of Celestial Seasonings.

Typography—"the eye is a creature of habit"

Good typography *helps* people read your copy, while bad typography prevents them from doing so.

Advertising agencies usually set their headlines in capital letters. This is a mistake. Professor Tinker of Stanford has established that capitals retard reading. They have no ascenders or descenders to help you recognize words, and tend to be read *letter by letter*.

The eye is a creature of habit. People are accustomed to reading books, magazines and newspapers in *lower case*.

Another way to make headlines hard to read is to superimpose them on your illustration.

Another mistake is to put a period at the end of headlines. Periods are also called full stops, because they stop the reader dead in his tracks. You will find no full stops at the end of headlines in newspapers.

Yet another common mistake is to set copy in a measure too wide or too narrow to be legible. People are accustomed to reading newspapers, which are set about 40 characters wide.

Which typefaces are easiest to read? Those that people are *accustomed* to reading, like the Century family, Caslon, Baskerville and Jenson. The more outlandish the typeface, the harder it is to read. The drama belongs in what you say, not in the typeface.

Sanserif faces like this are particularly difficult to read. Says John Updike, "Serifs exist for a purpose. They help the eye to pick up the shape of the letter. Piquant in little amounts, sanserif in page-size sheets repels readership as wax paper repels water; it has a sleazy, cloudy look."

Some art directors use copy as the raw material for designing queer shapes, thus making it illegible.

In a recent issue of a magazine I found 47 ads with the copy set in *reverse*—white type on a black background. It is almost impossible to read.

If you have to set *very long* copy, there are some typographical devices that increase its readership:

1. A subhead of two lines, between your headline and your body copy, heightens the reader's appetite for the feast to come.

2. If you start your body copy with a drop-initial, you increase readership by an average of 13 percent.

3. Limit your opening paragraph to a maximum of 11 words.

4. After two or three inches of copy, insert a crosshead, and thereafter throughout. Cross-heads keep the reader marching forward. Make some of them interrogative, to excite curiosity in the next run of copy.

5. When I was a boy, it was common practice to *square up* paragraphs. It is now known that widows—short lines—increase readership.

6. Set key paragraphs in bold face or italic.

7. Help the reader into your paragraphs with arrowheads, bullets, asterisks and marginal marks.

8. If you have a lot of unrelated facts to recite, don't use cumbersome connectives. Simply *number* them—as I am doing here.

Figure 15-3. Some principles of typography

9. What size type should you use?

<small>This is 5-point, and too small to read.</small>

This is 14-point, and too big.

This is 11-point, and about right.

10. If you use leading (line-spacing) between paragraphs, you increase readership by an average of 12 percent.

You may think that I exaggerate the importance of good typography. You may ask if I have ever heard a housewife say that she bought a new detergent because the ad was set in Caslon. No. But do you think an ad can sell if nobody can read it? You can't save souls in an empty church.

As Mies van der Rohe said of architecture, ''God is in the details.''

Figure 15-3.   Some principles of typography

Source: Adapted from ''Ogilvy on Advertising, Wanted: A Renaissance in Print Advertising,'' *Advertising Age*, August 1, 1983, p. M4ff. See also the book, *Ogilvy on Advertising* (New York: Crown Publishers, 1983), by the same author.

people and cost $150,000 or more. As suggested earlier, it begins with one person—the copywriter—but can involve significant creative inputs at the production stage as well. The two major tasks in television commercial production are filming and editing.

Filming generally is based on a storyboard and a list of specifications supplied by the advertising agency; a production house is the usual type of company involved in television commercial production. These are centered in large metropolitan areas such as New York, Chicago and Los Angeles, and many specialize in the business of producing television commercials.

Filming begins after all the necessary ingredients have been brought together. A director and/or producer will be assigned. A talent scout may be hired to interface with professional actors or actresses to be included in the commercial. A composer may be hired to develop an original score and musicians and singers to carry it out. The inclusion of a ''jingle'' in the commercial invariably leads to finding and using this type of talent.

The filming may be done in a fixed location studio. Often, however, it is necessary to move people and equipment to a location site where particular background scenes are called for—a forest, seaside cliffs, and so on. Filming is done in pieces and parts and later is put together and edited at the editing stage. The Green Giant commercial, for example, was made by building a Styrofoam model of a ''valley,'' superimposing animated characters, and then filming the feet and legs of a male model (the giant) standing over the whole thing.

In sum, producing a filmed (or videotaped) television commercial is a major complicated process. Even before filming starts, the producer using the storyboard guide and production notes (announcer preference, set sketches, ideas for props, musical requirements, and so on) gets involved in many activities. These include casting sessions to select the actors and/or announcer, set design sessions to work out exactly how the background will look, location discussions or trips to decide where the commercial will be shot, prop sessions to decide on various articles to be used, and arranging shooting schedules, recording sessions, and completion dates. All this must be done before filming begins, and these meetings are called "preproduction" meetings. Filming of individual scenes is usually not done in the sequence in which they appear in the final commercial. Also visual and sound tracks are usually not recorded at the same time.

Editing is required because much more footage is generated than is finally used. Several different camera angles will be shot, for example, to give the director some choice of the best possible ones to use. After the shooting begins, the film is quickly developed, often overnight, to provide rushes or dailies, which are hurried prints of inferior quality. These are used by the director to screen the preceding day's work, to select the best shots, and to decide whether further retakes are necessary before the set is torn down and the cast disbanded.

After the sound track is completed and the picture cut and edited, the two are combined into an answer print. There are usually several sound tracks, including the voice and music tracks, and often special sound effects tracks. A sound cutter "lays in" these tracks so they can be mixed. An audio engineer is then brought in to weave the various tracks together. An equally complicated series of editing operations takes place on the picture part of the track. When complete, it is brought together with the master sound track to produce the answer print. The whole process from storyboard to answer print usually takes seven to eight weeks. The answer print is used primarily to get agency and client approval. From it an appropriate number of release prints are generated and shipped to the networks and/or individual stations for broadcast. The release print is what is commonly referred to as the finished commercial. It is not uncommon to produce it in several versions, such as 15 seconds, 30 seconds, or 60 seconds, depending upon the media scheduling decisions. It is the release prints that are shipped to the broadcast media and aired.

The following section discusses the development of a new television commercial for American Express. The issues and complexities of television commercial production are nicely illustrated in this story. Note the importance given to minute details such as what the actor wears, the subtleties required in the father-son relationship, the 43 takes plus "dozens without sound," and the great stakes involved.

Behind the Scenes at an American Express Commercial*

The marketing executives from American Express Co. are unhappy. After months of research, prepreproduction meetings, preproduction meetings, casting sessions, budget audits, and other preparations for this moment, they arrive on location for filming of their television commercial—only to find the leading man wearing the wrong jacket.

In a big national ad campaign, little things like this count. "We believe that advertising is important enough that you want to get it right," says Diane Shaib, vice president for consumer marketing at American Express. For this commercial, getting it right is especially urgent: both the client and its agency, Ogilvy & Mather, have a lot riding on the outcome. American Express is eager to get more men in their twenties and thirties to sign up for its plastic charge card. Ogilvy needs to come up with a successful commercial after the failure of a recent string of American Express ads that the client pulled off the air.

*Mark N. Vamos. Reprinted from the May 20, 1985 issue of *Business Week* by special permission © 1985 by McGraw-Hill, Inc.

Both nervously await reaction to the 30-second ad, which cost about $100,000 and is now hitting the national airwaves.

Wardrobe Chaos.   Just days before the filming, the American Express marketers discuss the wardrobe with the agency. What will look more universal, they wonder—a blue blazer or a corduroy jacket? They are still pondering the question and leaning toward the blazer when they walk onto the set and find the actor wearing a dark corduroy jacket. Some of the scenes have already been shot, and the budget clock is ticking. Amid the controlled chaos of a commercial shoot, exasperation is rising behind polite smiles, urgent confabulations are held in corners, and higher authorities are summoned.

For more than ten years, American Express has been running its "Do you know me?" commercials, aimed at its traditional market: successful, older businessmen. Three years ago, however, AmEx decided to pursue the large number of younger women entering the work force and launched its "Interesting Lives" series. The first commercial, its "New Card" spot, showed a young woman taking her husband out to dinner to celebrate the arrival of her card, and it scored big. Women applied in droves. By last year, they held 27 percent of all AmEx green cards, up from 10 percent in the 1970s. The spot won awards and lavish praise for showing a strong, successful woman.

While that reaction startled American Express, subsequent audience research surprised the company even more. Instead of offending young men by showing a woman taking a man out to dinner, the commercial actually attracted them. "We're talking about three years ago—and markets outside of New York," says Shaib. "That's a bit shocking."

That's also when the trouble started. The company and its agency decided to extend the "Interesting Lives" campaign to attract young men by intention rather than by accident—in effect, to turn it into an all-purpose yuppie campaign. "The mission is to tweak their awareness of the card's appropriateness for them," says Shaib. Over the next three years, the company shot six new ads, but the only things they seemed to tweak were noses. One by one, as audience reaction arrived, AmEx pulled the ads. Two were so troublesome that they never even made it past the test-marketing stage. One showed a woman paying for dinner on a first date, the other a husband accompanying his wife on her business trip. Audience reactions included words such as "abrasive" and "castrating"—not exactly the message American Express wanted to convey. "It's very difficult these days to do ads with men and women as equals," sighs Kathleen O'Shaughnessy, a manager of marketing research at AmEx.

Early this year, the client and the agency agreed to try again, and Ogilvy wrote five new commercials. This time, however, AmEx decided to test the spots in rough form before any were produced, something it had not done before. Each ad was translated into color sketches that were transferred onto slides. Actors recorded the accompanying dialogue. With the roughs in hand, AmEx and Ogilvy headed into the field.

One-Way Mirror.   At 8 o'clock one evening in late February, nine men and a moderator sit around a gray conference table in midtown Manhattan. They are the targets of the campaign—young men who are eligible for an American Express card but haven't applied.

Each will receive $50 for participating in this focus group, the last of 11 such sessions held nationwide. Observing them from a darkened room behind a one-way mirror are 11 staffers from AmEx and Ogilvy, including account managers, researchers, and copywriters. Surprisingly, in a commercial aimed at men, all the observers are women.

Eugene Shore, a psychologist and president of Business Information Analysis Corp., a Pennsylvania research firm, shows the five rough commercials. He asks the focus group for comments and suggestions after each. Some win raves, others are panned. After one rough is shown, someone says, "If I saw this on TV, I'd just say, 'Boy, this is another one of those dumb commercials that make no sense.' "

Working with comments like these, the marketers have already narrowed the choice to two or three strong candidates, one of which is known as "Young Lawyer." It opens with father and son seated at a restaurant table. The dialogue concerns the son's career and how disappointed the father was when he didn't join the family law firm. But now that the son is "Mr. District Attorney," the father is proud of him. The son objects, saying he's only "an assistant to an assistant." He places his American Express card on the tray that the waiter puts on the table with the check. The father laughs, saying: "The pay must be getting better over at City Hall."

The lights come up, and Shore asks for reactions. "I feel this is pointed at the business community, because you have to be successful to have this card," says Stephen, an accountant. Tim, who works for a menswear designer, disagrees: "He says he's an assistant to an assistant. So maybe I can qualify." The women behind the mirror smile at this response. The line is a crucial one. To attract new cardholders, the commercial must convey accessibility—but not too much. The American Express card is prestige plastic. The ad can't make it seem as easy to get as MasterCard or Visa, which AmEx staffers contemptuously refer to as "shoppers' cards." As O'Shaughnessy, the market researcher, later puts it, "It's very difficult to communicate eligibility and at the same time maintain prestige. We're sort of talking out of both sides of our mouth."

"Too Northeast."   Over the next few weeks, Ogilvy staffers begin scouting locations for "Young Lawyer." They also hunt for a director with a flair for filming realistic dialogue. "This ad lives and dies on being able to cast two people who have believable rapport," says Ann Curry Marcato, the Ogilvy vice president responsible for producing the spot. And, Shore warns at the session, the father and son risk "coming across as WASP, bankclub, Harvard."

It is late March when the account management team from Ogilvy and two executives from American Express hold a preproduction meeting to go over the casting, wardrobe, location, and production schedule. That's when the problem of the corduroy jacket first surfaces. "The feedback we've been getting from the research is that the Midwest and West Coast don't respond because they read it as too Northeast," says K. Shelly Porges, director of special markets at AmEx. "Can we do something more cross-country?" Ogilvy's Marcato replies that the agency is aware of the problem, and the discussion moves to other topics.

Ed Bianchi, Marcato's choice for director, who once shot a Dr Pepper extravaganza set on a giant pinball machine, outlines his notion of how the commercial should unfold.

He plans to open with a wide shot, showing diners and waiters, and then cut to a close-up of the father and son. "We pick them out through the crowd so you really have the feeling of eavesdropping on them," he says.

Porges objects to opening with a wide shot crowded with 14 extras. "What makes this an interesting life, anyway? The quality of a relationship. What will a long shot add to that?" she asks. Paul Pracilio, a vice president and associate creative director at Ogilvy, replies: "We have 30 seconds to reach out of that tube and grab someone by the necktie. By cutting in to see them, it's a damn sight more exciting piece of film."

Happy Medium.   The discussion moves to the waiter who will bring the check. Since the ad must make the card seem upscale but still accessible, the waiter can't look as if he works at too ritzy a restaurant. "It must be above Brew Burger but below the 21 Club," says Porges. Director Bianchi suggests that the waiter appear early in the commercial, as the son is saying he's only an assistant to an assistant district attorney. "The action of the waiter bringing the check is a subtle hint of what this commercial is going to be about," he says. Porges objects again. "Because of the 'assistant to an assistant' line, the focus groups said, 'Gee, maybe I could get this card,' " she says. "Getting that part garbled would be disastrous to us."

Three days later, the film crew has converted Jerry's Restaurant in Manhattan into a madhouse. The sidewalk is a jumble of cables, reflecting panels, and tripods. In the dining room, 25 crew members mill about, carrying equipment and shouting. The father-and-son team sits at a table, repeating their lines. The entire commercial will be reshot from several angles, Bianchi explains, to give the editor the option of cutting from one perspective to another.

Representatives from Ogilvy and AmEx are at the back of the room, watching and making suggestions. Still more staffers are in another room, watching a video monitor. Director Bianchi calls for take after take. Frequently, a telephone rings or a bus rumbles past on 23rd Street, ruining the shot. For most of the takes, Bianchi sits next to the camera, his face pressed against the lens so he can see what it is seeing, and grins at the actors.

After 43 takes involving dialogue—and dozens more without sound—Bianchi is satisfied. But suddenly, he insists on one more close-up of the son pulling the charge card from his wallet. The executives from Ogilvy and American Express are crowded around a video monitor, staring intently as the image of the wallet fills the screen. The son's hand reaches over, pulls out the card, and pauses. It's a Visa card. Everyone laughs and goes home.

Tense Tryout.   A week later, the preliminary version of the commercial is ready. A dozen client and agency people sit in red bucket chairs in an eighth floor screening room at Ogilvy & Mather's New York office. Tension is in the air—not least because, after all the discussion of wide shots and extras, those scenes wound up on the cutting-room floor. "We were thrilled to find so much of the personality of the son and father coming through," Marcato explains as she introduces the commercial. "We thought that it would be strongest to stay up tight.'' The commercial is run several times. The ad seems a bit choppy, jumping from close-ups of the son to the father to the check to the wallet and, finally, to the card. The Ogilvy team waits for a reaction.

"I think you've captured them just as I always envisioned them,'' says Shaib, the AmEx marketing vice president. "But because of the number of cuts back and forth, I never feel like I'm intimate with them.'' She also points out that, with all the close-ups, the commercial never shows the father and son together. After some discussion, the Ogilvy representatives agree to reedit the commercial to include the wide shot that American Express had initially argued against.

AmEx executives say they are pleased with the final version, which includes the wide shot. All the research was worthwhile, they say, because it helped them avoid some pitfalls, such as making the father too stern or the son too wimpy. The father's line about his son's pay getting better, for example, was ultimately given to the son because some viewers saw it as a subtle putdown. Now, the marketers say, the father is distinguished but warm, and the son is the kind of likable but independent character with whom the target market can identify.

The ad, which first appeared on May 6, will run for six to eight weeks, after which American Express will assess its impact. The company thinks it has a winner, but there's one little thing that still bothers it a bit: the son is wearing a corduroy jacket.

THE CLIENT-AGENCY RELATIONSHIP

Selecting an Agency

Clients can begin an agency search for various reasons. First, they could put up their account for a "review," in which both the incumbent agency and invited new agencies could be asked to make presentations to retain or obtain the account. Such a review could be a regular periodic one, or be precipitated by some unhappiness with the quality of the creative work the client thinks it has been receiving from the incumbent agency, or be sparked by an unsolicited contact from one of the "new business" departments of a nonincumbent agency. Agencies often maintain special "new business" departments, with individuals (nicknamed "rainmakers") charged with the responsibility of getting new business. Sometimes the source of friction with the current agency could be a change in marketing strategy at the client, with a perception that the current agency is unable or unwilling to implement the new strategy. The dissatisfaction might be caused by poor sales or market share performance, or heightened competitive activity (leading to an agency change as a "quick fix"). Or it might be caused by disputes over agency compensation (sometimes initiated by the agency, which feels it is making too little money on the account). A frequent catalyst for change is the appointment of new marketing or advertising chief at the client, who brings a new perspective (and a different set of agency loyalties and contacts) to his or her new job (the "new broom" syndrome). Such personnel shifts are sometimes caused by a change in ownership of the client, such as merger or acquisition activity.[1]

New agencies making presentations often present speculative ("spec") campaigns, indicating what kind of campaign they would create if they had the account and demonstrating their knowledge and understanding of the client's business. The costs for researching, staffing, and creating these "spec" campaigns can run in the many hundreds of thousands of dollars; often, but not always, the client inviting the "spec" campaign will pay for part of these costs. Clients selecting a new agency are sometimes advised by one of several agency selection consulting firms. A study by Cagley showed that in making this selection, clients place high weight on the quality and number of people assigned to the account, their creative abilities, a perceived similarity of objectives and operating styles (including personal "chemistry"), the degree of understanding displayed by the agency of the client's business, the agency's reputation for integrity, the agency's reputation for making—and sticking up for—recommendations, and so on. Also important are the agency's size and stability, its servicing, strategic planning, market research and media buying abilities, and the compensation and cost-control aspects. Of course, the situational importance of these varies across clients and situations.[2] It is important to note at this point that a smart client will not simply select an agency that thinks exactly like the client personnel do, but rather will choose one that provides a complementary perspective.

Probably the most important aspect, however, is the absence of account conflicts. Clients will simply not give their account to an agency which already services a competitor—with the notion of a competitor sometimes being defined rather broadly (for example, Hallmark once switched its account from Young & Rubicam because Y&R had a part of the AT&T long-distance telephone account). The frequency of conflicts increases as the client business undergoes mergers and consolidations—we are rapidly reaching the stage where a handful of megacorporations in the consumer packaged goods fields have brands in almost every product category (e.g., Procter & Gamble/Richardson-Vicks/ Noxell, Philip Morris/General Foods/Kraft, Unilever/Chesebrough Pond's/Lipton, Nestlé/ Carnation, etc.). This tendency has accelerated as companies introduce more brands, in response to greater consumer segmentation. The agency response to such client consolidations has been to structure their agencies into "groups," with maximum autonomy: Interpublic, for example, operates as merely a "holding company" with three "autonomous" networks: McCann-Erikson, Lintas: Campbell-Ewald, and Lowe Partners. The idea is that a client should not object to another agency in the group having the account of a competitor, since there is no opportunity for the transfer of secrets across the agency groups in such a network, and no conflict of interest. Of course, this argument is not always successful.

The Ongoing Relationship: Making It Work

Once an agency has been selected, perhaps the most crucial aspect that can pull them apart is the perception on the client side that the agency is not contributing to the client's business growth. A client should not (and usually does not) hire an agency merely to support what the client thinks: the agency is being hired to bring its own unique talents and perspectives to the client's business, to do the kind of creative thinking that the client simply does not and cannot do in-house. A client who does not expect and reward an agency for fresh thinking is usually going to get terrible advertising.

However, the agency can only make such contributions if both the agency and client work hard to develop the right kind of relationship.[3] Good clients create a sense of partnership with the agency—sharing information, research, and sales data; trusting the agency; being honest with the agency; respecting the expertise of the agency; asking the agency to provide its best thinking and not to settle for safe and mediocre creative. Good clients ask for the agency to get totally immersed in the client's business (such as sales and factory visits) and make it easy and possible for the agency personnel to do so. The agency account executive should be expected to fight for the agency's recommendations regarding good creative, and not be a passive "yes-man" for the client. A good client does not treat the agency as a superior treats a subordinate, but rather as an equal partner, as a part of the client's own marketing organization. A good client treats the agency people with respect and does not squander the agency's resources through wasted motion. A good client accepts occasional agency mistakes—which will always occur—with good humor; an agency that never makes mistakes is probably not trying hard enough to be fresh in its creative product.

A key element of this relationship has to be the desire and willingness of the client to support creative work that is not simply "safe" but instead is bold and takes risks—as long as it is on strategy. This can happen only if the approval process is kept short and simple, without several layers of management, and without committees, each trying to rewrite the ad and nitpick different creative elements. The approval process needs to use, but not rely exclusively on, research, and the people making the approvals on the client side need to be trained to recognize and approve fresh but on-target creative work. A standard agency complaint is that most MBA brand managers are typically overly analytical, risk averse, and committee oriented and have little training in recognizing good creative work.[4] It is especially important that advertising not be written to please the client's top management only (and their spouses!). Such a process distorts the original vision of the ad and greatly hurts the morale of the creatives. The client should brief the agency clearly on what is required and obtain agreement—before creative work is done—on exactly what the ad is expected to shoot for. When the agency makes its presentations, criticism should be honest but not brutal; it should be constructive and tactful and depersonalized; it should focus not on the ad's elements but on failures to communicate the agreed-on strategy and message. Praise and reward should be often and plentiful (when it is deserved). The agency should be given the responsibility to take whatever decisions it feels are necessary to achieve its creative vision. While the client should ask for the best creative, the client also needs to stick, over the years, to an idea that is working, instead of asking for change for its own sake.

On the agency side, the agency needs to display a great ability to listen carefully to what the client needs are (including those needs and desires that are not fully articulated) and must appreciate the political ramifications of agency recommendations. Good creative ideas can come from anywhere—including the client—and the agency should be open-minded. The agency needs to take a leadership role in developing and pushing for high quality and bold creative work on the client's account. It is the agency's role to be intellectually honest, to be "of counsel," to offer an outside perspective that the client may not have. However, in standing up for what it believes is right, the agency should not be arrogant, and should not seek creative awards for their own sake but seek the kind of creative work that is appropriate to the client's strategic objectives. It is important that the agency not shuffle people—creative, account, and top management—from the client's account simply because it begins to take the client's business for granted. Great attention needs to be placed on creating and maintaining the chemistry and rapport in the day-to-day agency-client relationship.[5] Budgets, details and deadlines must be respected. There should be good communication with the client—clients hate unpleasant surprises!

One major source of friction in client-agency relationships is a client perception that the agency is charging costs unfairly[6] or is making too much money on the client's account. It is important for the agency not to treat the client's money wastefully, but it is equally important for the client not to nitpick on production and other expenses and to ensure that the agency makes adequate profit on the client's account. The basic compensation structures for an agency were discussed in Chapter 1; we will only repeat here that the trend is clearly away from the flat 15 percent commission on billings to a reduced commission, fee-plus-commission, or fee-only arrangements. The key idea, of course, is that an agency's compensation should match its work load. An agency that creates several campaigns for a client, or has to modify the ads frequently (as in an airline or retail account where prices change all the time), or does substantial new work on small-billing brands probably does not make enough money on a flat commission and deserves to negotiate additional fees. On the other hand, an agency that essentially does only maintenance work on long-running campaigns for big-billing brands should probably expect cost-conscious clients to negotiate lower commission rates with it. Fees and commissions both have advantages and disadvantages—while commissions are not tailored to the amount of work and can lead to agencies making biased recommendations on how much money the client should spend, fees can lead to too much client interference in agency operations, can lead to nitpicking and friction and can create a dangerous "meter-running" mentality in which the quality of work can get hurt. Many clients negotiate the right to inspect the agency's books annually for the client's account to see if it is making too much money on it.

More than the long-term compensation structure, it is the cost-plus expenses that the agency incurs on the client's account that are often the source of friction. Clients are usually accustomed to tight cost controls; many agency people, on the other hand, knowingly or unknowingly treat the client's money as someone else's money (which it is), money that can be freely spent. In this context, particular mention must be made of commercial production expenses. While it is true that these are usually very small proportions of a brand's overall budget—the brand may be spending $20 million, and three ads in the campaign may cost $450,000 to produce[7]—it is also true that ads are often produced to lavish production budgets, and this can breed resentment and a sense of wasteful spending in the client.

An ad's production costs go up when it requires a distant, high-cost shooting location, a high-priced director, expensive props, an expensive endorser, and when adhoc "on-location" changes are made in the ad, rather than in "preproduction" meetings.

Costs can be reduced by getting multiple bids from different production houses (which charge a 35 to 50 percent markup on their own costs) and by carefully scrutinizing every element of these bids, often with the assistance of consultants.[8] Here, it is important for the agency creatives to remember the cost implications when they write a commercial: the same message can often be communicated equally effectively at a much lower production cost (though it is also true that today's video-sophisticated consumers expect expensive, slick "production values" in today's TV commercials).

For example, consider the launch of a new type of motor oil, which (among other advantages) won't freeze at low temperatures. One possible ad in this situation might involve freezing a car in a block of ice, photographing it through time-lapse photography as the ice melts over 36 hours, then using special effects to show the motor oil's logo catching fire and the car bursting through an oversized paper logo, using expensive special effects photography. A second creative photographic possibility might be simply to open a commercial freezer locker to freeze a rose and an open can of the oil, then show a gloved hand squeezing the rose (which shatters) and then picking up the can of the oil (which pours easily). Clearly, the second ad will cost much less, yet be as effective. As the commercial production consultant Hooper White writes,[9] "production dollars are typed into the spot by the writer and drawn into it by the art director . . . cost control in production is a before-the-fact exercise . . . the most effective cost control is exercised by agency creative directors, not by outside consultants."

The Ongoing Relationship: Reviews and Audits

It is usually considered a good idea for the client to have a system of regular performance reviews, in which latent sources of dissatisfaction on both sides can be aired and, it is hoped, resolved. This way, if the agency's performance is unsatisfactory, the agency can take early remedial steps, instead of finding out by surprise one day that it has been fired. For example, if the client is unhappy with the quality of the creative output, the agency can bring a new creative team to work on the client's account, or have talent from the agency's other offices contribute ideas. This way, the client can get the fresh creative it wants, without sacrificing the entire, long-term relationship with its present agency. A set of criteria to be used in such audits has been proposed by Michell, consisting of a review of changes in the environment, of changes in organizational and individual relationships (communication, openness, and interpersonal styles, etc.).[10]

SUMMARY

Following the creative work on an assignment, and any advertising pretesting considered necessary, the ads have to be produced and sent out to the selected media to be "run." This production process involves various people, including many suppliers and vendors outside the advertising agency.

The production process differs by the medium involved. For print production, it involves typographers, engravers, and printing. The rough ad goes through actual typesetting of the verbal copy, photoengraving of the visual elements and the type, and the production of the plate or "mat" from which the actual printed copies will be run. For television production, it includes the casting of actors and actresses, the composing and production of music scores, the actual filming (using a director and support staff), and the editing and mixing of audio and video tracks. Such production usually involves the services of an external production house, selected after competitive bidding. Various "tactical" decisions made at this stage—the choice of exact typeface, the casting of key characters, the choice of musical elements—can have an enormous impact on the success of the actual ad.

Through this production process, and throughout the entire advertising planning and implementation process, the relationship between the advertising agency and the marketing client becomes vitally important. Clients select agencies that they believe have the talent, skills, experience, resources, insight into their businesses, and "personal chemistry" to service their needs effectively and to bring in a creative perspective that the clients themselves may lack. Avoiding client conflicts is a major criterion as well. Clients can get more from their agencies if they give them some creative autonomy, share information and objectives with them, treat them as partners in the entire marketing effort, and develop a fair and nondestructive ad approval process. Compensation and cost control are often sources of friction that need to be carefully monitored. The entire agency-client relationship should be carefully reviewed at annual (or other) intervals.

DISCUSSION QUESTIONS

1. In the American Express example in the chapter, should the client and agency really have been that concerned with the nature of the jacket worn by the actor?

2. Identify a television ad that you have seen recently that apparently required a huge production budget, and discuss ways in which the same creative idea might have been communicated as effectively without such expense.

3. If you were the chief executive officer of a corporation hiring an ad agency, how would you go about selecting one? What would you look for?

4. Why should a marketing company not simply produce all of its ads at an "in-house" agency staffed by company employees, to save money, rather than go to an outside agency that might cost it more money?

5. Describe three different compensation arrangements that might exist between a client and an agency, and discuss the pros and cons of each for (a) a large-budget advertiser and (b) a small-budget advertiser.

NOTES

1. Peter Doyle, Marcel Corstjens, and Paul Michell, "Signals of Vulnerability in Agency-Client Relationships," *Journal of Marketing*, 44(Fall) 1980, pp. 18–23.

2. James W. Cagley, "A Comparison of Advertising Agency Selection Factors: Advertiser and Agency Perceptions," *Journal of Advertising Research*, June/July 1986, pp. 39–43.

3. *Adweek,* "In Advertising, What Distinguishes a Great Client?" February 15, 1988, pp. 36–38, and *Marketing News,* "15 Ways to Use Your Ad Agency More Productively," March 18, 1983, p. 10–11.

4. *Advertising Age,* "Product Manager: Adman's Friend or Foe?" August 17, 1981, p. 43.

5. Daniel B. Wackman, Charles T. Salmon, and Caryn C. Salmon, "Developing an Advertising Agency-Client Relationship," *Journal of Advertising Research,* December 1986/January 1987, pp. 21–27.

6. Ibid., p. 25.

7. *Advertising Age,* "Spot Production Costs Drop 4%," October 26, 1987, p. 46.

8. *Advertising Age,* "Marketers Police TV Commercial Costs," April 3, 1989, p. 51.

9. Hooper White, "How to Raise Effectiveness, Lower Costs of TV Spots," *Advertising Age,* September 21, 1981, p. 64.

10. Paul C. N. Michell, "Auditing of Agency-Client Relationships," *Journal of Advertising Research,* December 1986/January 1987, pp. 29–41.

CASES FOR PART IV

PERDUE FOOD*

"It Takes a Tough Man to Make a Tender Chicken" was the theme of the advertising campaign developed for Perdue Foods, Inc., of Salisbury, Maryland, by its New York–based agency, Scali, McCabe, Sloves, Inc. The campaign often featured Mr. Frank Perdue, president of Perdue Foods, who had become something of a celebrity as a result in the New York market and elsewhere where the print and radio and TV ad campaign had been run. From an obscure position as one of several hundred companies raising broilers in 1968, Perdue Foods had become by the end of 1972 the largest producer of branded broilers in the United States, killing about 1.5 million birds each week, almost twice as many as when the new agency had acquired the account in 1971.

Such visibility attracted competitors as well as customers, and in February of 1973 a major competitor, Maryland Chicken Processors, Inc., launched a direct frontal attack on Perdue Chickens with ads in the New England trade press carrying the headline:

> Read how Otis Esham's Buddy Boy chicken is going to beat the pants off the other guy's chicken.

The "other guy," of course, was Frank Perdue, and the Buddy Boy trade ad even featured a back-of-the-head picture of Frank Perdue with the caption "the other guy." It was a no-holds-barred approach which made direct and frequent reference to Perdue chickens. For example, the trade ad began,

*This case was prepared as a basis for classroom discussion by Frederick E. Webster, Jr. Copyright © 1973 by the Trustees of Dartmouth College.

The other guy has been a friend and neighbor of ours for years, as well as a competitor.

To be truthful about it, our hat's off to him. In the past year or so, he's probably done more for the chicken business than any other guy we know.

With his help and the help of his fine New York advertising agency, the consumer is now beginning to realize that it's worth paying a few more pennies a pound to get the kind of fine, plump, golden-yellow chicken we produce down here on the Eastern Shore of Maryland.

What this means is that the days of footballing the price of chicken all over the lot are probably numbered.

The new name of the game is Profits, and that's not just profits for the chicken business but profits for you, too. So, as far as we are concerned, that other guy is doing a real good job.

But he's vulnerable.

The other guy is a spunky little guy (no offense intended, Frank) who loves to go on television and the radio and tell folks about the fine kind of chicken we produce down home.

You think those commercials are going to hurt us?

Uh-uh. They can't do anything but *help* us.

What those commercials are doing is making the consumer aware that a chicken that's good enough to carry the brand name of a proud producer is going to be a *better* chicken than the one that is only good enough to be acceptable to the U.S. government.

Well, the actual truth is, those commercials could just as well be talking about Otis Esham's fresh Buddy Boy chicken. Because Otis's methods of raising and processing chicken are just about identical to the other guy's.

Except for one very important thing and here's where we get to the part about how the other guy is vulnerable.

That was only the first of four columns in a double-page spread. The ad went on to say that "the other guy's" chickens are packed and shipped in ice and that as the ice melts "your chicken is going to begin to get all water-logged," whereas Buddy Boy chickens are quick-chilled to 30°F and shipped in refrigerated trucks. The ad reported that Purity Supreme, a major New England chain, had taken on the Buddy Boy product and that a "hot" Boston-based ad agency, Pearson and MacDonald, had been given the Buddy Boy account. The ad also featured pictures of Otis Esham (whose position was not disclosed[1]), Jack Ackerman, head meat buyer for Purity Supreme (with the caption "Jack Ackerman of Purity Supreme, a 'tough bird' "), Pearson and MacDonald, and a crate of dressed broilers showing the "old-fashioned 'ice-packed' method." The ad went on to explain that "By the time you're reading this, Otis Esham will be on the major Boston radio stations telling your customers about how his fresh Buddy Boy chicken is a better chicken because it's a chilled chicken." More information about media plans was given, and readers were given a telephone number to call collect in Parsonburg, Maryland, to talk with "Bubba Shelton, Otis Esham's right-hand man for sales."

An executive at Scali, McCabe, Sloves called this "one of the most blatant frontal assaults I have ever seen in advertising" as the account executive and top agency per-

[1]In point of fact, Esham was president of Maryland Chicken Processors, a family-owned business. Esham and Perdue had known each other all their lives; at one time they had owned abutting properties.

sonnel began to talk about their response. Three classes of action were being considered. Some favored simply ignoring the Buddy Boy campaign because "it can't hurt us, it can only help us." Others wanted to respond directly, with trade and consumer ads, to the charge that ice-packing was an inferior method and that chickens became "water-logged," because this was not true. A third group suggested that now was the time for an entirely new Perdue campaign to take the initiative away from Buddy Boy and go after entirely new segments.

Growth of Perdue Foods, Inc.

An article in *Esquire* magazine in April 1973 described chicken farming as "about the last free-enterprise industry in America. Chicken is produced in a no-holds-barred, rags-to-riches, no-control system, at the fascinating confluence of all the commercial strains in the land: the chicken is where the most volatile elements of the assembly line, of the farm and the field, and bid-and-ask all come together." Until 1968, Perdue was raising chickens for resale to other processors. In 1967, sales had been about $35 million, mainly from selling live birds, but the business also included one of the East Coast's largest grain storage and poultry feed milling operations, soybean processing mulch plants, a hatchery, and 600 farmers raising broilers under contract to Perdue.

A buyer's market existed in 1967, which had squeezed chicken profits. More and more processors were lining up their own contract growers and cutting out Perdue and other middlemen. As Frank Perdue noted, "The situation was good for processors. As in all commodities, profit depends on high volume and small margins. A processor's normal profit on chickens runs $\frac{1}{4}$ to $\frac{1}{2}$ cents per pound. But in 1967's market, processors were paying us 10 cents a pound for what cost us 14 cents to produce, and their profits were as much as 7 cents per pound.

As a result of these conditions, Frank Perdue decided to redesign his business to coordinate egg hatching, chick delivery and feeding, broiler processing, and overnight delivery to market and to develop his own brand. The aim was to develop a quality chicken that could demand premium prices. Special attention was devoted to development of exact feeding formulas which would optimize the chickens' growth rate and give the chicken a golden-colored skin preferred by consumers.

Over the next three years, Perdue began consumer advertising on a limited basis. Distribution was concentrated in New York, with a small percentage of other East Coast cities and as far west as Cleveland. The Perdue brand was identified by a tag on the wing of the processed chicken. Distribution was concentrated in butcher shops and smaller chain food outlets.

Perdue Advertising

As the new strategy of integrated production and profit differentiation began to prove itself in the form of increased sales and profit margins, Frank Perdue became increasingly concerned with the quality of his advertising. After a period of intensive reading on the subject and interviews with almost 50 agencies, Perdue selected Scali, McCabe, Sloves,

Inc., in April 1971. The agency immediately began to prepare for a major campaign to be launched in New York City in July. Over Frank Perdue's initial objections, the agency developed a campaign featuring him as the spokesman for the product.

The campaign focused on the quality of Perdue's product, often using subtle humor to make the point. The direction of the campaign is indicated in Exhibits 1 to 4, photo

---

EXHIBIT 1   Perdue Foods, Inc.

SCALI, McCABE, SLOVES INC.   TITLE: "MY CHICKENS EAT BETTER THAN PEOPLE"

CLIENT: PERDUE FOODS INC.   LENGTH: 30 SECONDS

PRODUCT: PERDUE CHICKENS   COMMERCIAL NO.: TV-PD-30-2C

1. FRANK PERDUE: A chicken is what it eats. And my chickens eat better than . . .

2. people do. I store my own grain and mix my own feed.

3. And give my Perdue chickens nothing but pure well water to drink.

4. That's why my chickens always have that healthy golden-yellow color.

5. If you want to eat as good as my chickens, you'll just have to eat my chickens.

6. That's really good.

EXHIBIT 2   Perdue Foods, Inc.

SCALI, McCABE, SLOVES, INC.
CLIENT: PERDUE FARMS   TITLE: "BUTCHER SHOP"
PRODUCT: CHICKEN   LENGTH: 10 SECONDS
                                                 COMM'L. NO.: TV-PD-10-9

1. FRANK PERDUE: I don't allow my superior chickens in just any store.

2. That's why you can only buy Perdue chickens in butcher shops and better markets.

3. I don't want to give my name a bad name.

EXHIBIT 3   Perdue Foods, Inc.

SCALI, M^cCABE, SLOVES INC.

CLIENT: PERDUE FOODS INC.

PRODUCT: PERDUE CHICKENS

TITLE: "CLEAN LIVIN' "

LENGTH: 30 SECONDS

COMMERCIAL NO.: TV-PD-30-3C

1. FRANK PERDUE: Nobody gets near my chickens unless they wear this fancy get-up.

2. This is not to protect people from my chickens.

3. It's to protect my chickens from people.

4. My competitors think I'm nuts to go through all this.

5. But why do you suppose my chickens always have that healthy golden-yellow color . . .

6. instead of a pale one. I'll tell you why. Clean livin'.

7. (SILENT)

---

boards of four TV commercials. Radio and newspaper advertising was also planned. A new wing tag was designed featuring the company name and a money-back guarantee of quality. In an early 60-second TV commercial, Frank Perdue made the following comments:

> When people ask me about my chickens, two questions invariably come up. The first is "Perdue, your chickens have such a great golden-yellow color it's almost unnatural. Do you dye them?" Honestly, there's absolutely nothing artificial about the color of my chickens. If you had a chicken and fed it good yellow corn, alfalfa, corn gluten, and marigold petals, it would just naturally be yellow. You can't go around dyeing chickens. They wouldn't stand for it.
>
> The other question is "Perdue, your chickens are so plump and juicy, do you give them hormone injections?" This one really gets my hackles up. I do nothing of the kind.

EXHIBIT 4   Perdue Foods, Inc.

SCALI, M^cCABE, SLOVES INC.

CLIENT: PERDUE FOODS INC.

PRODUCT: PERDUE CHICKENS

TITLE: "COMPETITION"

LENGTH: 30 SECONDS

COMMERCIAL NO.: TV-PD-30-5C

1. FRANK PERDUE: Knowing how good my chickens are isn't good enough for me.

2. So every week I have my people go out and buy cases of my competitors' birds.

3. We put them through the same rigid inspection that our own Perdue chickens have to . . .

4. go through. It costs me a lot of money. But it's worth it.

5. It's the only way I have of knowing that I'm ahead of these guys.

IT TAKES
A TOUGH MAN
TO MAKE
A TENDER CHICKEN.

PERDUE

6. How're we doing? Did we win yet?

When chickens eat and live as well as mine do, you don't have to resort to artificial techniques. . . .

In the first year with the new agency, all advertising expenditures were aimed at the consumer. Only after consumer awareness and preference had been created was trade advertising begun. By the end of the first year, Perdue had achieved distribution in more than half of all New York butcher shops and small retail food outlets. Consumer surveys showed well over 50 percent awareness of the Perdue brand. While financial information was not publicly available, Perdue said "you have to assume it paid off." Competitors estimated that Perdue's costs increased between 2 and 4 cents per pound due to promotional expenses. At the retail level, Perdue chickens were able to command a premium of 5 to 10 cents per pound. One out of every six chickens sold in the New York market carried the Perdue brand. Similar campaigns were launched in Hartford, Connecticut (March 1972), and Baltimore (April 1972). Sales in 1972 exceeded $80,000,000.

Perdue advertising attracted a good deal of public attention, partly due to the distinctiveness of Frank Perdue's presentation, which was described by one commentator as having the sincerity and fervor of a Southern preacher. Stories about the company and its advertising appeared in *Business Week* (September 16, 1972), *Newsweek* (October 16, 1972), and *Esquire* (April 1973), among other places.

The Boston Campaign

Perdue's Boston campaign was launched in December 1972, following the basic pattern now established. The Boston market was somewhat different from New York in that a high percentage of chicken sales occurred through chain store supermarkets, whereas in New York the majority was sold through butcher shops and independent food outlets.

Shortly thereafter, Otis Esham publicized his plans to advertise in Boston and even gave the exact dates on which consumer advertising would break. Perdue's immediate response had been to triple Gross Rating Points (GRP) TV and radio coverage and to contract for additional newspaper coverage on heavy food-buying days, in anticipation of Buddy Boy's campaign. Perdue's first radio ads ran on December 18 and TV ads began on January 15.

Now that Buddy Boy's first trade advertising had appeared early in February, executives at Scali, McCabe, Sloves were wondering what steps to take next. Esham was planning radio for the second week of February and TV was scheduled for the beginning of April. It would be possible for Scali, McCabe, Sloves to prepare television ads within 72 hours to refute the points about "water-logged" chickens in the Buddy Boy advertising.

A principal of Buddy Boy's agency, Terry MacDonald, was quoted as saying "We're going to kill them. They have brilliant advertising. But we have the product advantage."

Discussion Question

1. What action should Scali, McCabe, Sloves recommend to Frank Perdue?

LEVI STRAUSS & CO.*

Sue Swenson, a member of the research group at Foote, Cone & Belding/Honig, a San Francisco advertising agency, was reviewing four copy-testing techniques described in the appendix to Chapter 14. A meeting was scheduled with the Levi Strauss account group the next day to decide on which copy tests to employ on two new Levi's campaigns. The following week a similar meeting was scheduled involving a campaign for a new bar soap for another client. In each case the task was to determine which testing approach would be used to help make the final selection of which commercials to use in the campaigns. Sue knew that she would be expected to contribute to the discussion by pointing out the strengths and limitations of each test and to make her own recommendation.

Levi Strauss & Co. had grown from a firm serving the needs of miners in the Gold Rush era of the mid-1800s to a large sophisticated clothing company. In 1979 it had sales of over $2 billion drawn from an international and domestic operation. The domestic company, Levi Strauss USA, included six divisions: Jeanswear, Sportswear,

*Courtesy of Levi Strauss.

Womenswear, Youthwear, Activewear, and Accessories. In 1979, Levi Strauss was among the 100 largest advertisers, with expenditures of $38.5 million, primarily on television.

Concerning the Levi's campaigns, Swenson recognized that two very different campaigns were involved. The first was a corporate image campaign. The overall objective was to build and maintain Levi's brand image. The approach was to build around the concepts of "Quality" and "Heritage," the most meaningful, believable, and universal aspects of the Levi's corporate personality. Unlike competitors who claim quality as a product feature, Levi's 128-year heritage advertisements had an important additional dimension. More specifically, the advertising involved the following strategy:

1. *Heritage-quality*: communicate to male and female consumers, ages 12 to 49, that Levi's makes a wide variety of apparel products, all of which share in the company's 128-year commitment to quality.
2. *Variety-quality*: Communicate to male and female consumers, ages 12 to 49, that Levi's makes a wide variety of quality apparel products for the entire family.

Exhibit 1 shows one of the commercials from the pool that was to be tested for the corporate campaign.

The second campaign was for Levi's Action suits. In 1979, the Sportswear division responsible for Action suits spent approximately $6 million on network television commercials and co-op newspaper ads to introduce Actionwear slacks, which topped the sales of both leading brands of men's slacks, Haggar and Farah, in that year. The primary segment was middle-age males who often suffer from middle-age spread. Actionwear slacks, a blend of polyester and other fabrics with a stretchable waistline, were presented as a solution to the problem. The advertising objectives for the new campaign were guided by the following:

Focus: Levi's Action garments are comfortable dress clothes.
Benefits: Primary—comfortable
           Secondary—attractive, good looking, well made, long wearing
Reasons why:
1. Levi's Action slacks are comfortable because they have a hidden stretch waistband and expandable shell fabric.
2. Levi's Action suit jacket is comfortable because it has hidden stretch panels that let you move freely without binding.
3. The Levi's name implies quality and well-made clothes.

Brand character: Levi's Action clothing is sensible, good-value menswear manufactured by Levi Strauss & Co., a company dedicated to quality.

Exhibit 2 shows a commercial from the pool for the Levi Action campaign.

Swenson also knew that previous Levi's commercials had proved exceptionally memorable and effective, owing to their distinctive creative approach. In part, their ap-

EXHIBIT 1   A corporate commercial

LEVI'S® "ROUNDUP"

(Music) Yessir, this drive started over a hundred years ago, back in California.

Just a few head of Levi's Blue Jeans, and a lot of hard miles.

Across country that would've killed ordinary pants.

But Levi's? They thrived on it! If anything, the herd got stronger —and bigger.

First there was kid's Levi's. Ornery little critters...seems like nothing stops 'em.

Then there was gal's pants, and tops, and skirts. Purtiest things you ever set eyes on.

And just to prove they could make it in the big city, the herd bred a new strain called Levi's Sportswear.

Jackets, shirts, slacks... a bit fancy for this job, I reckon, but I do admire the way they're made.

Fact is, pride is why we put our name on everything in this herd.

Tells folks, "This here's ours!" If you like what you got, then c'mon back!

We'll be here. You see, fashions may change...

...but quality never goes out of style!

Courtesy of Levi Strauss & Co., Two Embarcadero Center, San Francisco, California 94106.

EXHIBIT 2 An Action Suit commercial

TV. 30 Sec.
Title: "Action Suit/Bus"

ANNCR: If a man's suit jacket fits
like a straight jacket . . .
WIFE: Hold on, Joe!
JOE: I can't raise my arms.

ANNCR: If his pants fit their worst
around his waist,
WIFE: Sit down.
JOE: I can't – these pants are too
tight.

ANNCR: Then he needs Levi's*
Action Suit . . . perhaps
the most comfortable suit
a man can wear.

ANNCR: The waistband strrrr-
retches to give more room
when you need it.

JOE: Comfortable.
ANNCR: The jacket lets you
move your arms without
binding.

JOE: I can sit.
OLD LADY: Hmmmmmmph!

JOE: I can stand, too.

ANNCR: Levi's Action Suit from
Levi's Sportswear.

Courtesy of Levi Strauss & Co., Two Embarcadero Center, San Francisco, California 94106.

---

peal lies in their ability to challenge the viewer's imagination. The advertising assumes that viewers are thoughtful and appreciate advertising that respects their judgments.

In preparing for the next day's meeting with the Levi account group, she decided to carefully review the notes on four copy-testing services prepared by a staff assistant at FCB/H (see Appendix, Chapter 14). The immediate problem was to decide which of the services to recommend for testing commercials from the two Levi's campaigns. She knew that similar issues would be raised in discussions with another of the agency's clients the following week concerning a national campaign for a bar-soap line extension. Positioning for the bar soap essentially involved a dual cleanliness-fragrance theme and a demonstration commercial focusing on these two copy points.

Discussion Questions

1. What copy-testing service or services should Sue Swenson recommend for testing the two Levi Strauss commercials?
2. What service or services should she recommend for testing the bar-soap commercial?

16

MEDIA STRATEGY: SETTING MEDIA BUDGETS

I know half the money I spend on advertising is wasted, but I can never find out which half.

John Wanamaker, founder of a department store

In our experience, 49% of the time TV advertising heavy-up plans successfully increased sales relative to a lower or "base" advertising weight level. In other words, [in these cases] brand sales showed a positive relationship to TV advertising spending.

George Garrick, of Information Resources, Inc., commenting in 1989 on the results of ten years of experience from BehaviorScan® field tests of TV advertising budgets

The amount of money spent on advertising varies widely among companies even within the same industry. For example, while Procter & Gamble was spending 11.8 percent of every sales dollar on advertising in 1989, Lever Brothers was spending only 8.1 percent, while Colgate-Palmolive was spending as much as 13.5 percent. In the retail industry, in that same year, while Sears spent 2.7 percent of sales on advertising and Penney's 2.5 percent, K Mart spent only 1.9 percent.[1] Furthermore, firms often change their advertising expenditures radically from year to year. What generates this wide variation in advertising expenditures among firms within the same industry and over time for the same firm? How do companies go about setting advertising budgets? How should they be setting or establishing their budgets? What set of models and techniques can be employed to improve their decision making? This chapter will be directed to these questions.

The importance of setting advertising budgets using careful analysis, rather than industry rules of thumb or "gut feel," cannot be overemphasized. Various studies have repeatedly shown that the average advertising elasticity—the expected percentage change in volume sales when the amount spent on advertising rises 1 percent—is small, about only 0.22 percent.[2] Clearly, this is only an average across brands, and ignores long-term effects, and has various other shortcomings as a measure of the value of advertising spending. However, it does suggest that at least some brands may be spending too much on advertising (while others may need to spend even more than they do now).[3] When you combine this observation with the fact that for many brands the advertising budget is the single largest discretionary expense, running into tens of millions of dollars, you should realize quickly that "fine-tuning" the advertising budget is an activity that is worth a fair amount of a brand manager's time.

MARGINAL ANALYSIS

The theoretical underpinning of an advertising-budget decision is based on economic marginal analysis and is easily expressed. A firm should continue to add to the advertising budget as long as the incremental expenditures are exceeded by the marginal revenue they generate (see Figure 16-1). As pointed out in Chapter 2, such a marginal analysis could theoretically be applied to the other components of the marketing mix as well, such as sales promotion, personal selling, distribution, and pricing. A resulting optimal expenditure level could then be obtained for each component, which collectively would be the marketing mix. If the sum of these expenditures exceeded the available resources, the marketing budget for each would have to be scaled down. Each area would be constrained on the basis of the marginal revenue generated by the last dollar in its budget. If, for example, the last dollar put into personal selling generated $2 of brand contribution, whereas the last dollar of advertising generated $3 of brand contribution, it would probably be desirable to shift money from personal selling to advertising. Of course, personal

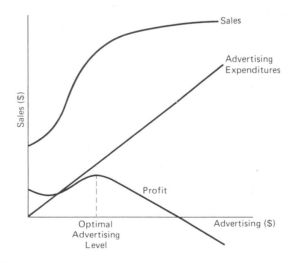

Figure 16-1.   Graph of sales, profit, and advertising curves used in marginal analysis

selling and advertising cannot absorb investments in small increments, but the principle of marginal analysis is still valid.

Some Difficulties in Applying Marginal Analysis

There are, unfortunately, some difficulties in applying marginal analysis in practice, as is the case with many other concepts from microeconomic theory. The assumption in the foregoing has been that it is appropriate to consider sales as a function of advertising expenditures, with advertising as the only input and immediate sales as the output. Such an assumption may be reasonable in some direct response advertising. However, in other situations, it is more tenuous. Even when it does seem reasonable, the determination of the shape and parameters of the response function (of sales, or contribution, responding to advertising) is no easy task. This will be clear when regression estimation techniques are presented in the latter part of this chapter. Furthermore, even when a certain response curve does accurately represent a certain situation, there is no guarantee that it will continue to be valid in the future. The conditions of the market, including the competitive environment, change. As a result, the nature and shape of the response function also can change.

The assumption that sales are determined solely by advertising expenditures is obviously faulty in practically all situations. The nature of the advertising campaign, the copy used, and the media selected will usually influence the shape of the response curve. A strong creative effort will evoke a different response than a tasteless, misdirected campaign, even if the same expenditure levels are involved. Indeed, tests by the Campbell Soup Company showed that the biggest sales-response changes can come not from varying how much advertising money you spend, but rather from where you spend it—the selection of target markets and media—and what you say in the ads (the message strategy).[4] Furthermore, it is difficult to sort out the effect of advertising from the effect of other forces that influence sales. Sales are, after all, a result of a company's total marketing and promotional effort as well as a number of environmental conditions, such as competitive actions and a host of economic, climatic, social, and cultural factors. If all factors including competitive activity remained constant except for advertising, it would be reasonable to consider advertising to be the only determinant of sales. The fact is, however, that such conditions do not hold in any real-world situation.

The dependent variable in the response function is sales—by implication, immediate sales. Although there are cases such as direct-mail advertising wherein the use of immediate sales is quite appropriate, in most instances there is a considerable lag between the time of the advertising and the time of the sales it might have helped stimulate. A consumer buying a car in June could have been affected by advertising for that car the previous fall. People may be affected by the reputation or image of a brand built up through advertising over a considerable period of time. Furthermore, advertising might attract buyers who become loyal customers for several years. Their immediate purchases may be only a small part of the value to the firm that enticed them to try the brand.

"Practical" Budget-Setting Analysis

There are, in general, two ways in which firms can react to the difficulty of determining the type of marginal analysis recommended by economic theory. They can, essentially, admit that the task is so formidable, at least given their expertise, that it is not worthwhile to pursue it and rely instead on other types of decision rules. Such rules may or may not reflect a marginal analysis. Some of these "decision rules" are discussed in the paragraphs that follow.

A second reaction is to attempt to determine a data-based "response function" (or graphical curve) relating advertising expenditure to sales, despite the difficulties. Once the shape of this curve is known, it can be used to determine the level of advertising that maximizes sales (or the profit contribution from sales). The argument is that, even if the result is imperfect, it might indeed provide some guidance, and the method at least has a theoretical basis. Furthermore, the exercise does not necessarily have to be expensive, so the risk is not excessive. The primary tools used in estimating such a response function are split-cable testing, field experimentation, regression analysis, and laboratory or field studies of the effects of increasing advertising frequency levels. These will be reviewed later in this chapter. (Another way of developing such a response function is simply to use managerial judgment, perhaps extracted with the assistance of a computer. Such techniques are sometimes labeled "decision calculus" techniques and are not described in this chapter because of their infrequent use).[5]

In the following sections, these two approaches will be more fully explored. Several frequently used "decision rules" used to set advertising budgets will first be examined. Then various attempts to estimate the response function using experimentation, regression analysis, and optimal repetition frequency analyses will be presented.

BUDGETING DECISION RULES

There are several "decision rules" on which many firms draw in making budget decisions.[6] Four such rules will be described. The rules are basically justified by arguing that budgets based on them are unlikely to be far from the actual optimal budget if a marginal analysis could be performed. In some cases, the rules are used in combination, the net budget being a compromise among several.

Percentage of Sales

One rule of thumb used in setting advertising budgets is the percentage of sales. Past sales or a forecast of future sales can be used as the base. A brand may have devoted 5 percent of its budget to advertising in the past. Thus, if the plan calls for doing $40 million worth of business next year, a $2 million advertising budget might be proposed. A similar decision could be based upon market share, or unit volume. For example, a brand could allocate $1 million for every share point it holds, or $2 for every case of the product it expects to sell.

The percentage-of-sales guide is the most common approach to setting advertising budgets. A 1981 survey of 55 of the 100 leading consumer advertisers found that over 70 percent reported using some version of the percentage-of-sales method,[7] as did a similar survey of 92 British companies.[8]

If a firm or brand has been successful over several years using the percentage-of-sales approach, it might be assumed that the decision rule yielded budgets reasonably close to the optimal, so there is little incentive to change to another approach in setting budgets. The rule does tend to make explicit the marketing mix decision, the allocation of the budget to the various elements of the marketing program. Furthermore, it provides comfort to a prudent financial executive who likes to know that her or his firm can afford the advertising. Finally, if competitors also use such a rule, it leads to a certain stability of advertising within the industry, which may be useful. If there is a ceiling on the size of the market, it is wise to avoid precipitating a war over advertising expenditures.

The major flaw in the method is that it does not rest on the premise that advertising can influence sales. In fact, sales or a sales estimate determine advertising expenditures. It can lead to excessive expenditures for large established brands and for over-the-hill brands that are basically servicing old loyal customers who will very likely continue to buy even if advertising support is withdrawn. It can, conversely, lead to inadequate budgets for promising healthy brands that could potentially become competitive with more advertising muscle.

The percentage-of-sales approach obviously needs to be modified in dynamic situations such as the following:

- When a brand is making a major repositioning move or reacting to one
- When a brand becomes established and dominant
- When a brand is just being introduced

Making a Move.   When a brand decides to make a move, a substantial increase in advertising might be necessary, an increase that may not be justified by the percentage-of-sales logic. For example, when Philip Morris purchased Miller beer in 1972 and initiated a campaign to reposition it and increase its share, the advertising budget was dramatically increased. Similarly, when the effects of the Miller effort became evident, the other beer companies had to consider breaking out of their percentage-of-sales routine and react to the Miller move.

Established Brand.   When a brand becomes established and dominant, it can usually start reducing the percentage of sales allocated to advertising. As brand name awareness becomes very high and the brand's image becomes very set, it is not usually necessary to advertise as heavily. Conversely, if a smaller brand is struggling to become known and is concerned about advertising at the minimal threshold level, it will often have to spend money at an artificially high percentage-of-sales level.

New Brand.   A new product, concept, or brand will have the special task of generating awareness and distribution from a zero level. As a result, it is usually necessary to make heavy investments in advertising during the first year or two of the brand's life. At Colgate-Palmolive, the guide is to base the advertising expenditures upon the total gross profit, which is the total sales less the product cost, as follows:[9]

- Advertising in first year equals twice the gross profit.
- Advertising in second year equals half the gross profit.
- Advertising in third and succeeding years equals 30 percent of the gross profit.

All You Can Afford

Firms with limited resources may decide to spend all that they can reasonably allocate to advertising after other unavoidable expenditures have been allocated. This rule usually ensures that they are not advertising too heavily, that advertising monies are not being wasted. It thus does have some logic. Of course, if the value of more advertising could be demonstrated, extra money could usually be raised, so the limitation may be somewhat artificial.

Some larger firms also use this rule. They start with the sales forecast and budget all expenditures, including profit, except advertising. The advertising budget is what is left over. About all that can be said about such a rule, which is actually used in too many situations, is that it generates a financial plan that usually looks neat and attractive in an accounting sense. However, it rests on the assumption that sales are independent of the advertising expenditures. There is no realization that advertising may influence sales. The only reason advertising is included is that its absence would be difficult to justify.

Competitive Parity

Another common guide is to adjust the advertising budget so that it is comparable to those of competitors. The logic is that the collective minds of the firms in the industry will probably generate advertising budgets that are somewhat close to the optimal. Everyone could not be too far from the optimal. Furthermore, any departure from the industry norms could precipitate a spending war.

The problem here is that there is no guarantee that a group of firms is spending at an optimal level. Insofar as their spending habits are constant over time, and assuming that market conditions change over time, they are probably not spending at the optimal level. Even if they are, it is likely that the situations of individual firms are sufficiently unique so that the practices of their competitors should not be followed. In particular, a new small firm in the field might not receive the proportionate amount of impact for its advertising that a large established firm receives. The success of the larger firm may be due to many other factors in addition to advertising. Furthermore, the method does not consider such questions as differences in effectiveness of various campaigns or the efficiency of media placement.

Objective and Task

Objective and task, more an approach to budgeting than a simple decision rule, is used by two-thirds of the largest advertisers.[10] An advertising objective is first established in specific terms. For example, a firm may decide to attempt to increase the awareness of its brand in a certain population segment to 50 percent. The tasks that are required to accomplish this objective are then detailed. They might involve the development of a particular advertising campaign exposing the relevant audience an average of five times. The cost of obtaining these exposures then becomes the advertising budget. This approach is logical in that it assumes that there is a causal flow from advertising to sales. In effect, it represents an effort to introduce intervening variables such as awareness or attitude, which will presumably be indicators of future sales as well as immediate sales.

The major problem with this approach is that the link between the objective and immediate and future sales is often not spelled out. Later in this chapter we will develop a framework for extending it in this direction so that it can indeed provide a logical, defensible basis for setting the advertising budget.

Budgeting Process in Large Firms

Figure 16-2 shows the organizational structure of a multibrand firm using a brand management system. Reporting to a marketing vice president are brand managers who are responsible for the profitability of the brand and managers of marketing functional areas such as sales, advertising, and marketing research. As mentioned in Chapter 1, some larger firms have added a layer of "category managers" to the decision-making process. Brand or category managers submit marketing plans, including an advertising budget, to the vice president of marketing, who must make investment trade-off decisions between brands and the marketing function programs. At some higher level these proposals must also compete with those from groups such as manufacturing and engineering. The whole process involves bargaining, persuasion, a fair amount of politics, and trade-off decisions.[11]

MARKET EXPERIMENTATION AND BUDGETING

A direct approach to estimating the sales response to advertising is to conduct field market experiments. Advertising expenditure levels are deliberately and systematically varied across areas. Sales changes are monitored through time, sometimes for several years, and related to advertising levels.

One of the best known sets of field experiments was conducted by Budweiser during the 1960s.[12] In one of its experiments seven advertising change treatments were used:

−100 percent (no advertising)
−50 percent
0 percent (advertising was unchanged)

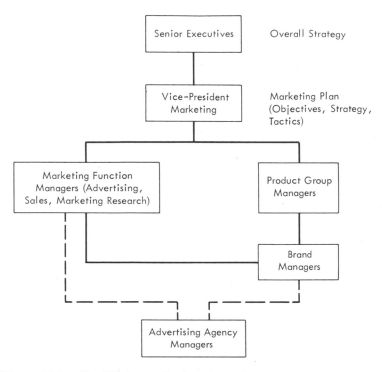

Figure 16-2. Simplified organization chart of a company employing the brand-management concept

+50 percent

+100 percent (the advertising expenditure was doubled)

+150 percent

+200 percent

Six marketing areas were assigned to each advertising treatment. The experiment ran for one year. Not only did "no advertising" result in the same sales level, but a −50 percent level actually resulted in a sales increase. One possible explanation was that there was a light-drinker segment for which reduced repetition was helpful. This experiment and others in the series resulted in substantial reductions in advertising expenditures, particularly on a per barrel basis, as Figure 16-3 illustrates.

Other published reports of advertising weight test experiments include a series of studies by the Campbell Soup Company, by the Defense Department for its Navy recruitment advertising, and by the Advertising Research Foundation for business-to-business advertising. During the period 1974 to 1979 the Campbell Soup Company conducted a series of advertising weight tests (as well as tests of creative strategy, media mix, and pricing) for V-8 cocktail vegetable juice.[13] It was found that a new creative strategy ("I could'a had a V-8"), when combined with a new media mix and a higher expenditure level, beat the old creative/media mix/spending level in being higher than the otherwise-

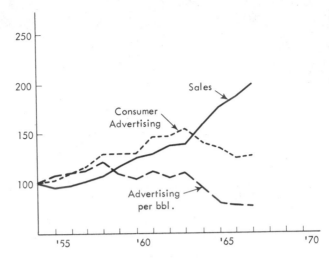

Figure 16-3.   Advertising and sales, Budweiser beer; index 1954 = 100

forecasted sales levels (as measured by warehouse withdrawal data, a gauge of sales into stores). Other tests, mainly involving Condensed and Chunky soups, Franco-American Pasta, and Swanson Frozen Foods, were also conducted; each lasted less than a year and used a small number of test markets (plus a matched control, "no change" market for comparison purposes).[14] Very few of these showed increases in advertising weight to "payout" in extra contribution, even when the advertising budgets were increased by 50 percent. However, once again, changes in creative strategy (such as pushing summer consumption of soups) and in media mix (trying to reach previously unreached consumers) were much more successful.

In trying to generalize from these Campbell Soup results, it is important to remember that these were old, well-established brands, such that it is very likely that their previous levels of advertising and brand awareness were likely to be close to "saturation" levels. Smaller, newer brands typically show a greater responsiveness to advertising weight increases than older brands, especially if the money is spent in geographical areas where market potentials are high but existing brand penetration is low.[15] However, it is still sobering to note that consumers do not respond swiftly to simply being told the same thing more often—it may be more fruitful to tell them something new and more interesting, and to tell it to people you haven't been telling it to before. The results of the Defense Department studies (conducted in 1978, over 26 media markets) also showed that Navy enlistments did not vary over a one-year experimental period when national Navy advertising was varied by amounts from −100 percent to +100 percent. However, variations in localized advertising, where copy was tailored to the individual market area, did make a difference.[16]

Finally, it is important to realize that such weight tests can be done for industrial (business-to-business) products as well. In a study conducted over the 1984–1986 period by the Advertising Research Foundation and the Association of Business Publishers, variations in the number of pages of advertising run for four industrial products were tested over a year.[17] Readers of controlled circulation business magazines in targeted customer companies saw ads for these products at three levels—low weight (under 8 pages), medium weight (e.g., 14 pages), and high weight (e.g., 28 pages). Obviously, these readers did not know of the variation in advertising weight; the sales and inquiries for these products from these companies were then related to the advertising levels. In general, the results confirmed that higher advertising did lead to more sales leads, more sales, and more profits, though the results took a while (four to six months) to emerge and did show a pattern of diminishing returns. It also appeared to be useful to increase advertising not only to the end users but also to the intermediary dealers.

Testing Advertising and Price

Sometimes it is useful to include marketing variables other than advertising in the experiment, particularly when the advertising response will depend on the levels of those other marketing variables. Eskin reports an experiment involving a new nutritional convenience food in which both advertising and price levels were tested.[18] A sample of 30 stores in each of four test cities was used. Two of the cities received a high advertising weight that was approximately twice that received by the other two cities. In addition, in each city the 30 test stores were split into three panels of 10 stores, each matched as to store size and other factors. Each of these matched panels received one of three price treatments: a base price below 50 cents, a price 10 cents above the base, and a price 20 cents above it. The test ran for six months. Each month the unit sales per store was measured. The experimental design is summarized at the top of Figure 16-4.

The results are summarized at the bottom of Figure 16-4. Clearly, the higher advertising was very effective when the base price was used. In contrast, increased advertising had almost no effect at the highest price. Prior to the test, the belief was that the best candidates for a national program were the combinations of high price and high advertising and low price and low advertising. The logic was that a high price was needed to provide margin to pay for the advertising. The test led to a very different conclusion, however—a low-price and high-advertising program.

In this case, the response to advertising depended upon the price level selected. If price had not been included in the experiment, a distorted impression might have emerged as to the advertising response. Inclusion of price, of course, also provided useful information about that marketing decision variable. In general, it is always very useful in an advertising field experiment to also measure the levels of other marketing variables that might impact on the sales results. The sales effects of such variables, called ''covariates,'' can then be statistically adjusted for in evaluating the effect of advertising weight (the ''manipulated variable'') on sales.

Problems with Market Experimentation

Experimental approaches are indeed useful as direct methods of obtaining information on sales-response curves. However, there are major problems associated with their use.

Test Design

Advertising:	Low Weight						High Weight					
	Market 1			Market 2			Market 3			Market 4		
Price:	Base	+10c	+20c	Base	+10c	+20c	Base	+10c	+20c	Base	+10c	+20c
N =	(10)	(10)	(10)	(10)	(10)	(10)	(10)	(10)	(10)	(10)	(10)	(10)
Month												
1												
2												
3												
4												
5												
6												

Total no. of observations = 720
Measure = total sales/per store/by month

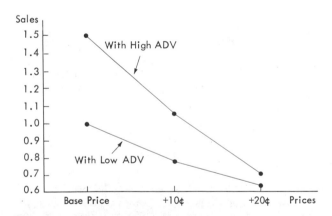

Figure 16-4.   An advertising and price experiment
Source: Adapted from Gerald Eskin, "A Case for Test Market Experiments, *Journal of Advertising Research,* 15, April 1975, pp. 29, 31.

Experimentation is inherently expensive. There are several types of costs to consider. First, there are the obvious direct costs of setting up the experiment and collecting and analyzing the results. Second is the fact that management decisions are delayed by the research. The researcher is often in a dilemma. On the one hand, validity considerations demand a longer experiment, often covering several repurchase cycles for the product. However, as the length increases, the timeliness of the results suffers. Furthermore, there is the very real likelihood that the situation will change (a major new product will emerge, for example) and the experimental results will not be applicable. Third, there is a security cost, particularly in new product contexts. Competitors will have access to the nature and results of your experiments. Finally, an advertising test will invariably involve excess advertising in some areas and less than optimal in others. The costs of either situation can be very significant.

Market experiments are never "controlled" as well as would be desirable; there are a litany of things that can "go wrong." The company's own sales force can work extra-hard during the test, making it difficult to draw conclusions about whether the source of the sales gain was the advertising weight change or the extra sales effort. The experimental cells can differ in more than just the amount of money being spent—the media mix and/or the creative might also vary, again making interpretation of test results difficult. Retailers can run out of stock because of logistical problems or because they did not anticipate the impact of more advertising. Distributors or retailers in "low advertising treatment areas" can mount their own advertising or promotion campaign to replace the national advertising being withdrawn. They are more concerned with their marketing position than with any experiment. Competitors' marketing efforts, including new product introductions, can confound the experiment. Further, competitors sometimes deliberately attempt to disrupt the test by radically changing some element of their competitive marketing strategy, such as their price or promotion effort.

Guidelines for Conducting Experiments

A list of guidelines for conducting experiments should include the following:

1. Use randomly selected control cities, areas, or stores so that the effects of advertising can be separated from all the other influences on sales. If possible, these control groups should be matched with the experimental groups on such dimensions as size, market share, or other sales-influencing variables (such as climate, in the case of soft drinks). For example, it would be useful to compare advertising levels across cities in which the advertised brand had comparable market share positions.
2. Use "before" as well as "after" measures. If sales as a result of the experiment can be compared with "last year's sales" or "last month's sales," the results will be much more sensitive. Sometimes it helps to compare sales after the experiment with the level of sales that would have been forecasted to occur if the experiment had not been run, using sophisticated forecasting methods that adjust for random and seasonal influences on sales, and so on.
3. Use substantial differences in advertising expenditures. Do not try to compare a 10 or 20 percent change in advertising; rather, look at 50 or 100 percent changes.
4. Test reduced advertising as well as increased advertising. The payoff at Budweiser was from the reduced advertising tests.
5. Control or at least monitor other variables that might affect the interpretation. For example, price or other marketing variables might be included in the experiment. Or the experiment might be repeated for large stores and small stores. Outside, uncontrollable factors—most notably, competitive behavior—should be monitored.

6. Make sure that the test is run for an adequate time. A full year is often required when a mature brand is involved. Not only does this provide data on effects on re-purchase (not just on initial trial), it also offers data on longer-term delayed, "carry-over" effects of advertising.

Split-Cable Testing

A relatively new and powerful technique for measuring advertising response is termed split-cable testing. Information Resources, Inc.'s (IRI) BehaviorScan is one of the several split-cable testing operations (SAMI/Burke and Nielsen being two others). Behavior-Scan maintains a 3,000-member consumer panel in each of nine cities (such as Pitts-field, Massachusetts, and Marion, Indiana). All panelists carry ID cards that they present to supermarkets and drugstores when buying. Their purchases are all monitored by IRI, as is in-store activity such as special prices, features, and displays. The panelists have a device connected to their TV set that allows BehaviorScan to monitor what channel is tuned and also to substitute one advertisement for another in what is called a "cut-in." Panelists are divided into groups of panelists who are indistinguishable except that they are exposed to different advertising. They live in the same neighborhoods and shop at the same stores. The advertising budget test simply involves setting the advertising ex-penditure (or weight) levels, assigning each to a group of panelists, and monitoring the results.

The ability to control exposure levels and to monitor purchase activity provides the potential to conduct experiments that, unlike field experiments, are tightly controlled. Since the same data source provides information on both advertising exposure and on ac-tual brand purchases, such data are often called "single-source" data, and this is a strong advantage. Further, access to shelf space is guaranteed, so there is little concern about distribution problems. In-store activities that can confound results are at least monitored. The tests are hidden from competitors, which reduces the chance of disruption. The exact number of advertising exposures is known. In a field test, even if the expenditure level were known, the number of exposures could vary enormously. Purchases can be moni-tored accurately on a daily basis. First (trial) purchases, repeat purchases, coupon re-demptions, and the time between purchases are all known.

Split-cable testing is certainly the state of the art and is undoubtedly the most ef-fective way to measure the response function. However, it is not without limitations. First, it is relatively expensive. The test itself will cost at least $100,000 and probably many times more in addition to the in-house cost of the advertiser and the agency.

Second, it is often necessary to run a test for at least six months and perhaps several years. The carryover impact can easily involve six or more purchase cycles, which can extend the test for a year. Further, the need to measure the impact on brand goodwill and loyalty may take longer to determine. In one test of a health care brand with a national budget of $15 million, it took two years before the sales of the low-advertising group, receiving the equivalent of a $10 million budget, declined.[19] After one year it was actually above the other group. With a lengthy test, there is always the danger that conditions may change making the results obsolete and outmoded.

Third, the experiments can actually be overcontrolled.[20] Since distribution is controlled, there is no measure of the ability of the advertising to influence distribution. Thus, effective advertising could easily affect the retailer's initial opinion and decision to stock the brand and the enthusiasm with which it is pushed. The retailers could be exposed to the advertising themselves, or they could be influenced by consumer reaction to it. Yet the split-cable tests really provide little information about such an impact.

Fourth, there is still doubt about the overall representativeness of the markets in which test market scanner data are available. While each service selects its test markets with care, and while tests are done on randomly selected consumers from within each test market panel, the fact remains that extrapolating to the entire United States from results based on a few test markets can be a hazardous undertaking.[21]

Finally, the tools are only now being developed to cope with, and analyze, the huge masses of data that single-source scanner data provide. Remember that every household is monitored for ad exposure every few seconds: a computer tape of data from these panels often contains literally millions of data records. Working with these data requires judgments on how to aggregate the information, across time periods, households, stores, brand varieties and pack sizes, and so on—and the results of the analysis often depend on the often arbitrary decisions on such aggregation. (Many analyses focus on effects on weekly sales at the store level.) We are only now learning how to work with such data, and they promise much potential.[22]

Despite these caveats, it is instructive to learn from the data base built up from Information Resources, Inc.'s BehaviorScan tests that about half (49 percent) of the 400 tests of increased advertising weight conducted by them between 1979 and 1989 showed a resulting increase in sales—more for new brands (59 percent of tests) than for old brands (46 percent of tests). The difference between new and old brands is even more striking when profit impact, rather than sales impact, is considered: 45 percent of the new brand tests "paid out" within a year, while only 20 percent of the established brand tests did so. However, when the cumulative profit effects into the second and third years after the test were also taken into account, the total profit impact almost doubles, and almost all the advertising tests that showed a significant sales effect also showed a significant profit effect.[23]

REGRESSION ANALYSIS FOR BUDGETING

Another approach to estimating the relationship between advertising and sales—the advertising-response curve—is to look at the historical patterns of sales and advertising. When advertising changed in the past, what happened to sales? Or if the advertising level differed in different sales areas, how did sales differ? Such an approach is relatively inexpensive, as it uses data in hand.

A systematic way to analyze such patterns is through the use of a statistical technique called multiple regression analysis. A typical regression model could attempt to predict sales in one time period with the following types of explanatory (or independent) variables:

- Sales in the preceding period
- Advertising in the current period
- Advertising in the previous period
- Advertising two periods back
- Other marketing variables, such as distribution or price, for this brand, as well as for competitive brands
- Some measure of the "quality" of the creative message (e.g., a copy-testing score)
- Measures of competitor advertising

Sales in the preceding period provide a measure of the existing market position that has probably been caused by the marketing program over a long period. Advertising nearly always has an impact in future periods, representing future purchase cycles. The inclusion of previous advertising expenditures thus provides an attempt to measure this carryover effect of advertising. The advertising response would be the sum of the current impact and the carryover effect. There are many statistical methods that attempt to capture this carryover effect, notably the use of the "Koyck" model (descriptions of which can be found in textbooks of econometric methods).

To isolate the impact of advertising spending it is necessary to include other marketing variables. First, it is useful (when possible) to try to separate the effect of advertising spending from the effect of copy quality. Second, it is important to include other marketing variables in the predictive model. Suppose, for example, that expenditures for sales promotion and advertising were potential causes of sales change. Unless such promotion was included in the model, the apparent advertising effect might really represent a promotion effect. Third, unless some measure of competitor advertising is also used, the apparent advertising impact may be distorted. An increase in advertising may have no impact on sales because competitor advertising increased dramatically. Without knowledge of competitor advertising, the advertising response might erroneously be thought to be low. One way of including competitive effects is obtain the actual figure for competitive advertising and include it as another independent (predictive) variable in the regression model. Another is to model this brand's market share as being dependent on its share of total category advertising (often called "share of voice").

One of the key problems facing the regression modeler is how best to model the "shape" of the relationship between advertising and sales—while typical regression computer programs assume a straight-line relationship between advertising and sales, this relationship is most often a curved, or "curvilinear," one. For instance, the responsiveness of sales to advertising may begin to decline after some level of advertising spending. This "diminishing returns" phenomenon is then better represented by a "downward-sloping" curve, in a graph where advertising levels are related to sales results. Alternatively, some modelers prefer to assume that the relationship is actually "S shaped:" in the beginning, when advertising budgets are low, sales do no not respond at all to advertising. Then we see a point of "increasing returns," as sales really begin to respond to increased advertising, as the ad budget exceeds some minimum "critical level" threshold. Finally, the curve begins to slope downward again, as once again the "diminishing returns" phase appears. Figure 16-5 depicts these three kinds of relationships. Statistical analysts attempt to capture these "nonlinear" (curved) possibilities in their regression models by predicting the log (or some other "transformation") of the sales figures by the log (or some other "transformation") of the advertising spending figure. Most studies of the shape of the actual advertising-sales relationship conclude that it is one of diminishing returns, though a few claim to find evidence of S-shaped relationships.[24]

Problems with Regression Analysis

Regression analysis is sometimes useful, but on the whole it has been disappointing. There are many problems associated with its use, so that this technique can either not be used at all, or requires the assistance of statistically skilled analysts. Perhaps the most difficult problem is to measure the carryover effect (which is also advertising's contribution to the brand's long-term equity or goodwill). The impact over one, two, or more periods simply gets swamped by all the other sources of sales variation.

There are several other difficulties associated with regression analysis modeling in general and with the problem of measuring the carryover effect in particular. Among them are the following

1. There is often little variation in advertising except that due to seasonable factors. Without variation in advertising it is not possible to detect the impact of changes in advertising on sales. This problem is severe when a brand is overadvertising and it is so far out on the advertising response curve that there is no response to any change in advertising. In that case an extreme drop in advertising would be needed to detect any response, and such a variation is simply not in the data.

2. The data may be faulty. For example, accounting sales data will represent shipments to retailers and not consumer purchases in response to advertising. Syndicated store movement data overcome this problem but are expensive and available only to consumer products firms. Accounting advertising data similarly represent billings by an

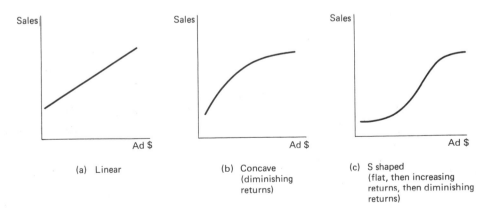

Figure 16-5. Three views about the advertising-sales relationship

agency and not exposures to ads. In fact, it is difficult to get any accurate measure of advertising exposures. Note further that any analysis of sales and advertising data covering a time period spanning several years needs somehow to adjust for inflation in media costs over time, as well as the changing population sizes that led to the sales figures. This sometimes leads to regressions in which per capita sales figures are predicted by inflation-adjusted media dollars.

3. Data describing other marketing variables are often not available or are expensive to obtain. Data describing competitor activities are rarely available.

4. Annual data really are inadequate since the immediate and carryover effect of advertising usually occurs in months, not years. In fact, statisticians have found that if the product is one that is bought frequently, say, every few weeks, then regressions using annual sales and advertising data can yield very misleading results. It is usually better to perform the analyses on "disaggregated" data, covering small units of time (such as months or quarters) and to do them separately for geographical markets that might show different relationships between advertising and sales.[25]

5. If a business uses the percentage-of-sales method of establishing a budget, a sales change could cause a change in advertising expenditures instead of the reverse (at least at the annual level). The nature of the causal relationship—advertising causing sales, or anticipated sales causing ad budgets—simply cannot be adequately disentangled by most regression analyses. This suggests that field or split-cable "weight test" experiments may be a better way of understanding how advertising affects sales, since a properly conducted experiment (one with a control group and with random assignment of test and control cells) permits causal conclusions.

STUDIES OF OPTIMAL REPETITION FREQUENCY

Yet another way to arriving at an advertising budget is to figure how many advertising exposures might be required per consumer to achieve the communications or advertising objective (the "frequency" needed per planning period—such as five exposures per four-week cycle). This can then be multiplied by the total number of consumers on whom that objective is sought to be achieved ("the reach" necessary, e.g., 10 million women ages 25 to 54). The product of these two numbers yields the total number of exposures necessary (in this case, 5 times 10 million, or 50 million exposures, per four-week cycle). This desired number of exposures can then be costed out, given a tentative media mix. For example, if it costs $25 to reach a thousand target women age 25 to 54 on prime time network TV (or about 2.5 cents per exposure), and $6 to reach them using daytime television (thus at about 0.6 cents per exposure), then a campaign split evenly between daytime and prime time TV would cost 1.55 cents per target exposure. (The data sources for such costs-per-thousand figures are described in the next chapter). For 50 million exposures every four weeks this would translate into $775,000 (50 million times 1.55 cents) every four weeks, or a little over 10 million dollars in media costs for a year of 13 such four-week cycles.

It should be immediately apparent that this is an extension of the "objectives and task" method of setting advertising budgets outlined earlier in this chapter. In the paragraphs that follow, we will describe further some research that is useful in answering the question of "What should be the appropriate frequency level?" As far as the target reach figures are concerned, these should be derived by working backward from marketing objectives involving incremental sales. For instance, if a packaged-goods company wished to sell another 10 million units of shampoo in the coming year, it might use previous research (or simply management's own judgment) to make the following series of calculations:

Need to sell an additional 10 million units of shampoo.

Every regular customer buys, on average, 10 units a year.

Therefore need to gain 1 million new regular customers.

For every person who becomes a new regular customer, need to get 2 to try our shampoo (i.e., we have a 50 percent regular repurchase rate among triers).

Therefore need to get 2 million new triers.

For every person who tries our brand, need to get 5 people to rate it as the brand of shampoo that comes first to mind (i.e., we have 20 percent trial among people for whom we are the shampoo brand that comes to mind first).

Therefore need to make 10 million target consumers have "top-of-mind awareness" of our shampoo.

The question that we are then faced, of course, is: How many exposures do we need to create (and maintain) such top-of-mind awareness, per four-week cycle or some other time frame, such as the purchasing cycle for that product? (In some other situation, we might be dealing with creating favorable attitudes rather than top-of-mind awareness, but the principle is the same.) We thus need to know something about how many exposures are necessary to lead to creating or maintaining awareness or favorable attitudes.

How Many Exposures?

Michael J. Naples, now president of the Advertising Research Foundation, conducted an extensive review of industry studies of repetition and concluded that, in general, around three exposures within a purchase cycle are about adequate to lead to or maintain the desired level of brand awareness or brand attitudes. Naples found that simply delivering one exposure to a target consumer within a purchase cycle usually was not enough; more than three exposures, on the other hand, usually led to diminishing returns, at least as far as recall was concerned. While this was an average tendency, smaller brands appeared to require (and benefit from) higher frequency more than larger brands did.[26]

Herbert Krugman, a General Electric manager and prominent advertising theorist, also suggests that a level of about three exposures is needed. He suggests that insights into the needed levels of repetition can be gained by considering the difference between the first, second, and third exposures.[27] In his conceptualization, there is no such thing as a fourth exposure.

The first exposure elicits a "What is it?" type of response. The audience member tries to understand the nature of the communication and, if possible, categorizes it as being of no further interest.

The second exposure, if not blocked out, produces several effects. One, particularly in television or radio advertising, is a continuation of the "What is it?" response. The first exposure may not have been adequate to gain an understanding of what it was. (In fact, some television copy-testing systems require at least two exposures for this very reason.) Another response is an evaluative "What of it?" response. The audience member will attempt to determine if it is relevant and convincing. The message will be evaluated. Associated with both responses could be an "Aha, I've seen this before" reaction.

The third exposure is basically a reminder in case the audience member has not yet acted on the message. Any additional exposure is just another third exposure, replicating the third-exposure experience. Thus, Krugman implies that only three exposures are required. However, it is not quite that simple, because some audience segments may, after the first exposure, screen the advertisement out until they are ready to process another exposure. This phenomenon is particularly prevalent in television advertising where there is low involvement. A potential purchase or a use experience may stimulate an audience member to be receptive to a second-exposure experience. As a result, several actual exposures might be needed before a "second-exposure" experience occurs. The effect of multiple exposures is not to generate a cumulative impact on an individual audience member, but to capture more second- and third-exposure experiences.

As a practical suggestion to General Electric managers, Krugman advised that they start with an objective of exposing two-thirds of their target audience at least twice and not more than four times per month. This advice is compatible with the concept that at least two exposures are needed and that any exposure over four is wasted since the second-exposure experience will have occurred for most of the audience.

A third source for a recommendation of using three or four exposures per planning cycle is the fact that this is the most frequently used level of "effective frequency" used by advertising agencies.[28] The concept of "effective exposure" was put forth in 1977 by advertising researcher Alvin Achenbaum.[29] In essence, the idea is that there is a minimum threshold of necessary exposures, below which the connection between the message and the consumer is simply not established strongly enough. Below this "effective frequency" level, therefore, exposures are wasted; people reached with less than this number of exposures—typically, but not always, three or four exposures per purchase cycle—have not been "effectively reached." Advertising agencies make widespread use of the "effective frequency" concept.[30]

While the concept of "effective frequency" is concerned most about the *minimum* level of exposures necessary, the concept of "wear-out" is concerned with the *maximum* number of exposures that should be used for any particular ad execution in a certain period of time. ("Wear-in," in contrast, is concerned with how soon a message makes its initial impact.) Wear-out occurs when successive exposures no longer have a positive impact on the audience. Indeed, the marginal impact can turn negative. The determination of the optimal frequency thus involves an understanding and an ability to predict when wear-in and wear-out will occur.

One of the first psychologists to study wear-out empirically was Ebbinghaus.[31] In a series of experiments reported in 1902, he related retention to repetition. He had a single subject (himself) learn a series of nonsense syllables by oral repetition. He found that diminishing returns set in as the number of repetitions increased. Since that time wear-out has been documented in a variety of field and laboratory studies by psychologists and advertising researchers. As repetitions build, advertising researchers have found that attention to the commercial, recall of the copy points, awareness of the advertised brand, brand attitude, and purchase intention will build, then level off, and ultimately decline.

One explanation for the wear-out phenomenon is that the audience stops attending to the advertising.[32] They may feel that they have already absorbed the information, or they may become bored. One study found that exposure repetition ultimately generated a significant decline in brand-name recall, but that this decline could be reversed when attention to the advertisement was experimentally induced.[33]

Another explanation of wear-out is that excessive exposure generates irritation. The audience, which accepts advertisements as a necessary part of print or broadcast media, may resent being exposed to the same advertisement many times. Psychologists Cacioppo and Petty monitored people's verbalized response to a persuasive written communication.[34] They found that the production of support arguments increased and then decreased with exposure. The number of negative thoughts, however, declined after the first few exposures but then increased as repetitions mounted. To combat wear-out, then, it is necessary to attempt to reduce inattention/boredom and irritation and/or to maximize the degree of "learning" from the ad that continues to occur despite repeated exposure.

One approach to fighting wear-out is to provide advertisements that reward the audience in some way. Information that is valued (features of a personal computer) could be provided. Humor can stimulate attention and liking (but it should be noted that humorous ads can wear-out even faster than straight ads, if consumers get tired of the jokes). Entertainment value can also come from creative approaches using music, dancing, action, or drama, and any of these can forestall wear-out. In fact, there is research to suggest that "emotional" ads wear-out less quickly than more "rational" ads, and that more "complex" ads wear-out more slowly than simpler ads that are "learned" very quickly. The exact pattern of wear-out is complex, depending on the measure being tracked (recall? attitudes?), the type of the ad, the spacing (timing and distribution) of the exposures, and so on.[35]

Wear-out can also be combated by spacing commercial exposures over time and by running multiple executions of the same campaign theme. Another one of the findings of Ebbinghaus was that spaced repetitions were more effective than the same number massed together.[36] Calder and Sternthal conducted an experiment involving three commercial exposures embedded in a one-hour adventure show in up to six sessions.[37] The pronounced wear-out found was substantially reduced when the advertising consisted of three commercials rather than a single one. When multiple media are used, variety is naturally introduced, which again will allow a higher level of repetition.

When Is More Frequency Needed?

Clearly, the research-based recommendation just made—that three or four exposures per four-week cycle is often appropriate—is an "average"; some situations call for more, others for less. The research on wear-in and wear-out provides some insights into the nature of the situations when higher levels of frequency may be justified. Higher levels of frequency may be warranted when the message is more interesting, such as with new brand launches, new messages, new ads; when the message is more complex; and when the message is more reliant on moods or imagery for its effectiveness. The level of frequency should be less when nothing new was being said, when a simple message was being put across, and so on. In particular, advertising that aims to develop associations between the brand and feelings, activities, or people will require more repetition than advertising that is designed to communicate information. Transformational advertising (advertising to transform the use experience, discussed in Chapter 7), for example, can require heavy repetition that continues over years or even decades. Such advertising fortunately is often entertaining and/or well liked, and thus heavy repetition involving multiple campaign executions and variations can be tolerated. Research also shows that messages that are better at generating recall, or more persuasive, are "received" by consumers faster, thus necessitating lower advertising spending.[38]

Batra and Ray, in a laboratory experiment, argued and showed that both wear-in and wear-out occur faster when the consumer has a higher level of involvement in the product category and/or knows more about it. In such situations, the consumer extracts information from the ad in earlier exposures, so that later exposures are essentially "wasted" as far as the advertiser is concerned. More exposure does not lead to more favorable attitudes—in fact, it may even lead to a downturn in such attitudes, since the highly involved consumers, having already learned what the ad has to say, may now find it irritating and tiresome. When the consumer is less involved or less knowledgeable, however, higher levels of repetition are warranted, since they do lead to increasing attitudes and purchase intentions.[39] A graph from their study is presented in Figure 16-6.

The complexity and size of the communication and persuasion task will also affect the repetitions needed. For example, a task that involves establishing a new brand name and communicating a complex new service will undoubtedly require heavy repetition as well as multiple executions. Another of the classic Ebbinghaus findings was that as the number of items to be communicated increased, the number of repetitions necessary to attain a certain level of learning also increased.[40]

Ostrow, a senior advertising executive with Young & Rubicam, suggested that heavier repetition would be required when[41]

- A new brand is involved.
- A smaller, less well-known brand is involved. A dominant brand will need less frequency because it will already have a high level of recognition and acceptance.
- A low level of brand loyalty has been achieved. A brand with a high level of purchase loyalty and attitude commitment will require less repetition.

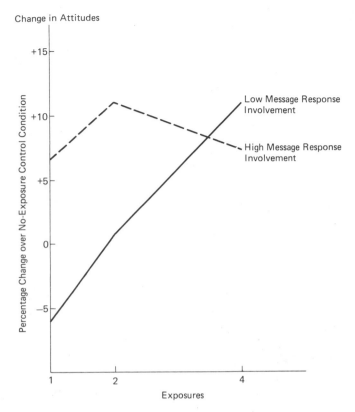

Figure 16-6.   Effect of repetition frequency on attitudes as a function of involvement level

Source: Batra and Ray, *Identifying Opportunities for Repetition Minimization,* Marketing Science Institute, Cambridge, Report No. 84-108, 1984.

- The purchase and use cycle is relatively long. Products with short purchase and use cycles generally need more repetition.
- When the target audience is less involved and less motivated to process the information or when it has less ability to process it (because of a lack of background information or because of a lack of mental skills).
- When there exists a great deal of clutter to break through. Of particular importance is the level of competitive advertising. It may be necessary to increase repetition to break through the presence of competitor advertising.

In defining what the optimal frequency level should be for a particular brand, it makes most sense to perform analysis on the sales history for that brand, perhaps using single-source scanner data. One such recent analysis in Britain found, across 15 frequently purchased packaged goods (such as coffee, tea, detergents, margarine, and cereals) that a frequency of four or more exposures per four weeks seemed to make sense.[42] It should always be remembered in such analyses that if diminishing returns set in after the consumer has *viewed* four exposures, the advertiser may need to actually schedule and run two or three times that many—actual viewing (what the research talks about) and "opportunities-to-see" (what advertisers actually pay for) are two different things.

Using these guidelines, then, an advertiser can determine what an appropriate level of frequency is, for the brand being considered. When combined with a level of target reach that makes sense from a marketing point of view, this can lead to a "bottom-up" estimate of the advertising budget required. Either this method, or the use of split-cable or field experiments, or of regression, should yield an estimate of an ad budget that makes more logical sense than the other decision rules discussed earlier in the chapter—though the latter are clearly easier to use, and thus used more in practice.

SUMMARY

The theoretical underpinning of the advertising budget is based on marginal analysis and is easily expressed. A firm should continue to add to its advertising budget as long as the incremental expenditures are exceeded by the marginal revenue they generate. The determination of the functional relationship between advertising expenditures and sales, which is at the heart of marginal analysis, is most difficult for several reasons. First, the assumption that advertising expenditures affect immediate sales is often faulty. Second, the determination of the shape and parameters of the relationship is no easy task. Finally, the relationship changes through time.

Practical decision makers, in response to the problems of marginal analysis, have used several decision rules. The most widely used approach, which bases the advertising budget on some "percentage of sales," can lead to excessive expenditures for well-established brands and inadequate expenditures for new and promising brands.

Setting ad budgets requires determination of the sales response to advertising. One approach is to conduct field experiments by varying advertising levels in different test stores, cities, or areas. Field experiments encouraged Budweiser to reduce advertising in the 1960s. They tend to be costly both in money and time. Further, many factors can confound or mask the results, such as actions of retailers and competitors, the inability to deliver precise levels of advertising to test cities, and the impact of other marketing variables.

Another approach is split-cable testing, wherein advertising seen by matched panels of consumers is controlled and their purchases are monitored via store scanner systems. Split-cable testing scores high on validity and control but is fairly expensive, provides little information of the impact of the advertising on retailers, and can take from six months to two years, depending on the difficulty of measuring long-term effects.

A third approach, regression analysis, works with existing data and is thus inexpensive. However, it too has its problems, because of the lack of variability of the advertising data, the lack of data on confounding factors such as competitor actions and other marketing variables, the arbitrariness of the aggregation decisions necessary, the difficulty of measuring the long-term impact of advertising, and others.

Advertising budgets can also be based upon an analysis of how many advertising exposures might be required per consumer to achieve the communications objective—a modified "objective and task" approach to budget setting. The key is to determine how many exposures are needed. A frequent rule of thumb is that three or four exposures per purchase cycle are needed in most contexts. However, this is only an average. In specific situations the maturity of the brand, the involvement level of consumers, the need to avoid wear-out, the complexity of the communication task, and the nature of associations being created, and other factors are needed to decide the optimal frequency. This can then be used, along with a reach target, to determine total budget needs.

DISCUSSION QUESTIONS

1. At the chapter outset, some large advertising expenditure differences were observed between firms in the same industry. Why?

2. In Figure 16-1, why is the sales curve S shaped? Explain the gradually accelerating section on the lower half of the curve and the flattening out section on the upper half. Discuss the significance of this shape from the viewpoint of (a) a company, (b) an industry, and (c) the economy as a whole.

3. What is the percentage-of-sales budgeting approach? Why is it so widely used? Under what circumstances might it be inappropriate? Why?

4. What assumptions underlie the "all-you-can-afford" and "competitive-parity" approaches to setting advertising budgets?

5. Contact someone in a firm that does a significant amount of advertising. What advertising budget-setting decision rule do they use? To what extent is the budget decision arrived at by the "bargaining process" referred to in connection with Figure 16-2?

6. Design a field experiment that would provide input data for the sales response to advertising function for a company selling men's razor blades. How much would the experiment likely cost? Identify other variables that might affect sales in your chosen test markets. What is the role, if any, of "laboratory experimentation" in this context?

7. Repeat question 6 for a company selling technical instruments used in scientific laboratories and hospitals. How would the design differ? Should "industrial marketing" companies attempt to identify sales-response functions in connection with their advertising activities?

8. Which kinds of firms are likely to invest in advertising and sales experiments? Why are experiments used infrequently? What are the problems and limitations of experiments? Why are experiments involving tests of reduced advertising expenditures so rare?

9. Suppose that you were a brand manager and had developed an experiment involving four Midwest test cities in which four levels of advertising expenditure were used over a six-month period. The resulting sales were compared with the sales during the same six months of the previous year. During your presentation to top management, you run into two challenges. First, the executive vice president claims that the budget levels suggested by the model will not apply to your campaign in the East because response to advertising is different in that part of the country. Second, the advertising manager claims that the new campaign will have a much higher response than previous advertising and consequently the model output is of no relevance. How would you respond to these questions?

10. What are the two most important attributes of a split-cable test? In what sense might a split-cable test be overcontrolling? Under what circumstances would you worry about such a problem? What are the other disadvantages of split-cable testing?

11. What is the difference between a marginal analysis and a regression analysis?

12. Why might a regression model fit the data better if the log of advertising expenditures is used as the independent variable instead of the advertising expenditures?

13. Why would a regression analysis of a three-year sequence of monthly advertising expenditures and market share of a detergent be a less sensitive and valid way to determine advertising response than an experiment?

14. Suppose that you are attempting to get housewives to try your new gourmet vegetable dish and have divided housewives into two groups—those interested in kitchens and those not so interested. Using your own subjective reasoning, estimate the probability of each group's trying the product after zero, one, three, five, and ten advertising exposures during a three-month period.

15. How might that repetition function in question 14 be affected by whether the ad was in color, whether it used short or long copy, and in what vehicle the ad appeared?

16. What are the factors that should contribute to wear-out? Illustrate your answer with specific examples of commercials that you can recall. What are some ads that you have not tired of even though might have seen them 50 times? And which ones have you come to hate when repeated? Why?

NOTES

1. *Advertising Age,* September 26, 1990.

2. See David A. Aaker and James M. Carman, "Are Your Overadvertising?" *Journal of Advertising Research,* 22, August/September 1982, pp. 57–70, and Gert Assmus, John U. Farley, and Donald R. Lehmann, "How Advertising Affects Sales: Meta-analysis of Econometric Results," *Journal of Marketing Research,* 21 (1), 1984, pp. 65–74. The 0.22 figure comes from Assmus et al.

3. For a debate on the value of looking at such elasticities, see Simon Broadbent, "What Is a 'Small Advertising Elasticity?" *Journal of Advertising Research,* August/September 1989, pp. 37–39, and accompanying articles.

4. J. O. Eastlack, Jr., and Ambar G. Rao, "Advertising Experiments in the Campbell Soup Company," *Marketing Science,* 8(1), Winter 1989, pp. 57–71.

5. For descriptions and applications of decision calculus advertising budgeting models, see John D. C. Little, "Models and Managers: The Concept of a Decision Calculus," *Management Science,* 16, 1970, pp. B466–485; John D. C. Little, "BRANDAID: A Marketing Mix Model, Part I: Structure," *Operations Research,* 23, 1975, pp. 628–655; and Amiya Basu and Rajeev Batra, "ADSPLIT: A Multi-Brand Advertising Budget Allocation Model," *Journal of Advertising,* 17(1), 1988, pp. 44–51.

6. For some recent studies of how various advertisers set advertising budgets, see Colin Gilligan, "How British Advertisers Set Budgets," *Journal of Advertising Research,* 17, February 1977, pp. 47–49; Charles H. Patti and Vincent Blasko, "Budgeting Practices of Big Advertisers," *Journal of Advertising Research,* 21, December 1981, pp. 23–29; K. M. Lancaster and J. A. Stern, "Computer-Based Advertising Budgeting Practices of Leading U.S. Consumer Advertisers," *Journal of Advertising,* 12(4), 1983, pp. 4–9; and Nigel Piercy, "Advertising Budgeting: Process and Structure as Explanatory Variables," *Journal of Advertising,* 16(2), 1987, pp. 34–40.

7. Patti and Blasko, "Budgeting Practices of Big Advertisers."

8. Gilligan, "How British Advertisers Set Budgets."

9. Barbara Brady, June Connolly, Les Quok, Karen Wachtel, and Peter Weiss, "Bright 'N Soft," Unpublished paper, 1979.

10. Patti and Blasko, "Budgeting Practices."

11. Piercy, "Advertising Budgeting: Process and Structure as Explanatory Variables."

12. Russell L. Ackoff and James R. Emshoff, "Advertising Research at Anheuser-Busch, Inc. (1963–68)," *Sloan Management Review,* Winter 1975, pp. 1–15.

13. Joseph O. Eastlack, Jr., and Ambar G. Rao, "Modeling Response to Advertising and Pricing Changes for V-8 Cocktail Vegetable Juice," *Marketing Science,* 5(3), Summer 1986, pp. 245–259.

14. Eastlack and Rao, "Conducting Advertising Experiments in the Real World," "The Campbell Soup Company Experience," 1989.

15. Ibid.

16. V. P. Carroll, A. G. Rao, H. L. Lee, A Shapiro, and B. L. Bayus, "The Navy Enlistment Marketing Experiment," *Marketing Science,* 4(4), Fall 1985, pp. 352–374.

17. Michael J. Naples and Rolf M. Wulfsberg, "The Bottom Line: Does Industrial Advertising Sell?" *Journal of Advertising Research,* pp. RC4–RC16.

18. Gerald J. Eskin, "A Case for Test Market Experiments," *Journal of Advertising Research,* 15, April 1975, pp. 27–33.

19. Reg Rhodes, "What AdTel Has Learned," Paper presented to the American Marketing Association's New York Chapter, March 22, 1977.

20. Paul W. Farris and David J. Rcibstein, "Overcontrol in Advertising Experiments," *Journal of Advertising Research,* 24, June/July 1984, pp. 37–44.

21. *Adweek's Marketing Week,* January 23, 1989, p. 24.

22. *Adweek's Marketing Week,* January 23, 1989, p. 24.

23. George Garrick, "Properly Evaluating the Role of TV Advertising," Paper presented at the Advertising Research Foundation 35th Annual Conference, New York, April 1989.

24. Julian A. Simon and Johan Arndt, "The Shape of the Advertising Response Function," *Journal of Advertising Research,* 20 (4), 1980, pp. 11–28; Robert L. Steiner, "The Paradox of Increasing Returns to Advertising," *Journal of Advertising Research,* February/March 1987, pp. 45–53; and John D. C. Little, "Aggregate Advertising Models: The State of the Art," *Operations Research,* 27, 1979, pp. 629–667.

25. A. G. Rao and P. B. Miller, "Advertising/Sales Response Functions," *Journal of Advertising Research,* 15, 1975, pp. 82–92.

26. Michael J. Naples, *Effective Frequency: The Relationship Between Frequency and Advertising Effectiveness* (New York: Association of National Advertisers, 1979), p. 79.

27. Herbert E. Krugman, "What Makes Advertising Effective?" *Harvard Business Review,* March/April 1975, pp. 96–103.

28. Kent M. Lancaster, Peggy J. Kreshel, and Joya R. Harris, "Estimating the Impact of Advertising Media Plans: Media Executives Describe Weighting and Timing Factors," *Journal of Advertising,* 15, September 1986, pp. 21–29, 45; and Peggy J. Kreshel, Kent M. Lancaster, and Margaret A. Toomey, "How Leading Advertisers Perceive Effective Reach and Frequency," *Journal of Advertising,* 14 (3), 1985, pp. 32–38, 51.

29. Alvin Achenbaum, "Effective Exposure: A New Way of Evaluating Media," Address before the Association of National Advertisers Media Workshop, New York, 1977.

30. For further references on the effective frequency concept, see Peter B. Turk, "Effective Frequency Report," *Journal of Advertising Research,* April/May 1988, pp. 55–59.

31. Hermann Ebbinghaus, *Grundzuge der Psychologie* (Leipzig: Viet, 1902).

32. Bobby J. Calder and Brian Sternthal, "Television Commercial Wearout: An Information Processing View," *Journal of Marketing Research,* 17, May 1980, pp. 173–186.

33. Charles S. Craig, Brian Sternthal, and Clark Leavitt, "Advertising Wearout: An Experimental Analysis," *Journal of Marketing Research,* 13, November 1976, pp. 365–372.

34. John Cacioppo and Richard Petty, "Effects of Message Repetition and Position on Cognitive Response, Recall and Persuasion," *Journal of Personality and Social Psychology,* 37, January 1979, pp. 97–109.

35. For a review, see Cornelia Pechmann and David W. Stewart, "Advertising Repetition: A Critical Review of Wearin and Wearout," *Current Issues and Research in Advertising,* Vol. 11, 1978, pp. 285–329.

36. Ebbinghaus, *Grundzuge der Psychologie.*

37. Calder and Sternthal, "Television Commercial Wearout."

38. Margaret Henderson Blair, "An Empirical Investigation of Advertising Wearin and Wearout," *Journal of Advertising Research,* December 1987/January 1988, pp. 45–50.

39. Rajeev Batra and Michael L. Ray, "Situational Effects of Advertising Repetition," *Journal of Consumer Research,* 12, March 1986, pp. 432–445.

40. Ebbinghaus, *Grundzuge der Psychologie.*

41. Joseph W. Ostrow, "Setting Frequency Levels: An Art or a Science?" *Journal of Advertising Research,* 24, August/September 1984, pp. I9–I11.

42. Phil Gullen and Hugh Johnson, "Relating Product Purchasing and TV Viewing," *Journal of Advertising Research,* December 1986/January 1987, pp. 9–19.

APPENDIX

A MODEL OF ADAPTIVE CONTROL

A model that uses experimental data as an explicit input to the budget decision was developed by John D. C. Little, a professor at MIT.* It recognizes that the relationship between advertising and sales changes over time with changing market conditions. As a result, the advertising budget decision should be updated accordingly.

*John D. C. Little, "A Model of Adaptive Control of Promotional Spending," *Operations Research,* 14, November–December 1966, pp. 175–97.

The adaptive-control model starts by assuming a response curve and finding an optimal level of advertising expenditure, as in Exhibit 1. If the decision maker were confident about an estimate of the response function and if he or she believes it would not change over time, the problem would be solved. However, under more realistic conditions, it becomes desirable to obtain more information about the response curve. In particular, it is worthwhile to experiment by advertising at nonoptimal levels in a few test markets to gain such information. The new information from the experiments is added to the existing information on the sales response function to determine the current optimal advertising expenditure rate.

EXHIBIT 1   Sales experiment

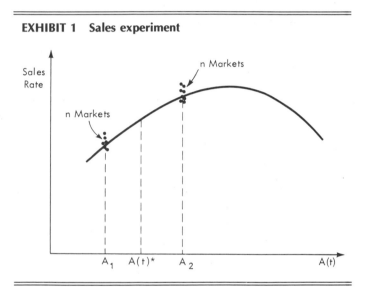

Assume that the advertising sales response function can be described by a specific mathematical function such as the following quadratic function:

$$S(A) = \alpha + \beta A - \gamma A^2 \tag{1}$$

where $S(A)$ = sales

A = advertising expenditures

α, β, γ = parameters

The first two terms in equation (1) represent the familiar straight-line, linear relationship. The third term adds a curvature. An example of equation (1) is the upside-down "U" shown in Exhibit 1.

If M is the gross margin of the product, then profit, P, will be

$$P = MS(A) - A \tag{2}$$

The value of advertising expenditures, $A*$, that will maximize equation (2) can be found graphically or algebraically.[1]

Little has argued that the optimal advertising rate is relatively insensitive to γ as long as the parameter is set within reasonable bounds. Thus, Little assumes that γ is known and constant. He argues, however, that β is not likely to stay constant through time. Changes in competitive activity, product changes, changes in the quality of advertising, or shifts in economic conditions can result in changes in response β.

Exhibit 1 shows the nature of a sales experiment to derive estimates of β. It assumes at a particular time, t, the advertising rate $A(t)*$ is considered to be optimal. All markets with the exception of a set receiving a lower rate, A_1, and a set receiving a higher rate, A_2, are subjected to this level of advertising.[2] The sales rate in the groups of markets at A_1 and A_2 provides information from which a revised estimate of the parameter β can be derived.[3]

Little compared the results of a computer-simulation version of the adaptive-control model with four other modeling alternatives. The model compared particularly well when contrasted with the results of assuming a constant advertising rate. These comparisons can be made by calculating how much the loss in profits would be in each case relative to having perfect information on the respective functions. In one case of assuming a constant

---

[1]Substituting equation (1) into equation (2) yields

$$P = M\alpha + M\beta A - M\gamma A^2 - A$$

Taking the derivative of P with respect to A and setting it equal to zero,

$$M\beta - 2M\gamma A - 1 = 0$$

Solving for A.

$$A* = \frac{M\beta - 1}{2M\gamma}$$

[2]The optimal gap between A_1 and A_2 and optimal number of test markets to use can be calculated. See Little, "Model of Adaptive Control," pp. 128–130.

[3]Letting S_1 and S_2 be the observed mean sales rates in the groups of markets at A_1 and A_2, respectively, the experimental mean for (t) can be calculated as follows:

$$\hat{\beta}(t) = \frac{1}{A_1 - A_2} (\bar{S}_2 + \gamma A_2^2 - \bar{S}_1 - \gamma A_1^2)$$

The β to be used in determining the budget for the next time period, $t + 1$, is termed $\beta(t + 1)$. It is a weighted average of the β used in the current time period $\beta(t)$ and the estimate of β obtained from the experiment, $\hat{\beta}(t)$.

$$\beta(t + 1) = a\beta(t) + (1 - a)\hat{\beta}(t)$$

Thus, the decision rule defining the advertising rate in the next time period, $A(t + 1)*$, is

$$A(t + 1)* = \frac{M\beta(t + 1) - 1}{2M\gamma}$$

If the experiment were very accurate, a small value of a could be used and heavy reliance placed on the current experiment. If the accuracy of the experiment were low, a large value of a would be appropriate. In this case, the current rate would depend mostly on the rate used in the preceding time period, which in turn represents a summary of all past experience up to that time.

rate, for example, losses amounted to 28.7 percent compared with only 1.5 percent for the adaptive-model formulation.

This model illustrates, among other things, the advantages of attempting to make objective measurements of relevant parameter values through experimental procedures and stresses the importance of repeated measurements. It is above all based on a recognition that an advertising manager faces a constantly changing environment and that he or she must adapt both plans and budget to the changing conditions. Many companies in effect are continuously experimenting and engaging in these types of marketing research studies, even though they may not be guided by formal decision rules. Although such research is bound to be costly, the effort is often worthwhile. The adaptive-control model provides an approach to answering the question of how much should be invested in such research, as well as how much to invest in advertising at any particular time.

17

MEDIA TACTICS: ALLOCATING MEDIA BUDGETS

But do the people in Maine have anything to say to the people in Texas?
Mark Twain when informed that the telegraph
cable had been stretched all the way from
Maine to Texas

Once the decision has been made on how much money to spend in an advertising campaign—using the approaches discussed in the last chapter—the next class of decisions has to do with how that money should be spent. Should we spend more of the money in television or magazines? Within magazines, should we advertise in *Cosmopolitan* or *Vogue*, or both? Should a two-page advertisement be used or would a single-page advertisement be better? Should our television spot be in prime time or during daytime programming? Should it be 15 seconds or 30 seconds? Such questions need to be addressed in the development of the media plan, the focus of this chapter.

The media plan identifies and details the media schedule that is to be used. A media schedule specifies how the media budget is to be spent. Although the level of detail of a media schedule can vary, it can include the specification of up to four types of media factors:

1. *Media class*: a type of medium, such as television, radio, newspapers, magazines, billboards, and direct mail.
2. *Media vehicles*: provides the immediate environment for the advertisement. For example, within the media class of television there are various vehicles, such as NBC News and ABC's "Monday Night Football," and within the media class of magazines there are *Esquire, Time, TV Guide,* and *Vogue.*
3. *Media option*: a detailed description of an advertisement's characteristics other than the copy and the artwork used. It specifies, in addition to the media vehicle, such advertisement characteristics as size (full page or half page), length (15 second or 30 second or 60 second), color (black and white or four color), or location (inside front cover or interior location).

4. *Scheduling and timing*:   how media options are scheduled over time. Among the strategy alternatives are (a) *flighting*, periods of total inactivity; (b) *continuous*, advertising spread evenly through time; and (c) *pulsing,* a continuous base augmented by intermittent bursts of heavy advertising. Timing decisions include the selection of specific issues (the August 17 issue of *Time)* or time slots (the second World Series game).

The media schedule will at a minimum specify the number of planned insertions in each media vehicle. A more detailed media schedule also specifies the other details of a media option, such as size or length and the timing of the advertisement insertions. For example, one media schedule might include ten network commercials on daytime television and two advertisements in *Time, Women's Day,* and *Newsweek* all in the first quarter of the year. A more detailed media schedule might specify 60-second commercials and two-page advertisements and that all the advertising was to be placed during the first week in February.

Even for small media budgets there can be literally thousands, even millions, of possible media schedules from which to choose. The task is to select a media plan from this set that will be relatively effective. In making this selection the media planner will usually first select a limited set of media possibilities. From this set the planner will then attempt to develop and evaluate a limited number of media schedules, often using computerized media models as well as judgment. Finally, once the media plan is completely specified, the desired media time (or space) must be bought and prices negotiated with the media owner. This process is also briefly discussed at the end of the chapter.

The selection of the most effective media schedule is based upon both quantitative and qualitative criteria. That is, the media planner attempts first to ensure that, for the available budget, the advertiser is obtaining the maximum number of advertising exposures—to the target segments—at the lowest possible cost. Such analysis requires working with huge masses of data on the audiences of the media vehicles and the costs involved in using these vehicles. Computer programs are often used to assist in such quantitative analyses. After this number-crunching, however, qualitative judgments have to be applied as well, for a computer cannot completely take into account the qualitative aspects of a particular media buy (for example, the "excitement" value of running a TV ad on the Super Bowl telecast). In addition, judgments also have to be applied in running the computer programs, in determining what these programs should attempt to "optimize," such as the desired level of exposures (frequency) and the number of people potentially exposed to the message (reach). These principles, and this process, will be discussed in this chapter, and then illustrated in the context of a media plan of The Broiler.

MEDIA CLASS DECISIONS

The first media allocation decision, that of allocating the budget over various media, is one that is made on both quantitative and qualitative criteria.

Quantitatively, data are collected on just how many people in the target market can be reached through that media class (such as radio, or newspapers, or daytime television).

The source of such data is often a source like Simmons or MRI (which are both described shortly). Radio, for example, is a terrific medium to reach business commuters through "drive-time" or to reach teenagers. Television's great strength is as a "mass medium," since it delivers very broad reach at low cost (per thousand people reached, not necessarily per television spot. While a single network prime-time 30-second spot can cost as much as $185,000, this is actually cheap on a per-person-reached basis, since that one single spot will be potentially exposed to almost 13 million homes.) While TV reaches mass audiences, magazines and direct mail are excellent in reaching narrowly defined target segments. Radio, too, reaches narrow segments—no single radio station usually has more than 2 to 3 percent of the audience in a market—and since the listeners of a particular radio station tend to be loyal, a radio campaign is useful in building high levels of frequency against them. Newspapers (and spot television) make geographical targeting possible.

Qualitatively, the most important considerations have to do with the "fit" between the medium and the creative execution. Television, because it can show action using both audio and visual, can make an impact that simply is not possible in other media. For some types of advertising, such as emotional or image advertising, or product demonstrations, this type of impact can be critical to the copy approach. On the other hand, television is a passive medium, and is not really suited to copy with high factual content. Neither is outdoor, which can only be used for name recognition purposes, since billboards cannot really communicate much information in the few seconds that they are viewed. Radio can involve the listener by getting him or her to use imagination to visualize stimuli (but radio ads still have much poorer recall than ads in other media, because of the higher clutter). Print, especially the magazine medium, is more suitable for long and complex messages. Magazines generally offer better color reproduction than newspapers. Because of their association with news stories, however, newspapers could have a sense of objectivity and a spirit of being current that could rub off on the advertisements in the right context.

A second set of qualitative criteria has to do with production logistics. Ads in network TV and magazines often require long "lead times"—they usually have to be submitted to the network or publisher weeks in advance of when they actually appear, making it difficult to use them in situations when the copy might have to be changed on short notice. Radio and newspapers are much more flexible on this score, and also have the advantage of lower production costs, so that they are frequently utilized by retailers, banks, airlines, and other businesses where rapid price changes need to be communicated at short notice. When news has to be communicated rapidly to a target market, broadcast media (TV, radio) and newspapers also have another relevant advantage over magazines or direct mail: while the former will reach their targets almost immediately (called a "fast cume"), the latter will take a while—often a couple of weeks—for their messages to get read and acted upon (a "slow cume").

A third set of qualitative criteria has to do with the competitive setting. Often, when faced with a high-spending competitor, it makes sense to use another medium than that used by the competitor, to avoid being "swamped" by the competitor's advertising. Alternatively, it may make sense to use the same medium, but to schedule one's own ads at a different time of year. Ultimately, the final choice of media classes involves reconciling these different quantitative and qualitative criteria, using managerial judgment.

MEDIA VEHICLE DECISIONS

The first consideration in making a media vehicle decision is simply the number of exposures that can be obtained, and for what cost. These quantitative considerations are later supplemented by various qualitative ones, such as the suitability of a particular editorial environment to a particular ad, which we shall discuss later in this section.

Media Terminology

Table 17-1 shows the type of information used by the media planners at the J. Walter Thompson agency in selecting magazines. The first column is the *unit cost* of a full-page color advertisement. The second column shows the total *audience* (also called *readership*), in millions, obtained by the magazine. Note that the total audience is much higher than the *circulation* because of the substantial numbers who read a magazine that someone else bought. The third column is the basic counting statistic, *cost per thousand* or CPM. It is the cost per thousand audience members. Thus, the CPM for *Good Housekeeping* is $1.20, which means that it cost $1.20 to reach 1,000 members of the *Good Housekeeping* audience. The circulation trend figure allows media planners to project the CPM number into the future. As a practical matter, there is a lag of several months and perhaps even a year between the media decision and the placement of the advertisements, so such trends can be significant. However, magazines will often guarantee a certain circulation level (called a *rate base*) and will refund part of the payment if the circulation does not achieve the guaranteed level.

It is, of course, of no value to obtain audience members if they are not exposed to the advertisements or the media options. It is advertisement exposures that are of ultimate interest, not vehicle exposures. If there is reason to believe that advertisement readership among some vehicles is higher than others, the basic CPM figures should be adjusted accordingly. In Table 17-1, the fourth column is an effort to measure page exposure. It is based upon the survey question, "How many pages out of ten did you open in this particular copy of the magazine?" The result is a crude indicator of page exposure as opposed to vehicle exposure. Sometimes a subjective opinion as to how seriously audience members look at the advertisements is helpful. Some magazines, for example, are actually bought by some because their advertisements provide information about home decorating, fashion, instrumentation technology, or some other specialized area of interest.

In buying television, the basic unit of counting is the *gross rating point* or GRP. A commercial's *rating* is the percentage of the potential audience (such as "all women aged 25–54") that are tuned in to the commercial. For a national buy, the audience could be all U.S. homes with television. (The number of *homes using television*, HUT, at any given time period is always smaller than the total number of homes with television, and is usually expressed as a percentage of the latter.) However, the concept of ratings will apply for audiences defined by region (the Los Angeles area) or by any other means (for example, adults from 18 to 35). If the commercial is associated with a program, its rating would be the rating of the program. If it is not associated with a program, it would be the

TABLE 17-1. Selecting Magazines

	Unit cost ($1,000s)	Total audience (millions)	Cost per thousand CPM[a]	Percent mag. exposed	Circulation		Target segment			In home		Target concern index	Compact. pages	Reader opinion	Other considerations
					PRESENT	TREND	%	MILLIONS	CPM[a]	% AUD.	CPM[a]				
Good House-keeping	$27.9	23.2	$1.20	62	5.6	+ 1%	21[b]	10.1[c]	2.74	57[d]	4.87[c]	123[f]	14[g]	91	Seal of Approval
Glamour	11.3	5.6	2.02	54	1.7	+ 4	6	2.9	3.88	41	9.46	NA	5	63	Pers. card
Cosmopolitan	13.0	7.5	1.73	63	1.9	+14	7	3.3	3.92	41	9.56	NA	NA	74	Singles aud.
Family Circle	36.0	18.9	1.90	66	8.3	+ 8	18	9.0	4.00	69	5.80	121	4	56	Practical
Woman's Day	34.9	19.2	1.82	67	7.9	+ 5	16	7.9	4.43	63	7.03	118	6	60	Practical
Redbook	26.2	13.7	1.91	66	4.8	– 1	11	5.5	4.79	58	8.26	136	0	79	Mommas aud.
Mademoiselle	7.5	3.0	2.50	58	.8	+ 1	3	1.5	4.95	35	14.14	NA	1	67	Pers. card
Parents	17.4	5.5	3.16	46	2.0	+ 1	5	2.4	7.25	60	12.08	130	10	74	Environment

Source: Adapted from "Numbers Aren't Everything," *Media Decisions*, 10, June 1975, p. 69.

[a] Cost per thousand.

[b] The percent of the target segment covered by the magazine.

[c] The number of the target segment covered by the magazine.

[d] The percent of the magazine's audience exposed in the home.

[e] Cost per thousand considering only the in-home audience.

[f] The extent to which the editorial content reaches out to the target segment.

[g] Compatible pages—the number of editorial pages devoted during the past year to the relevant subject.

502

average rating during that time period. The highest rated period is prime time, followed by the period just prior to prime time, termed the early fringe.

Just as any particular TV program has a rating, it also has a *share* of the total number of households watching any TV program during that time period. Thus, suppose that during the 7 to 7.15 time period last Thursday, 60 million TV sets were watching any TV program, of the 100 million TV households that could potentially be actually watching TV. Then the HUT for that time period is 60, or 60 percent. Suppose the TV program *Cheers* had, at that time, 20 million households tuned into it. Then the share for *Cheers* is 33 (20 million divided by 60 million), but its rating (expressed with respect to households) is 20 (20 million divided by 100 million). Mathematically, a program's rating always equals its share multiplied by the HUT.

To obtain total gross rating points for a media schedule, the ratings of the commercials are summed. For example, the following schedule in which a commercial is run 17 times in a one-week period yields 142 GRPs:

3 showings in a time slot with a 12 rating = 36 GRP

4 showings in a time slot with a 4 rating = 16 GRP

10 showings in a time slot with a 9 rating = 90 GRP

Total for the week = 142 GRP

The number of different people reached through this three-program media schedule depends on the *duplication* between the three programs. If there was absolutely no duplication, then the total ratings achieved would be 12 plus 4 plus 9, or 25, meaning that 25 percent of the target population would have seen the ad at least once. In reality, since we do have duplication, this total number of people exposed to the ad at least once will be somewhat less. If it was 25 percent, however, the average member of the audience will be exposed 5.68 times (142 divided by 25), although many, of course, will not be exposed at all and others will be exposed up to 17 times, since there are 17 potential opportunities to be exposed. (The concept of an *exposure distribution* will be explained shortly.)

One measure of the efficiency of a given program or time slot will be the *cost per rating point* (CPRP): cost per rating point = CPRP = cost of a commercial/divided by the rating points delivered by that commercial.

Reach and Frequency

At this stage it is appropriate to introduce the two most basic terms in media planning: *reach* and *frequency*. Reach refers to the number of people or households that will be exposed to an advertising schedule *at least once* over a specified period of time (usually, but not necessarily, a four-week time period). Very importantly, a person who sees the same ad twice (such as the people in our television example, who could have seen it up to 17 times) is not counted twice (or more), but just once. *Cumulative audience* is a more restrictive term, used to designate the reach of two or more issues of the same media vehicle—here the duplication being subtracted out is the "internal overlap" of people who see or read two issues or shows of the same media (such as reading two weekly issues of the same weekly magazine, or watching two weekly episodes of the same TV situation comedy). In such situations, the number of *new* (nonduplicated) readers or viewers picked up by the media vehicle in its second issue or show is called its *accumulation*. When the duplication being subtracted out is one between two or more different media vehicles—what one might call "external overlap," such as that between one week's issues of *Time* and *Newsweek*—the term *net coverage* is sometimes used as the relevant reach descriptor.

The term "reach" thus almost always refers to "unduplicated reach," net both of "internal" and "external" duplication. However, since in almost every media schedule there many people who see an ad more than once, frequency refers to the number of times someone sees the ad. "*Average frequency*" thus refers to the average number of times a person or household is exposed to a schedule. Thus, since GRPs refer to the total number of exposures delivered, and reach is the unduplicated number of people who got those exposures, GRPs equals the average frequency multiplied by the reach (where the reach is measured in terms of rating points).

In our television example earlier, our reach was 25 rating points (for the case of no duplication between the three TV programs), and our average frequency was 5.68, for the total figure of 142 GRPs delivered in that week. For a magazine buy, a schedule that bought one ad each in magazine A (readership of 28 million people) and magazine B (readership of 22 million people) would generate 50 million exposures (sometimes called *opportunities-to-see*, or OTS.). If 10 million of these people read both magazines A *and* B, we might have 10 million duplicated readers, or a reach of 40 million. Thus our average frequency here is 50 million OTS divided by 40 million reach, or 1.25, over the relevant time period.

Since the number of GRPs or OTS you can buy is directly related to how much money you spend, this brings us to the most basic media planning question: for a given budget that can buy a given number of GRPs or OTS do we want to increase reach or increase frequency? For a given budget, there is always a trade-off between increasing reach or increasing frequency. Some criteria for setting the desired frequency levels were discussed in the last chapter. For some campaigns, reach will be critical. For example, a campaign to gain awareness of a new product may need to reach a substantial portion of the market to be successful. Furthermore, a punchy awareness advertisement may not require many repetitions. Another campaign involving a series of advertisements designed to communicate product details may require many exposures, as may an image campaign. In that case the frequency could be a very important characteristic of a proposed media schedule.

Qualifiers on Basic Reach and Frequency

Qualifying Reach.   The first refinement of the counting-exposures approach to media vehicle selection is to consider the types of people being exposed. A primary issue in developing advertising objectives is to specify the target segment or segments. It will be of little value to deliver an audience containing people not in a target segment.

In Table 17-1, the seventh column shows the percentage of the target audience that is covered by the magazine. The eighth column is the total target audience reached by the magazine, and the ninth is the CPM, only including the target audience. Such a figure, that includes only the target audience, is sometimes called the *effective audience*. *Good Housekeeping* is still the most efficient magazine, but now *Glamour*'s cost looks better relative to the other alternatives than it did when the total audience was considered.

In Chapter 4, various alternative segmentation variables were discussed. Recall that product usage is often useful as a segmentation variable. The heavy user of cosmetics, for example, might be an attractive segment for a cosmetics company. In such a case, vehicle audiences would be desired that included a higher percentage of heavy cosmetic users. Another segmentation variable often useful is life-style. Thus a life-style profile of vehicle audiences would also be helpful to a media planner with such a target segment.

Later in this chapter, the available media data will be discussed in more detail. It turns out that data such as product usage and life-style profiles are available, but that demographic data on vehicle audiences is much more complete, convenient, and inexpensive. Thus, if a target segment is defined in terms of demographics, the task of matching the target segment to a vehicle audience is much easier. For example, an automobile firm may be targeting on the young adult market or on the senior citizen market. When other segmentation variables are employed, it is usually possible to describe the target segment, for example, heavy users of credit cards, in terms of demographics so that the media demographic information can be employed. One study, however, showed that such an indirect approach (going through demographics) sacrificed considerable efficiency. It is more direct, and probably more accurate, to evaluate alternative media vehicles in terms of how many target segment consumers they reach, using syndicated media sources that permit such evaluations.

When several target segments are involved, it might be useful to weight each formally as to its relative value. Thus a computer component manufacturer might have as a primary segment design engineers and maintenance engineers, and buyers might represent secondary segments. Weights could then be attached to each group, and a media vehicle's total reach might be evaluated in terms of the weighted sum of the individual groups reached.

Qualifying Frequency.   The exposure-counting approach to media decisions implicitly assumes that all exposures to an individual will have equal impact. Thus ten exposures to one individual is as desirable as two exposures to each of five people or one exposure to each of ten people. Clearly, there may be a need to achieve some minimum ("threshold" or "critical mass") level of frequency against every reached individual, below which that person would not have been "effectively" reached. Such a frequency level is often called *effective frequency*. At the higher end of the frequency scale, the value of successive exposure will eventually diminish, at least within some time period. If the number of exposures is excessive, the audience can become annoyed, and the impact of future exposures may actually be negative. Because of the need to consider both the minimum "threshold" exposure levels needed, and the "maximum" exposure levels that should not be exceeded, the media planner needs not just an "average frequency" number but an entire *frequency distribution*. Such a frequency distribution specifies the exact number (or percentage) number of people exposed once, twice, three times, four times, and so on.

Very often these frequency distributions are statistically estimated using assumptions about the "shape" of the distribution, and carry names such as the "beta binomial" distribution (BBD).[1] The estimation of the frequency distribution is more complex than the estimation of the reach and frequency, but there are still a variety of approaches available. One of the fastest and most inexpensive was first suggested by Metheringham and is usually termed the Metheringham method. The inputs required are the reach of each of the vehicles, the duplication between each pair of vehicles and the duplication between two insertions in the same vehicle. The output is a frequency distribution. The key assumption is essentially that all vehicles are identical with respect to reach and duplication with other vehicles. Thus, the method essentially averages all the input reach data and the duplication data. The method works quite well when only one vehicle is involved or when, for example, only daytime television spots are involved. However, it works much less well when a more realistic schedule involving several different vehicles is to be evaluated. The following is an example of a frequency distribution for a media insertion schedule involving two insertions in each of three magazines:

Number of exposures	Frequency distribution	Audience
0	0.22	198,000
1	0.15	135,000
2	0.25	225,000
3	0.18	162,000
4	0.10	90,000
5	0.02	18,000
6	0.08	72,000
Total	1.00	900,000

The frequency distribution thus provides a much more detailed portrayal than reach and average frequency. The noticeable bulge at 0 and 6 is actually characteristic of many frequency distributions. They essentially reflect those who tend not to read many magazines and those who tend to read many.

A variety of frequency distributions can generate the same reach and average frequency values, which have very different implications. The implicit assumption behind the consideration of frequency distributions is that the number of exposures that an individual receives matters. It is often helpful to make that assumption explicit by specifying the value of successive exposures. Some illustrative alternatives are shown in Table 17-2. Set A implies that the reach is the only value of a media schedule of interest. It indicates the need is to expose audience members once, and anything more is of no value. Set B implies that all exposures have equal value. Set C suggests that exposures will have equal impact until three exposures are obtained, and then they will have no value. The remaining sets have different assumptions. Clearly, the value given to different exposures matters in the calculations of what the level of reach really is--for instance, if exposure

TABLE 17-2.   Value of Successive Exposures

	RELATIVE VALUE					
Exposure	A	B	C	D	E	F
0						
1	1	1	1	0	1	1
2	0	1	1	0	1	0.9
3	0	1	1	1	0.7	0.8
4	0	1	0	1	0.5	0.7
5	0	1	0	1	0.3	0.5
6	0	1	0	1	0	0.5
7	0	1	0	1	0	0.5
8	0	1	0	0	0	0.2
9	0	1	0	0	0	0.2
10	0	1	0	0	0	0

levels below 3 are considered of no value, then our reach should be defined not as the number of people receiving at least one exposure, but as the number of people receiving at least three exposures. Some media people call the level of reach using the "effective frequency" as the cutoff level the *effective reach* level.

The development of assumptions regarding the value of successive exposures must consider the timing of the exposures, because forgetting can occur between them. It is further complicated because of the differences among people appeals, the month of the year, product characteristics, and other factors. Some people require more exposures than others. Some campaigns wear well, and others tend to obtain maximum impact rapidly. Thus the decision on how to evaluate a particular frequency distribution, and set a particular effective frequency level, must be made with great care.

Measuring Print Vehicle Audiences

Circulation data for print media are most easily obtained from the Audit Bureau of Circulations. Such print vehicle circulation data, however, neglect "pass-along" readers both inside and outside the home. Thus, to measure a vehicle's audience (or readership), it is necessary to apply approaches such as recent reading, reading habit, and through-the-book, to a randomly selected population sample.

In recent reading, respondents are asked whether they looked at a copy within the past week for a weekly publication or during the last month if it was a monthly publication. One problem is that the survey is unlikely to represent an "average" week, so there is a seasonality factor to consider. Also, a reader could read several issues in one week and be incorrectly reported as not being a reader in another week. Another concern is the tendency to exaggerate readership of prestige magazines and to minimize readership of vehicles that do not match people's self-image. Still another is the forgetting factor. One study found that 50 of 166 people who were observed reading magazines in a doctor's office said they had never read the magazine they had been observed reading.

The reading-habit method, which asks respondents how many issues out of the last four they personally read or looked into, is also sensitive to memory difficulties. In particular, it is difficult to discriminate between reading the same issue several times and reading several issues.

The through-the-book approach attempts to reduce the memory factor. Respondents are shown a copy of a specific issue of a magazine that he or she reads and asked whether several articles were read and if they were interesting. The respondent is then asked if he or she read that issue. The approach, which requires an expensive personal interview, is sensitive to the issue age. A too-recent issue will miss later readers. A too-old issue risks forgetting.

The two major audience-measuring services are Mediamark (MRI) and Simmons (SMRB). Simmons interviews 19,000 people each year and produces annual reports; MRI interviews 20,000 people and produces twice-yearly reports. Both services obtain data on between 3 and 4,000 brands in over 500 product categories that are analyzed on a national plus geographic basis. In addition to providing demographic and psychographic data on brand and category usage, each service provides media data—including duplication and accumulation data—that cover TV, radio, magazines, newspapers, outdoor, and Yellow Pages. The data are available both in printed volumes and on computer tape (for customized analyses). An example of a page from Simmons is shown in Table 17-3.

Since these two services use different methods in estimating readership, they often yield different estimates of readership for different magazines (called "books" by media planners), and differences between the two have sparked sharp controversy through the years. Table 17-4 shows a comparison of the audience estimates based on the two techniques.

For newspapers, readership data—based on telephone interviews—are available from both Simmons and from another service called Scarborough Research. Both contact over 60,000 adults every year, in over 50 markets nationwide, and provide estimates of the number of adult readers by weekday and for Sunday editions. Demographic breakdowns are provided, as are estimates of cumulative reach.

Measuring Broadcast Vehicle Audience

The principal methods of obtaining audience data for broadcast media are the people-meter and the diary.

The principal source of national television ratings is the Nielsen Television Index, National Audience Demographics (NTI-NAD). The NTI consists of approximately 2,000 households, matched according to U.S. national statistics, that agree to have an electronic device called a *people-meter* attached to their TV sets. The people-meter is a small unit placed on top of or beside the television set, recording what channel is viewed at what time, for every half-minute during every 24-hour period. Eight sets of lights on the set are used to indicate which member of the household—including visitors—is watching; these lights can be turned on or off using a remote device, and those watching are meant to turn them on when they start watching and off when they stop. Data from the people-meter are sent periodically by telephone to the Nielsen central offices, where they are related to each person's age, sex, and so on that Nielsen collects separately and keeps on file. In addition, Nielsen meters New York, Los Angeles, and Chicago to provide local ratings in these areas on a next-day basis. Nielsen also reports HUT, the percentage of all television homes whose set is in use.

People-meters have the advantage, over the previously used television meters called audimeters, of providing information not only about how many people are watching a TV program, but also about who they are, in terms of age and sex, and so on. Prior to 1987, Nielsen used two samples of people in its national panel: one of people with the audimeters, which simply recorded what channel the program was tuned to at different points of time when the set was on, and a second "diary" panel, in which panelists with known age and sex characteristics self-reported their viewing. The data from both sources were then combined. Today, the people-meters provide both kinds of data simultaneously. However, these people-meters too have their problems: people consciously and actively have to turn the meters on and off when they enter or exit the room where the TV is on, and this can be bothersome. The search is now on for "passive" people-meters, devices that will automatically record who is watching, using sophisticated optics and/or other techniques such as sonar and infra-red heat-sensing.[2]

Weekly diaries provide the basic data gathering instrument for local television ratings. Nielsen and Arbitron, its competitor, both monitor over 200 local markets (which Arbitron calls ADI, or "areas of dominant influence," and Nielsen calls DMA, or "designated market area"). The sample size of the Nielsen effort (called the Nielsen Station Index, or NSI) ranges from 2,200 households in New York to several hundred in the smallest markets. Monthly reports are provided from four to seven times a year depending on the size of the market. During three "sweep" months of November, February, and May, over 200 markets are covered by both Nielsen and Arbitron. Over the course of a year's time, over 800,000 households will be involved in a television diary panel for one of the two services.

Similarly, diaries are also used to collect quarter-hour estimates of radio listenership, by Arbitron (for 256 local radio markets). Data from Birch can be used to supplement the Arbitron data, in markets not adequately served by Arbitron, typically in metro areas. Another service called RADAR (for Radio's All-Dimension Audience Research) collects listenership data for the national radio networks, using 8,000 telephone interviews to get recall of radio programs listened to. These data for both radio and local TV provide total size and demographic breakdowns for each station/program for every quarter hour, as well as estimates of the relevant cumulative audience, for one-week and beyond.

The quality of diary data can vary. Some respondents do not fill it out during the day but try to recall viewing activity. As a result, fringe programming generally does not fare as well from the diary as it does from the electronic meters. Another problem is that the homemaker is often the one who fills it out and is often not conversant with children's shows and lesser known programs. The major diary problem is thus probably nonresponse bias. It has been suggested that the diary panel tends to understate the younger audience. The cooperation rate among the 18- to 24-year-old group is especially low.

TABLE 17-3. Magazine Readership as Reported by Simmons

Magazine	COST PER PAGE[b] (1000s)		AUDIENCE IN 1,000s[a]				BUYING STYLE				
	B&W	4-Color	Adults	Female	Age 18–34	Household income over 25,000	Brand loyal	Ecologist	Economy minded	Planner	Style conscious
Total adults (millions)			155.8	81.1	63.1	41.3	40.2	43.5	60.2	67.7	36.0
1. American Baby	$15.7	$21.7	2,308	1,963	1,902	575	636	659	918	880	701
2. Better Homes	51.9	62.8	21,579	16,684	7,815	7,123	6,340	6,439	9,318	10,243	6,399
3. Bon Appetit	11.0	15.7	3,000	2,306	1,206	1,610	941	801	1,074	1,413	1,145
4. Business Week	17.4	26.1	4,147	913	1,770	2,557	1,291	815	1,465	1,878	1,012
5. Car and Driver	13.9	21.3	2,720	539	1,961	1,159	748	767	1,158	1,461	778
6. Ebony	12.9	19.9	6,925	3,639	4,029	1,461	1,716	2,020	2,678	3,036	2,034
7. Family Health	6.2	8.7	3,325	2,281	1,205	1,035	1,016	1,028	1,465	1,690	938
8. Fortune	17.9	27.3	2,190	583	889	1,541	688	425	609	904	486
9. Golf	10.3	15.5	2,283	628	902	1,266	686	568	839	996	794
10. Gourmet	7.0	12.5	2,263	1,573	670	1,126	639	725	773	1,006	773
11. Guns & Ammo	5.3	8.6	2,898	299	1,815	975	797	1,092	1,313	1,478	684
12. House & Garden	14.8	21.8	7,917	6,061	3,071	2,998	2,624	2,374	3,383	3,643	2,792
13. Mademoiselle	8.8	12.8	3,620	3,415	2,180	1,332	1,065	1,111	1,657	1,832	1,656
14. McCall's	42.5	52.2	18,372	16,266	7,143	5,753	5,131	5,577	7,930	8,672	6,023
15. Money Mag.	11.4	17.9	3,691	1,663	1,768	1,927	1,040	958	1,395	1,900	1,001
16. Motor Trend	12.4	19.8	3,358	422	1,926	1,159	823	834	1,303	1,554	721
17. Ms.	6.5	8.7	1,375	1,211	991	360	317	486	475	712	425
18. Nat'l. Lampoon	6.7	9.9	3,348	759	2,845	1,377	995	912	785	1,225	737
19. Newsweek	33.2	51.7	17,197	6,893	8,827	7,370	5,046	4,422	5,713	7,855	4,582

20. New Yorker	8.3	13.2	3,008	1,412	1,433	1,509	1,078	863	1,099	1,490	855
21. Outdoor Life	14.8	21.4	5,438	1,133	2,784	1,748	1,448	1,937	2,410	2,640	1,236
22. People	23.0	29.5	18,138	10,641	10,992	6,162	4,888	5,296	6,228	8,112	5,230
23. Playboy	36.2	50.6	13,932	2,749	9,596	4,910	3,523	3,729	4,713	5,965	3,334
24. Playgirl	6.6	8.8	2,110	1,253	1,384	546	526	613	786	1,007	513
25. Reader's Digest	74.6	89.6	39,283	22,303	12,942	12,769	11,360	10,802	15,618	17,937	9,611
26. Road & Track	10.7	16.8	2,454	405	1,761	1,098	589	657	752	1,264	474
27. Rolling Stone	9.1	13.7	2,780	943	2,552	911	663	834	910	1,249	621
28. Seventeen	10.5	15.2	5,259	4,484	3,230	1,573	1,132	1,607	2,266	2,492	1,849
29. Smithsonian	17.5	21.9	4,952	2,404	1,665	2,730	1,630	1,475	1,420	2,321	1,083
30. Sport	13.3	19.4	6,116	1,231	3,816	1,890	1,552	1,488	2,115	2,908	1,722
31. Sports Afield	7.0	10.0	5,318	1,137	2,330	1,982	1,818	1,491	2,193	2,451	1,079
32. Sunset	14.2	19.7	5,227	3,446	1,778	2,317	1,585	1,441	1,827	2,509	1,163
33. Time	45.1	70.3	20,180	8,269	9,854	8,782	5,786	5,192	6,606	9,049	5,032
34. Travel/Holiday	5.9	8.4	1,139	570	299	471	365	397	479	599	332
35. True Story	9.8	12.8	5,925	5,294	3,297	801	1,565	1,946	2,865	2,538	1,665
36. TV Guide	58.8	69.5	42,236	23,389	20,984	11,223	11,130	12,532	16,249	18,818	10,695
37. U.S. News	21.9	34.6	8,635	2,724	3,288	4,112	2,563	2,119	3,310	4,343	2,267
38. Vogue	10.4	15.2	5,755	5,192	2,825	2,194	1,775	1,970	2,495	2,824	2,367
39. Woman's Day	49.9	59.8	18,225	16,606	7,008	5,523	5,121	5,427	7,746	8,876	5,835
40. Working Woman	5.2	7.4	974	941	518	437	756	288	320	597	313

[a]Source: "The 1979 Study of Media and Markets—Multi-Media Audiences: Adults," Simmons Market Research Bureau, 1979.

[b]Source: Consumer Magazine and Farm Publication Rates and Data, Standard Rate & Data Service, November 27, 1980. Shown are the costs of a one-page single-insertion advertisement.

TABLE 17-4.   Total Adult Readers Comparison

Magazine	Mediamark	Simmons
Time	25,701,000	20,035,000
Newsweek	23,640,000	16,453,000
U.S. News	11,586,000	8,733,000
Family Circle	32,143,000	18,255,000
McCall's	24,641,000	17,287,000
Ladies Home Journal	21,920,000	12,971,000
Harper's Bazaar	3,574,000	3,301,000
Playboy	21,401,000	15,584,000

Source: Adapted from Leah Rozen, ''Reader Data Still Don't Jibe,'' *Advertising Age,* October 6, 1980, p. 118.

Other Media Data

In addition to estimates of the viewership, readership, and listenership of individual media vehicles, various other sources of media information also become useful in developing a media plan. These include estimates of how much your competitive brands are spending, by major medium and by geographical area, obtained through services such as the *Leading National Advertisers* (LNA) Reports (for all media), *Media Records* (for newspapers), the *Rome Report* (for business and trade publications), *Broadcast Advertisers Report* (for television and radio), and so on. Media planners also rely on the *Standard Rate and Data Service* (SRDS) volumes for information on pricing and costs of different media vehicles. Background information on advertisers and advertising agencies is available in the *Standard Directory of Advertisers* and the *Standard Directory of Advertising Agencies*, the so-called ''red books,'' in addition to the annual issues put out by *Advertising Age* magazine. Information about the potential buying power of different geographical areas is provided, among others, by the rankings and ''Surveys of Buying Power'' put out by *Sales Management* magazine. Many advertising agencies also issue annual guidebooks providing averages of costs and audiences, for use in ''quick and dirty'' estimation by their clients and internal staff.

Using Computerized Media Planning Models

Clearly, making media decisions can be difficult. There are usually a huge number of alternative feasible schedules, and huge masses of cost, audience size, and duplication data. (Chapter One provided details of the vast number of media options available, and the advertising trends across those media.) Duplication data are usually only available for each pair of media vehicles (such as *Time* with *Newsweek*), and ways have to be found to estimate the total unduplicated reach in schedules with tens or hundreds of media vehicles, not just two. It is no wonder that simple CPM measures are often all that are relied on. A better way to cope with this complexity, however, is to use a formal media computer model that will develop estimates of total duplication and then search for the ''best'' media schedule, given a budget constraint and facts (data) about the vehicles under consideration. Such media selection models have undergone an extensive evolution over the past 30 years, and may be classified into three main types.

The first major category of models use mathematical optimization techniques, such as linear, nonlinear, integer, dynamic, or goal programming, and attempt to maximize reach (or some other objective function) within budget (and other) constraints. The first such widely heralded model was developed in 1961 by the BBDO advertising agency, and there have been various refinements since then. However, these models have all suffered from various severe limitations and are thus not widely used today. Their demise led to the second major category of models, called simulation models. In essence, these operate on real exposure data (obtained from a sample of consumers) and "simulate" what the reach and frequency exposures would be among these consumers for given media schedules. The frequency exposures obtained are sometimes also combined with a judgment-based response function, and the schedule with the highest response is then judged the most promising. Models in this category include the CAM model developed in Britain in the late 1960s, and various others since then. Their weakness is their inability to evaluate a large number of schedules, which becomes extremely computer intensive; they are therefore typically used with only a few "candidate" schedules. Companies such as Interactive Marketing Services (IMS) and Telmar use such approaches, through which agencies can evaluate different schedules. The third type of model is called "heuristic," meaning it develops a reasonably superior, but not necessarily "optimal," solution for a media planning problem. An example would be Young & Rubicam's "High Assay" model of 1962, which added vehicles to a schedule based on marginal contribution (in cost per thousand, adjusting for various other factors). Other published models have included Little and Lodish's MEDIAC, Aaker's ADMOD, and so on. Fuller descriptions of these and other computer media models are found in a review by Rust.[3]

It is easily seen why such computer models can be valuable to a media planner, who can quickly see the trade-offs between cost, reach, and frequency for different alternative media schedules under consideration. It is important always to remember, however, that a media planner (or client) should not be seduced by the seeming objectivity of numbers on a computer printout. These numbers have to be modified for various qualitative, judgmental criteria, to which we now turn.

Qualitative Media Vehicle Source Effects

Media vehicle source effects are a measure of the qualitative value of the media vehicle. The concept is that an exposure in one vehicle might have more impact than an exposure of the same advertisement in another vehicle. For example, an advertisement for a women's dress line in *Vogue* might make more of an impact on those exposed than the same advertisement in *True Confessions,* even if the audiences were the same. Similarly, it is claimed that *Esquire* provides an above-average vehicle for men's fashions because it is an appropriate environment for this type of advertising. The differential impact could be caused by editorial environment, physical reproduction qualities, or audience involvement. (Similar source effects can apply to entire media classes, such as television versus newspapers, but these are not discussed here.)

In Table 17-1 several approaches to the measurement of the vehicle source effect are illustrated. The target concentration index reflects the degree to which the editorial product reaches out to the target segment, people who have traveled overseas for example. Each magazine is scored subjectively on this basis. The concept is that if the editorial content is involving, the advertisement will be read with more intensity. A more objective measure is the number of compatible pages, the editorial pages that the magazine has devoted during the last year to the subject in question, such as foreign travel. The reader opinion column is based upon the number of readers who indicate that the magazine is "very important in my life" or is "one of my favorites" or "find considerable interest in its advertising pages." The Table 17-1 in-home columns indicate the percentage of the magazine's audience who read the magazine in their home. It may be that the in-home reader is less distracted and more likely to read an advertisement more thoroughly than an out-of-home reader.

There is general agreement that there does exist a vehicle source effect. As early as 1962, the Alfred Politz research organization demonstrated that an advertisement in *McCall's* would generate higher "quality" image and brand-preference ratings than identical ads placed in general readership magazines.[4] The determination of the vehicle source effect will obviously depend on the campaign objectives. An awareness objective will involve different source-effect considerations than communication or image-oriented objectives. However, there are at least five vehicle attributes that are often relevant considerations: unbiasedness, expertness, prestige, mood created, and involvement.

Unbiasedness.   If advertising concerned with political or social issues is considered, the position of the vehicle may indeed affect the communications. For example, an advertisement opposing gun control in the publication of an organization such as the National Rifle Association may be more likely to appear biased than if the same advertisement appeared in another vehicle.

Expertness.   Advertisements can usually be expected to reflect the degree of expertise associated with the area of interest of the vehicle in which they appear. Thus, the magazine *World Tennis* is seen by its readers as a reliable source of information regarding new product developments in tennis, new playing techniques, new types of tennis court surfaces, and so on. The editors and writers are recognized authorities in competitive and instructive tennis. A reader, therefore, comes to the magazine willing to accept information from this source. The concept is that the reader's mental set does not change when he or she moves from an article in *World Tennis* to an advertisement describing a new racket used by Boris Becker.

Prestige.   A vehicle's prestige is a third attribute commonly considered to be important for some product. The *New Yorker* has an exclusiveness and aloofness that might be expected to generate a similar feeling toward products advertised in it. Thus, if a product is endeavoring to build a status image, it may well be useful to advertise it in a high-status vehicle.

A study by Gert Assmus provides an interesting approach toward identifying the components of the vehicle source effect and demonstrates the relevance of the prestige dimension.[5] In his study, 125 people associated with media planning in the medical field rated six medical journals as to the journal's vehicle source effect and as to the extent to which the journals were perceived to have each of 16 attributes. He found substantial differences in the vehicle source effect ratings. Furthermore, the three attributes that were the strongest predictors of the overall vehicle source effect rating were useful editorial content, prestige, and reference value. A knowledge of these elements could be of value in attempting to assign vehicle source weights in the medical context.

Mood Created.   The influence of a vehicle's prestige may be viewed as working through the mood it creates among its readers. The concept is that a vehicle-induced mood will affect the impact of a commercial communication. In our context, if we were advertising a Daiquiri mix, we would like to know what mood is associated with a positive attitude toward this product. Then an attempt would be made to determine which vehicles tend to provide such a mood. If any media or vehicles uniquely provided such a mood, they might well also provide more effective exposure than other vehicles. Such an argument could lead to the use of women's glamor magazines for lipsticks, powders, and perfumes, *Family Health* for nutrition-oriented advertisements, and *Sports Illustrated* for advertisements that relate to sports and exercise.

A concept related to mood is that a vehicle should harmonize with the product. Crane reported that depth interviews conducted by one advertiser suggest that men's products are best advertised on Westerns and with "assertive" commercials, whereas food products call for commercials using emotional appeals and appearing on situation comedies. Although these findings may reflect respondents' knowledge of current practices rather than any more basic tendencies, Schwerin's findings tend to support these conclusions. Food commercials, Schwerin reports, fit well with situation comedies but do poorly in a mystery, adventure, or Western context. Analgesics do well both in adult Westerns and situation comedies.[6]

Audience Involvement.   An involving vehicle should generate a superior commercial exposure than a vehicle that is not very interesting to the audience. Agency executives Barclay, Doub, and McMurtrey found that in daytime programming, commercials in serial programs generated more recall and attentiveness than other program types, and situation comedies fared least well. However, Soldow and Principe, in a forced-exposure lab setting, compared commercials in a low-involving program ("Brady Bunch," a situation comedy) with the same commercials in a high-involving program ("Baretta," an action program).[7] The low-involving environment was actually superior with respect to buying intentions and brand and sales message recall. Their findings suggest that a program can be so suspenseful and involving that it detracts from the advertising impact.

Other Dimensions.   Wolfe and his associates reported on an advertising agency that studied vehicle effects and concluded that three factors should be "included within a qualitative publication index: competitive advertising volume (defined as number of pages), editorial content (defined as percentage of space devoted to subjects pertaining to the product), and editorial quality (defined as the ratio of editorial pages to total pages)."[8]

Vehicle Source Effects and Copy Approaches

A study by Aaker and Brown illustrates that the nature of vehicle source effects will depend on the copy approach used.[9] Four print advertisements represented two copy approaches—image and "reason why." One image advertisement for dinnerware had almost no copy but used a picture of a bride and groom with a headline indicating that the queen of England had used similar dinnerware on her wedding table. The reason-why advertisement for comparably priced dinnerware, shown in Figure 17-1, used copy indicating that the product was durable, ovenproof, and safe in a dishwasher. A second product category, spices, also contributed an image and a reason-why advertisement. The reason-why spice advertisement included a recipe, noted the unique bottle shape, and included a coupon for a spice rack. The image spice advertisement showed a noted cookbook author who stressed the importance of using top-rated spices.

A survey of 30 housewives rated 18 magazines as to their prestigiousness and expertness with respect to cooking, foods, and kitchenware. Two magazines, *Vogue* and the *New Yorker,* were rated as prestigious and ranked low on the expert scale. Two others, *Better Homes and Gardens* and *Sunset,* were considered as expert but not prestigious.

Another sample of 64 housewives was shown a series of four folders, each with a cover page from one of the four test magazines. Each folder had three advertisements, including one of the test advertisements. Among the questions asked of the respondent about each advertisement were questions concerning perceived product price, product quality, and product reliability, all of which were expected to measure the ability of the image advertisements to affect perceived quality.

The hypothesis was that the image advertisements would perform better in prestige magazines than in expert magazines with respect to these image-oriented measures, but that the reverse would occur with reason-why advertisements. The results are summarized in Figure 17-2 for nonusers of the advertised brand who are more sensitive to the advertising. Clearly the hypotheses are confirmed. The study indicates clearly that the vehicle source effects are sensitive to the type of advertising used.

MEDIA OPTION DECISIONS

The media planner is really concerned with advertisement audience size rather than vehicle audience size. Thus, in addition to selecting particular media vehicles, decisions also have to be made about the particular "unit" of advertising that is to be employed—15-second versus 30-second TV commercial, half-page versus full-page ad, inside page magazine ad versus back cover magazine ad, black-and-white versus four-color ad, and so on.

One measurement approach to making such decisions in magazines is to use average Starch scores or Starch ad norms. In the Starch survey, respondents are taken through a

Figure 17-1. A reason-why advertisement
Courtesy of The Carborundum Company.

magazine and, for each advertisement, are asked if they saw it in the issue. The *noted* score is the percentage who answer affirmatively. Two companion measures are *seen/ associated* (note the name of the advertiser) and *read most* (read more than 50 percent of

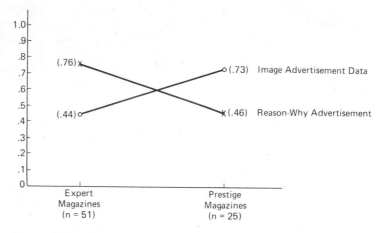

Figure 17-2.   Ratings of product quality (nonusers of advertised brand)

the copy). The Starch measure dates back to 1923 and has been applied consistently since that early start. One indication of advertisement exposure for a vehicle would be the average Starch noted scores for the full-page advertisements contained in it.

Studies using the Starch data indicate that advertisement exposure will depend on the product class, the involvement of the segment in the product class, and on such media-option variables as the size and color of the advertisement, position, and copy approach.

Advertisement Size and Color.   Trohdahl and Jones determined that the size determines 40 percent of the variation in newspaper advertisement readership.[10] Since doubling the advertisement size falls short of doubling the readership, the use of larger advertisements needs to be justified on impact rather than audience-size grounds. Similarly, research on recall of TV commercials of different length has found that, at least in the short-run, 15-second commercials provide greater than half (70 or 80 percent) of the recall of 30-second spots.[11] Starch has concluded that readership scores of full-page magazine advertisements using four colors are about 85 percent higher than are scores of half-page advertisements using four colors.[12] However, the use of four colors only generates about 50 percent more readership than black and white for one-page and two-page advertisements.

Advertisement Location.   Starch has concluded that advertisements on the back of a magazine will attract about 65 percent more readers than will those toward the middle. Advertisements on the inside front and back covers will attract about 30 percent more readers. Similarly, research by Webb and Ray on TV clutter has shown that TV spots that are at the beginning or the end of a string or pod of commercials—rather than being in the middle of the pod—do better on recall, and are hurt less by increased amounts of advertising clutter.[13]

Copy Execution.   Starch found that advertisements very similar to the editorial matter of a magazine suffer somewhat in the noted score but gain 50 percent in terms of the read-most measure. Similarly, the use of comic continuity advertising—the use of panels like a comic strip—receive slightly less noted scores but substantially better read-most scores.

SCHEDULING/TIMING DECISIONS

Decisions on how best to "space out" ads over time are based essentially on assumptions about how the advertising objective being aimed at (e.g., recall, or attitudes) *respond* to the presence of advertising exposures and *decay* when such advertising is absent. Based on these assumptions, the advertiser typically chooses from among three patterns of distributing the planned ads over a given time period: (1) *flighting*, burst of advertising alternated with periods of total inactivity, (2) *continuous or even*, advertising spread evenly through the campaign time period, and (3) *pulsing*, a continuous base augmented by intermittent bursts of heavy advertising.

If, for example, it is believed that attitudes require heavy advertising to change (because of possible S-shaped response function), but that such attitudes do not then decay rapidly once they are changed, such beliefs would suggest the need for flighting if changing attitudes was the advertising objective. Heavy bursts would be needed to change attitudes, and periods of no advertising could be risked because the changed attitudes would not decay rapidly. In contrast, if it was believed that recall both responded easily to advertising, and decayed rapidly if there was no advertising, then a recall-increasing ad campaign would probably need to be continuous. You need to be advertising all the time so as not to see recall drop off dangerously, but such advertising could be at a low frequency level since recall would respond even at these low levels.[14] Of course, such conceptual arguments would need to be modified for several pragmatic considerations: the needs of product seasonality, the need to avoid going head to head against a larger competitor, and the need to coordinate advertising pulses with scheduled sales promotion events, for example.

Several studies exist that have empirically examined the shape of the response and decay functions for recall (fewer studies have looked at attitudes). A host of studies, including the Ebbinghaus experiments, have confirmed the commonsense notion that recall declines over time and that this decline is greatest at the outset and diminishes over time. Agency researcher Zielske conducted a field experiment that is regarded as a classic study of repetition and forgetting.[15] Two groups of women, randomly selected from a telephone directory, were mailed 13 different advertisements from the same newspaper advertising campaign for an ingredient food. One group received an advertisement weekly for 13 weeks. The other group received the same 13 mailings but at intervals of four weeks during the year. Throughout the year, aided only by mention of the product class, recall was measured by telephone interviews. No single person was interviewed in person more than once. A person can become sensitized to the advertisement after an interview; if a person has been interviewed twice, the second interview would usually be biased. The results of the study are shown in Figure 17-3 with the learning and forgetting process graphically displayed.

Zielske's data are usually interpreted to mean that a flight or pulse of ads leads to a higher (temporary) peak in recall, while a continuous (evenly spaced) timing strategy would be better for products that required the maximization of average weekly recall (not simply a one-time higher peak in recall). Note also that the flighted schedule led to greater and more rapid subsequent fall-of in recall than the even schedule. While the flighting schedule led to a higher one-time peak, it is very important to note that the total number of "recall-weeks" (the number of weeks multiplied by the appropriate recall rate) was higher under the even schedule, especially if the data are not "smoothed" (as they have in the graph presented here).[16] Similar results were later found by Strong, who used a computer simulation model (built on data from a two field experiments, including Zielske's original experiment); a flighting schedule led to higher peak recall than a more even schedule.[17]

Lodish, one of the developers of the MEDIAC media planning model, estimated the forgetting function using data from a study of advertising retention in five magazines by

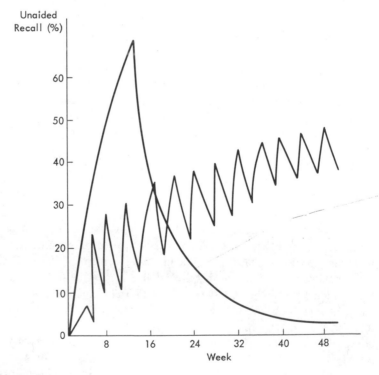

Figure 17-3.   The 1958 repetition study

Source: Adapted from Hubert A. Zielske, "The Remembering and Forgetting of Advertising," *Journal of Marketing,* American Marketing Association, 23, January 1959, pp. 239–243.

W. R. Simmons.[18] The retention measured was the ability of readers of a specific issue to distinguish among advertisements that appeared in that issue and ones that did not. Lodish found that the retention measure fell by 25 percent each week. Strong, in his simulation, found that recall fell by over 45 percent per week and that the decay over several weeks was proportional to the square root of the number of weeks since last exposure.[19]

Zielske and Henry later examined 17 tracking studies involving six established products.[20] A tracking study is a repeated survey over time to track a measure such as awareness. Unaided recall of television advertising copy was the measure in this case. The recall level varied from 10 to 16 percent and the weekly GRP ranged from 40 to 200. A regression analysis yielded the following model:

$$\Delta A_t = 0.30 W_t - 0.10 A_{t-1}$$

where ΔA_t = percentage-point change in unaided recall in week t
W_t = gross rating points received in week t
A_{t-1} = unaided recall level in week $t - 1$

The first term indicates, for example, that 100 GRP per week will, on the average, produce three percentage points of unaided recall. The second term in the formula represents the average forgetting rate. For example, if recall in the prior week had been at the 15 percent level, then in the absence of further advertising, recall would be expected to drop to 13.5 percent. Thus, from one week to the next, just 10 percent would be forgotten. That, of course, is less than the 25 or 45 percent found by Lodish and Strong in their studies, demonstrating that these decay functions will be unique to the situation involved.

The point of these efforts to estimate parameters is not so much to indicate specific "universal" parameter values but rather to illustrate approaches that can be taken to estimate functions in given contexts. Further, it is vital to note that the response and decay function parameters are very likely a function also of the measure being modeled—recognition, recall, and attitudes are each likely to behave differently. We know much more about recall than about recognition or attitudes, though it would be reasonable to speculate that the last two would decline more slowly over time than would recall.[21]

It should be noted, in conclusion, that the superiority of flighting or pulsing in maximizing peak levels of recall has been examined not only in the field experiments described earlier, but also in many of the mathematical models built by management scientists, in which an "optimal" (recall- or profit-maximizing) scheduling strategy is sought. Not surprisingly, the answers obtained depend on the assumptions made about the shape of the decay function.[22]

Media Buying/Organization

Once a final media schedule is determined, using the criteria just discussed, the actual negotiation and buying of the media units (television and radio time, magazine and newspaper space, etc.) have to occur. While the buying of media was traditionally done by the advertising agency that did the creative work on the account, this pattern has recently begun to change. Some clients have begun to consolidate all the media buying for all their accounts (brands) at one agency, rather than spread it over several agencies. Others have separated the media buying task from the creative one and have the media buying done either in-house or through a media-buying service (after modifying the fee structure appropriately for the agency that does the creative work).

The underlying reason for these changes has been the negotiating benefit, to the client, of buying a bigger dollar amount of media time or space from each media supplier. The rates for media are rarely fixed in stone, though they may appear to be so when described on a rate card. Broadcast media, and increasingly magazines as well, undertake a negotiation process with agencies and clients taking into account the total size of the media buy as well as the supply-and-demand situation at the time of negotiation. These negotiations determine not just the dollar amounts to be paid but also the particulars of favored page (or time) placement, and so on.

Since negotiations are involved, the expertise of the agency media buyers obviously matters a lot. For this reason, advertising agencies and media buying services have media buying units in which media buyers specialize according to the medium and the geographical areas involved. Thus network TV buys are typically made by a different media buyer than one who specializes in local TV stations in, say, Los Angeles. Radio buyers and Print buyers are also different people, as are those who perform media research and media planning functions. In dealing with local (nonnational) media, a media buyer typically deals with a "media rep" firm that represents that local station or newspaper nationally rather than with that local media vehicle directly.

These negotiations are complex, and media buys are made at different rates depending on the conditions involved. Network television time, for instance, can either be bought several months ahead by a high-volume buyer wanting a deal covering an entire season (called an "upfront" buy) or bought in the quarter of the year when the ad will air (a "scatter" buy). If bought in the upfront market, the advertiser often receives an exposure-size guarantee—the number of people guaranteed to watch the show—but is limited in terms of cancellation flexibility. If the network fails to deliver the promised audience, or if the airing of an ad is somehow botched, the network is typically obliged to "make good" by offering extra time free of charge to make up for the shortfall. If the buy is made in the scatter market, the price paid depends on the supply-and-demand situation at that time: television time, like airline seats and hotel rooms, is a perishable commodity, and prices can move up and down very rapidly depending on how eager the two sides are to consummate the transaction.

The price paid also varies with the specificity of the schedule: the rates are higher if the advertiser wants his spot to run at a fixed time of day, or fixed page location, rather than anywhere (the latter is called *run of paper*, or ROP, in newspapers, and *run of time* on radio). Further, as if this was not complex enough, the media vehicle reserves the right to yank your spot off the air if all you pay is a lower "preemptible" rate, than a higher "nonpreemptible" rate. This complexity is one reason why media buying is best done by seasoned media buying professionals.

THE MEDIA PLAN FOR THE BROILER

Now that we have discussed the complete media planning, scheduling, and buying process, it is useful to see what an actual media plan might look like. A simulated television plan for one of the leading fast-food chains, The Broiler, is shown in Figure 17-4. The total advertising and promotional budget is around $250 million, of which well over one-half is earmarked for television. The television plan illustrates a segmentation strategy and several types of scheduling alternatives.

The children segment, including teens, is an important market. The Broiler has always lagged McDonald's with respect to children but has made inroads with the St. Bernard advertising spokesman. The St. Bernard's campaign with additional characters and a "fun" theme is planned. As the figure indicates, national buys of 140 GRP per week will be supported by 300 GRPs per week on local television. Six Saturday morning pulses were planned during the year. In such a pulse, 30-second commercials would appear every half-hour from 8:30 A.M. to the conclusion of children's Saturday programming.

The young adult market, the 18- to 34-year-olds is another important segment for The Broiler. Research showed that within this segment, it was leading on the product quality dimension. For example, in terms of having hot and tasty food, The Broiler received a 88 percent rating, about 20 to 30 points above its rivals. Ratings for "value" were much weaker. The strategy was to lead from strength by focusing upon the product quality dimension. To attract this segment, the media plan suggested 500 to 600 GRPs per week for the adult segment. Five adult pulses were planned, each of which will translate into a 30-second spot every 30 minutes on each network during prime time.

The plan called for advertising to focus upon certain themes for relatively long periods and to be linked to simple, tested promotions. For example, a hamburger theme was to be used in January and February. In March and April, the emphasis was to be on breakfasts, supported by a breakfast promotion.

Research indicated that The Broiler had not penetrated the heavy-user group sufficiently, the group that accounts for 50 percent of the total market. Thus, more attention was focused upon the heavy user segment, especially blacks, Hispanics, and the 10- to 17-year-old set. The prime-time adult schedule included spots featuring blacks. The effort toward blacks also included *Ebony* and *Jet* magazines and black radio. The Hispanic thrust used Spanish television.

Women were to be reached not only by the daytime national media effort, but by a $2 million campaign in *Family Circle, Good Housekeeping,* and *People.*[23]

SUMMARY

The selection of the type of medium, such as television, radio, or magazines, will depend in part upon the number of people in the target audience that the medium can deliver, as well as compatibility with the needs of the creative message, needs regarding timing and flexibility, and so on.

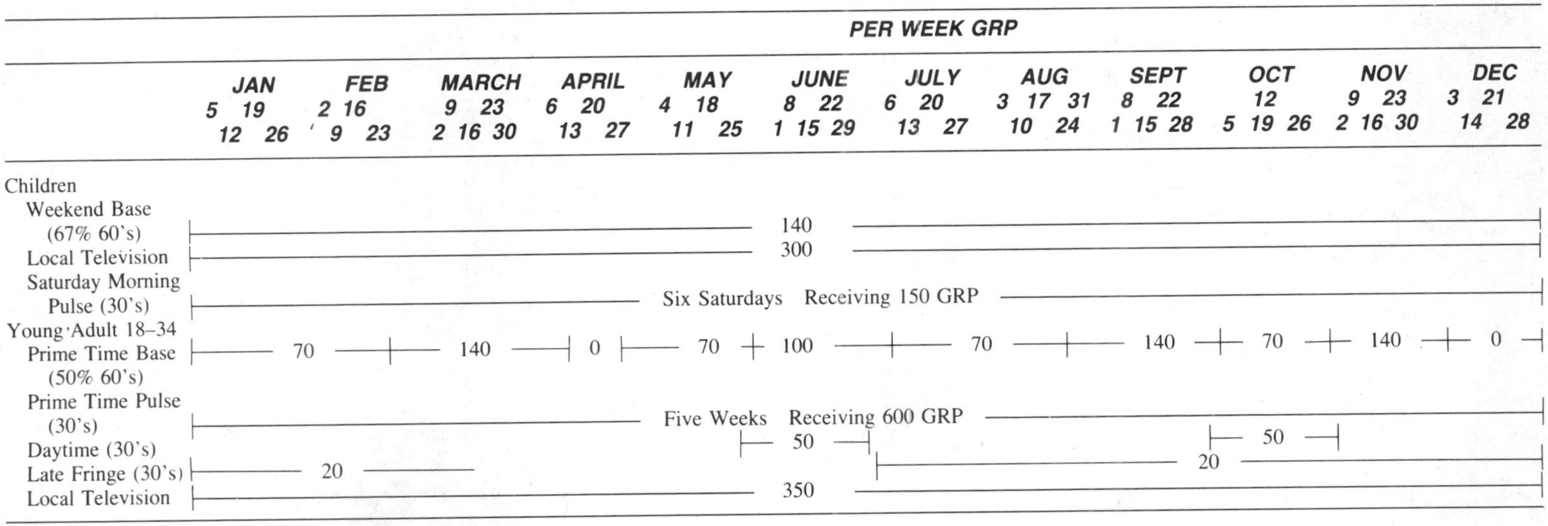

PER WEEK GRP

	JAN 5 19 / 12 26	FEB 2 16 / 9 23	MARCH 9 23 / 2 16 30	APRIL 6 20 / 13 27	MAY 4 18 / 11 25	JUNE 8 22 / 1 15 29	JULY 6 20 / 13 27	AUG 3 17 31 / 10 24	SEPT 8 22 / 1 15 28	OCT 12 / 5 19 26	NOV 9 23 / 2 16 30	DEC 3 21 / 14 28

Children
Weekend Base (67% 60's) — 140
Local Television — 300
Saturday Morning Pulse (30's) — Six Saturdays Receiving 150 GRP

Young/Adult 18-34
Prime Time Base (50% 60's) — 70 ... 140 ... 0 ... 70 ... 100 ... 70 ... 140 ... 140 ... 70 ... 140 ... 0
Prime Time Pulse (30's) — Five Weeks Receiving 600 GRP
Daytime (30's) — 50 ... 50 ... 20
Late Fringe (30's) — 20
Local Television — 350

¹ Late fringe is the two hour period following prime time.

Figure 17-4. National television media plan for The Broiler

A basic concern in determining which specific media vehicle to select is cost per thousand or CPM for print and gross rating point or GRP for television, both of which are a measure of total exposures per dollar cost. However, it is usually useful also to measure reach (the number of people exposed at least once) and average frequency (the average number of exposures per exposed person). Exposure decisions add precision to an understanding of what the media plan is actually delivering.

Data sources were discussed. One approach to measuring print readership is recent reading, asking people whether they read a magazine last month. The people-meter attaches to TV sets and monitors the stations watched in order to obtain measures of television program viewing. In some contexts, it can be relevant to evaluate vehicles in terms of their expertness, prestige, mood, and audience involvement.

Decisions as to media options, for example, the size and color for print ads and length for TV and radio ads, must also be made as do decisions as to scheduling/timing, the use of flighting, pulsing, or continuous advertising. The actual buying can be done by the advertising agency or by a specialized media buying organization.

DISCUSSION QUESTIONS

1. A basic component of a media model objective function involves counting exposures generated by an insertion schedule. The remaining components introduced in this chapter attempt to qualify the exposures, the potential worth of the audience member, and so on. How else might you want to qualify exposures? What other components might be added to the list?

2. Comment on the media plan for the Broiler. What would the "value of successive exposure" function look like? How would you go about deciding upon the mix of 60- and 30-second commercials?

3. You are an advertising manager for a new line of package marking devices for use by retail food stores. Your advertising is designed to create awareness among chain store managers. Two schedules with equal cost are proposed. One uses many trade journals and will reach 10,000 store managers with a frequency of 1.1. The other reaches fewer journals and will reach 4,000 with a frequency of 5.4. Which of these two alternatives is superior? What other factors should be considered?

4. In a survey of housewives, the readership of the *Atlantic Monthly* was exaggerated and the readership of *Modern Romance* seemed much less than circulation figures indicated. Why would respondents incorrectly report their readership in this manner? Can you think of any measure, perhaps unobtrusive, to avoid this bias?

5. Of the recent-reading and through-the-book methods, which do you prefer? Why?

6. What are the limitations of the people-meter?

7. Generate vehicle source-effect values for a set of magazines or TV programs using your own subjective judgment, assuming a product and an advertising objective. For example, suppose that a product-effectiveness ad was generated for an electric frypan

and the magazine alternatives were *Women's Day, TV Guide, Vogue, Elle, McCall's,* and *Time.* Justify your set of values.

8. Under what circumstances would it be effective to pulse advertising rather than spreading it out evenly? Evaluate the strategy of The Broiler to engage in ten or so television pulse campaigns during the year.

9. What are the advantages of using a media buying organization?

10. Given the data in Table 17-3, select media vehicles using CPM figures for (a) all adults and (b) females only.

NOTES

1. For an excellent technical review, see Roland Rust, *Advertising Media Models: A Practical Guide* (Lexington, MA: Lexington Books, 1986).

2. *Business Week,* June 18, 1990, p. 27, and Daozheng Lu and David A. Kiewit, "Passive People Meters: A First Step," *Journal of Advertising Research,* June/July 1987, pp.9–14.

3. Rust, *Advertising Media Models.*

4. *A Measurement of Advertising Effectiveness: The Influence of Audience Selectivity and Editorial Environment,* report by Alfred Politz, Inc., November 1962.

5. Gert Assmus, "An Empirical Investigation into the Perception of Vehicle Source Effects," *Journal of Advertising,* Winter 1978, pp. 4–10.

6. Lauren E. Crane, "How Product, Appeal and Program Affect Attitudes Towards Commercials," *Journal of Advertising Research,* 4, March 1964, p. 15.

7. Gary F. Soldow and Victor Principe, "Response to Commercials as a Function of Program Context," *Journal of Advertising Research,* 21, April 1981, pp. 59–64.

8. Harry D. Wolfe, James K. Brown, G. Clark Thompson, and Steven H. Greenberg, *Evaluating Media* (New York: National Industrial Conference Board, 1966), p. 85.

9. David A. Aaker and Philip K. Brown, "Evaluating Vehicle Source Effects," *Journal of Advertising Research,* 12, August 1972, pp. 11–16.

10. Verling Trohdahl and Robert Jones, "Predictors of Newspaper Advertising Viewership," *Journal of Advertising Research,* 5, March 1965, pp. 23–27.

11. Michael L. Ray and Peter H. Webb, "Three Prescriptions for Clutter," *Journal of Advertising Research,* February/March 1986, p. 69.

12. Daniel Starch, *Measuring Advertising Readership and Results* (New York: McGraw-Hill, 1966), p. 61.

13. Peter H. Webb and Michael L. Ray, "Effects of TV Clutter," *Journal of Advertising Research,* 9, 3 (1979), pp. 7–12.

14. For a conceptual development of this idea, see Rajeev Batra and Michael L. Ray, "Advertising Situations: The Implications of Differential Involvement and Accompanying Affect Responses," in R. J. Harris, ed., *Information Processing Research in Advertising* (Hillsdale, NJ: Erlbaum, 1983), pp. 127–151.

15. Herbert A. Zielske, "The Remembering and Forgetting of Advertising," *Journal of Marketing,* 23, March 1959, pp. 239–243.

16. Julian L. Simon, "What Do Zielske's Real Data Really Show About Pulsing?" *Journal of Marketing Research,* 16, August 1979, pp. 415–420.

17. Edward C. Strong, "The Spacing and Timing of Advertising," *Journal of Advertising Research,* 17 (6), December 1977, pp. 25–31.

18. Leonard M. Lodish, "Empirical Studies on Individual Responses to Exposure Patterns," *Journal of Marketing Research*, 8, May 1971, pp. 214–216.

19. Edward C. Strong, "The Use of Field Experimental Observations in Estimating Advertising Recall," *Journal of Marketing Research*, 11 November 1974, pp. 369–378.

20. Hubert A. Zielske and Walter A. Henry, "Remembering and Forgetting Television Ads," *Journal of Advertising Research*, 20, April 1980, pp. 7–13.

21. Regarding the decay and testing of recognition, see Herbert Krugman, "Memory Without Recall, Exposure Without Perception," *Journal of Advertising Research*, 17, August 1977, pp. 7–12, and Surendra N. Singh and Michael L. Rothschild, "Recognition as a Measure of Learning from Television Commercials," *Journal of Marketing Research*, 20, August 1983, pp. 235–248.

22. See, for instance, M. W. Sasieni, "Optimal Advertising Strategies," *Marketing Science*, 8 (4), 1989, pp. 358–370; H. Simon, "ADPULS: An Advertising Model with Wearout and Pulsation," *Journal of Marketing Research*, 19 (October 1982), pp. 352–363; V. Mahajan and E. Muller, "Advertising Pulsing Policies for Generating Awareness for New Products," *Marketing Science*, 5 (Spring 1986), pp. 89–111; and T. I. Seidman, S. P. Sethi, and N. A. Derzko, "Dynamics and Optimization of a Distributed Sales-Advertising Model," *Journal of Optimization Theory and Applications*, 52(3), pp. 443–462.

23. For a similar plan, see "McDonald's 1979 Plan: Beat Back the Competition," *Advertising Age*, February 19, 1979, p. 1.

CASE FOR PART V

PACIFIC TELEPHONE & TELEGRAPH COMPANY*

For some years prior to 1972, PT&T had been concerned about the steadily rising rate of user calls for directory assistance (DA). Directory assistance service, for which the company did not charge, was expensive and cost the company in the neighborhood of $40 to $50 million per year. In one city alone, for example, daily volume of DA calls had increased in the peak month of September from 47,000 calls per day in 1969 to a projected 59,000 calls per day in 1972. Operators' attempts to use polite phrases in asking customers to reduce the incidence of DA dialing had not been successful. Other educational programs, internal control programs, and some limited advertising had been tried, but volume of DA calls continued to rise.

The company decided in 1971 to develop a stronger and more direct advertising campaign and to test its effects in one market. Fresno, California, was chosen as the test city, and an eight-week advertising program was designed, made up of two television spots, radio spots, newspaper ads, and bill inserts. The principal themes of the ads were "Dial it yourself" and "The $40 million phone call." The campaign cost $14,000.

A summary of the essential procedure and phases of the study follows.

*Courtesy of Pacific Telephone and Telegraph Company.

Phase I, Pre-Ad Campaign

An attitude survey of Fresno residents was run during May and June 1972 to determine attitudes and opinions about the company's cost of providing DA service and about possible charges for DA service. A total of 337 Fresno customers were interviewed by telephone.

Phase II, Ad Campaign

The campaign was run for two months, July and August 1972, and involved television and radio spots, newspaper ads, and a special bill insert. Advertising emphasized the cost of providing the service, the number of calls made for numbers in the directory, and points like, "If you're concerned about the cost of your telephone service, please look up numbers in the phone book whenever you can."

Phase III, Post-Ad Campaign

Phase III consisted of two additional studies: (1) an advertising awareness survey done in September to determine coverage of the advertising among heavy residence DA users and (2) a post-ad campaign attitude survey, also done in September. The awareness survey involved 604 heavy-usage customers stratified by two-usage levels. One-half of the sample was randomly drawn from heavy users making 21 to 60 calls and one-half from very heavy users making 61 or more calls during May and June. The post-ad attitude survey was a telephone interview study of 333 residence customers, following the same procedures that had been used in the pre-ad phase. In all phases, detailed call tracking was established in four Fresno prefixes. Two of these prefixes had predominantly residential customers, and the other two had predominantly business customers. These data provided the primary information by which the company attempted to trace the effects of the advertising campaign on the actual behavior of customers with respect to DA rates.

Exhibit 1 shows monthly DA call volume in Fresno from January 1969 to November 1972. There is a marked regularity of seasonal patterning from year to year, and on this basis the company had forecast a projected volume without advertising. In September 1972, for example, the peak month of DA calls, the projection was about 59,000. Exhibit 1 shows that actual volume following the July-August campaign was only about 53,000, and the long-term growth pattern appeared to have been broken. The company calculated that the average volume decrease for the five months, July-November, was 9 percent.

Exhibit 2 shows that the trend in Fresno did not occur on a companywide basis during the period. The company overall was experiencing a growth rate during the period of about 7 percent over 1971, whereas Fresno, starting in August, showed a decrease to below 1971 volume. Some other highlights from the awareness and attitude study phase of the study were as follows:

1. Among heavy users, ad recall was very high, about 75 percent. Four out of ten heavy users who had seen or heard advertising said that they used the directory more often than they did before seeing the ads; they acknowledged that exposure to the advertising was what motivated them to make fewer DA calls.

EXHIBIT 1   Fresno directory assistance average business day volume

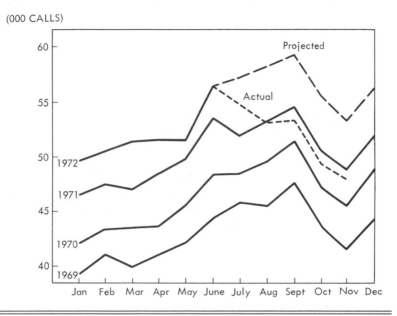

**EXHIBIT 2   Increase in average business day directory
assistance volume, comparison of PT&T and Fresno
(Percentage change from 1971 to 1972)**

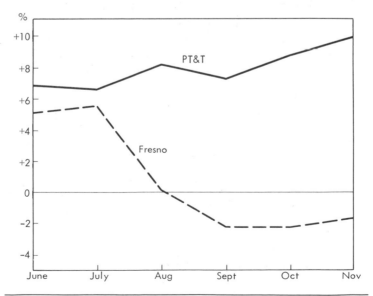

2. Some favorable shifts in attitudes and opinions about the cost of providing DA service and about possible DA charges were revealed in the attitude surveys. After the advertising, more people (26 percent versus 38 percent) said that DA service "costs a lot" for the company to provide. In the post-ad campaign survey, more people (48 percent versus 60 percent) said they would look up local numbers in the directory. This shift occurred almost entirely among respondents who said that they had seen or heard the test advertising. Finally, fewer respondents in the post-ad campaign survey felt that their reaction to the idea of a DA charge was "completely unreasonable" (43 percent versus 34 percent). These studies also provided valuable information on some of the demographic and life-style characteristics of heavy DA users compared with the general population; the heavy users tended to be younger, self-employed people in professional or managerial positions.

The results of the Fresno test were encouraging to company executives. It appeared that in Fresno the advertising campaign had had a significant and dramatic effect on call volume. An analysis was made of the cost savings resulting from the campaign in Fresno, and it was determined that, excluding overhead and equipment expenses, the company had saved $44,000 in wage and salary benefits over a five-month period as a result of the decreased volume. If the 9 percent call rate reduction could be maintained for one year, the savings would be $106,000. The production and media costs of the campaign were calculated to be $14,000.

Marketing Decisions

In the spring of 1972, the marketing planning group was attempting to determine what action should be taken for the coming year. A proposal vigorously put forward by one executive was that the company impose a minimal charge for DA assistance, which would be added to a customer's regular monthly bill, even though such a charge would be resisted by customers and the public utilities commission which would have to approve it. Another executive suggested that a systemwide campaign be developed along the lines of the Fresno campaign and be launched in the fall of 1972. It was estimated that throughout the system there were about 1 million DA calls daily and that the annual expense for operators and equipment handling these calls was about $55 million.

Although nobody knew precisely what a systemwide campaign would cost, the company's advertising agency had suggested that it would be about $500,000. The head of the marketing research group suggested a third alternative. He proposed that the company set aside additional funds for continued research on advertising effects on DA call volume and, in effect, repeat the Fresno experiment in other test markets before proceeding with a systemwide campaign or imposing a charge for the service. These executives were aware of the increasing amount of publicity being generated at the time by citizen groups against advertising by utility companies. Many of these groups were arguing that, because of the environmental and energy crisis, public utilities should be restricted from advertising. They claimed funds should be used to reduce customer telephone charges rather than be wasted on activities like advertising.

Discussion Questions

1. Based on the figures given in the case, what is the economic value to the company of the advertising expenditures invested in the Fresno test market?

2. All other considerations aside, and assuming that a decision is made to launch a systemwide advertising campaign, how much money should the company invest in such a campaign?

3. In your own words, describe the Fresno test market experiment.

4. What problems do you see in the experimental design? How would you have changed it?

5. Discuss the assumption that the savings in Fresno could be projected to cover the full year.

6. What action should the marketing planning group have taken in the spring of 1972?

18

ADVERTISING REGULATION

Consumers have a considerable tolerance for exaggeration and puffery
in advertising. . . . They undoubtedly expect advertisements to be
biased and to present merchandise in an attractive light.

Neil Borden, 1942, professor of advertising,
Harvard University

Advertising has a responsibility within our economic system to provide information on new and existing products and services. Most of what is purchased is advertised. Thus, the economic health of both buyers and competitors is affected if the advertising system is injected with false or misleading claims. The result can be a misallocation of resources, disappointed or even injured buyers, and damaged competitors.

There is no question that false and misleading advertising should be prevented and that the government needs to play a key role through the FTC, state and local regulation, and the courts. It is, however, not a simple task because there are a host of issues that need to be addressed.

One central issue is the definitional one—what is deception? When Blatz claims that it is "Milwaukee's finest beer," is deception involved when many (particularly other Milwaukee brewers) argue that other beers are superior? What does "finest" mean? One advertisement claimed that a hair dye would color hair permanently. If someone exposed to the advertisement believed that the dye would hold for hair not yet grown and thus a single dye would last for decades, is the claim deceptive?

There are other issues as well. How many people need to misunderstand before deception is involved? When there is disagreement about what is deception, who should decide? How can dishonest and careless advertisers be detected, prosecuted, and punished? To what extent can self-regulation be relied upon? What are appropriate remedies? These questions and others make the issue of deception a complex area for an advertiser, the media, and the government.

In the following sections, the history of regulation will be briefly sketched. The concept of deception will then be considered. The role of advertising research will then be examined followed by a discussion of the remedies available to the FTC when deception is found. Finally, the matter of lawsuits and self-regulation will be considered.

HISTORY OF FEDERAL REGULATION OF ADVERTISING

In 1914, the Federal Trade Commission Act was passed, which created the federal agency that has had the primary responsibility for the regulation of advertising. Section 5 of the FTC Act contained this prohibition: "Unfair methods of competition in commerce are hereby declared unlawful." The aim was to provide an agency that could deal with restraints of trade more effectively than had the Sherman antitrust law. The problem of deceptive advertising was not a target of the FTC Act. Millstein, a legal scholar, observes: "The most important development in the long history of the FTC's prohibition of false advertising was that the FTC concerned itself with the problem in the first place."[1] In many respects it was a fortuitous accident.

The FTC became concerned with deceptive advertising because of its effect upon competition. In the first test case in 1919 the FTC moved against Sears, Roebuck.[2] Sears had advertised that their prices for sugar and tea were lower than competitors because of their larger buying power. The claim was found to be false, but the FTC action was upheld, not because of subsequent damage caused the consumer but by the fact that smaller competitors could be injured. Thus for many years, advertising regulation was largely concentrated on the need to protect small firms and competitors rather than consumers themselves.

In 1931, in the landmark *FTC* v. *Raladam* case, the Supreme Court specifically held that the FTC could not prohibit false advertising if there is no evidence of injury to a competitor.[3] The ruling struck a decisive blow in that it stopped any movement in the direction of protecting the consuming public directly. However, it was a blessing in disguise for it helped to mobilize support for redefining the powers of the FTC. The ultimate result was the Wheeler-Lea Amendment passed in 1938, which amended Section 5 of the FTC Act to read as follows: "Unfair methods of competition in commerce and unfair or deceptive actions or practices in commerce are hereby declared unlawful." Thus the obligation to demonstrate that injury to competition occurred was removed. The issue then was not a jurisdictional one but rather how to move forward against deceptive advertising.

A basic issue in the enforcement of these laws against deceptive advertising, to which we now turn, is how to define and identify deception.

WHAT IS DECEPTIVE ADVERTISING?

Conceptually, deception exists when an advertisement is introduced into the perceptual process of some audience and the output of that perceptual process (1) differs from the reality of the situation and (2) affects buying behavior to the detriment of the consumer. The input itself may be determined to contain falsehoods. The more difficult and perhaps more common case, however, is when the input, the advertisement, is not obviously false, but the perceptual process generates an impression that is deceptive. A disclaimer may not pass through the attention filter or the message may be misinterpreted.

Legally, the definition of deception has evolved over the years since the Wheeler-Lea Amendment was passed. Refinements have been caused by the FTC in its decisions in individual cases and in its Trade Regulation Rules, which cover unlawful trade practices of entire industries. The FTC positions can be appealed to the courts, which ultimately provide the legal definition of deceptive advertising.

To provide guidance in the face of a history of sometimes conflicting decisions regarding deception, the FTC in 1983 decided to go on record with a formal position. Although somewhat controversial (it was passed on a 3-to-2 vote), it does represent an important effort to define deception. Dividing the definition into its three major components, it states that deception will be found if

1. there is a misrepresentation, omission, or practice that is likely to mislead.
2. the consumer is acting responsibly (or reasonably) in the circumstances.
3. to the consumer's detriment [that is, the practice] is material and consumer injury is likely because consumers are likely to have chosen differently but for the deception.[4]

Although some argue that this definition only codifies the body of law that preceded it, most observers suggested that the definition involves two major changes from prior positions which make it harder for a ad to qualify as deceptive.[5] First, the deception must be likely to mislead while the prior understanding was that it need only have a tendency or capacity to mislead. Second, the deception must occur in consumers acting responsibly or reasonably in the circumstances rather than simply a substantial number of consumers (even if they are naive and unthinking). Thus, the consumer is charged with at least some minimal responsibility in interpreting the advertising.

In the following discussion, we will look more closely at these three dimensions of deceptive advertising.

A Misrepresentation or Omission

There are a variety of ways in which misrepresentation or omissions can occur:

Suggesting that a small difference is important. A Lorillard ad that correctly claimed that its cigarette was the lowest level of tar and nicotine in a cigarette test reported in *Reader's Digest* was ruled deceptive because the differences between Lorillard's Kent and several other brands was insignificant and meaningless.[6]

Implying that a test is scientifically conducted. A television commercial for a car wax used flaming gasoline on an automobile to demonstrate that the wax could withstand intense heat.[7] However, because the gasoline was only burning for a few seconds, no significant heat was generated and the test really proved nothing.

Using an ambiguous or easily confused phrase. The use of the phrase "government supported" could be interpreted as "government approved" and was therefore challenged.[8] In another case the FTC held that a toothpaste claim that it "fights decay" could be interpreted as a claim that it provides complete protection and was therefore deceptive.[9]

Implying a benefit that does not exist. An aspirin substitute, Efficen, was truthfully advertised as containing no aspirin. However, the FTC charged that the no aspirin claim implied incorrectly that the product would not have Aspirin's side effects.[10]

Implying that a product benefit is unique to a brand. A FTC complaint against Wonder Bread argued that Wonder Bread's claim that its brand build bodies 12 ways falsely implied that Wonder Bread was unique with respect to such a claim. Although this charge was subsequently dropped, it does illustrate one possible way in which the definition of deception could be broadened.[11] Interestingly, Hunt-Wesson Foods, soon after the Wonder Bread complaint was filed, developed a policy of avoiding advertising brands that are virtually similar to their competitors.

Implying that a benefit is needed. Gainesburgers once advertised that its product contained all the milk protein your dog needs. It was true that the product had milk protein that competitors did not. But it was also true that dogs need little or no milk protein. The FTC argued that the line "Every BODY Needs Milk" incorrectly implied that good health required regular milk consumption.

Incorrectly implying that an endorser uses and advocates the brand. Advertisements implied that an acne medication was superior and had cured Pat Boone's daughter's acne when neither claim was true.[12] Pat Boone, the endorser, was ordered to return his remuneration to users. An endorser in general only need inform the audience that payment is involved when there is an implication that no payment is involved. Procter & Gamble, however, was judged to imply incorrectly that washing machine manufactures distributed P&G detergents with their machines because they endorsed the brands rather than the fact that they were paid to do so.

Omitting a needed qualification. The FTC can require that a more complete disclosure be made to correct a misconception. Thus Geritol was required to indicate that the "tired feeling" it was supposed to help was possibly due to factors that the product could not treat effectively.[13] Similarly, baldness cures have been required to indicate that baldness usually is hereditary and untreatable. Toys usually are assumed to be safe. Therefore, toy manufacturers have a special responsibility to point out possible unsafe aspects of their toys.

It is interesting to consider how far pressure from the FTC for complete disclosure could go. There are a wide variety of advertised brands that differ little in substance from competitors. It is a common practice to associate a brand with an attribute of the product class. Should the brand be required to state in its advertisement that all brands are virtually identical in this respect? For example, an aspirin advertisement may emphasize the product's pain-relieving quality without mentioning that all aspirin-based brands will have a similar effect.

Making a claim without substantiation. The FTC can require advertisers to substantiate claims made with respect to safety, performance, efficacy, quality, or comparative price when such claims will be relied on by a consumer who lacks the ability or knowledge to independently judge their validity. Firestone was ordered to stop advertising that its tires "stop 25% faster," and Fedders was told to stop calling its reserve cooling system "unique" when it was unable to support these claims with valid test or survey data. Inadequate substantiation is considered an unfair (as opposed to deceptive) action by the FTC.

Puffery

A rather well-established rule of law is that "trade puffing" is permissible. Puffing takes two general forms. The first is a subjective statement of opinion about a product's quality, using such terms as "best or greatest." Nearly all advertisements contain some measure of puffery. "You can't get any closer"(Norelco), "Try something better" (J&B Scotch), "Gas gives you a better deal" (American Gas Association), "Live better electrically" (Edison Electric Institution), "State Farm is all you need to know about insurance," "Super Shell." None of these statements has been proved to be true, but neither have they been proved false. They all involve some measure of exaggeration.

In 1946, the court set aside the FTC ruling in the *Carlay* case that a weight-reduction plan involving Ayds candy, which claimed to be "easy" to follow, was deceptive. The court noted that "what was said was clearly justifiable . . . under those cases recognizing that such words as 'easy,' 'perfect,' 'amazing,' 'prime,' 'wonderful,' and 'excellent' are regarded in law as mere puffing or dealer's talk upon which no charge of misrepresentation can be based." [14]

The second form of puffery is an exaggeration extended to the point of outright spoof that is obviously not true. A Green Giant is obviously fictitious, and even if he were real, he wouldn't be talking the way he does. In the 1927 *Ostermoor* case, the court pointed to the puffery argument in denying that a mattress company was deceptive in using an illustration appearing to depict that the inner filling of a mattress would expand to 35 inches when in fact it would expand only 3 to 6 inches. [15]

Preston and Johnson and later Preston examine the puffery issue and declare that although it is well established in law, it is at the same time somewhat vulnerable and has been often denied. [16] For example, in the *Tanners Shoe Company* case, the FTC denied the puffery defense, declaring that

> it was stipulated that it is not literally true that respondents' shoes will assure comfort or a perfect fit to all individuals. However, respondents contend that such representations constitute legitimate trade puffery and are not false representations within the meaning of the law. . . . The representation that the product provides support where it is most needed clearly carries an orthopedic or health connotation, and it is undisputed that respondents' shoes are not orthopedic . . . but are stock shoes. It would appear that such a representation is false in attributing to the product a quality which it does not possess rather than exaggerating a quality which it has. [17]

Who Is Deceived—The Reasonable Consumer?

Who is it that is to be protected? The FTC has historically taken the extreme position that essentially all are to be protected, in particular those who are naive, trusting, and of low intelligence.

In 1944 this position was graphically illustrated by two cases. In the *Charles of the Ritz* case, the FTC found that the trademark "Rejuvenescence" was associated with a foundation makeup cream in a manner that promised the restoration of a youthful complexion.[18] Some, including those ignorant, unthinking, and credulous, might believe that the product could actually cause youth to be restored. In *Gelb* v. *FTC*, the FTC prohibited the claim that a hair-coloring product could color hair permanently.[19] Its position was that some might believe that even new hair would have the desired new color.

The 1955 *Kirchner* case provided some relief to the charge that no deception can exist.[20] It involved a swimming aid and the claim that when the device was worn under a swimming suit it was "thin and invisible." The commission decided that buyers who were not "foolish or feebleminded" would be unlikely to take this claim literally, noting

> Perhaps a few misguided would believe, for example, that all "Danish pastry" is made in Denmark. Is it, therefore, an actual deception to advertise "Danish pastry" when it is made in this country? Of course not. A representation does not become "false and deceptive" merely because it will be unreasonably misunderstood by an insignificant and unrepresentative segment of the class of persons to whom the representation is addressed.[21]

The *Kirchner* case also indicated that advertising aimed at particularity susceptible groups will be evaluated with respect to that group. Thus, when children are the target, deception will be evaluated with respect to them. One case was decided on the basis of the advertising impact on a "busy businessman." This refinement is interesting because it recognizes that people may perceive stimuli differently, depending on the situational context.

As noted, in 1983, the FTC narrowed its definition of deception in an important way. Previously an advertisement was held to be deceptive if it "has the tendency or capacity to deceive a substantial number of consumers in a material way." However, in the *Cliffdale* case, the proper test for finding deception was whether the claim is "material and likely to mislead consumers acting 'reasonably' under the circumstances." The key word is "reasonably." A mail-order company, Cliffdale Associates, had advertised an automobile fuel economy device, the $12.95 BallMatic Valve, which made deceptive performance claims. The FTC concluded that consumers acting reasonably would not be materially affected.

Materiality of the Falsehood

For an advertisement to be deceptive, it must contain a material untruth, that is, one capable of affecting purchase decisions. It should be likely that the advertisement will cause public injury. Millstein explains:

> "Public injury" does not mean that a consumer must actually suffer damage, or that it must be shown that goods purchased are unequal to the value expended. Rather, "public injury" results if the advertisement has a tendency to induce action (such as the purchase itself) detrimental to the consumer that might not otherwise have been taken. If such action could not have been induced by the claim (even though false), there is no "public injury." This

requirement comports with the express provision of Section 15 of the FTC Act, as amended, that the advertisement must be misleading in a material respect to be actionable.[22]

Courts and the FTC have ruled that only mock-ups and props that were intended to demonstrate visually a quality that was material to the sale of a product would be prohibited. If the demonstration would not affect consumer's decisions, then even if it were misrepresented, it would not be deceptive. Thus, mashed potatoes could be used in television commercials in scenes depicting ice cream consumption (ice cream will melt too rapidly under lights) if the texture and color of the prop were not emphasized as selling points of the product.

DETERMINING DECEPTION USING ADVERTISING RESEARCH

The crucial issue in deceptive advertising is often the determination of how the advertising claims are perceived by consumers and what impact such perceptions have on consumer behavior. Since these issues are also central to copy testing and to the evaluation of an advertising campaign, it would be natural for the FTC and the courts to avail themselves of the methodologies of advertising research. Until the late 1960s, however, there was actually little consumer research employed in this context.

Several factors inhibited the use of consumer research on perceptions.

1. The FTC simply was not required by the courts to develop evidence—subjective judgment was held as adequate.

2. The use of independently commissioned survey research is somewhat inconsistent with the traditional adversary system of justice wherein each side submits arguments and evidence to support a position. To an attorney, agreeing to a carefully conceived and conducted survey might be too much like calling a prestigious witness without knowing which side his or her testimony will support.

3. There are methodological difficulties and pitfalls in any study. The population must be defined, a defensible sampling plan created, and questions designed to pass tests of unbiasedness and validity. Additional pressures on any research design are created in the legal context by opposing lawyers and experts who will try to discredit it. Some early survey efforts were extremely flawed with small, unrepresentative samples and naive questionnaires.

4. Defendants have lacked motivation to introduce survey evidence, as it would tend to be used against them. In the 1963 *Benrus Watch* case a survey showed that 86 percent correctly interpreted an ad, but the FTC used the fact that 14 percent had been deceived as evidence against Benrus.[23]

Over the years, the reluctance to use consumer research to determine how advertising is perceived and how it impacts has gradually eroded for two reasons. First, the consumer research community has both advanced their methods and worked to apply them in the legal setting. Several prominent consumer researchers have worked in the FTC, for example, and thereby have helped show how research methods can be applied to determine the impact of deception upon perceptions, beliefs, and behavior. Second, the courts, seeing the power of consumer evidence especially as to perceptions, have begun to look for such evidence and be suspicious when it is missing or flawed.

What Is an Acceptable Level of Misperception?

A key lingering issue had been the determination of the ''acceptable'' level of misperception. In general, levels under 5 percent are considered too low. However, as the *Benrus Watch* case illustrates, levels of 15 to 20 percent have been deemed high enough to support a finding that deception exists. In the 1972 *Firestone Tire* case, the FTC concluded that if 10 percent of the audience perceived the claim that Safety Champion tire was free of any defects and safe under any conditions, that level was substantial.[24] How extensive must the deception be before deception is determined to exist?

To develop a guideline as to what level of miscomprehension should be expected in an average ad, the American Association of Advertising Agencies sponsored a study, reviewed in Chapter 8. A set 60 of television ads were exposed to respondents who were asked six true/false questions about each (and a series of editorial messages). A remarkably consistent finding (both using ads and the editorial messages) was that 30 percent of the content was miscomprehended. The implication is that any baseline under 30 percent is unfair and unrealistic.

Others have concluded that a close examination of the study suggests that any baseline measure should be less than 30 percent. First, the study involved a single exposure to a broad audience in an artificial situation, whereas most advertising involves multiple exposures in natural settings involving a target audience.[25] Second, some of the questions were ambiguous, poorly worded, or immaterial. Third, the measure used may not be appropriate. Other measures, based upon unaided recall, for example, might generate much lower levels. In addition, there is a concern that the study focused upon literal miscomprehension while much of deception involves claims that are literally true.

Preston and Richards also makes the case that some miscomprehension is eradicable and should not be considered a baseline given that nothing can be done about.[26] For example, ''I don't have no bananas'' is ambiguous but could be easily revised to remove the ambiguity. The use of ''the pain reliever doctors recommend most'' could have been replace with ''aspirin'' and reduced substantially the ''miscomprehension.'' Another name could have been selected so that the brand Aspercreme was not incorrectly perceived to contain aspirin.

There is no question that miscomprehension does occur. The question is: What should the ''baseline'' level be in a particular context? The standard will surely depend on the context. If health and safety are involved, only very low or even zero levels of misperception might be tolerated. However, if the ''danger'' in buying the wrong soap or toothpaste is modest, higher levels could be tolerated.

REMEDIES

The FTC has a variety of remedies at its disposal. One task is to select the remedy most appropriate to the situation. Among the remedies are the cease-and-desist order, restitution, affirmative disclosure, and corrective advertising.

Cease-and-Desist Orders

The cease-and-desist order, which prohibits the respondent from engaging any more in the deceptive practice, is actually the only formal procedure established by the FTC Act for enforcing its prohibition of "deceptive acts and practices." It has been criticized as being a command to "go and sin no more," which has little practical effect. Due to procedural delays, it is not uncommon for several years to elapse between the filing of the complaint and the issuance of the order. In one extreme case, it took 16 years for the commission to get the "Liver" out of Carter's Little Liver Pills.[27] During the delay, the advertising can go on. By the time the cease-and-desist order is issued, the advertising may have served its purpose and another campaign may be underway anyway.

Restitution

Restitution means that the consumer is compensated for any damage. For example, the FTC required a mail-order company to make restitution in the form of full refunds for its skin cream, diet plans, vitamin supplements, and other products that had advertised claims not adequately substantiated.[28] Restitution is rarely considered because of its severity.

Affirmative Disclosures

If an advertisement has provided insufficient information to the consumer, an affirmative disclosure might be issued.[29] Affirmative disclosures require "clear and conspicuous" disclosure of the omitted information. Often the involved information relates to deficiencies or limitations of the product or service possibly relating to matters of health or safety. Kenrec Sports, Inc., was ordered to disclose certain limitations to its swimming aid, such as that the device is not a life preserver and should always be used in shallow water.[30] Medi-Hair International was required for one year to devote at least 15 percent of each advertisement for its baldness concealment system to the limitations and drawbacks of the system.

Corrective Advertising

Corrective advertising requires advertisers to rectify past deception by making suitable statements in future commercials.[31] The concept is illustrated by the 1971 Profile Bread case, the first case for which corrective advertising was a part of the remedy.[32] The consent order agreed to by Continental Baking specified that 25 percent of the next year's

Profile Bread advertising had to support a FTC-approved correct message, such as one featuring Julia Meade, which read in part

> Hi, Julia Meade for Profile Bread. Like all mothers, I'm concerned about nutrition and balanced meals. So, I'd like to clear up any misunderstanding you may have about Profile Bread from its advertising or even its name.
>
> Does Profile have fewer calories than any other brands? No. Profile has about the same per ounce as other brands. To be exact, Profile has seven fewer calories per slice. That's because Profile is sliced thinner. But eating Profile will not cause you to lose weight. A reduction of seven calories is insignificant. It's total calories and balanced nutrition that count. And Profile can help you achieve a balanced meal because . . .[33]

There was some evidence that the sales of Profile Bread suffered as a result of the corrective advertising.

The 1975 FTC corrective advertising order against Warner-Lambert's Listerine is important because it was appealed all the way to the Supreme Court.[34] Listerine had advertised for over 50 years that gargling with Listerine mouthwash helped prevent colds and sore throats by killing germs. They were required by the courts to include the statement, "Listerine will not help prevent colds or sore throats or lessen their severity" in $10 million of advertising, which was equal to the average annual expenditure during a prior 10-year period.

Listerine implemented the order by embedding the statement in a commercial featuring two couples, each with a husband finding himself having "onion breath." One couple used Scope and the other Listerine. The wife using Scope sniffed her husband's breath and said that she didn't know that "clinical tests prove Listerine fights onion breath better than Scope." The other replied, "We always knew." The corrective disclosure appeared midway in the 30-second spot as follows: "While Listerine will not help prevent colds or sore throats or lessen their severity, breath tests prove Listerine fights onion breath better than Scope."

Three field studies basically found that the corrective advertising had a modest impact. In day-after-recall tests, only 5 percent mentioned the corrective message when asked to describe the ad; it was the fourth most recalled message in the ad.[35] Two studies focused on before-after changes in beliefs about Listerine. One, using four waves of telephone interviews, found a reduction of about 20 percent in overall deceptive beliefs about Listerine's effectiveness.[36] The other, an FTC study, consisted of seven waves of questionnaire mailings which garnered 10,000 returned questionnaires (a 70 percent response rate) from the Market Facts consumer panel.[37] Beliefs that Listerine is effective for colds and sore throats fell about 11 percent (14 percent for Listerine users). The amount of mouthwash used for colds and sore throats dropped 40 percent. Thus, a substantial level of misperception about Listerine effectiveness remained after the campaign.

The Listerine case clearly established the FTC's authority to order corrective advertising, but it also served to raise some important issues. Any remedy should be nonpunitive in nature and should be the least burdensome remedy. How do you determine whether the corrective advertising is generating damage to sales or image that would not be necessary to correcting the misperceptions? A remedy should preserve the First

Amendment right to express ideas. What about those ideas that are counter to the corrective message's claims? Can an advertiser simply decide to stop advertising, thereby avoiding corrective advertising?

One problem with corrective advertising is that it has usually resulted in lawyers writing copy and insisting that it be run some arbitrary length of time. Wilkie has observed that the much more sensible approach would be to give the advertisers a communication task and let them achieve it any way that they can.[38]

Such an approach was partially applied in the Hawaiian Punch case.[39] Hawaiian Punch used a catchy jingle, "Seven Natural Fruit Juices in Hawaiian Punch," together with fruit photos even though it contains only 11 to 15 percent fruit juice. Hawaiian Punch agreed to disclose the actual fruit juice content of the product ("contains not less than 11 percent natural fruit juice"). The disclosure was to run until a specified survey found that 67 percent of fruit drink purchasers are aware that Hawaiian Punch contained less than 20 percent natural fruit juice. A series of 17 semiannual telephone surveys indicated that relevant perceptions were slow to change.[40] Over the 1974–1982 period, the proportion of consumers who believed that Hawaiian Punch had 20 percent or less fruit juice increased from 20 percent (1974) to 40 percent (1975) to 50 percent (1982). The target was reached only after nine years of advertising.

The implementation of the communication objective approach to corrective advertising will always face difficulties. The problem of ascertaining how misperception and its effect are to be measured and the appropriate target level of misperception that should be obtained reappears in this context. Judgments on such questions are required to set communication objectives. Obviously, a zero misperception level is not generally feasible. Yet regulators and the general public to which they must answer have difficulty accepting realistic standards. A key is to know whether the advertiser is making a good faith effort toward the objective. Copy testing could logically be used to address this point, but the parties would have to agree in advance on relevant and suitable tests, a difficult prospect. Another problem is the cost of measuring deception over time. The tracking required to measure the impact of the commercials—no problem for large advertisers, who do that anyway—could be costly for smaller advertisers and may require the government to share some of the costs.

Corrective advertising has only rarely been considered since the Listerine case largely because of the difficulties in deciding upon the target objective. However, it remains an important option especially because conceptually it serves to focus attention on what are usually the central issues in deception cases.

COMPETITOR LAWSUITS

Another mechanism that inhibits deceptive advertising is the possibility that competitors will sue, charging that false advertising has caused them damage. In one case, a suit was successfully brought by Honeywell against a competitor who supplied replacement parts to Honeywell's safety control systems and had incorrectly claimed that its products had comparable quality and ease of replacement to that of Honeywell.

During the last decade, the 1946 Lanham Trademark Act has been broadened to provide the basis for suits in which a competitor has been disparaged in an comparative ad. In one visible case a rental firm, Jartran, ran a series of ads that was judged to have damaged U-Haul.[41] In one, a special introductory Jartran price was compared to U-Haul's usual price, implying a price difference that did not exist. In another, older smaller U-Haul trucks were compared to new larger Jartran trucks, incorrectly implying a difference between the average truck in the two fleets.

In most cases, the relief is an injunction to stop the offending practice. However, the a wide range of remedies exit. In the Jartran case, the firm was ordered to replace $6 million in lost U-Haul profits and another $13.6 million to compensate for U-Haul's corrective advertising outlay. Another $20 million was assessed because the action was willful and malicious.

SELF-REGULATION

Self-regulation is another vehicle to combat deceptive advertising by national advertisers. In place in the United States since 1971, the effort is intended to provide a fast, flexible alternative to FTC and the courts. Complaints from consumers or competitors are investigated by the National Advertising Division (NAD), an arm of the Council of Better Business Bureaus (CBBB). In evaluating a complaint, NAD normally requests that the advertiser submit substantiation for the claims made in the challenged advertisements. If the complaint is judged to be justified, the advertiser is requested to modify or withdrawal the challenged advertising. The finding can be appealed to a panel drawn mostly from the advertising industry.

The self-regulation process does provide remedies in a meaningful number of cases—perhaps 100 decisions each year are brought. Although the penalties are relatively minor—it can generate negative publicity, refer the case to the FTC, and suggest major media deny access to the offender—as a practical matter nearly all advertisers accept its findings. Its biggest value, however, is probably to provide a forum to establish standards for advertisers and to make visible issues regarding deception in advertising.[42]

In one series of 11 rulings by the NAB, three involved claims that were substantiated.[43] For example, Revlon supplied independent research to support its claim that Colorsilk, a hair-coloring product, promises color that is rich, true, and lasting and hair that feels silkier and looks healthier.

The other eight companies either modified or discontinued their advertising. Curtis Mathes failed to mention that labor charges were not included when advertising the four-year limited warranty on its television sets. Hall of Music in television advertisements offered over 80 of the world's greatest masterpieces in a two-album collection. The NAD was concerned that the consumer might believe that he or she was getting the entire selection instead of excerpts. Louis Marx in television advertisements for Big Wheel, a ride-on toy, used the disclaimer, "assembly required." The children's unit of NAD felt that simpler wording is needed for child-directed advertisements. E. J. Brach advertised that "We still use fresh, natural ingredients, so Brach's tastes better than other candy." The NAD indicated that some clarification was required since some artificial coloring and flavoring is used.

SUMMARY

Conceptually, deception exists when an advertisement is input to the perceptual process of some audience and the output of that perceptual process (1) differs from the reality of the situation and (2) affects buying behavior to the detriment of the consumer. The legal definition has been influenced by a 1983 formal FTC position which stated that deception will be found if there is a misrepresentation or omission that is likely to mislead a consumer acting responsibly to the consumer's detriment.

A misrepresentation or omission can occur because of an ambiguous phrase or when the ad contains the incorrect implication that:

- Small differences are important.
- A test is conducted scientifically.
- A benefit exists, is needed, or is unique to a brand.
- An endorser uses and/or advocates the brand.
- A claim does not require a qualification.
- A claim is substantiated.

Puffing, the subjective statement of opinion concerning a product's quality, using terms such as "best," is permissible. However, the definition of what is puffery has been narrowed over time.

The 1983 FTC statement narrowed the definition of deception from "having the capacity to deceive a substantial number of consumers in a material way" to "material and likely to mislead consumers acting 'reasonably' under the circumstances." Thus the "unthinking and credulous" seem no longer to be protected but the requirement that the advertising affect the consumer remains.

Consumer research was rarely used in deception cases until the 1970s because the FTC subjective judgment was deemed adequate, legal adversaries would not be comfortable agreeing to allow a study to prove deception, of methodological difficulties, and because defendants feared that consumer research would be used against them. A key issue is to determine the acceptable level of misperception. The AAAA study based upon single exposures to ads found that around 28 percent of claims made in commercials are misperceived, about the same level found in other television programming. The appropriate level will clearly be a function of the situation and the measure used.

The FTC has several available remedies. Cease-and-desist orders prohibit the respondent from engaging further in the deceptive practice. Restitution provides compensation to those deceived. Affirmative disclosure requires that missing information be disclosed in a clear and conspicuous manner. Corrective advertising seeks to eliminate the effects of prior misleading advertising. Efforts to employ corrective advertising by requiring the insertion of some phrase in the ads generally has little impact. A more useful remedy would be to demand corrective advertising aimed at some communication objective. The difficulty is to establish that objective.

Deception in advertising can also be controlled by competitor lawsuits and by self-regulation. The Lanham Trademark Act has been used as a vehicle to combat damage caused when a competitor is disparaged unfairly in a comparative ad. The advertising industry has developed an ambitious program of self-regulation, which rests largely on the support of the industry itself that has provided relatively fast and effective results in comparison to action using the FTC or the courts.

DISCUSSION QUESTIONS

1. In your judgment, are the following deceptive?
   (a) The Geritol case (tired blood)
   (b) Wonder Bread (the implied uniqueness issue)
   (c) Efficen (implying a benefit that doesn't exist)
2. For the advertisements in question 1, how would you use advertising research to help determine whether deception is present?
3. All advertisements have the capacity to deceive some audience members. For example, if you just showed a picture of a glass of milk, some people would believe that the advertisement was falsely implying that everyone must drink at least one glass of milk a day because that belief has been ingrained in them. Comment.
4. Evaluate the following proposals:
   (a) Advertising for brands that are, for all practical purposes, identical to competitors' should be eliminated.
   (b) The use of live models or spokespeople should be eliminated.
   (c) Only the product itself, with no background scenes, can be shown in an advertisement.
5. The FTC is concerned about the use of endorsements by celebrities or experts (as opposed to the use of spokesperson or a "slice-of-life" dramatization). What guidelines would you suggest that would help ensure that such advertisements would not be deceptive? Illustrate how your guidelines would apply by considering examples.
6. If a brand is not substantially different from its competitors, should its advertisements state that fact? What would be the effect of such a rule?
7. Pornography, which is protected by free speech guarantees, is judged by whether the average person applying contemporary community standards believes the dominant theme appeals to prurient interests. What is the standard applied to advertising? Is that appropriate? Should the rights of business to inform be specified by the FTC? What guidelines should be used in interpreting surveys designed to measure deception?

8. If the FTC holds that inadequate substantiation exists for an advertising claim, they have held responsible not only the manufacturer but also the agency preparing the advertising, the retailer running it, and the celebrity used in the advertisement to endorse the product. Comment on this policy.

9. Identify three advertisements that contain claims that should have prior substantiation.

10. In some corrective advertising proposals, a one-year period and 25 percent of advertising budgets were suggested as the extent of the corrective advertising effort. How should the percentage and the time period be determined? How should it vary with products and situation? Give examples.

11. How would you determine if the National Advertising Review Board is effective at resolving complaints concerning deceptive advertising? If its concern is broadened to include issues of taste, how do you think it will perform in that regard? How would you then measure performance?

12. In a survey of 200 people, 90 percent recognized the *Good Housekeeping* Seal, 50 percent relied upon it for purchasing decisions, and 29 percent believed that the product met federal quality and safety standards, but no one interviewed recognized that the seal was given only to advertisers. Should such a seal be continued? What role does it have in consumer decision making?

13. Consider question 5 in Chapter 19 regarding an advertising code for children.

14. Some argue that comparative advertisements in which one or more competitors are explicitly named are unfair to competitors and tend to be deceptive and therefore should be illegal. Such advertisements are, in fact, illegal in France, Belgium, Spain, and Italy. Comment.

15. Comment on the AAAA study of miscomprehension levels. Does 28 percent provide a benchmark level of miscomprehension to be used in deceptive advertising cases?

NOTES

1. Ira M. Millstein, "The Federal Trade Commission and False Advertising," *Columbia Law Review,* 64, March 1964, p. 439.

2. *Sears, Roebuck & Co.* v. *FTC,* 258 Fed. 307 (7th Cir. 1919).

3. *FTC* v. *Raladam Co.,* 258 U.S. 643 (1931).

4. FTC (1983) at 689–690. For an excellent analysis of this statement, see Gary T. Ford and John E. Calfee, "Recent Developments in FTC Policy on Deception," *Journal of Marketing, 50,* July 1986, pp. 82–103.

5. Thomas C. Kinnear and Ann R. Root, "The FTC and Deceptive Advertising in the 1980s: Are Consumers Being Adequately Protected?" *Journal of Public Policy & Marketing,* 1988, pp. 40–48.

6. *P. Lorillard Co.* v. *FTC,* 186 F.2d 52 (4th Cir. 1950).

7. Hutchinson Chem. Corp., 55 FTC 1942 (1959).

8. *FTC* v. *Sterling Drug, Inc.,* 215 F.Supp. 327, 330 (S.D.N.Y.), aff'd 317 F.2d 699 (2d Cir. 1963).

9. Bristol-Myers Co., 46 FTC 162 (1949), aff'd 185 F.2d 58 (4th Cir. 1950).

10. Ivan L. Preston, Communication Research in the Prosecution of Deceptive Advertising,'' Lecture given at the University of Texas, May, 1986.

11. "FTC to Issue Consent in Wonder Case," *Advertising Age,* November 5, 1973, p. 1.

12. Amy Freedland, "Truth or Consequences: Deceptive Advertising Laws and Policies of the Twentieth Century," Unpublished paper, University of Michigan, Ann Arbor, 1990.

13. J. B. Williams Co., 3 Trade Reg. Rep. 17. 339 (FTC Dkt. No. 8547, 1965), appeal docketed, No. 16, 969 (6th Cir. 1965).

14. *Carlay* v. *FTC,* 153 F.2d 493, 496 (1946).

15. *Ostermoor & Co.* v. *FTC,* 16 F.2d 962 (2d Cir. 1927).

16. Ivan L. Preston and Ralph H. Johnson, "Puffery: A Vulnerable (?) Feature of Advertising," Paper presented at the annual convention of the Association for Education in Journalism, University of South Carolina, August 1971, and Ivan L. Preston, "The FTC's Handling of Puffery and Other Selling Claims Made 'By Implication,' " *Journal of Business Research,* June 1977, pp. 155–181.

17. Tanners Shoe Company, 53 FTC Decisions 1137 (1957).

18. *Charles of the Ritz Dist. Corp.* v. *FTC,* 143 F.2d 676 (2d Cir. 1944).

19. *Gelb* v. *FTC,* 144 F.2d 580 (2d Cir. 1944).

20. Trade Reg. Rep. 16664 (FTC, November 7, 1963).

21. Ibid., at 21539-40.

22. Millstein, "False Advertising," p. 438.

23. Benrus Watch Co., 3 Trade Reg. Rep. 16541 (FTC, July 31, 1963).

24. Firestone Tire, 81 FTC Decisions 298, 1972.

25. Gary T. Ford and Richard Yalch, "Viewer Miscomprehension of Televised Communication—A Comment," *Journal of Marketing,* 46, Fall 1982, pp. 27–31.

26. Ivan L. Preston and Jeff I. Richards, "Consumer Miscomprehension as a Challenge to FTC Prosecutions of Deceptive Advertising," *The John Marshall Law Review,* Spring 1986, pp. 605–635.

27. *Carter Products, Inc.* v. *FTC,* 186 F.2d 821 (7th Cir. 1951).

28. Dorothy Cohen, "The FTC's Advertising Substantiation Program," *Journal of Marketing,* Winter 1980, pp. 26–35.

29. Robert F. Wilkes and James B. Wilcox, "Recent FTC Actions: Implications for the Advertising Strategist," *Journal of Marketing,* 38, January 1974.

30. Kenrec Sports, Inc., et al., 3 Trade Reg. Rep. 19. 971 (1972).

31. For an excellent review of corrective advertising from which much of this section draws, see William L. Wilkie, Dennis L. McNeill, and Michael B. Mazis, "Marketing's 'Scarlet Letter': The Theory and Practice of Corrective Advertising," *Journal of Marketing,* 48, Spring 1984, pp. 11–31.

32. ITT Continental Baking Co. (1973), 8860, 83 FTC 865.

33. Ibid.

34. Warner-Lambert (1975), 8891, 86 FTC 1398.

35. Michael B. Mazis, Dennis L. McNeill, and Kenneth Bernhardt, "Day After Recall of Listerine Corrective Commercials," Working paper (Washington, D.C.: American University, 1981).

36. Gary M. Armstrong, Metin N. Gurol, and Frederick A. Russ, "Detecting and Correcting Deceptive Advertising," *Journal of Consumer Research,* 6, December 1979, pp. 237–246.

37. Michael B. Mazis, "The Effects of FTC's Listerine Corrective Advertising Order," a report to the FTC, Washington, D.C., 1981.

38. William L. Wilkie, *Consumer Research and Corrective Advertising* (Cambridge, MA: Marketing Science Institute, 1973).

39. RJR Foods, Inc. (1973), C2424 (July 13).

40. Thomas C. Kinnear, James Taylor, and Odee Gur-Arie, "Affirmative Disclosure: Long-Term Monitoring of Residual Effects," *Journal of Business Policy and Marketing*, 2, forthcoming.

41. *U-Haul Int'l, Inc., v. Jartran, Inc.*, 601 F.Supp. 1140 (1984), aff'd 793 F.2d 1034 (9th Cir. 1986).

42. Jean J. Boddewyn, "Advertising Self-regulation: True Purpose and Limits," *Journal of Advertising*, 18, (2), 1989, pp. 19–27.

43. "Pillsbury Loses Some Brownie Points at NAD," *Advertising Age*, March 17, 1980, p. 10.

19

ADVERTISING AND SOCIETY

Nine-tenths and more of advertising is largely competitive wrangling as
to the relative merits of two undistinguishable compounds. In a truly
functional society, 90 percent of people employed by advertising would
be able to engage in "productive occupations."

Stuart Chase, *Tragedy of Waste*, 1925

Advertising is more than advertisements alone. It is an institutional
part of our society, a social force affecting and affected by our style
of life.

Raymond Bauer and Stephen Greyser,
Advertising in America

For decades, indeed centuries, broad social and economic issues have been raised concerning the role of advertising in society. In 1759, Dr. Samuel Johnson suggested that advertisers had moral and social questions to consider:

> The trade of advertising is now so near to perfection, it is not easy to propose any improvement. But as every art ought to be exercised in due subordination to the publick good, I cannot but propose it as a moral question to these matters of the publick ear. Whether they do not sometimes play too wantonly with our passions.[1]

Since then advertising has been studied, analyzed, defended, and attacked by individuals representing a wide spectrum of professional interests, including economists, sociologists, politicians, businessmen, novelists, and historians.

A STRUCTURING OF THE ISSUES

The central issues of advertising and society can be divided into three categories, as depicted in Figure 19-1. The first category represents the nature and content of the advertising to which people are exposed. Is the practice of advertising inherently unethical?

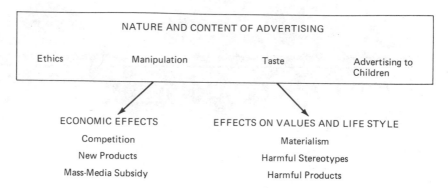

Figure 19-1.   Structuring the issues

Are appeals used that manipulate consumers against their will? There are a variety of issues associated with taste. Is advertising too repetitious, too silly, too preoccupied with sex? Does it irritate or offend the audience member? Finally, there are questions about the fairness of advertising to children, especially when the sugar products involved could adversely affect their health. In essence, this category, the nature and content of advertising, considers the means rather than the ends of advertising, the means being the copy and media tactics used.

The remaining two categories represent the aggregate effects of advertising on society as a whole. These are often called secondary consequences or effects. One of these is the effect on society's values and life-styles. There are those who believe that advertising competes with or dominates such other socialization agents as literature, plays, music, the church, the home, and the school; that it fosters materialism at the expense of other basic values; that it may serve to reinforce sexual or racial discrimination; or that it promotes harmful products. The second is the effect of advertising on society's economic well-being and on the efficiency of the operation of the economic system. To what extent can the power of advertising lead to the control of the market by a few firms, which will weaken competition and raise consumer prices? What is the economic value of advertising as an efficient mechanism for communicating the existence of new products? To what extent does it subsidize mass media?

NATURE AND CONTENT OF ADVERTISING

Ethics

Ethics in advertising is a topic of ongoing concern to many people both inside and outside of the field. For example, a book-length treatment of the subject was published by F. P. Bishop in 1949.[2] It has received increased attention in recent years because of other practices of business and government which have aroused public ire and indignation: stock market scandals, insider trading on Wall Street, the collapse of savings and loan associations resulting from unethical (but not necessarily illegal) behavior, junk bonds, defense procurement, and crooked politicians. Kanter,[3] argues that events such as these have produced a nation of cynics and that this cynicism spills over into people's views toward advertising. Many are challenging the ethics of agency executives who accept commissions for developing advertising to sell cigarettes, for example. Hunt and Chonko[4] found that agency executives are not as concerned about the ethics of their behavior as they are about agency/client/vendor relations, and the effectiveness of the advertising message. Dubinsky and Loken[5] have developed a model which attempts to organize issues of ethics in advertising.

There is considerable overlap between what many consider to be ethical issues in advertising and the issues of manipulation, taste, and advertising's effects on values and life-styles reviewed in this chapter. In what follows, we will therefore consider ethics from these various viewpoints. In the next section, for example, we review motivation research in the context of the manipulation issue. Although the motivation research user may not have absolute power over consumers, there are still ethical questions associated with its use—indeed, with the use of many forms of market research—that are most relevant. Is the practice of conducting depth interviews to attempt to isolate hidden motives acceptable? It is one thing to probe in an analyst's office for medical reasons but another to do so in the home or laboratory for commercial reasons. Can interviewers be sure that such an experience will not do psychological harm? And what about the common situation wherein a respondent is not told the actual purpose of the interview? These issues really focus on the research effort itself.

Does Advertising Manipulate?

Perhaps the essence of a free marketplace and a free society is the freedom to make decisions of various kinds, or in this context, the freedom to select or not select a particular brand. There are those who fear that this freedom is circumscribed by the "power" of advertising—that advertising is so effective it can manipulate a buyer into making a decision against his or her will or at least against his or her best interests in allocating his financial resources.

The argument takes several forms. First, there is concern with the use of motivation research, the appeal to motives at the subconscious level. Second, there is the use of indirect emotional appeals. Finally, there is the more general claim of the power of scientific advertising to persuade—to make people believe things and behave in ways that are not in their own or society's best interests.

Motivation Research.   Motivation research is an approach that draws on the Freudian psychoanalytic model of consumer decision making. It assumes that important buying motives are subconscious in that a respondent cannot elucidate them when asked an opinion of a brand or a product class. Thus, a person may dislike prunes because of a subconscious association of prunes with old age or parental authority but may not consciously realize the existence of this association and its relevance to purchasing decisions. A consumer may actually prefer a cake mix that requires the addition of an egg because it subconsciously satisfies the need to contribute to the baking process, although she or he consciously believes that the only reason is that a fresh egg adds quality.

Motivation research made a strong impact on marketing in the 1950s; many saw it as a decisive and powerful marketing tool. Furthermore, it received widespread attention beyond marketing professionals by such books as Vance Packard's *The Hidden Persuaders*.[6] The result was a feeling that advertising could indeed identify subconscious motives and, by playing on these motives, influence an unsuspecting public. The result was an Orwellian specter of the consumer's subconscious being exposed and manipulated without his or her knowledge.

The concept of the consumer being manipulated at the subconscious level reached its zenith with a subliminal 1956 advertising experiment by James Vicary. In a movie theater, he flashed the phrases, "Drink Coke" and "Hungry, Eat popcorn" on the screen every 5 seconds.[7] The phrases were exposed for 1/3,000th of a second, well below threshold levels. The tests, which covered a six-week period, were reported to have increased cola sales by 57 percent and popcorn sales by 18 percent. The concept of subliminal advertising operating at the subconscious level really suggested manipulation. However, this test lacked even rudimentary controls and has not been replicated. Furthermore, many other tests of subliminal communication in an advertising context have had negative results. There is therefore an overwhelming consensus among the advertising professional community that subliminal perception simply does not work.

Saegert,[8] however, has suggested that perhaps this conclusion might be premature. One marketing study did generate significantly greater "thirst ratings" by subjects exposed subliminally to the word "Coke" than other subjects exposed to a nonsense syllable word. Furthermore, psychologists have been able to increase indications of existing traits like depression, homosexuality, and stuttering by subliminal stimuli, but only where these traits already existed in the subjects.[9] Clearly, these studies only raise the possibility that subliminal communication might be able to bring unconscious motives to the surface, not that it could create or change motives.

We now know that motivation research, for better or worse, was oversold, and that motivation research knowledge does not give an advertiser anything approaching total control over an audience. Motivation research does have a role to play in developing effective advertisements, however. It has been particularly useful in providing insight, in suggesting copy alternatives, and in helping creative people avoid approaches that will precipitate undesirable reactions. Most people probably make choices most of the time for reasons they are aware of, particularly in situations in which real economic risk is involved. Unlike the situation of having the receiver totally under the control of the persuader, popularized in brainwashing experiments, advertising does not control a receiver's options. Although marketing professionals have accepted the reduced scope of motivation research, the layperson is still haunted by the spector of the "hidden persuaders."

Emotional Appeals. The communication of factual information about a product's primary function is usually accepted as being of value to the consumer. However, when advertising utilizes appeals or associations that go beyond such a basic communication task, the charge of manipulation via "emotional appeals" is raised. Scitovsky declared

To the extent that it (advertising) provides information about the existence of available (buyer) alternatives, advertising always renders the market more perfect. If advertising is mainly suggestive and confined to emotional appeal, however, it is likely to impede rational comparison and choice, thus rendering the market less perfect.[10]

The implication is that consumers will be led to make less than optimal decisions by such emotional appeals. The FTC reviewed several hundred proposed television commercials. FTC Commissioner Mary Gardiner Jones observed

A typical theme running through these commercials is to hold the product out as the pathway to success and happiness and the antidote to what is otherwise a drab, boring or lonely life. Thus dishwashing liquids are advertised as sweeping away the dullness of life. They are the housewife's pathroad to beauty and romantic excitement. Their use will make the whole world soft and gentle. Bath soaps have a similar rejuvenating capacity. Use of these products is associated with cool sophistication, weddings, traveling and entertainment, enjoyment of life at its unhampered best. Some bath soap advertisers stress the sensual success which will immediately accrue to the user, others the ability of the product to resolve all husband and wife crises and still others the health and exuberance or the happy family do-it-togetherness which will be engendered by the product.[11]

These observations are related to issues of deception. The line between artistic license and deception is something hard to draw. Is an advertisement an innocent, entertaining exaggeration that few will take seriously, or is it really capable of deceiving? The last chapter reviewed these and other related issues. Jones's observations also involve some definitional issues. How should such basic concepts as product, needs, rationality, and information be defined? Bauer and Greyser have noted that different advertising spokespersons, for convenience labeled businesspeople and business critics, have radically different perceptions of these key concepts.[12]

Consider the word "product." The critic views a product as an entity with only one primary identifiable function. Thus, an automobile is a transportation device. The businessperson is concerned with a product's secondary function, because it may represent the dimensions upon which the product differentiation rests. The automobile's appearance might provide a mechanism by which the individual can express his or her personality. High horsepower and superior handling may provide an outlet for an individual's desire for excitement.

Another key concept is "need." The critic sees consumer needs as corresponding to a product's primary function. Thus, there is a need for transportation, nutrition, and recreation. The businessperson, on the other hand, takes a much broader view of consumer needs, considering any product attribute or appeal on which real product differentiation can be based as reflecting legitimate needs—needs that are strong enough to affect purchase decisions.

Two other central concepts are rationality and information. The critic sees any decision that results in an efficient matching of product to needs, as he or she defines these terms, as rational. Information that serves to enhance rational decision making is good information. The businessperson contends that any decision a consumer makes to serve his or her own perceived self-interest is rational. Information, then, is any data or argument that will truthfully put forth the attractiveness of a product in the context of a consumer's own buying criteria.

In part, the resolution of these different perspectives will inevitably involve value judgments and honest differences in premises. To some extent, however, they involve assumptions about consumer decision making and utility theory that should be amenable to research. The challenge is to identify clearly, using a common vocabulary, the value judgments that are required and to isolate precisely the empirical questions.

Power of Modern Advertising.   There also exists a somewhat more general claim that advertisers have the raw power to manipulate consumers. Many companies have the capacity to obtain large numbers of advertisement exposures. Furthermore, some observers believe that these companies can utilize highly sophisticated, scientific techniques to make such advertising effective.

This book has, in fact, attempted to marshal scientific knowledge from theory and practice. The reader should by now be painfully aware of the limitations of the most sophisticated approaches available. The fact is that consumer-choice behavior is determined by many factors in addition to advertising—the advice of friends, decisions and life-styles of family members, news stories, prices, distribution variables, and on and on. Advertising is but one of many variables, and it has a limited role. It can communicate the existence of a new automobile and perhaps induce a visit to a dealer, but it can rarely make the final sale. It can explain the advantages of a toothpaste and perhaps be influential in getting some people to try the brand, but it has little impact on their decision to repurchase it. There is an inexhaustible number of examples of huge promotional efforts for products that failed. If advertising had the power that some attribute to it, many of these products would still be with us.

Taste

Some critics feel that advertising is objectionable because the creative effort behind it is not in good taste. This type of objection was explored in a massive study conducted in the mid-1960s.[13] More than 1,500 people were asked to list those advertisements that they found annoying, enjoyable, informative, or offensive. Of the more than 9,000 advertisements involved, 23 percent were labeled as annoying and 5 percent as offensive. Although a portion of these advertisements irritated respondents because they were considered deceptive, the majority were so categorized for reasons related to questions of taste.

Advertising may not be omnipotent, but many contend that it is too omnipresent or intrusive. More than 42 percent of the annoying advertisements in the foregoing study were considered too loud, too long, too repetitious, or involved unpleasant voices, music, or people. Another 31 percent had content that was considered silly, unreal, boring, or depressing. Nearly one-fourth of the offensive advertisements were considered inappropriate for children. More than one-fourth of the offensive advertisements involved such products as liquor or cigarettes. A study by Aaker and Bruzzone found of 524 prime-time television commercials the top eight most irritating commercials were the eight commercials for feminine hygiene products like tampons.[14] Commercials for women's undergarments and hemorrhoid products were close behind. Clearly there is a strong product class effect with respect to irritation with television advertising.

The Appeal.   In an open letter to the *Detroit News* entitled, "You Dirty Old Ad Men Make Me Sick," a reader took issue with the use of sex in advertising. In making her case, she described several advertisements:

> A love goddess runs down the beach, waves nibbling at her toes, her blond streaked hair sweeping back behind wide, expectant eyes. A flimsy garment clings to every supple curve. She runs faster, arms open, until finally she throws herself breathlessly into HIS arms. . . . Where's this scene? Right in your living room, that's where. Wild and passionately aroused, she can't stop herself. She runs her fingers through his hair, knocks his glasses off, and kisses him and kisses him again. . . . Who's watching? Your nine-year-old daughter as she sits on her stuffed panda bear and wipes jelly off her face.[15]

The letter received considerable response from advertising professionals. Some argued that advertisements, as long as they are not obscene, reflect society and its collective life-styles. They observed that nudity and the risque are part of the contemporary world in which advertising is embedded. Others agreed that sex is overused and suggested that effective advertising can be created without titillating.

One problem is that television commercials have to create attention and communicate a message—and accomplish all this in 30 or even 15 seconds—a demanding task, indeed. Another problem is that television reaches large, broad audiences. It is one thing to use a risque approach in *Playboy* magazine and quite another to use it on prime-time television when the likelihood of offending is much greater.

Fear appeals have also been criticized. The intent of the fear appeal is to create anxiety that can supposedly be alleviated by an available product (insurance against a fire or a safe tire to prevent accidents) or action (stop smoking). There exists the possibility that such appeals may create emotional disturbances or a long-run anxiety condition in some audience members. The cumulative effects of such advertising may be highly undesirable to some, although it can also be argued that they quickly cease to have any significant degree of emotional impact, and the audience soon becomes immune to the messages.

Intrusiveness.   To some people, advertising, especially television advertising, is often like a visitor who has overstayed his welcome. It becomes an intrusion. Greyser postulates a life cycle wherein an advertising campaign moves with repetition from a period of effectiveness, and presumably audience acceptance, to a period of irritation.[16] The cycle contains the following stages:

1. Exposure to the message on several occasions prior to serious attention (given some basic interest in the product)
2. Interest in the advertisement on either substantive (informative) or stimulus (enjoyment) grounds
3. Continued but declining attention to the advertisement on such grounds
4. Mental tune-out of the advertisement on grounds of familiarity
5. Increasing re-awareness of the advertisement, now as a negative stimulus (an irritant)
6. Growing irritation

The number of exposures between the start of a campaign and the stage of growing irritation is obviously a key variable. On what factors will it depend? An important factor, of course, is the intensity of the campaign itself. Bursts of advertising that generate many exposures over a short time period will undoubtedly run a high risk of irritation. A second factor involves other advertising to which the audience is exposed. The cycle will be shorter if different brands and even different product classes use similar approaches. Advertisements involving similar demonstrations, spokespeople, jingles, or animation may be difficult to separate in the mind of an audience member. Campaigns for beer, soda, and menthol cigarettes, for example, have been perceived as being highly similar. Product usage and brand preferences are two additional factors affecting the cycle time period. Greyser noted that

> consumers dislike only 21 percent of the advertisements for products used (19 percent annoying, 2 percent offensive), whereas they dislike 37 percent of advertisements for products they don't use (29 percent annoying, 8 percent offensive). For brand preferrers the tendency is even more marked: only 7 percent of advertisements for one's favorite brand are disliked compared with 76 percent of the advertisements for "brands wouldn't buy" (only product users included).[17]

Still another factor is the entertainment value of the advertisement. Campaigns using advertisements with high entertainment value have demonstrated their ability to survive heavy repetition. An important issue is the determination of the link between liking and effectiveness. There is some evidence that the very pleasant and the very unpleasant advertisements are more effective than those in between. A disliked commercial may attract attention and communicate better than a bland commercial. Further, the negative feeling toward the ad may not get attached to the brand. The nature of the relationship will undoubtedly depend on the audience, the product, and other variables. Furthermore, there are several definitional and measurement problems involved.

The result is a decrease in the long-run effectiveness of advertising. It is in the best interests of advertisers to be concerned not only with the irritation caused by specific campaigns, but also with that caused by the impression of advertising in general. Twenty- or 30-second television spots may be cost effective for the brand but less so when the total impression of a cluttered media is considered.

Advertising to Children

In 1977 the FTC was stimulated to examine television advertising to children. A FTC staff report recommended that

- All television advertising be banned for any product which is directed to or seen by audiences composed of a significant proportion of children who are too young to understand the selling purpose of the advertising.
- Either balance televised advertising for sugared food products directed to or seen by audiences composed of a significant proportion of older children with nutritional and or health disclosures funded by advertisers or ban it completely.

These proposals, which were intensely debated, were ultimately defeated in part because of changes in the political environment in the early 1980s. However, the issues remain, and parent and consumer groups are still concerned and active.

The proposals were based upon several facts and judgments. First, children between the ages of 2 and 11 spend about 25 hours per week watching television and see approximately 20,000 ads per year. About 7,000 of these ads are for highly sugared products. Second, there is evidence that some preschool children cannot differentiate between commercials and programming, cannot understand the selling intent of commercials, and cannot distinguish between fantasy and reality. Third, children between the ages of 7 and 12 have difficulty balancing appeals of highly sugared products with long-term health risks—by age 2 about one-half of children have diseased gums and decayed teeth. Fourth, there are no counterads for fruit and vegetables. Fifth, much of children's advertising is deceptive in that it omits significant information, such as the complexity and safety of operating toys. Opposition to the proposals marshaled their own facts and judgments. First, banning television advertising to protect those children who do not understand the selling intent of commercials will deny advertisers the right of free speech to communicate with other audience members, who, in fact, constitute the great majority of the audience for most children's programs. Second, the FTC does not have the professional competence to serve as a ''national nanny'' deciding to what children should not be exposed. Parents are generally both more competent and involved to help children interpret information and make decisions. Third, there is no evidence of a relationship between television exposure and the incidence of tooth decay. Further, there is very little evidence that eating the most heavily advertised products will cause tooth decay. Fourth, there is evidence that children are aware that fruits and vegetables are more nutritious than highly sugared foods.

The controversy has generated an on-going stream of research on the effects of children's advertising. Goldberg and Gorn[18] in a series of experiments generally confirm that advertising can influence children to select the advertised product (highly sugared cereals, candy, etc.) over more nutritious products. In one experiment,[19] for example, children who viewed candy commercials picked significantly more candy over fruit as snacks. Eliminating the candy commercials proved as effective in encouraging selection of fruit as did exposing the children to fruit commercials or nutritional public service announcements. Macklin,[20] in studies of preschoolers, found in contrast to some widely held beliefs, that some were able to comprehend the informational role of TV advertising. Brucks, Armstrong, and Goldberg[21] had 9- to 10-year-olds verbalize their thoughts while watching commercials reasoning that the number of counterarguments produced would indicate the child's use of cognitive defenses. It was found that counterarguing occurred, but only when a cue was present to activate the process.

EFFECTS ON VALUES AND LIFE-STYLES

Advertising by its very nature receives wide exposure. Furthermore, it presumably has an effect on what people buy and thus on their activities. Because of this exposure and because of its role as a persuasive vehicle, it is argued that it has an impact on the values and life-styles of society and that this impact has its negative as well as positive side. Pollay[22] in an article titled, "Quality of Life in the Padded Sell..," for example, states

> Earlier it was argued . . . that appeals to mass markets tended to promote conformity; appeals to status promote envy, pride and social competitiveness; appeals to fears promote anxiety; appeals to newness promote disrespect for tradition, durability, experience, or history; appeals to youth promote reduced family authority; appeals to sexuality promote promiscuity; and so forth. Transcending all of these specifics is the tendency of ads to appeal to consumers as individuals, isolated as an audience from their family, friends, or peers, and encouraged to "look out for number 1" or to be "Me! I'm the one!" The appeal to individualism with a creed of greed undermines community, cooperation, charity, and compassion.[23]

The key issues are what values and life-styles are to be encouraged as healthy, which are to be avoided, and what relative impact or influence advertising has on them. Despite their difficulty and their relationship to deep philosophical questions, they are well worth addressing to illuminate judgments and assumptions about our market system and society that are too often glossed over.[24]

It is interesting that the issues are hotly debated at the international level, and that countries, particularly Third World countries, are vitally interested in them. The United Nations' UNESCO organization, for example, put together a sixteen member commission to study the "totality of communication problems in modern society."[25] The commission's report, which became known as the *MacBride Report* (named after the Irish diplomat Sean MacBride who headed the commission), produced 82 recommendations directed largely at the potential dangers of advertising and the needs for controls on advertising practices. As might be expected, reactions to the report were highly polarized with support largely coming from Third World countries and opposition coming from industry representatives in developed countries.

Three issues that have attracted particular attention are the relationship of advertising to materialism, the role that advertising has played in creating harmful stereotypes of women and ethnic minorities, and the possible contribution of advertising in promoting harmful products.

Materialism

Materialism is defined as the tendency to give undue importance to material interests. Presumably there is a corresponding lessening of importance to nonmaterial interests such as love, freedom, and intellectual pursuits.

Bauer and Greyser argue, however, that although people do spend their resources on material things, they do so in the pursuit of nonmaterial goals.[26] They buy camping equipment to achieve a communion with nature, music systems to understand the classic composers, and an automobile for social status. The distinctive aspect of our society is not the possession of material goods, but the extent to which material goods are used to attain nonmaterial goals. Bauer and Greyser thus raise the issue of whether material goods are a means to an end rather than an end in themselves. In making such an evaluation it is useful to consider how people in other cultures fulfill nonmaterial goals. The leader in a primitive culture may satisfy a need for status in a different way from someone in our culture, but is the means used really that relevant? Russell Belk and others[27] have begun a systematic series of studies into materialism in American society showing its manifestations in advertising, comic books, television programming, swap meets, and the role of consuming and consumption in many facets of life generally.

Does advertising create or foster materialism or merely reflect values and attitudes that are created by more significant sociological forces? Mary Gardiner Jones develops the argument that advertising, especially television advertising, is a contributing force:

> The conscious appeal in the television commercial . . . is essentially materialistic. Central to the message of the television commercial is the premise that it is the acquisition of things which will gratify our basic and inner needs and aspirations. It is the message of the commercial that all of the major problems confronting an individual can be instantly eliminated by the application of some external force—the use of a product. Externally derived solutions are thus made the prescription for life's difficulties. Television gives no recognition to the individual's essential responsibility for at least a part of his condition or to the importance to the individual of proving his own capacity to deal with life's problems. In the world of the television commercial all of life's problems and difficulties, all of our individual yearnings, hopes—and fears—can yield instantly to a material solution and one which can work instantly without any effort, skill or trouble on our part.[28]

Associating advertising with materialism, of course, does not demonstrate a causal link, as Commissioner Jones would be the first to recognize. In fact, such a link is impossible to prove or disprove. It is true that advertising and the products advertised are a part of our culture and thus contribute to it in some way. It is also true, however, that advertising does not have the power to dominate other forces (family, church, literature, and so on) that contribute to the values of society.

Promoting Stereotypes

The accusation that advertising has contributed to the role stereotyping of women and ethnic minorities has been supported by several studies. In 729 advertisements appearing in 1970, none showed women in a professional capacity, whereas 35 of them so portrayed men.[29] The authors concluded that the advertisements reflected the stereotype that women do not do important things, are dependent on men, are regarded by men primarily as sex objects, and should be in the home. Kassarjian, a UCLA psychologist, examined print advertising in 1946, 1956, and 1965 and found that only one-third of 1 percent of the advertisements contained blacks, that the blacks in the ads of the 1940s were in a low-status role, that the blacks of the 1960s tended to be entertainers, and that the appearance of blacks as true peers was sparse.[30]

A host of questions are raised. Does role stereotyping continue in advertising? What negative impact does advertising have in creating stereotypes, or what positive force does it have in breaking them down? In the absence of definitive answers to these questions, what should the advertisers' position be? Should countering role stereotypes be one objective of advertising? It is known that role portrayals of women in advertising which are consistent with the roles played by women in the viewing audience is more effective than when the roles are inconsistent. Thus, advertising showing women in traditional roles is less effective with an audience of professional women, and vice versa.[31]

Promoting Harmful Products

There is a national concern with the problems of alcohol and cigarettes. Local legislators have increased taxes to around 45 percent of total alcohol sales and toughened drunk driving laws. Happy Hours have been banned in several states. Twenty-three states have complied with a federal law to increase the drinking age to 21 or lose highway funds. The Surgeon General's report on tobacco and lung cancer has lead to a wave of calls for increased legislation and proposals to ban cigarette advertising.

Concerning alcohol, a group calling itself SMART (Stop Merchandising Alcohol on Radio and Television) has proposed a ban on wine and beer advertising. There have been other less severe proposals as well. Some have suggested counterads which would dramatically ''advertise'' the health disadvantages of drinking. Similar movements against cigarettes were effective and led to the banning of cigarette advertising on television. Others have proposed that beer advertising (like wine advertising) stop using sports figures in their advertising. There is already a ban on the use of active athletes and actual drinking in beer commercials.

The basic argument is that alcohol, like cigarettes, is a ''harmful'' product. Alcohol is unhealthy for the individual and is indirectly responsible for injuries and deaths resulting from drunk drivers. Why encourage people to use alcohol via advertising? The use of sports stars whom kids admire suggests that alcohol is not only harmless but that it is associated with fun-loving, healthy people.

There are a variety of counterarguments. First, there is no evidence that advertising, which is geared toward brand choice rather than increasing consumption, affects total alcohol consumption.[32] Across-country studies do not indicate that those countries, such as Finland and Norway, which already ban alcohol advertising on television have lower consumption than other countries, such as the United Kingdom, which do not. Over time, observations are similar. Beer advertising has increased substantially in the first half of the 1980s, while sales dropped around 12 percent in the same time period. On the other hand, per capita alcohol consumption has risen during the past 30 years at the same rate as in Western Europe, without, of course, any advertising. In addition to this basic counterargument, there is also the suggestion that

- A ban of advertising would prohibit product innovation that may be helpful. For example, firms have introduced products such as the wine coolers and the low-alcohol beers.
- The real goal is to return to alcohol prohibition, which did not work—it only created a revenue source for gangsters and made lawbreakers of the rank and file of America.
- Many other products could be criticized on similar grounds. Should advertising for automobiles be banned when high performance and sportiness is stressed since they could contribute to reckless driving?

An interesting study by Schuster and Powell[33] showed that the Sloan-Kettering Report linking cancer and smoking, warning labels on cigarettes, and implementation of the Fairness Doctrine which gave equal time to antismoking messages in the 1950s and 1960s, all resulted in declines in cigarette consumption. However, in all cases, the declines were short-lived and consumption would generally recover and continue upward a year or so after the announcements. In contrast, the outright banning of cigarette advertising on radio and television in 1970 had little negative impact on cigarette consumption. In fact consumption increased after the ban was put into effect. Thus, outlawing advertising in the case of either cigarettes or alcohol may not be the most effective way of handling the problem.

ECONOMIC EFFECTS OF ADVERTISING

It is unreasonable to separate the economic and social impact of advertising. The social issues, by themselves, tend to focus on the negative aspects of advertising—its intrusiveness, content that is in bad taste, and the possibly undesirable impact on values and lifestyles. If advertising were regarded solely on these grounds, it would be difficult to defend, despite the fact that much advertising is entertaining, some may even be of real artistic value, and some is directed toward supporting causes that are universally praised. Advertising is basically an economic institution. It performs an economic function for an advertiser, affects economic decisions of the audience, and is an integral part of the whole economic system. Thus an economic evaluation should accompany other types of appraisal of advertising. Here are some of the economic benefits of advertising.

Providing Informational Utility

Advertising that distributes information to consumers that can help them make better economic decisions than they would in the absence of that information provides a positive economic service. Of course, any advertising that, by deception or any other means, induces consumers to make suboptimal decisions provides a corresponding negative economic service. Some advertising is of more value than others along this dimension. Classified advertising, advertising for retail stores, catalog advertising, and much of industrial advertising are usually sought out because of their informational value.

A study by Aaker and Norris of 524 prime-time television commercials suggests that even television advertising is perceived as informative by substantial groups of people.[34] On the average 18.1 percent of respondents (approximately 500 per commercial) checked the word informative from a list of 20 adjectives when asked to describe the commercial. The percentage was over 20 when snack and beverage items were excluded.

Advertising and Brand Names

Advertising plays an important role in establishing and maintaining brand names.[35] A brand name identifies the source of a product and provides a construct by which a buyer can store information about that source. Such a construct is of little consequence in product lines like screws or shoelaces, wherein the perceived differences among brands are minor, or in products like greeting cards, which can be evaluated relatively competently by the buyer. For products like automobiles, appliances, or men's shirts, however, which have relatively high levels of perceived quality differences among brands and which are difficult to evaluate by inspection, the brand name plays an important role in the buying process. A buyer can reasonably assume that a manufacturer willing to risk large sums of money to tell about a product is not likely to let poor product quality damage the investment.

The concept of *brand equity* was introduced in Chapter 8 to highlight the value of branding and brand names. Brand equity implies that brand names can add value to a product independent of any other production or marketing activities. Just adding the name Coca-Cola, for example, to a new soda drink adds value to the drink. The measurement of the value of the equity in a brand name is a challenging task which has become of particular importance for corporate mergers and acquisitions.

Media Support

Advertising provides more than 60 percent of the cost of periodicals, more than 70 percent of the cost of newspapers, and nearly 100 percent of the cost of radio and television.[36] For their support of the commercial television stations, advertisers receive approximately 15 percent of the airtime.[37] Of course, a pay television system could be developed or public funds could be used, but either alternative would cost the consumer something in direct cash outlays or increased taxes.

Employment

In his 1925 book on the tragedy of waste, Stuart Chase stated that in a truly functional society 90 percent of the people employed by advertising would be able to engage in "productive occupations." There are many who would disagree with Chase's view that advertising is an unproductive occupation. It assumes, for example, that only production (or form utility) and not marketing (time, place, and possession utility) is productive. There are few in today's world that would argue that marketing has no role to play or does not add value. There is little question that advertising provides employment for significant numbers of people in both the United States and in other advanced industrialized countries. A million or more jobs are probably associated with the creation, production and delivery of advertising in the United States alone.

Distribution Costs

Advertising is part of a total marketing program; it does not operate in isolation. Its function is usually to communicate to large audiences, and it often performs this function very efficiently. Without advertising, the communication function would still remain but would probably have to be accomplished in some other way by retailers, salespeople, and so on. The alternative in many situations could cost significantly more.

In 1964, cookie companies spent only 2.2 percent of sales on advertising, whereas cereal companies spent 14.9 percent.[38] However, the cookie companies spent 22.1 percent of sales on other selling and distribution costs, compared with 12.1 percent of sales for cereal companies. Cookie companies employed routemen to deliver goods and service the shelves. Cereal companies, however, had created sufficient consumer demand so that the retailer found it worthwhile to monitor the stock and the firms were relieved of this marketing expense. In this instance, then, it can be argued that cookie companies shifted marketing cost from advertising to other marketing activities and that an evaluation of their advertising expenses in isolation would be deceptive.

Effect on Business Cycles

Advertising could theoretically be a tool to alleviate the extremes of the business cycle. A knowledgeable businessperson, anticipating a booming economy and capacity production, should reduce advertising expenditures. Conversely, when the economy is weak and orders are needed, many firms should increase their advertising. Since the extremes of a business cycle cause inflation or unemployment, any mechanism to stabilize conditions would be an economic benefit. The problem is that many advertisers, especially those who tend to set their advertising budgets at a fixed percentage of sales, actually increase advertising when times are good and decrease it when sales are weak. These firms may thus actually increase the extremes of the business cycle instead of decreasing them. Simon reviewed the literature and concluded that this tendency actually dominates—advertising expenditures generally follow the same course as the business cycle.[39] He also concluded that the potential of advertising to affect the business cycle is small, since decisions such as inventory investment are much stronger determinants of the nature of economic cycles. The evidence to date is that advertising has a negative though small impact in reducing the extremes of the business cycle.

Providing Product Utility

Advertising, by generating associations between products and moods, life-styles, and activities, can add to the utility a buyer receives from the product. Most people do not buy cars solely to move from one point to another, but to achieve a feeling of independence, to express a personality, or to establish a certain mood or feeling. Evaluating the amount of utility, if any, that advertising adds to a product returns us to the fundamental issue raised earlier of the definition of such terms as "need" and "product." In a recent study of the contributions of advertising to productivity, the American Association of Advertising Agencies, argues that innovation and high technology, as a primary source of productivity, should not be focused solely on cost reduction, but rather on "innovation for higher value."[40] Figure 19-2 shows an advertisement announcing the results of the study. The focus is on considering the total product. The argument is that the consumer's conceptual perception of the product is as significant as the physical characteristics and should be considered a product ingredient. As stated in the report,

> This mingling of the tangible (malt, hops, barley) with the "elusive" (positioning, brand image, perceptions) is a challenge to all managers, not just those in the marketing disciplines. Today, the *conceptual* nature of added value is no longer limited to product categories like beer, fast food, perfume, or Scotch whiskey. On the contrary: *Conceptual value added*— the perceptions of a product's unique, singular fit into a consumer's personal system of wants, needs, and values—is increasingly becoming the single most powerful discriminator in every category.[41]

Encouraging New Products

Advertising encourages product development by providing an economical way to inform potential buyers of the resulting new products or product improvements. In many situations, innovation requires large research and development expenditures and substantial investments in production facilities that might be difficult to justify if advertising could not be efficiently employed to communicate the existence of the innovation. In this respect, advertising encourages product competition. It can also encourage development of improvements in basic skills and health habits such as the Barbara Bush appeal to stimulate reading shown in Figure 19-3.

The development of new products and the improvement of existing products can mean an expanding economy with more jobs and investment opportunities and a buyer selection that is continually improving in breadth and quality. However, as Borden stated in his classic study of the economic effects of advertising, published in 1942, an expanding set of product options can be disadvantageous for the buyer, especially when they reflect minor differentiation of existing products that add little real utility.[42]

UNTIL NOW, THE VALUE OF ADVERTISING WAS SOMETHING EVEN ITS STRONGEST SUPPORTERS COULDN'T PUT INTO NUMBERS.

They could cite success stories of advertising going into a market, how this was followed by a shift in purchase patterns, in market share, in immediate sales.

But no one expressed the value of advertising as return-on-investment until The Strategic Planning Institute did its PIMS (Profit Impact of Market Strategy) study* with the Ogilvy Center for Research and Development.

It found that advertising nearly doubled R.O.I.! (See graph on the left.)

Brands that advertise much more than their competitors enjoy an average R.O.I. of 32 percent. Brands that advertise much less than their competitors average 17 percent.

This is the first systematic evidence linking advertising, profitability, and growth. It draws on more than 700 consumer businesses in North America and Europe, spanning the years 1970 to 1986—years of both rapid and slow inflation, both good and bad years of the business cycle.

The graph on the lower right shows further evidence. It represents the competitive performance of two actual brands over a 10-year period, as analyzed by Robert M. Prentice, an advertising and marketing consultant. He distinguishes between consumer-franchise-building (CFB) activities (whether advertising or promotion) and non-CFB activities.

Brand A used predominantly price-incentive promotions. Brand B spent approximately the same amount, but most of the money went into consumer-franchise-building activities—particularly advertising and promotion.

In the first year, the two brands were nearly even in their category. But after 10 years in which they took dramatically contrasting approaches to the spending of marketing funds, they ended up in remarkably different positions.

Brand B had become a resounding success, not only in terms of its sales performance versus Brand A, but also in terms of its contributing profits to the company.

For brand franchise owners and managers, the insight into how advertising contributes to profitability will be just as interesting as how much it contributes.

For more information, you can write to The Committee on the Value of Advertising, Department A, American Association of Advertising Agencies, 666 Third Avenue, New York, New York 10017.

Now that there's finally proof of advertising's true value, there's only one thing you need to do. Take advantage of it.

*© 1987 The Strategic Planning Institute, Cambridge, MA

AAAA

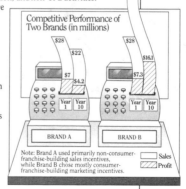

Figure 19-2. The AAAA advertisement

Courtesy of American Association of Advertising Agencies, Inc.

Figure 19-3. An advertisement to encourage people to read
Courtesy of Magazine Publishers of America.

Public Service Advertising

Public service advertising discussed in Chapter 1 can be considered in this context as a force for improving society and alleviating social problems. The value of advertising by Federal government and other nonprofit agencies to help reduce crime, prevent forest fires, stem environmental pollution, and other worthwhile causes, exceeds the value of advertising by many of the largest private advertisers. Figure 19-4 shows an effective recycling advertisement sponsored by the Environmental Defense Fund and the Advertising Council.

ADVERTISING AND COMPETITION

The existence of vigorous competition is important to a market economy. Competitive forces lead to real product innovation, the efficient distribution of goods, and the absence of inflated prices. The question is: What impact does advertising have on competition?[43] There have been hypotheses put forth indicating that advertising can actually decrease the level of competition. For example, it is argued that heavy advertising expenditures in many industries generate strong brand loyalty that tends to create barriers to potential competitors. The hypothesized result is fewer competitors, less competition, and higher prices. Fortunately, these hypotheses have been examined theoretically and empirically by economists, and, although few definitive conclusions are yet available, it is now possible to structure the argument, identify some key issues, and marshall some empirical studies that bear on these issues.

Market Concentration

One measure of competition within an industry is the degree to which the sales of the industry are concentrated in the hands of a few firms. The specific construct is the concentration ratio the share of the industry sales held by the four largest firms. When the concentration ratio exceeds 50 percent, price competition is theorized to be less vigorous and high prices result. Among the many industries that would qualify under this criterion are automobiles, aircraft, electric lamps, flat glass, primary aluminum, and household refrigerators and freezers.[44]

The concentration ratio as an indicator of market concentration and competition has intuitive appeal and is convenient, but conceptual and theoretical problems are associated with it. The main problem is in defining the industry meaningfully. Theoretically, an industry should include all brands from which buyer choice is made. Such a judgment is not easy to make. Does the cereal industry include instant breakfast, breakfast squares, and pop tarts? Do aluminum companies compete only with one another or do they also compete with copper and steel companies? Should import competition be included? What about industries in which regional brands are important such as the cement industry which has a low concentration nationally but a high concentration in regional markets? The definitional problem is compounded by the fact that most empirical studies are based on

TAKE A FEW MINUTES TO GO THROUGH YOUR GARBAGE.

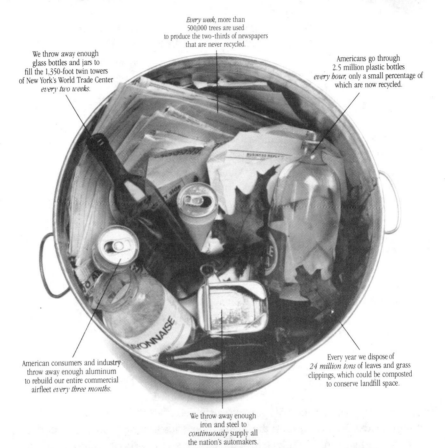

Every week, more than 500,000 trees are used to produce the two-thirds of newspapers that are never recycled.

We throw away enough glass bottles and jars to fill the 1,350-foot twin towers of New York's World Trade Center *every two weeks*.

Americans go through 2.5 million plastic bottles *every hour*, only a small percentage of which are now recycled.

American consumers and industry throw away enough aluminum to rebuild our entire commercial airfleet *every three months*.

Every year we dispose of *24 million tons* of leaves and grass clippings, which could be composted to conserve landfill space.

We throw away enough iron and steel to *continuously* supply all the nation's automakers.

The ordinary bag of trash you throw away is slowly becoming a serious problem for everybody.

Because the fact is, not only are we running out of resources to make the products we need, we're running out of places to put what's left over.

Write the Environmental Defense Fund at: 257 Park Avenue South, New York, NY 10010, for a free brochure that will tell you virtually everything

you'll need to know about recycling.

One thing's for certain, the few minutes you take to learn how to recycle will spare us all a lot of garbage later.

IF YOU'RE NOT RECYCLING SM
YOU'RE THROWING IT ALL AWAY. EDF ™ Ad Council

© 1988 EDF

ENVIRONMENTAL DEFENSE FUND CAMPAIGN
MAGAZINE AD NO. EDF-2801-90—7" x 10" (110 Screen)
Volunteer Agency: Deutsch, Inc., Campaign Director: Harry E. Davis, DuPont Co.

Figure 19-4. A recycling advertisement
Courtesy of The Advertising Council.

the Standard Industry Classification (SIC) of the U.S. Census Bureau whose categories are somewhat arbitrary. Another problem with the four-firm concentration ratio is that it does not reflect the distribution of market shares among firms. It is thus now largely replaced with HHI (the Herfindahl-Hirschman Index), which is the sum of the squares of the market shares of all the competitors. For example, the HHI of a four-firm industry would be 2500 if all had 25 percent shares but would be twice as much if one firm had a 70 percent market share.

A Causal Model

Figure 19-5 provides a simplified causal model that summarizes various hypotheses suggesting that advertising contributes to a reduction of competition in the marketplace. The model introduces several crucial constructs such as market concentration, barriers to entry, and product differentiation. The arrows represent hypothesized causal relationships among these constructs. After presenting these hypotheses, some counterarguments will be raised and several relevant empirical studies will be examined.

The central construct in the model is market concentration. The basic argument is that when concentration exists, there is little incentive to engage in vigorous price competition since any price decrease would be immediately neutralized by a similar price change by the other major competitors. A direct result, therefore, is higher prices and profits.

With price competition inhibited, there is a hypothesized incentive to advertise heavily, since a competitor will not be likely to duplicate an advertising campaign. An advertising campaign that duplicates a competitor's is rarely successful. Thus, one result of concentration is thought to be heavy, noninformative advertising, the cost of which is

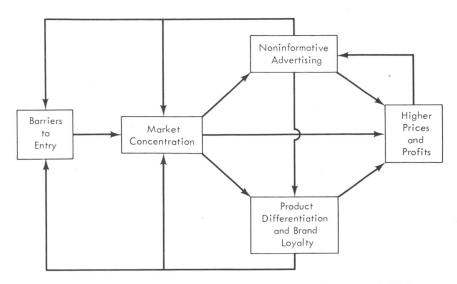

Figure 19-5. Market concentration: some hypothesized causes and effects

passed on to the buyer in the form of higher prices. The reduced price of private label brands is cited as evidence of such higher prices.

Another hypothesized effect of concentration is the attempt, by advertising and minor product changes, to differentiate products that are essentially identical with respect to their primary function. Differentiated products can generate brand loyalty and thus escape vigorous price competition. The result is another link to higher prices and profits. Product differentiation can be a highly desirable response to diverse market needs and wants and is not bad per se. As Scherer points out,

> The relevant question for economic analysis is not . . . whether product differentiation is a good thing but rather, how much product differentiation there should be, and whether certain market conditions might lead to excessive or inadequate differentiation. . . . Product differentiation activities most often singled out for a vote of public disapproval include image differentiation created or reinforced through intensive advertising.[45]

The higher profits are not considered earned rewards of product innovation but the result of market power. The issue of the definition of a product is, of course, central (recall the earlier discussion on the definition of product and related terms).

Concentration is said to be perpetuated and increased by the existence of barriers to entry that prevent or at least discourage potential competitors from entering the market. Advertising is thought by some to generate entry barriers directly and through the product differentiation it generates. The purpose of product differentiation is presumably to develop a reason for a buyer to buy one brand over another, to generate brand loyalty. This brand loyalty is hypothesized to be a barrier to entry.[46]

Advertising is also hypothesized to generate entry barriers by providing the larger advertiser in some industries with two kinds of advantages over a smaller competitor. First, the large advertiser is thought to receive preferential treatment by the media with respect to the cost and selection of advertising space. Second, a threshold level of advertising is hypothesized to exist, below which advertising would be ineffective simply because the exposure frequency would be too low to communicate. When this threshold level is high, the cost of entering a market—and thus the risk—becomes excessive.[47]

Notice that, to the extent that advertising and product differentiation place the small competitor at a disadvantage, it not only represents a barrier to entry of new competitors, but could also impede the growth of existing ones, thereby increasing the level of concentration. If existing competitors weaken and perhaps disappear, the concentration, and thus the market power, of those remaining could be increased.

One additional feature of Figure 19-2 should be emphasized. The existence of higher prices and margins tends to generate advertising since it ''pays'' to advertise high-margin products. Thus, the feedback from higher prices to advertising. The result is that an ever-increasing cycle of concentration-profitability-advertising concentration, and so on, is created.

Advertising, then, is not only considered an effect of concentration generating economic waste, it is also an important cause. The argument is that it helps create ''artificial'' product differentiation that, in turn, creates brand loyalty—a major entry barrier.

Furthermore, it has the potential of discouraging a small competitor by increasing the market risk and by placing him at a cost disadvantage.

Kessides,[48] in a cross-industry study of the entry-deterring effects of advertising concludes that there are two countervailing effects of advertising on entry. On the one hand, advertising impedes entry because it gives rise to a sunk cost barrier. On the other hand, it reduces the perceived risk of entry. Industries with high advertising intensities are more prone to entry than lower-intensity industries. The reduction in perceived risk of entry with advertising present appears to outweigh the other effects. Advertising promotes entry in the large majority of industries, but can retard it in a few.

The advertising of physician services has become the focus of studies of advertising and entry in recent years. Advertising in this industry was banned prior to 1982. The FTC played the major role in forbidding the ban on advertising by the American Medical Association. The result has been that advertising of physician services has increased from about 5 percent in 1982 to about 20 percent by 1987. Rizzo and Zeckhauser[49] surveyed almost 2,000 physicians who answered questions about their advertising policies and concluded that advertising inhibited entry into the physician market. However, it was also found that experienced physicians for which advertising would have the greatest benefit advertised less. In general, they were reluctant to have themselves or their practices associated with advertising. Thus, to this point in the evolution of the industry, advertising may have facilitated entry. The authors conclude that advertising will be more of a barrier to entry when advertising acceptance increases among well-established physicians.

The Cereal Industry

The cereal industry provides a good vehicle to illustrate the argument further, as it has frequently been used as an example by those observers concerned with concentration. Scanlon summarized the case against the cereal industry.[50] He pointed out that the three largest firms in the industry, Kellogg, General Foods, and General Mills, account for about 85 percent of industry sales, and all but about 2 percent of the balance is held by the next three largest firms. Thus, the concentration level is indeed high. Scanlon further suggested that the concentration is caused by advertising levels that have operated at approximately 15 percent of sales for the three largest firms. Turning to market performance, he observed that the industry profits are high and that product quality is low, as evidenced by the nutritional shortcomings of breakfast cereal, particularly of the more popular, heavily advertised brands. Scanlon estimated that cereal prices were 25 percent higher than they would be if the industry were not concentrated. He claimed that there were no natural production scale economies to justify the concentration, that a brand volume of 1 percent of industry sales would represent an efficient production level.

These arguments have not gone unchallenged. Stern and Dunfee found that the four largest cereal brands (as opposed to firms) controlled only 29.7 percent of the market in 1964, down from 37.5 percent in 1954.[51] These statistics could indicate the existence of significant interbrand competition that may (or may not) provide a similar market situation as more interfirm competition. They also pointed out that two other indexes of competition had increased over time. One, total cereal consumption, increased 10 percent between 1960 and 1970, despite rises in cereal prices that exceeded the inflation rate. The other was new product introductions. Of course, a question arises whether the new brands represented real consumer benefits or whether they were instead only minor variations of existing products designed to replace competitive brands.[52]

Ippolito and Mathios[53] focused on the cereal market in a period in which information developed about the health benefits of fiber. Advertising of fiber health claims was banned until Kellogg succeeded in challenging the restrictions in 1984 even though the health effects of fiber were well known from about the mid-1970s. The authors argued that advertising should contribute a large portion to the public stock of information about the relations between fiber and health, that information from producers in the form of advertising should reach a larger portion of the public than government information, and that competition among firms should lead to voluntary disclosure of product information as well as development of new products. They conclude that consumers react to new relevant information, but that there are considerable costs in acquiring and processing the information. Advertising plays a role in both providing relevant information and in reducing costs to the consumer of acquiring and processing it.

Concentration and Prices

A viable level of competition and relatively low prices might exist with high levels of concentration in at least two situations. The first is when it is feasible to enter the market on a local or regional scale. Brands that dominate the market nationally may be vulnerable in a local market where buyer tastes and needs may be somewhat unique. Furthermore, while the cost of a national entry may be large, the cost of reaching a small geographic segment may be more modest.

The second type of situation is where there exists what Galbraith termed countervailing power on the buyer side.[54] If concentration exists on the buyer side, it can counter the market power of a few sellers. Thus, Sears, Roebuck, Montgomery Ward, and the major automobile companies can extract price concessions from the tire companies. A&P, Safeway, and the other large grocery chains are in a position to gain price reductions from grocery manufacturers.

Empirical Studies

Several of the hypotheses imbedded in the model represented in Figure 19-5 have been explored empirically. Some associations have been found, but the associations often have alternative explanations. Several of the relevant studies will be examined. The intent is to suggest generalizations where they emerge and to illuminate the issues further.

Advertising and Prices.   A very basic question is what impact advertising has upon prices. Buzzell and Farris found that firms with higher relative prices advertise their products more intensively than do those with lower prices.[55] They controlled for product quality by using judgments of perceived quality made by the managers of the involved products. Farris and Albion review this study and several others and conclude that there is a relationship between advertising and pricing.[56] However, they caution that several factors need to be considered in making interpretations. First, a higher price could simply reflect higher quality and the controls for quality are difficult to make. Second, consumers would probably demand lower prices for a nonadvertised product as it is not obvious how unadvertised products could compete in the same market with a lack of advertising being their sole distinguishing feature. Finally, the relative prices of advertised and unadvertised brands are less important than the absolute or average price level of a product category that would prevail in the absence of advertising. It is by no means clear that the average price is higher when some brands are heavily advertised. The argument that advertising can support the entry of new "low-cost" brands is supported by research on eyeglass retailing. Benham found that eyeglass prices were 25 to 30 percent higher in states with total advertising bans presumably because the entry of high-volume, low-priced retailers is inhibited.[57] Krishnamurthi and Raj using data from a split-cable AdTel television test concluded that increased advertising lowers price sensitivity. Effects were examined by segment. The effect was stronger in the high-price-sensitivity segment than in the low-price segment.[58]

The relation between price advertising and product quality has also been studied. Rogersen[59] developed a model of the welfare implications of price advertising of professional services. Professional services have a high content of intangible attributes, one of which is quality. Quality can only be appreciated through consumption of the service. It is assumed that advertising conveys true price information, but that consumers must visit the producer to verify quality. It is concluded that advertising serves as a signal of product quality through price. The higher the price, the higher is the incentive for producing high quality because repeat business is valuable. Price advertising of professional services may thus increase welfare by giving firms incentives to differentiate through choosing different qualities and providing consumers with a signal of product quality.

Advertising and Profitability.   The evidence of an association between advertising and profitability is stronger. Economists Comanor and Wilson, in an influential study, attempted to explain interindustry differences in profit rates.[60] They examined the return on equity after taxes of 41 consumer-goods industries, using both the advertising-sales (A/S) ratio and the average advertising expenditures of the major firms as indicators of advertising intensity. Although they did not find high correlation (only 0.10) between four-firm concentration ratios and the A/S ratio, they did determine, using a regression model, that both advertising measures were significantly related to profitability. They concluded that industries with high advertising outlays earned approximately 50 percent more than other industries. They further attributed much of the profitability differential to entry barriers created by advertising expenditures, arguing that such a cross-sectional study (as contrasted with a time-series study) tends to emphasize the long-run difference among industries and thus should reflect basic structural characteristics like concentration. At least for manufacturing industries, this basic finding has been consistently found in several studies using different samples and measures.[61] Thomas argues that there are three bases for large, above-normal profits of firms in industries with heavy advertising: advertising durability, economies of scale, and heterogeneity (best selling brands have lower per unit marketing costs). Heterogeneity is found to be the most important explanation of supra-normal profits, whereas both durability of advertising and economies of scale were found to have little effect. Thomas thus suggests that high profits constitute rent to brands of high quality.[62]

However, such speculation on causal explanations for the association is naturally less than definitive. It may be, for example, that there are industry characteristics that could jointly cause profits and a tendency to rely on advertising. Or it may be that advertising in some industries is often a more economically efficient means of marketing than any other marketing alternative. From this perspective, the finding that firms in an industry who use advertising compared with those that do not (or use it less) are more profitable is not surprising. In such instances, the nature of the causal link might be quite different from what is implied by Comanor and Wilson.

Advertising and Brand Stability.   Brand loyalty, created in part by advertising, is hypothesized to be a barrier to entry and thus to competition.[63] If such a hypothesis holds, relatively stable brand shares might be expected in industries with extensive advertising. In an early study, Telser examined the leading brands of various product categories in 1948 and 1959 and found an inverse relationship between product class advertising intensity and the stability of the market share of the leading brands.[64] He suggested that the advertising helped to encourage new brand introductions, which, in turn, contributed to the lack of brand stability. New brand introductions, of course, are far different from the entry of new competitors.

Remedies

The problem of the relation of advertising to concentration and competition has been studied in some detail. Yet it is still far from clear whether advertising has any independent causal effect on concentration. However, even if it is assumed to have an effect, the question remains of what remedy might be useful in altering the effect. The issue, in part, is if the argument represented by Figure 19-5 is accepted, what should be done about it? In particular, are additional restrictions on advertising appropriate?

Assume, for example, that some advertising actually does encourage concentration and results in anticompetitive effects and that therefore some restraints could be justified. The problem is: Which part of whose advertising results in anticompetitive effects? Should restrictions be placed on the cereal industry or only on its largest firms? Or should any restraints apply to the entire food industry? What kinds of restraints? Should advertising actually be banned in some industries? What impact would that have on new product development?

There are restraints on some advertising now. Certain services like legal and medical services are restricted in the way they can be advertised. In most states, the prices of prescription drugs cannot be advertised. There are restraints with respect to certain media. Liquor and cigarettes cannot be advertised on television. It is instructive to review these situations and to consider whether the reasons for the restrictions are defensible and whether they have had undesirable, unanticipated consequences. Sheldon and

Doroodian[65] studied the effects of cigarette advertising on demand and the reaction of consumers and industry to government health warnings during the 1952–1984 period. It was concluded that industry advertising increases consumption, that industry increases advertising in response to health warnings, and that when an advertising medium is removed (through a ban) total industry advertising is reduced. Holak and Srinivas,[66] using the cigarette industry's advertising ban of 1970 as a natural experiment, found substantial differences in elasticity and inertia between pre- and postban periods. Demand becomes more inelastic with respect to advertising fluctuations if television and radio can no longer be used as media vehicles. Thus, a ban on advertising can have both positive and negative effects. The consumption of products such as cigarettes may be reduced overall or for certain segments (even this conclusion, however, is controversial[67]). But because brand loyalty levels increase after a ban is imposed, a ban may serve as a barrier to entry. In other words, simply banning advertising in an attempt to reduce demand for products like cigarettes may be ineffective.

It might be possible for the government to restrict advertising levels in certain industries. Restrictions could take the form of mandatory controls on the rates at which firms could increase their advertising budgets. It could even include a provision for firms to decrease their level of advertising. A problem with any such proposal is that it would work to the disadvantage of the small, vigorous firm that is trying to compete with larger organizations and of the innovative firm that must announce new product developments. If the absolute level of advertising were controlled, the smaller firms would not be inhibited, but the large firms would be penalized simply because of their size. Furthermore, there is the sticky issue of determining the exact level of advertising expenditures that would be desirable in any given context. There is precedent for such a move, however. In 1966, the Monopolies Commission in Great Britain recommended a 40 percent cut in advertising expenditures of the leading detergent companies and a 20 percent reduction in wholesale prices. However, partly because of threats to move some of their operations to the European continent, an alternative proposal was adopted. The two involved companies agreed to introduce new, less promoted detergents, priced 20 percent below existing brands.[68]

There have been proposals made to place a tax on advertising or to reduce the tax deduction allowed for advertising over a certain amount.[69] It presumably would not affect the small competitor who would not be advertising at the affected level. Of course, the determination of the amount of reduction and the level at which the reduction would be applicable would be difficult to fix. Furthermore, companies could alter their marketing mix in ways to shift the advertising dollar to other forms of promotion that might have an impact similar to that of advertising. Also, any such plan would discriminate against those companies that tend to rely on advertising in favor of companies like Avon, for example, that rely mainly on direct selling.

The practical question of the nature of the remedy and how it should be implemented needs to be more formally introduced into the analysis. It is tempting to propose a remedy that will seem to rectify obvious problems. However, in many cases, the remedy can be worse than the original problem. The Robinson-Patman Act, for example, has in the eyes of some greatly inhibited price competition instead of encouraging it.

SUMMARY

There are three categories of issues concerning advertising and society. Two of them represent the aggregate effects of advertising on society's value and life-styles and on society's economic well-being. The third focuses on the nature and content of advertising. It involves issues of ethics, manipulation, taste, and advertising to children.

There has been considerable interest in the question of advertising and ethics in the past decade because of many questionable business and government practices which have been brought to public attention generally. Whether it is "ethical" to participate in advertising cigarettes in view of new medical findings on the link between cigarette smoking and cancer is an example. It is clear that advertising ethics and other social and economic issues of advertising are heavily intertwined. Consider the argument that advertising manipulates consumers. First, there is concern that advertisers, using subconscious motives uncovered by motivation research, can manipulate an unwilling consumer. Although it is now recognized by professionals that the power of motivation research is limited, some ethical questions about its use still remain. Second, there is a concern with the use of "emotional" appeals. The key issue is the definition of a product. Is a product an entity with one or more primary functions or does it involve any dimension relevant to the consumer when she or he makes a purchase decision? Finally, there is the more general concern with the power represented by the volume of advertising and the skill of the people who create it.

Some advertising is criticized on the basis of taste—that it uses appeals that are offensive, that the content is annoying, or that it is simply too intrusive. Some critics object to the use of sex appeals, especially when children may be exposed to the advertising. Others are concerned with the use of fear appeals. The irritation life cycle is conceptualized to help understand the intrusive quality of advertising. An FTC proposal to ban all television advertising to preschool children and all sugar product television advertising to older children was seriously and vigorously debated.

It is argued that advertising has a negative impact on values and life-styles of society. The key issues are what values and life-styles are to be avoided and what relative impact or influence does advertising have on them. What is materialism and is it bad or is it merely a means to various goals? What role does (and should) advertising have in promoting or combating stereotypes? Does beer and wine advertising promote alcoholism and drunk driving?

It is unreasonable to separate the economic and social effects of advertising. Advertising is basically an economic institution, and any overall appraisal of advertising should include an analysis of its economic impact. Advertising provides economic value to society in many ways. It enhances buyer decision making by providing information and by supporting brand names. It provides an efficient means for firms to communicate with their customers. Such a function is particularly important in the introduction of new products. By generating various product associations, advertising can add to the utility a buyer receives from a product. It provides employment, supports the various media, and has the potential to reduce extremes in the levels of consumer buying.

A central issue is the impact that advertising has on competition. It is argued that heavy advertising expenditures in some industries generate product differentiation among products that are essentially identical. This product differentiation provides the basis for brand loyalties that represent a significant barrier to potential competitors. It is also hypothesized that in these industries heavy advertising expenditures are needed for successful competition. Such large expenditure levels represent another barrier to entry of new competitors. With the entry of new competitors inhibited, there is a tendency for industries to become more concentrated over time—to have fewer competitors. The result is a reduction in vigorous competition, higher prices, and excessive profits. Advertising in such industries is regarded as noninformative; its role is to shift buyers around among "identical" products and is thus largely an economic waste.

The implications of these hypotheses have been studied by economists. They have found evidence of association between advertising and concentration, but, on balance, the association is weaker than might be expected. The evidence of association between advertising and profitability is somewhat stronger. There is considerable controversy concerning the macroeconomic effects of advertising, and scholars can be found who vigorously defend one side or the other. Issues are both theoretical, concerning questions of causation and inference, and methodological involving measurement of difficult constructs such as concentration and market boundaries.

The practical question of what remedies seem appropriate needs to be formally introduced into the analysis. Among the proposed remedies are that advertising in some industries be limited or prohibited or that a tax be applied to advertising. Remedies that are defensible and will not cause more problems than they solve are not easy to develop. Many studies have been done on the effects of eliminating cigarette advertising without a definitive conclusion being reached that such a public policy will result in more harm or more good.

DISCUSSION QUESTIONS

1. Suppose that a motivation research study found that housewives disliked a certain transparent, clinging, wrapping material because of their basic dislike of cooking, which was subconsciously transferred to the material. As a result, nonkitchen uses were emphasized in the advertising. Is this manipulation? In the research, the housewives were told only that the aim of the study was to determine their attitudes toward housekeeping in general. Was such a guise ethical?

2. Define the terms "need," "product," "information," and "rationality." Does a commercial showing a group of people enjoying a cola drink communicate information? Is it an appropriate appeal? Consider other examples. Is manipulation involved?

3. Richard Avedon, a photographer and consultant to agencies and clients, helped develop for Calvin Klein jeans a very controversial set of television commercials. They featured the 15-year-old actress-model Brooke Shields in a variety of sultry, sophisticated, suggestive commercials. In one, Brooke Shields says in a suggestive manner,

''Nothing comes between me and my Calvins.'' In another controversial television commercial for a men's fragrance, a man wearing a pajama bottom is seen getting out of bed and discussing the previous night by phone with a woman who had slept with him.

(a) Do you feel that such advertising is effective? In what way?

(b) Would you run such advertising on network television if you felt it was effective if you were an advertiser? If you were an agency whose client had insisted on it?

(c) If you were a CBS censor, would you allow it on your network?

4. Suppose you are the president of a major consumer food company. A church group claiming to represent 2.5 million members is attempting to reduce the ''excessive violence, sex, and profanity'' on television. The members have informed you that they are boycotting all products advertised on eight programs, including ''Miami Vice'' and ''Dallas,'' and expect that their boycott will cost you $20 million in sales. What would your response be? Do you feel that you should have a policy concerning such programming? Would you screen episodes of such programs and selectively avoid episodes that are particularly objectionable'?

5. Take a position on the FTC proposals regarding television advertising to children. What about banning the advertising of sugar products directed at children under 12'? Would you prefer that food advertisers to children fund ''counterads'' geared to promote nutrition? What about cutting back Saturday morning kids' advertising to four minutes per hour? Would you alter or add to the following partial listing of the provisions of a Canadian broadcasting code for children?

(a) Product characteristics should not be exaggerated.

(b) Results from a craft or kit that an average child could not obtain should not be shown.

(c) Undue pressure to buy or to urge parents to buy should be avoided.

(d) A commercial should not be repeated during a program.

(e) Program personalities will not do commercials on their own programs.

(f) Well-known persons other than actors will not endorse products.

(g) Price information should be clear and complete.

(h) Messages must not reflect disdain for parents or casually portray undesirable family living habits.

(i) Advertising must not imply that product possession makes the owner superior.

(j) The media should contribute directly or indirectly to sound and safe habits.

6. Should there be similar codes for other society groups such as senior citizens or ethnic minorities?

7. What is materialism? It has been said that our society emphasizes the use of material goods to attain nonmaterial goals. Comment. Is America too materialistic? What is advertising's role in establishing values and life-styles? How does a nation go about changing its values?

8. Should advertisers be concerned about minority stereotypes developed in advertisements? Why? If you were an agency president, how would you develop a policy and set of procedures in this regard?

9. In your view, should beer advertisers be banned from using sports figures in their ads? What about the use of image advertising in general? Should beer and wine advertising be banned from television and radio advertising? From all advertising? What about the use of ''power/sportiness'' appeals in automobile advertising? Should beer advertisers stop all college and sports promotions?

10. In an open letter to the makers of Alka-Seltzer, the following questions were posed by Ries, Cappiello, Colwell, a New York advertising agency: Why did you spend $23 million to promote a product that everyone knows about? Why did you spend $23 million to promote a product that is mostly bicarbonate and aspirin? Why not put some of that money into your laboratories? Why not develop new products that are worth advertising? Comment.

11. What would be the economic effect of a ban on all advertising? Of a ban on radio and television advertising?

12. What is the definition of a market? What is the distinction between the compact car market and the automobile market? Campbell had 8 percent of the dry-soup market in 1962 versus 57 percent for Lipton and 16 percent for Wyler's. Should an analyst focus on the soup market or the dry-soup market?

13. The concentration ratio in the beer industry went from 21 percent in 1947 to 34 percent in 1963. Yet the fact that Pabst was third in 1952, ninth in 1957, and third again in 1962 indicates that the industry was far from stable. Furthermore, regional brands like Lone-Star and Pearl, two Texas brands that forced a national brand out of their market, compete very effectively with national brands and require only a regional advertising budget. Comment.

14. What is the economic impact of advertising? When will it generate lower prices? Under what conditions will it increase prices? Evaluate the causal model represented in Figure 19-5.

15. If you were the chairman of an advertising agency with a cigarette account would you drop the account after hearing the Surgeon General's report on smoking and health?

16. It has been proposed by Ralph Nader that a 100 percent tax be applied on all advertising expenditures in excess of a percentage specified for different companies by the FTC. Evaluate this proposal. How else might large advertising expenditures be reduced? What would be the effect of a law outlawing advertising in the cigarette industry? In the detergent industry (in which 11 percent of sales is spent on advertising)?

NOTES

1. *The Works of Samuel Johnson*, LL.D., IV (Oxford: Talboys and Wheeler, 1825), p. 269. For a contemporary book, see Roxanne Hovland and Gary B. Wilcox, eds., *Advertising in Society: Classic and Contemporary Readings on Advertising's Role in Society* (Chicago: NTC Business Books, 1989).

2. F. P. Bishop, *The Ethics of Advertising* (Longdon: Robert Hale, 1949).

3. Donald L. Kanter, "Cynical Marketers at Work," *Journal of Advertising Research*, December/January, 1988–89, pp. 28–34.

4. S. D. Hunt and L. B. Chonko, *Journal of Advertising*, 16 (4) 1987, pp. 16–24. See also, L. B. Chonko and S. D. Hunt (1985), "Ethics and Marketing Management: An Empirical Examination," *Journal of Business Research*, 13, August 1985, pp. 339–359; O. C. Ferrell and L. G. Gresham, "A Contingency Framework for Understanding Ethical Decision Making in Marketing," *Journal of Marketing* 29, Summer 1985, pp. 87–96; and D. M. Krugman and O. C. Ferrell, "The Organizational Ethics of Advertising: Corporate and Agency Views," *Journal of Advertising*, 10 (1), 1981, pp. 21–30ff.

5. Alan J. Dubinsky and Barbara Loken, "Analyzing Ethical Decision Making in Marketing," *Journal of Business Research*, 19, 1989, pp. 83–107.

6. Vance Packard, *The Hidden Persuaders* (New York: Pocket Books, 1957).

7. William L. Wilkie, *Consumer Research* (New York: John Wiley, 1986), p. 377.

8. Joel Saegert, "Another Look at Subliminal Perception," *Journal of Advertising Research*, 19, February 1979, pp. 55–57.

9. Del Hawkens, "The Effects of Subliminal Stimulation on Drive Level and Brand Preference," *Journal of Marketing Research*, 7, August 1970, pp. 322–326.

10. Tibor Scitovsky, *Welfare and Competition* (Homewood, IL: Richard D. Irwin, 1951), pp. 401–402.

11. Mary Gardiner Jones, "The Cultural and Social Impact of Advertising on American Society," *Arizona State Law Journal*, 3, 1970.

12. Raymond A. Bauer and Stephen A. Greyser, "The Dialogue That Never Happens," *Harvard Business Review*, 50, January/February 1969, pp. 122–128.

13. Raymond A. Bauer and Stephen A. Greyser, *Advertising in America: The Consumer View* (Boston: Division of Research, Graduate School of Business Administration, Harvard University, 1968).

14. David A. Aaker and Donald Bruzzone, "What Causes Irritation in Television Advertising," Spring 1985, pp. 47–57.

15. Kathy McMeel, "You Dirty Old Ad Men Make Me Sick," *Advertising Age*, December 1, 1969, p. 28.

16. Stephen A. Greyser, "Irritation in Advertising," *Journal of Advertising Research*, 13, February 1973, p. 8.

17. Ibid., p. 6.

18. See, for example, Marvin E. Goldberg and Gerald J. Gorn, "Children's Reactions to Television Advertising: An Experimental Approach," *Journal of Consumer Research* 1, September 1977, pp. 69–75, and "Some Unintended Consequences of TV Advertising to Children," *Journal of Consumer Research*, 5, June 1978, pp. 22–29 by the same authors.

19. Gerald J. Gorn and Marvin E. Goldberg, "Behavioral Evidence of the Effects of Televised Food Messages on Children," *Journal of Consumer Research*, 9, September 1982, pp. 200–205.

20. M. Carole Macklin, "Preschoolers' Understanding of the Informational Function of Television Advertising," *Journal of Consumer Research*, 14, September 1987, pp. 229–239.

21. Merrie Brucks, Gary M. Armstrong, and Marvin E. Goldberg, "Children's Use of Cognitive Defenses Against Television Advertising: A Cognitive Response Approach," *Journal of Consumer Research*, 14, March 1988, pp. 471–482.

22. Richard M. Pollay, "Quality of Life in the Padded Sell: Common Criticism of Advertising's Cultural Character and International Public Policies," in James H. Leigh and Claude R. Martin, Jr., eds., *Current Issues and Research in Advertising* (Ann Arbor: University of Michigan Press, 1986), pp. 173–250.

23. Ibid., p. 196. See also Richard W. Pollay, "The Distorted Mirror: Reflections on the Unintended Consequences of Advertising," *Journal of Marketing*, 50, April 1986, pp. 18–36, and Morris B. Holbrook, "Mirror, Mirror, on the Wall, What's Unfair in the Reflections of Advertising?" *Journal of Marketing*, 51, July 1987, pp. 95–103.

24. J. G. Myers, *Social Issues in Advertising* (New York: American Association of Advertising Agencies Educational Foundation, 1972).

25. Kusum Singh and Bertram Gross, " 'MacBride': The Report and the Response," *Journal of Communications*, 31, October 1981, pp. 104–117.

26. Bauer and Greyser, "The Dialogue That Never Happens."

27. Russell W. Belk, "Materialism: Trait Aspects of Living in the Material World," *Journal of Consumer Research*, 12, December 1985, pp. 265–280, and Morris B. Holbrook and Elizabeth C. Hirschman, "The Experiential Aspects of Consumption: Consumer Fantasies, Feelings, and Fun," *Journal of Consumer Research*, 9, September 1982, pp. 132–140.

28. Mary Gardiner Jones, "The Cultural and Social Impact of Advertising on American Society," presented to the Trade Regulation Roundtable of the Association of American Law Schools, San Francisco, December 1969, pp. 13–14.

29. Alice E. Courtney and Sarah Wemick Lockeretz, "A Woman's Place: An Analysis of the Roles Portrayed by Women in Magazine Advertisements," *Journal of Marketing Research*, 8, February 1971, pp. 92–95.

30. Harold H. Kassarjian, "The Negro and American Advertising, 1946–65," *Journal of Marketing Research*, 6, February 1969, pp. 29–39.

31. Thomas W. Leigh, Arno J. Rethans, and Tamatha R. Whitney, "Role Portrayals of Women in Advertising: Cognitive Responses and Advertising Effectiveness," *Journal of Advertising Research*, October/November 1987, pp. 54–63.

32. "Whole World Is Watching U.S. Alcohol Ad Debate," *Advertising Age*, February 11, 1985, p. 70.

33. Camille P. Schuster and Christine P. Powell, "Comparison of Cigarette and Alcohol Advertising Controversies," *Journal of Advertising*, 16 (2), 1987, pp. 26–33. See also Avery M. Abernethy and Jesse E. Teel, "Advertising Regulation's Effect upon Demand for Cigarettes," *Journal of Advertising*, 15 (4) 1986, pp. 51–55, and George P. Moschis (1989), "Point of View: Cigarette Advertising and Young Smokers," *Journal of Advertising Research*, April/May 1989, pp. 51–60.

34. David A. Aaker and Donald Norris, "Characteristics of Television Commercials Perceived as Informative," *Journal of Advertising Research*, February 1982.

35. Phillip Nelson, "Advertising as Information," *Journal of Political Economy*, 82, July/August 1974, pp. 729–754.

36. Fritz Machlup, *The Production and Distribution of Knowledge in the United States* (Princeton, NJ: Princeton University Press, 1962), p. 265.

37. Julian L. Simon, *Issues in the Economics of Advertising* (Urbana: University of Illinois Press, 1970), p. 276.

38. "Grocery Manufacturing," Technical Study No. 6, National Commission on Food Marketing, June 1966, p. 147.

39. Simon, *Issues in the Economics of Advertising*.

40. Committee on the Value of Advertising, American Association of Advertising Agencies, *The Value Side of Productivity: A Key to Competitive Survival in the 1990's* (New York: AAAA, 1990).

41. Ibid., p. 21.

42. Neil H. Borden, *The Economic Effects of Advertising* (Homewood, IL: Richard D. Irwin, 1942), p. 609.

43. For a recent book-length treatment of the subject, see Robert E. McAuliffe, *Advertising, Competition, and Public Policy: Theories and New Evidence* (Lexington, MA: Lexington Books, 1987). McAuliffe addresses advertising as a barrier to entry, questions of correlation and causality, measurement issues, and implications for public policy.

44. Frederic M. Scherer, *Industrial Market Structure and Economic Performance* (Boston: Houghton Mifflin, 1980), p. 62.

45. Ibid., p. 375.

46. For a model of advertising and entry, see Richard Schmalensee, "Advertising and Entry Deterrence: An Exploratory Model," Working Paper, Alfred Sloan School of Management, Cambridge: Massachusetts Institute of Technology, 1982.

47. Paul D. Scanlon, "Oligopoly and 'Deceptive' Advertising: The Cereal Industry Affair," *Antitrust Law & Economics Review,* 3, Spring 1970, p. 101.

48. J. N. Kessides, "Advertising, Sunk Cost, and Barriers to Entry," *The Review of Economics and Statistics,* February 1986.

49. John A. Rizzo and Richard J. Zeckhauser, "Advertising and Entry: The Case of Physician Services," *Journal of Political Economy,* 98, June 1990, pp. 476–500.

50. Scanlon, "Oligopoly and 'Deceptive' Advertising," pp. 99–110.

51. Louis W. Stern and Thomas W. Dunfee, "Public Policy Implications of Non-price Marketing and De-Oligopolization in the Cereal Industry," in Fred C. Allvine, ed., *Public Policy and Marketing Practices* (Chicago: American Marketing Association, 1973), pp. 271–287.

52. See also Paul N. Bloom, "The Cereal Companies: Monopolists or Super Marketers?" *MSU Business Topics,* Summer 1978, pp. 41–49.

53. P. M. Ippolito and A. D. Mathios, "Information, Advertising, and Health Choice: A Study of the Cereal Market," *Rand Journal of Economics,* Vol. 21, Autumn 1990.

54. John K. Galbraith, *American Capitalism: The Concept of Countervailing Power* (Boston: Houghton Mifflin, 1956).

55. Robert D. Buzzell and Paul W. Farris, "Marketing Costs in Consumer Goods Industries," Marketing Science Institute, Report N. 76-111, August 1976.

56. Paul W. Farris and Mark S. Albion, "The Impact of Advertising on the Price of Consumer Products," *Journal of Marketing,* 44, Summer 1980, pp. 17–35.

57. Lee Benham, "The Effect of Advertising on the Price of Consumer Products," *Journal of Marketing,* 44, Summer 1980, pp. 17–35, and Lee Benham, "The Effect of Advertising on the Price of Eyeglasses," *The Journal of Law and Economics,* 15, October 1972, pp. 337–352.

58. Lakshman Krishnamurthi and S. P. Raj, "The Effect of Advertising on Consumer Price Sensitivity," *Journal of Marketing Research,* 22, May 1985, pp. 119–129.

59. W. P. Rogersen, "Price Advertising and the Deterioration of Product Quality," *Review of Economic Studies,* 55, 1988, pp. 215–229.

60. William S. Comanor and Thomas A. Wilson, "Advertising, Market Structure and Performance," *Review of Economics and Statistics,* 49, November 1967, pp. 423–440.

61. Scherer, Industrial Market Structure and Economic Performance, p. 286.

62. L. G. Thomas, "Advertising in Consumer Goods Industries: Durability, Economies of Scale, and Heterogeneity," *The Journal of Law and Economics,* April 1989.

63. Richard Schmalensee, "Brand Loyalty and Barriers to Entry," *Southern Economic Journal,* 40, April 1974, pp. 579–588.

64. Lester G. Telser, "Advertising and Competition," *Journal of Political Economy,* December 1964, pp. 537–562.

65. B. J. Sheldon and K. Doroodian, "A Simultaneous Model of Cigarette Advertising: Effects on Demand and Industry Response to Public Policy," *The Review of Economics and Statistics,* November 1989.

66. Susan L. Holak and Srinivas K. Reddy, "Effects of a Television and Radio Advertising Ban: A Study of the Cigarette Industry," *Journal of Marketing,* 50, October 1986, pp. 219–227.

67. James L. Hamilton, "The Demand for Cigarettes: Advertising, the Health Scare and the Cigarette Advertising Ban," *Review of Economics and Statistics,* 54, 1972, pp. 401–411, and Lynne Schneider, Benjamin Klein, and Kevin M. Murphy, "Governmental Regulation of Cigarette Health Information," *Journal of Law and Economics,* 24, December 1981, pp. 575–612.

68. Scherer, Industrial Market Structure, p. 404.

69. Robert C. Pace, "The Story of the Florida Tax on Advertising," *International Journal of Advertising,* 7, 1988, pp. 283–292.

INDEX

Note: italics indicate illustrated ads/storyboards